RUNNING
LINUX

ifconfig

ifconfig ✓

RUNNING

LINUX

MATT WELSH AND **LAR KAUFMAN**

O'REILLY & ASSOCIATES, INC.

103 MORRIS STREET, SUITE A

SEBASTOPOL, CA 95472

Running Linux
by Matt Welsh and Lar Kaufman

Editor: Andy Oram

Production Editor: Stephen Spainhour

Printing History:

February 1995:   First Edition.

This book is printed on acid-free paper with 85% recycled content, 15% post-consumer waste. O'Reilly & Associates is committed to using paper with the highest recycled content available consistent with high quality.

ISBN: 1-56592-100-3   [4/95]

TABLE OF CONTENTS

CHAPTER TWO

CHAPTER FIVE

POWER TOOLS _____ 205

CHAPTER SIX

PROGRAMMING WITH LINUX

FIGURES

PREFACE

This is a book about Linux, a free implementation of UNIX for personal computers. Linux is one of the most significant achievements of free software, and it has the potential to completely change the face of the PC operating system world. In this book, we will take you from the comfort of your own home on a journey across the often treacherous landscape of UNIX.

There is very little else that you need for your trip. The following three items may come in handy: a towel, a strong cup of coffee, and (optionally) a computer. In the first chapter we will detail the precise hardware requirements for this computer, but for the time being any metaphysical representation of a computer slightly more advanced than, say, an abacus, will do.

This book is for the adventurer and the entrepreneur. Linux itself is somewhat of a rebellion against the world of commercial software. The world of Linux is not a planned or organized one. You must expect the unexpected. You must always yield to the driving force behind free software: that being the desire—no, *need*—to develop and maintain the most succinct and powerful system anywhere. To put it in a nutshell: you must hack.

My own adventures with Linux began several years ago, when the system was still in its infancy. Binaries would break when a new kernel was released, there were no shared libraries, and the idea of TCP/IP or X Window System support was a good-natured joke among developers. Nobody had any idea that Linux would make it this far. With all of its advances, however, the system retains the hackish spirit from whence it emerged. Development today is no less dynamic and exciting than it was in the early, pioneering days—in fact, the enormous popularity of the system has made it more so.

In writing this book, I wanted to make Linux a real choice for the masses of personal computer users who find themselves trapped within the limitations of commercial operating systems (need I name names?). Because of the cooperative nature of the system, certain aspects of Linux can be confusing or apparently ad hoc. In this book, I've tried to condense as much wisdom as possible, based on correspondence with thousands of Linux users worldwide. I think that in this book you'll find everything that you need to know to get the most out of your Linux system.

Why People Like Linux

Why on earth would you want to run Linux? Good question. What you have now works, doesn't it? Or, maybe it doesn't. Maybe you're just itching for something different, or maybe you're tired of a 640K memory limit although you have 20 MB of RAM. Here are a few reasons why people are switching to Linux:

- It's free. That is, Linux is a freely redistributable clone of the UNIX operating system (OS). You can get it free from someone who has it, or download it from an Internet site or a bulletin board system (BBS), or you can buy it at a reasonable price from a vendor who has packaged it (probably with added value) and who may also provide support services.

- It's popular. It runs on the inexpensive Intel 386/486/Pentium PC architecture and supports a broad range of video cards, audio cards, CD-ROM drives, disk drives, and other devices. Linux can be used on EISA, Localbus, or PCI systems as well. Linux is now being ported to other platforms, including the Motorola 680x0, DEC ALPHA, PowerPC, and SPARC processors. Other architectures are also targeted and development projects are underway.

  There are some very busy Internet newsgroups where Linux is discussed by an international community of users and developers, as well as email mailing lists and Fidonet Echo conferences. Even major commercial software developers have enthusiastically developed applications on Linux, including, for example, Novell Corporation (owners of UNIX System Laboratories), who ported the popular NetWare package to it.

- It's powerful. You will be pleased to see how fast the system runs, even with many processes running and with multiple windows open. Linux makes excellent use of the hardware. Many commercial operating systems (namely MS-DOS) make very little use of the advanced multitasking capabilities of the 80x86 processor. Linux is native to this architecture and uses them all. A Linux machine with a reasonably fast processor and a sufficient amount of RAM can perform as well, or better, than expensive UNIX workstations.

- It is of good quality, and runs high-quality software applications. Linux is being developed publicly with hundreds of programmers and users refining it, but with the individual vision and focus of its originator, Linus Torvalds. It incorporates the work of universities, companies, and individuals in the form of highly developed compilers, editors, utilities, and scripts that have been developed over the last quarter century. Unlike other new operating systems,

Linux already has an enormous base of applications freely available for your use, from major scientific applications, to multimedia tools, to games.

- It has full UNIX features. Linux is a true multi-user, multitasking operating system. It uses the X Window System graphical user interface (GUI) and offers several different easy-to-use, configurable window managers. Full networking support (TCP/IP, SLIP, PPP, UUCP, among others) is available.

- It's highly compatible with MS-DOS and Windows. You can install Linux along with other disk partitions that contain MS-DOS or other operating systems. Linux can directly access MS-DOS files from the floppy or hard drive. Developers are working on emulators for both MS-DOS and Windows, so that you can eventually run your favorite commercial applications from Linux. Linux does *not* run under MS-DOS, Windows, or any other operating system—it is completely independent of them, but features have been added to allow the separate systems to work together.

- It is small. The basic OS will run on 2 MB of system memory, and a carefully configured system complete with GUI and window manager will run well on 4 MB. A good basic distribution will fit in 40 MB of disk storage. (If this seems like a lot of disk space, it's because Linux provides a lot of utilities.) The minimal system for a full Linux implementation is probably a 16 mHz 386SX system with 4 MB of RAM using a common graphics coprocessor video card. To really appreciate the power of the system and the GUI, however, you will need a faster machine and nice video hardware. But everything from the lowest-end 386SX to the highest-end Pentium is supported.

- It is big. Some of the larger distributions fill more than 250 MB of uncompressed disk storage in binary files alone. (Full source code is freely available for Linux, and it is available prepared for your installation from diskette or CD from a number of sources.) The number of powerful utilities and applications ported to Linux grows constantly. You could probably fill a gigabyte hard disk with them, even without loading up on graphics and audio files.

  Most Linux users can run a complete system in 100MB or so of diskspace. This includes all of the basics, as well as the nice extras such as the X Window System environment, text processing tools, and development utilities such as compilers and libraries. But if you're a real power user, much more is available.

- It's supported. The biggest line of support is the Internet and its many thousands of Linux newsgroup participants, but you can also contract for support from an independent company, or buy a supported version of Linux from one of its distributors.

- It's documented. There is this book (an excellent start!). The Linux development community established the Linux Documentation Project (LDP) early on, to facilitate the development of Linux. The LDP has several books in electronic form that you can print or access on your computer. Additionally, other books are being brought out by various publishers in several countries. Finally, once you get over a few installation humps, Linux is pretty much like any other UNIX system, so general books about UNIX use and administration will give you all the help you need.

- You can use Linux. We're eager to show you what you need to know, in this book! We think you will like it.

Organization of This Book

Each chapter of this book contains a big chunk of information. It takes you into a world of material that could easily take up several books. But we move quickly through the topics you need to know.

Chapter 1, *Introduction to Linux*, tries to draw together many different threads. It explains why Linux came to be, and what makes it different from other versions of UNIX as well as other operating systems for personal computers.

Chapter 2, *Obtaining and Installing Linux*, is a comprehensive tutorial on installing and configuring Linux on your system. It discusses how to obtain Linux, preparations to make before installing the software, the installation procedure itself, and basic system configuration.

Chapter 3, *Basic UNIX Commands and Concepts*, offers a system administrator's introduction to UNIX, for people who need one. It is intended to give you enough tools to let you perform the basic tasks that you need to do throughout the book. Basic commands are covered, along with some tips for administrators and some concepts you should know.

Chapter 4, *Essential System Management*, covers system administration and maintenance. This is perhaps the most important and useful chapter of the book; it covers user account management, backups, software upgrading, building a new kernel, and more.

Chapter 5, *Power Tools*, introduces you to the most popular and commonly-used tools on Linux. You'll learn how to use a text editor, install and configure the X Window System, and do other useful everyday tasks.

Chapter 6, *Programming with Linux*, is for programmers. Besides tools for C programming and debugging, it introduces other popular languages such as Perl and Tcl/Tk.

Chapter 7, *Networking and Communications*, tells you how to set up your all-important connection to the outside world. It shows you how to configure your system so it can work on a local area network, in case you are in an organization that has one. SLIP, electronic mail, and World Wide Web server configuration are also discussed.

Appendix A, *Sources of Linux Information*, tells you about other useful documentation for Linux and other sources of help.

Appendix B, *Linux Vendor List*, provides a list of vendors who distribute Linux on CD-ROM, diskette, or other media.

Appendix C, *FTP Tutorial and Site List*, tells you how to use the File Transfer Protocol on the Internet to obtain the Linux software itself or Linux-related documents. This appendix also lists important Linux FTP archive sites.

Appendix D, *Bulletin Board Access to Linux*, is a listing of bulletin board systems (BBSes) that carry Linux files.

Appendix E, *The GNU General Public License*, contains the license under which Linux (as well as a lot of other free software) is copyrighted (or as some people like to say, "copylefted").

The Bibliography lists a number of books, HOWTOs, and Internet RFCs of interest to Linux users and administrators.

Conventions Used in This Book

The following is a list of the typographical conventions used in this book.

Bold	is used for machine names, hostnames, or site names, for user names and IDs, and for occasional emphasis.
Italic	is used for file and directory names, program and command names, command-line options, email addresses and path names, and to emphasize new terms.
`Constant Width`	is used in examples to show the contents of files or the output from commands, and to indicate environment variables and keywords that appear in code.
`Constant Italic`	is used to indicate variable options, keywords, or text that the user is to replace with an actual value.
`Constant Bold`	is used in examples to show commands or other text that should be typed literally by the user.

The bomb icon in the left margin is for Caution: you can make a mistake here that hurts your system or is hard to recover from.

[0]Biblio
Chapter 0
manpage(1)

The book icon indicates a reference to another part of this book or to another source of information. The citation string (or strings) underneath the book may be either a number and key for a book, HOWTO article, or RFC listed in the Bibliography; a pointer to another chapter or appendix in this book; or a referral to a particular program's manual page.

Acknowledgments

This book is the result of many people's efforts, and as expected it would be impossible to list them all here. First of all, I would like to thank Andy Oram, who did an excellent job of editing, writing, and whip-cracking to get this book into shape. Apart from being the overall editor, Andy contributed the UNIX tutorial chapter as well as material for the X section. It was Andy who approached me about writing for O'Reilly in the first place, and he has demonstrated the patience of a saint when waiting for my updates to trickle in.

Those of you who are already familiar with Linux may notice that some portions of this book, such as the introductory and installation chapters, have been released as part of *Linux Installation and Getting Started*, a free book available via the Internet. O'Reilly allowed me to release those portions (originally written for this book) to the I&GS, so they could benefit the Internet-based Linux community and I could get feedback and corrections from its readership. Thanks to everyone who contributed edits to those sections.

I would also like to thank the following people for their work on the Linux operating system—without all of them, there wouldn't be anything to write a book about: Linus Torvalds, Donald Becker, Alan Cox, Remy Card, Ted T'so, H.J. Lu, Ross Biro, Drew Eckhardt, Ed Carp, Eric Youngdale, Fred van Kempen, Steven Tweedie, Patrick Volkerding, and all of the other hackers, from the kernel grunts to the lowly docos, too numerous to mention here.

Special thanks to the following people for their contributions to the Linux Documentation Project, general friendliness, or the occasional donation to keep me going: Phil Hughes, Melinda McBride, Bill Hahn, Dan Irving, Michael Johnston, Joel Goldberger, Michael K. Johnson, Adam Richter, Roman Yanovsky, Jon Magid, Erik Troan, Lars Wirzenius, Olaf Kirch, and Anna Clark.

Finally, a big round of virtual applause to the editing, production, and management staff at O'Reilly & Associates for their interest and aid in Linux material. Stephen Spainhour diligently copyedited and helmed the production of the book, with help from Clairemarie Fisher O'Leary, Ellen Siever, Sheryl Avruch, Kismet McDonough, and Donna Woonteiler. Edie Freedman created the cover and found the pictures for the chapter headings (based on an idea of Lar's). Jennifer Niederst designed the interior layout and provided the little marginal icons for the cross-references. Chris Reilley and Hannah Dyer made all the figures. Thanks for the cowboy, guys.

If you have questions, comments, or corrections for this book, please feel free to get in touch with the authors. Matt Welsh can be reached on the Internet at *mdw@sunsite.unc.edu*. Lar Kaufman can be reached at *lark@conserve.org*.

CHAPTER ONE
INTRODUCTION
TO LINUX

This is a book about Linux, a free UNIX clone for personal computer systems that supports full multitasking, the X Window System, TCP/IP networking, and much more. Hang tight and read on—in the pages that follow we describe the system in agonizing detail.

Linux has generated more excitement in the computer field than any other development of the past several years. Its surprisingly fast spread and the loyalty it inspires recall the excitement of do-it-yourself computing that used to characterize earlier advances in computer technology. Ironically, it succeeds by rejuvenating one of the oldest operating systems still in widespread use, UNIX. Linux is both a new technology and an old one.

In narrow technical terms, Linux is just the operating system kernel, offering the basic services of process scheduling, virtual memory, file management, and device I/O. In other words, Linux itself is the lowest-level part of the operating system.

However, most people use the term "Linux" to refer to the complete system—the kernel along with the many applications which it runs: a complete development and work environment including compilers, editors, graphical interfaces, text processors, games, and more.

This book will be your guide to Linux's shifting and many-faceted world. Linux has developed into the operating system for businesses, education, and personal productivity, and this book will help you get the most out of it.

Linux can turn any 386, 486, or Pentium PC into a workstation. It will give you the full power of UNIX at your fingertips. Businesses are installing Linux on entire networks of machines, using the operating system to manage financial and hospital records, a distributed-user computing environment, telecommunications, and more. Universities worldwide are using Linux for teaching courses on operating systems programming and design. And, of course, computing enthusiasts everywhere are using Linux at home, for programming, document production, and all-around hacking.

What makes Linux so different is that it is a *free* implementation of UNIX. It was and still is developed by a group of volunteers, primarily on the Internet, who exchange code, report bugs, and fix problems in an open-ended environment. Anyone is welcome to join in the Linux development effort: all it takes is interest in hacking a free UNIX clone and some kind of programming know-how. The book that you hold in your hands is your tour guide.

In this book, we assume that you're comfortable with a personal computer (running any operating system, such as MS-DOS or Windows), and that you're willing to do some experimentation and hacking to get everything working correctly. Linux is somewhat more complex than the "plug and play" operating systems available in the PC world, but with this book as your guide we hope you'll find that setting up and running your own Linux system is quite easy and a great deal of fun.

About This Book

This book is an overview and entry-level guide to the Linux system. We attempt to present enough general and interesting information on a number of topics to satisfy UNIX novices and wizards alike. This book should provide sufficient material for almost anyone to install and use Linux and get the most out of it. Instead of covering many of the volatile technical details, those things which tend to change with rapid development, we give you enough background to find out more on your own.

Linux is not difficult to install and use. However, as with any implementation of UNIX, there is often some black magic involved to get everything working correctly. We hope that this book will get you on the Linux tour bus and show you how groovy this operating system can be.

In this book, we cover the following topics:

- What is Linux? The design and philosophy of this unique operating system, and what it can do for you.

- All the details of what is needed to run Linux, including suggestions on what kind of hardware configuration is recommended for a complete system.

- How to obtain and install Linux. Because there are many distributions of the Linux system, we include general information which should be adequate to install any release.

- For new users, an introduction to the UNIX system including an overview of the most important commands and concepts.

- The care and feeding of the Linux system, including system administration and maintenance, upgrading the system, and how to fix things when they don't work.

- Getting the most out of your Linux system, with "power tools" such as TEX, Emacs, the X Window System, and more.

- The Linux programming environment. The tools of the trade for programming and developing software on the Linux system, including C, C++, Perl, shell scripts, and more esoteric languages such as Tcl/Tk.

- Using Linux for telecommunications and networking, including TCP/IP, UUCP, and SLIP. We also talk about configuring electronic mail, as well as a World Wide Web server on your Linux system.

This book is for the personal computer user who wishes to get the most out of their system with Linux. Our purpose is to provide enough information to get new users up and running, and able to do everything that they can do under other personal computer operating systems, and more, under Linux. We talk about everything from the basics to installation to systems administration to programming to networking.

Chapter 3
Chapter 4

While much of the discussion in this book is not overly technical, it helps to have previous experience with another UNIX system. For those who don't have UNIX experience, we have included a short tutorial in Chapter 3, *Basic UNIX Commands and Concepts*, for new users. Chapter 4, *Essential System Management*, is a complete chapter on systems administration, which should help even seasoned UNIX users in running a Linux system.

If you are new to UNIX, you'll want to pick up a more complete guide to UNIX basics. We don't dwell for long on the fundamentals, instead preferring to skip to the fun parts of the system. At any rate, while this book should be enough to get you running, more information on running UNIX will be essential for most readers. See Appendix A, *Sources of Linux Information*, for a list of sources of information.

A Brief History of Linux

UNIX is one of the most popular operating systems worldwide because of its large support base and distribution. It was originally developed as a multitasking system for minicomputers and mainframes in the mid-1970's. But it has since grown to become one of the most widely used operating systems anywhere, despite its sometimes confusing interface and lack of central standardization.

The real reason for UNIX's popularity? Many hackers feel that UNIX is the Right Thing—the One True Operating System. Hence, the development of Linux by an expanding group of UNIX hackers who want to get their hands dirty with their own system.

Versions of UNIX exist for many systems—ranging from personal computers to supercomputers such as the Cray Y-MP. Most versions of UNIX for personal computers are quite expensive and cumbersome. At the time of this writing, a one-machine version of AT&T's System V for the 386 runs at about US $1500.

Linux is a freely distributable version of UNIX developed primarily by Linus Torvalds[*] at the University of Helsinki in Finland. Linux was developed with the help of many UNIX programmers and wizards across the Internet, allowing anyone with enough know-how and gumption the ability to develop and change the system. The Linux kernel uses no code from AT&T or any other proprietary source, and much of the software available for Linux is developed by the GNU project at the Free Software Foundation in Cambridge, Massachusetts. However, programmers all over the world have contributed to the growing pool of Linux software.

Linux was originally developed as a hobby project by Linus. It was inspired by Minix, a small UNIX system developed by Andy Tanenbaum, and the first discussions about Linux were on the Usenet newsgroup *comp.os.minix*. These discussions were concerned mostly with the development of a small, academic UNIX system for Minix users who wanted more.

The very early development of Linux dealt mostly with the task-switching features of the 80386 protected-mode interface, all written in assembly code. Linus writes:

> After that it was plain sailing: hairy coding still, but I had some devices, and debugging was easier. I started using C at this stage, and it certainly speeds up development. This is also when I start to get serious about my megalomaniac ideas to make "a better Minix than Minix." I was hoping I'd be able to recompile *gcc* under Linux some day...

> Two months for basic setup, but then only slightly longer until I had a disk-driver (seriously buggy, but it happened to work on my machine) and a small filesystem. That was about when I made 0.01 available [around late August of 1991]: it wasn't pretty, it had no floppy driver, and it couldn't do much anything. I don't think anybody ever compiled that version. But by then I was hooked, and didn't want to stop until I could chuck out Minix.

No announcement was ever made for Linux version 0.01. The 0.01 sources weren't even executable: they contained only the bare rudiments of the kernel source and assumed that you had access to a Minix machine to compile and play with them.

On 5 October 1991, Linus announced the first "official" version of Linux, version 0.02. At this point, Linus was able to run *bash* (the GNU Bourne Again Shell) and *gcc* (the GNU C compiler), but not very much else was working. Again, this was intended as a hacker's system. The primary focus was kernel development—none of the issues of user support, documentation, distribution, and so on had even

---

[*] His Internet email address, should you have something pressing to say about the kernel, is *torvalds@kruuna.helsinki.fi*.

been addressed. Today, the Linux community still seems to treat these ergonomic issues as secondary to the "real programming"—kernel development.

Linus wrote in *comp.os.minix*,

> Do you pine for the nice days of Minix-1.1, when men were men and wrote their own device drivers? Are you without a nice project and just dying to cut your teeth on a OS you can try to modify for your needs? Are you finding it frustrating when everything works on Minix? No more all-nighters to get a nifty program working? Then this post might be just for you.
>
> As I mentioned a month ago, I'm working on a free version of a Minix-lookalike for AT-386 computers. It has finally reached the stage where it's even usable (though may not be depending on what you want), and I am willing to put out the sources for wider distribution. It is just version 0.02... but I've successfully run *bash*, *gcc*, GNU *make*, GNU *sed*, *compress*, etc. under it.

After version 0.03, Linus bumped the version number up to 0.10, as more people started to work on the system. After several further revisions, Linus increased the version number to 0.95, to reflect his expectation that the system was ready for an "official" release very soon. (Generally, software is not assigned the version number 1.0 until it is theoretically complete or bug-free.) This was in March of 1992. Almost a year and a half later, in late December of 1993, the Linux kernel was still at version 0.99.pl14—asymptotically approaching 1.0. As of the time of this writing, the current kernel version is 1.1 patchlevel 52, and 1.2 is right around the corner.

Linux could not have come into being without the GNU tools created by the Free Software Foundation. Their *gcc* compiler, which we'll discuss in a later chapter, gave life to Linus Torvalds's code. GNU tools have been intertwined with the development of Linux from the beginning.

Berkeley UNIX (BSD) has also played an important role in Linux—not so much in its creation, but in providing the tools that make it popular. Most of the utilities that come with Linux distributions are ported from BSD. Networking daemons and utilities are particularly important. The kernel networking code for Linux was developed from the ground up (two or three times, in fact), but the daemons and utilities are vintage BSD.

Today, Linux is a complete UNIX clone, capable of running the X Window System, TCP/IP, Emacs, UUCP, mail and news software, you name it. Almost all of the major free software packages have been ported to Linux, and commercial software is becoming available. Much more hardware is supported than in original versions of the kernel. Many people have executed benchmarks on 80486 Linux systems and found them comparable with mid-range workstations from Sun Microsystems and Digital Equipment Corporation. Who would have ever guessed that this "little" UNIX clone would have grown up to take on the entire world of personal computing?

Who's Using Linux?

Application developers, network providers, kernel hackers, multimedia authors—these are a few of the categories of people who find that Linux has a particular charm.

UNIX programmers are increasingly using Linux because of its cost—they can pick up a complete programming environment for a few dollars and run it on cheap PC hardware—and because it offers a great basis for portable programs. It's a modern operating system that is POSIX-compliant and looks a lot like System V, so code that works on Linux should work on other contemporary systems. Linux on a modest PC runs faster than many UNIX workstations.

Networking is one of Linux's strengths. It has been adopted with gusto by people who run community networks like Free-Nets, or who want to connect non-profit organizations or loose communities of users through UUCP. Linux makes a good hub for such networks. Since Linux also supports NFS and NIS, you can easily merge a personal computer into a corporate or academic network with other UNIX machines. It is easy to share files, support remote logins, and run windows on other systems.

Kernel hackers were the first to come to Linux—in fact, the ones who helped Linus Torvalds create Linux—and are still a formidable community. If you want to try tuning buffer sizes and the number of table entries to make your applications run a little faster, Linux is one of your best choices. You'll get a lot of sympathy on the net when things go wrong, too.

Finally, Linux is becoming an exciting forum for multimedia. This is because it is compatible with an enormous amount of hardware such as sound cards. Several programming environments, the Andrew Toolkit being the best-known, have been ported to Linux.

As a "real-world" example of Linux's use within the computing community, Linux systems have traveled the high seas of the North Pacific, managing telecommunications and data analysis for an oceanographic research vessel. Linux systems are being used at research stations in Antarctica. As a more mundane example, perhaps, several hospitals are using Linux to maintain patient records. One of the reviewers of this book puts it to use in the U.S. Marine Corps. Linux is proving to be as reliable and useful as other implementations of UNIX.

So Linux is spreading out in many directions. Even naive end-users can certainly enjoy it if they get the support that universities and corporations typically provide their computer users. Configuration and maintenance require some dedication. But Linux proves to be cost-effective, powerful, and empowering for people who like having that extra control over their environments.

System Features

Linux supports most of the features found in other implementations of UNIX, plus quite a few that aren't found elsewhere. This section is a nickel tour of the Linux kernel features.

Linux is a complete multitasking, multi-user operating system (just like all other versions of UNIX). This means that many users can be logged into the same machine at once, running multiple programs simultaneously.

The Linux system is mostly compatible with a number of UNIX standards (inasmuch as UNIX has standards) on the source level, including IEEE POSIX.1, System V, and BSD features. It was developed with source portability in mind: therefore, you will probably find commonly-used features in the Linux system that are shared across multiple implementations. A great deal of free UNIX software available on the Internet and elsewhere compiles on Linux out of the box. In addition, all source code for the Linux system, including the kernel, device drivers, libraries, user programs, and development tools, is freely distributable.

Other specific internal features of Linux include POSIX job control (used by shells such as *csh* and *bash*), pseudoterminals (*pty* devices), and support for national or customized keyboards using dynamically-loadable keyboard drivers. Linux also supports *virtual consoles*, which allow you to switch between multiple login sessions from the system console in text mode. Users of the *screen* program will find the Linux virtual console implementation familiar.

Chapter 2
Chapter 4

Linux supports various filesystem types for storing data. Some filesystems, such as the *ext2fs* filesystem, have been developed specifically for Linux. Other filesystem types, such as the Minix-1 and Xenix filesystems, are also supported. The MS-DOS filesystem has been implemented as well, allowing you to access MS-DOS files on hard drive or floppy directly. The ISO 9660 CD-ROM filesystem type, which reads all standard formats of CD-ROMs, is also supported. We'll talk more about filesystems in Chapter 2, *Obtaining and Installing Linux*, and Chapter 4.

Chapter 7

Linux provides a complete implementation of TCP/IP networking. This includes device drivers for many popular Ethernet cards, SLIP (Serial Line Internet Protocol, allowing you to access a TCP/IP network via a serial connection), PLIP (Parallel Line Internet Protocol), PPP (Point-to-Point Protocol), NFS (Network File System), and so on. The complete range of TCP/IP clients and services is supported, such as FTP, Telnet, NNTP, and SMTP. We'll talk more about networking in Chapter 7, *Networking and Communications*.

The *kernel* is the guts of the operating system itself—it is the code that controls the interface between user programs and hardware devices, the scheduling of processes to achieve multitasking, and many other aspects of the system. The kernel is not a separate process running on the system—instead, you can think of the kernel as a set of routines, constantly in memory, which every process has access to. Kernel routines can be called in a number of ways. One direct method to utilize the kernel is for a process to execute a *system call*, which is a function that causes the kernel to execute some code on behalf of the process. For example, the *read* system call will read data from a file descriptor. To the programmer, this looks like another C function, but in actuality the code for *read* is contained within the kernel.

Kernel code is also executed in other situations. For example, when a hardware device issues an interrupt, the interrupt handler is found within the kernel. When a process takes an action that requires it to wait for results, the kernel steps in and puts the process to sleep, scheduling another process in its place. Similarly, the kernel switches control between processes rapidly, using the clock interrupt (and other means) to trigger a switch from one process to another. This is basically how multitasking is accomplished.

The Linux kernel is known as a "monolithic" kernel, in that all device drivers are part of the kernel proper. Some operating systems employ a "microkernel" architecture whereby device drivers and other code are loaded and executed on demand, and not necessarily always in memory. There are advantages and disadvantages to both designs—the monolithic architecture is more common among UNIX implementations, and is the design employed by classic kernel designs such as BSD. Linux does support loadable device drivers (which can be loaded and unloaded from memory through user commands), which is the subject of the section "Loadable Device Drivers" in Chapter 4.

The kernel is able to emulate 387-FPU instructions itself, so that systems without a math coprocessor can run programs that require floating-point math instructions.

The Linux kernel is developed to use the special protected-mode features of the Intel 80x86 processors. In particular, Linux makes use of the protected-mode descriptor-based memory management paradigm and many of the other advanced features of these processors. Anyone familiar with 80386 protected-mode programming knows that this chip was designed for a multitasking system such as UNIX (or, actually, Multics). Linux exploits this functionality.

The Linux kernel supports demand-paged loaded executables. That is, only those segments of a program that are actually used are read into memory from disk. Also, copy-on-write pages are shared among executables. This means that if several instances of a program are running at once, they will share pages in physical memory, reducing overall memory usage.

In order to increase the amount of available memory, Linux also implements disk paging: that is, up to 256 megabytes of "swap space"[*] can be allocated on disk. When the system requires more physical memory, it will swap out inactive pages to disk, thus allowing you to run larger applications and support more users at

---

[*] Swap space is inappropriately named: entire processes are not swapped, but rather individual pages. Of course, in many cases entire processes will be swapped out, but this is not necessarily always the case.

once. However, swap is no substitute for physical RAM—it is much slower due to the time required to access the disk.

The kernel also implements a unified memory pool for user programs and disk cache. In this way, all free memory is used for caching, and the cache is reduced when running large programs.

Executables use dynamically linked shared libraries, meaning that executables share common library code in a single library file found on disk, not unlike the SunOS shared library mechanism. This allows executable files to occupy much less space on disk, especially those that use many library functions. There are also statically linked libraries for those who wish to use object debugging or maintain "complete" executables without the need for shared libraries to be in place. Linux shared libraries are dynamically linked at run time, allowing the programmer to replace modules of the libraries with their own routines.

Chapter 6

To facilitate debugging, the Linux kernel does core dumps for post-mortem analysis. Using a core dump and an executable linked with debugging support, you can determine what caused a program to crash. We'll talk about this in Chapter 6, *Programming with Linux.*

Software Features

In this section, we'll introduce you to many of the software applications available for Linux, and talk about a number of common computing tasks. After all, the most important part of the system is the wide range of software available for it. It is even more impressive that most of this software is freely distributable.

Basic Commands and Utilities

Virtually every utility that you would expect to find on standard implementations of UNIX has been ported to Linux. This includes basic commands such as *ls, awk, tr, sed, bc, more,* and so on. You name it, Linux has it. Therefore, you can expect your familiar working environment on other UNIX systems to be duplicated on Linux. All of the standard commands and utilities are there. (Novice Linux users should see Chapter 3 for an introduction to these basic UNIX commands.)

Chapter 3

Many text editors are available, including *vi, ex, pico,* and *jove,* as well as GNU Emacs and variants such as Lucid Emacs (which incorporates extensions for use under the X Window System) and *joe.* Whatever text editor you're accustomed to using has more than likely been ported to Linux.

The choice of a text editor is an interesting one. Many UNIX users still use "simple" editors such as *vi* (in fact, the author wrote this book using *vi* under Linux). However, *vi* has many limitations, due to its age, and more modern (and complex) editors such as Emacs are gaining popularity. Emacs supports a complete LISP-based macro language and interpreter, a powerful command syntax, and other

Chapter 5

fun-filled extensions. Emacs macro packages exist to allow you to read electronic mail and news, edit the contents of directories, and even engage in an artificially intelligent psychotherapy session (indispensable for stressed-out Linux hackers). In Chapter 5, *Power Tools*, we include a complete *vi* tutorial and describe Emacs in detail.

One interesting note is that most of the basic Linux utilities are GNU software. These GNU utilities support advanced features not found in the standard versions from BSD or AT&T. For example, GNU's version of the *vi* editor, *elvis*, includes a structured macro language, which differs from the original AT&T implementation. However, the GNU utilities strive to remain compatible with their BSD and System V counterparts. Many people consider the GNU versions of these programs superior to the originals.

The most important utility to many users is the *shell*. The shell is a program that reads and executes commands from the user. In addition, many shells provide features such as *job control* (allowing the user to manage several running processes at once—not as Orwellian as it sounds), input and output redirection, and a command language for writing *shell scripts*. A shell script is a file containing a program in the shell command language, analogous to a "batch file" under MS-DOS.

There are many types of shells available for Linux. The most important difference between shells is the command language. For example, the C shell (*csh*) uses a command language somewhat like the C programming language. The classic Bourne shell uses a different command language. One's choice of a shell is often based on the command language that it provides. The shell that you use defines, to some extent, your working environment under Linux.

No matter what UNIX shell you're accustomed to, some version of it has probably been ported to Linux. The most popular shell is the GNU Bourne Again Shell (*bash*), a Bourne shell variant that includes many advanced features, such as job control, command history, command and filename completion, an Emacs-like interface for editing the command line, and powerful extensions to the standard Bourne shell language. Another popular shell is *tcsh*, a version of the C Shell with advanced functionality similar to that found in *bash*. Other shells include the Korn shell (*ksh*), BSD's *ash*, *zsh*, a small Bourne-like shell, and *rc*, the Plan 9 shell.

What's so important about these basic utilities? Linux gives you the unique opportunity to tailor a custom system to your needs. For example, if you're the only person who uses your system, and you prefer to exclusively use the *vi* editor and the *bash* shell, there's no reason to install other editors or shells. The "do it yourself" attitude is prevalent among Linux hackers and users.

Text Processing and Word Processing

Almost every computer user has a need for some kind of document preparation system. (How many computer enthusiasts do you know who still use pen and paper? Not many, we'll wager.) In the PC world, *word processing* is the norm: it involves editing and manipulating text (often in a "What-You-See-Is-What-You-Get" (*WYSIWYG*) environment) and producing printed copies of the text, complete with figures, tables, and other garnishes.

In the UNIX world, *text processing* is much more common, which is quite different than the classical concept of word processing. With a text processing system, text is entered by the author using a "typesetting language," which describes how the text should be formatted. Instead of entering the text within a special word processing environment, the source may be modified with any text editor such as *vi* or Emacs. Once the source text (in the typesetting language) is complete, the user formats the text with a separate program, which converts the source to a format suitable for printing. This is somewhat analogous to programming in a language such as C, and "compiling" the document into a printable form.

There are many text processing systems available for Linux. One is *groff*, the GNU version of the classic *troff* text formatter originally developed by Bell Labs and still used on many UNIX systems worldwide. Another modern text processing system is TEX, developed by Donald Knuth of computer science fame. Dialects of TEX, such as LATEX, are also available.

Text processors such as TEX and *groff* differ mostly in the syntax of their formatting languages. The choice of one formatting system over another is also based upon what utilities are available to satisfy your needs, as well as personal taste.

For example, some people consider the *groff* formatting language to be a bit obscure, so they use TEX, which is more readable by humans. However, *groff* is capable of producing plain ASCII output, viewable on a terminal, while TEX is intended primarily for output to a printing device. Still, various programs exist to produce plain ASCII from TEX-formatted documents, or to convert TEX to *groff*, for example.

Another text processing system is Texinfo, an extension to TEX used for software documentation by the Free Software Foundation. Texinfo is capable of producing a printed document, or an online-browsable hypertext "Info" document from a single source file. Info files are the main format of documentation used by GNU software such as Emacs.

Text processors are used widely in the computing community for producing papers, theses, magazine articles, and books (in fact, this book was written in LATEX and printed from *groff*). The ability to process the source language as a plain text file opens the door to many extensions to the text processor itself. Because source documents are not stored in an obscure format, readable only by a particular word processor, programmers are able to write parsers and translators for the formatting language, extending the system.

What does such a formatting language look like? In general, the formatting language source consists mostly of the text itself, along with "control codes" to produce a particular effect, such as changing fonts, setting margins, creating lists, and so on.

As an example, take the following text:

Mr. Torvalds:

We are very upset with your current plans to implement *post-hypnotic suggestion* in the **Linux** terminal driver code. We feel this way for three reasons:

1. Planting subliminal messages in the terminal driver is not only immoral, it is a waste of time;

2. It has been proven that "post-hypnotic suggestions" are ineffective when used upon unsuspecting UNIX hackers;

3. We have already implemented high-voltage electric shocks, as a security measure, in the code for `login`.

We hope you will reconsider.

This text would appear in the LATEX formatting language as the following:

```
Mr. Torvalds:

We are very upset with your current plans to implement {\em post-hypnotic
suggestion\/} in the {\bf Linux} terminal driver code. We feel this
way for three reasons:
\begin{enumerate}
\item Planting subliminal messages in the terminal driver is not only
     immoral, it is a waste of time;
\item It has been proven that ``post-hypnotic suggestions'' are ineffective
     when used upon unsuspecting UNIX hackers;
\item We have already implemented high-voltage electric shocks, as a
     security measure, in the code for {\tt login}.
\end{enumerate}
We hope you will reconsider.
```

The author enters the above "source" text using any text editor, and generates the formatted output by processing the source with LATEX. At first glance, the typesetting language may appear to be obscure, but it's actually quite easy to learn. Using a text processing system enforces typographical standards when writing. For example, all enumerated lists within a document will look the same, unless the author modifies the definition of the enumerated list "environment." The primary goal is to allow the author to concentrate on writing the actual text, instead of worrying about typesetting conventions.

WYSIWYG word processors are attractive for many reasons; they provide a powerful (and sometimes complex) visual interface for editing the document. However, this interface is inherently limited to those aspects of text layout that are accessible to the user. For example, many word processors provide a special "format language" for producing complicated expressions such as mathematical formulae. This is identical text processing, albeit on a much smaller scale.

The subtle benefit of text processing is that the system allows you to specify exactly what you mean. Also, text processing systems allow you to edit the source text with any text editor, and the source is easily converted to other formats. The tradeoff for this flexibility and power is the lack of a WYSIWYG interface.

Many users of word processors are used to seeing the formatted text as they edit it. On the other hand, when writing with a text processor, one generally does not worry about how the text will appear when formatted. The writer learns to expect how the text should look from the formatting commands used in the source.

There are programs which allow you to view the formatted document on a graphics display before printing. For example, the *xdvi* program displays a "device independent" file generated by the TEX system under the X Window System. Other software applications, such as *xfig*, provide a WYSIWYG graphics interface for drawing figures and diagrams, which are subsequently converted to the text processing language for inclusion in your document.

Admittedly, text processors such as *nroff* were around long before word processing was available. However, many people still prefer to use text processing, because it is more versatile and independent of a graphics environment. In either case, the *idoc* word processor is also available for Linux, and before long we expect to see commercial word processors becoming available as well. If you absolutely don't want to give up word processing for text processing, you can always run MS-DOS, or some other operating system, in addition to Linux.

There are many other text processing utilities available. The powerful METAFONT system, used to design fonts for TEX, is included with the Linux port of TEX. Other programs include *ispell*, an interactive spell checker and corrector; *makeindex*, used for generating indices in LATEX documents; and many *groff* and TEX-based macro packages for formatting various types of documents and mathematical texts. Conversion programs are available to translate between TEX or *groff* source and a myriad of other formats.

In Chapter 5 we discuss LATEX, *groff*, and other text-formatting tools in detail.

Chapter 5

Programming Languages and Utilities

Linux provides a complete UNIX programming environment, including all of the standard libraries, programming tools, compilers, and debuggers that you would expect to find on other UNIX systems. Within the UNIX software development world, applications and systems programming is usually done in C or C++. The standard C and C++ compiler for Linux is GNU's *gcc*, which is an advanced, modern compiler supporting many options. It is also capable of compiling C++ (including AT&T 3.0 features) as well as Objective-C, another object-oriented dialect of C.

Besides C and C++, many other compiled and interpreted programming languages have been ported to Linux, such as Smalltalk, FORTRAN, Pascal, LISP, Scheme, and Ada (if you're masochistic enough to program in Ada—we're not going to stop you). In addition, various assemblers for writing protected-mode 80386 code are available, as are UNIX hacking favorites such as Perl (the script language to end all script languages) and Tcl/Tk (a shell-like command processing system that includes support for developing simple X Window System applications).

The advanced *gdb* debugger has been ported, which allows you to step through a program to find bugs, or examine the cause for a crash using a core dump. *gprof*, a profiling utility, will give you performance statistics for your program, letting you know where your program is spending most of its time executing. The Emacs text editor provides an interactive editing and compilation environment for various programming languages. Other tools include GNU *make* and *imake*, used to manage compilation of large applications, and RCS, a system for source locking and revision control.

Linux is ideal for developing UNIX applications. It provides a modern programming environment with all of the bells and whistles. Professional UNIX programmers and system administrators can use Linux to develop software at home, and then transfer the software to UNIX systems at work. This not only can save a great deal of time and money, but will also let you work in the comfort of your own home.[*] Computer science students can use Linux to learn UNIX programming and to explore other aspects of the system, such as kernel architecture.

With Linux, not only do you have access to the complete set of libraries and programming utilities, but you also have the complete kernel and library source code at your fingertips.

Chapter 6

Chapter 6 is devoted to the programming languages and tools available for Linux.

The X Window System

The X Window System is the standard graphics interface for UNIX machines. It is a powerful environment supporting many applications. Using X, the user can have multiple terminal windows on the screen at once, each one containing a different login session. A pointing device such as a mouse is generally used with the X interface.

Many X-specific applications have been written, such as games, graphics utilities, programming and documentation tools, and so on. With Linux and X, your system is a bona fide workstation. Coupled with TCP/IP networking, you can even display X applications running on other machines on your Linux display, as is possible with other systems running X.

The X Window System was originally developed at MIT and is freely distributable. However, may commercial vendors have distributed proprietary enhancements to the original X software. The version of X available for Linux is known as XFree86, a port of X11R6 made freely distributable for 80386-based UNIX systems such as

---

* The author uses his Linux system to develop and test X applications at home, which can be directly compiled on workstations elsewhere.

Linux. XFree86 supports a wide range of video hardware, including VGA, Super VGA, and a number of accelerated video adaptors. This is a complete distribution of the X software, containing the X server itself, many applications and utilities, programming libraries, and documentation.

Standard X applications include *xterm* (a terminal emulator used for most text-based applications within an X window), *xdm* (the X Session Manager, which handles logins), *xclock* (a simple clock display), *xman* (an X-based manual page reader), and more. The many X applications available for Linux are too numerous to mention here, but the base XFree86 distribution includes the "standard" applications found in the original MIT release. Many others are available separately, and theoretically any application written for X should compile cleanly under Linux.

The look and feel of the X interface is controlled to a large extent by the *window manager*. This friendly program is in charge of the placement of windows, the user interface for resizing, iconifying, and moving windows, the appearance of window frames, and so on. The standard XFree86 distribution includes *twm*, the classic MIT window manager, although more advanced window managers such as the Open Look Virtual Window Manager (*olvwm*) are available as well. One window manager that is popular among Linux users is *fvwm*. This is a small window manager, requiring less than half of the memory used by *twm*. It provides a 3-D appearance for windows, as well as a virtual desktop—if the user moves the mouse to the edge of the screen, the entire desktop is shifted as if the display were much larger than it actually is. *fvwm* is greatly customizable and allows all functions to be accessed from the keyboard as well as from the mouse. Many Linux distributions use *fvwm* as the standard window manager.

The XFree86 distribution contains programming libraries and include files for those wily programmers who wish to develop X applications. Various widget sets, such as Athena, Open Look, and Xaw3D, are supported. All of the standard fonts, bitmaps, manual pages, and documentation are included. PEX (a programming interface for 3-D graphics) is also supported.

Many X applications programmers use the proprietary Motif widget set for development. Several vendors sell single and multiple-user licenses for a binary version of Motif for Linux. Because Motif itself is relatively expensive, not many Linux users own it. However, binaries statically linked with Motif routines may be freely distributed. Therefore, if you write a program using Motif and wish to distribute it freely, you may provide a binary so that users without Motif can use the program.

The only major caveats with X are the hardware and memory requirements. A 386 with 4 megabytes of RAM is capable of running X, but 8 megabytes or more of physical RAM are needed to use it comfortably. A faster processor is nice to have as well, but having enough physical RAM is much more important. In addition, to achieve really slick video performance, an accelerated video card (such as a local bus S3-chipset card) is strongly recommended. Performance ratings in excess of

140,000 xstones have been achieved with Linux and XFree86. With sufficient hardware, you'll find that running X and Linux is as fast, or faster, than running X on other UNIX workstations.

Chapter 5

In Chapter 5, we'll discuss how to install and use the X Window System on your Linux machine.

Networking

Interested in communicating with the world? Yes? No? Maybe? Linux supports the two primary networking protocols for UNIX systems: TCP/IP and UUCP. TCP/IP (Transmission Control Protocol/Internet Protocol, for acronym aficionados) is the set of networking paradigms that allow systems all over the world to communicate on a single network known as the Internet. With Linux, TCP/IP, and a connection to the network, you can communicate with users and machines across the Internet via electronic mail, Usenet news, file transfers with FTP, and more. There are many Linux systems currently on the Internet.

Most TCP/IP networks use Ethernet as the physical network transport. Linux supports many popular Ethernet cards and interfaces for personal computers, including the D-Link pocket Ethernet adaptor for laptops.

However, because not everyone has an Ethernet drop at home, Linux also supports SLIP (Serial Line Internet Protocol), which allows you to connect to the Internet via modem. In order to use SLIP, you'll need to have access to a SLIP server, a machine connected to the network which allows dial-in access. Many businesses and universities provide such SLIP servers. In fact, if your Linux system has an Ethernet connection as well as a modem, you can configure it as a SLIP server for other hosts.

NFS (Network File System) allows your system to seamlessly share files with other machines on the network. FTP (File Transfer Protocol) allows you to use *sendmail* and *smail*, which are systems for sending and receiving electronic mail using the SMTP protocol; NNTP-based electronic news systems such as C News and INN; *telnet*, *rlogin*, and *rsh*, which allow you to log in and execute commands on other machines on the network; and *finger*, which allows you to get information on other Internet users. There are tons of TCP/IP-based applications and protocols out there.

A full range of mail and news readers are available for Linux, such as *Elm*, *Pine*, *rn*, *nn*, and *tin*. Whatever your preference, you can configure your Linux system to send and receive electronic mail and news from all over the world.

If you have experience with TCP/IP applications on other UNIX systems, Linux will be very familiar to you. The system provides a standard socket programming interface, so virtually any program that uses TCP/IP can be ported to Linux. The Linux X server also supports TCP/IP, allowing you to display applications running on other systems on your Linux display.

Chapter 7

In Chapter 7, we'll discuss the configuration and setup of TCP/IP, including SLIP, for Linux. We'll also discuss configuration of mail software.

UUCP (UNIX-to-UNIX Copy) is an older mechanism used to transfer files. UUCP machines are connected to each other over phone lines via modem, but UUCP is able to transport over a TCP/IP network as well. If you do not have access to a TCP/IP network or a SLIP server, you can configure your system to send and receive files and electronic mail using UUCP. See Chapter 7, where we discuss UUCP concepts and configuration.

Telecommunications and BBS Software

If you have a modem, you will be able to communicate with other machines using one of the telecommunications packages available for Linux. Many people use telecommunications software to access bulletin board systems (BBSes), as well as commercial online services such as Prodigy, CompuServe, and America On-Line. Other people use their modems to connect to a UNIX system at work or school. You can even use your modem and Linux system to send and receive facsimiles. Telecommunications software under Linux is very similar to that found under MS-DOS or other operating systems. Anyone who has ever used a telecommunications package will find the Linux equivalent familiar.

Chapter 7

One of the most popular communications packages for Linux is Seyon, an X application providing a customizable, ergonomic interface, with built-in support for various file transfer protocols such as Kermit, Zmodem, and so on. Other telecommunications programs include C-Kermit, *pcomm*, and *minicom*. These are similar to communications programs found on other operating systems and are quite easy to use. We discuss Kermit and ZModem in more detail in the section "File Transfer and Remote Terminal Software" in Chapter 7.

If you do not have access to a SLIP server (see the previous section), you can use *term* to multiplex your serial line. *term* will allow you to open multiple login sessions over the modem connection to a remote machine. *term* will also allow you to redirect X client connections to your local X server through the serial line, allowing you to display remote X applications on your Linux system. Another software package, KA9Q, implements a similar SLIP-like interface.

Running a bulletin board system (BBS) is a favorite hobby (and means of income) for many people. Linux supports a wide range of BBS software, most of which is more powerful than what is available for other operating systems. With a phone line, a modem, and Linux, you can turn your system into a BBS, providing dial-in access to your system to users worldwide. BBS software for Linux includes XBBS and the UniBoard BBS packages.

Most BBS software locks the user into a menu-based system where only certain functions and applications are available. An alternative to BBS access is full UNIX access, which would allow users to dial into your system and log in as a regular user. While this would require a fair amount of maintenance on the part of the system administrator, it can be done, and providing public UNIX access from your Linux system is not difficult to do. Along with a TCP/IP network, you can provide electronic mail and news access to users on your system.

If you do not have access to a TCP/IP network or UUCP feed, Linux will also allow you to communicate with a number of BBS networks, such as FidoNet, with which you can exchange electronic news and mail via the phone line.

Interfacing with MS-DOS

Various utilities exist to interface with the world of MS-DOS. The most well-known application is the Linux MS-DOS Emulator, which allows you to run many MS-DOS applications directly from Linux. Although Linux and MS-DOS are completely different operating systems, the 80386 protected-mode environment allows certain tasks to behave as if they were running in 8086-emulation mode, as MS-DOS applications do.

The MS-DOS emulator is still under development, yet many popular applications run under it. Understandably, however, MS-DOS applications that use bizarre or esoteric features of the system may never be supported, because it is only an emulator. For example, you wouldn't expect to be able to run any programs which use 80386 protected-mode features, such as Microsoft Windows (in 386 enhanced mode, that is).

Applications that run successfully under the Linux MS-DOS Emulator include 4DOS (a command interpreter), Foxpro 2.0, Harvard Graphics, MathCad, Stacker 3.1, Turbo Assembler, Turbo C/C++, Turbo Pascal, Microsoft Windows 3.0 (in *real* mode), and WordPerfect 5.1. Standard MS-DOS commands and utilities (such as *PKZIP*, and so on) work with the emulator as well.

The MS-DOS Emulator is meant mostly as an ad hoc solution for those people who need MS-DOS only for a few applications, but use Linux for everything else. It's not meant to be a complete implementation of MS-DOS. Of course, if the Emulator doesn't satisfy your needs, you can always run MS-DOS as well as Linux on the same system. Using the LILO boot loader, you can specify at boot time which operating system to start. Linux can coexist with other operating systems, such as OS/2, as well.

Linux provides a seamless interface for transferring files between Linux and MS-DOS. You can mount an MS-DOS partition or floppy under Linux, and directly access MS-DOS files as you would any other.

Currently under development is a project known as WINE—a Microsoft Windows emulator for the X Window System under Linux. Once WINE is complete, users will be able to run Microsoft Windows applications directly from Linux. This is similar to the proprietary WABI Windows emulator from Sun Microsystems. At the time of this writing, WINE is still in the early stages of development, but the outlook is good.

Chapter 5

We'll show you how to use the MS-DOS emulator in the section "Linux, DOS, and Foreign OS Compatibility" in Chapter 5, along with other juicy ways to interface Linux with MS-DOS.

Other Applications

A host of miscellaneous applications are available for Linux, as one would expect from such a hodgepodge operating system. Linux's primary focus is currently for personal UNIX computing, but this is rapidly changing. Business and scientific software is expanding, and commercial software vendors are beginning to contribute to the growing pool of applications.

Several relational databases are available for Linux, including Postgres, Ingres, and Mbase. These are full-featured, professional client/server database applications similar to those found on other UNIX platforms. *rdb*, a commercial database system, is available as well.

Scientific computing applications include FELT (a finite element analysis tool), *gnuplot* (a plotting and data analysis application), Octave (a symbolic mathematics package, similar to MATLAB), *xspread* (a spreadsheet calculator), *xfractint* (an X-based port of the popular Fractint fractal generator), *xlispstat* (a statistics package), and more. Other applications include Spice (a circuit design and analysis tool) and Khoros (an image/digital signal processing and visualization system).

Of course, there are many more such applications that have been, and can be, ported to run on Linux. Whatever your field, porting UNIX-based applications to Linux should be straightforward. Linux provides a complete UNIX programming interface, sufficient to serve as the base for any scientific application.

As with any operating system, Linux has its share of games. These include classic text-based dungeon games such as Nethack and Moria; MUDs (multi-user dungeons, which allow many users to interact in a text-based adventure) such as DikuMUD and TinyMUD; and a slew of X games such as *xtetris*, *netrek*, and *Xboard* (the X11 front-end to *gnuchess*). The popular shoot-em-up arcade-style Doom has also been ported to Linux.

For audiophiles, Linux has support for various sound cards and related software, such as CDplayer (a program which can control a CD-ROM drive as a conventional CD player, surprisingly enough), MIDI sequencers and editors (allowing you to compose music for playback through a synthesizer or other MIDI-controlled instrument), and sound editors for digitized sounds.

Linux
Software Map

Can't find the application you're looking for? The Linux Software Map, described in Appendix A, contains a list of many software packages that have been written and ported to Linux. While this list is far from complete, it contains a great deal of software. Take a look at it just to see the enormous amount of material that has already been ported—the size of the map is itself a wonderful advertisement for Linux. Another way to find Linux applications is to look at the *INDEX* files found on Linux FTP sites, if you have Internet access. Just by poking around you'll find a great deal of software just waiting to be played with.

If you absolutely can't find what you need, you can always attempt to port the application from another platform to Linux. Or, if all else fails, you can write the application yourself.

If it's a commercial application you're looking for, there may be a free "clone" available. Or, you can encourage the software company to consider releasing a Linux binary version. Several individuals have contacted software companies, asking them to port their applications to Linux, and have met with various degrees of success.

About Linux's Copyright

Linux is covered by what is known as the GNU *General Public License*, or *GPL*. The GPL was developed for the GNU project by the Free Software Foundation. It makes a number of provisions for the distribution and modification of "free software." "Free" in this sense refers to freedom, not just cost. The GPL has always been subject to misinterpretation, and we hope that this summary will help you to understand the extent and goals of the GPL and its effect on Linux. A complete copy of the GPL is included in Appendix E, *The GNU General Public License*.

Appendix E

Originally, Linus Torvalds released Linux under a license more restrictive than the GPL, which allowed the software to be freely distributed and modified, but prevented any money changing hands for its distribution and use. The GPL allows people to sell and make profit from free software, but does not allow them to restrict the right for others to distribute the software in any way.

First, it should be explained that "free software" covered by the GPL is *not* in the public domain. Public domain software is software that is not copyrighted, and is literally owned by the public. Software covered by the GPL, on the other hand, is copyrighted to the author or authors. This means that the software is protected by standard international copyright laws and that the author of the software is legally defined. Just because the software may be freely distributed does not mean that it is in the public domain.

GPL-licensed software is also not "shareware." Generally, "shareware" software is owned and copyrighted by the author, but the author requires users to send in money for its use after distribution. On the other hand, software covered by the GPL may be distributed and used free of charge.

The GPL also allows people to take and modify free software, and distribute their own versions of the software. However, any derived works from GPL software must also be covered by the GPL. In other words, a company could not take Linux, modify it, and sell it under a restrictive license. If any software is derived from Linux, that software must be covered by the GPL as well.

People and organizations can distribute GPL software for a fee, and even make a profit from its sale and distribution. However, in selling GPL software, the distributor cannot take those rights away from the purchaser; that is, if you purchase GPL software from some source, you may distribute the software for free, or sell it yourself as well.

This might sound like a contradiction at first. Why sell software for profit when the GPL allows anyone to obtain it for free? As an example, let's say that some company decided to bundle a large amount of free software on a CD-ROM and distribute it. That company would need to charge for the overhead of producing and distributing the CD-ROM, and the company may even decide to make profit from the sales of software. This is allowed by the GPL.

Organizations that sell free software must follow certain restrictions set forth in the GPL. First, they cannot restrict the rights of users who purchase the software. This means that if you buy a CD-ROM of GPL software, you can copy and distribute that CD-ROM free of charge, or resell it yourself. Secondly, distributors must make it obvious to users that the software is indeed covered by the GPL. Thirdly, distributors must provide, free of charge, the complete source code for the software being distributed. This will allow anyone who purchases GPL software to make modifications of that software.

Allowing a company to distribute and sell free software is a very good thing. Not everyone has access to the Internet to download software, such as Linux, for free. The GPL allows companies to sell and distribute software to those people who do not have free (cost-wise) access to the software. For example, many organizations sell Linux on diskette, tape, or CD-ROM via mail order, and make profit from these sales. The developers of Linux may never see any of this profit; that is the understanding that is reached between the developer and the distributor when software is licensed by the GPL. In other words, Linus knew that companies may wish to sell Linux, and that he may not see a penny of the profits from those sales.

In the free software world, the important issue is not money. The goal of free software is always to develop and distribute fantastic software and to allow anyone to obtain and use it. In the next section, we'll discuss how this applies to the development of Linux.

The Design and Philosophy of Linux

When new users encounter Linux, they often have a few misconceptions and false expectations of the system. Linux is a unique operating system, and it is important to understand its philosophy and design in order to use it effectively. Time enough for a soapbox. Even if you are an aged UNIX guru, what follows is probably of interest to you.

In commercial UNIX development houses, the entire system is developed with a rigorous policy of quality assurance, source and revision control systems, documentation, and bug reporting and resolution. Developers are not allowed to add features or to change key sections of code on a whim: they must validate the change as a response to a bug report and consequently "check in" all changes to the source control system, so that the changes can be backed out if necessary. Each developer is assigned one or more parts of the system code, and only that developer may alter those sections of the code while it is "checked out."

Internally, the quality assurance department runs rigorous regression test suites on each new pass of the operating system and reports any bugs. It is the responsibility of the developers to fix these bugs as reported. A complicated system of statistical analysis is employed to ensure that a certain percentage of bugs are fixed before the next release, and that the operating system as a whole passes certain release criteria.

In all, the process used by commercial UNIX developers to maintain and support their code is very complicated, and quite reasonably so. The company must have quantitative proof that the next revision of the operating system is ready to be shipped; hence the gathering and analysis of statistics about the operating system's performance. It is a big job to develop a commercial UNIX system, often large enough to employ hundreds (if not thousands) of programmers, testers, documenters, and administrative personnel. Of course, no two commercial UNIX vendors are alike, but you get the general picture.

With Linux, you can throw out the entire concept of organized development, source control systems, structured bug reporting, or statistical analysis. Linux is, and more than likely always will be, a hacker's operating system.[*]

Linux is primarily developed as a group effort by volunteers on the Internet from all over the world. There is no single organization responsible for developing the system. For the most part, the Linux community communicates via various mailing lists and Usenet newsgroups. A number of conventions have sprung up around the development effort: for example, anyone wishing to have their code included in the "official" kernel should mail it to Linus Torvalds. He will test it and include it in the kernel (as long as it doesn't break things or go against the overall design of the system, he will more than likely include it).

The system itself is designed with a very open-ended, feature-minded approach. While recently the number of new features and critical changes to the system has diminished, the general rule is that a new version of the kernel will be released about every few months (sometimes even more frequently than this). Of course, this is a very rough figure; it depends on a several factors including the number of bugs to be fixed, the amount of feedback from users testing pre-release versions of the code, and the amount of sleep that Linus has had this week.

---

[*] What I mean by "hacker" is a feverishly dedicated programmer, a person who enjoys exploiting computers and generally doing interesting things with them. This is in contrast to the common connotation of "hacker" as a computer wrongdoer or outlaw.

Suffice it to say that not every single bug has been fixed, and not every problem ironed out between releases. As long as the system appears to be free of critical or oft-manifesting bugs, it is considered "stable" and new revisions will be released. The thrust behind Linux development is not an effort to release perfect, bug-free code; it is to develop a free implementation of UNIX. Linux is for the developers, more than anyone else.

Anyone who has a new feature or software application to add to the system generally makes it available in an "alpha" stage—that is, a stage for testing by those brave or unwary users who want to bash out problems with the initial code. Because the Linux community is largely based on the Internet, alpha software is usually uploaded to one or more of the various Linux FTP sites (see Appendix A) and a message posted to one of the Linux Usenet newsgroups about how to get and test the code. Users who download and test alpha software can then mail results, bug fixes, or questions to the author.

Appendix A

After the initial problems in the alpha code have been fixed, the code enters a "beta" stage, in which it is usually considered stable but not complete (that is, it works, but not all of the features may be present). Otherwise, it may go directly to a "final" stage in which the software is considered complete and usable. For kernel code, once it is complete, the developer may ask Linus to include it in the standard kernel, or as an optional add-on feature to the kernel.

Keep in mind that these are only conventions—not rules. Some people feel so confident with their software that they don't need to release an alpha or test version. It is always up to the developer to make these decisions.

You might be amazed that such a nonstructured system of volunteers programming and debugging a complete UNIX system could get anything done at all. As it turns out, it is one of the most efficient and motivated development efforts ever employed. The entire Linux kernel was written *from scratch*, without employing any code from proprietary sources. A great deal of work was put forth by volunteers to port all the free software under the sun to the Linux system. Libraries were written and ported, filesystems developed, and hardware drivers written for many popular devices.

The Linux software is generally released as a *distribution*, which is a set of prepackaged software making up an entire system. It would be quite difficult for most users to build a complete system from the ground up, starting with the kernel, adding utilities, and installing all of the necessary software by hand. Instead, there are a number of software distributions including everything that you need to install and run a complete system. Again, there is no standard distribution—there are many, each with their own advantages and disadvantages. We'll talk more about the various available Linux distributions in Appendix B, *Linux Vendor List.*

Appendix B

Despite the completeness of the Linux software, you will still need a bit of UNIX know-how to install and run a complete system. No distribution of Linux is completely bug-free, so you may be required to fix small problems by hand after installation.

Hints for UNIX Novices

Installing and using your own Linux system does not require a great deal of background in UNIX. In fact, many UNIX novices successfully install Linux on their systems. This is a worthwhile learning experience, but keep in mind that it can be very frustrating to some. If you're lucky, you will be able to install and start using your Linux system without any UNIX background. However, once you are ready to delve into the more complex tasks of running Linux—installing new software, recompiling the kernel, and so forth—having background knowledge in UNIX is going to be a necessity.

Chapter 3
Chapter 4

Fortunately, by running your own Linux system you will be able to learn the essentials of UNIX necessary for these tasks. This book contains a good deal of information to help you get started. Chapter 3 is a tutorial covering UNIX basics, and Chapter 4 contains information on Linux system administration. You may wish to read these chapters before you attempt to install Linux at all—the information contained therein will prove to be invaluable should you run into problems.

Nobody can expect to go from being a UNIX novice to a UNIX system administrator overnight. No implementation of UNIX is expected to run trouble and maintenance free. You must be aptly prepared for the journey which lies ahead. Otherwise, if you're new to UNIX, you may very well become overly frustrated with the system.

Hints for UNIX Gurus

Even those people with years of UNIX programming and system administration experience may need assistance before they are able to pick up and install Linux. There are still aspects of the system that UNIX wizards will need to be familiar with before diving in. For one thing, Linux is not a commercial UNIX system. It does not attempt to uphold the same standards as other UNIX systems you may have come across. To be more specific, while stability is an important factor in the development of Linux, it is not the *only* factor.

More important, perhaps, is functionality. In many cases, new code will make it into the standard kernel even though it is still buggy and not functionally complete. The assumption is that it is more important to release code which users can test and use than delay a release until it is "complete." As an example, WINE (the Microsoft Windows Emulator for Linux) had an "official" alpha release before it was completely tested. In this way, the Linux community at large had a chance to work with the code, test it, and help develop it, while those who found the alpha code "good enough" for their needs could use it. Commercial UNIX vendors rarely, if ever, release software in this manner.

If you have been a UNIX system administrator for more than a decade, and have used every commercial UNIX system under the Sun (no pun intended), Linux may take some getting used to. The system is very modern and dynamic. A new kernel release is made approximately every few months. New software is constantly being released. One day your system may be completely up to date with the current trend, and the next day the same system is considered to be in the Stone Age.

With all of this dynamic activity, how can you be expected to keep up with the ever-changing Linux world? For the most part, it is best to upgrade incrementally; that is, upgrade only those parts of the system that *need* upgrading, and then only when you think an upgrade is necessary. For example, if you never use Emacs, there is little reason to continuously install every new release of Emacs on your system. Furthermore, even if you are an avid Emacs user, there is usually no reason to upgrade it unless you find that some feature is missing that is in the next release. There is little or no reason to always be on top of the newest version of software.

We hope that Linux will meet or exceed your expectations of a home-brew UNIX system. At the very core of Linux is the spirit of free software, of constant development and growth. The Linux community favors expansion over stability, and that is a difficult concept to swallow for many people, especially those steeped in the world of commercial UNIX. You cannot expect Linux to be perfect; nothing ever is in the free software world. However, we believe that Linux really is as complete and useful as any other implementation of UNIX.

Differences Between Linux and Other Operating Systems

It is important to understand the differences between Linux and other operating systems, such as MS-DOS, OS/2, and other implementations of UNIX for the personal computer. First of all, it should be made clear that Linux will coexist happily with other operating systems on the same machine—that is, you can run MS-DOS and OS/2 along with Linux on the same system without problems. There are even ways to interact between the various operating systems, as we'll see.

Why Use Linux?

Why use Linux instead of a well-known, well-tested, and well-documented commercial operating system? We could give you a thousand reasons. One of the most important, however, is that Linux is an excellent choice for personal UNIX computing. If you're a UNIX software developer, why use MS-DOS at home? Linux will allow you to develop and test UNIX software on your PC, including database and X applications. If you're a student, chances are that your university computing system runs UNIX. With Linux, you can run your own UNIX system and tailor it to your own needs. Installing and running Linux is also an excellent way to learn UNIX if you don't have access to other UNIX machines.

But let's not lose perspective. Linux isn't just for personal UNIX users. It is robust and complete enough to handle large tasks, as well as distributed computing needs. Many businesses—especially small ones—are moving to Linux in lieu of other UNIX-based workstation environments. Universities are finding Linux to be perfect for teaching courses in operating systems design. Larger commercial software vendors are starting to realize the opportunities that a free operating system can provide.

Linux Versus MS-DOS

It's not uncommon to run both Linux and MS-DOS on the same system. Many Linux users rely on MS-DOS for applications such as word processing. While Linux provides its own analogues for these applications (for example, TEX), there are various reasons why a particular user would want to run MS-DOS as well as Linux. If your entire dissertation is written using WordPerfect for MS-DOS, you may not be able to easily convert it to TEX or some other format. There are many commercial applications for MS-DOS that aren't available for Linux, and there's no reason why you can't use both.

As you might know, MS-DOS does not fully utilize the functionality of the 80x86 processor. On the other hand, Linux runs completely in the processor's protected mode and exploits all of the features of the processor. You can directly access all of your available memory (and beyond, using virtual RAM).

We could debate the pros and cons of MS-DOS and Linux for pages on end. However, suffice it to say that Linux and MS-DOS are completely different entities. MS-DOS is inexpensive (compared to other commercial operating systems) and has a strong foothold in the PC computing world. No other operating system for the PC has reached the level of popularity of MS-DOS—largely because the cost of these other operating systems is unapproachable to most personal computer users. Very few PC users can imagine spending $1000 or more on the operating system alone. Linux, however, is free, and you finally have the chance to decide.

We will allow you to make your own judgments of Linux and MS-DOS based on your expectations and needs. Linux is not for everybody. If you have always wanted to run a complete UNIX system at home, without the high cost of other UNIX implementations for the PC, Linux may be what you're looking for.

There are tools available to allow you to interact between Linux and MS-DOS. For example, it is easy to access MS-DOS files from Linux. There is also an MS-DOS emulator available, which allows you to run many popular MS-DOS applications. A Microsoft Windows emulator is currently under development.

Linux Versus the Other Guys

A number of other advanced operating systems are on the rise in the PC world. Specifically, IBM's OS/2 and Microsoft's Windows NT are becoming very popular as more users move away from MS-DOS.

Both OS/2 and Windows NT are full multitasking operating systems, much like Linux. Technically, OS/2, Windows NT, and Linux are quite similar: they support roughly the same features in terms of user interface, networking, security, and so forth. However, the real difference between Linux and the Other Guys is the fact that Linux is a version of UNIX and hence benefits from the contributions of the UNIX community at large.

What makes UNIX so important? Not only is it the most popular operating system for multi-user machines, it is also the foundation for the majority of the free software world. Nearly all of the free software available on the Internet is written specifically for UNIX systems. (The Internet itself is largely UNIX-based.)

There are many implementations of UNIX from many vendors, and no single organization is responsible for distribution. There is a large push in the UNIX community for standardization in the form of open systems, but no single corporation controls this design. Hence, any vendor (or, as it turns out, any hacker) may implement these standards in an implementation of UNIX.

OS/2 and Windows NT, on the other hand, are proprietary systems. The interface and design are controlled by a single corporation, and only that corporation may implement that design. (Don't expect to see a free version of OS/2 anytime in the near future.) In one sense, this kind of organization is beneficial: it sets a strict standard for the programming and user interface unlike that found even in the open systems community. OS/2 is OS/2 wherever you go—the same holds for Windows NT.

However, the UNIX interface is constantly developing and changing. Several organizations are attempting to standardize the programming model, but the task is very difficult. Linux, in particular, is mostly compliant with the POSIX.1 standard for the UNIX programming interface. As time goes on, it is expected that the system will adhere to other such standards, but standardization is not the primary issue in the Linux development community.

Other Implementations of UNIX

There are several other implementations of UNIX for the 80x86. The 80x86 architecture lends itself to the UNIX design, and a number of vendors have taken advantage of this.

In terms of features, other implementations of UNIX for the PC are quite similar to Linux. You will see that almost all commercial versions of UNIX support roughly the same software, programming environment, and networking features. However, there are some strong differences between Linux and commercial versions of UNIX.

First of all, Linux supports a different range of hardware from commercial implementations. In general, Linux supports the most well-known hardware devices, but support is still limited to that hardware which developers actually have access to. Commercial UNIX vendors generally have a wider support base and tend to support more hardware, although Linux is not far behind. We'll cover the hardware requirements for Linux in the next section.

Appendix A

Secondly, commercial implementations of UNIX usually come bundled with a complete set of documentation as well as user support from the vendor. In contrast, most of the documentation for Linux is limited to documents available on the Internet—and books such as this one. In the section "Sources of Linux Information" we list sources of Linux documentation and other information. Appendix A also provides some useful details.

As far as stability and robustness are concerned, many users have reported that Linux is at least as stable as commercial UNIX systems. Linux is still under development, and certain features (such TCP/IP networking) are less stable but improve as time goes by.

Appendix B

The most important factor to consider for many users is price. The Linux software is free if you have access to the Internet (or another computer network) and can download it. If you do not have access to such a network, you may need to purchase it via mail order on diskette, tape, or CD-ROM (see Appendix B). Of course, you may copy Linux from a friend who may already have the software, or share the cost of purchasing it with someone else. If you are planning to install Linux on a large number of machines, you need only purchase a single copy of the software—Linux is not distributed on a "single machine" license.

The value of commercial UNIX implementations should not be demeaned: along with the price of the software itself, one usually pays for documentation, support, and assurance of quality. These are very important factors for large institutions, but personal computer users may not require these benefits. In any case, many businesses and universities are finding that running Linux in a lab of inexpensive personal computers is preferable to running a commercial version of UNIX in a lab of workstations. Linux can provide the functionality of a workstation on PC hardware at a fraction of the cost.

There are other free or inexpensive implementations of UNIX for the 80x86. One of the most well known is FreeBSD, an implementation and port of BSD UNIX for the 386. FreeBSD is comparable to Linux in many ways, but which one is "better" depends on your own personal needs and expectations. The only strong distinction that we can make is that Linux is developed openly (where any volunteer can aid in the development process), while FreeBSD is developed within a closed team of programmers who maintain the system. Because of this, serious philosophical and design differences exist between the two projects. The goals of the two projects are entirely different: the goal of Linux is to develop a complete UNIX system from scratch (and have a lot of fun in the process), and the goal of FreeBSD is in part to modify the existing BSD code for use on the 386.

NetBSD is another port of the BSD NET/2 distribution to a number of machines, including the 386. NetBSD has a slightly more open development structure, and is comparable to FreeBSD in many respects.

Appendix E

Another project of note is HURD, an effort by the Free Software Foundation to develop and distribute a free version of UNIX for many platforms. Contact the Free Software Foundation (the address is given in Appendix E) for more information about this project. At the time of this writing, HURD is still in early stages of development.

Other inexpensive versions of UNIX exist as well, such as Coherent (available for about $99) and Minix (an academic but useful UNIX clone upon which the early development of Linux was based). Some of these implementations are of mostly academic interest, while others are full-fledged systems for real productivity. But many personal UNIX users are moving to Linux.

Hardware Requirements

Now you must be convinced of how wonderful Linux is, and all of the great things that it can do for you. However, before you rush out and install the software, you need to be aware of the hardware requirements and limitations that Linux has.

Keep in mind that Linux was developed by its users. This means, for the most part, that the hardware supported by Linux is only the hardware which the users and developers actually have access to. As it turns out, most of the popular hardware and peripherals for 80x86 systems are supported (in fact, Linux supports more hardware than some commercial implementations of UNIX). However, some of the more obscure and esoteric devices aren't supported yet. As time goes on, a wider range of hardware is supported, so if your favorite devices aren't listed here, chances are that support for them is forthcoming.

Another drawback for hardware support under Linux is that many companies have decided to keep the hardware interface proprietary. The upshot of this is that volunteer Linux developers simply can't write drivers for those devices (if they could, those drivers would be owned by the company that owned the interface, which would violate the GPL). The companies that maintain proprietary interfaces write their own drivers for operating systems such as MS-DOS and Microsoft Windows; the end user (that's you) never needs to know about the interface. Unfortunately, this does not allow Linux developers to write drivers for those devices.

There is very little that can be done about the situation. In some cases, programmers have attempted to write hackish drivers based on assumptions about the interface. In other cases, developers will work with the company in question and attempt to obtain information about the device interface, with varying degrees of success.

[69] Hardware
HOWTO

In the following sections, we'll attempt to summarize the hardware requirements for Linux. The Linux Hardware HOWTO (see the section "Sources of Linux Information" for an explanation of HOWTOs) contains a more complete listing of hardware supported by Linux.

Disclaimer: A good deal of hardware support for Linux is currently in the development stage. Some distributions may or may not support these experimental features. This section primarily lists hardware that has been supported for some time and is known to be stable. When in doubt, consult the documentation for the distribution of Linux you are using (see the section "Distributions of Linux" in Chapter 2) for more information on Linux distributions).

Chapter 2

Motherboard and CPU Requirements

Linux currently supports systems with an Intel 80386, 80486, or Pentium CPU. This includes all variations on this CPU type, such as the 386SX, 486SX, 486DX, and 486DX2. Non-Intel "clones," such as AMD and Cyrix processors, work with Linux as well.

If you have an 80386 or 80486SX, you may also wish to use a math coprocessor, although one isn't required (the Linux kernel can do FPU emulation if you do not have a math coprocessor). All standard FPU couplings are supported, such as IIT, Cyrix FasMath, and Intel coprocessors.

The system motherboard must use ISA, EISA, or PCI bus architecture. These terms define how the system interfaces with peripherals and other components on the main bus. Most systems sold today are either ISA or EISA bus. IBM's MicroChannel (MCA) bus, found on machines such as the IBM PS/2, is not currently supported.

Systems that use a local bus architecture (for faster video and disk access) are supported as well. It is suggested that you have a standard local bus architecture such as the VESA Local Bus (VLB).

Memory Requirements

Linux requires very little memory to run compared to other advanced operating systems. You should have at the very least 2 megabytes of RAM; however, it is strongly suggested that you have 4 megabytes. The more memory you have, the faster the system will run.

Linux can support the full 32-bit address range of the 80x86; in other words, it will utilize all of your RAM automatically.

Linux will run happily with only 4 megabytes of RAM, including all of the bells and whistles such as the X Window System, Emacs, and so on. However, having more memory is almost as important as having a faster processor. Eight megabytes is more than enough for personal use; 16 megabytes or more may be needed if you are expecting a heavy user load on the system.

Most Linux users allocate a portion of their hard drive as swap space, which is used as virtual RAM. Even if you have a great deal of physical RAM in your machine, you may wish to use swap space. While swap space is no replacement for actual physical RAM, it can allow your system to run larger applications by swapping out inactive portions of code to disk. The amount of swap space that you should allocate depends on several factors; we'll come back to this question in the section "Linux Partition Requirements" in Chapter 2.

Chapter 2

Hard Drive Controller Requirements

You do not need to have a hard drive to run Linux; you can run a minimal system completely from floppy. However, this is slow and very limited, and many users have access to hard drive storage anyway. You must have an AT-standard (16-bit) controller. There is support in the kernel for XT-standard (8-bit) controllers; however, most controllers used today are AT-standard. Linux should support all MFM, RLL, and IDE controllers. Most, but not all, ESDI controllers are supported—only those which do ST506 hardware emulation.

The general rule for non-SCSI hard drive and floppy controllers is that if you can access the drive from MS-DOS or another operating system, you should be able to access it from Linux.

Linux also supports a number of popular SCSI drive controllers, although support for SCSI is more limited because of the wide range of controller interface standards. Supported SCSI controllers include the Adaptec AHA1542B, AHA1542C, AHA1742A (BIOS version 1.34), AHA1522, AHA1740, AHA1740 (SCSI-2 controller, BIOS 1.34 in Enhanced mode); Future Domain 1680, TMC-850, TMC-950; Seagate ST-02; UltraStor SCSI; and Western Digital WD7000FASST. Clones that are based on these cards should work as well.

Hard Drive Space Requirements

Of course, to install Linux, you'll need to have some amount of free space on your hard drive. Linux will support multiple hard drives in the same machine; you can allocate space for Linux across multiple drives if necessary.

The *amount* of hard drive space that you will require depends greatly on your needs and the amount of software that you're installing. Linux is relatively small as UNIX implementations go; you could run a complete system in 10 to 20 megabytes of space on your drive. However, if you want to have room for expansion, and for larger packages such as the X Window System, you will need more space. If you plan to allow multiple users to use the machine, you will need to allocate storage for their files.

Chapter 2

Also, unless you have a large amount of physical RAM (16 megabytes or more), you will more than likely want to allocate swap space to be used as virtual RAM. We will discuss all of the details of installing and using swap space in the section "Linux Partition Requirements" in Chapter 2.

Each distribution of Linux usually comes with some literature that should help you to gauge the precise amount of required storage depending on the amount of software you plan to install. You can run a minimal system with less than 20 megabytes; a complete system with all of the bells and whistles in 80 megabytes or less; and a very large system with room for many users and space for future expansion in the range of 100-150 megabytes. Again, these figures are meant only as a ballpark approximation; you will have to look at your own needs and goals in order to determine your specific storage requirements.

Monitor and Video Adapter Requirements

Linux supports all standard Hercules, CGA, EGA, VGA, IBM monochrome, and Super VGA video cards and monitors for the default text-based interface. In general, if the video card and monitor coupling works under another operating system such as MS-DOS, it should work fine with Linux. Original IBM CGA cards suffer from "snow" under Linux, which is not pleasant to use.

Chapter 5

Graphical environments such as the X Window System have video hardware requirements of their own. Instead of listing these requirements here, we relegate the discussion to the section "Hardware Requirements" in Chapter 5. In short, to run the X Window System on your Linux machine, you will need one of the video cards listed in that section.

Miscellaneous Hardware

The above sections described the hardware required to run a Linux system. However, most users have a number of "optional" devices such as tape and CD-ROM storage, sound boards, and so on, and are interested in whether or not this hardware is supported by Linux. Read on.

Mice and other pointing devices

For the most part, you will be using a mouse only under a graphical environment such as the X Window System. However, several Linux applications not associated with a graphics environment do make use of the mouse.

Linux supports all standard serial mice, including Logitech, MM series, Mouseman, Microsoft (2-button), and Mouse Systems (3-button). Linux also supports Microsoft, Logitech, and ATIXL busmice. The PS/2 mouse interface is supported as well.

All other pointing devices, such as trackballs, which emulate the above mice, should work as well.

CD-ROM storage

Almost all CD-ROM drives use the SCSI interface. As long as you have a SCSI adaptor supported by Linux, then your CD-ROM drive should work. A number of CD-ROM drives have been verified to work under Linux, including the NEC CDR-74, Sony CDU-541, and Texel DM-3024. The Sony internal CDU-31a and the Mitsumi CD-ROM drives are supported by Linux as well.

Linux supports the standard ISO-9660 filesystem for CD-ROMs.

Tape drives

There are several types of tape drives available on the market. Most of them use the SCSI interface, all of which should be supported by Linux. Among the verified SCSI tape drives are the Sankyo CP150SE; Tandberg 3600; and Wangtek 5525ES, 5150ES, and 5099EN with the PC36 adaptor. Other QIC-02 drives should be supported as well.

Drivers are currently under development for various other tape devices, such as Colorado drives, which hang off of the floppy controller.

Printers

Linux supports the complete range of parallel printers. If you are able to access your printer via the parallel port from MS-DOS or another operating system, you should be able to access it from Linux as well. The Linux printing software consists of the UNIX standard *lp* and *lpr* software. This software also allows you to print remotely via the network, if you have one available.

Modems

As with printer support, Linux supports the full range of serial modems, both internal and external. There is a great deal of telecommunications software available for Linux, including Kermit, *pcomm*, *minicom*, and Seyon. If your modem is accessible from another operating system on the same machine, you should be able to access it from Linux with no difficulty.

Ethernet Cards

Many popular Ethernet cards and LAN adapters are supported by Linux. These include:

- 3com 3c503, 3c503/16

- Novell NE1000, NE2000

- Western Digital WD8003, WD8013

- Hewlett-Packard HP27245, HP27247, HP27250

- D-Link DE-600

The following clones are reported to work:

- LANNET LEC-45

- Alta Combo

- Artisoft LANtastic AE-2

- Asante Etherpak 2001/2003,

- D-Link Ethernet II

- LTC E-NET/16 P/N 8300-200-002

- Network Solutions HE-203,

- SVEC 4 Dimension Ethernet

- 4-Dimension FD0490 EtherBoard 16

Clones which are compatible with any of the above cards should work as well.

Sources of Linux Information

As you have probably guessed, there are many sources of information about Linux available apart from this book. In particular, there are a number of books, not specific to Linux but rather about UNIX in general, that will be of importance, especially to those readers without previous UNIX experience. If you are new to the UNIX world, we seriously suggest that you take the time to peruse one of these books before you attempt to brave the jungles of Linux. Specifically, the book *Learning the UNIX Operating System*, by Grace Todino and John Strang, is a good place to start.

[7] Learning
UNIX

Many of the following sources of information are available online in some electronic form. That is, you must have access to an online network, such as the Internet, Usenet, or Fidonet. If you do not have online access to any of this material, you might be able to find someone kind enough to give you hardcopies of the documents in question. Read on.

Online Documents

If you have access to the Internet, you can get many Linux documents via anonymous FTP from archive sites all over the world. If you do not have direct Internet access, these documents may still be available to you; many Linux distributions on CD-ROM contain all of the documents mentioned here. Also, they are distributed

Appendix D

on many other networks, such as Fidonet and CompuServe. See Appendix D, *Bulletin Board Access to Linux*, for a list of BBSes that carry Linux materials.

Appendix C

If you are able to send mail to Internet sites, you may be able to retrieve these files using one of the FTPMAIL servers which will electronically mail you the documents or files from FTP archive sites. See Appendix C, *FTP Tutorial and Site List*, for more information on using FTPMAIL.

There are a great number of FTP archive sites that carry Linux software and related documents. A list of well-known Linux archive sites is given in Appendix C. In order to reduce network traffic, you should always use the FTP site that is geographically (network-wise) closest to you.

Appendix A

Appendix A contains a listing of some of the Linux documents that are available via anonymous FTP. The filenames will differ depending on the archive site in question; most sites keep Linux-related documents in the *docs* subdirectory of their Linux archive space. For example, on the FTP site **sunsite.unc.edu**, Linux files are stored in the directory */pub/Linux*, with Linux-related documentation being found in */pub/Linux/docs*.

Examples of available online documents are the Linux FAQ, a collection of frequently asked questions about Linux; the Linux HOWTO documents, each describing a specific aspect of the system—including the Installation HOWTO, the Printing HOWTO, and the Ethernet HOWTO; and the Linux META-FAQ, a list of other sources of Linux information on the Internet.

Most of these documents are also regularly posted to one or more Linux-related Usenet newsgroups; see the section "Usenet Newsgroups" below.

Linux on the World Wide Web

The Linux Documentation Home Page is available to World Wide Web users at the URL:

```
http://sunsite.unc.edu/mdw/linux.html
```

This page contains many HOWTOs and other documents in HTML format, as well as pointers to other sites of interest to Linux users.

Books and Other Published Works

At this time, there are few published works specifically about Linux. Most noteworthy are the books from the Linux Documentation Project, a project carried out over the Internet to write and distribute a bona fide set of "manuals" for Linux. These manuals are analogues to the documentation sets available with commercial versions of UNIX: they cover everything from installing Linux to using and running the system, programming, networking, kernel development, and more.

Appendix A

The Linux Documentation Project manuals are available via anonymous FTP from the Internet, as well as via mail order from several sources. Appendix A lists the manuals that are available and covers the means of obtaining them in detail. O'Reilly & Associates, among others, has published the *Linux Network Administrator's Guide*.

There are not many books specifically about Linux currently available. However, there are a large number of books about UNIX in general which are certainly applicable to Linux—as far as using and programming the system is concerned, Linux does not differ greatly from other implementations of UNIX. In short, almost everything you want to know about using and programming Linux can be found in sources meant for a general UNIX audience. In fact, this book is meant to be complemented by the large library of UNIX books currently available; here, we present the most important Linux-specific details and hope that you will look to other sources for more in-depth information.

Armed with a number of good books about using UNIX, as well as the book you hold in your hands, you should be able to tackle just about anything. Appendix A includes a list of highly recommended UNIX books, for UNIX newcomers and UNIX wizards alike.

Appendix B

There is also a monthly magazine about Linux called the *Linux Journal*. It is distributed worldwide, and is an excellent way to keep in touch with the many goings-on in the Linux community—especially if you do not have access to Usenet news (see below). See Appendix B for information on subscribing to the *Linux Journal*.

Usenet Newsgroups

Usenet is a worldwide electronic news and discussion forum with a heavy contingent of so-called "newsgroups"—discussion areas devoted to a particular topic. Much of the development of Linux has been done over the waves of the Internet and Usenet, and not surprisingly there are a number of Usenet newsgroups available for discussions about Linux.

The original Linux newsgroup was *alt.os.linux*, and was created to move some of the discussions about Linux out of *comp.os.minix* and the various mailing lists. Soon, the traffic on *alt.os.linux* grew to be large enough that a newsgroup in the *comp* hierarchy was warranted; a vote was taken in February of 1992, and *comp.os.linux* was created.

comp.os.linux quickly became one of the most popular (and loudest) Usenet groups—more popular than any other *comp.os* group. In December of 1992, a vote was taken to split the newsgroup in order to reduce traffic; only *comp.os.linux.announce* passed this vote. In July of 1993, the group was finally split into the new hierarchy. Almost 2000 people voted in the *comp.os.linux* reorganization, making it one of the largest Usenet Call For Votes ever. The Linux newsgroups were reorganized again, in December 1994, to reflect the changing needs of the growing readership. At this time *comp.os.linux.announce* is one of the most popular Usenet newsgroups overall.

If you do not have direct Usenet access, but are able to send and receive electronic mail from the Internet, there are mail-to-news gateways available for each of the newsgroups below.

comp.os.linux.announce

> *comp.os.linux.announce* is a moderated newsgroup for announcements and important postings about the Linux system (such as bug reports, important patches to software, and so on). If you read any Linux newsgroups at all, read this one. Often, the important postings in this group are not crossposted to other groups. This group also contains periodic postings about Linux, including many of the online documents described in the last section and listed in Appendix A.

Appendix A

> Postings to this newsgroup must be approved by the moderators, Matt Welsh and Lars Wirzenius. If you wish to submit an article to this group, in most cases you can simply post the article as you normally would (using Pnews or whatever posting software that you have available); the news software will automatically forward the article to the moderators for approval. However, if your news system is not set up correctly, you may need to mail the article directly; the submission address is *linux-announce@tc.cornell.edu.*

comp.os.linux.answers

> This is another moderated newsgroup, used for posting periodic information about Linux such as FAQ lists, HOWTO documents, and other relatively long articles. These articles are not posted to *comp.os.linux.announce* because they are often too large for people with slow or expensive newsfeeds to handle.

> If you have a periodic posting that should be approved for posting on this newsgroup, contact Matt Welsh at *mdw@sunsite.unc.edu.*

> The rest of the Linux newsgroups listed below are unmoderated.

comp.os.linux.setup

> This newsgroup is for questions and discussion about installing and running a Linux system, most commonly in an active, multi-user environment. Any discussion about administrative issues of Linux (such as packaging software, making backups, handling users, and so on), installation of the software, and related topics is welcome here.

comp.os.linux.development.system

> This is a newsgroup for discussions about development of the•Linux system. All issues related to kernel and system software development should be discussed here. For example, if you are writing a kernel driver and need help with certain aspects of the programming, this would be the place to ask. This newsgroup is also for discussions about the direction and goals behind the

Linux development effort, as described (somewhat) in the section "The Design and Philosophy of Linux."

It should be noted that this newsgroup is not (technically) for discussions about development of software *for* Linux, but rather for discussions of development *of* Linux. That is, issues dealing with applications programming under Linux should be discussed in the newsgroup *comp.os.linux.development.apps*; *comp.os.linux.development.system* is about developing the Linux system itself, including the kernel, system libraries, and so on.

comp.os.linux.development.apps
This newsgroup is for discussions related to developing or porting applications for Linux. By *applications* we mean any user-level software from the smallest utility to the largest software package. Low-level system software should be discussed in *comp.os.linux.development.system*.

comp.os.linux.hardware
This newsgroup is devoted to discussions of hardware support or problems under Linux. If you can't get Linux working with your Foobaz, Inc. Ethernet Hub/Food Processor unit, you might want to post here.

comp.os.linux.networking
All discussions about networking under Linux (including TCP/IP, SLIP, PPP, UUCP, and other protocols) should be posted here. This can include discussion of hardware issues (such as how to configure a particular Ethernet card), but *comp.os.linux.hardware* is available for those topics as well.

comp.os.linux.x
This newsgroup is for discussions about installing, configuring, and running the X Window System software (such as XFree86) under Linux. There is another newsgroup, *comp.windows.x.i386unix* also devoted to this topic, but many Linux users don't seem to know about that group. If you have problems with the X Window System that are specifically Linux-related, you can post here. Note that general X-related questions should be posted in one of the *comp.windows.x* groups.

comp.os.linux.advocacy
This newsgroup is available to let you flame other personal computer operating systems to a crisp. If you really, really hate MS-DOS, FreeBSD, OS/2, or Windows NT, this is the place for you. This doesn't necessarily mean that anybody will listen, of course.

comp.os.linux.misc
This newsgroup is for all discussion which doesn't quite fit into the other available Linux groups. Any nontechnical or metadiscourse about the Linux system should remain in *comp.os.linux.misc*. Flame wars should generally be directed to another group, such as *comp.os.linux.advocacy*.

It should be noted that the newsgroup *comp.os.linux*, which was originally the only Linux group, has been superseded by the new hierarchy of groups. If you have access to *comp.os.linux*, but not to the newer Linux groups listed above, encourage your news administrator to create the new groups on your system.

Internet Mailing Lists

If you have access to Internet electronic mail, you can participate in a number of mailing lists even if you do not have Usenet access. If you are not directly on the Internet, you can join one of these mailing lists as long as you are able to exchange electronic mail with the Internet. (For example, UUCP, FidoNET, CompuServe, and other networks all have access to Internet mail.)

The "Linux Activists" mailing list is primarily for Linux developers and people interested in aiding the development process. This is a "multi-channel" mailing list, in which you join one or more "channels" based on your particular interests. Some of the available channels include: NORMAL, for general Linux-related issues; KERNEL, for kernel development; GCC, for discussions relating to the *gcc* compiler and library development; NET, for discussions about the TCP/IP networking code; DOC, for issues relating to writing and distributing Linux documentation; and more.

For more information about the Linux Activists mailing list, send mail to *linux-activists@niksula.hut.fi*. You will receive a list of currently available channels, including information on how to subscribe and unsubscribe to particular channels on the list.

Quite a few special-purpose mailing lists about and for Linux exist as well. The best way to find out about these is to watch the Linux Usenet newsgroups for announcements, as well as to read the list of publicly-available mailing lists, periodically posted to the Usenet group *news.answers*.

Getting Help

You will undoubtedly require some degree of assistance during your adventures in the Linux world. Even the most wizardly of UNIX wizards is occasionally stumped by some quirk or feature of Linux, and it's important to know how and where to find help when you need it.

The primary means of getting help in the Linux world are via Internet mailing lists and Usenet newsgroups. If you don't have online access to these sources, you might be able to find comparable Linux discussion forums on other online services, such as on local BBSes, CompuServe, and so on.

A number of businesses are providing commercial support for Linux. You can pay a "subscription fee" which will allow you to call the consultants for help with your

Appendix B

Linux problems. Appendix B contains a list of Linux vendors, some of which provide commercial support. However, if you have access to Usenet and Internet mail, you may find the free support found there to be just as useful.

Keeping the following suggestions in mind will greatly improve your experiences with Linux and will guarantee you more success in finding help to your problems.

Appendix A

Consult all available documentation first! The first thing you should do when encountering a problem is consult the various sources of information listed in the previous section and Appendix A. These documents were laboriously written for people like you—people who need help with the Linux system. Even books written for UNIX in general are applicable to Linux, and you should take advantage of them. More than likely, you will find the answer to your problems somewhere in this documentation, as impossible as it may seem.

If you have access to Usenet news or any of the Linux-related mailing lists, be sure to actually *read* the information there before posting for help with your problem. Many times, solutions to common problems are not easy to find in documentation, and instead are well-covered in the newsgroups and mailing lists devoted to Linux. If you only post to these groups, and don't actually read them, you are asking for trouble.

Learn to appreciate self-maintenance. In most cases, it is preferable to do as much independent research and investigation into the problem as possible before seeking outside help. After all, you asked for it by running Linux in the first place! Remember that Linux is all about hacking and fixing problems yourself. It is not a commercial operating system, nor does it try to look like one. Hacking won't kill you. In fact, it will teach you a great deal about the system to investigate and solve problems yourself—maybe even enough to one day call yourself a Linux guru. Learn to appreciate the value of hacking the system, and how to fix problems yourself. You can't expect to run a complete, home-brew Linux system without some degree of handiwork.

Remain calm. It is vital to refrain from getting frustrated with the system, at all costs. Nothing is earned by taking an axe—or worse, a powerful electromagnet—to your Linux system in a fit of anger. The authors have found that a large punching bag or similar inanimate object is a wonderful way to relieve the occasional stress attack. As Linux matures and distributions become more reliable, we hope that this problem will go away. However, even commercial UNIX implementations can be tricky at times. When all else fails, sit back, take a few deep breaths, and go after the problem again when you feel relaxed. Your mind and conscience will be clearer.

Refrain from posting spuriously. Many people make the mistake of posting or mailing messages pleading for help prematurely. When encountering a problem, do not—we repeat, do *not*—rush immediately to your nearest terminal and post a message to one of the Linux Usenet newsgroups. Often, you will catch your own mistake five minutes later and find yourself in the curious situation of defending your own sanity in a public forum. Before posting anything to any of the Linux mailing lists or newsgroups, first attempt to resolve the problem yourself and be absolutely certain what the problem is. Does your system not respond when switched on? Perhaps the machine is unplugged.

If you do post for help, make it worthwhile. If all else fails, you may wish to post a message for help in any of the number of electronic forums dedicated to Linux, such as Usenet newsgroups and mailing lists. When posting, remember that the people reading your post are not there to help you. The network is not your personal consulting service. Therefore, it is important to remain as polite, terse, and informative as possible.

How can one accomplish this? First, you should include as much (relevant) information about your system and your problem as possible. Posting the simple request "I cannot seem to get email to work" will probably get you nowhere unless you include information on your system, what software you are using, what you have attempted to do so far, and what the results were. When including technical information, it is usually a good idea to include general information on the version(s) of your software (Linux kernel version, for example), as well as a brief summary of your hardware configuration. However, don't overdo it—including information on the brand and type of monitor that you have probably is irrelevant if you're trying to configure networking software.

Secondly, remember that you need to make some attempt—however feeble—at solving your problem before you go to the Net. If you have never attempted to set up electronic mail, for instance, and first decide to ask folks on the Net how to go about doing it, you are making a big mistake. There are a number of documents available (see the section "Sources of Linux Information" in this chapter) on how to get started with many common tasks under Linux. The idea is to get as far along as possible on your own and *then* ask for help if and when you get stuck.

Also remember that the people reading your message, however helpful, may occasionally get frustrated by seeing the same problem over and over again. Be sure to actually read the Linux newsgroups and mailing lists before posting your problems. Many times, the solution to your problem has been discussed repeatedly, and all that's required to find it is to browse the current messages.

Lastly, when posting to electronic newsgroups and mailing lists, try to be as polite as possible. It is much more effective and worthwhile to be polite, direct, and informative—more people will be willing to help you if you master a humble tone. To be sure, the flame war is an art form across many forms of electronic communication, but don't allow that to preoccupy your time and other people's. The network is an excellent way to get help with your Linux problems—but it is important to know how to use the network *effectively*.

CHAPTER TWO

OBTAINING AND
INSTALLING LINUX

Ⅰn this chapter, we'll describe how to obtain the Linux software, in the form of one of the various pre-packaged distributions, and how to install the distribution that you choose.

As we have mentioned, there is no single "official" distribution of the Linux software; there are, in fact, many distributions, each of which serves a particular purpose and set of goals. These distributions are available via anonymous FTP from the Internet, on BBS systems worldwide, and via mail on diskette, tape, and CD-ROM.

Here, we present a general overview of the installation process. Each distribution has its own specific installation instructions, but armed with the concepts presented here you should be able to feel your way through any installation. Appendix A, *Sources of Linux Information*, lists sources of information for installation instructions and other help, if you're at a total loss.

Appendix A

Distributions of Linux

Because Linux is free software, no single organization or entity is responsible for releasing and distributing the software. Therefore, anyone is free to put together and distribute the Linux software, as long as the restrictions in the GPL are observed. The upshot of this is that there are many distributions of Linux, available via anonymous FTP or mail order.

You are now faced with the task of deciding upon a particular distribution of Linux that suits your needs. Not all distributions are alike. Many of them come with just about all of the software you'd need to run a complete system—and then some. Other Linux distributions are "small" distributions intended for users without copious amounts of diskspace. Many distributions contain only the core Linux software, and you are expected to install larger software packages, such as the X

Chapter 4

Window System, yourself. (In Chapter 4, *Essential System Management*, we'll show you how.)

[64] Distri-
bution HOWTO

The Linux Distribution HOWTO contains a list of Linux distributions available via the Internet as well as mail order. Appendix B, *Linux Vendor List*, also lists contact addresses for a number of Linux mail-order vendors.

Appendix B

How can you decide among all of these distributions? If you have access to Usenet news, or another computer conferencing system, you might want to ask there for personal opinions from people who have installed Linux. Even better, if you know someone who has installed Linux, ask them for help and advice. In actuality, most of the popular Linux distributions contain roughly the same set of software, so the distribution that you select is more or less arbitrary.

Getting Linux from the Internet

Appendix C

If you have access to the Internet, the easiest way to obtain Linux is via anony-mous FTP.[*] Appendix C lists a number of FTP archive sites which carry Linux soft-ware. One of these is **sunsite.unc.edu**, and the various Linux distributions can be found there in the directory */pub/Linux/distributions*.

Many distributions are released via anonymous FTP as a set of disk images. That is, the distribution consists of a set of files, and each file contains the binary image of a floppy. In order to copy the contents of the image file onto the floppy, you can use the RAWRITE.EXE program under MS-DOS. This program copies, block-for-block, the contents of a file to a floppy, without regard for disk format.[†] Also be aware that this is a labor-intensive way of installing Linux: the distribution can easily come to more than 50 diskettes.

RAWRITE.EXE is available on the various Linux FTP sites, including **sun-site.unc.edu** in the directory */pub/Linux/system/Install/rawwrite*.

Therefore, in many cases, you simply download the set of diskette images, and use RAWRITE.EXE with each image in turn to create a set of diskettes. You boot from the so-called "boot diskette," and you're ready to roll. The software is usually installed directly from the floppies, although some distributions allow you to install from an MS-DOS partition on your hard drive. Some distributions allow you to install over a TCP/IP network. The documentation for each distribution should describe these installation methods if they are available.

---

[*] If you do not have direct Internet access, you can obtain Linux via the *ftpmail* service, provided that you have the ability to exchange email with the Internet. See Appendix C, *FTP Tutorial and Site List*, for details.

[†] If you have access to a UNIX workstation with a floppy drive, you can also use the *dd* command to copy the file image directly to the floppy. A command such as *dd of=/dev/rfd0 if=foo bs=18k* will "raw write" the contents of the file *foo* to the floppy device on a Sun workstation. Consult your local UNIX gurus for more information on your system's floppy devices and the use of *dd*.

Other Linux distributions are installed from a set of MS-DOS formatted floppies. For example, the Slackware distribution of Linux requires RAWRITE.EXE only for the boot and root diskettes. The rest of the diskettes are copied to MS-DOS formatted diskettes using the MS-DOS COPY command. The system installs the software directly from the MS-DOS floppies. This saves you the trouble of having to use RAWRITE.EXE for many image files, although it requires you to have access to an MS-DOS system to create the diskettes.

Each distribution of Linux available via anonymous FTP should include a *README* file describing how to download and prepare the diskettes for installation. Be sure to read all of the available documentation for the release that you are using.

When downloading the Linux software, be sure to use *binary* mode for all file transfers (with most FTP clients, the command *binary* enables this mode).

Getting Linux from Other Online Sources

If you have access to another computer network such as CompuServe or Prodigy, there may be a means to download the Linux software from these sources. In addition, many bulletin board (BBS) systems carry Linux software. Not all Linux distributions are available from these computer networks, however—many of them, especially the various CD-ROM distributions, are available only via mail order.

Getting Linux via Mail Order

Appendix B

If you don't have Internet or BBS access, you can get many Linux distributions via mail order on diskette, tape, or CD-ROM. Appendix B lists a number of these distributors. Many of them accept credit cards as well as international orders, so if you're not in the United States or Canada, you still should be able to obtain Linux in this way.

Linux is free software, but distributors are allowed by the GPL to charge a fee for it. Therefore, ordering Linux via mail order might cost you between US $30 and US $150, depending on the distribution. However, if you know someone who has already purchased or downloaded a release of Linux, you are free to borrow or copy their software for your own use. Linux distributors are not allowed to restrict the license or redistribution of the software in any way. If you are thinking about installing an entire lab of machines with Linux, for example, you only need to purchase a single copy of one of the distributions, which can be used to install all of the machines.

Preparing to Install Linux

After you have obtained a distribution of Linux, you're ready to prepare your system for installation. This takes a certain degree of planning, especially if you're already running other operating systems. In the following sections we'll describe how to plan for the Linux installation.

Installation Overview

While each release of Linux is different, in general the method used to install the software is as follows:

1. **Repartition your hard drive(s).** If you have other operating systems already installed, you will need to repartition the drives in order to allocate space for Linux. This is discussed in the section "Repartitioning Your Drives" below.

2. **Boot the Linux installation media.** Each distribution of Linux has some kind of installation media—usually a "boot floppy"—which is used to install the software. Booting this media will either present you with some kind of installation program, which will step you through the Linux installation, or allow you to install the software by hand.

3. **Create Linux partitions.** After repartitioning to allocate space for Linux, you create Linux partitions on that empty space. This is accomplished with the Linux *fdisk* program, covered in the section "Creating Linux Partitions."

4. **Create filesystems and swap space.** At this point, you will create one or more *filesystems*, used to store files, on the newly-created partitions. In addition, if you plan to use swap space, you will create the swap space on one of your Linux partitions. This is covered in the sections "Creating the Swap Space" and "Creating the Filesystems."

5. **Install the software on the new filesystems.** Finally, you will install the Linux software on your newly-created filesystems. After this, it's smooth sailing—if all goes well. This is covered in the section "Installing the Software." Later, in the section "Running Into Trouble," we describe what to do if anything goes wrong.

Many distributions of Linux provide an installation program, which will step you through the installation process and automate one or more of the above steps for you. Keep in mind throughout this chapter that any number of the above steps may be automated for you, depending on the distribution.

Important hint: While preparing to install Linux, the best advice that we can give is to *take notes* during the entire procedure. Write down everything that you do, everything that you type, and everything that you see that might be out of the ordinary. The idea here is simple: if (or when!) you run into trouble, you want to be able to retrace your steps and find out what went wrong. Installing Linux isn't difficult, but there are many details to remember. You want to have a record of all of these details so that you can experiment with other methods if something goes wrong. Also, keeping a notebook of your Linux installation experience is useful when you want to ask other people for help, for example, when posting a message to one of the Linux-related Usenet groups. Your notebook is also something that you'll want to show to your grandchildren someday.[*]

Repartitioning Concepts

In general, hard drives are divided into *partitions,* where a single partition is devoted to a single operating system. For example, on one hard drive, you may have several separate partitions—one devoted to, say, MS-DOS, another to OS/2, and another to Linux.

If you already have other software installed on your system, you may need to resize those partitions in order to free up space for Linux. You will then create one or more Linux partitions on the resulting free space for storing the Linux software and swap space. We call this process *repartitioning.*

Many MS-DOS systems utilize a single partition inhabiting the entire drive. To MS-DOS, this partition is known as C:. If you have more than one partition, MS-DOS names them D:, E:, and so on. In a way, each partition acts like a separate hard drive.

On the first sector of the disk is a *master boot record* along with a *partition table.* The boot record (as the name implies) is used to boot the system. The partition table contains information about the locations and sizes of your partitions.

There are three kinds of partitions: *primary, extended,* and *logical.* Of these, primary partitions are used most often. However, because of a limit in the size of the partition table, you can only have four primary partitions on any given drive.

The way around this four-partition limit is to use an extended partition. An extended partition doesn't hold any data by itself; instead, it acts as a "container" for logical partitions. Therefore, you could create one extended partition, covering the entire drive, and within it create many logical partitions. However, you may have only one extended partition per drive.

Linux Partition Requirements

Before we explain how to repartition your drives, you need to have an idea of how much space you will be allocating for Linux. We will be discussing how to create these partitions later, in the section "Creating Linux Partitions."

---

[*] The author shamefully admits that he kept a notebook of all of his tribulations with Linux for the first few months of working with the system. It is now gathering dust on his bookshelf.

On UNIX systems, files are stored on a *filesystem*, which is essentially a section of the hard drive (or other medium, such as CD-ROM or diskette) formatted to hold files. Each filesystem is associated with a specific part of the directory tree; for example, on many systems, there is a filesystem for all of the files in the directory */usr*, another for */tmp*, and so on. The *root filesystem* is the primary filesystem, which corresponds to the topmost directory, /.

Under Linux, each filesystem lives on a separate partition on the hard drive. For instance, if you have a filesystem for / and another for */usr*, you will need two partitions to hold the two filesystems.

Before you install Linux, you will need to prepare filesystems for storing the Linux software. You must have at least one filesystem (the root filesystem), and therefore one partition, allocated to Linux. Many Linux users opt to store all of their files on the root filesystem, which is in most cases easier to manage than several filesystems and partitions.

However, you may create multiple filesystems for Linux if you wish—for example, you may want to use separate filesystems for */usr* and */home*. Those readers with UNIX system administration experience will know how to use multiple filesystems creatively. In the section "Creating Filesystems" of Chapter 4, we discuss the use of multiple partitions and filesystems.

Chapter 4

Why use more than one filesystem? The most commonly stated reason is safety; if, for some reason, one of your filesystems is damaged, the others will (usually) be unharmed. On the other hand, if you store all of your files on the root filesystem, and for some reason the filesystem is damaged, then you may lose all of your files in one fell swoop. This is, however, rather uncommon; if you back up the system regularly, you should be quite safe.[*]

Another reason to use multiple filesystems is to divvy up storage between multiple hard drives. If you have, say, 40 megabytes free on one hard drive, and 50 megabytes free on another, you might want to create a 40-megabyte root filesystem on the first drive and a 50-megabyte */usr* filesystem on the other. Currently it is not possible for a single filesystem to span multiple drives; if your free hard drive storage is fragmented between drives you will need to use multiple filesystems to utilize it all.

In summary, Linux requires at least one partition, for the root filesystem. If you wish to create multiple filesystems, you will need a separate partition for each additional filesystem. Some distributions of Linux automatically create partitions and filesystems for you, so you may not need to worry about these issues at all.

Another issue to consider when planning your partitions is swap space. You have two options. The first is to use a *swap file* which exists on one of your Linux filesystems. You will create the swap file for use as virtual RAM after you install

---

[*] The author uses a single 200-megabyte filesystem for all of his Linux files and hasn't had any problems (so far).

the software. The second option is to create a *swap partition*, an individual partition to be used only as swap space. Most people use a swap partition instead of a swap file.

A single swap file or partition may be up to 16 megabytes in size. If you wish to use more than 16 megabytes of swap, you can create multiple swap partitions or files—up to eight in all. For example, if you need 32 megabytes of swap, you can create two 16-megabyte swap partitions.

Setting up a swap partition is covered in the section "Creating the Swap Space," and setting up a swap file in the section "Managing Swap Space" in Chapter 4.

Chapter 4

Therefore, in general, you will create at least two partitions for Linux: one for use as the root filesystem, and the other for use as swap space. There are, of course, many variations on the above, but this is the minimal setup. You are not required to use swap space with Linux, but if you have less than 16 megabytes of physical RAM it is strongly suggested that you do.

Of course, you need to be aware of how much *space* these partitions will require. The size of your Linux filesystems (containing the software itself) depends greatly on how much software you're installing and what distribution of Linux you are using. Hopefully, the documentation that came with your distribution will give you an approximation of the space requirements. A small Linux system can use 20 megabytes or less; a larger system anywhere from 80 to 100 megabytes, or more. Keep in mind that in addition to the space required by the software itself, you need to allocate extra space for user directories, room for future expansion, and so forth.

The size of your swap partition (should you elect to use one) depends on how much virtual RAM you require. A rule of thumb is to use a swap partition that is twice the space of your physical RAM; for example, if you have 4 megabytes of physical RAM, an 8-megabyte swap partition should suffice. Of course, this is mere speculation—the actual amount of swap space that you require depends on the software you will be running. If you have a great deal of physical RAM (say, 16 megabytes or more), you may not wish to use swap space at all.

Important note: Because of BIOS limitations, it is usually not possible to boot from partitions using cylinders numbered over 1023. Therefore, when setting aside space for Linux, keep in mind that you may not want to use a partition in the >1023-cylinder range for your Linux root filesystem. Linux can still *use* partitions with cylinders numbered over 1023, but you may not be able to *boot* Linux from such a partition. This advice may seem premature, but it is important to know while planning your drive layout.

If you absolutely must use a partition with cylinders numbered over 1023 for your Linux root filesystem, you can always boot Linux from floppy. This is not so bad, actually—it takes only a few seconds longer to boot than from the hard drive. At any rate, it's always an option.

Repartitioning Your Drives

In this section, we'll describe how to resize your current partitions (if any) to make space for Linux. If you are installing Linux on a "clean" hard drive, you can skip this section and proceed to the section "Installing the Linux Software."

The usual way to resize an existing partition is to delete it (thus destroying all of the data on that partition) and recreate it. Before repartitioning your drives, *back up your system*. After resizing the partitions, you can reinstall your original software from the backup. However, there are several programs available for MS-DOS that are able to resize partitions nondestructively. One of these is known as FIPS and can be found on many Linux FTP sites.

Also, keep in mind that because you'll be shrinking your original partitions, you may not have space to reinstall everything. In this case, you need to delete enough unwanted software to allow the rest to fit on the smaller partitions.

The program used to repartition is known as *fdisk*. Each operating system has its own analogue of this program; for example, under MS-DOS, it is invoked with the FDISK command. You should consult your documentation for whatever operating systems you are currently running for information on repartitioning. Here, we'll discuss how to resize partitions for MS-DOS using FDISK, but this information should be easily extrapolated to other operating systems.

The *fdisk* program (on any operating system) is responsible for reading the partition table on a given drive and manipulating it to add or delete partitions. However, some versions of *fdisk* do more than this, such as adding information to the beginning of a new partition to make it usable by a certain operating system. For this reason, you should usually only create partitions for an operating system with the version of *fdisk* that comes with it. You can't create MS-DOS partitions with Linux *fdisk*—partitions created in this way can't be used correctly by MS-DOS. Similarly, MS-DOS *fdisk* may not be able to recognize Linux partitions. As long as you have a version of *fdisk* for each operating system that you use, you should be fine. (Note that not all systems name this program *fdisk*—some refer to it as a "disk manager" or "volume manager.")

Later, in the section "Creating Linux Partitions," we describe how to create Linux partitions, but for now we are concerned with resizing your current ones.

Please consult the documentation for your current operating systems before repartitioning your drive. This section is meant to be a general overview of the process; there are many subtleties that we do not cover here. You can lose all of the software on your system if you do not repartition the drive correctly.

Let's say that you have a single hard drive on your system, currently devoted entirely to MS-DOS. Hence, your drive consists of a single MS-DOS partition, commonly known as C:. Because this repartitioning method will destroy the data on that partition, you need to create a bootable MS-DOS "system disk," which contains everything necessary to run FDISK and restore the software from backup after the repartitioning is complete.

In many cases, you can use the MS-DOS installation disks for this purpose. However, if you need to create your own system disk, format a floppy with the command

    FORMAT /s A:

Copy onto this floppy all of the necessary MS-DOS utilities (usually most of the software in the directory \DOS on your drive), as well as the programs FORMAT.COM and FDISK.EXE. You should now be able to boot this floppy, and run the command

    FDISK C:

to start up FDISK.

Use of FDISK should be self-explanatory, but consult the MS-DOS documentation for details. When you start FDISK, use the menu option to display the partition table, and *write down* the information displayed there. It is important to keep a record of your original setup in case you want to back out of the Linux installation.

To delete an existing partition, choose the FDISK menu option "Delete an MS-DOS Partition or Logical DOS Drive." Specify the type of partition that you wish to delete (primary, extended, or logical) and the number of the partition. Verify all of the warnings. Poof!

To create a new (smaller) partition for MS-DOS, just choose the FDISK option "Create an MS-DOS Partition or Logical DOS Drive." Specify the type of partition (primary, extended, or logical), and the size of the partition to create (specified in megabytes). FDISK should create the partition, and you're ready to roll.

After you're done using FDISK, you should exit the program and reformat any new partitions. For example, if you resized the first DOS partition on your drive (c:) you should run the command

    FORMAT /s C:

You may now reinstall your original software from backup.

Installing the Linux Software

After you have resized your existing partitions to make space for Linux, you are ready to install the software. Here is a brief overview of the procedure:

- Boot the Linux installation media.

- Run *fdisk* under Linux to create Linux partitions.

- Run *mke2fs* and *mkswap* to create Linux filesystems and swap space.

- Install the Linux software.

- Finally, either install the LILO boot loader on your hard drive, or create a boot floppy in order to boot your new Linux system.

As we have said, one (or more) of these steps may be automated for you by the installation procedure, depending on the distribution of Linux you are using. Please consult the documentation for your distribution for specific instructions.

Booting Linux

The first step is to boot the Linux installation media. In most cases, this is a "boot floppy," which contains a small Linux system. Upon booting the floppy, you will be presented with an installation menu of some kind which will lead you through the steps of installing the software. On other distributions, you will be presented with a login prompt when booting this floppy. Here, you usually log in as **root** or **install** to begin the installation process.

The documentation that comes with your particular distribution will explain what is necessary to boot Linux from the installation media.

Most distributions of Linux use a boot floppy that allows you to enter hardware parameters at a boot prompt to force hardware detection of various devices. For example, if your SCSI controller is not detected when booting the floppy, you will need to reboot and specify the hardware parameters (such as I/O address and IRQ) at the boot prompt.

Likewise, IBM PS/1, ThinkPad, and ValuePoint machines do not store drive geometry in the CMOS, so you must specify it at boot time.

The boot prompt is often displayed automatically when booting the boot floppy. This is the case for the Slackware distribution. Other distributions require you to hold down the Shift or Control key while booting the floppy. If successful, you should see the prompt

    boot:

and possibly other messages.

To try booting without any special parameters, just press Enter at the boot prompt.

Watch the messages as the system boots. If you have an SCSI controller, you should see a listing of the SCSI hosts detected. If you see the message

    SCSI: 0 hosts

then your SCSI controller was not detected, and you will have to use the hardware detection procedure we'll describe in a moment.

Also, the system will display information on the drive partitions and devices detected. If any of this information is incorrect or missing, you will have to force hardware detection.

On the other hand, if all goes well and your hardware seems to be detected, you can skip to the following section, "Drives and Partitions Under Linux."

To force hardware detection, you must enter the appropriate parameters at the boot prompt, using the following syntax:

    ramdisk *parameters...*

There are a number of such parameters available; here are some of the most common.

hd=*cylinders,heads, sectors*
  Specify the hard drive geometry. Required for systems such as the IBM PS/1, ValuePoint, and ThinkPad. For example, if your drive has 683 cylinders, 16 heads, and 32 sectors per track, use

    ramdisk hd=683,16,32

tmc8xx=*memaddr,irq*
  Specify address and IRQ for BIOS-less Future Domain TMC-8xx SCSI controller. For example,

    ramdisk tmc8xx=0xca000,5

  The 0x prefix must be used for all values given in hexadecimal. This is true for all of the following options.

st0x=*memaddr,irq*
  Specify address and IRQ for BIOS-less Seagate ST02 controller.

t128=*memaddr,irq*
  Specify address and IRQ for BIOS-less Trantor T128B controller.

ncr5380=*port,irq,dma*
  Specify port, IRQ, and DMA channel for generic NCR5380 controller.

aha152x=*port,irq,scsi_id,*1
  Specify port, IRQ, and SCSI ID for BIOS-less AIC-6260 controllers. This includes Adaptec 1510, 152x, and Soundblaster-SCSI controllers.

For each of these, you must enter *ramdisk* followed by the parameter that you wish to use.

[70] SCSI HOWTO [72] CD-ROM HOWTO

If you have questions about these boot-time options, please read the Linux SCSI HOWTO, which should be available on any Linux FTP archive site, as well as the Linux CD-ROM HOWTO. These documents describe hardware compatibility in much more detail.

Drives and Partitions Under Linux

Many distributions require you to create Linux partitions by hand using the *fdisk* program. Others may automatically create partitions for you. Either way, you should know the following information about Linux partitions and device names.

Drives and partitions under Linux are given different names from their counterparts under other operating systems. Under MS-DOS, floppy drives are referred to as A: and B:, while hard drive partitions are named C:, D:, and so on. Under Linux, the naming convention is quite different.

Device drivers, found in the directory */dev*, are used to communicate with devices on your system (such as hard drives, mice, and so on). For example, if you have a mouse on your system, you access it through the driver */dev/mouse*. Floppy drives, hard drives, and individual partitions are all given individual device drivers of their own. Don't worry about the device driver interface for now; it is important only to understand how the various devices are named in order to use them. The section "Device Files" in Chapter 4 talks more about devices.

Chapter 4

Table 2-1 lists the names of these various device drivers.

Table 2–1: Linux Partition Names

Device	Name
First floppy (A:)	*/dev/fd0*
Second floppy (B:)	*/dev/fd1*
First hard drive (entire drive)	*/dev/hda*
First hard drive, primary partition 1	*/dev/hda1*
First hard drive, primary partition 2	*/dev/hda2*
First hard drive, primary partition 3	*/dev/hda3*
First hard drive, primary partition 4	*/dev/hda4*
First hard drive, logical partition 1	*/dev/hda5*
First hard drive, logical partition 2	*/dev/hda6*
etc.	
Second hard drive (entire drive)	*/dev/hdb*
Second hard drive, primary partition 1	*/dev/hdb1*
etc.	
First SCSI hard drive (entire drive)	*/dev/sda*
First SCSI hard drive, primary partition 1	*/dev/sda1*
etc.	
Second SCSI hard drive (entire drive)	*/dev/sdb*
Second SCSI hard drive, primary partition 1	*/dev/sdb1*
etc.	

A few notes about this table. */dev/fd0* corresponds to the first floppy drive (A: under MS-DOS) and */dev/fd1* corresponds to the second floppy (B:).

Also, SCSI hard drives are named differently from other drives. IDE, MFM, and RLL drives are accessed through the devices */dev/hda*, */dev/hdb*, and so on. The individual partitions on the drive */dev/hda* are */dev/hda1*, */dev/hda2*, and so on. However, SCSI drives are named */dev/sda*, */dev/sdb*, etc., with partition names such as */dev/sda1* and */dev/sda2*.

[extended partition is treated as primary]

Most systems, of course, do not have four primary partitions. But the names */dev/hda1* through */dev/hda4* are still reserved for these partitions; they cannot be used to name logical partitions.

Here's an example. Let's say that you have a single IDE hard drive, with three primary partitions. The first two are set aside for MS-DOS, and the third is an extended partition which contains two logical partitions, both for use by Linux. The devices referring to these partitions would be:

Device	Name
First MS-DOS partition (C:)	*/dev/hda1*
Second MS-DOS partition (D:)	*/dev/hda2*
Extended partition	*(/dev/hda3)* — *extended partition.*
First Linux logical partition	*/dev/hda5*
Second Linux logical partition	*/dev/hda6*

Note that */dev/hda4* is skipped; it corresponds to the fourth primary partition, which we don't have in this example. Logical partitions are named consecutively starting with */dev/hda5*.

Creating Linux Partitions

Now you are ready to create Linux partitions with the *fdisk* command. In general, you will need to create at least one partition for the Linux software itself and another partition for swap space.

After booting the installation media, run *fdisk* by typing

```
fdisk drive
```

where *drive* is the Linux device name of the drive you plan to add partitions to (see Table 2-1). For instance, if you want to run *fdisk* on the first SCSI disk in your system, use the command *fdisk /dev/sda*. */dev/hda* (the first IDE drive) is the default if you don't specify one.

If you are creating Linux partitions on more than one drive, run *fdisk* once for each drive.

```
# fdisk /dev/hda

Command (m for help):
```

Here *fdisk* is waiting for a command; you can type m to get a list of options.

```
Command (m for help): m
Command action
   a   toggle a bootable flag
   d   delete a partition
   l   list known partition types
   m   print this menu
   n   add a new partition
   p   print the partition table
   q   quit without saving changes
   t   change a partition's system id
   u   change display/entry units
   v   verify the partition table
   w   write table to disk and exit
   x   extra functionality (experts only)

Command (m for help):
```

The n command is used to create a new partition. Most of the other options you won't need to worry about. To quit *fdisk* without saving any changes, use the q command. To quit *fdisk* and write the changes to the partition table to disk, use the w command.

The first thing you should do is display your current partition table and write the information down, for later reference. Use the p command.

```
Command (m for help): p
Disk /dev/hda: 16 heads, 38 sectors, 683 cylinders
Units = cylinders of 608 * 512 bytes
    Device Boot  Begin   Start    End  Blocks   Id  System
/dev/hda1    *       1       1    203   61693    6  DOS 16-bit >=32M

Command (m for help):
```

In this example, we have a single MS-DOS partition on */dev/hda1*, which is 61693 blocks (about 60 megs).[*] This partition starts at cylinder number 1 and ends on cylinder 203. We have a total of 683 cylinders in this disk; so there are 480 cylinders left to create Linux partitions on.

To create a new partition, use the n command. In this example, we'll create two primary partitions (*/dev/hda2* and */dev/hda3*) for Linux.

```
Command (m for help): n
Command action
   e   extended
   p   primary partition (1-4)
   p
```

Here, *fdisk* is asking the type of the partition to create: extended or primary. In our example, we're creating only primary partitions, so we choose p.

---

[*] A block, under Linux, is 1024 bytes.

```
Partition number (1-4):
```

fdisk will then ask for the number of the partition to create; since partition 1 is already used, our first Linux partition will be number 2.

```
Partition number (1-4): 2
First cylinder (204-683):
```

Now enter the starting cylinder number of the partition. Since cylinders 204 through 683 are unused, we'll use the first available one (numbered 204). There's no reason to leave empty space between partitions.

```
First cylinder (204-683): 204
Last cylinder or +size or +sizeM or +sizeK (204-683):
```

fdisk is asking for the size of the partition to create. We can either specify an ending cylinder number, or a size in bytes, kilobytes, or megabytes. Since we want our partition to be 80 megs in size, we specify +80M. When specifying a partition size in this way, *fdisk* will round the actual partition size to the nearest number of cylinders.

```
Last cylinder or +size or +sizeM or +sizeK (204-683): +80M

Warning: Linux cannot currently use 33090 sectors of this partition
```

If you see a warning message such as this, it can be ignored. *fdisk* prints the warning because it's an older program, and dates before the time that Linux partitions were allowed to be larger than 64 megabytes.

Now we're ready to create our second Linux partition. For sake of demonstration, we'll create it with a size of 10 megabytes.

```
Command (m for help): n
Command action
   e   extended
   p   primary partition (1-4)
p
Partition number (1-4): 3
First cylinder (474-683): 474
Last cylinder or +size or +sizeM or +sizeK (474-683): +10M
```

At last, we'll display the partition table. Again, write down all of this information—especially the block sizes of your new partitions. You'll need to know the sizes of the partitions when creating filesystems, later. Also, verify that none of your partitions overlap.

```
Command (m for help): p

Disk /dev/hda: 16 heads, 38 sectors, 683 cylinders
Units = cylinders of 608 * 512 bytes
    Device Boot  Begin   Start    End  Blocks   Id  System
/dev/hda1    *       1       1    203   61693    6  DOS 16-bit >=32M
```

```
/dev/hda2          204       204       473    82080   81   Linux/MINIX
/dev/hda3          474       474       507    10336   81   Linux/MINIX
```

As you can see, */dev/hda2* is now a partition of size 82080 blocks (which corresponds to about 80 megabytes), and */dev/hda3* is 10336 blocks (about 10 megs).

Note that many distributions (such as Slackware) require you to use the t command in *fdisk* to change the type of the swap partition to "Linux swap," which is usually numbered 82. You can use the L command to print a list of known partition type codes, and then use t to set the type of the swap partition to that which corresponds to "Linux swap."

This way the installation software will be able to automatically find your swap partitions based on type. If the installation software doesn't seem to recognize your swap partition, you might want to re-run *fdisk* and use the t command on the partition in question.

In the example above, the remaining cylinders on the disk (numbered 508 to 683) are unused. You may wish to leave unused space on the disk, in case you wish to create additional partitions later.

Finally, we use the w command to write the changes to disk and exit *fdisk*.

```
Command (m for help): w

#
```

Keep in mind that none of the changes you make while running *fdisk* will take effect until you give the w command, so you can toy with different configurations and save them when you're done. Also, if you want to quit *fdisk* at any time without saving the changes, use the q command. Remember that you shouldn't modify partitions for operating systems other than Linux with the Linux *fdisk* program.

You may not be able to boot Linux from a partition using cylinders numbered over 1023. Therefore, you should try to create your Linux root partition within the sub-1024 cylinder range. Again, if this is impossible, you can simply boot Linux from floppy.

Some Linux distributions require you to reboot the system after running *fdisk*. This is to allow the changes to the partition table to take effect before installing the software. Newer versions of *fdisk* automatically update the partition information in the kernel, so rebooting isn't necessary. To be on the safe side, after running *fdisk* you should reboot the installation media, as before, before proceeding.

Creating the Swap Space

Chapter 4

If you are planning to use a swap partition for virtual RAM, you're ready to prepare it for use.[*] In the section "Managing Swap Space" of Chapter 4, we discuss the preparation of a swap file, in case you don't want to use an individual partition.

Many distributions require you to create and activate swap space before installing the software. If you have a small amount of physical RAM, the installation procedure may not be successful unless you have some amount of swap space enabled.

The command used to prepare a swap partition is *mkswap*, and it takes the form

```
mkswap -c partition size
```

where *partition* is the name of the swap partition and *size* is the size of the partition in blocks.[†] For example, if your swap partition is */dev/hda3* and is 10336 blocks in size, use the command

```
# mkswap -c /dev/hda3 10336
```

The *-c* option tells *mkswap* to check for bad blocks on the partition when creating the swap space.

If you are using multiple swap partitions, you will need to execute the appropriate *mkswap* command for each partition.

After formatting the swap space, you need to enable it for use by the system. Usually, the system automatically enables swap space at boot time. However, because you have not yet installed the Linux software, you need to enable it by hand.

The command to enable swap space is *swapon*, and it takes the form

```
swapon partition
```

In the example above, to enable the swap space on */dev/hda3*, we use the command

```
# swapon /dev/hda3
```

Creating the Filesystems

Before you can use your Linux partitions to store files, you must create *filesystems* on them. Creating a filesystem is analogous to formatting a partition under MS-DOS or other operating systems. We discussed filesystems briefly in the section "Linux Partition Requirements."

---

* Again, some distributions of Linux will prepare the swap space automatically for you, or via an installation menu option.

† This is the size as reported by *fdisk*, using the p menu option. A block under Linux is 1024 bytes.

There are several types of filesystems available for Linux. Each filesystem type has its own format and set of characteristics (such as filename length, maximum file size, and so on). Linux also supports several "third-party" filesystem types such as the MS-DOS filesystem.

The most commonly used filesystem type is the *Second Extended Filesystem*, or *ext2fs*. The *ext2fs* is one of the most efficient and flexible filesystems; it allows filenames up to 256 characters and filesystem sizes of up to 4 terabytes. In the section "Filesystem Types" in Chapter 4, we'll discuss the various filesystem types available for Linux. Initially, however, we suggest that you use the *ext2fs* filesystem.

Chapter 4

To create an *ext2fs* filesystem, use the command

```
mke2fs -c partition size
```

where *partition* is the name of the partition, and *size* is the size of the partition in blocks. For example, to create an 82080-block filesystem on */dev/hda2*, use the command

```
# mke2fs -c /dev/hda2 82080
```

If you're using multiple filesystems for Linux, you'll need to use the appropriate *mke2fs* command for each filesystem.

If you have encountered any problems at this point, see the section "Running Into Trouble" at the end of this chapter.

Installing the Software

Finally, you are ready to install the software on your system. Every distribution has a different mechanism for doing this. Many distributions have a self-contained program that will step you through the installation. On other distributions, you will have to *mount* your filesystems in a certain subdirectory (such as */mnt*) and copy the software to them by hand. On CD-ROM distributions, you may be given the option to install a portion of the software on your hard drives, and leave most of the software on the CD-ROM.

Some distributions offer several different ways to install the software. For example, you may be able to install the software directly from an MS-DOS partition on your hard drive, instead of from floppies. Or you may be able to install over a TCP/IP network via FTP or NFS. See your distribution's documentation for details.

For example, the Slackware distribution only requires you to do the following:

1.   Create partitions with *fdisk*.

2.   Optionally create swap space with *mkswap* and *swapon* (if you have 4 megs or less of RAM).

3.   Run the *setup* program. *setup* leads you through a very self-explanatory menu system to install the software.

The exact method used to install the Linux software differs greatly with each distribution. We're hoping that installing the Linux software should be self-explanatory, as it is with most distributions.

Creating the Boot Floppy or Installing LILO

Every distribution provides some means of booting your new Linux system after you have installed the software. In many cases, the installation procedure will create a "boot floppy," which contains a Linux kernel configured to use your newly-created root filesystem. In order to boot Linux, you would boot from this floppy and control would be transferred to your hard drive after booting. On other distributions, this "boot floppy" is the installation floppy itself.

Many distributions give you the option of installing LILO on your hard drive. LILO is a program that resides on your drive's master boot record. It is able to boot a number of operating systems, including MS-DOS and Linux, and allows you to select at startup time which to boot.

In order for LILO to be installed successfully, it needs to know a good deal of information about your drive configuration—for example, which partitions contain which operating systems, how to boot each operating system, and so on. Many distributions, when installing LILO, attempt to "guess" at the appropriate parameters for your configuration. Although it's not often, the automated LILO installation provided by some distributions can fail and leave your master boot record in shambles (although it's very doubtful that any damage to the actual data on your hard drive will take place). In particular, if you use OS/2's Boot Manager, you should *not* install LILO using the automated procedure—there are special instructions for using LILO with the Boot Manager, which will be covered later.

In many cases, it is best to use a boot floppy until you have a chance to configure LILO yourself, by hand. If you're feeling exceptionally trustworthy, though, you can go ahead with the automated LILO installation if it is provided with your distribution.

Chapter 4

In the section "Using LILO" of Chapter 4, we'll cover in detail how to configure and install LILO for your particular setup.

If everything goes well, then congratulations! You have just installed Linux on your system. Go have a Diet Coke or something—you deserve it.

In case you did run into any trouble, the section "Running Into Trouble" describes the most common sticking points for Linux installations, and how to get around them.

Additional Installation Procedures

Some distributions of Linux provide a number of additional installation procedures, allowing you to configure various software packages such as TCP/IP networking, the X Window System, and so on. If you are provided with these configuration options during installation, you may wish to read ahead in this book for more information on how to configure this software. Otherwise, you should put off these installation procedures until you have a complete understanding of how to configure the software.

It's up to you; if all else fails, just go with the flow and see what happens. It's very doubtful that anything that you do incorrectly now cannot be undone in the future. (Knock on wood.)

Postinstallation Procedures

After you have completed installing the Linux software, you should be able to reboot the system, log in as **root**, and begin exploring the system. (Each distribution has a different method for doing this—follow the instructions given by the distribution.)

Before you strike out on your own, however, there are some tasks which are most conveniently done at this point that may save you a lot of grief later. Some of these tasks are trivial if you have the right hardware and Linux distribution; others may involve a little research on your part, and you may decide to postpone them until later.

Creating a User Account

In order to start using your system, you'll need to create a user account for yourself. Eventually, if you plan to have other users on your system, you'll create user accounts for them as well. But before you begin to explore you need at least one account.

Why is this? Every Linux system has several pre-installed accounts, such as **root**. The **root** account, however, is intended exclusively for administrative purposes. As **root** you have all kinds of privileges and can access all files on your system.

However, using **root** can be dangerous, especially if you're new to Linux. Because there are no restrictions on what **root** can do, it's all too easy to mistype a command and inadvertently delete files, damage your filesystem, and so on. You should log in as **root** only when you need to perform system administration tasks, such as fixing configuration files, installing new software, and so on. See the section "Running the System" in Chapter 4 for details.

Chapter 4

For normal usage, you should create a standard user account. UNIX systems have built-in security which prevents users from deleting other users' files, corrupting important resources such as system configuration files, and so on. As a regular user you'll be protecting yourself from your own mistakes. This is especially true for users without UNIX system administration experience.

Many Linux distributions provide tools for creating new accounts. These programs are usually called *useradd* or *adduser*. As **root**, invoking one of these commands should present you with a usage summary for the command, and creating a new account should be fairly self-explanatory.

Other distributions, such as the Yggdrasil LGX CD-ROM, provide a generic system administration tool for various tasks, one of which is creating a new user account. The *control-panel* command under LGX will start up this tool.

If all else fails, you can create an account by hand. Usually, all that is required to create an account is:

- Edit the file */etc/passwd* to add the new user.

- Optionally edit the file */etc/shadow* to specify "shadow password" attributes for the new user.

- Create the user's home directory.

- Copy skeleton configuration files (such as *.bashrc*) to the new user's home directory. These can sometimes be found in the directory */etc/skel*.

Chapter 4

We don't want to go into great detail here—the particulars of creating a new user account can be found in virtually every book on UNIX system administration (see the Bibliography for suggested reading). We also talk about creating users in the section "Managing User Accounts" in Chapter 4. With luck, there will be a tool provided to take care of these details for you.

Keep in mind that to set or change the password on the new account, you can use the *passwd* command. For example, to change the password for the user **duck**, issue the following command:

```
# passwd duck
```

This will set or change the password for duck. If you execute the *passwd* command as **root**, it will not prompt you for the original password. In this way, if you have forgotten your old password, but can still log in as **root**, you can reset it.

Getting Online Help

Linux provides online help in the form of manual pages—or "man pages" for short. Throughout this book, we'll be directing you to look at the manual pages for particular commands to get more information. Manual pages describe programs and applications on the system in detail. It's important for you to learn right off how to access this online documentation in case you get into a bind.

To get online help for a particular command, use the *man* command. For example, to get information on the *passwd* command, use the command

```
$ man passwd
```

This should present you with the manual page for *passwd*.

Usually, manual pages are provided as an optional package with most distributions, so they won't be available unless you have opted to install them. In addition, certain manual pages may be missing or incomplete on your system. It depends on how complete your distribution is, and how up-to-date the manual pages are at the time.

Chapter 3

Linux manual pages also document system calls, library functions, configuration file formats, and kernel internals. In the section "Manual Pages" of Chapter 3, *Basic UNIX Commands and Concepts*, we'll describe their use in more detail.

Editing /etc/fstab

In order to ensure that all of your Linux filesystems will be available when you reboot the system, you may need to edit the file */etc/fstab*, which describes your filesystems. Many distributions automatically generate the */etc/fstab* file for you during installation, so all may be well. However, if you have additional filesystems that were not used during the installation process, you may need to add them to */etc/fstab* in order to make them available. Swap partitions should be included in */etc/fstab* as well.

In order to access a filesystem, it must be *mounted*. Mounting a filesystem associates that filesystem with a particular directory. For example, the root filesystem is mounted on */*, the */usr* filesystem on */usr*, and so on. (If you did not create a separate filesystem for */usr*, all files under */usr* will be stored on the root filesystem.)

Chapter 4

We don't want to smother you with technical details here, but it is important to understand how to make your filesystems available before exploring the system. For more details on mounting filesystems, see the section "Mounting Filesystems" in Chapter 4, or any book on UNIX system administration.

The root filesystem is automatically mounted on */* when you boot Linux. However, your other filesystems must be mounted individually. Usually, this is accomplished by the command

```
mount -av
```

in the system startup file */etc/rc*. This tells the *mount* command to mount any filesystems listed in the file */etc/fstab*. Therefore, in order to have your filesystems mounted automatically at boot time, you need to include them in */etc/fstab*. (Of course, you could always mount the filesystems by hand, using the *mount* command after booting, but this is unnecessary work.)

Here is a sample */etc/fstab* file. In this example, the root filesystem is on */dev/hda1*, the */home* filesystem is on */dev/hdb2*, and the swap partition is */dev/hdb1*.

```
# /etc/fstab
# device        directory    type    options
#
/dev/hda1       /            ext2    defaults
/dev/hdb2       /home        ext2    defaults
/dev/hdb1       none         swap    sw
/proc           /proc        proc    defaults
```

The lines beginning with the "#" character are comments. Also, you'll notice an additional entry for */proc*. */proc* is a "virtual filesystem" used to gather process information by commands such as *ps*.

As you can see, */etc/fstab* consists of a series of lines. The first field of each line is the device name of the partition (such as */dev/hda1*). The second field is the *mount point*—the directory where the filesystem is mounted. The third field is the type. Linux *ext2fs* filesystems should use ext2 for this field. swap should be used for swap partitions. The fourth field is for mounting options. You should use defaults in this field for filesystems, and sw for swap partitions.

Using this example as a model, you should be able to add entries for any filesystems that are not already listed in the */etc/fstab* file.

How do we add entries to the file? The easiest way is to edit the file, as **root**, using an editor such as *vi* or Emacs. We won't get into the use of text editors here—*vi* and Emacs are both covered at the beginning of Chapter 5, *Power Tools*.

Chapter 5

After editing the file, you'll need to issue the command

```
# /etc/mount -a
```

or reboot for the changes to take effect.

If you're stuck at this point, don't be alarmed. We suggest that UNIX novices do some reading on basic UNIX usage and system administration. Most of the remainder of this book is going to assume familiarity with these basics, so don't say we didn't warn you.

Shutting Down the System

You should never reboot or shutdown your Linux system by pressing the reset switch or with the old "Vulcan Nerve Pinch"—that is, by pressing Ctrl-Alt-Del in unison. You shouldn't simply switch off the power, either. As with most UNIX systems, Linux caches disk writes in memory. Therefore, if you suddenly reboot the system without shutting down "cleanly," you can corrupt the data on your drives.

The easiest way to shut down the system is with the *shutdown* command. As an example, to shutdown and reboot the system immediately, use the following command as **root**:

```
# shutdown -r now
```

This will cleanly reboot your system. The manual page for *shutdown* describes the other command-line arguments that are available.

Running Into Trouble

Almost everyone runs into some kind of snag or hangup when attempting to install Linux the first time. Most of the time, the problem is caused by a simple misunderstanding. Sometimes, however, it can be something more serious, such as an oversight by one of the developers, or a bug.

This section will describe some of the most common installation problems, and how to solve them. If your installation appears to be successful, but you received unexpected error messages during the installation, these are described here as well.

Problems with Booting the Installation Media

When attempting to boot the installation media for the first time, you may encounter a number of problems. These are listed below. Note that the following problems are *not* related to booting your newly-installed Linux system. See the section "Problems After Installing Linux" for information on these kinds of pitfalls.

- **Floppy or media error when attempting to boot.**

  The most popular cause for this kind of problem is a corrupt boot floppy. Either the floppy is physically damaged, in which case you should re-create the disk with a *brand new* floppy, or the data on the floppy is bad, in which case you should verify that you downloaded and transferred the data to the floppy correctly. In many cases, simply re-creating the boot floppy will solve your problems. Retrace your steps and try again.

  If you received your boot floppy from a mail order vendor or some other distributor, instead of downloading and creating it yourself, contact the distributor and ask for a new boot floppy—but only after verifying that this is indeed the problem.

- **System "hangs" during boot or after booting.**

  After the installation media boots, you will see a number of messages from the kernel itself, indicating which devices were detected and configured. After this, you will usually be presented with a login prompt, allowing you to proceed with installation (some distributions instead drop you right into an installation program of some kind). The system may appear to "hang" during several of these steps. Be patient; loading software from floppy is very slow. In many cases, the system has not hung at all, but is merely taking a long time. Verify that there is no drive or system activity for at least several minutes before assuming that the system is hung.

1. After booting from the LILO prompt, the system must load the kernel image from floppy. This may take several seconds; you will know that things are going well if the floppy drive light is still on.

2. While the kernel boots, SCSI devices must be probed for. If you do not have any SCSI devices installed, the system will "hang" for up to 15 seconds while the SCSI probe continues; this usually occurs after the line

   ```
   lp_init: lp1 exists (0), using polling driver
   ```

   appears on your screen.

3. After the kernel is finished booting, control is transferred to the system bootup files on the floppy. Finally, you will be presented with a login prompt, or be dropped into an installation program. If you are presented with a login prompt such as

   ```
   Linux login:
   ```

   you should then log in (usually as **root** or **install**—this varies with each distribution). After entering the username, the system may pause for 20 seconds or more while the installation program or shell is being loaded from floppy. Again, the floppy drive light should be on. Don't assume that the system is hung.

Any of the above items may be the source of your problem. However, it is possible that the system actually may "hang" while booting, which can be due to several causes. First of all, you may not have enough available RAM to boot the installation media. (See the following item for information on disabling the ramdisk to free up memory.)

Chapter 1

Hardware incompatibility causes many system hangs. The section "Hardware Requirements" in Chapter 1, *Introduction to Linux*, presents an overview of supported hardware under Linux. Even if your hardware is supported, you may run into problems with incompatible hardware configurations which are causing the system to hang. See the section "Hardware Problems" below, for a discussion of hardware incompatibilities.

- **System reports out-of-memory errors while attempting to boot or install the software.**

This item deals with the amount of RAM that you have available. On systems with 4 megabytes of RAM or less, you may run into trouble booting the installation media or installing the software itself. This is because many distributions use a "ramdisk," which is a filesystem loaded directly into RAM, for operations while using the installation media. The entire image of the installation boot floppy, for example, may be loaded into a ramdisk, which may require more than a megabyte of RAM.

The solution to this problem is to disable the ramdisk option when booting the install media. Each release has a different procedure for doing this; on the SLS release, for example, you type "`floppy`" at the LILO prompt when booting the *a1* disk. See your distribution's documentation for details.

You may not see an "out of memory" error when attempting to boot or install the software; instead, the system may unexpectedly hang, or fail to boot. If your system hangs, and none of the explanations in the previous section seem to be the cause, try disabling the ramdisk.

Keep in mind that Linux itself requires at least 2 megabytes of RAM to run at all; some distributions of Linux require 4 megabytes or more.

- **The system reports an error such as permission denied or file not found while booting.**

  This is an indication that your installation bootup media is corrupt. If you attempt to boot from the installation media (and you're sure that you're doing everything correctly), you should not see any errors such as this. Contact the distributor of your Linux software and find out about the problem, and perhaps obtain another copy of the boot media if necessary. If you downloaded the bootup disk yourself, try re-creating the bootup disk, and see if this solves your problem.

- **The system reports the error VFS: Unable to mount root when booting.**

  This error message means that the root filesystem (found on the boot media itself), could not be found. This means that either your boot media is corrupt in some way, or that you are not booting the system correctly.

  For example, many CD-ROM distributions require that you have the CD-ROM in the drive when booting. Also be sure that the CD-ROM drive is on, and check for any activity. It's also possible that the system is not locating your CD-ROM drive at boot time; see the section "Hardware Problems" for more information.

  If you're sure that you are booting the system correctly, then your bootup media may indeed be corrupt. This is a very uncommon problem, so try other solutions before attempting to use another boot floppy or tape.

Hardware Problems

The most common problem encountered when attempting to install or use Linux is an incompatibility with hardware. Even if all of your hardware is supported by

Linux, a misconfiguration or hardware conflict can sometimes cause strange results—your devices may not be detected at boot time, or the system may hang.

It is important to isolate these hardware problems if you suspect that they may be the source of your trouble. In the following sections we will describe some common hardware problems and how to resolve them.

Isolating hardware problems

If you experience a problem that you believe to be hardware-related, the first thing that you should to do is attempt to isolate the problem. This means eliminating all possible variables and (usually) taking the system apart, piece-by-piece, until the offending piece of hardware is isolated.

This is not as frightening as it may sound. Basically, you should remove all nonessential hardware from your system, and then determine which device is actually causing the trouble—possibly by reinserting each device, one at a time. This means that you should remove all hardware other than the floppy and video controllers, and of course the keyboard. Even innocent-looking devices such as mouse controllers can wreak unknown havoc on your peace of mind unless you consider them nonessential.

Chapter 1

For example, let's say that the system hangs during the Ethernet board detection sequence at boot time. You might hypothesize that there is a conflict or problem with the Ethernet board in your machine. The quick and easy way to find out is to pull the Ethernet board, and try booting again. If everything goes well, then you know that either the Ethernet board is not supported by Linux (see the section "Hardware Requirements" in Chapter 1 for a list of compatible boards), or there is an address or IRQ conflict with the board.

"Address or IRQ conflict?" What on earth does that mean? All devices in your machine use an IRQ, or *interrupt request line*, to tell the system that they need something done on their behalf. You can think of the IRQ as a cord that the device tugs when it needs the system to take care of some pending request. If more than one device is tugging on the same cord, the kernel won't be able to determine which device it needs to service. Instant mayhem.

Therefore, be sure that all of your installed devices are using unique IRQ lines. In general, the IRQ for a device can be set by jumpers on the card; see the documentation for the particular device for details. Some devices do not require the use of an IRQ at all, but it is suggested that you configure them to use one if possible (the Seagate ST01 and ST02 SCSI controllers being good examples).

In some cases, the kernel provided on your installation media is configured to use a certain IRQ for certain devices. For example, on some distributions of Linux, the kernel is preconfigured to use IRQ 5 for the TMC-950 SCSI controller, the Mitsumi CD-ROM controller, and the bus mouse driver. If you want to use two or more of these devices, you'll need first to install Linux with only one of these devices

Chapter 4

enabled, then recompile the kernel in order to change the default IRQ for one of them. (See the section "Building a New Kernel" in Chapter 4 for information on recompiling the kernel.)

Another area where hardware conflicts can arise is with DMA (*direct memory access*) channels, I/O addresses, and shared memory addresses. All of these terms describe mechanisms through which the system interfaces with hardware devices. Some Ethernet boards, for example, use a shared memory address as well as an IRQ to interface with the system. If any of these are in conflict with other devices, then the system may behave unexpectedly. You should be able to change the DMA channel, I/O, or shared memory addresses for your various devices with jumper settings. (Unfortunately, some devices don't allow you to change these settings.)

The documentation for your various hardware devices should specify the IRQ, DMA channel, I/O address, or shared memory address that the devices use, and how to configure them. Again, the simple way to get around these problems is just to temporarily disable the conflicting devices until you have time to determine the cause of the problem.

Table 2-2 is a list of IRQ and DMA channels used by various "standard" devices found on most systems. Almost all systems will have some of these devices, so you should avoid setting the IRQ or DMA of other devices in conflict with these values.

Table 2-2: Common Device Settings

Device	I/O Address	IRQ	DMA
ttyS0 (*COM1*)	3f8	4	n/a
ttyS1 (*COM2*)	2f8	3	n/a
ttyS2 (*COM3*)	3e8	4	n/a
ttyS3 (*COM4*)	2e8	3	n/a
lp0 (*LPT1*)	378 – 37f	7	n/a
lp1 (*LPT2*)	278 – 27f	5	n/a
fd0, fd1 (floppies 1 and 2)	3f0 – 3f7	6	2
fd2, fd3 (floppies 3 and 4)	370 – 377	10	3

Problems recognizing hard drive or controller

When Linux boots, you should see a series of messages on your screen such as:

```
Console: colour EGA+ 80x25, 8 virtual consoles
Serial driver version 3.96 with no serial options enabled
tty00 at 0x03f8 (irq = 4) is a 16450
tty03 at 0x02e8 (irq = 3) is a 16550A
lp_init: lp1 exists (0), using polling driver
...
```

Here, the kernel is detecting the various hardware devices present on your system. At some point, you should see the line

```
Partition check:
```

followed by a list of recognized partitions, for example:

```
Partition check:
  hda: hda1 hda2
  hdb: hdb1 hdb2 hdb3
```

If, for some reason, your drives or partitions are not recognized, then you will not be able to access them in any way.

There are several conditions that can cause this to happen:

- **Hard drive or controller not supported.** If you are using a hard drive controller (IDE, SCSI, or otherwise) that is not supported by Linux, the kernel will not recognize your partitions at boot time.

- **Drive or controller improperly configured.** Even if your controller is supported by Linux, it may not be configured correctly. (This is particularly a problem for SCSI controllers; most non-SCSI controllers should work fine without any additional configuration.)

  Refer to the documentation for your hard drive and/or controller for information on solving these kinds of problems. In particular, many hard drives will need to have a jumper set if they are to be used as a "slave" drive (for example, as the second hard drive). The acid test for this kind of condition is to boot up MS-DOS, or some other operating system, known to work with your drive and controller. If you can access the drive and controller from another operating system, then it is not a problem with your hardware configuration.

  See the section "Isolating hardware problems" above for information on resolving possible device conflicts, and the section "Problems with SCSI controllers and devices" below for information on configuring SCSI devices.

- **Controller properly configured, but not detected.** Some BIOS-less SCSI controllers require the user to specify information about the controller at boot time. The section "Problems with SCSI controllers and devices" below describes how to force hardware detection for these controllers.

- **Hard drive geometry not recognized.** Some systems, such as the IBM PS/ValuePoint, do not store hard drive geometry information in the CMOS memory, where Linux expects to find it. Also, certain SCSI controllers need to be told where to find drive geometry in order for Linux to recognize the layout of your drive.

Most distributions provide a bootup option to specify the drive geometry. In general, when booting the installation media, you can specify the drive geometry at the LILO boot prompt with a command such as:

```
boot: linux hd=cylinders,heads,sectors
```

where *cylinders*, *heads*, and *sectors* correspond to the number of cylinders, heads, and sectors per track for your hard drive.

After installing the Linux software, you will be able to install LILO, allowing you to boot from the hard drive. At that time, you can specify the drive geometry to the LILO installation procedure, making it unnecessary to enter the drive geometry each time you boot. See the section "Using LILO" in Chapter 4 for more about LILO.

Chapter 4

Problems with SCSI controllers and devices

Presented here are some of the most common problems with SCSI controllers and devices such as CD-ROMs, hard drives, and tape drives. If you are having problems getting Linux to recognize your drive or controller, read on.

[70] SCSI
HOWTO

The Linux SCSI HOWTO (see Appendix A) contains much useful information on SCSI devices in addition to that listed here. SCSI can be particularly tricky to configure at times.

- **A SCSI device is detected at all possible ID's.** This is caused by strapping the device to the same address as the controller. You need to change the jumper settings so that the drive uses a different address from the controller itself.

- **Linux reports sense errors, even if the devices are known to be error-free.** This can be caused by bad cables or by bad termination. If your SCSI bus is not terminated at both ends, you may have errors accessing SCSI devices. When in doubt, always check your cables.

- **SCSI devices report timeout errors.** This is usually caused by a conflict with IRQ, DMA, or device addresses. Also check that interrupts are enabled correctly on your controller.

- **SCSI controllers using BIOS are not detected.** Detection of controllers using BIOS will fail if the BIOS is disabled, or if your controller's "signature" is not recognized by the kernel. See the Linux SCSI HOWTO for more information about this.

- **Controllers using memory-mapped I/O do not work.** This is caused when the memory-mapped I/O ports are incorrectly cached. Either mark the board's address space as uncacheable in the XCMOS settings, or disable cache altogether.

- **When partitioning, you get a warning that "cylinders > 1024," or you are unable to boot from a partition using cylinders numbered above 1023.** BIOS limits the number of cylinders to 1024, and any partition using cylinders numbered above this won't be accessible from the BIOS. As far as Linux is concerned, this affects only booting; once the system has booted you should be able to access the partition. Your options are to either boot Linux from a boot floppy, or boot from a partition using cylinders numbered below 1024. See the section "Creating the Boot Floppy or Installing LILO" for information on creating a boot diskette or installing LILO.

- **CD-ROM drive or other removable media devices are not recognized at boot time**. Try booting with a CD-ROM (or disk) in the drive. This is necessary for some devices.

If your SCSI controller is not recognized, you may need to force hardware detection at boot time. This is particularly important for BIOS-less SCSI controllers. Most distributions allow you to specify the controller IRQ and shared memory address when booting the installation media. For example, if you are using a TMC-8xx controller, you may be able to enter

```
boot: linux tmx8xx=interrupt,memory-address
```

at the LILO boot prompt, where *interrupt* is the IRQ of controller, and *memory-address* is the shared memory address. Whether or not you will be able to do this depends on the distribution of Linux you are using; consult your documentation for details.

Problems Installing the Software

Actually installing the Linux software should be quite trouble-free, if you're lucky. The only problems that you might experience would be related to corrupt installation media or lack of space on your Linux filesystems. Here is a list of these common problems.

- **System reports "Read error, file not found," or other errors while attempting to install the software**. This is indicative of a problem with your installation media. If you are installing from floppy, keep in mind that floppies are quite susceptible to media errors of this type. Be sure to use brand-new, newly-formatted floppies. If you have an MS-DOS partition on your drive, many Linux distributions allow you to install the software from the hard drive. This may be faster and more reliable than using floppies.

  If you are using a CD-ROM, be sure to check the disk for scratches, dust, or other problems that might cause media errors.

  The cause of the problem may be that the media is in the incorrect format. For example, if using floppies, many Linux distributions require that the floppies be formatted in high-density MS-DOS format. (The boot floppy is the exception; it is not in MS-DOS format in most cases.) If all else fails, either obtain a new set of floppies, or recreate the floppies (using new diskettes) if you downloaded the software yourself.

- **System reports errors such as "tar: read error" or "gzip: not in gzip format".** This problem is usually caused by corrupt files on the installation media itself. In other words, your floppy may be error-free, but the data on the floppy is in some way corrupted. For example, if you downloaded the Linux software using text mode, rather than binary mode, then your files will be corrupt, and unreadable by the installation software. The section "Downloading Files" in Appendix C explains how to set the right mode.

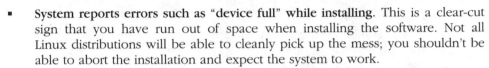
Appendix C

- **System reports errors such as "device full" while installing.** This is a clear-cut sign that you have run out of space when installing the software. Not all Linux distributions will be able to cleanly pick up the mess; you shouldn't be able to abort the installation and expect the system to work.

The solution is usually to re-create your filesystems (with the *mke2fs* command) which will delete the partially-installed software. You can then attempt to re-install the software, this time selecting a smaller amount of software to install. In other cases, you may need to start completely from scratch, and rethink your partition and filesystem sizes.

- **System reports errors such as "read_intr: 0x10" while accessing the hard drive.** This is usually an indication of bad blocks on your drive. However, if you receive these errors while using *mkswap* or *mke2fs*, the system may be having trouble accessing your drive. This can either be a hardware problem (see the section "Hardware Problems"), or it might be a case of poorly specified geometry. If you used the

      hd=cylinders,heads,sectors

  option at boot time to force detection of your drive geometry, and incorrectly specified the geometry, you could receive this error. This can also happen if your drive geometry is incorrectly specified in the system CMOS.

- **System reports errors such as "file not found" or "permission denied".** This problem can occur if not all of the necessary files are present on the installation media (see the next paragraph) or if there is a permissions problem with the installation software. For example, some distributions of Linux have been known to have bugs in the installation software itself. These are usually fixed very rapidly and are quite infrequent. If you suspect that the distribution software contains bugs, and you're sure that you have not done anything wrong, contact the maintainer of the distribution to report the bug.

If you have other strange errors when installing Linux (especially if you downloaded the software yourself), be sure that you actually obtained all of the necessary files when downloading. For example, some people use the FTP command

      mget *.*

when downloading the Linux software via FTP. This will download only those files that contain a ".." in their filenames; if there are any files without the "." you will miss them. The correct command to use in this case is

```
mget *
```

The best advice is to retrace your steps when something goes wrong. You may think that you have done everything correctly, when in fact you forgot a small but important step somewhere along the way. In many cases, just attempting to re-download or re-install the Linux software can solve the problem. Don't beat your head against the wall any longer than you have to!

Also, if Linux unexpectedly hangs during installation, there may be a hardware problem of some kind. See the section "Hardware Problems" for hints.

Problems After Installing Linux

You've spent an entire afternoon installing Linux. In order to make space for it, you wiped your MS-DOS and OS/2 partitions, and tearfully deleted your copies of SimCity and Wing Commander. You reboot the system, and nothing happens. Or, even worse, *something* happens, but it's not what should happen. What do you do?

In the section "Problems with Booting the Installation Media," we covered some of the most common problems that can occur when booting the Linux installation media—many of those problems may apply here. In addition, you may be victim to one of the following maladies.

Problems booting Linux from floppy

If you are using a floppy to boot Linux, you may need to specify the location of your Linux root partition at boot time. This is especially true if you are using the original installation floppy itself, and not a custom boot floppy created during installation.

While booting the floppy, hold down the Shift or Control key. This should present you with a boot menu; press Tab to see a list of available options. For example, many distributions allow you to type

```
boot: linux hd=partition
```

at the boot menu, where *partition* is the name of the Linux root partition, such as */dev/hda2*. Consult the documentation for your distribution for details.

Problems booting Linux from the hard drive

If you opted to install LILO, instead of creating a boot floppy, then you should be able to boot Linux from the hard drive. However, the automated LILO installation procedure used by many distributions is not always perfect. It may make incorrect assumptions about your partition layout, in which case you will need to re-install LILO to get everything right. Installing LILO is covered in the section "Using LILO" in Chapter 4.

- **System reports "Drive not bootable—Please insert system disk."** You will get this error message if the hard drive's master boot record is corrupt in some way. In most cases, it's harmless, and everything else on your drive is still intact. There are several ways around this:

  1. While partitioning your drive using *fdisk*, you may have deleted the partition that was marked as "active." MS-DOS and other operating systems attempt to boot the "active" partition at boot time (Linux pays no attention to whether the partition is "active" or not). You may be able to boot MS-DOS from floppy and run FDISK to set the active flag on your MS-DOS partition, and all will be well.

     Another command to try (with MS-DOS 5.0 and higher) is

     ```
     FDISK /MBR
     ```

     [handwritten: presumably from boot floppy !! if HD not bootable !!]

     This command will attempt to rebuild the hard drive master boot record for booting MS-DOS, overwriting LILO. If you no longer have MS-DOS on your hard drive, you'll need to boot Linux from floppy and attempt to install LILO later.

  2. If you created an MS-DOS partition using Linux's version of *fdisk*, or vice versa, you may get this error. You should create MS-DOS partitions only by using MS-DOS's version of FDISK. (The same applies to operating systems other than MS-DOS.) The best solution here is either to start from scratch and repartition the drive correctly, or to merely delete and re-create the offending partitions using the correct version of *fdisk*.

  3. The LILO installation procedure may have failed. In this case, you should boot either from your Linux boot floppy (if you have one), or from the original installation media. Either of these should provide options for specifying the Linux root partition to use when booting. Hold down the Shift or Control key at boot time, and press Tab from the boot menu for a list of options.

- **When booting the system from the hard drive, MS-DOS (or another operating system) starts instead of Linux.** First of all, be sure that you actually installed LILO when installing the Linux software. If not, then the system will still boot MS-DOS (or whatever other operating system you may have) when you attempt to boot from the hard drive. In order to boot Linux from the hard drive, you will need to install LILO (see the section "Using LILO" in Chapter 4).

  On the other hand, if you *did* install LILO, and another operating system boots instead of Linux, then you have LILO configured to boot that other operating system by default. While the system is booting, hold down the Shift or Control key, and press Tab at the boot prompt. This should present you with a list of possible operating systems to boot; select the appropriate option (usually just "`linux`") to boot Linux.

If you wish to select Linux as the default operating system to boot, you will need to re-install LILO.

It also may be possible that you attempted to install LILO, but the installation procedure failed in some way. See the previous item.

Problems logging in

After booting Linux, you should be presented with a login prompt, like so:

```
Linux login:
```

At this point, either the distribution's documentation or the system itself will tell you what to do. For many distributions, you simply log in as **root**, with no password. Other possible usernames to try are **guest** or **test**.

Most newly-installed Linux systems should not require a password for the initial login. However, if you are asked to enter a password, there may be a problem. First, try using a password equivalent to the username; that is, if you are logging in as **root**, use "`root`" as the password.

If you simply can't log in, consult your distribution's documentation; the username and password to use may be buried in there somewhere. The username and password may have been given to you during the installation procedure, or they may be printed on the login banner.

One cause of this password impasse may be a problem with installing the Linux login and initialization files. If this is the case, you may need to reinstall (at least parts of) the Linux software, or boot your installation media and attempt to fix the problem by hand.

Problems using the system

If login is successful, you should be presented with a shell prompt (such as # or $) and can happily roam around your system. The next step in this case is to try the procedures in Chapter 3. However, there are some initial problems with using the system that sometimes creep up.

The most common initial configuration problem is incorrect file or directory permissions. This can cause the error message

```
Shell-init: permission denied
```

to be printed after logging in (in fact, any time you see the message "`permission denied`" you can be fairly certain that it is a problem with file permissions).

In many cases, it's a simple matter of using the *chmod* command to fix the permissions of the appropriate files or directories. For example, some distributions of Linux once used the (incorrect) file mode 0644 for the root directory (/). The fix was to issue the command

```
# chmod 755 /
```

Chapter 3

as **root**. (File permissions are covered by the section "File Ownership and Permissions" in Chapter 3.) However, in order to issue this command, you needed to boot from the installation media and mount your Linux root filesystem by hand—a hairy task for most newcomers.

Chapter 1

As you use the system, you may run into places where file and directory permissions are incorrect, or software does not work as configured. Welcome to the world of Linux! While most distributions are quite trouble-free, you can't expect them to be perfect. We don't want to cover all of those problems here. Instead, throughout the book we help you to solve many of these configuration problems by teaching you how to find them and fix them yourself. In Chapter 1, we discussed this philosophy in some detail. In Chapter 4, we give hints for fixing many of these common configuration problems.

CHAPTER THREE
BASIC UNIX COMMANDS AND CONCEPTS

I f you've come to Linux from MS-DOS or another non-UNIX operating system, you have a steep learning curve ahead of you. We might as well be candid on this point. UNIX is a world all its own.

In this chapter we're going to introduce the rudiments of UNIX for those readers who have never had exposure to this operating system. If you are coming from MS-DOS, Microsoft Windows, or other environments, the information in this chapter will be absolutely vital to you. Unlike other operating systems, UNIX is not at all intuitive. Many of the commands have seemingly odd names or syntax, the reasons for which usually date back many years to the early days of this system. And, although many of the commands may appear to be similar to their MS-DOS counterparts, there are important differences.

There are dozens of other books that cover basic UNIX usage. You should be able to go to the computer section of any chain bookstore and find at least three or four of them on the shelf. (A few that we like are listed in the Bibliography.) However, most of these books cover UNIX from the point of view of someone sitting down at a workstation or terminal connected to a large mainframe—not someone who is running their own UNIX system on a personal computer!

Also, these books often dwell upon the more mundane aspects of UNIX—boring text-manipulation commands such as *awk*, *tr*, and *sed*, most of which you will never need unless you get into doing some serious UNIX trickery. In fact, many UNIX books talk about the original *ed* line editor, which has long been made obsolete by *vi* and Emacs. Therefore, although many of the UNIX books available today contain a great deal of useful information, many of them contain pages upon pages of humdrum material that you could probably care less about at this point.

Instead of getting into the dark mesh of text processing, shell syntax, and other issues, in this chapter we strive to cover the basic commands needed to get you up to speed with the system, if you're coming from a non-UNIX environment. This chapter is far from complete—a real beginner's UNIX tutorial would take an entire book. It's our hope that this chapter will give you enough to keep you going in your adventures with Linux, and that you'll invest in one of the aforementioned UNIX books once you have a need to do so. We'll give you enough UNIX background to make your terminal usable, keep track of jobs, and enter essential commands.

Chapter 4

Chapter 4, *Essential System Management*, contains material on system administration and maintenance. This is by far the most important chapter for anyone running their own Linux system. If you are completely new to UNIX, the material found in Chapter 4 should be easy to follow given the tutorial here.

Chapter 5

One big job we don't cover in this chapter is how to edit files. It's one of the first things you need to learn on any operating system. The two most popular editors for Linux, *vi* and Emacs, are discussed at the beginning of Chapter 5, *Power Tools*.

Logging In

Let's assume that your installation went completely smoothly and you are facing the prompt

```
Linux login:
```

Many Linux users are not so lucky; they have to perform some heavy tinkering when the system is still in a raw state, or in single-user mode. But for now we'll talk about logging into a functioning Linux system.

Logging in, of course, distinguishes one user from another. It lets several people work on the same system at once, and makes sure that you are the only person to have access to your files.

You may have installed Linux at home and be thinking right now, "Big deal. No one else shares this system with me, and I'd just as soon not have to log in." But logging in under your personal account also provides a certain degree of protection—your account won't have the ability to destroy or remove important system files. The system administration account (covered in the next chapter) is used for such touchy matters.

You were probably asked to set up a login account for yourself when you installed Linux. If you have such an account, type the name you chose at the `Linux login:` prompt. If you don't have an account yet, type `root` because that account is certain to exist. Some distributions may also set up an account called **install** or some other name, for fooling around when you first install the system.

Now you see

```
Password:
```

and you need to enter the correct password. The terminal turns off echoing for this operation, so that nobody looking at the screen can read your password. If the prompt does not appear, you should add a password to protect yourself from other people's tampering; we'll go into this later.

By the way, both the name and the password are case-sensitive. Check to make sure the Caps Lock key is not set, because typing ROOT instead of root will not work.

When you have successfully logged in, you will see a prompt. If you're **root** this may be a simple

```
#
```

For other users, the prompt is usually a dollar sign. The prompt may also contain the name you assigned to your system, or the directory you're in currently. Whatever appears here, you are now ready to enter commands. We say that you are at the "shell level," and that the prompt you see is the "shell prompt." This is because you are running a program called the shell that handles your commands. Right now we can ignore the shell, but later in this chapter we'll find out that it does a number of useful things for us.

As we show commands in this chapter, we'll show the prompt simply as $. So if you see

```
$ pwd
```

it means that the shell prints $ and that pwd is what you're supposed to enter.

Setting a Password

If you don't already have a password, we recommend you set one. Just enter the command *passwd*. The command will prompt you for the old password (to make sure you're you) and then prompt you twice for the new one. Why twice? To make sure you enter it without typos.

There are standard guidelines for choosing passwords so that they're hard for other people to guess. Some systems even check your password and reject any that don't meet the minimal criteria. For instance, it is often said that you should have at least six characters in the password. Furthermore, you should mix uppercase and lowercase characters, or include characters other than letters and digits.

To change your password, just enter the *passwd* command again.

Virtual Consoles

As a multiprocessing system, Linux gives you a number of interesting ways to do several things at once. You can start a long software installation and then switch to reading mail or compiling a program. This should be a major part of Linux's appeal to MS-DOS users (although the newest Microsoft Windows has finally come to grips with multiprocessing, too).

Most Linux users, when they want this asynchronous access, will employ the X Window System. But before you get X running you can do something similar through virtual consoles. This feature is specific to Linux; it is not provided by other UNIX systems.

To try out virtual consoles, just hold down the Alt key and press one of the function keys F1 through F8. As you press each function key, you see a totally new screen complete with a login prompt. You can log in to different virtual consoles just as if you were two different people, and switch between them to carry out different activities. You can even run a complete X session in each console.

Popular Commands

The number of commands on a typical UNIX system is enough to fill a couple hundred reference pages. And you can add new commands too. The commands we'll tell you about here are just enough to navigate and to see what you have on the system.

Directories

Like MS-DOS, and virtually every modern computer system, UNIX files are organized into a hierarchical directory structure. UNIX imposes no rules about where files have to be, but conventions have grown up over the years. Thus, on Linux you'll find a directory called */home* where each user's files are placed. Each user has a subdirectory under */home*. So if your login name is **mdw**, your personal files are located in */home/mdw*. This is called your home directory. You can, of course, create more subdirectories under it.

As you can see, the components of a directory are separated by slashes. The term *pathname* is often used to refer to this slash-separated list.

What directory is */home* in? The directory named */* of course. This is called the root directory. We have already mentioned it when setting up file systems.

When you log in, the system puts you in your home directory. To verify this, use the "print working directory" or *pwd* command:

```
$ pwd
/home/mdw
```

The system confirms that you're in */home/mdw*.

You certainly won't have much fun if you have to stay in one directory all the time. Now try using another command, *cd*, to move to another directory.

```
$ cd /usr/bin
$ pwd
/usr/bin
$ cd
```

Where are we now? A *cd* with no arguments returns us to our home directory. By the way, the home directory is often represented by a tilde (~). So the string ~/*programs* means that *programs* is located right under your home directory.

While we're thinking about it, let's make a directory called ~/*programs*. From your home directory, you can enter either

```
$ mkdir programs
```

or the full pathname

```
$ mkdir /home/mdw/programs
```

Now change to that directory:

```
$ cd programs
$ pwd
/home/mdw/programs
```

The special character sequence .. refers to "the directory just above the current one." So you can move back up to your home directory through:

```
$ cd ..
```

The opposite of *mkdir* is *rmdir*, which removes directories:

```
$ rmdir programs
```

Similarly, the *rm* command deletes files. We won't show it here, because we haven't yet shown how to create a file. You generally use the *vi* or Emacs editor for that (see Chapter 5), but some of the activities later in this chapter will create files too.

Listing Files

Enter *ls* to see what is in a directory. Issued without an argument, it shows the contents of the current directory. You can include an argument to see a different directory:

```
$ ls /home
```

Some systems have a fancy *ls* that displays special files—such as directories and executable files—in bold, or even in different colors. If you want to change the default colors, edit the file */etc/DIR_COLORS*, or create a copy of it in your home directory named *.dir_colors* and edit that.

Like most UNIX commands, *ls* can be controlled by options that start with a hyphen (–). Make sure that you type a space before the hyphen. One useful option for *ls* is *–a* for "all," which will reveal to you riches that you never imagined in your home directory:

```
$ cd
$ ls -a
.                        .bashrc                  .fvwmrc
..                       .emacs                   .xinitrc
.bash_history            .exrc
```

The single dot refers to the current directory, and the double dot to the directory right above it. But what are those other files beginning with a period? They are called hidden files. Putting a period in front of their names keeps them from being shown during a normal *ls* command. Many programs employ hidden files for user options—things about their default behavior that you want to change. For instance, you can put commands in the file *.Xdefaults* to alter how programs using the X Window System operate. So most of the time you can forget these files exist, but when you're configuring your system you'll find them very important. We'll list some of them later.

Another useful *ls* option is *–l* for "long." It shows extra information about the files. Figure 3-1 shows typical output, and what each field means.

We'll discuss the permissions, owner, and group fields later in this chapter, in the section "File Ownership and Permissions." The command also shows the size of each file and when it was last modified.

Viewing Files, More or Less

One way to look at a file is to invoke an editor, such as

```
$ emacs .bashrc
```

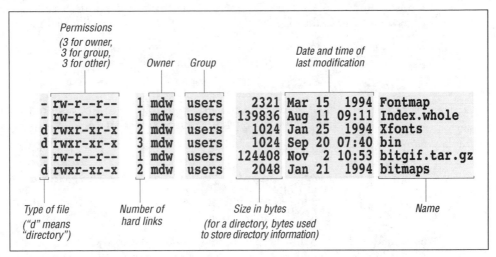

Figure 3–1. Output of ls –l

But if you just want to scan it quickly, rather than edit it, other commands are quicker. The simplest is the strangely-named *cat* command:

```
$ cat .bashrc
```

But a long file will scroll by too fast for you to see, so most people use the *more* command instead.

```
$ more .bashrc
```

This prints a screenful at a time, and waits for you to press the space bar before printing more. *more* has a lot of powerful options. For instance, you can search for a string in the file: press the slash key (/), type the string, and press Return.

A popular variation on the *more* command is called *less*. It has even more powerful features, like the ability to move backward in the file (just press b).

Symbolic Links

Sometimes you want to keep a file in one place and pretend it is another. This is done most often by a system administrator, not a user. For instance, you might keep several versions of a program around, called *prog.0.9, prog.1.1,* and so on, but use the name *prog* to refer to the version you're using currently. Or you may have a file installed in one partition because you have disk space for it there, but the program that uses the file needs it to be in a different partition because the pathname is hard-coded into the program.

UNIX provides *links* to handle these situations. In this section we'll examine the *symbolic link*, which is the most flexible and popular type. A symbolic link is a kind of dummy file that just points to another file. If you edit or read or execute the symbolic link, the system is smart enough to give you the real file instead.

Let's take the *prog* example. You want to create a link named *prog* that points to the actual file, which is named *prog.1.1*. Enter the command:

```
$ ln -s prog.1.1 prog
```

Now you've created a new file named *prog* that is kind of a dummy file—if you run it, you're really running *prog.1.1*. Let's look at what ls -l has to say about the file:

```
$ ls -l prog
lrwxrwxrwx   2 mdw      users          8 Nov 17 14:35 prog -> prog.1.1
```

The l at the beginning of the line shows that the file is a link, and the little -> indicates the real file that the link points to.

Symbolic links are really simple, once you get used to the idea of one file pointing to another. You'll encounter links all the time when installing software packages.

Shells

As we said before, logging in to the system puts you into a shell. So does opening an *xterm* window in X. The shell interprets and executes all of your commands. Let's look a bit at different shells before we keep going, because they're going to affect some of the material coming up.

If it seems confusing that UNIX offers many different shells, just accept it as an effect of evolution. Believe us, you wouldn't want to be stuck using the very first shell developed for UNIX, the Bourne shell. While it was a very powerful user interface for its day (the mid-1970's), it lacked a lot of useful features for interactive use—including the ones shown in this section. So other shells have been developed over time, and you can now choose the one that best suits your way of working.

Some of the shells available on Linux are:

bash
> Bourne Again shell. The most commonly used shell on Linux. POSIX-compliant, compatible with Bourne shell, created and distributed by the GNU project (Free Software Foundation). Offers command-line editing.

csh
> C shell. Developed at Berkeley. Mostly compatible with the Bourne shell for interactive use, but has a very different interface for programming. Does not offer command-line editing, although it does have a sophisticated alternative called history substitution.

ksh

> Korn shell. Perhaps the most popular on UNIX systems generally, and was the first to introduce modern shell techniques (including some borrowed from the C shell) into the Bourne shell. Compatible with Bourne shell. Offers command-line editing.

sh Bourne shell. The original shell. Does not offer command-line editing.

tcsh

> Enhanced C shell. Offers command-line editing.

zsh

> Z shell. The newest of the shells. Compatible with Bourne shell. Offers command-line editing.

Try the following command in order to find out what your shell is. It prints out the full pathname where the shell is located. Don't forget to type the dollar sign.

```
$ echo $SHELL
```

Probably you are running *bash*, the Bourne Again Shell. If you're running something else, this might be a good time to change to *bash*. It's powerful, POSIX-compliant, well-supported, and very popular on Linux. Use the *chsh* command to change your shell:

```
$ chsh
Enter password: Type your password here—this is for security's sake
The current shell is: /bin/sh
You can choose one of the following:
1: /bin/sh
2: /bin/bash
Enter a number between 1 and 2: 2
Shell changed.
```

There are a couple of ways to view the differences between shells.

One is to distinguish Bourne-compatible shells from *csh*-compatible shells. This will be of interest to you when you start to program with the shell—which is also known as writing shell scripts. The Bourne shell and C shell have different programming constructs. Most people now agree that the Bourne shell is better, and there are many UNIX utilities that recognize only the Bourne shell.

Another way to categorize shells is those that offer command-line editing (all the newer ones) versus those that do not. *sh* and *csh* lack this useful feature.

When you combine the two criteria—being compatible with the Bourne shell, and offering command-line editing—your best choice comes down to *bash*, *ksh*, or *zsh*. Try out several shells before you make your choice—it helps to know more than one, in case you find yourself on a system that limits your choice of shells someday.

Useful Keys and How to Get Them to Work

When you type a command, pressing the Backspace key should remove the last character. Ctrl-U should delete the whole line.* When you have finished a command and it is executing, Ctrl-C should abort it, and Ctrl-Z should suspend it. (When you want to resume the program, enter *fg* for "foreground.")

If any of these keys fail to work, your terminal is not configured right for some reason. You can fix it through the *stty* command. Use the syntax

    stty *function key*

where *function* is what you want to do, and *key* is the key that you press. Specify a control key by putting a circumflex (ˆ) in front of the key.

Here is a set of sample commands to set up the functions described earlier:

```
$ stty erase ^H
$ stty kill ^U
$ stty intr ^C
$ stty susp ^Z
```

The first control key shown, ˆH, represents the ASCII code generated by the Backspace key.

By the way, you can generate a listing of your current terminal settings by entering *stty −a*. But that doesn't mean you can understand the output! *stty* is a very complicated command with many uses, some of which require a lot of knowledge about terminals.

Typing Shortcuts

If you've been following along this tutorial at the terminal, you may be tired of typing the same things over and over again. It can be particularly annoying when you make a mistake and have to start over again. Here is where the shell really makes life easier. It doesn't make UNIX as simple as a point-and-click interface, but it can help you work really fast in a command environment.

This section discusses command-line editing. The tips here work if your shell is *bash*, *ksh*, *tcsh*, or *zsh*.

The idea of command-line editing is to treat the last fifty or so lines you typed as a buffer in an editor. You can move around these lines and change them the way you'd edit a document. Every time you press the return key, the shell executes the current line.

---

* Ctrl-U means hold down the Control key and press u.

Word Completion

First, let's try something simple that can save you a lot of time. Type the following, without pressing the Return key.

```
$ cd /usr/inc
```

Now press the Tab key. The shell will add lude to complete the name of the directory */usr/include*. Now you can press the Return key, and the command will execute.

The criteria for specifying a filename is "minimal completion." Type just enough characters to distinguish a name from all the others in that directory. The shell can find the name and complete it—up to and including a slash, if the name is a directory.

You can use completion on commands too. For instance, if you type

```
$ ema
```

and press the Tab key, the shell will add the cs to make emacs (unless some other command in your path begins with ema).

What if there are multiple files that match what you've typed? If they all start with the same characters, the shell completes the word up to the point where names differ. Beyond that, most shells do nothing. *bash* has a neat enhancement: if you press the Tab key twice, it displays all the possible completions. For instance, if you enter

```
$ cd /usr/l
```

and press the Tab key twice, *bash* prints something like

```
lib         local
```

Moving Around Among Commands

Press the up arrow, and the command you typed previously appears. The up arrow takes you back through the command history, while the down arrow takes you forward. If you want to change a character on the current line, use the left or right arrow keys.

As an example, suppose you tried to execute

```
$ mroe .bashrc
```

Of course, you typed mroe instead of more. To correct the command, call it back by pressing the up arrow. Then press the left arrow until the cursor lies over the o in mroe. You could use the Backspace key to remove the o and r and retype them correctly. But here's an even neater shortcut: just press Ctrl-T. It will reverse o and r, and you can then press the Return key to execute the command.

Many other keys exist for command-line editing. But the basics shown here will do quite a bit for you. If you learn the Emacs editor, you will find that most keys work the same way in the shell. And if you're a *vi* fan, you can set up your shell so that it uses *vi* key bindings instead of Emacs bindings. In *bash*, *ksh*, or *zsh*, enter the command:

```
$ export VISUAL=vi
```

In *tcsh* enter:

```
$ setenv VISUAL vi
```

Filename Expansion

Another way to save time in your commands is to use special characters to abbreviate filenames. You can specify many files at once by using these characters. This feature of the shell is sometimes called "globbing."

MS-DOS provides a few crude features of this type. You can use a question mark to mean "any character" and an asterisk to mean "any string of characters." UNIX provides these wildcards too, but in a much more robust and rigorous way.

Let's say you have a directory containing the following C source files:

```
$ ls
inv1jig.c    inv2jig.c    inv3jig.c    invinitjig.c    invpar.c
```

To list the three files containing digits in their names, you could enter:

```
$ ls inv?jig.c
inv1jig.c    inv2jig.c    inv3jig.c
```

The shell looks for a single character to replace the question mark. Thus, it displays *inv1jig.c*, *inv2jig.c*, and *inv3jig.c*, but not *invjiginit.c* because that name contains too many characters.

If you're not interested in the second file, you can specify the ones you want using brackets:

```
$ ls inv[13]jig.c
inv1jig.c    inv3jig.c
```

If any single character within the brackets matches a file, that file is displayed. You can also put a range of characters in the brackets:

```
$ ls inv[1-3]jig.c
inv1jig.c    inv2jig.c    inv3jig.c
```

Now we're back to displaying all three files. The hyphen means "match any character from 1 through 3, inclusive." You could ask for any numeric character by specifying 0-9, and any alphabetic character by specifying [a-zA-Z]. In the latter case, two ranges are required because the shell is case-sensitive. The order used, by the way, is that of the ASCII character set.

Suppose you want to see the init file, too. Now you can use an asterisk, because you want to match any number of characters between the inv and the jig:

```
$ ls inv*jig.c
inv1jig.c    inv2jig.c    inv3jig.c    invinitjig.c
```

The asterisk actually means "zero or more characters," so if a file named *invjig.c* existed, it would be shown, too.

Unlike MS-DOS, the UNIX shells let you combine special characters and normal characters any way you want. Let's say you want to look for any source (*.c*) or object (*.o*) file that contains a digit. The resulting name combines all the expansions we've studied in this section!

```
$ ls *[0-9]*.[co]
```

Filename expansion is very useful in shell scripts (programs), where you don't always know exactly how many files exist. For instance, you might want to process multiple log files named *log001*, *log002*, and so on. No matter how many there are, the expression *log** will match them all.

One final warning: filename expansion is not quite the same as regular expressions, which are used by many utilities to specify groups of strings. Regular expressions are beyond the scope of this book, but are described by many books that explain UNIX utilities.

Saving Your Output

System administrators (and other human beings too) see a lot of critical messages fly by on the computer screen. It's often important to save these messages so you can scrutinize them later, or (all too often) send them to a friend who can figure out what went wrong. So in this section we'll explain a little bit about redirection, a powerful feature provided by UNIX shells. If you come from MS-DOS, you have probably seen a similar but more limited type of redirection.

If you put a greater-than sign (>) and a filename after any command, the output of the command will be sent to that file. For instance, to capture the output of *ls*, you can enter

```
$ ls /usr/bin > ~/Binaries
```

A listing of */usr/bin* will be stored in your home directory in a file named *Binaries*. If *Binaries* had already existed, the > would wipe out what was there and replace it with the output of the *ls* command. Overwriting a current file is a common user error. If your shell is *csh* or *tcsh*, you can prevent overwriting through the command:

```
$ set noclobber
```

And in *bash* you can achieve the same effect by entering:

```
$ noclobber=1          It doesn't have to be 1, anything will have the same effect.
```

Another (and perhaps more useful) way to prevent overwriting is to append new output. For instance, having saved a listing of */usr/bin*, suppose we now want to add the contents of */bin*. We can append it to the end of the *Binaries* file by specifying two greater-than signs:

```
$ ls /bin >> ~/Binaries
```

You will find the technique of output redirection very useful when running a utility many times and saving the output for troubleshooting.

There are actually two output streams from most UNIX programs. One is called the standard output, and the other is the standard error. If you're a C programmer you'll recognize these: the standard error is the file named *stderr* to which you print messages.

The > character does not redirect the standard error. It's useful when you want to save legitimate output without mucking up a file with error messages. But what if the error messages are what you want to save? This is quite common during troubleshooting.

The solution is to use a greater-than sign followed by an ampersand. (This construct works in every shell except the original Bourne shell.) It redirects both the standard output and the standard error. For instance:

```
$ gcc invinitjig.c >& error-msg
```

This command saves all the messages from the *gcc* compiler in a file named *error-msg*. (Of course, the object code is not saved there. It's stored in *invinitjig.o* as always.) On the Bourne shell and *bash* you can also say it slightly differently:

```
$ gcc invinitjig.c &> error-msg
```

Now let's get really fancy. Suppose you want to save the error messages but not the regular output—the standard error but not the standard output. In the Bourne-compatible shells you can do this by entering:

```
$ gcc invinitjig.c 2> error-msg
```

The shell arbitrarily assigns the number 1 to the standard output and the number 2 to the standard error. So the above command saves only the standard error.

Finally, suppose you want to throw away the standard output—keep it from appearing on your screen. The solution is to redirect it to a special file called

/dev/null. (You've heard people say things like "Send your criticisms to /dev/null"? Well, this is where the phrase came from.) The */dev* directory is where UNIX systems store special files that refer to terminals, tape drives, and other devices. But */dev/null* is unique; it's a place you can send things so that they disappear into a black hole. For instance, the following command saves the standard error and throws away the standard output:

```
$ gcc invinitjig.c 2>error-msg >/dev/null
```

So now you should be able to isolate exactly the output you want.

In case you've wondered whether < means anything to the shell—yes, it does. It causes commands to take their input from a file. But most commands allow you to specify input files on their command lines anyway, so this "input redirection" is rarely necessary.

Sometimes you want one utility to operate on the output of another utility. For instance, you can use the *sort* command to put the output of other commands into a more useful order. A crude way to do this would be to save output from one command in a file, and then run *sort* on it. For instance:

```
$ du > du_output
$ sort -n du_output
```

but UNIX provides a much more succinct and efficient way to do it using a *pipe.* Just place a vertical bar between the first command and the second:

```
$ du | sort -n
```

The shell sends all the input from the *du* program to the *sort* program.

In the example above, *du* stands for "disk usage" and shows how many blocks each file occupies under the current directory. Normally its output is in a somewhat random order:

```
$ du
10        ./zoneinfo/Australia
13        ./zoneinfo/US
9         ./zoneinfo/Canada
4         ./zoneinfo/Mexico
5         ./zoneinfo/Brazil
3         ./zoneinfo/Chile
20        ./zoneinfo/SystemV
118       ./zoneinfo
298       ./ghostscript/doc
183       ./ghostscript/examples
3289      ./ghostscript/fonts
          .
          .
          .
```

So we have decided to run it through *sort* with the *−n* and *−r* options. The *−n* option means "sort in numerical order" instead of the default ASCII sort, and the *−r* option means "reverse the usual order" so that the highest number appears first. The result is output that quickly shows you which directories and files hog the most space:

```
$ du | sort -rn
34368       .
16005       ./emacs
16003       ./emacs/19.25
13326       ./emacs/19.25/lisp
4039        ./ghostscript
3289        ./ghostscript/fonts
            .
            .
            .
```

Since there are so many files, we had better use a second pipe to send output through the *more* command (one of the most common uses of pipes):

```
$ du | sort -rn | more
34368       .
16005       ./emacs
16003       ./emacs/19.25
13326       ./emacs/19.25/lisp
4039        ./ghostscript
3289        ./ghostscript/fonts
            .
            .
            .
```

What Is a Command?

We've said that UNIX offers a huge number of commands, and that you can add new ones. This makes it radically different from most operating systems, which contain a strictly limited table of commands. So what are UNIX commands, and how are they stored?

On UNIX, a command is simply a file. For instance, the *ls* command is a binary file located in the directory *bin*. So, instead of *ls*, you could enter the full pathname, also known as the *absolute pathname*:

```
$ /bin/ls
```

This makes UNIX very flexible and powerful. To provide a new utility, a system administrator can simply install it in a standard directory where commands are located. There can also be different versions of a command—for instance, you can offer a new version of a utility for testing in one place, while leaving the old version in another place, and users can choose the one they want.

Here's a common problem: sometimes you enter a command that you expect to be on the system, but you receive a message such as "Not found." The problem may be that the command is located in a directory that your shell is not searching. The list of directories where your shell looks for commands is called your path. Enter the following to see what your path is (remember the dollar sign!):

```
$ echo $PATH
/usr/local/bin:/usr/bin:/bin:/usr/bin/X11:/usr/lib/uucp:.
```

This takes a little careful eyeballing. The output is a series of pathnames separated by colons. The first pathname, for this particular user, is */usr/local/bin*. The second is */usr/bin*, and so on. So if two versions of a command exist, one in */usr/local/bin* and the other in */usr/bin*, the one in */usr/local/bin* will execute.

The last pathname in this example is simply a dot; it refers to the current directory. Unlike MS-DOS, UNIX does not look automatically in your current directory. You have to tell it to explicitly, as shown here. Some people think it's a bad idea to look in the current directory, for security reasons. (A cracker who gets into your account might copy a malicious program to one of your working directories.)

If a command is not found, you have to figure out where it is on the system, and add that directory to your path. The manual page should tell you where it is. Let's say you find it in */usr/sbin*, where a number of system administration commands are installed. You realize that you need access to these system administration commands, so you enter the following. Note that the first PATH doesn't have a dollar sign, but the second one does.

```
$ export PATH=$PATH:/usr/sbin
```

This makes */usr/sbin* the last directory to be searched. The command is saying, "Make my path equal to the old path plus */usr/sbin*."

Actually, the command above works for some shells but not others. It's fine for most Linux users, who are working in a Bourne-compatible shell like *bash*. But if you use *csh* or *tcsh* you need to issue the following command instead:

```
set path = ( $PATH /usr/sbin )
```

Finally, there are a few commands that are not files. *cd* is one. Most of these commands affect the shell itself, and therefore have to be understood and executed by the shell. Because they are part of the shell they are called built-in commands.

Putting a Command in the Background

Before the X Window System, which makes it easy to run multiple programs at once, UNIX users took advantage of UNIX's multitasking features by simply putting an ampersand at the end of commands.

```
$ gcc invinitjig.c &
[1] 21457
```

The ampersand puts the command into the background, meaning that the shell prompt comes back and you can continue to execute other commands while the *gcc* command is compiling your program. The [1] is a job number that is assigned to your command. The 21457 is a process ID, which we'll discuss later. Job numbers are assigned to background commands in order, and therefore are easier to remember and type than process IDs.

Of course, multitasking does not come for free. The more commands you put into the background, the slower your system runs as it tries to interleave their execution.

You wouldn't want to put a command in the background if it requires user input. If you do so, you see an error message like:

```
Stopped (tty input)
```

You can solve this problem by bringing the job back into the foreground through the *fg* command. If you have many commands in the background, you can choose one of them by its job number or its process ID. For our long-lived *gcc* command, the following commands are equivalent:

```
$ fg %1
$ fg 21457
```

Don't forget the percent sign on the job number; that's what distinguishes job numbers from process IDs.

To get rid of a command in the background, issue a *kill* command:

```
$ kill %1
```

Manual Pages

The most empowering information you can get is how to conduct your own research. Following this precept, we will now tell you about the online help system that comes built in to UNIX systems. It is called manual pages, or man pages for short.

Actually, manual pages are not quite the boon they ought to be. This is because they are short and take a lot of UNIX background for granted. Each one focuses on a particular command, and rarely helps you decide why you should use that command. Still, they are critical. Commands can vary slightly on different UNIX systems, and the manual pages are the most reliable way to find out what your system does. The Linux Documentation Project deserves a lot of credit for the incredible number of hours they have put into creating manual pages.

To find out about a command, enter a command like:

```
$ man ls
```

Manual pages are divided into different sections depending on what they are for. User commands are in section 1, UNIX system calls in section 2, and so on. The sections that will interest you most are 1, 4 (file formats), and 8 (system administration commands). When you view manual pages online, these sections are merely conceptual; you can optionally specify them when you are searching for a command:

```
$ man 1 ls
```

But if you consult a hard copy manual, you'll find it divided into actual sections according to the numbering scheme. Sometimes an entry in two different sections can have the same name. (For instance, *chmod* is both a command and a system call.) So you will sometimes see the name of a manual page followed by the section number in parentheses, as in "*ls(1)*."

Look near the top of a manual page. The first heading is NAME. Under it is a brief one-line description of the item. These descriptions can be valuable if you're not quite sure what you're looking for. Think of a word related to what you want, and specify it in an *apropos* command.

whatis database requires to be created by running /usr/sbin/makewhatis first!! i.e. before apropos will work

```
$ apropos edit
```

The above command shows you all the manual pages that have something to do with editing. It's a very simple algorithm: *apropos* simply prints out all the NAME lines that contain the string you ask for.

Chapter 5

An X Window System application, *xman*, also helps you browse manual pages. It is described in the section "xman: a point-and-click interface to manual pages" in Chapter 5.

Like commands, manual pages are sometimes installed in strange places. For instance, you may install some site-specific programs in the directory */usr/local*, and put their manual pages in */usr/local/man*. The *man* command will not automatically look in */usr/local/man*, so when you ask for a manual page you may get the message "No manual entry." Fix this by specifying all the top *man* directories in a variable called MANPATH. For example (you have to put in the actual directories where the manual pages are on your system):

```
$ export MANPATH=/usr/man:/usr/local/man
```

The syntax is like PATH, described earlier in this chapter. Each two directories are separated by a colon. If your shell is *csh* or *tcsh*, you need to say:

```
$ setenv MANPATH /usr/man:/usr/local/man
```

Have you read some manual pages, and still found yourself confused? They're not meant to be introductions to new topics. Get yourself a good beginner's book about UNIX, and come back to manual pages gradually as you become more comfortable on the system. Then they'll be irreplaceable.

File Ownership and Permissions

Ownership and permissions are central to security. It's important to get them right, even when you're the only user, because odd things can happen if you don't. For the files that users create and use daily, these things usually work without much thought (although it's still useful to know the concepts). For system administration, matters are not so easy. Assign the wrong ownership or permission, and you might get into a frustrating bind like not being able to read your mail. In general, the message

```
Permission denied
```

means that someone has assigned an ownership or permission that restricts access more than you want.

What Permissions Mean

Permissions refer to the ways in which someone can use a file. There are three such permissions under UNIX:

- *Read* permission means you can look at the file's contents.

- *Write* permission means you can change or delete the file.

- *Execute* permission means you can run the file as a program.

When each file is created, the system assigns some default permissions that work most of the time. For instance, it gives you both read and write permission, but most of the world has only read permission. If you have a reason to be paranoid, you can set things up so that other people have no permissions at all.

Additionally, most utilities know how to assign permissions. For instance, when the compiler creates an executable program, it automatically assigns executable permission. When you check a file out of RCS without locking it, you get only read permission (because you're not expected to change the file), but if you lock the file, you get read and write permission (you're expected to edit it and check it back in). We'll discuss RCS in the section "Revision Control Tools" in Chapter 6, *Programming with Linux.*

Chapter 6

There are times when defaults don't work, though. For instance, if you create a shell script or perl program, you'll have to assign executable permission yourself so that you can run it. We'll show how to do that later in this section, after we get through the basic concepts.

Permissions have different meanings for a directory:

- Read permission means you can list the contents of that directory.

- Write permission means you can add or remove files in the directory.

- Execute permission means you can list information about the files in that directory.

Don't worry about the difference between read and execute permission for directories—basically, they go together. Assign both, or neither.

Chapter 4

Note that, if you allow people to add files to a directory, you also let them remove files. The two privileges go together when you assign write permission. However, there is a way you can let users share a directory and keep them from deleting each other's files. See the section "Upgrading Other Software" in Chapter 4.

There are more files on UNIX systems than the plain files and directories we've talked about so far. These are special files (devices), sockets, symbolic links, and so forth, each type observing its own rules. But you don't need to know the details on each type.

Owners and Groups

Now, who gets these permissions? To allow people to work together, UNIX has three levels of permission: owner, group, and other. The "other" covers everybody who has access to the system and who isn't the owner or a member of the group.

The idea behind having groups to is to give a set of users, like a team of programmers, access to a file. For instance, a programmer creating source code may reserve write permission to herself, but allow members of her group to have read access through a group permission. As for "other," it might have no permission at all. (You think your source code is *that* good?)

Chapter 4

Each file has an owner and a group. The owner is generally the user who created the file. Each user also belongs to a default group, and that group is assigned to every file the user creates. You can create many groups, though, and assign each user to multiple groups. By changing the group assigned to a file, you can give access to any collection of people you want. We'll discuss groups more when we get to the section "The Group File" in Chapter 4.

Now we have all the elements of our security system: three permissions (read, write, execute) and three levels (user, group, other). Let's looks at some typical files and see what permissions are assigned.

Figure 3-2 shows a typical executable program. We generated this output by executing *ls* with the −*l* option.

Two useful facts stand right out: the owner of the file is an author of this book and your faithful guide, **mdw**, while the group is **lib** (perhaps a group created for

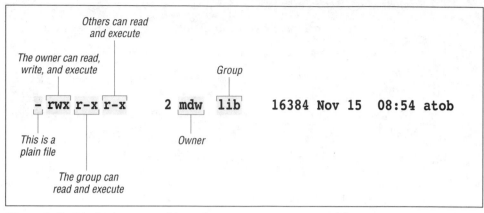

Figure 3-2. Displaying ownership and permissions

programmers working on libraries). But the key information about permissions is encrypted in the set of letters on the left side of the display.

The first character is a hyphen, indicating that this is a plain file. The next three bits apply to the owner; as we would expect, **mdw** has all three permissions. The next three bits apply to members of the group: they can read the file (not too useful for a binary file) and execute it, but they can't write to it because the field that should contain a w contains a hyphen instead. And the last three bits apply to "other"; they have the same permissions in this case as the group.

As another exercise, here is a file checked out of RCS with a lock:

```
-rw-r--r--   2 mdw      lib           878 Aug  7 19:28 tools.tex
```

The only difference between this file and Figure 3-2 is that the x bits in this case have been replaced by hyphens. No one needs to have execute permission because the file is not meant to be executed; it's just text.

One more example—a typical directory:

```
drwxr-xr-x   2 mdw      lib           512 Jul 17 18:23 perl
```

The left-most bit is now a d, to show that this is a directory. The executable bits are back, because you want people to see the contents of the directory.

Files can be in some obscure states that aren't covered here; see the *ls* manual page for gory details. But now it's time to see how you can change ownership and permissions.

Changing the Owner, Group, and Permissions

As we said, most of the time you can get by with the default security that the system gives you. But there are always exceptions, particularly for system administrators. To take a simple example, suppose you are creating a directory under */home* for a new user. You have to create everything as **root**, but when you're done you have to change the ownership to the user—otherwise, that user won't be able to use the files! (Fortunately, if you use the *adduser* command discussed in the section "Creating Accounts" in Chapter 4, it takes care of ownership for you.)

Chapter 4

Similarly, there are certain utilities such as UUCP and News that have their own users. No one ever logs in as **uucp** or **news**, but those users and groups must exist so that the utilities can do their job in a secure manner. In general, the last step when installing software is usually to change the owner, group, and permissions as the documentation tells you to do.

The *chown* command changes the owner of a file, and the *chgrp* command changes the group. So after installing some software named *sampsoft*, you might change both the owner and the group to **bin** by executing:

```
# chown bin sampsoft
# chgrp bin sampsoft
```

These work because you are installing software as **root**, and so you can issue *chown* and *chgrp* on any file, anytime. If you were not **root**, there's a subtle problem with the above commands. After you changed the owner, you wouldn't have permission to change the group! Nor could you change permissions, move the file to another directory, or do anything else. So if you're not running as **root**, save the change of ownership as the last thing you do to a file—then you have to say good-bye.

The syntax for changing permissions is more complicated. The permissions can also be called the file's "mode," and the command that changes them is *chmod*. Let's start our exploration of this command through a simple example—say that you've written a neat program in Perl or Tcl named *header*, and you want to be able to execute it.

```
$ chmod +x header
```

The plus sign means "add a permission," and the x indicates which permission to add.

If you want to remove execute permission, use a minus sign in place of a plus:

```
$ chmod -x header
```

The command just shown assigns permissions to all levels—user, group, and other. Let's say that you are secretly into software hoarding, and don't want anybody to use the command but yourself. (No, that's too cruel—let's say instead that you think the script is buggy and want to protect other people from hurting themselves until you've exercised it.) You can assign execute permission just to yourself through the command:

```
$ chmod u+x header
```

Whatever goes before the plus sign is the level of permission, and whatever goes after is the type of permission. Group permission is g and other is o. So to assign permission to both yourself and the file's group, enter

```
$ chmod ug+x header
```

Multiple types of permissions can also be assigned:

```
$ chmod ug+rwx header
```

There are a few more shortcuts that you can learn from the *chmod* manual page in order to impress someone looking over your shoulder, but they don't offer any functionality besides what we've just shown.

As arcane as the syntax of the mode argument may seem, there's another syntax that is even more complicated. We have to describe it though, for several reasons. First of all, there are several situations that cannot be covered by the syntax we've just shown, called "symbolic mode." Second, people often use the other syntax, called "absolute mode," in their documentation. Finally, there are times that you may actually find the absolute mode more convenient.

To understand absolute mode, you have to think in terms of bits. And in octal notation. Don't worry, it's not too hard. A typical mode contains three characters, corresponding to the three levels of permission (user, group, and other). These levels are illustrated in Figure 3-3. Within each level, there are three bits corresponding to read, write, and execute permission.

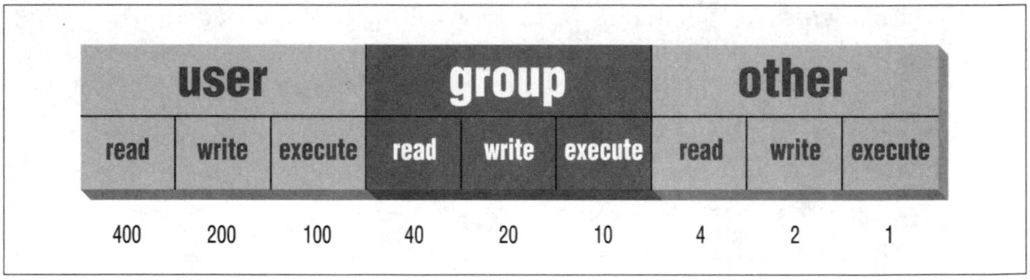

user			group			other		
read	write	execute	read	write	execute	read	write	execute
400	200	100	40	20	10	4	2	1

Figure 3-3: Bits in absolute mode

Let's say you want to give yourself read permission, and no permission to anybody else. You want to specify just the bit represented by the number 400. So the *chmod* command would be:

```
$ chmod 400 header
```

To give read permission to everybody, choose the correct bit from each level: 400 for yourself, 40 for your group, and 4 for other. The full command is:

```
$ chmod 444 header
```

This is like using a mode +r, except that it simultaneously removes any write or execute permission. (To be precise, it's just like a mode of =r, which we didn't mention earlier. The equal sign means "assign these rights, and no others.")

To give read and execute permission to everybody, you have to add up the read and execute bits. 400 plus 100 is 500, for instance. So the corresponding command is:

```
$ chmod 555 header
```

which is the same as =rx. To give someone full access, you would specify that digit as a 7—the sum of 4, 2, and 1.

One final trick: how to set the default mode that is assigned to each file you create (with a text editor, the > redirection operator, and so on). This is done by executing a *umask* command, or putting one in your shell's start-up file. This file might be called *.bashrc*, *.cshrc*, or something else depending on the shell you use (we'll discuss shells in the next section).

The *umask* command takes an argument like the absolute mode in *chmod*, but the meaning of the bits is inverted. You have to determine the access you want to grant for user, group, and other, and subtract each digit from 7. That gives you a three-digit mask.

For instance, say you want yourself to have all permissions (7), your group to have read and execute permissions (5), and others to have no permissions (0). Subtract each bit from 7 and you get 0 for yourself, 2 for your group, and 7 for other. So the command to put in your start-up file is:

```
umask 027
```

A strange technique, but it works. The *chmod* command looks at the mask when it interprets your mode; for instance, if you assign the mode +x to a file, it will assign execute permission for you and your group, but will exclude others because the mask doesn't permit them to have any access.

Start-up Files

Configuration is a strong element of UNIX. This probably stems from two traits commonly found in hackers: they want total control over their environment, and they strive to minimize the number of keystrokes and other hand movements they have to perform. So all the major utilities on UNIX—editors, mailers, debuggers, X Window System clients—provide files that let you override their default behaviors in a bewildering number of ways.

Start-up files are usually in your home directory. Their names begin with a period, which keeps the *ls* command from displaying them under normal circumstances. None of the files are required; all the affected programs are smart enough to use defaults when the file does not exist. But everyone finds it useful to have the start-up files. Here are some common ones:

.bashrc
> For the *bash* shell. The file is a shell script, which means it can contain commands and other programming constructs.

.bash_profile
> For the *bash* shell. Another shell script. The difference between this and *.bashrc* is that *.bash_profile* runs only when you log in. It was originally designed so you could separate interactive shells from those run by background processors like *cron* (discussed in the next chapter). But it is not too useful on modern computers with the X Window System, because when you open a new *xterm* window, only *.bashrc* runs. If you start up a window with the command *xterm –ls*, it will run *.bash_profile*, too.

.cshrc
> For the C shell or *tcsh*. The file is a shell script, using C shell constructs.

.login
> For the C shell or *tcsh*. The file is a shell script, using C shell constructs. Like *.bash_profile* in the *bash* shell, this runs only when you log in.

.emacs
> For the Emacs editor. Consists of Lisp functions. See the section "Tailoring Emacs" in Chapter 5.

Chapter 5

.exrc
> For the *vi* editor (also known as *ex*). Each line is an editor command. See "Extending vi" in Chapter 5.

.fvwmrc
> For the *fvwm* window manager. Consists of special commands interpreted by *fvwm*. A sample file is shown in the section "Configuring fvwm" in Chapter 5.

.twmrc

For the *twm* window manager. Consists of special commands interpreted by *twm.*

.newsrc

For news readers. Contains a list of all newsgroups offered at the site.

.Xdefaults

For programs using the X Window System. Each line specifies a resource (usually the name of a program and some property of that program) along with the value that resource should take. This file is described in "The X resource database" in Chapter 5.

.xinitrc

For the X Window System. Consists of shell commands that run whenever you log into an X session. See the section "Customizing Your X Environment" in Chapter 5 for details on using this file.

Important Directories

You already know about */home*, where user files are stored. As a system administrator and programmer, several other directories will be important to you. Here are a few, along with their contents.

/bin

The most essential UNIX commands, such as *ls.*

/usr/bin

Other commands. The distinction between */bin* and */usr/bin* is arbitrary; it was a convenient way to split up commands on early UNIX systems that had small disks.

/usr/sbin

Commands used by the superuser for system administration.

/boot

Where the kernel, and other files used during booting, are sometimes stored.

/etc

Files used by subsystems such as networking, NFS, and mail. Typically these contain tables of network services, disks to mount, and so on.

/var

Administrative files, such as log files, used by various utilities.

/var/spool

Temporary storage for files being printed, sent by UUCP, and so on.

/usr/lib
> Standard libraries, such as *libc.a*. When you link a program, the linker always searches here for the libraries specified in –*l* options.

/usr/lib/X11
> The X Window System distribution. Contains the libraries used by X clients, as well as fonts, sample resources files and other important parts of the X package.

/usr/include
> Standard location of include files used in C programs, such as *<stdio.h>*.

/usr/src
> Location of sources to programs built on the system.

/etc/skel
> Sample start-up files that you can place in the home directories for new users.

Programs That Serve You

We're including this section because you should start to be interested in what's running on your system behind your back.

Many modern computer activities are too complex to be satisfied by simply looking at a file or some other static resource. They need to interact with another running process.

Appendix C

For instance, take *ftp*, which you may have used to download Linux. (It is described in Appendix C, *FTP Tutorial and Site List.*) When you *ftp* to another system, another program has to be running on that system to accept your connection and interpret your commands. So there's a program running on that system called *ftpd*. The "d" in the name stands for *daemon*, which is a quaint UNIX term for a server that runs in the background all the time. Most daemons handle network activities.

You've probably heard of the buzzword *client/server* enough to make you sick, but here it is in action—has been in action for years, on UNIX.

Daemons start up when the system is booted. To see how they get started, look in the */etc/inittab* and */etc/inetd.conf* files. We won't go into their formats here. But each line in these files lists a program that runs when the system starts.

For instance, in */etc/inittab* you will see one or more lines with the string getty or agetty. This is the program that listens at a terminal (tty) waiting for a user to log in. It's the program that displays the "login :" prompt we talked about at the beginning of this chapter.

The */etc/inetd.conf* file represents a more complicated way of running programs— another level of indirection. The idea behind */etc/inetd.conf* is that it would waste a lot of system resources if a dozen or more daemons were spinning idly, waiting for a request to come over the network. So instead, the system starts a single daemon named *inetd*. All the daemons in the */etc/inetd.conf* file also start up, but are suspended in a state where they use very little of the precious system tables. When a request comes in over the network, *inetd* figures out which daemon it's for and wakes up that daemon just long enough to handle the request.

In the next section, we'll show you how to see which daemons are running on your system. There's a daemon for every service offered by the system to other systems on a network—*fingerd* to handle remote *finger* requests, *rwhod* to handle *rwho* requests, and so on. A few daemons also handle non-networking services, such as *lpd*, which prints files.

Processes

At the heart of UNIX lies the concept of a process. Understanding this concept will help you keep control of your login session as a user. If you are also a system administrator, the concept is even more important.

A process is an independently-running program that has its own set of resources. For instance, we showed in an earlier section how you could direct the output of a program to a file, while your shell continued to direct output to your screen. The reason that the shell and the other program can send output to different places is that they are separate processes.

On UNIX, the finite resources of the system, like the memory and the disks, are managed by one all-powerful program called the kernel. Everything else on the system is a process.

Thus, before you log in, your terminal is monitored by a *getty* process as mentioned earlier. After you log in, the *getty* process dies (a new one is started by the kernel when you log out) and your terminal is managed by your shell, a different process. The shell then creates a new process each time you enter a command. The creation of a new process is called *forking*, because one process splits into two.

If you are using the X Window System, each process starts up one or more windows. Thus, the window you are typing commands into is owned by an *xterm* process. That process forks a shell to run within the window. And that shell forks yet more processes as you enter commands.

To see the processes you are running, enter the command *ps*. Figure 3-4 shows some typical output and what each field means. You may be surprised how many processes you are running, especially if you are using X. One of the processes is the *ps* command itself, which of course dies as soon as the output is displayed.

```
$   ps
     PID     TTY     STAT     TIME     COMMAND
    1663     pp3     S        0:01     -bash
    1672     pp3     T        0:07     emacs
    1676     pp3     R        0:00     ps
```

PID – *Process ID (used to kill a process)*   **TIME** – *CPU time used so far*
TTY – *Controlling terminal*   **COMMAND** – *Command running*
STAT – *State*

Figure 3–4. Output of ps command

The first field in the *ps* output is a unique identifier for the process. If you have a runaway process that you can't get rid of through Ctrl-C or other means, you can kill it by going to a different virtual console or X window and entering:

```
$ kill process-id
```

The TTY field shows the terminal the process is running on, if any. (Everything run from my shell uses my terminal, of course, but background daemons don't have a terminal.)

The STAT field shows what state the process is in. The shell is currently suspended, so this field shows an S. An Emacs editing session is running, but it's suspended using Ctrl-Z. This is shown by the T in its STAT field. The last process shown is the *ps* that is generating all this input; it's state of course is R because it is running.

The TIME field shows how much CPU time the processes have used. Since both *bash* and Emacs are interactive, they actually don't use much of the CPU.

You aren't restricted to seeing your own processes. Look for a minute at all the processes on the system. The *–a* option stands for "all processes," while the *–x* option includes processes that have no controlling terminal (such as daemons started at run time).

```
$ ps -ax | more
```

Now you can see the daemons that we mentioned in the previous section. And here, with a breathtaking view of the entire UNIX system at work, we end this chapter.

CHAPTER FOUR
ESSENTIAL SYSTEM MANAGEMENT

I f you're running your own Linux system, one of the first tasks at hand is to learn the ropes of system administration. You won't be able to get by for long without having to perform some kind of system maintenance, software upgrade, or mere tweaking necessary to keep things in running order.

Running a Linux system is not unlike riding and taking care of a motorcycle.[*] Many motorcycle hobbyists prefer caring for their own equipment—routinely cleaning the points, replacing worn-out parts, and so forth. Linux gives you the opportunity to experience the same kind of "hands-on" maintenance with a complex operating system.

While a passionate administrator can spend any amount of time tuning it for performance, you really have to perform administration only when a major change occurs—you install a new disk, a new user comes on the system, or a power failure causes the system to go down unexpectedly. We discuss all these situations in this chapter.

Another common Linux activity is building the kernel. Although it's particularly important on Linux because the kernel is still being upgraded regularly, the activity of rebuilding the operating system is well known to other UNIX administrators and even administrators on some non-UNIX systems. Your system supports a limited number of devices and other kernel objects, so you can make the kernel much smaller and more efficient by taking out the ones you don't need.

Linux is surprisingly accessible, in all respects—from the more mundane tasks of upgrading shared libraries to the more esoteric such as mucking about with the

---

* At least this author attests a strong correspondence between Linux system administration and Robert Pirsig's *Zen and the Art of Motorcycle Maintenance*. Does Linux have the Buddha nature?

kernel. Because all of the source code is available, and the body of Linux developers and users has traditionally been of the hackish breed, systems maintenance is not only a part of daily life but also a great learning experience. Trust us—there's nothing like telling your friends how you upgraded from X11R5 to X11R6 in less than half an hour, and all the while you were recompiling the kernel to support the ISO 9660 filesystem. (They may have no idea what you're talking about, in which case you can give them a copy of this book.)

In this chapter we will explore your Linux system from the mechanic's point of view—showing you what's under the hood, as it were—and explain how to take care of it all, including software upgrades, managing users, filesystems, and other resources, taking backups, and what to do in emergencies. If you've never used a UNIX system before, we'll also take you for a test drive and show you the basics of running and using the system.

Once you put the right entries in start-up files, your Linux system will, for the most part, run itself. As long as you're happy with the system configuration and the software that's running on it, very little work will be necessary on your part. However, we'd like to encourage Linux users to experiment with their system and customize it to taste. Very little about Linux is carved in stone, and if something doesn't work the way that you'd like it to, you should be able to change that. For instance, if you'd rather read blinking green text on a cyan background, rather than the traditional white-on-black, we'll show you how to configure that. As long as you promise not to let anyone know who told you.

It should be noted that many Linux systems include fancy tools to simplify many system administration tasks. These tools can do everything from managing user accounts to creating filesystems to doing your laundry. These utilities can either make your life easier or more difficult, depending on how you look at them. In this chapter we present the "guts" of system administration, demonstrating the tools that should be available on any Linux system (and indeed nearly all UNIX systems). These are the core of the system administrator's toolbox: the metaphorical hammer, screwdriver, and socket wrench that you can rely on to get the job done. If you'd rather use the 40-horsepower circular saw, feel free—but it's always nice to know how to use the hand tools in case the power goes out.

[56] Unix
Sys. Admin
[57]
Essential
Sys. Admin

Good follow-on books, should you wish to investigate more topics in UNIX system administration, include the *Unix System Administration Handbook* by Nemeth, Snyder, and Seebass, and *Essential System Administration* by Frisch.

Running the System

Being the system administrator for any UNIX system requires a certain degree of responsibility and care. This is equally true for Linux, even if you're the only user on your system.

Many of the system administrator's tasks are done by logging into the **root** account. This account has special properties on UNIX systems—specifically, the usual file permissions and other security mechanisms simply don't apply to **root**. That is, **root** can access and modify any file on the system—no matter who it belongs to. Whereas normal users can't damage the system (say, by corrupting filesystems or touching other users' files), **root** has no such restrictions.

Why does the UNIX system have security in the first place? The most obvious reason for this is to allow users to choose how they wish their own files to be accessed. By changing file permission bits (with the *chmod* command), users can specify that certain files should only be readable, writable, or executable by certain groups of other users, or no other users at all. This helps to ensure privacy and integrity of data—you wouldn't want other users to read your personal mailbox, for example, or to edit the source code for an important program behind your back.

The UNIX security mechanisms also prevent users from damaging the system. The system restricts access to many of the raw device files (accessed via */dev*—more on this in the section "Device Files") corresponding to hardware such as your hard drives. If normal users could read and write directly to the disk drive device, they could wreak all kinds of havoc—say, by completely overwriting the contents of the drive. Instead, the system requires normal users to access the drives via the filesystem—where security is enforced via the file permission bits described above.

It is important to note that not all kinds of "damage" that can be caused are necessarily malevolent. System security is more of a means to protect users from their own natural mistakes and misunderstandings rather than to enforce a police state on the system. And, in fact, on many systems security is rather lax—UNIX security is designed to foster the sharing of data between groups of users who may be, say, cooperating on a project. The system allows users to be assigned to groups, and file permissions may be set for an entire group. For instance, one development project might have free read and write permission to a series of files, while at the same time other users are prevented from modifying those files. With your own personal files, you get to decide how public or private the access permissions should be.

The UNIX security mechanism also prevents normal users from performing certain actions, such as calling certain system calls within a program. For example, there is a system call which will cause the system to halt, called by programs such as *shutdown* (more on this later in the chapter) to reboot the system. If normal users could call this function within their programs, they could accidentally (or purposefully) halt the system at any time.

In many cases you have to bypass the UNIX security mechanisms in order to perform system maintenance or upgrades. This is what the **root** account is for. Because no such restrictions apply to **root**, it is very easy for a knowledgeable system administrator to get work done without worrying about the usual file permissions or other limitations.

The usual way to log in as **root** is with the *su* command. *su* allows you to assume the identification of another user—for example,

```
su andy
```

will prompt you for the password for **andy**, and if it is correct will set your user ID to that of **andy**. Without a username argument, *su* will prompt you for the **root** password, validating your user ID as **root**. Once you are finished using the root account, you log out in the usual way and are returned to your own mortal identity.

Why not simply log in as **root**, from the usual login prompt? As we'll see, this is desirable in some instances, but most of the time it's best to use *su* after logging in as yourself. On a system with many users, use of *su* records a message such as

```
Nov  1 19:28:50 loomer su: mdw on /dev/ttyp1
```

in the system logs, such as */var/adm/messages* (we'll talk more about these files later). This message indicates that the user **mdw** successfully issued a *su* command, in this case for **root**. If you were to log in directly as **root**, no such message would appear in the logs; you wouldn't be able to tell which user was mucking about with the root account. This is important if there are multiple administrators on the machine: it is often desirable to find out who used *su*, and when.

The root account can be considered a magic wand—both a very useful and potentially dangerous tool. Fumbling the magic words which you invoke while holding this wand can wreak unspeakable damage on your system. For example, the simple eight-character sequence *rm –rf /* will delete every file on your system, if executed as **root**, and if you're not paying attention. Does this problem seem farfetched? Not at all. You might be trying to delete an old directory, such as */usr/src/oldp*, and accidently slip in a space after the first slash, producing:

```
rm –rf / usr/src/oldp
```

Another common mistake is to confuse the arguments for commands such as *dd*, a command which is often used to copy large chunks of data from one place to another. For instance, in order to save the first 1024 bytes of data from the device */dev/hda* (which contains the partition table and boot record for that drive), one might use the command

```
dd if=/dev/hda of=/tmp/stuff bs=1k count=1
```

However, if we reverse `if` and `of` in the above command, something quite different happens: The contents of */tmp/stuff* are written to the top of */dev/hda*. If */tmp/stuff* contains garbage or incorrect data, you've just succeeded in hosing your partition table and possibly a filesystem superblock. Welcome to the wonderful world of system administration!

The point here is that you should sit on your hands before executing any command as **root**. Stare at the command for a minute before pressing Enter, and make sure that it makes sense. If you're not sure of the arguments and syntax of the command, quickly check the manual pages or try the command in a safe environment before firing it off. Otherwise you'll learn these lessons the hard way—mistakes made as **root** can be disastrous.

In many cases the prompt for the root account differs from that for normal users—classically, the **root** prompt contains a hash mark (#), while normal user prompts contain $ or %. (Of course, use of this convention is up to you—it is utilized on many UNIX systems, however.) Although the prompt may remind you that you are wielding the **root** magic wand, it is not uncommon for users to forget this or accidentally enter a command in the wrong window or virtual console.

Like any powerful tool, the root account can also be abused. It is important, as the system administrator, to protect the root password, and if you give it out at all, to give it only to those users whom you trust (or who can be held responsible for their actions on the system). If you're the only user of your Linux system, this certainly doesn't apply—unless, of course, your system is connected to a network, or allows dial-in login access.

The primary benefit of not sharing the root account with other users is not so much that the potential for abuse is diminished (although this is certainly the case). Even more important is that if you're the one person with the ability to use the root account, you have complete knowledge of how the system is configured. If anyone were able to, say, modify important system files (as we'll talk about in this chapter), then the system configuration could be changed behind your back, and your assumptions about how things work would be incorrect. Having one system administrator act as the arbiter for the system configuration means that one person always knows what's going on.

Also, allowing other people to have the root password means that it's much more likely that someone will eventually make a mistake using the root account. Although each person with knowledge of the root password may be trusted, anybody can make mistakes. If you're the only system administrator, you have only yourself to blame for making the inevitable human mistakes as **root**.

That being said, let's dive into the actual tasks of system administration under Linux. Buckle your seatbelt.

Booting the System

There are several ways of booting Linux on your system. The most common methods involve booting from the hard drive, or using a boot floppy. In many cases the installation procedure will have configured one or both of these for you; in any case, it's important to understand how to configure booting for yourself.

Using a Boot Floppy

Traditionally, a Linux "boot floppy" simply contains a kernel image, which is loaded into memory when the floppy is booted on the system.* The kernel image is usually compressed, using the same algorithm as the *gzip* compression program (more on this in the section "Building the Kernel"). This allows the kernel, which may be a megabyte or more in size, to require only a few hundred kilobytes of diskspace. Part of the kernel code is not compressed—this part contains the routines necessary to uncompress the kernel from the disk image and load it into memory. Therefore, the kernel actually "bootstraps" itself at boot time by uncompressing into memory.

A number of parameters are stored in the kernel image. Among these parameters is the name of the device to use as the root filesystem once the kernel boots. Another parameter is the text mode to use for the system console. All of these parameters may be modified using the *rdev* command, which we'll discuss later in the section.

After the kernel has started, it attempts to mount a filesystem on the root device hard-coded in the kernel image itself. This will serve as the root filesystem—that is, the filesystem on /. The section "Managing Filesystems" discusses filesystems in more detail; all that you need to know for now is that the kernel image must contain the name of your root filesystem device. If the kernel can't mount a filesystem on this device, it gives up, issuing a kernel "panic" message. (Essentially, a *kernel panic* is a fatal error signaled by the kernel itself. A panic will occur whenever the kernel is terminally confused and can't continue with execution. For example, if there is a bug in the kernel itself, a panic might occur when it attempts to access memory which doesn't exist. We'll talk about kernel panics more in the section "What To Do in an Emergency.")

The root device stored in the kernel image is that of your root filesystem, on the hard drive. This means that once the kernel boots, it mounts a hard drive partition as the root filesystem, and all control transfers to the hard drive. Once the kernel is loaded into memory, it stays there—the boot floppy need not be accessed again (until you reboot the system, of course).

Many Linux distributions create a boot floppy for you in this way when installing the system. Using a boot floppy is an easy way to boot Linux if you don't want to bother booting from the hard drive. (For example, OS/2's or Windows NT's boot managers are somewhat difficult to configure for booting Linux. We'll talk about this in the next section.) Once the kernel has booted from the floppy, you are free to use the floppy drive for other purposes. *(of kernal image only)*

---

* A Linux boot floppy may instead contain a LILO boot record, which will cause the system to boot a <u>kernel</u> from the hard drive. We'll discuss this in the next section, when we talk about LILO.

Given a kernel image, you can create your own boot floppy. On many Linux systems, the kernel itself is stored in the file */boot/vmlinuz.** This is not a universal convention, however; other Linux systems store the kernel in */vmlinuz* or */vmlinux*, others in a file such as */Image*. (If you have multiple kernel images, you can use LILO to select which one to boot. See the next section.) Note that newly-installed Linux systems may not have a kernel image on the hard drive, if a boot floppy was created for you. In any case, you can build your own kernel. It's usually a good idea to do this anyway—you will be able to "customize" the kernel to only include those drivers for your particular hardware. See the section "Building the Kernel" later in the chapter for details.

All right. Let's say that you have a kernel image in the file */boot/vmlinuz*. To create a boot floppy, the first step is to use *rdev* to set the root device to that of your Linux root filesystem. (If you built the kernel yourself, this should be already set to the correct value, but it can't hurt to check with *rdev*.) We discussed how to create the root device in the sections "Drives and Partitions Under Linux" and "Creating Linux Partitions" in Chapter 2, *Obtaining and Installing Linux*.

Chapter 2

As **root**, use *rdev –h* to print a usage message. As you will see, there are many supported options, allowing you to specify the root device (our task here), the swap device, RAMdisk size, and so on. For the most part you needn't concern yourself with these options now.

If we use the command *rdev /boot/vmlinuz*, the root device encoded in the kernel found in */boot/vmlinuz* will be printed:

```
courgette:/# rdev /boot/vmlinuz
Root device /dev/hda1
```

If this is incorrect, and the Linux root filesystem is actually on */dev/hda3*, we should use the command

```
courgette:/# rdev /boot/vmlinuz /dev/hda3
courgette:/#
```

rdev is the strong silent type; nothing is printed when you set the root device, so run *rdev /boot/vmlinuz* again to check that it is set correctly.

Now you're ready to create the boot floppy. For best results use a brand-new, formatted floppy. You can format the floppy under MS-DOS or using *fdformat* under Linux; this will lay down the sector and track information so that the system can auto-detect the size of the floppy. (See the section "Managing Filesystems" later for more on using floppies.)

---

* Why the silly filename? On many UNIX systems, the kernel is stored in a file named */vmunix*. Naturally, Linux has to be different and names its kernel images *vmlinux*, and places them in the directory */boot* to get them out of the root directory. The name *vmlinuz* was adopted to differentiate compressed kernel images from uncompressed images. Actually, the name and location of the kernel don't matter a bit, as long as you either have a boot floppy containing a kernel, or LILO knows how to find the kernel image.

To create the boot diskette you can use *dd* to copy the kernel image to the diskette, as in:

```
courgette:/# dd if=/boot/vmlinuz of=/dev/fd0 bs=8192
```

If you're interested in *dd*, the manual page will be illustrative; in brief, this copies the input file (*if* option) named */boot/vmlinuz* to the output file (*of* option) named */dev/fd0* (the first floppy device), using a block size (*bs*) of 8192 bytes. Of course, the plebian *cp* can be used as well, but we UNIX sysadmins love to use cryptic commands to complete relatively simple tasks. That's what separates us from mortal users!

Your boot floppy should now be ready to go. You can shut down the system (see the section "Shutting Down the System") and boot with it, and if all goes well your Linux system should boot as it usually does. It might be a good idea to make an extra boot floppy as a spare, and in the section "What To Do in an Emergency," we describe methods by which boot floppies can be used to recover from disaster.

Using LILO

LILO (which stands for *Linux Loader*) is a general-purpose boot manager which can boot whatever operating systems you have installed on your machine, including Linux. There are dozens of ways to configure LILO. Here we're going to discuss the two most common methods—installing LILO on the master boot record of your hard drive, and installing LILO as a secondary boot loader for Linux only.

LILO is the most common way to boot Linux from the hard drive. (By the expression "boot from the hard drive," we mean that the kernel itself is stored on the hard drive and no boot floppy is required, but remember that even when you use a boot floppy, control is transferred to the hard drive once the kernel is loaded into memory.) If LILO is installed on your drive's master boot record, or MBR, it is the first code to run when the hard drive is booted. LILO can then boot other operating systems—such as Linux or MS-DOS—and allow you to select between them at boot time.

However, both OS/2 and Windows NT have boot managers of their own, which occupy the MBR. If you are using one of these systems, in order to boot Linux from the hard drive you may have to install LILO as the "secondary" boot loader for Linux only. In this case LILO is installed on the boot record for just your Linux root partition, and the boot manager software (for OS/2 or NT) takes care of executing LILO from there when you wish to boot Linux.

As we'll see, however, both the OS/2 and NT boot managers are somewhat uncooperative when it comes to booting LILO. This is a poor design decision, and if you must absolutely use one of these boot managers, it might be easier to boot Linux from floppy instead. Read on.

Before proceeding we should note that a number of Linux distributions are capable of configuring and installing LILO when you first install the Linux software. However, it's often best to configure LILO yourself, just to ensure that everything is done correctly.

The /etc/lilo.conf file

The first step in configuring LILO is to set up the LILO configuration file, which is often stored in */etc/lilo.conf*. (On other systems the file may be found in */boot/lilo.conf* or */etc/lilo/config*.)

We are going to walk through a sample *lilo.conf* file. You can use this file as a base for your own *lilo.conf*, and edit it for your own system.

The first section of this file sets up some basic parameters.

```
boot = /dev/hda
compact
install = /boot/boot.b
map = /boot/map
```

The boot line sets the name of the device where LILO should install itself in the boot record. In this case, we want to install LILO in the master boot record of */dev/hda*, the first non-SCSI hard drive. If you're booting from a SCSI hard drive, use a device name such as */dev/sda* instead. If you give a partition device name (such as */dev/hda2*), instead of a drive device, LILO will be installed as a secondary boot loader on the named partition. We'll talk about this in more detail later.

The compact line tells LILO to perform some optimization; always use this unless you are seriously hacking on your LILO configuration. Likewise, always use the install and map lines as shown. install names the file containing the boot sector to use on the MBR, and map specifies the "map file" that LILO creates when installed. These files should be in the directory */boot*, although on other systems they may be found in */etc/lilo*. */boot/map* won't be created until you install LILO for the first time.

Now, for each operating system that we wish LILO to boot, we add a stanza to */etc/lilo.conf*. For example, a Linux stanza might look like this:

```
# Stanza for Linux with root partition on ./dev/hda2.
image = /boot/vmlinuz    # Location of kernel
   label = linux         # Name of OS (for the LILO boot menu)
   root = /dev/hda2      # Location of root partition
   vga = ask             # Ask for VGA text mode at boot time
```

The image line specifies the name of the kernel image. Subfields include label, which gives this stanza a name for use with the LILO boot menu (more on this below); root, which specifies the Linux root partition; and vga, which specifies the VGA text mode to use for the system console.

Valid modes for vga are normal (for standard 80x25 display), extended (for extended text mode, usually 132x44 or 132x60), ask (to be prompted for a mode at boot time), or an integer (such as 1, 2, or 3). The integer corresponds to the number of the mode that you select when using ask. The exact text modes available depend on your video card; use vga = ask to get a list.

If you have multiple Linux kernels that you wish to boot—for example, if you're doing some kernel debugging—you can add an image... stanza for each one. The only required subfield of the image stanza is label. If you don't specify **root** or vga, the defaults that are coded into the kernel image itself using *rdev* will be used. If you do specify **root** or vga, these override the values that you may have set using *rdev*. Therefore, if you are booting Linux using LILO there's no need to use *rdev*; the LILO configuration file sets these boot parameters for you.

A stanza for booting MS-DOS would look like the following:

```
# Stanza for MSDOS partition on /dev/hda1.
other = /dev/hda1    # Location of partition
    table = /dev/hda  # Location of partition table for /dev/hda2
    label = msdos     # Name of OS (for boot menu)
```

You would use an identical stanza to boot OS/2 from LILO (using a different label line, of course).

If you wish to boot an MS-DOS that is located on the second drive, you should add the line

```
loader = /boot/any_d.b
```

to the MS-DOS other... stanza. For OS/2 partitions on the second drive, add the line

```
loader = /boot/os2_d.b
```

There are many more options available for LILO configuration. The LILO distribution itself (found on most Linux FTP sites and distributions) includes an extensive manual describing them all. The above should suffice for most systems, however.

Once you have your */etc/lilo.conf* ready, you can run the command

```
/sbin/lilo
```

as **root**. This should display information such as the following:

```
courgette:/# /sbin/lilo
Added linux
Added msdos
courgette:/#
```

Using the *−v* switch with *lilo* will print more diagnostic information should something go wrong; also, using the *−C* option will allow you to specify a configuration file other than */etc/lilo.conf*.

Once this is done you're ready to shut down your system (again, see the section "Shutting Down the System" for details), reboot, and try it out. The first operating system stanza listed in */etc/lilo.conf* will be booted by default. To select one of the other kernels or operating systems listed in */etc/lilo.conf*, hold down the Shift or Control key while the system boots. This should present you with a LILO boot prompt:

```
boot:
```

Here, you can press Tab to get a list of available boot options:

```
boot: tab-key
linux msdos
```

These are the names given with `label` lines in */etc/lilo.conf*. Enter the appropriate label and that operating system will boot. In this case, entering `msdos` will cause MS-DOS to boot from */dev/hda1*, as we specified in the *lilo.conf* file.

Using LILO as a secondary boot loader

If you're using the OS/2 or Windows NT boot manager, or don't want LILO to inhabit the master boot record of your drive, you can configure LILO as a secondary boot loader, which will live on the boot record of just your Linux root partition.

To do this, simply change the `boot = ...` line of */etc/lilo.conf*, as above, to the name of the Linux root partition. For example,

```
boot = /dev/hda2
```

will install LILO on the boot record of */dev/hda2*, to boot Linux only. Note that this works only for primary partitions on the hard drive (that is, not extended or logical partitions).

In order to boot Linux in this way, the Linux root partition should be marked as "active" in the partition table. This can be done using *fdisk* under Linux or MS-DOS. When booting the system, the BIOS will read the boot record of the "active" partition to start Linux.

If you are using OS/2's or Windows NT's boot manager, you should install LILO in this way, and then tell the boot manager that it can boot another operating system from that partition on your hard drive. The method for doing this depends on the boot manager in question; see your documentation for details.

LILO is known to work with OS/2's Boot Manager, but getting things to work well is not always easy. The problem is that OS/2 Boot Manager won't even recognize your partitions created with Linux *fdisk*. The way around this problem is to create the Linux partitions using OS/2's *fdisk*, and format them (say, as an MS-DOS FAT partition) first. Now OS/2 will recognize the partitions, and you can use the Linux *fdisk* command to set the types of the partitions to `Linux native` and `Linux swap`,

Chapter 2

as described in the section "Creating Linux Partitions" in Chapter 2. You can then install Linux on these partitions, install LILO on the boot record of your Linux root partition, and (hopefully) all will be well.

Why are we telling you this now? Because OS/2's Boot Manager is broken with respect to booting operating systems that it doesn't know about. Instead of using OS/2 Boot Manager, you can install LILO on the MBR of your drive and have it boot OS/2, using an other... stanza in the */etc/lilo.conf* file as you would with MS-DOS. Another option is to simply boot Linux from floppy—or, even better, not to use OS/2 at all. But let's not get carried away.

Specifying boot time options

When you first installed Linux, more than likely you booted a floppy which gave you the now-familiar LILO boot prompt. At this prompt you can enter several boot time options, such as

```
hd=cylinders,heads,sectors
```

to specify the hard drive geometry. Each time you boot Linux, it may be necessary to specify these parameters in order for your hardware to be detected correctly, as described in the section "Booting Linux" in Chapter 2.

Chapter 2

If you are using LILO to boot Linux from the hard drive, you can specify these parameters in */etc/lilo.conf* instead of entering them at the boot prompt each time. To the Linux stanza of the *lilo.conf* file, just add a line such as

```
append = "hd=683,16,38"
```

This will cause the system to behave as though hd=683,16,38 were entered at the LILO boot prompt. If you wish to specify multiple boot options, you can do so with a single append line, as in

```
append = "hd=683,16,38 hd=64,32,202"
```

In this case we specify the geometry for the first and second hard drives, respectively.

Note that you need to use such boot options only if the kernel doesn't detect your hardware at boot time. You should already know if this is necessary, based on your experiences with installing Linux; in general you should have to use an append line in *lilo.conf* only if you had to specify these boot options when first booting the Linux installation media.

There are a number of other boot time options available. Most of them deal with hardware detection, which has already been discussed in Chapter 2. However, the following additional options may also be useful to you:

single
>   Boot the system in single-user mode; skip all of the system configuration and start a root shell on the console. See the section "What To Do in an Emergency" for hints on using this.

root=*partition*
>   Attempt to mount the named *partition* as the Linux root filesystem. This will override any value given in */etc/lilo.conf*.

ro   Mount the root filesystem as read-only. This is usually done in order to run *fsck*; see the section "Checking and Repairing Filesystems."

ramdisk=*size*
>   Specify a size, in bytes, for the RAMdisk device. This will override any value in */etc/lilo.conf*. Most users need not worry about using the RAMdisk; it's useful primarily for installation.

vga=*mode*
>   Set the VGA display mode. This will override any value in */etc/lilo.conf*. Valid modes are normal, extended, ask, or an integer. This is equivalent to the vga = values used in *lilo.conf*; see the section "The /etc/lilo.conf file" above.

Any of these options can be entered by hand at the LILO boot prompt, or specified with the append option in */etc/lilo.conf*.

LILO includes complete documentation that describes all of the configuration options available. On many Linux systems this documentation can be found in */usr/src/lilo*. If you can't seem to find anything, grab the LILO distribution from one of the Linux archive sites, or ask your Linux vendor to provide the sources and documentation for LILO. This documentation includes a manual that describes all of the concepts of booting and using LILO in detail, as well as a *README* file that contains excerpts from this manual, formatted as plain text.

Removing LILO

If you have LILO installed on your master boot record (MBR), the easiest way to remove it is to use MS-DOS FDISK. The command

```
FDISK /MBR
```

will run FDISK and overwrite the MBR with a valid MS-DOS boot record.

LILO saves backup copies of your original boot record in the files */boot/boot.0300* (for IDE drives) and */boot/boot.0800* (for SCSI drives). These files contain the MBR of the drive before LILO was installed. You can use the *dd* command to replace the boot record on the drive with this backup copy. For example,

```
dd if=/boot/boot.0300 of=/dev/hda bs=446 count=1
```

will copy the first 446 bytes of the file */boot/boot.0300* to */dev/hda*. Even though the files are 512 bytes in size, only the first 446 bytes should be copied back to the MBR.

Be *very careful* when using this command! This is one of those cases where blindly executing commands that you find in a book can cause real trouble if you're not sure of what you're doing. Only use this method as a last resort and only if you're certain that the files */boot/boot.0300* or */boot/boot.0800* contain the boot record that you want. Many distributions of Linux come installed with bogus versions of these two files; you might need to delete them before you install LILO.

The LILO documentation contains further hints for removing LILO and debugging your LILO configuration.

System Startup and Initialization

In this section we're going to talk about exactly what happens when the system boots. Understanding this process and the files involved is important for performing various kinds of system configuration.

Kernel Boot Messages

The first step is booting the kernel. As described in the previous section, this can be done from floppy or hard drive. As the kernel loads into memory, it will print messages to the system console such as:

```
20480 bytes for swap cache allocated
Console: colour EGA+ 80x25, 8 virtual consoles
Serial driver version 4.00 with no serial options enabled
tty00 at 0x03f8 (irq = 4) is a 16450
tty01 at 0x02f8 (irq = 3) is a 16450
tty03 at 0x02e8 (irq = 3) is a 16550A
snd2 <SoundBlaster Pro 3.2> at 0x220 irq 5 drq 1
snd1 <Yamaha OPL-3 FM> at 0x388 irq 0 drq 0
Drive 0: CR-52x-x (2.11)
SBPCD: 1 SoundBlaster CD-ROM drive(s) at 0x0230.
Calibrating delay loop.. ok - 33.22 BogoMips
Memory: 19312k/20480k available (476k kernel code, 384k reserved, 308k data)
This processor honours the WP bit even when in supervisor mode. Good.
Floppy drive(s): fd0 is 1.44M
Swansea University Computer Society NET3.016
Checking 386/387 coupling... Ok, fpu using exception 16 error reporting.
Linux version 1.1.37 (root@loomer) #4 Fri Sep 30 00:08:33 EDT 1994
Partition check:
  hda: Maxtor 7213 AT (202MB IDE w/64KB Cache, MaxMult=32, CHS=683/16/38)
  hda: hda1 hda2
  hdb: WDC AC140M (40MB IDE w/31KB Cache, MaxMult=8, CHS=977/5/17)
  hdb: hdb1 hdb2
```

These messages are all printed by the kernel itself, as each device driver is initialized. The exact messages printed depend on what drivers are compiled into your kernel and what hardware you have on your system. Here's a quick rundown on what they mean.

First, we see that 20 kilobytes have been allocated by the kernel for the "swap cache," which is used to speed up operations when swapping pages to and from disk (more on this later in the chapter). Then the console type is printed; note that this has to do only with the text mode being used by the kernel, not the capabilities of your video card. (Even an SVGA video card is reported as EGA+ as far as the console text mode is concerned.)

The serial device driver is then initialized, which prints information on each detected serial port. A line such as

```
tty00 at 0x03f8 (irq = 4) is a 16450
```

means that the first serial device (*/dev/tty00*, or COM1) was detected at address 0x03f8, IRQ 4, using 16450 UART functions.

Next, the soundcard driver is initialized; the names and addresses for the various sound devices are printed. In this case, a SoundBlaster Pro soundcard is detected, along with a SoundBlaster Pro CD-ROM drive.

The next message printed is the "BogoMips" calculation for your processor. This is an utterly bogus (hence the name) measurement of processor speed, which is used to obtain optimal performance in delay loops for several device drivers. The kernel also prints information on the system memory.

```
Memory: 19312k/20480k available (476k kernel code, 384k reserved, 308k data)
```

Here, we see that 19312K of RAM are available for the system to use. This means that the kernel itself is using 1168K.

The floppy driver is initialized, as are the network drivers. The system shown above has no network devices installed; if you have an Ethernet card, additional information will be printed.

Finally, the IDE hard disk driver is initialized, and the type of each IDE drive is printed, along with a list of detected partitions.

Depending on your hardware, other messages will be printed in addition to those given above. For example, parallel port and SCSI drivers will be initialized at this point, if you have them.

These messages are printed to the console at boot time, but are usually saved in the system log files as well.

init and inittab

Once the device drivers are initialized, the kernel executes the program *init,* which is found in */etc, /bin,* or */sbin* (it's */sbin/init* on most systems).

init is a general-purpose program that spawns new processes and restarts certain programs when they exit. For example, each virtual console has a *getty* process running on it, started by *init.* When you exit from a login session on one of the virtual consoles, the *getty* process exits, and *init* starts a new one, allowing you to log in again.

init is also responsible for running a number of programs and scripts when the system boots. Everything that *init* does is controlled by the file */etc/inittab.* Each line in this file is of the format

    code:runlevels:action:command

code is a unique one or two-character sequence used to identify this entry in the file. Several of the entries must have a particular code to work correctly; more on this later.

runlevels is the list of "runlevels" in which this entry should be executed. A run-level is simply a number or letter that specifies the current system state, as far as *init* is concerned. For example, when the system runlevel is changed to 3, all entries in */etc/inittab* containing 3 in the runlevels field will be executed. Run-levels are a useful way to group entries in */etc/inittab* together. For example, you might want to say that runlevel 1 executes only the bare minimum of configuration scripts, runlevel 2 executes everything in runlevel 1 plus networking configuration, runlevel 3 executes everything in levels 1 and 2 plus dial-in login access, and so forth.

For the most part, you don't need to concern yourself with runlevels. When the system boots, the default runlevel (as set in */etc/inittab*) is entered. On most systems, this is runlevel 5. Unless you have a particular need to bring up the system without executing all of the configuration scripts described here, use the default runlevel for everything.

The command field is the command that *init* will execute for this entry. The action field tells *init* how to handle this entry; for example, whether to execute the given command once, or to respawn the command whenever it exits.

Let's take a look at a sample */etc/inittab,* in Example 4-1.

Example 4-1: Sample /etc/inittab file

```
# Set the default runlevel to five
id:5:initdefault:

# Execute /etc/rc.d/rc.S when the system boots
si:S:sysinit:/etc/rc.d/rc.S
```

Example 4-1: Sample /etc/inittab file (continued)

```
# Run this script when entering runlevel S (single-user mode)
su:S:wait:/etc/rc.d/rc.K

# Run this script for all other runlevels (multi-user mode)
rc:12345:wait:/etc/rc.d/rc.M

# Executed when we press ctrl-alt-delete
ca::ctrlaltdel:/sbin/shutdown -t3 -rf now

# Start agetty for virtual consoles 1 through 6
c1:12345:respawn:/sbin/agetty 38400 tty1
c2:12345:respawn:/sbin/agetty 38400 tty2
c3:45:respawn:/sbin/agetty 38400 tty3
c4:45:respawn:/sbin/agetty 38400 tty4
c5:45:respawn:/sbin/agetty 38400 tty5
c6:45:respawn:/sbin/agetty 38400 tty6
```

The exact contents of */etc/inittab* depend on your system and the distribution of Linux that you have installed.

First, we see that the default runlevel is set to 5. The action field for this entry is initdefault, which causes the given *runlevel* to be set to the default. That's the runlevel normally used whenever the system boots. You can override the default with any level you want by running *init* manually (which you might do when debugging your configuration). LILO can also boot in single-user mode (runlevel S)—see the section "Specifying boot time options."

The next entry tells *init* to execute the script */etc/rc.d/rc.S* when the system boots. (The action field is sysinit, which specifies that this entry should be executed when *init* is first started at system boot.) This file is simply a shell script containing commands to handle basic system initialization; for example, swapping is enabled, filesystems are checked and mounted, and the system clock is synchronized with the CMOS clock. You can take a look at this file on your system; we'll be talking more about the commands contained therein later in the chapter. See the sections "Managing Filesystems" and "Managing Swap Space."

Next, we see that the script *rc.K* is executed when entering runlevel S, for single-user mode. *rc.K* usually contains commands to unmount filesystems and disable swapping, allowing the system administrator to perform maintenance on them if necessary. The action field here is wait, which tells *init* to execute the given *command*, and to wait for it to complete execution before doing anything else.

Likewise, the script *rc.M* is executed for runlevels 1 through 5, which correspond to "multi-user" modes. How you differentiate these runlevels from each other is up to you; on many systems there's no difference between them. *rc.M* contains most of the remaining system configuration commands, such as setting the console screensaver, setting the system hostname, initializing networking, and starting various daemons such as *syslogd* (the system login daemon) and *lpd* (the printer daemon). Again, you can take a look at this file to see what commands are executed on your system.

On many systems, *rc.M* may execute other scripts found in */etc/rc.d*. Most noteworthy is *rc.local*, which contains "local" configuration—whatever commands you'd like to add to the system startup routine for convenience or fun. Of course, you're free to modify scripts such as *rc.M* directly, but using a different script— *rc.local*—for your personal changes to the system keeps those changes logically separate from the configuration included in the original distribution. This is mostly a matter of taste, and makes no technical difference.

The next entry, labeled ca, is executed when the key combination Ctrl-Alt-Del (also known as the "Vulcan Nerve Pinch") is pressed on the console. This key combination produces an interrupt that will usually reboot the system. Under Linux, this interrupt is caught and sent to *init*, which executes the entry with the action field of ctrlaltdel. The command shown here, */sbin/shutdown –t3 –rf now*, will do a "safe" reboot of the system. (See the next section, "Shutting Down the System.") This way we protect the system from sudden reboot when Ctrl-Alt-Del is pressed.

Finally, the *inittab* file includes entries that execute */sbin/agetty* for the first six virtual consoles. *agetty* is one of the several *getty* variants available for Linux. *getty* is a program that opens a terminal device (such as a virtual console, or a serial line), sets various parameters for the terminal driver, and executes */bin/login* to initiate a login session on that terminal. Therefore, to allow logins on a given virtual console, you must be running *getty* or *agetty* on it. *agetty* is the version used on a number of Linux systems, but others use *getty*, which has a slightly different syntax. See the manual pages for *getty* and *agetty* on your system.

agetty takes two arguments: a baud rate and a device name. The port names for Linux virtual consoles are */dev/tty1*, */dev/tty2*, and so forth. *agetty* assumes that the given device name is relative to */dev*. The baud rate for virtual consoles should generally be 38400.

Note that the action field for each *agetty* entry is respawn. This means that *init* should restart the command given in the entry when the *agetty* process dies, which is every time a user logs out.

Now you should be familiar with *init*, but the various files and commands in */etc/rc.d*, which do all of the work, remain a mystery. We can't delve into these files without more background on other system administration tasks, such as managing filesystems. Read on, and hopefully by the end of this chapter all should be clear.

Single-user Mode

Most of the time, you operate the system in multi-user mode so that users can log in. But there is a special state called *single-user mode*, where UNIX is running but there is no login prompt. When you're in single-user mode, you're basically super-user (**root**). You may have to enter this mode during installation, if something goes wrong. It's also important for certain routine system administration tasks, like checking corrupted file systems. (This is not fun. Try not to corrupt your file system. For instance, always shut down the system through a *shutdown* command before you turn off the power. This is described in the section "Shutting Down the System.")

Under single-user mode, the system is nearly useless; very little configuration is done, filesystems are unmounted, and so forth. This is necessary for recovering from certain kinds of system problems; see the section "What To Do in an Emergency" for details.

Note that UNIX is still a multiprocessing system, even in single-user mode. You can run multiple programs at once. Servers can run in the background, so that special functions such as the network can operate. But if your system supports more than one terminal, only the console can be used. And the X Window System cannot run.

Shutting Down the System

Fortunately, shutting down the Linux system is much simpler than booting and startup. However, it's not just a matter of hitting the reset switch. Linux, like all UNIX systems, buffers disk reads and writes in memory. This means that disk writes are delayed until absolutely necessary, and multiple reads on the same disk block will be served directly from RAM. This greatly increases performance as disks are extremely slow relative to the CPU.

The problem is that if the system were to be suddenly powered down or rebooted, the buffers in memory would not be written to disk, and data could be lost or corrupted. */sbin/update* is a program started from */etc/rc.d/rc.S* on most systems; it syncs the contents of the disk buffers every thirty seconds to prevent serious damage from occurring should the system crash. However, to be completely safe, the system needs to undergo a "safe" shutdown before rebooting. This will not only ensure that disk buffers are properly synchronized, but also allow all running processes to cleanly exit.

shutdown is the general, all-purpose command used to halt or reboot the system. As **root**, you can issue the command

```
/sbin/shutdown -r +10
```

to cause the system to reboot in ten minutes. The *—r* switch indicates that the system should be rebooted after shutdown, and +10 is the amount of time to wait (in minutes) until shutting down. The system will print a warning message to all active terminals, counting down until the shutdown time. You can add your own warning message by including it on the command line, as in:

```
/sbin/shutdown -r +10 "Rebooting to try new kernel"
```

You can also specify an absolute time to shutdown, as in

```
/sbin/shutdown -r 13:00
```

to reboot at 1:00 pm. Likewise, you can say

```
/sbin/shutdown -r now
```

to reboot immediately (after the safe shutdown process).

Using the *—h* switch, instead of *—r*, will cause the system to simply be halted after shutdown—you can then turn off the system power without fear of losing data.

As we saw in the previous section, you can have *init* catch the Ctrl-Alt-Del key sequence and execute a *shutdown* command in response to it. If you're used to rebooting your system in this way it might be good idea to check that your */etc/inittab* contains a `ctrlaltdel` entry. Note that you should never reboot your Linux system by pressing the system power switch, or the reboot switch on the front panel of your machine. Unless the system is flat-out hung (a rare occurrence), you should always use *shutdown*. The great thing about a multiprocessing system is that one program may hang, but you can almost always switch to another window or virtual console to recover.

shutdown provides a number of other options. The *—c* switch will cancel a currently-running *shutdown*. (Of course, you can kill the process by hand using *kill*, but *shutdown —c* might be easier.) The *—k* switch will print the warning messages but not actually shutdown the system. See the manual page for *shutdown* if you're interested in the gory details.

shutdown(8)

Managing User Accounts

Even if you're the only actual human being who uses your Linux system, understanding how to manage user accounts is important—even more so if your system hosts multiple users.

User accounts serve a number of purposes on UNIX systems. Most prominently, they give the system a way to distinguish between different people who use the system, for reasons of identification and security. Each user has a personal

Chapter 3

account, with a separate username and password. As discussed in the section "File Ownership and Permissions" in Chapter 3, *Basic UNIX Commands and Concepts*, users may set permissions on their files, allowing or restricting access to them by other users. Each file on the system is "owned" by a particular user, who may set the permissions for that file. User accounts are used to authenticate access to the system—only those people with accounts may access the machine. Also, accounts are used to identify users, for the purpose of keeping system logs, tagging electronic mail messages with the name of the sender, and so forth.

Apart from personal accounts, there are users on the system that provide administrative functions. As we've seen, the **root** account is to be used by the system administrator to perform maintenance—but usually not for personal system use. Such accounts are accessed using the *su* command, allowing another account to be accessed after logging in through a personal account.

Other accounts on the system may not be set aside for human interaction at all. These accounts are generally used by system daemons, which must access files on the system through a specific user ID other than **root** or one of the personal user accounts. For example, if you configure your system to receive a newsfeed from another site, the news daemon must store news articles in a spool directory that anyone can access, but only one user (the news daemon) can write to. No human being is associated with the **news** account—it is an "imaginary" user set aside for the news daemon only.

One of the permissions bits that can be set on executables is the *setuid* bit, which causes the program to be executed with the permissions of the owner of that file. For example, if the news daemon were owned by the user **news**, and the setuid bit set on the executable, it would run as if by the user **news**. **news** would have write access to the news spool directory, and all other users would have read access to the articles stored there. This is a security feature. News programs can give users just the right amount of access to the news spool directory, but no one can just play around there.

As the system administrator, it will be your job to create and manage accounts for all of the users (real and virtual) on your machine. This is actually a painless, hands-off task in most cases, but it's important to understand how it works.

The passwd File

Every account on the system has an entry in the file */etc/passwd*. This file contains entries, one line per user, that specify several attributes for each account, such as the username, real name, and so forth.

Each entry in this file is of the format

```
username:password:uid:gid:gecos:homedir:shell
```

username is a unique character string, identifying the account. For personal accounts, this is the name under which the user logs in. On most systems this is limited to 8 alphanumeric characters—for example, **larry** or **kirsten**.

password is an encrypted representation of the user's password. This field is set using the *passwd* program to set the account's password—it uses a one-way encryption scheme which is difficult (but not impossible) to break. You don't set this by hand; the *passwd* program does it for you. Note, however, that if the first character of the *passwd* field is * (an asterisk), the account is "disabled"—the system will not allow logins as this user. See the section "Creating Accounts."

uid is the user ID, a unique integer which the system uses to identify the account. The system uses the *uid* field internally when dealing with process and file permissions—it's easier and more compact to deal with integers than byte strings. Therefore, both the *uid* and the *username* identify a particular account: the *uid* is more important to the system, while *username* is more convenient for humans.

gid is the group ID, an integer referring to the user's default group, found in the file */etc/group*. See the section "The Group File," below.

gecos contains miscellaneous information about the user, such as the user's real name, and optional "location information" such as the user's office address or phone number. This information is used by programs such as *mail* and *finger* to identify users on the system; we'll talk more about it below. By the way, *gecos* is a historical name dating back to the 1970's; it stands for *General Electric Comprehensive Operating System*. GECOS has nothing to do with UNIX, except that this field was originally added to */etc/passwd* to provide compatibility with some of its services. Just in case you needed to know.

homedir is the user's home directory. This is usually a directory owned by the user for his or her own personal use; more on this below. When the user first logs in, his or her shell finds its current working directory in the named *homedir*.

shell is the name of the program to run when the user logs in; in most cases this is the full pathname of a shell, such as */bin/bash* or */bin/tcsh*.

Many of the above fields are optional; the only required fields are *username*, *uid*, *gid*, and *homedir*. Most user accounts will have all fields filled in, but "imaginary" or administrative accounts may use only a few of them.

Here are two sample entries that you might find in */etc/passwd*:

```
root:ZxPsI9ZjiVd9Y:0:0:The root of all evil:/root:/bin/bash
aclark:BjDf5hBysDsii:104:50:Anna Clark:/home/aclark:/bin/bash
```

The first entry is for the **root** account. First of all, notice that the *uid* of **root** is zero. This is what makes **root root**—the system knows that uid 0 is "special" and that it does not have the usual security restrictions. The gid of **root** is also zip, which is mostly a convention. Many of the files on the system are owned by **root** and the **root** group, which have a uid and gid of zero, respectively. More on groups in a minute.

Chapter 3

On many systems, **root** uses the "home directory" */root*, or just */*. This is not usually relevant, because you will most often use *su* to access **root** from your own account. Also, it is tradition to use a Bourne-shell variant (in this case */bin/bash*) for the **root** account, although you can use C shell if you like. (Shells are discussed in the section "Shells" in Chapter 3.) Be careful, though—Bourne shells and C shells have differing syntax, and switching between them when using **root** can be confusing and lead to mistakes.

The second entry is for an actual human being, username **aclark**. In this case, the *uid* is 104. The *uid* field can technically be any unique integer; on many systems, it's customary to have user accounts numbered 100 and above, and administrative accounts in the sub-100 range. The *gid* is 50, which just means that **aclark** is in whatever group is numbered 50 in the */etc/group* file. Hang on to your horses; groups are covered in the next section.

Home directories are often found in */home*, and named after the username of their owner. This is, for the most part, a useful convention to avoid confusion when finding a particular user's home directory, but you can technically place a home directory anywhere. You should observe the directory layout used on your system, however.

Note that as the system administrator, it's not usually necessary to modify the */etc/passwd* file directly. There are several programs available which can help you create and maintain user accounts; see the section "Creating Accounts," below.

The Group File

User groups are a convenient way to logically organize sets of user accounts, and allow users to share files within their group or groups. Each file on the system has both a user and a group owner associated with it. Using *ls −l*, you can see the owner and group for a particular file, as in:

```
rutabaga% ls -l boiler.tex
-rwxrw-r--   1 mdw      megabozo    10316 Oct  6 20:19 boiler.tex
rutabaga%
```

This file is owned by the user **mdw** and belongs to the **megabozo** group. We can see from the file permissions that **mdw** has read, write, and execute access to the file, that anyone in the **megabozo** group has read and write access, and that all other users have read access only.

This doesn't mean that **mdw** is in the **megabozo** group—it simply means that the file may be accessed, as shown by the permissions bits, by anyone in the **megabozo** group (which may or may not include **mdw**—judge for yourself).

This way files can be shared among groups of users, and permissions can be specified separately for the owner of the file, the group to which the file belongs, and everyone else. An introduction to permissions appears in the section "File Ownership and Permissions" in Chapter 3.

Every user is assigned to at least one group, that specified in the *gid* field of the */etc/passwd* file. However, a user can be a member of multiple groups. The file */etc/group* contains a one-line entry for each group on the system, very similar in nature to */etc/passwd*. The format of this file is

```
groupname:password:gid:members
```

Here, *groupname* is a character string identifying the group; it is the group name printed when using commands such as *ls –l.*

password is an optional password associated with the group, which allows users not in this group to access the group with the *newsgroup* command. See below.

gid is the group ID used by the system to refer to the group; it is the number used in the *gid* field of */etc/passwd* to specify a user's default group.

members is a comma-separated list of usernames, identifying those users who are members of this group, but who have a different *gid* in */etc/passwd*. That is, this list need not contain those users who have this group set as their "default" group in */etc/passwd*—it's only for users who are additional members of the group.

For example, */etc/group* might contain the following entries:

```
root:*:0:
bin:*:1:root,daemon
users:*:50:
bozo:*:51:linus,mdw
megabozo:*:52:kibo
```

The first entries, for the groups **root** and **bin**, are administrative groups, similar in nature to the "imaginary" accounts used on the system. Many files are owned by groups such as **root** and **bin**. The other groups are for user accounts. Like user IDs, the group ID values for user groups are often placed in ranges above 50 or 100.

The *password* field of the *group* file is something of a curiosity. It isn't used much, but in conjunction with the *newsgroup* program it will allow users who aren't members of a particular group to assume that group ID, if they have the password. For example, using the command

```
rutabaga% newsgroup bozo
Password: password for group bozo
rutabaga%
```

will start a new shell with the group ID of **bozo**. If the *password* field is blank, or the first character is an asterisk, you will receive a `permission denied` error if you attempt to *newsgroup* to that group.

However, the *password* field of the *group* file is seldom used, and is really not necessary. (In fact, most systems don't provide tools to set the password for a group; you could use *passwd* to set the password for a dummy user in */etc/passwd* and copy the encrypted *password* field to */etc/group.*) Instead, you can make a user a member of multiple groups simply by including the username in the `members` field for each additional group. In the above example, the users **linus** and **mdw** are members of the **bozo** group, as well as whatever group they are assigned to in the */etc/passwd* file. If we wanted to add **linus** to the **megabozo** group as well, we'd change the last line of the example above to:

```
megabozo:*:52:kibo,linus
```

The command *groups* will tell you which groups you belong to, as in:

```
rutabaga% groups
users bozo
```

Giving a list of usernames to *groups* will list the groups that each user in the list belongs to.

When you log in, you are automatically assigned to the group ID given in */etc/passwd*, as well as any additional groups for which you're listed in */etc/group.* This means that you have "group access" to any files on the system with a group ID contained in your list of groups. In this case, the group permission bits (set with *chmod g+...*) for those files apply to you. (Unless you're the owner, in which case the owner permission bits apply, instead.)

Now that you know the ins and outs of groups, how should you assign groups on your system? This is really a matter of style, and depends on how your system will be used. For systems with just one or a handful of users, it's easiest to have a single group (called, say, **users**) to which all personal user accounts belong. Note that all of the system groups—those groups contained within */etc/group* when the system is first installed—should probably be left alone. Various daemons and programs may depend upon them.

If you have a number of users on your machine, there are several ways to organize groups. For example, an educational institution may have separate groups for **students**, **faculty**, and **staff**. A software company might have different groups for each design team. On other systems, each user is placed into a separate group, named identically to the username. This keeps each pigeon in its own hole, so to speak, and allows users to share files with a particular group. However, adding a user to an additional group usually requires the system administrator to intervene (by editing */etc/group*). It's really up to you.

Creating Accounts

Creating a user account requires several steps: adding an entry to */etc/passwd*, creating the user's home directory, and setting up the user's default configuration files (such as *.bashrc*) in their home directory. Luckily, you don't have to perform these steps by hand; nearly all Linux systems include a program called *adduser* to do this for you.

Running *adduser* as **root** should work as follows. Just enter the requested information at the prompts; many of the prompts have reasonable defaults which you can select by pressing Enter.

```
Adding a new user. The username should not exceed 8 characters
in length, or you many run into problems later.

Enter login name for new account (^C to quit): norbert

Editing information for new user [norbert]

Full Name: Norbert Ebersol
GID [100]: 51

Checking for an available UID after 500
First unused uid is 501

UID [501]: (enter)
Home Directory [/home/norbert]: (enter)
Shell [/bin/bash]: (enter)
Password [norbert]: (norbert's password)

Information for new user [norbert]:
Home directory: [/home/norbert] Shell: [/bin/bash]
Password: [(norbert's password)] uid: [501] gid: [51]

Is this correct? [y/N]: y

Adding login [norbert] and making directory [/home/norbert]
Adding the files from the /etc/skel directory:
./.emacs -> /home/norbert/./.emacs
./.kermrc -> /home/norbert/./.kermrc
./.bashrc -> /home/norbert/./.bashrc
```

There should be no surprises here; just enter the information as requested or choose the defaults. Note that *adduser* uses 100 as the default group ID, and looks for the first unused user ID after 500. It should be safe to go along with these defaults; in the above example we used a group ID of 51 and the default user ID of 501.

After the account is created, the files from */etc/skel* are copied to the user's home directory. */etc/skel* contains the "skeleton" files for a new account; they are the default configuration files (such as *.emacs* and *.bashrc*) for the new user. Feel free to place other files here if your new user accounts should have them.

After this is done, the new account is ready to roll—**norbert** can log in, using the password set using *adduser*. New users should always change their own passwords, using *passwd*, immediately after logging in for the first time. This is to guarantee security.

root can set the password for any user on the system. For example, the command

```
passwd norbert
```

will prompt for a new password for **norbert**, without asking for the original password. Note, however, that you must know the root password in order to change it. If you forget the root password entirely, you can boot Linux into a root shell, in single-user mode, or from an "emergency floppy," and clear the *password* field of the */etc/passwd* entry for **root**. See the section "What To Do in an Emergency."

Some Linux systems provide the command-line–driven *useradd* instead of *adduser*. This program requires you to provide all of the relevant information as command-line arguments. If you can't locate *adduser* and are stuck with *useradd*, see the manual pages, which should help you out.

Deleting and Disabling Accounts

Deleting a user account is much easier than creating one; this is the well-known concept of entropy at work. To delete an account, you must remove the user's entry in */etc/passwd*, remove any references to the user in */etc/group*, and delete the user's home directory, as well as any additional files created or owned by the user. For example, if the user has an incoming mailbox in */var/spool/mail*, it must be deleted as well.

The command *userdel* (the yin to *useradd*'s yang) will delete an account and the account's home directory. For example,

```
userdel -r norbert
```

will remove the recently-created account for **norbert**. The *-r* option forces the home directory to be removed as well. Other files associated with the user—for example, the incoming mailbox, *crontab* files, and so forth—must be removed by hand. Usually these are quite insignificant and can be left around. By the end of this chapter you should know where these files are, if they exist. A quick way to find the files associated with a particular user is through the command

```
find / -user username -ls
```

This will give an *ls –l* listing of each file owned by *username*. Of course, to use this, the account associated with *username* must still have an entry in */etc/passwd*. If you deleted the account, use the *–uid num* argument instead, where *num* is the numeric user ID of the dearly departed user.

Temporarily (or not-so-temporarily) disabling a user account, for whatever reason, is even simpler. You can either remove the user's entry in */etc/passwd* (leaving the home directory and other files intact), or add an asterisk to the first character of the *password* field of the */etc/passwd* entry, as so:

```
aclark:*BjDf5hBysDsii:104:50:Anna Clark:/home/aclark:/bin/bash
```

This will disallow logins to the account in question.

Modifying User Accounts

Modifying attributes of user accounts and groups is usually a simple matter of editing */etc/passwd* and */etc/group*. Many systems provide commands such as *usermod* and *groupmod* which do just this; it's often easier to edit the files by hand.

To change a user's password, you should use the *passwd* command, which will prompt for a password, encrypt it, and store the encrypted password the in */etc/passwd* file.

If you need to change the user ID of an existing account, you can do this by editing the *uid* field of */etc/passwd* directly. However, you should also *chown* the files owned by the user to that of the new *uid*. For example,

```
chown -R aclark /home/aclark
```

will set the ownership for all files in the home directory used by **aclark** back to **aclark**, if you changed the *uid* for this account. If *ls –l* prints a numeric user ID, instead of a username, this means that there is no username associated with the *uid* owning the files. Use *chown* to fix this.

Archive and Compression Utilities

There are dozens of utilities available for UNIX systems for archiving and compressing files, in many shapes and forms. Some of these (such as *tar* and *compress*) date back to the earliest days of UNIX; others (such as *gzip*) are relative newcomers. The main goal of these utilities is to archive files (that is, to pack many files together into a single file, for easy transportation or backup) and to compress files (to reduce the amount of diskspace required to store a particular file or set of files).

In this section we're going to discuss the most common file formats and utilities that you're likely to run into. For instance, a near-universal convention in the UNIX world is to transport files or software as a *tar* archive, compressed using *compress* or *gzip*. In order to create or unpack these files yourself, you'll need to know the tools of the trade. The tools are most often used when installing new software, or creating backups—the subject of the following two sections in this chapter.

Using gzip

gzip is a fast and efficient compression program distributed by the GNU project. The basic function of *gzip* is to take a file, compress it, save the compressed version as *filename.gz*, and remove the original, uncompressed file. The original file is removed only if *gzip* is successful; it is very difficult to accidentally delete a file in this manner. Of course, being GNU software, *gzip* has more options than you want to think about, and many aspects of its behavior can be modified using command-line options.

First, let's say that we have a large file named *garbage.txt*:

```
rutabaga% ls -l garbage.txt
-rw-r--r--   1 mdw      hack        312996 Nov 17 21:44 garbage.txt
```

To compress this file using *gzip*, we simply use the command:

```
gzip garbage.txt
```

This replaces *garbage.txt* with the compressed file *garbage.txt.gz*. What we end up with is the following:

```
rutabaga% gzip garbage.txt
rutabaga% ls -l garbage.txt.gz
-rw-r--r--   1 mdw      hack        103441 Nov 17 21:44 garbage.txt.gz
```

Note that *garbage.txt* is removed when *gzip* completes.

You can give *gzip* a list of filenames; it will compress each file in the list, storing each with a *.gz* extension. (Unlike the *zip* program for UNIX and MS-DOS systems, *gzip* will not, by default, compress several files into a single *.gz* archive. That's what *tar* is for; see the next section.)

How efficiently a file is compressed depends upon its format and contents. For example, many graphics file formats (such as GIF and JPEG) are already well compressed, and *gzip* will have little or no effect upon such files. Files that compress well usually include plain text files and binary files such as executables and libraries.

You can get information on a gzipped file using *gzip –l*. For example,

```
rutabaga% gzip -l garbage.txt.gz
compressed  uncompr. ratio uncompressed_name
   103115    312996  67.0% garbage.txt
```

To get our original file back from the compressed version, we use *gunzip*, as in

```
gunzip garbage.txt.gz
```

After doing this, we obtain:

```
rutabaga% gunzip garbage.txt.gz
rutabaga% ls -l garbage.txt
-rw-r--r--   1 mdw        hack        312996 Nov 17 21:44 garbage.txt
```

Which is identical to the original file. Note that when you *gunzip* a file, the compressed version is removed once the uncompression is complete.

gzip stores the name of the original, uncompressed file in the compressed version. This way, if the compressed filename (including the *.gz* extension) is too long for the filesystem type (say, you're compressing a file on an MS-DOS filesystem with 8.3 filenames), the original filename can be restored using *gunzip*, even if the compressed file had a truncated name.

To uncompress a file to its original filename, use the *–N* option with *gunzip*. For example,

```
rutabaga% gzip garbage.txt
rutabaga% mv garbage.txt.gz rubbish.txt.gz
```

If we were to *gunzip rubbish.txt.gz* at this point, the uncompressed file would be named *rubbish.txt*, after the new (compressed) filename. However, with the *–N* option, we obtain:

```
rutabaga% gunzip -N rubbish.txt.gz
rutabaga% ls -l garbage.txt
-rw-r--r--   1 mdw        hack        312996 Nov 17 21:44 garbage.txt
```

gzip and *gunzip* can also compress or uncompress data from standard input and output. If *gzip* is given no filenames to compress, it attempts to compress data read from standard input. Likewise, if you use the *–c* option with *gunzip*, it will write uncompressed data to standard output. For example, you could pipe the output of a command to *gzip* to compress the output stream and save it to a file in one step, as in:

```
rutabaga% ls -laR $HOME | gzip > filelist.gz
```

This will produce a recursive directory listing of your home directory and save it in the compressed file *filelist.gz*. You can display the contents of this file with the command:

```
rutabaga% gunzip -c filelist.gz | more
```

which will uncompress *filelist.gz* and pipe the output to the *more* command. When you use *gunzip –c*, the file on disk remains compressed.

The *zcat* command is identical to *gunzip –c*. You can think of this as a version of *cat* for compressed files.

When compressing files, you can use one of the options *–1*, *–2*, ... through *–9* to specify the speed and quality of the compression used. *–1* (also *--fast*) specifies the fastest method, which compresses the files less compactly, while −9 (also --*best*) uses the slowest but best compression method. If you don't specify one of these options the default is −6. None of these options has any bearing on how you use *gunzip*; *gunzip* will be able to uncompress the file no matter what speed option you use.

gzip is relatively new in the UNIX world. The compression programs used on most UNIX systems are *compress* and *uncompress*, which were included in the original Berkeley versions of UNIX. *compress* and *uncompress* are very much like *gzip* and *gunzip*, respectively; *compress* saves compressed files as *filename.Z* as opposed to *filename.gz*, and uses a slightly less efficient compression algorithm.

However, the free software community has been moving to *gzip* for several reasons. First of all, *gzip* works better. Secondly, there has been a patent dispute over the compression algorithm used by *compress*—the results of which could prevent third parties from implementing the *compress* algorithm on their own. Because of this, the Free Software Foundation urged a move to *gzip*, which at least the Linux community has embraced. *gzip* has been ported to many architectures, and many others are following suit. Happily, *gunzip* is able to uncompress the *.Z* format files produced by *compress*.

The bottom line is that you should use *gzip*/*gunzip* for your compression needs. If you encounter a file with the extension *.Z*, it was probably produced by *compress*, and *gunzip* can uncompress it for you.

Earlier versions of *gzip* used *.z* (lowercase!) instead of *.gz* as the compressed-filename extension. Because of the potential confusion with *.Z*, this was changed. At any rate, *gunzip* retains backwards-compatibility with a number of filename extensions and file types.

Using tar

tar is a general-purpose archiving utility capable of packing many files into a single archive file, retaining information such as file permissions and ownership. The name *tar* stands for *tape archive*, because the tool was originally used to archive files as backups on tape. However, use of *tar* is not at all restricted to making tape backups, as we'll see.

The format of the *tar* command is

```
tar functionoptions files...
```

where `function` is a single letter indicating the operation to perform, `options` is a list of (single-letter) options to that function, and `files` is the list of files to pack or unpack in an archive. (Note that `function` is not separated from `options` by any space.)

function can be one of:

- c, to create a new archive;

- x, to extract files from an archive;

- t, to list the contents of an archive;

- r, to append files to the end of an archive;

- u, to update files that are newer than those in the archive;

- d, to compare files in the archive to those in the filesystem.

You'll rarely use most of these ~~options~~ functions; the most commonly used are c, x, and t.

The most common *options* are:

- v, to print verbose information when packing or unpacking archives;

- k, to keep any existing files when extracting—that is, to not overwrite any existing files which are contained within the tar file.

- f *filename*, to specify that the tar file to be read or written is *filename*.

There are others, which we will cover later in this section.

Although the *tar* syntax might appear complex at first, in practice it's quite simple. For example, say we have a directory named *mt*, containing these files:

```
rutabaga% ls -l mt
total 37
-rw-r--r--   1 root      root             24 Sep 21  1993 Makefile
-rw-r--r--   1 root      root            847 Sep 21  1993 README
-rwxr-xr-x   1 root      root           9220 Nov 16 19:03 mt
-rw-r--r--   1 root      root           2775 Aug  7  1993 mt.1
-rw-r--r--   1 root      root           6421 Aug  7  1993 mt.c
-rw-r--r--   1 root      root           3948 Nov 16 19:02 mt.o
-rw-r--r--   1 root      root          11204 Sep  5  1993 st_info.txt
```

We wish to pack the contents of this directory into a single *tar* archive. To do this, we use the command

```
tar cf mt.tar mt
```

The first argument to *tar* is the *function* (here, c, for create) followed by any *options*. Here, we use the one option *f mt.tar*, to specify that the resulting tar archive should be named *mt.tar*. The last argument is the name of the file(s) to archive; in this case, we give the name of a directory, in which case *tar* packs all of the files in that directory into the archive.

Note that the first argument to *tar* must be a function letter followed by a list of options. Because of this, there's no reason to use a dash (–) to precede the options as many UNIX commands require. *tar* will allow you to use a dash, as in

```
tar -cf mt.tar mt
```

but it's really not necessary. In some versions of *tar*, the first letter must be the *function*, as in c, t, or x. In other versions the order of letters does not matter.

It is often a good idea to use the v option with *tar*; this will list each file as it is archived. For example,

```
rutabaga% tar cvf mt.tar mt
mt/
mt/st_info.txt
mt/README
mt/mt.1
mt/Makefile
mt/mt.c
mt/mt.o
mt/mt
```

If you use v multiple times, additional information will be printed, as in

```
rutabaga% tar cvvf mt.tar mt
drwxr-xr-x root/root        0 Nov 16 19:03 1994 mt/
-rw-r--r-- root/root    11204 Sep  5 13:10 1993 mt/st_info.txt
-rw-r--r-- root/root      847 Sep 21 16:37 1993 mt/README
-rw-r--r-- root/root     2775 Aug  7 09:50 1993 mt/mt.1
-rw-r--r-- root/root       24 Sep 21 16:03 1993 mt/Makefile
-rw-r--r-- root/root     6421 Aug  7 09:50 1993 mt/mt.c
-rw-r--r-- root/root     3948 Nov 16 19:02 1994 mt/mt.o
-rwxr-xr-x root/root     9220 Nov 16 19:03 1994 mt/mt
```

This is especially useful to let you verify that *tar* is doing the right thing.

In some versions of *tar*, f must be the last letter in the list of options. This is because *tar* expects the f option to be followed by a filename—the name of the tar file to read from or write to. If you don't specify f *filename* at all, *tar* assumes for historical reasons that it should use the device */dev/rmt0* (that is, the first tape drive). In the section "Making Backups" we'll talk about using *tar* in conjunction with a tape drive to make backups.

Now, we can give the file *mt.tar* to other people, and they can extract it on their own system. To do this, they would use the command

```
tar xvf mt.tar
```

This will create the subdirectory *mt* and place all of the files listed above into it, with the same ownership and permissions as found on the original system. The x option stands for "extract." The v option is used again here to list each file as it is extracted. This will produce:

```
courgette% tar xvf mt.tar
mt/
mt/st_info.txt
mt/README
```

```
mt/mt.1
mt/Makefile
mt/mt.c
mt/mt.o
mt/mt
```

We can see that *tar* saves the pathname of each file relative to the location in which the tar file was originally created. That is, when we created the archive using *tar cf mt.tar mt*, the only input filename that we specified was *mt*, the name of the directory containing the files. Therefore, *tar* stores the directory itself and all of the files below that directory in the tar file. When we extract the tar file, the directory *mt* is created and the files placed into it, the exact inverse of what was done to create the archive.

By default, *tar* extracts all tar files relative to the current directory in which you execute *tar*. For example, if you were to pack up the contents of your */bin* directory with the command

```
tar cvf bin.tar /bin
```

tar would give the warning

```
tar: Removing leading / from absolute path names in the archive.
```

What this means is that the files are stored in the archive within the subdirectory *bin*. When this tar file is extracted, the directory *bin* will be created *in the working directory of tar*—not as */bin* on the system where the extraction is being done. This is very important, and is meant to prevent terrible mistakes when extracting tar files. Otherwise, extracting a tar file packed as, say, */bin*, would trash the contents of your */bin* directory when you extracted it. If you really wanted to extract such a tar file into */bin*, you would extract it from the root directory, */*. You can override this behavior using the P option when packing tar files, but it's not recommended that you do so.

Another way to create the tar file *mt.tar* would have been to *cd* into the *mt* directory itself, and use a command such as

```
tar cvf mt.tar *
```

This way the *mt* subdirectory would not be stored in the tar file; when extracted, the files would be placed directly in your current working directory. One fine point of *tar* etiquette is to always pack tar files so that they contain a subdirectory, as we did in the first example with *tar cvf mt.tar mt*. Therefore, when the archive is extracted, the subdirectory will be created and any files placed there. This way you can ensure that the files won't be placed directly in your current working directory—they will be tucked out of the way and prevent confusion. This also saves the person doing the extraction the trouble of having to create a separate directory (should they wish to do so) to unpack the tar file. Of course, there are plenty of situations in which you wouldn't want to do this. So much for etiquette.

When creating archives, you can, of course, give *tar* a list of files or directories to pack into the archive. In the first example we have given *tar* the single directory *mt*, but in the above paragraph we used the wildcard *, which the shell expands into the list of filenames in the current directory.

Before extracting a tar file, it's usually a good idea to take a look at its table of contents to determine how it was packed. This way you can determine if you do need to create a subdirectory yourself within which to unpack the archive. A command such as

    tar tvf *tarfile*

will list the table of contents for the named *tarfile*. Note that when using the t function, only one v is required to get the long file listing, as seen below:

```
courgette% tar tvf mt.tar
drwxr-xr-x root/root          0 Nov 16 19:03 1994 mt/
-rw-r--r-- root/root      11204 Sep  5 13:10 1993 mt/st_info.txt
-rw-r--r-- root/root        847 Sep 21 16:37 1993 mt/README
-rw-r--r-- root/root       2775 Aug  7 09:50 1993 mt/mt.1
-rw-r--r-- root/root         24 Sep 21 16:03 1993 mt/Makefile
-rw-r--r-- root/root       6421 Aug  7 09:50 1993 mt/mt.c
-rw-r--r-- root/root       3948 Nov 16 19:02 1994 mt/mt.o
-rwxr-xr-x root/root       9220 Nov 16 19:03 1994 mt/mt
```

No extraction is being done here; we're just displaying the archive's table of contents. We can see from the filenames that this file was packed with all files in the subdirectory *mt*, so that when we extract the tar file the directory *mt* will be created, and the files placed there.

You can also extract individual files from a tar archive. To do this, use the command

    tar xvf *tarfile files*

where *files* is the list of files to extract. As we've seen, if you don't specify any *files*, *tar* extracts the entire archive.

When specifying individual files to extract, you must give the full pathname as it is stored in the tar file. For example, if we wanted to grab just the file *mt.c* from the above archive *mt.tar*, we'd use the command

    tar xvf mt.tar mt/mt.c

This would create the subdirectory *mt* and place the file *mt.c* within it.

tar has many more options than those mentioned here. These are the features that you're likely to use most of the time, but GNU *tar* in particular has extensions which make it ideal for creating backups and the like. See the *tar* manual page and the following section for more information.

Using tar with gzip

tar does not compress the data stored in its archives in any way. If you are creating a tar file from three 200K files, you'll end up with an archive of about 600K. It is common practice to compress tar archives with *gzip* (or the older *compress* program). You could create a gzipped tar file using the commands:

```
tar cvf tarfile files...
gzip -9 tarfile
```

But that's so cumbersome, and requires you to have enough space to store the uncompressed *tar* file before you *gzip* it.

A much trickier way to accomplish the same task is to use an interesting feature of *tar* which allows you to write an archive to standard output. If you specify – as the tar file to read or write, the data will be read from or written to standard input or output. For example, we can create a gzipped tar file using the command

```
tar cvf - files... | gzip -9 > tarfile.tar.gz
```

Here, *tar* creates an archive from the named `files` and writes it to standard output; next, *gzip* reads the data from standard input, compresses it, and writes the result to its own standard output; finally, we redirect the gzipped tar file to *tarfile.tar.gz*.

We could extract such a tar file using the command

```
gunzip -9c tarfile.tar.gz | tar xvf -
```

gunzip uncompresses the named archive file, writes the result to standard output, which is read by *tar* on standard input and extracted. Isn't UNIX fun?

Of course, both of the above commands are rather cumbersome to type. Luckily, the GNU version of *tar* provides the z option which automatically creates or extracts gzipped archives. (We saved the discussion of this option until now, so you'd truly appreciate its convenience.) For example, we could use the commands

```
tar cvzf tarfile.tar.gz files...
```

and

```
tar xvzf tarfile.tar.gz
```

to create and extract gzipped tar files. Note that you should name the files created in this way with the *.tar.gz* filename extensions, to make their format obvious. The z option works just as well with other tar functions such as t.

Only the GNU version of *tar* supports the z option; if you are using *tar* on another UNIX system, you may have to use one of the longer commands given above to accomplish the same tasks. Nearly all Linux systems use GNU *tar*.

Keeping the above in mind, you could write short shell scripts or aliases to handle cookbook tar file creation and extraction for you. Under *bash*, you could include the following functions in your *.bashrc*:

```
tarc () { tar czvf $1.tar.gz $1 }
tarx () { tar xzvf $1 }
tart () { tar tzvf $1 }
```

With these functions, to create a gzipped tar file from a single directory, you could use the command

```
tarc directory
```

The resulting archive file would be named *directory.tar.gz*. (Be sure that there's no trailing slash on the directory name; otherwise the archive will be created as *.tar.gz* within the given *directory*.) To list the table of contents of a gzipped tar file, just use

```
tart file.tar.gz
```

Or, to extract such an archive, use

```
tarx file.tar.gz
```

tar Tricks

Because *tar* saves the ownership and permissions of files in the archive, and retains the full directory structure, as well as symbolic and hard links, using *tar* is an excellent way to copy or move an entire directory tree from one place to another on the same system (or even between different systems, as we'll see). Using the – syntax described above, you can write a tar file to standard output, which is read and extracted on standard input elsewhere.

For example, say that we have a directory containing two subdirectories: *from-stuff* and *to-stuff*. *from-stuff* contains an entire tree of files, symbolic links, and so forth—something which is very difficult to mirror precisely using a recursive *cp*. In order to mirror the entire tree beneath *from-stuff* to *to-stuff*, we could use the commands

```
cd from-stuff
tar cf - . | (cd ../to-stuff; tar xvf -)
```

Simple and elegant, right? We start in the directory *from-stuff* and create a tar file of the current directory, which is written to standard output. This archive is read by a subshell (the commands contained within parentheses); the subshell does a *cd* to the target directory, *../to-stuff* (relative to *from-stuff*, that is), and then runs *tar xvf*, reading from standard input. No tar file is ever written to disk; the data is sent entirely via pipe from one *tar* process to another. The second *tar* process has the v option which will print each file as it's extracted; in this way we can verify that the command is working as expected.

In fact, you could transfer directory trees from one machine to another (via the network) using this trick; just include an appropriate *rsh* command within the sub-shell on the right side of the pipe. The remote shell would execute *tar* to read the archive on its standard input. (Actually, GNU *tar* has facilities to automatically read or write tar files from other machines over the network; see the *tar* manual page for details.)

tar(1)

Making Backups

Taking backups of your system is a very important way to protect yourself from data corruption or loss in case you have problems with your hardware, or make a mistake such as deleting important files inadvertently. During your experiences with Linux, you're likely to make quite a few customizations to the system which can't be restored by simply reinstalling from your original installation media. However, if you happen to have your original Linux floppies or CD-ROM handy, it may not be necessary to back up your entire system. Your original installation media already serves as an excellent backup.

Under Linux, as with any UNIX-like system, you can make mistakes while logged in as **root** that would make it impossible to boot the system or log in. Many new-comers approach such a problem by reinstalling the system entirely from backup, or worse, from scratch. This is seldom if ever necessary. In the section "What To Do in an Emergency" we'll talk about what to do in these cases.

If you do experience data loss, it is sometimes possible to recover that data using the filesystem maintenance tools described in the section "Checking and Repairing Filesystems." Unlike some other operating systems, however, it's generally not possible to "undelete" a file that has been removed by *rm*, or overwritten by a careless *cp* or *mv* command (for example, copying one file over another destroys the file copied over). In these extreme cases backups are key to recovering from problems.

Backups are usually made to tape or floppy. Neither medium is 100% reliable, although tape is much more dependable than floppy in the long term. There are many tools available that can help you to make backups. In the simplest case, you can use a combination of *gzip* and *tar* to back up files from your hard drive to floppy or tape. This is the best method to use when you make only occasional backups, no more often than, say, once a month.

If you have numerous users on your system, or make frequent changes to the system configuration, it might make more sense to employ an incremental backup scheme. Under such a scheme, you would take a "full backup" of the system only about once a month. Then, every week, you would back up only those files which changed in the last week. Likewise, each night, you could back up just those files which changed over the previous 24 hours. There are several tools which exist to aid you in the task of backing up in this fashion.

The idea behind an incremental backup is that it is much more efficient to take backups in small steps—you use fewer diskettes or tapes, and the weekly and nightly backups are much shorter and easier to run. This makes it easier to back up more often—you have a backup that is at most a day old. If you were to, say, accidentally delete your entire system, you would restore it from backup in the following manner:

1. Restore from the most recent monthly backup. Say, if you wiped the system on July 17th, you would restore the July 1 full backup. Your system now reflects the state of files when the July 1 backup was made.

2. Restore from each of the weekly backups made so far this month. In our case, we could restore from the two weekly backups from July 7th and 14th. Restoring each weekly backup updates all of the files which changed during that week.

3. Restore from each of the daily backups during the last week, that is, since the last weekly backup. In this case, we would restore the daily backups from July 15th and 16th. The system now looks as it did when the daily backup was taken on July 16th; no more than a day's worth of files have been lost.

Depending on the size of your system, the full monthly backup might require 200 megabytes or more of backup storage—at most one tape, with today's tape media, but quite a few floppies. However, the weekly and daily backups would generally require much less storage space. Depending on how your system is used, you might decide to take the weekly backup on Sunday night and not bother with daily backups for the weekend.

One important characteristic that backups should (usually) have is the ability to select individual files from the backup for restoration. This way, if you accidentally delete a single file or group of files, you can simply restore those files without having to do a full system restoration. Depending on how you take backups, however, this task will be either very easy or painfully difficult.

In this section, we're going to talk about the use of *tar*, *gzip*, and a few related tools for taking backups to floppy and tape. We'll even cover the use of floppy and tape drives in the bargain. These tools allow you to take backups more or less "by hand"—you can automate the process by writing shell scripts and even schedule your backups to run automatically during the night using *cron*. All you have to do is flip tapes. There are other software packages out there that provide a nice menu-driven interface for creating backups, restoring specific files from backup, and so forth. Many of these packages are, in fact, nice front-ends to *tar* and *gzip*. You can decide for yourself what kind of backup system suits you best.

Simple Backups

The simplest means of taking a backup is to use *tar* to archive all of the files on the system, or only those files in a set of specific directories. Before you do this, however, you need to decide what files to back up. Do you need to back up every file on the system? This is very rarely necessary, especially if you have your original installation disks or CD-ROM. If you have made important changes to the system, but everything else is as just the way it was found on your installation media, you could get by only archiving those files which you have made changes to. Over time, however, it is very difficult to keep track of such changes.

Chapter 5

In general, you will be making changes to the system configuration files in */etc*. There are other configuration files as well, and it can't hurt to archive directories such as */usr/lib*, */usr/X11R6/lib/X11* (which contains the XFree86 configuration files, as we'll see in the section "Installing XFree86" of Chapter 5, *Power Tools*), and so forth.

You should also back up your kernel sources (if you have upgraded or built your own kernel); these are found in */usr/src/linux*.

During your Linux adventures it's a good idea to keep notes on what features of the system you've made changes to so you can make intelligent choices when taking backups. If you're truly paranoid, go ahead and backup the whole system—that can't hurt, but the cost of backup media might.

Chapter 7

Of course, you should also back up the home directories for each user on the system; these are generally found in */home*. If you have your system configured to receive electronic mail (see the section "The smail Mail Transport Agent" in Chapter 7, *Networking and Communications*), you might want to back up the incoming mail files for each user. Many people tend to keep old and "important" electronic mail in their incoming mail spool, and it's not difficult to accidentally corrupt one of these files through a mailer error or other mistake. These files are usually found in */var/spool/mail*.

Backing up to tape

Assuming that you know what files or directories to back up, you're ready to roll. The *tar* command can be used directly, as we've seen in the section "Using tar," to make a backup. For example, the command

```
tar cvf /dev/rft0 /usr/src /etc /home
```

will archive all of the files from */usr/src*, */etc*, and */home* to */dev/rft0*. */dev/rft0* is the first "floppy tape" device—that is, for the type of tape drive which hangs off of the floppy controller. Many popular tape drives for the PC use this interface. If you have a SCSI tape drive, the device names are */dev/st0*, */dev/st1*, and so forth, based on the drive number. Those tape drives with another type of interface have their own device names; you can determine these by looking at the documentation for the device driver in the kernel.

You can then read the archive back from the tape using a command such as

```
tar xvf /dev/rft0
```

This is exactly as if you were dealing with a tar file on disk, as seen in the section "Archive and Compression Utilities."

When using the tape drive, the tape is seen as a stream that may be read from or written to in one direction only. Once *tar* completes, the tape device will be closed, and the tape will rewind. You don't create a filesystem on a tape, nor do you mount it or attempt to access the data on it as files. You simply treat the tape device itself as a single "file" to create or extract archives from.

Be sure that your tapes are formatted before you use them. This ensures that the beginning-of-tape marker and bad blocks information has been written to the tape. At the time of this writing, no tools exist for formatting QIC-80 tapes (those used with floppy tape drivers) under Linux; you'll have to format tapes under MS-DOS or use preformatted tapes.

Creating one tar file per tape might be wasteful if the archive requires but a fraction of the capacity of the tape. In order to place more than one file on a tape, you must first prevent the tape from rewinding after each use, and you must have a way to position the tape to the next "file marker," both for tar file creation and for its extraction.

The way to do this is to use the non-rewinding tape devices, which are named */dev/nrft0, /dev/nrft1*, and so on for floppy tape drivers, and */dev/nrst0, /dev/nrst1*, etc. for SCSI tapes. When this device is used for reading or writing, the tape will not be rewound when the device is closed (that is, once *tar* has completed). You can then use *tar* again to add another archive to the tape. The two tar files on the tape won't have anything to do with each other. Of course, if you later overwrite the first tar file, you may overwrite the second file or leave an undesirable gap between the first and second files (which may be interpreted as garbage). In general, don't attempt to replace just one file on a tape that has multiple files on it.

Using the non-rewinding tape device, you can add as many files to the tape as space permits. In order to rewind the tape after use, use the *mt* command. *mt* is a general-purpose command that performs a number of functions with the tape drive.

For example, the command

```
mt /dev/nrft0 rewind
```

rewinds the tape in the first floppy-tape device. (In this case, you can use the corresponding rewinding tape device as well; however, the tape will rewind just as a side-effect of the tape device being closed.)

Similarly,

```
mt /dev/nrft0 reten
```

will retension the tape, by winding it to the end and then rewinding it.

When reading files on a multiple-file tape, you must use the non-rewinding tape device with *tar*, and the *mt* command to position the tape to the appropriate file.

For example, to skip to the next file on the tape, use the command

```
mt /dev/nrft0 fsf 1
```

This skips over one file on the tape. Similarly, to skip over two files, use

```
mt /dev/nrft0 fsf 2
```

mt(1)

Be sure to use the appropriate non-rewinding tape device with *mt*. Note that this command does not move to "file number two" on the tape; it skips over the next two files based on the current tape position. Just use *mt* to rewind the tape if you're not sure where the tape is currently positioned. You can also skip back; see the *mt* manual page for a complete list of options.

You need to use *mt* every time you read a multi-file tape. Using *tar* twice in succession to read two archive files usually won't work; this is because *tar* doesn't recognize the "file marker" placed on the tape between files. Once the first *tar* completes, the tape is positioned at the beginning of the file marker. Using *tar* immediately will give you an error message, because *tar* will attempt to read the file marker. After reading one file from a tape, just use

```
mt device fsf 1
```

to move to the next file.

Backing up to floppy

Just as we saw in the last section, the command

```
tar cvf /dev/fd0 /usr/src /etc /home
```

makes a backup of */usr/src*, */etc*, and */home* to */dev/fd0*, the first floppy device. You can then read the backup using a command such as

```
tar xvf /dev/fd0
```

Again, this treats the floppy just as if you were dealing with a file on disk. You don't create a filesystem on the floppy or attempt to mount it.

Because floppies have a rather limited storage capacity, GNU *tar* allows you to create a "multi-volume" archive. (This feature applies to tapes, as well, but is far more useful in the case of floppies.) With this feature, *tar* will prompt you to insert a new volume after reading or writing each floppy. To use this feature, simply provide the M option to *tar*, as in

```
tar cvMf /dev/fd0 /usr/src /etc /home
```

Be sure to label your floppies well, and don't get them out of order when attempting to restore the archive.

One caveat of this feature is that it doesn't support the automatic *gzip* compression provided by the z option (as seen in the previous section). However, there are various reasons why you may not want to compress your backups created with *tar*, as discussed below. At any rate, you can create your own multi-volume backups using *tar* and *gzip* in conjunction with a program that can read and write data to a sequence of floppies (or tapes, what have you), prompting for each in succession. One such program is *backflops*, available on several Linux distributions and on the FTP archive sites. A do-it-yourself way to accomplish the same thing would be to write the backup archive to a disk file and use *dd* or a similar command to write the archive as individual chunks to each floppy. If you're brave enough to try this, you can figure it out for yourself.

To gzip, or not to gzip?

There are good arguments both for and against compression of *tar* archives when making backups. The overall problem at hand is that neither *tar* nor *gzip* is particularly fault-tolerant, no matter how convenient they are. Although compression using *gzip* can greatly reduce the amount of backup media required to store an archive, compressing entire *tar* files as they are written to floppy or tape makes the backup prone to complete loss if even one block of the archive is corrupted— say, through a media error (not uncommon in the case of floppies and tapes). Most compression algorithms, *gzip* included, depend on the coherency of data across many bytes in order to achieve compression. If any data within a compressed archive is corrupt, *gunzip* may not be able to uncompress the file at all, making it completely unreadable to *tar*.

This is much worse than if the tar file were uncompressed on the tape. Although *tar* doesn't provide much protection against data corruption within an archive, if there is minimal corruption within a tar file, you will usually be able to recover most of the archived files with little trouble, or at least those files up until the corruption occurs. Although far from perfect, it's much better than losing your entire backup.

A better solution would be to use an archiving tool other than *tar* to make backups. There are several options available. *cpio* is an archiving utility that packs files together, similar in fashion to *tar*. However, because of the simpler storage method used by *cpio*, it can recover cleanly from data corruption in an archive. (It still doesn't handle errors well on gzipped files.)

The best solution may be to use a tool such as *afio*. *afio* supports multi-volume backups and is similar in some respects to *cpio*. However, *afio* includes compression, and is more reliable because each individual file is compressed. This means that if data on an archive is corrupted, the damage can be isolated to individual files, instead of the entire backup.

These tools should be available with your Linux distribution, as well as from all of the Internet-based Linux archives. A number of other backup utilities, with varying degrees of popularity and usability, have been developed or ported for Linux. If you're serious about backups, you should look into them.[*]

Incremental Backups

Incremental backups, as described earlier in this section, are a good way to keep your system backups up to date. For example, you can take nightly backups of only those files that changed in the last 24 hours, weekly backups of all files that changed in the last week, and monthly backups of the entire system.

You can create incremental backups using the tools mentioned above: *tar*, *gzip*, *cpio*, and so on. The first step in creating an incremental backup is to produce a list of files that changed since a certain amount of time ago. This is easily done with the *find* command.[†]

For example, to produce a list of all files that were modified in the last 24 hours, we can use the command

```
find / -mtime 1 -print > /tmp/filelist.daily
```

The first argument to *find* is the directory to start from—here, /, the root directory. The *-mtime 1* option tells *find* to locate all files that changed in the last 24 hours, and *-print* causes these filenames to be printed to standard output. We redirect standard output to a file for later use.

Likewise, to locate all files that changed in the last week, use

```
find / -mtime 7 -print > /tmp/filelist.weekly
```

Note that if you use *find* in this way, it will traverse all mounted filesystems. If you have a CD-ROM mounted, for example, *find* will attempt to locate all files on the CD-ROM as well (which you probably do not wish to backup). The *-prune* option can be used to exclude certain directories from the walk performed by *find* across the system; or, you can use *find* multiple times with a first argument other than /. See the manual page for *find* for details.

find(1)

Now you have produced a list of files to back up. Previously, when using *tar*, we have specified the files to archive on the command line. However, this list of files

---

* Of course, this section was written after the author took the first backup of his Linux system in nearly four years of use!

† If you're not familiar with *find*, bocome so soon. *find* is a great way to do things such as locate files across many directories which have certain filenames, permissions, or modification times. *find* can even execute a program for each file that it locates. In short, *find* is your friend, and all good system administrators know how to use it well.

may be much too long for a single command line (which is usually limited to around 2048 characters), and the list itself is contained within a file.

We can use the *–T* option with *tar* to specify a file containing a list of files for *tar* to back up. In order to use this option we'll have to use an alternate syntax to *tar* in which all options are specified explicitly with dashes. For example, to back up the files listed in *tmp/filelist.daily* to the device */dev/rft0*, use the command

```
tar -cv -T /tmp/filelist.daily -f /dev/rft0
```

You can now write a short shell script that will automatically produce the list of files and back them up using *tar*. You can use *cron* to cause the script to be executed nightly at a certain time; all you have to do is make sure there's a tape in the drive. You can write similar scripts for your weekly and monthly backups. *cron* is covered in the section "Scheduling Jobs Using cron," later in the chapter.

Upgrading Software

Linux is a fast-moving target. Because of the cooperative nature of the project, new software is always becoming available, and programs are constantly being updated with newer versions. This is especially true of the Linux kernel, which has many groups of people working on it. During the development process, it's not uncommon for a new kernel patch to be released on a nightly basis. While other parts of the system may not be as dynamic, the same principles apply.

With this constant development, how can you possibly hope to stay on top of the most recent versions of your system software? The short answer is, you can't. While there are people out there who have a need to stay current with, say, the nightly kernel patch release, for the most part there's no reason to bother upgrading your software this often. In this section we're going to talk about why and when to upgrade, and show you how to upgrade several important parts of the system.

When should you upgrade? In general, you should consider upgrading a portion of your system only when you have a demonstrated *need* to upgrade. For example, if you hear of a new release of some application that fixes important bugs (that is, those bugs which actually affect your personal use of the application), you might want to consider upgrading that application. If the new version of the program provides new features that you might find useful, or has a performance boost over your present version, it's also a good idea to upgrade. However, upgrading just for the sake of having the newest version of a particular program is probably silly.

Upgrading can sometimes be a painful thing to do. For example, you might want to upgrade a program that requires the newest versions of the compiler, libraries, and other software in order to run. Upgrading this program will also require you to upgrade several other parts of the system, which can be a time-consuming process. On the other hand, this can be seen as an argument for keeping your software up to date—if your compiler and libraries are current, upgrading the program in question won't be a problem.

Chapter 1

How can you find out about new versions of Linux software? The best way is to watch the USENET newsgroup *comp.os.linux.announce* (see the section "Usenet Newsgroups" in Chapter 1, *Introduction to Linux*) where announcements of new software releases and other important information are posted. If you have Internet access, you can then download the software via FTP and install it on your system.

If you don't have access to USENET or the Internet, the best way to keep in touch with recent developments is to pay for a CD-ROM subscription Here you receive an updated copy of the various Linux FTP sites, on CD-ROM, every couple of months. This service is available from a number of Linux vendors. It's a good thing to have, even if you have Internet access.

This brings us to another issue—what's the best upgrade method? Some people feel that it's easier to completely upgrade the system by reinstalling everything from scratch whenever a new version of their favorite distribution (say, Slackware) is released. This way you don't have to worry about various versions of the software working together. For those without Internet access, this may indeed be the easiest method—if you receive a new CD-ROM only once every two months, a great deal of your software may be out of date.

It's our opinion, however, that reinstallation is not a good upgrade plan at all. Most of the current Linux distributions are not meant to be upgraded in this way, and a complete reinstallation may be very complex or time-consuming. Also, if you plan to upgrade in this manner, you generally lose all of your own modifications and customizations to the system, and you'll have to make backups of your user's home directories and any other important files that would be deleted during a reinstallation. Many novices choose this upgrade path because it's the easiest one to follow. In actuality, not much changes from release to release, so a complete reinstallation is usually unnecessary and can be avoided with a little upgrading know-how.

In this section we'll show you how to upgrade various pieces of your system individually. We'll show you how to upgrade your system libraries and compiler, as well as give you a generic method for installing new software. In the section "Building a New Kernel," we'll talk about building a new kernel.

Upgrading Libraries

Most of the programs on a Linux system are compiled to use shared libraries. These libraries contain useful functions common to many programs. Instead of storing a copy of these routines in each program that calls them, the libraries are contained in files on the system that are read by all programs at run time. That is, when a program is executed, the code from the program file itself is read, followed by any routines from the shared library files. This saves a great deal of disk space—only one copy of the library routines is stored on disk.

In some instances, it's necessary to compile a program to have its own copy of the library routines, instead of using the routines from the shared libraries. (This is sometimes necessary for debugging a program.) We say that programs built in this way are *statically linked*, while programs built to use shared libraries are *dynamically linked.*

Therefore, dynamically linked executables depend upon the presence of the shared libraries on disk. Shared libraries are implemented in such a way that the programs compiled to use them generally don't depend on the version of the libraries that are available. This means that you can upgrade your shared libraries, and all programs that are built to use those libraries will automatically use the new routines. (There is an exception: If major changes are made to a library, the old programs won't work with the new library. You'll know that this is the case because the major version number is different—we'll explain more below. In this case, you keep both the old libraries and new libraries around. All of your old executables will continue to use the old libraries, and any new programs that are compiled will use the new libraries.)

When you build a program to use shared libraries, a piece of code is added to the program that causes it to execute *ld.so*, the dynamic linker, when the program is started. *ld.so* is responsible for finding the shared libraries that the program needs and loading the routines into memory. Dynamically-linked programs are also linked against "stub" routines, which simply take the place of the actual shared library routines in the executable. *ld.so* replaces the stub routine with the code from the libraries when the program is executed.

The *ldd* command can be used to list the shared libraries on which a given executable depends. For example,

```
rutabaga% ldd /usr/bin/X11/xterm
        libXaw.so.6 (DLL Jump 6.0) => /usr/X11R6/lib/libXaw.so.6.0
        libXt.so.6 (DLL Jump 6.0) => /usr/X11R6/lib/libXt.so.6.0
        libX11.so.6 (DLL Jump 6.0) => /usr/X11R6/lib/libX11.so.6.0
        libc.so.4 (DLL Jump 4.5pl26) => /lib/libc.so.4.5.26
```

Here, we see that the *xterm* program depends on the four shared libraries *libXaw*, *libXt*, *libX11*, and *libc*. (The first three are related to the X Window System, and the last is the standard C library.) We also see the version numbers of the libraries for which the program was compiled (that is, the version of the stub routines used), and the name of the file which contains each shared library. This is the file that *ld.so* will find when the program is executed.

In order to use a shared library, the version of the stub routines (in the executable) must be compatible with the version of the shared libraries. Basically, a library is compatible if its major version number matches that of the stub routines. The major version number is the part before the first period in the version number; in 6.0, the major number is 6. This way, if a program was compiled with version 6.0 of the stub routines, shared library versions 6.1, 6.2, and so forth could be

Chapter 6

used by the executable. In the section "More Fun with Libraries" of Chapter 6, *Programming with Linux*, we describe how to use shared libraries with your own programs.

The file */etc/ld.so.conf* contains a list of directories that *ld.so* will search to find shared library files. An example of such a file is

```
/usr/lib
/usr/local/lib
/usr/X11R6/lib
```

ld.so always looks in */lib* and */usr/lib*, regardless of the contents of *ld.so.conf.* Usually, there's no reason to modify this file, and the environment variable LD_LIBRARY_PATH can be used to add additional directories to this search path (for example, if you have your own private shared libraries which shouldn't be used system-wide). However, if you do add entries to */etc/ld.so.conf,* be sure to use the command

```
ldconfig
```

which will re-generate the shared library cache from the *ld.so* search path. This cache is used by *ld.so* to quickly find libraries at run time without actually having to search the directories on its path. Check the manual pages for *ld.so* and *ldconfig* for more.

Now that you understand how shared libraries are used, let's move on to upgrading them. The two libraries that are most commonly updated are *libc* (the standard C library) and *libm* (the math library).[*] For each shared library, there are three separate files:

at compile-time
(link)

library.a

This is the static version of the library. When a program is statically linked, routines are copied from this file directly into the executable, so the executable contains its own copy of the library routines. If a program is statically linked, neither of the following two files are used for this library.

library.sa

at link-time

This is the shared library stub. When a program is dynamically linked, a stub from this file is copied into the executable for each routine used in the library. At run time, this stub is replaced, in memory, by the actual routine from the shared library. If a program is dynamically linked, the *library.a* file is not used for this library.

---

[*] At the time of this writing, the Linux community is making a move to ELF, a different file format for executables and shared libraries. ELF will affect some of the material in this section—for example, the *libm* library may not be shared. However, nearly all of the material presented here should be valid under ELF.

library.so.version
>   This is the shared library image itself. When a dynamically-linked program is executed, *ld.so* copies the routines for this library from this file into memory.

For the *libc* library, you'll have files such as *libc.a*, *libc.sa*, and *libc.so.4.5.26*. The *.a* and *.sa* files are generally kept in */usr/lib*. When you compile a program either the *.a* or *.sa* file is used for linking, and the compiler looks in */usr/lib* by default. If you have your own libraries, you can keep these files anywhere, and control where the linker looks with the *−L* option to the compiler. See the section "More Fun with Libraries" in Chapter 6 for details.

The shared library image, *library.so.version*, is kept in */lib* for most system-wide libraries. Shared library images can be found in any of the directories which *ld.so* will search at run time—this includes */lib*, */usr/lib*, and the files listed in *ld.so.conf*. See the *ld.so* manual page for details.

If you look in */lib*, you'll see a collection of files such as the following:

```
lrwxrwxrwx  1 root     root          14 Oct 23 13:25 libc.so.4 -> libc.so.4.5.26
-rwxr-xr-x  1 root     root      623620 Oct 23 13:24 libc.so.4.5.26
lrwxrwxrwx  1 root     root          15 Oct 17 22:17 libvga.so.1 -> libvga.so.1.1.7
-rwxr-xr-x  1 root     root      128004 Oct 17 22:17 libvga.so.1.1.7
```

Here, we see the shared library images for two libraries—*libc* and *libvga*. Note that each image has a symbolic link to it, named *library.so.major*, where *major* is the major version number of the library. The minor number is omitted because *ld.so* searches for a library only by its major version number. When *ld.so* sees a program that has been compiled with the stubs for version 4.5.26 of *libc*, it looks for a file called *libc.so.4* in its search path. Here, */lib/libc.so.4* is a symbolic link to */lib/libc.so.4.5.26*, the actual version of the library that we have installed.

When you upgrade a library, you must replace the *.a*, *.sa*, and *.so.version* files corresponding to the library. The first two are easy: just copy over them with the new versions. However, you must use some caution when replacing the shared library image, *.so.version*. This is because most of the programs on the system depend upon those images, so you can't simply delete them or rename them. To put this another way, the symbolic link *library.so.major* must *always* point to a valid library image. To accomplish this, you'll first copy the new image file to */lib*, and then change the symbolic link to point to the new file in one step, using *ln −sf*. This is demonstrated below.

Let's say that you're upgrading from version 4.5.26 of the *libc* library to version 4.6. You should have the files *libc.a*, *libc.sa*, and *libc.so.4.6*. First, copy the *.a* and *.sa* files to the appropriate location, overwriting the old versions:

```
rutabaga# cp libc.a /usr/lib
rutabaga# cp libc.sa /usr/lib
```

[handwritten note: because .a & .sa files are only used at ~~install too~~ compile time, for new programs using the new libraries.]

157

Now, copy the new image file to */lib* (or wherever the library image should be):

```
rutabaga# cp libc.so.4.6 /lib
```

Now, if you use the command *ls –l /lib/libc** you should see something like:

```
lrwxrwxrwx  1 root     root           14 Oct 23 13:25 libc.so.4 -> libc.so.4.5.26
-rwxr-xr-x  1 root     root       623620 Oct 23 13:24 libc.so.4.5.26
-rwxr-xr-x  1 root     root       720310 Nov 16 11:02 libc.so.4.6
```

To update the symbolic link to point to the new library, we use the command

```
rutabaga# ln -sf /lib/libc.so.4.6 /lib/libc.so.4
```

This gives us:

```
lrwxrwxrwx  1 root     root           14 Oct 23 13:25 libc.so.4 -> /lib/libc.so.4.6
-rwxr-xr-x  1 root     root       623620 Oct 23 13:24 libc.so.4.5.26
-rwxr-xr-x  1 root     root       720310 Nov 16 11:02 libc.so.4.6
```

new & old
libraries — version no.
same

Now the old image file, *libc.so.4.5.26*, can be safely removed. You *must* use *ln –sf*
to replace the symbolic link in one step, especially when updating libraries such
as *libc*. If you were to remove the symbolic link first, and then attempt to use *ln –s*
to add it again, more than likely *ln* would not be able to execute because the symbolic link is gone, and as far as *ld.so* is concerned, the *libc* library can't be found.
Once the link is gone, nearly all of the programs on your system will be unable to
execute. Be very careful when updating shared library images.

Whenever you upgrade or add a library to the system, it's not a bad idea to run
ldconfig to re-generate the library cache used by *ld.so*. In some cases a new library
may not be recognized by *ld.so* until you run *ldconfig*.

One question remains—where can you obtain the new versions of libraries? Several of the basic system libraries (*libc*, *libm*, and so on) can be downloaded from
the directory */pub/Linux/GCC* on **sunsite.unc.edu**. It contains the Linux versions of
the *gcc* compiler, libraries, include files, and other utilities. Each file there should
have a *README* or *release* file that describes what to do and how to install it.
Other libraries are maintained and archived separately. At any rate, all libraries that
you install should include the *.a*, *.sa*, and *.so.version* files, as well as a set of
include files for use with the compiler.

Upgrading the Compiler

One other important part of the system to keep up to date is the C compiler and
related utilities. These include *gcc* (the GNU C and C++ compiler itself), the linker,
the assembler, the C preprocessor, and various include files and libraries used by
the compiler itself. All of these are included in the Linux *gcc* distribution. Usually,
a new version of *gcc* is released along with new versions of the *libc* library and
include files, and each requires the other.

You can find the current *gcc* release for Linux on the various FTP archives, including */pub/Linux/GCC* on **sunsite.unc.edu**. The release notes there should tell you what to do. Usually, upgrading the compiler is a simple matter of unpacking several tar files as **root**, and possibly removing some additional files. If you don't have Internet access, you can obtain the newest compiler from CD-ROM archives of the FTP sites, as described above.

To find out what version of *gcc* you have, use the command

```
gcc -v
```

This should tell you something like

```
Reading specs from /usr/lib/gcc-lib/i486-linux/2.5.8/specs
gcc version 2.5.8
```

Note that *gcc* itself is just a front-end to the actual compiler and code-generation tools found under

```
/usr/lib/gcc-lib/machine/version
```

Chapter 6

gcc (usually in */usr/bin*) can be used with multiple versions of the compiler proper, with the −*V* option. In the section "Programming with gcc" in Chapter 6 we describe the use of *gcc* in detail.

Upgrading Other Software

Of course, you'll have to periodically upgrade other pieces of your system. As discussed above, it's usually easier and best to upgrade only those applications that you have a need to upgrade. For example, if you never use Emacs on your own system, why bother keeping up-to-date with the most recent version of Emacs? For that matter, you may not need to stay completely current with those applications that you do use often. If something works for you, there's little need to upgrade.

In order to upgrade other applications, you'll have to obtain the newest release of the software. This is usually available as a gzipped or compressed tar file. Such a package could come in several forms. The most common are *binary distributions*, in which the binaries and related files are archived and ready to unpack on your system, and *source distributions*, in which the source code (or portions of the source code) for the software is provided, and you have to issue commands to compile and install it on your system.

Shared libraries make distributing software in binary form very easy; as long as you have a version of the libraries installed that is compatible with the library stubs used to build the program, you're set. However, in many cases it is easier (and a good idea) to release a program as source. Not only does this make the source code available to you for inspection and further development, but it allows you to build the application specifically for your system, with your own libraries. Many programs allow you to specify certain options at compile-time, such as selectively including various features in the program when built. This kind of customization isn't possible if you get prebuilt binaries.

There's also a security issue at play when installing binaries without source code. Although, on UNIX systems, viruses are nearly unheard of,[*] it's not difficult to write a "Trojan Horse," a program which appears to do something useful, but in actuality causes damage to the system. For example, someone could write an application that includes the "feature" of deleting all files in the home directory of the user executing the program. Because the program would be running with the permissions of the user executing it, the program itself has the ability to do this kind of damage. (Of course, the UNIX security mechanism prevents damage being done to other users' files, or to any important system files owned by **root**.)

While having source won't necessarily prevent this from happening (do you read the source code for every program you compile on your system?), at least it gives you a way to verify what the program is really doing. A programmer would have to make a certain effort to prevent such a Trojan Horse from being discovered—but if you install binaries blindly, you are setting yourself up for trouble.

At any rate, dealing with source and binary distributions of software is quite simple. If the package is released as a tar file, first use the *tar t* option to determine how the files have been archived. In the case of binary distributions, you may be able to unpack the tar file directly on your system, say from / or */usr*. When doing this, be sure to delete any old versions of the program and its support files (those that aren't overwritten by the new tar file). If the old executable comes before the new one on your path, you'll continue to run the old version unless you remove it.

Source distributions are a bit trickier. First, you must unpack the sources into a directory of their own. Most systems use */usr/src* for just this. Because you usually don't have to be **root** to build a software package (you will usually require **root** permissions to install the program once compiled!), it might be a good idea to make */usr/src* writeable by all users, with the command

```
chmod 1777 /usr/src
```

This will allow any user to create subdirectories of */usr/src* and place files there. The first 1 in the mode is the "sticky" bit, which prevents users from deleting each other's subdirectories.

You can now create a subdirectory of */usr/src* and unpack the tar file there, or you can unpack the tar file directly from */usr/src* if the archive contains a subdirectory of its own.

---

[*] A "virus" in the classic sense is a program which attaches to a "host," which will run when the host is executed. On UNIX systems, this usually requires root privileges to do any harm, and if programmers could obtain such privileges, they probably wouldn't bother with a virus.

Once the sources are available, the next step is to read any *README* files or installation notes included with the sources. Nearly all packages include such documentation. The basic method used to build most programs is:

Chapter 6

1. Check the *Makefile*. This file contains instructions for *make*, which is used to control the compiler to build programs. Many applications require you to edit minor aspects of the *Makefile* for your own system; this should be self-explanatory. The installation notes will tell you if you have to do this. If you need more help with the *Makefile*, read the section "Makefiles" in Chapter 6.

2. Possibly edit other files associated with the program. Some applications require you to edit a file named *config.h*; again, this will be explained in the installation instructions.

3. Possibly run a configuration script. Such a script is used to determine what facilities are available on your system, which is necessary to build more complex applications. You'll know if you have to do this.

4. Run *make*. Generally, this will execute the appropriate compilation commands as given in the makefile. In many cases you'll have to give a "target" to *make*, as in *make all* or *make install*. These are two common targets; the former is usually not necessary, but can be used to build all targets listed in a makefile (for example, if the package includes several programs, but only one is compiled by default); the latter is often used to install the executables and support files on the system after compilation. For this reason, *make install* is usually run as **root**.

You might have problems compiling or installing new software on your system, especially if the program in question hasn't been tested under Linux, or depends on other software that you don't have installed. In Chapter 6 we talk about the compiler, *make*, and related tools in detail.

Most software packages include manual pages and other files, in addition to the source and executables. The installation script (if there is one) will place these files in the appropriate location. In the case of manual pages, you'll find files with names such as *foobar.1* or *foobar.man*. These files are (usually) *nroff* source files, which are formatted to produce the human-readable pages displayed by the *man* command. If the manual page source has a numeric extension, such as *.1*, copy it to the directory */usr/man/man1*, where *1* is the number used in the filename extension. (This corresponds to the manual "section" number; for most user programs, it is 1.) If the file has an extension such as *.man*, it will usually suffice to copy the file to */usr/man/man1*, renaming the *.man* extension to *.1*.

Building a New Kernel

Rebuilding the kernel sounds like a pastime for hackers, but it is an important skill for any system administrator. First, you will want to rebuild the kernel on your system to eliminate the device drivers that you don't need. This will reduce the amount of memory used by the kernel itself—as described in the section "Managing Swap Space," the kernel is always present in memory, and the memory that it uses is not able to be reclaimed for use by programs if necessary.

You will also need to occasionally upgrade your kernel to a newer version. As with any other piece of your system, if you know of important bug fixes or new features in a kernel release, you may want to upgrade to pick them up. Those people who are actively developing kernel code will also need to keep their kernel up-to-date in case changes are made to the code they are working on. Sometimes, it is necessary to upgrade your kernel to use a new version of the compiler or libraries. Some applications (such as the X Window System software) require a certain kernel version to run.

You can find out what kernel version you are running through the command *uname –a*. This should produce something like

```
rutabaga% uname -a
Linux rutabaga 1.1.37 #6 Wed Nov 16 17:50:50 EST 1994 i486
```

uname(1)

Here, we see a machine running version 1.1.37 of the kernel, which was last compiled on November 16. We see other information as well, such as the hostname of the machine, the number of times that this kernel has been compiled (six), and the fact that the machine is an 80486. The manual page for *uname* can tell you more.

The Linux kernel is a many-tentacled beast. Many groups of people work on different pieces of it, and some parts of the code are a patchwork of ideas meeting different design goals. Overall, however, the kernel code is clean and uniform, and those interested in exploring its innards should have little trouble doing so. However, because of the great amount of development going on with the kernel, new releases are made very rapidly—sometimes daily! The chief reason for this is that nearly all device drivers are contained within the kernel code, and every time someone updates a driver, a new release will be necessary. As the Linux community moves towards loadable device drivers, the maintainers of those drivers can release them independently of the main kernel, alleviating the necessity of such rapid updates.

Currently, Linus Torvalds maintains the "official" kernel release. Although the General Public License allows anyone to modify and re-release the kernel under the same copyright, Linus's maintenance of an "official" kernel is a very helpful convention, which keeps version numbers uniform and allows everyone to be on equal footing when talking about kernel revisions. In order for a bug fix or new feature to be included in the kernel, all one must do is send it to Linus, who will usually incorporate the change as long as it doesn't break anything.

Kernel version numbers follow the convention

```
major.minor.patchlevel
```

major is the major version number, which rarely changes, *minor* is the minor version number, which indicates the current "strain" of the kernel release, and *patchlevel* is the number of the patch to the current kernel version. Some examples of kernel versions are 1.0.5, (patchlevel 5 of kernel version 1.0), and 1.1.52 (patchlevel 52 of kernel version 1.1).

By convention, even-numbered kernel versions (1.0, 1.2, 1.4, and so on) are "stable" releases, patches for which will contain only bug fixes and no new features. Odd-numbered kernel versions (1.1, 1.3, 1.5, and so on) are "development" releases, patches for which contain whatever new code developers wish to add and bug fixes for that code. When a development kernel matures to the point where it is stable enough for wide use, it is renamed to have the next highest (even) minor version number, and the development cycle begins again.

For example, kernel versions 1.0 and 1.1 were worked on concurrently. Patches made to 1.0 were bug fixes—meant only to correct problems in the existing code. Patches to 1.1 included bug fixes as well as a great deal of new code—new device drivers, new features, and so on. When kernel version 1.1 was stable enough (around version 1.1.65), it was renamed to 1.2, and a copy made and named version 1.3. Development continued with versions 1.2 and 1.3. 1.2 would be the new "stable" kernel while 1.3 was a development kernel for new features.

Note that this version-numbering convention applies only to Linus's official kernel release, and only to kernel versions after 1.0. Prior to 1.0 (by the time you read this book, this will be ancient history), there was only one "current" kernel version and patches were consistently made to it. The kernel development community has found that having two concurrent kernel versions allows those who want to experiment to use the development kernel, and those who need a reliable platform to stick with the stable kernel. In this way, if the development kernel is seriously broken by new code, it shouldn't affect those who are running the newest stable kernel. The general rule is that you should use development kernels if only you want to be on the leading edge of new features and are willing to risk problems with your system. Use the development kernels at your own risk.

On your system, the kernel sources live in */usr/src/linux*. If you are going to rebuild your kernel only from the current sources, you don't need to obtain any files or apply any patches. If you wish to upgrade your kernel to a new version, you'll need to follow the instructions in the following section.

Obtaining Kernel Sources

The official kernel is released as a gzipped tar file, containing the sources along with a series of patch files—one per patchlevel. The tar file contains the source for the unpatched revision; for example, there is a tar file containing the sources for

Chapter 6

kernel version 1.1 with no patches applied. Each subsequent patchlevel is released as a patch file (produced using *diff*), which can be applied using the *patch* program. In the section "Patching Files" in Chapter 6 we describe the use of *patch* in detail.

Let's say that you're upgrading to kernel version 1.1 patchlevel 15. You'll need the sources for 1.1 (the file might be named *v1.1.0.tar.gz*) and the patches for patchlevels 1 through 15. These files would be named *patch1*, *patch2*, and so forth. (You do need *all* of the patchfiles up to the version that you're upgrading to. Usually, these patchfiles are rather small, and are gzipped on the archive sites.) All of these files can be found in the *kernel* directory of the Linux FTP archive sites; for example, on **sunsite.unc.edu** the directory containing the 1.1 sources and patches is */pub/Linux/kernel/v1.1*.

Unpacking the sources

First, you need to unpack the source tar file from */usr/src*. You can do this with commands such as

```
rutabaga# cd /usr/src
rutabaga# cp linux linux.old
rutabaga# tar xzf v1.1.0.tar.gz
```

This will save your old kernel source tree as */usr/src/linux.old* and create */usr/src/linux*, containing the new sources. Note that the tar file containing the sources *does* include the *linux* subdirectory.

You should keep your current kernel sources in the directory */usr/src/linux*. This is because there are two symbolic links—*/usr/include/linux* and */usr/include/asm*—that point into the current kernel source tree to provide certain header files when compiling programs. (You should always have your kernel sources available so that programs using these include files can be compiled.) If you want to keep several kernel source trees around, just be sure that */usr/src/linux* points to the most recent one.

Applying patches

If you are applying any patch files, you will use the *patch* program. Let's say that you have the files *patch1.gz* through *patch15.gz*, which are gzipped. These patches should be applied from */usr/src*. That doesn't mean that the patchfiles themselves should be located there, but rather that *patch* should be executed from */usr/src*. For each patchfile, you can use the command

```
gunzip -c patchfile | patch -p0
```

from */usr/src*. The *–p0* option tells *patch* that it shouldn't strip any part of the filenames contained within the patchfile.

You must apply each patch in numerical order by patchlevel. This is very important. Note that using a wildcard such as *patch** will *not* work—this is because the * wildcard uses ASCII order, not numeric order. (Otherwise you'd get *patch1* followed by *patch10* and *patch11*, as opposed to *patch2* and *patch3*.) It is best to run the above command for each patchfile in succession, by hand. This way you can ensure that you're doing things in the right order.

You shouldn't encounter problems when patching your source tree in this way, unless you try to apply patches out of order or apply a patch more than once. Check the *patch* manual page if you do encounter trouble. If all else fails remove the new kernel source tree and start over from the original tar file.

To double-check that the patches were applied successfully, use the commands

```
find /usr/src/linux -follow -name "*.rej" -print
find /usr/src/linux -follow -name "*#" -print
```

This will list any files that are "rejected" portions of the patch process. If any such files exist, they contain sections of the patchfile that could not be applied for some reason. Look into these, and if there's any doubt start over from scratch. You *cannot* expect your kernel to compile or work correctly if the patch process did not complete successfully and without rejections.

Building the Kernel

Whether or not you've upgraded your kernel sources, you're ready to build a new kernel. The primary reason to do this is either to simply upgrade, or to trim down your current kernel, excluding device drivers for which you have no need.

There are six steps to building the kernel, and they should be quite painless:

1. Run *make config*, which will ask you various questions about which drivers you wish to include.

2. Run *make dep*, to gather dependencies for each source file and include them in the various Makefiles.

3. If you have built a kernel from this source tree before, run *make clean* to clear all of the old object files and force a complete rebuild.

4. Run *make* to build the kernel itself.

5. Go have a coffee (or two, depending on the speed of your machine and amount of available memory).

6. Install the new kernel image, either on a boot floppy or via LILO.

All of these commands are executed from */usr/src*, except for Step 5, which you can do anywhere.

There is a *README* included in the kernel sources, which should be located as */usr/src/linux/README* on your system. Read it. It contains up-to-date notes on kernel compilation, which may be more current than the information presented here. Be sure to follow the steps described there, using the descriptions given below as a guide. *or manrconfig or xlconfig.*

The first step is to run *make config*. This executes a script that will ask you a set of yes/no questions about which drivers to include in the kernel. There are defaults for each question, but be careful—the defaults probably don't correspond to what you want. Running *make config* prints some prompts, which are shown below.

Simply answer each question, either by pressing Enter for the default, or pressing y or n (followed by Enter). Not all of the questions have a yes/no answer; you may be asked to enter a number or some other value. Your answers to each question will become the default the next time you build the kernel from this source tree.

```
/bin/sh Configure
*
* General setup
*
Kernel math emulation (CONFIG_MATH_EMULATION) [n]
Normal harddisk support (CONFIG_BLK_DEV_HD) [y]
XT harddisk support (CONFIG_BLK_DEV_XD) [n]
Networking support (CONFIG_NET) [n]
Limit memory to low 16MB (CONFIG_MAX_16M) [n]
System V IPC (CONFIG_SYSVIPC) [y]
Use -m486 flag for 486-specific optimizations (CONFIG_M486) [y]
   ... and so on ...
The linux kernel is now hopefully configured for your setup.
Check the top-level Makefile for additional configuration,
and do a 'make dep ; make clean' if you want to be sure all
the files are correctly re-made
```

The questions should be rather straightforward, if you understand the hardware present on your machine. The following questions are found in the kernel configuration for version 1.1. If you have applied other patches, additional questions might appear—the same is true for later versions of the kernel.

Kernel math emulation

> Answer yes to this item if you do *not* have a floating-point coprocessor in your machine. This is necessary for the kernel to emulate the presence of a math coprocessor.

Normal harddisk support

> Almost everyone should answer yes to this; it enables drivers for all of the standard hard disk types.

XT harddisk support

Answer yes to this only if you have an older XT disk controller. Most people won't need this.

Networking support

Answer yes to this if you want any kind of TCP/IP, Ethernet, loopback, or SLIP support in your kernel. In Chapter 7, we talk about this in detail.

Chapter 7

Limit memory to low 16MB

Even if you have less than 16 megabytes, you'll probably want to answer no to this. This option is provided to get around problems that some systems have accessing memory above 16MB.

System V IPC

Answering yes to this option includes kernel support for System V interprocess communication (IPC) functions, such as *msgrcv* and *msgsnd*. Some programs ported from System V require this; you could answer yes unless you have a strong aversion to these features.

Use -m486 flag for 486-specific optimizations

If you have an 80486 or Pentium processor, you should answer yes to this. Even if you have a 386, answering yes to this option can't hurt. It simply optimizes the compilation of the kernel code in some places for the 486 and Pentium chips.

SCSI support

If you have a SCSI controller of any kind, answer yes to this option. You will be asked a series of question about the specific SCSI devices on your system; be sure you know what type of hardware you have installed. If you don't have any SCSI hardware, you should answer no to this option; it will greatly reduce the size of the compiled kernel.

CD-ROM drivers

This is a series of questions dealing with the specific non-SCSI CD-ROM drivers supported by the kernel, such as the Sony CDU31A/33A, Mitsumi, SoundBlaster Pro CD-ROM, and so on.

Filesystems

This is a series of questions for each filesystem type supported by the kernel. As discussed in the section "Managing Filesystems," there are a number of filesystem types supported by the system, and you can pick and choose which ones to include in the kernel. Nearly all systems should include support for the Minix, Second Extended, and */proc* filesystems. You should include support for the MS-DOS filesystem if you want to access your MS-DOS files directly from Linux, and the ISO 9660 filesystem to access files on a CD-ROM (most of which are encoded in this way).

Parallel printer support
This includes support for various parallel-port routines necessary for using printers. Answer yes if you plan to use a parallel printer with your machine.

Mouse support
Various types of mice (particularly "busmice," which have an interface other than through the serial port), require their own kernel drivers. You will be asked questions about several of these mice types, such as the Logitech, PS/2, and Microsoft busmouse. Answer yes to the appropriate questions if you have any of these furry cheese-loving creatures.

Selection (cut and paste for virtual consoles)
selection is an interesting tool that allows you to use the mouse to cut and paste text between virtual consoles, similar in nature to using *xterm*. If you are restricted to the text-only environment this can be a very useful feature. *selection* should have a manual page on your system; it is included with most Linux distributions. *selection* itself runs as a daemon program to control the mouse support, but it requires some kernel support for accessing the virtual console buffers. Answer yes to this question if you'd like to use this feature.

Tape support
Various types of tape drivers are supported by the kernel, and you'll be asked questions about each of them. These include the QIC-02 and QIC-117 tape drivers; the latter is used for "floppy tape" controllers, the primary driver for which is a loadable module. See the section "Loadable Device Drivers" and the Linux Ftape HOWTO for more details.

[71] Ftape
HOWTO

Sound card support
Answering yes to this option will present you with several questions about your sound card, which drivers you wish to have installed, and other details such as the IRQ and address of the sound hardware.

Kernel profiling support
Enabling this option will turn on features in the kernel that will profile its performance and provide other information useful for debugging the system. These features require some overhead and can cause the system to run more slowly; you should answer no to this option unless you're working on a specific kernel problem.

After running *make config*, you'll be asked to edit "the top-level Makefile," which means */usr/src/linux/Makefile*. In most cases, it's not at all necessary to do this. If you wanted to alter some of the compilation options for the kernel, or change the default root device or SVGA mode, you could edit the Makefile to accomplish this. Setting the root device and SVGA mode can easily be done by running *rdev* on a compiled kernel image, as we saw in the section "Using a Boot Floppy."

The next step is to run *make dep*. This issues a series of commands that will walk through the directory tree and gather dependencies for source files, adding information to the various Makefiles for them. (If you really want to know what's going on here: this adds rules for the Makefile so that certain code will be recompiled if, say, a header file included by a source file changes.) This step should take five or ten minutes at most to complete.

If you wish to force a complete recompile of the kernel, you should issue *make clean* at this point. This will remove all object files produced from a previous build from this source tree. If you have never built the kernel from this tree, you're probably safe skipping this step (although it can't hurt). If you are tweaking minor parts of the kernel you might want to avoid this step so that only those files that have changed will be recompiled. At any rate, running *make clean* simply ensures that the entire kernel will be recompiled "from scratch," and if you're in any doubt, use this command to be on the safe side.

Now you're ready to compile the kernel. This is done with the command *make*, with no arguments. It is best to build your kernel on a lightly-loaded system, with most of your memory free for the compilation. If other users are accessing the system, or if you're trying to run any large applications yourself (such as the X Window System, or another compilation), the build may slow to a crawl. The key here is memory. A slower processor will complete the kernel compilation just as rapidly as a faster one, given enough RAM for the task.

The kernel compilation can take anywhere from 10 minutes to many hours, depending on your hardware. There is a great deal of code—well over a megabyte—in the entire kernel, so this should come as no surprise. Slower systems with 4 megabytes (or less) of RAM can expect to take several hours for a complete rebuild; faster machines with more memory can complete in less than half an hour. Your mileage will most assuredly vary.

If any errors or warnings occur while compiling, you cannot expect the resulting kernel to work correctly for you; in most cases (but not all) the build will halt if an error occurs. Such errors can be the result of incorrectly applying patches, problems with the *make config* and *make dep* steps, or actual bugs in the code. In the "stock" kernels, this latter case is very rare, but is more common if you're working with development code or new drivers under testing. If you have any doubt remove the kernel source tree altogether and start over from scratch.

When the compilation is complete, you will be left with the file *zImage*, in */usr/src/linux*. The kernel is so named because it is the executable image of the kernel, and it has been internally compressed using the *gzip* algorithm. When the kernel boots, it will uncompress itself into memory—don't attempt to use *gzip* or *gunzip* on *zImage* yourself! The kernel requires much less diskspace when compressed in this way, allowing kernel images to fit on a floppy.

You should now run *rdev* on the new kernel image to verify that the root filesystem device, console SVGA mode, and other parameters have been set correctly. This is described in the section "Using a Boot Floppy" earlier in the chapter.

With your new kernel in hand, you're ready to configure it for booting. This involves either placing the kernel image on a boot floppy, or configuring LILO to boot the kernel from the hard drive. These topics are discussed in the section "Booting the System." To use the new kernel, configure it for booting in one of these ways, and reboot the system.

Loadable Device Drivers

Traditionally, device drivers have been included as part of the kernel. There are several reasons for this. First of all, nearly all device drivers require the special hardware access provided by being part of the kernel code. Such hardware access can't be obtained easily through a user program. Also, device drivers are much easier to implement as part of the kernel—such drivers would have complete access to the data structures and other routines in the kernel, and could call them freely.

There are several problems with a conglomerate kernel containing all drivers in this way. First of all, it requires the system administrator to rebuild the kernel in order to selectively include device drivers, as we saw in the previous section. Also, this mechanism lends itself to sloppy programming on the part of the driver writers: there's nothing stopping a programmer from writing code that is not completely modular—code which, for example, directly accesses data private to other parts of the kernel. The cooperative nature of the Linux kernel development compounds this problem, and not all parts of the code are as neatly contained as they should be. This can make it more difficult to maintain and debug the code.

In an effort to move away from this paradigm, the Linux kernel supports loadable device drivers—device drivers that are added to or removed from memory at run time, with a series of commands. Such drivers are still part of the kernel, but they are compiled separately and enabled only when loaded. Loadable device drivers, or *modules*, are generally loaded into memory using commands in one of the boot-time *rc* scripts.

Modules provide a cleaner interface for writing drivers. To some extent, they require the code to be somewhat modular and to follow a certain coding convention. (Note that this doesn't actually prevent a programmer from abusing the convention and writing non-modular code. Once the module has been loaded, it is just as free to wreak havoc as if it were compiled directly into the kernel.) Using modules makes drivers easier to debug—you can simply unload a module, re-compile it, and re-load it without having to reboot the system or rebuild the kernel as a whole. Modules can be used for other parts of the kernel, such as filesystem types, in addition to device drivers.

[71] Ftape
HOWTO

Several device drivers under Linux are implemented as modules. One of the most popular is the "floppy tape" driver (or *ftape* driver), for tape drives that connect to the floppy controller, such as the Colorado Memory Jumbo 120/250 models. If you plan to use this driver on your system, you'll need to know how to build, load, and unload modules. See the Linux Ftape-HOWTO for more about these devices and supported hardware.

The first thing you'll need is the *modules* package, which contains the commands used to load and unload modules from the kernel. On the FTP archive sites, this is usually found as *modules.tar.gz* in the directory where the kernel sources are kept. This package contains the sources to the commands *insmod*, *rmmod*, and *lsmod*. Most Linux distributions include these commands (found in *sbin*). If you already have these commands installed, you probably don't need to get the *modules* package. However, it can't hurt to get the package and rebuild these commands, to be sure that you have the most up-to-date version.

To rebuild these commands, unpack *modules.tar.gz* (say, in a subdirectory of */usr/src*). Follow the installation instructions contained there; usually all you have to do is execute *make* followed by *make install* (as **root**). The three commands will now be installed in */sbin* and ready to use.

The next thing you'll need is a module to play with. A good example of this is the floppy tape driver described earlier. This is available on most FTP archive sites as *ftape-version.tar.gz*; unpack this tar file and follow the notes in the *README* file to compile the driver.

A module is simply a single object file containing all of the code for the driver. For example, the *ftape* module might be called *ftape.o*. On many systems, the modules themselves are stored in the directory */boot* (this might not be the best location, but modules are generally loaded at boot time). You might have several modules installed on your system already; look for files with the filename extension *.o* in */boot*.

Once you have a compiled module, you can load it using the command

    insmod *module*

where *module* is the name of the module object file. For example:

    insmod /boot/ftape.o

will install the *ftape* driver, if it is found in that file.

Once a module is installed, it may display some information to the console (as well as to the system logs), indicating that it is initialized. For example, the *ftape* driver might display the following:

```
ftape v1.14 29/10/94 (c) 1993, 1994 Bas Laarhoven (bas@vimec.nl)
  QIC-117 driver for QIC-40 and QIC-80 tape drives
[000] kernel-interface.c (init_module) - installing QIC-117 ftape driver....
[001] kernel-interface.c (init_module) - 3 tape_buffers @ 001B8000.
[002]  calibr.c (time_inb) - inb() duration: 1436 nsec.
[003]  calibr.c (calibrate) - TC for `udelay()' = 2944 nsec. (at 2049 counts).
[004]  calibr.c (calibrate) - TC for `fdc_wait()' = 2857 nsec. (at 2049 counts).
```

The exact messages printed depend on the module, of course. Each module should come with ample documentation describing just what it does and how to debug it if there are problems—at the time of this writing, modules are a relatively new feature and the details change rapidly.*

You can list the drivers that are loaded with the command *lsmod*, as in

```
rutabaga% lsmod
Module:          #pages:
ftape             40
```

The memory usage of the module is displayed as well; under Linux, a page is 4 kilobytes. The *ftape* driver here is using 160K of memory.

A module can be unloaded from memory using the *rmmod* command. For example,

```
rmmod ftape
```

The argument to *rmmod* is the name of the driver as it appears in the *lsmod* listing.

Once you have modules working to your satisfaction, you can include the appropriate *insmod* commands in one of the *rc* scripts executed at boot time. One of your *rc* scripts might already include a place where *insmod* commands can be added, depending on your distribution.

The implementation of modules has been developing over the last few months (this being written in late 1994). At this time, you must rebuild a module any time you upgrade your kernel to a new version or patchlevel. (Rebuilding your kernel, but keeping the same kernel version, doesn't require you to do this.) This is done to ensure that the module will be compatible with the kernel version that you're using. If you attempt to load a module with a newer or older kernel than it was compiled for, *insmod* will complain and not allow the module to be loaded. When rebuilding a module, you must be running the kernel that it will be used under. Therefore, when upgrading your kernel, upgrade and reboot the new kernel first, then rebuild your modules and load them.

Managing Filesystems

To UNIX systems, a *filesystem* is some device (such as a hard drive, floppy, or CD-ROM) that is formatted to store files. Filesystems can be found on hard drives, floppies, CD-ROMs, and other storage media that permits random access. (Most notably, a tape allows only sequential access, and therefore can't contain a filesystem per se.)

The exact format and means by which the files are stored is not important; the system provides a common interface for all *filesystem types* which it recognizes. Under Linux, filesystem types include the Second Extended Filesystem, or *ext2fs*, which

---

* Note that the *ftape* driver also requires that the kernel be built with QIC-117 support enabled; this is usually done via the *make config* step.

you probably use to store Linux files; the MS-DOS filesystem, which allows files on MS-DOS partitions and floppies to be accessed under Linux; and several others, including the ISO 9660 filesystem used by CD-ROM.

Each of these filesystem types has a very different underlying format for storing data. However, when you access any filesystem under Linux, the system presents the data as files arranged into a hierarchy of directories, along with owner and group IDs, permissions bits, and the other characteristics that you're familiar with.

In fact, information on file ownership, permissions, and so forth is provided only by filesystem types that are meant to be used for storing Linux files. For filesystem types that don't store this information, the kernel drivers used to access these filesystems "fake" the information. For example, the MS-DOS filesystem has no concept of file ownership; therefore, all files are presented as if they were owned by **root**. This way, above a certain level, all filesystem types look alike, and each file has certain attributes associated with it. Whether or not this data is actually used in the underlying filesystem is another matter altogether.

As the system administrator, you will need to know how to create filesystems should you want to store Linux files on a floppy or add additional filesystems to your hard drives. You'll also need to know how to use the various tools to check and maintain filesystems should data corruption occur. Also, you'll need to know the commands and files used to access filesystems, for example, those on floppy or CD-ROM.

Filesystem Types

Table 4-1 lists the filesystem types supported by the Linux kernel, as of November 1994. New filesystem types are always being added to the system, and experimental drivers for several filesystems not listed here are available. To find out what filesystem types your kernel supports, look at the kernel source tree, in the directory */usr/src/linux/fs*. You can select which filesystem types to support when building your kernel; see the section "Building the Kernel" earlier in this chapter.

Table 4-1: Linux Filesystem Types

Filesystem	Type Name	Description
Second Extended Filesystem	*ext2*	Most common Linux filesystem
Extended Filesystem	*ext*	Superseded by *ext2*
Minix Filesystem	*minix*	Original Minix filesystem; rarely used
Xia Filesystem	*xia*	Like *ext2*, but rarely used
UMSDOS Filesystem	*umsdos*	Used to install Linux on an MS-DOS partition
MS-DOS Filesystem	*msdos*	Used to access MS-DOS files

Table 4-1: Linux Filesystem Types (continued)

Filesystem	Type Name	Description
HPFS Filesystem	*hpfs*	Read-only access for HPFS partitions (DoubleSpace)
/proc Filesystem	*proc*	Provides process information for *ps*
ISO 9660 Filesystem	*iso9660*	Used by most CD-ROMs
Xenix Filesystem	*xenix*	Used to access files from Xenix
System V Filesystem	*sysv*	Used to access files from System V variants
Coherent Filesystem	*coherent*	Used to access files from Coherent

Each filesystem type has its own own attributes and limitations; for example, the MS-DOS filesystem restricts filenames to eight characters plus a three-character extension, and should be used only to access existing MS-DOS floppies or partitions. For most of your work with Linux, you'll use the Second Extended Filesystem, which was developed primarily for Linux, supports 256-character filenames, a 4-terabyte maximum filesystem size, and a slew of other goodies. Earlier Linux systems used the now-depreciated Extended and Minix filesystems. (The Minix filesystem was originally used for several reasons. First of all, Linux was originally cross-compiled under Minix. Also, Linus was quite familiar with the Minix filesystem, and it was straightforward to implement in the original kernels.) The Xia filesystem is not unlike the Second Extended filesystem, but development on it has come to a virtual standstill, and it hasn't gained much popularity.

The UMSDOS filesystem is used to install Linux under a private directory of an existing MS-DOS partition. This is a good way for new users to try out Linux without repartitioning. The MS-DOS filesystem, on the other hand, is used to access MS-DOS files directly. The HPFS filesystem is used to access files that have been compressed under MS-DOS using a program such as Stacker or DoubleSpace. At the time of this writing, the HPFS support under Linux is limited to read-only access.

/proc is a virtual filesystem—that is, no actual disk space is associated with it. If you look in the directory */proc*, you'll see a number of "files" and "directories," the contents of which change as time progresses. The kernel provides system statistics and process information through the */proc* filesystem; when you attempt to access any files in */proc*, the kernel recognizes this and produces some data to satisfy your read request. None of these "files" and "directories" are stored on disk;

they're crafted by the kernel as an easy way to access this information from programs such as *ps* and *top*.[*]

The ISO 9660 filesystem (previously known as the High Sierra Filesystem, and abbreviated *hsfs* on other UNIX systems), is used by most CD-ROMs. Like MS-DOS, this filesystem type restricts filename length and stores only limited information about each file. However, most CD-ROMs provide the Rock Ridge Extensions to ISO 9660, which allow the kernel filesystem driver to assign long filenames, ownerships, and permissions to each file. The net result is that accessing an ISO 9660 CD-ROM under MS-DOS will give you 8.3-format filenames, but under Linux will give you the "true," complete filenames.

Finally, we have three filesystem types corresponding to other UNIX variants found on the personal computer: Xenix, System V, and Coherent. (These are actually handled by the same kernel driver, with slightly different parameters for each). If you have filesystems created under one of these formats, you'll be able to access the files from Linux.

Mounting Filesystems

In order to access any filesystem under Linux, you must *mount* it on a certain directory. This makes the files on the filesystem appear as though they reside in the given directory, allowing you to access them.

The *mount* command is used to do this, and usually must be executed as **root**. (As we'll see below, ordinary users can use *mount* if the device is listed in the */etc/fstab* file.) The format of this command is

```
mount -t type device mount-point
```

mount -t iso9660 /dev/sbpcd
=> /mnt/cdrom

where *type* is the type name of the filesystem as given in Table 4-1, *device* is the physical device where the filesystem resides (the device file in */dev*), and *mount-point* is the directory to mount the filesystem on. You have to create the directory before issuing *mount*.

For example, if you have a second extended filesystem on the partition */dev/hda3*, and wish to mount it on the directory */mnt*, use the command

```
mount -t ext2 /dev/hda2 /mnt
```

If all goes well you should be able to access the filesystem under */mnt*.

---

[*] Note that the */proc* filesystem under Linux is not of the same format as the */proc* filesystem under SVR4 (say, Solaris 2.x). Under SVR4, each running process has a single "file" entry in */proc*, which can be opened and treated with certain *ioctl()* calls to obtain process information. On the contrary, Linux provides most of its information in */proc* through *read()* and *write()* requests.

Likewise, to mount a filesystem contained on a floppy, we can use the command

```
mount -t msdos /dev/fd0 /mnt
```

This will make the files available on an MS-DOS format floppy under */mnt.*

There are many options to the *mount* command, which can be specified with the −*o* switch. For example, the MS-DOS, ISO 9660, and HPFS filesystems support "auto-conversion" of text files from MS-DOS format (which contain CR-LF at the end of each line), to UNIX format (which contain merely a newline at the end of each line). Using a command such as

```
mount -o conv=auto -t msdos /dev/fd0 /mnt
```

will turn on this conversion for files that don't have a filename extension that could be associated with a binary file (such as *.exe, .bin,* and so forth).

One common option to mount is −*o ro* (or, equivalently, −*r*) which mounts the filesystem as read-only. All write access to such a filesystem will be met with a "permission denied" error. Mounting a filesystem as read-only is necessary for media, such as CD-ROM, that are non-writeable. Attempting to mount a CD-ROM without the −*r* option will give you the cryptic error message:

```
mount: block device /dev/cdrom is not permitted on its filesystem
```

Use a command such as

```
mount -t iso9660 -r /dev/cdrom /mnt
```

instead. This is also necessary if you are trying to mount a floppy that has the write-protect tab in place.

The *mount* manual page lists all of the mounting options which are available. Not all of them are of immediate interest, but you might have a need for some of them, someday.

The inverse of mounting a filesystem is, naturally, unmounting it. Unmounting a filesystem has two effects: It syncs the system's buffers with the actual contents of the filesystem on disk, and makes the filesystem no longer available from its mount point. You are then free to mount another filesystem on that mount point.

Unmounting is done with the *umount* command (note that the first "n" is missing from the word "unmount"), as in:

```
umount /dev/fd0
```

to unmount the filesystem on */dev/fd0.* Similarly, to unmount whatever filesystem is currently mounted on a particular directory, use a command such as

```
umount /mnt
```

It is important to note that removable media, including floppies and CD-ROMs, should not be removed from the drive or swapped for another disk while mounted. This will cause the system's information on the device to be out of sync with what's actually there, and could lead to no end of trouble. Whenever you want to switch a floppy or CD-ROM, unmount it first, using the *umount* command, and then remount the device.

Reads and writes to filesystems on floppy are buffered in memory as they are for hard drives. This means that when you read or write data to a floppy, there may not be any immediate drive activity. The system handles I/O on the floppy asynchronously, and reads or writes data only when absolutely necessary. So if you copy a small file to a floppy, but the drive light doesn't come on, don't panic—the data will be written eventually. You can use the command

```
sync
```

to force the system to write all filesystem buffers to disk, causing a physical write of any buffered data. Unmounting a filesystem causes this to happen as well.

If you wish to allow mortal users to mount and unmount certain devices, you have two options. The first option is to include the user option for the device in */etc/fstab* (described later in this section). This will allow any user to use the *mount* and *umount* command for a given device. Another option is to use one of the mount front-ends available for Linux. These programs run setuid **root** and allow ordinary users to mount certain devices. In general, you wouldn't want normal users mounting and unmounting a hard drive partition, but use of CD-ROM and floppy drives might be more lenient on your system.

There are quite a few things that can go wrong when attempting to mount a filesystem. Unfortunately, the *mount* command will give you the same error message in response to a number of problems:

```
mount: wrong fs type, /dev/cdrom already mounted, /mnt busy, or other error
```

wrong fs type is simple enough: this means that you may have specified the wrong *type* to *mount*. If you don't specify a type, *–t minix* is assumed, under Linux systems.

device already mounted means just that: that the device is already mounted on another directory. You can find out what devices are mounted, and where, using the *mount* command with no arguments:

```
rutabaga# mount
/dev/hda2 on / type ext2 (rw)
/dev/hda3 on /msdos type msdos (rw)
/dev/cdrom on /cdrom type iso9660 (ro)
/proc on /proc type proc (rw,none)
```

Here, we see two hard drive partitions, one of type *ext2* and the other of type *msdos*, a CD-ROM mounted on */cdrom*, and the */proc* filesystem. The last field of each line (for example, (rw)) lists the options under which the filesystem is mounted. More on these soon.

Note that the CD-ROM device is mounted in */cdrom*. If you use your CD-ROM often, it's convenient to create the directory */cdrom* and mount the device there. */mnt* is generally used to temporarily mount filesystems such as floppies.

The error *mount-point* busy is rather odd. Essentially, it means that there is some activity taking place under *mount-point* that prevents you from mounting a filesystem there. Usually, this means that there is an open file under this directory, or some process has its current working directory beneath *mount-point*. When using *mount*, be sure that your root shell is not within *mount-point*; do a *cd /* to get to the top-level directory. Or, another filesystem could be mounted with the same *mount-point*. Use *mount* with no arguments to find out.

Of course, other error isn't very helpful. There are several other cases in which *mount* could fail. If the filesystem in question has data or media errors of some kind, *mount* may report that it is unable to read the filesystem's *superblock*, which is (under UNIX-like filesystems) the portion of the filesystem that stores information on the files, and attributes for the filesystem as a whole. If you attempt to mount a CD-ROM or floppy, and there's no CD-ROM or floppy in the drive, you will receive an error message such as

```
mount: /dev/cdrom is not a valid block device
```

Floppies are especially prone to physical defects (more so than you might initially think), and CD-ROMs can suffer from dust, scratches, fingerprints, being inserted upside-down, that kind of thing. (If you attempt to mount your Stan Rogers CD as ISO 9660 format, you will likely run into similar problems.)

Also, be sure that the mount point that you're trying to use (such as */mnt*) exists. If not, you can simply create it with the *mkdir* command.

If you have problems mounting or accessing a filesystem, data on the filesystem may be corrupt. There are several tools which can help to repair certain filesystem types under Linux; see the section "Checking and Repairing Filesystems" below.

The system automatically mounts several filesystems when the system boots. This is handled by the file */etc/fstab*, which includes an entry for each filesystem which should be mounted at boot time. Each line in this file is of the format

```
device mount-point type options
```

Here, *device*, *mount-point*, and *type* are equivalent to their meanings in the *mount* command, and *options* is a comma-separated list of options that you would use with the −*o* switch to *mount*.

A sample */etc/fstab* is shown in Example 4-2.

Example 4-2: Sample /etc/fstab file

```
# device         directory      type      options
/dev/hda2        /              ext2      defaults
/dev/hda3        /msdos         msdos     defaults
/dev/cdrom       /cdrom         iso9660   ro
/proc            /proc          proc      none

/dev/hda1        none           swap      sw
```

add to /etc/fstab

to access
CD-ROM
(Panasonic, here)

The last line of this file specifies a swap partition. This is described in the section "Managing Swap Space."

mount(8)

The *mount* manual page lists the possible values for *options*; if you wish to specify more than one option, you can list them with separating commas and no whitespace, as in:

```
/dev/cdrom       /cdrom         iso9660   ro,user
```

The user option allows users other than **root** to mount the filesystem. If this option is present, a user can execute a command such as

```
mount /cdrom
```

to mount the device. Note that if you specify only a device or mount point (not both) to *mount*, it will look up the device or mount point in */etc/fstab* and mount the device with the parameters given there. This allows you to mount devices listed in */etc/fstab* with ease.

The option defaults should be used for most filesystems; it enables a number of other options, such as rw (read-write access), async (buffer I/O to the filesystem in memory asynchronously), and so forth. Unless you have a specific need to modify one of these parameters, use defaults for most filesystems, and ro for read-only devices such as CD-ROMs.

The command *mount –a* will mount all filesystems listed in */etc/fstab*. This command is executed at boot time by one of the scripts found in */etc/rc.d*, usually *rc.S*. This way, all filesystems listed in */etc/fstab* will be made available when the system starts up; your hard drive partitions, CD-ROM drive, and so forth will all be mounted.

There is an exception to this: the *root filesystem*. The root filesystem, mounted on /, usually contains the file */etc/fstab* as well as the scripts in */etc/rc.d*. In order for these to be available, the kernel itself must mount the root filesystem directly at boot time. The device containing the root filesystem is coded into the kernel image, and can be altered using the *rdev* command (see "Using a Boot Floppy"). While booting, the kernel attempts to mount this device as the root filesystem, trying several filesystem types in succession (first Minix, then Extended, and so forth). If at boot time, the kernel prints an error message such as

```
VFS: Unable to mount root fs
```

this means that one of the following has happened:

- The root device coded into the kernel is incorrect.

- The kernel does not have support compiled in for the filesystem type of the root device. (See "Building the Kernel" for more details. This is usually relevant only if you build your own kernel.)

- The root device is corrupt in some way.

In any of these cases, the kernel can't proceed and panics. See "What To Do in an Emergency" for clues on what to do in this situation. If filesystem corruption is the problem, this can usually be repaired; see "Checking and Repairing Filesystems."

A filesystem does not need to be listed in */etc/fstab* in order to be mounted, but it does need to be listed there in order to be mounted "automatically" by *mount −a*, or to use the user mount option.

Creating Filesystems

A filesystem can be created using the *mkfs* command. Creating a filesystem is analogous to "formatting" a partition or floppy, allowing it to store files.

Each filesystem type has its own *mkfs* command associated with it—for example, MS-DOS filesystems may be created using *mkfs.msdos*, Second Extended filesystems using *mkfs.ext2*, and so forth. The program *mkfs* itself is a front-end which can create a filesystem of any type, by executing the appropriate version of *mkfs* for that type.[*]

When you installed Linux, you may have created filesystems by hand using a command such as *mke2fs*. (If not, then the installation software created the filesystems for you.) In fact, *mke2fs* is equivalent to *mkfs.ext2*. The programs are the same (and on many systems, one is a symbolic link to the other), but the *mkfs.fs-type* filename is used to make it easier for *mkfs* to execute the appropriate filesystem-type specific program. If you don't have the *mkfs* front-end, you can use *mke2fs* or *mkfs.ext2* directly.

Assuming that you're using the *mkfs* front-end, a filesystem can be created using the command

---

[*] Historically, under Linux the *mkfs* command created a Minix filesystem. On newer Linux systems, *mkfs* is a front-end for any filesystem type, and Minix filesystems are created using *mkfs.minix*.

```
mkfs -t type device blocks
```

where *type* is the type of filesystem to create, given in Table 4-1, *device* is the device on which to create the filesystem (such as */dev/fd0*, for a floppy), and *blocks* is the size of the filesystem, in 1024-byte blocks.

For example, to create an *ext2* filesystem on a floppy, we can use the command

```
mkfs -t ext2 /dev/fd0 1440
```

Here, *blocks* is 1440, which specifies a 1.44 megabyte, high-density 3.5 inch floppy. You could create an MS-DOS floppy using *−t msdos* instead.

We can now mount the floppy, as described in the previous section, copy files to it, and so forth. Remember to unmount the floppy before removing it from the drive.

Creating a filesystem will delete *all* data on the corresponding physical device (floppy, hard drive partition, whatever). *mkfs* will usually *not* prompt you before creating a filesystem, so be absolutely sure that you know what you're doing.

Chapter 2

Creating a filesystem on a hard drive partition is done exactly as shown above, except that you would use the partition name, such as */dev/hda2*, as the *device*. Don't try to create a filesystem on a device such as */dev/hda*. This refers to the entire drive, not just a single partition on the drive. You can create partitions using *fdisk*, as described in the section "Creating Linux Partitions" in Chapter 2.

You should be especially careful when creating filesystems on hard drive partitions. Be absolutely sure that the *device* and *size* arguments are correct. If you enter the wrong *device*, you could end up destroying the data on your current filesystems, and if you specify the wrong *size*, you could overwrite data on other partitions. Be sure that *size* corresponds to the partition size as reported by Linux *fdisk*.

When creating filesystems on floppies, it's usually best to do a low-level format first. This lays down the sector and track information on the floppy so that its size can be automatically detected using the devices */dev/fd0* or */dev/fd1*. One way to do a low-level format is with the MS-DOS FORMAT command; another way is with the Linux program *fdformat*. For example, to format the diskette in the first floppy drive, use the command

```
rutabaga# fdformat /dev/fd0
Double-sided, 80 tracks, 18 sec/track. Total capacity 1440 kB.
Formatting ... done
Verifying ... done
```

Using the *−n* option to *fdformat* will skip the verification step.

Each filesystem-specific version of *mkfs* supports several options that you might find useful. Most types support the *−c* option, which causes the physical media to be checked for bad blocks while creating the filesystem. If bad blocks are found, they will be marked and avoided when writing data to the filesystem. In order to use these type-specific options, include them after the *–t type* option to *mkfs*, as so:

```
mkfs -t type -c device blocks
```

To determine what options are available, see the manual page for the type-specific version of *mkfs*. (For example, for the Second Extended filesystem, see *mke2fs*.) Most types support *–c* for bad block checking, and *–v* for verbose output.

You may not have all of the available type-specific versions of *mkfs* installed. If this is the case, *mkfs* will fail when you try to create a filesystem of a type for which you have no *mkfs.type*. Nearly all filesystem types supported by Linux have a corresponding *mkfs.type* available, somewhere.

If you run into trouble using *mkfs*, it's possible that Linux is having problems accessing the physical device. In the case of a floppy, this might just mean a bad floppy. In the case of a hard drive, it could be more serious—for example, the disk device driver in the kernel might be having problems reading your drive. This could be a hardware problem, or a simple matter of your drive geometry being specified incorrectly. See the manual pages for the various versions of *mkfs*, and read the sections in Chapter 2 on troubleshooting installation problems. They apply equally here.

Chapter 2

Checking and Repairing Filesystems

It is sometimes necessary to check your Linux filesystems for consistency, and repair them if there are any errors or lost data. Such errors commonly result from a system crash or loss of power, where the kernel isn't able to sync the filesystem buffer cache with the contents of the disk. In most cases, such errors are relatively minor. However, if the system were to crash while writing a large file, that file may be lost and the blocks associated with it marked as "in use," when in fact there is no file entry corresponding to them. In other cases, errors can be caused by accidentally writing data directly to the hard drive device (such as */dev/hda*), or one of the partitions.

The program *fsck* is used to check filesystems and correct any problems that may be found. Like *mkfs*, *fsck* is a front-end for a filesystem-type–specific *fsck.type*, such as *fsck.ext2* for Second Extended filesystems. (As with *mkfs.ext2*, *fsck.ext2* is a symbolic link to *e2fsck*, either of which you could execute directly if the *fsck* front-end is not installed.)

Use of *fsck* is quite simple; the format of the command is

```
fsck -t type device
```

where *type* is the type of filesystem to repair, as given in Table 4-1, and *device* is the device (drive partition or floppy) on which the filesystem resides.

For example, to check an *ext2* filesystem on */dev/hda2*, we use:

```
rutabaga# fsck -t ext2 /dev/hda2
Parallelizing fsck version 0.5a (5-Apr-94)
e2fsck 0.5a, 5-Apr-94 for EXT2 FS 0.5, 94/03/10
/dev/hda2 is mounted.  Do you really want to continue (y/n)? yes

/dev/hda2 has reached maximal mount count, check forced.
Pass 1: Checking inodes, blocks, and sizes
Pass 2: Checking directory structure
Pass 3: Checking directory connectivity
Pass 4: Check reference counts.
Pass 5: Checking group summary information.

Free blocks count wrong for group 3 (3331, counted=3396).  FIXED
Free blocks count wrong for group 4 (1983, counted=2597).  FIXED
Free blocks count wrong (29643, counted=30341).  FIXED
Inode bitmap differences: -8280.  FIXED
Free inodes count wrong for group #4 (1405, counted=1406).  FIXED
Free inodes count wrong (34522, counted=34523).  FIXED

/dev/hda2: ***** FILE SYSTEM WAS MODIFIED *****
/dev/hda2: ***** REBOOT LINUX *****
/dev/hda2: 13285/47808 files, 160875/191216 blocks
```

[handwritten: fsck -f forces check!!]

First of all, note that the system asks for confirmation before checking a mounted filesystem. If any errors are found and corrected while using *fsck*, you'll have to reboot the system if the filesystem is mounted. This is because the changes made by *fsck* may not be propagated back to the system's internal knowledge of the filesystem layout. In general, it's not a good idea to check mounted filesystems.

As we can see, several problems were found, and corrected, and because this filesystem was mounted the system informs us that the machine should be rebooted.

How can you check filesystems while they are unmounted? With the exception of the root filesystem, you can simply *umount* any filesystems before running *fsck* on them. The root filesystem, however, can't be unmounted. One way to check your root filesystem while it's unmounted is to use a boot/root diskette combination, such as the installation diskettes used by your Linux distribution. This way, the root filesystem is contained on a floppy, and the root filesystem (on your hard drive) remains unmounted, and you can check it from there. See "What To Do in an Emergency" for more details about this.

Another way to check the root filesystem is to mount it read-only. This can be done using the option ro from the LILO boot prompt (see the section "Specifying boot time options"). However, other parts of your system configuration (for example, the programs executed by */etc/init* at boot time) may require write access to the root filesystem, so you can't boot the system normally or these programs will fail. To boot the system with the root filesystem mounted as read-only you might

want to boot the system in to single-user mode as well (using the boot option single). This will prevent any additional system configuration at boot time—you can
then check the root filesystem and reboot the system normally.

To cause the root filesystem to be mounted read-only, you can either use the ro
boot option, or use *rdev* to set the read-only flag in the kernel image itself.

Many Linux systems automatically check the filesystems at boot time. This is usually done by executing *fsck* from */etc/rc.d/rc.S* (*fsck* is described in "Checking and
Repairing Filesystems"). When this is done, the system usually mounts the root
filesystem initially as read-only, uses *fsck* to check it, and then uses the command

```
mount -w -o remount /
```

The *-o remount* option causes the given filesystem to be "remounted" with the
new parameters; in this case, the *-w* option (equivalent to *-o rw*) causes the
filesystem to be mounted read-write. The net result is that the root filesystem is
remounted with read-write access.

When *fsck* is executed at boot time, it checks all filesystems other than root before
they are mounted. Once *fsck* completes, the other filesystems are mounted using
mount. Check out the files in */etc/rc.d*, especially *rc.S* (if present on your system),
to see how this is done. If you want to disable this feature on your system, comment out the lines in the appropriate */etc/rc.d* file that execute *fsck*.

There are several options that you can pass to the type-specific *fsck*. Most types
support the options *-a*, which automatically confirms any prompts which *fsck.type*
may display; *-c*, which does bad-block checking, as with *mkfs*; and *-v*, which
prints verbose information during the check operation. These options should be
given after the *-ttype* argument to *fsck*, as in:

```
fsck -t type -v device
```

to run *fsck* with verbose output.

See the manual pages for *fsck* and *e2fsck* for more information.

Not all filesystem types supported by Linux have a *fsck* variant available. To check
and repair MS-DOS filesystems you should use a tool under MS-DOS, such as the
Norton Utilities, to accomplish this task. You should be able to find versions of
fsck for the Second Extended filesystem, Minix filesystem, and Xia filesystem at
least.

Later in the chapter, in the section "What To Do in an Emergency," we provide
additional information on checking filesystems and recovering from disaster. *fsck*
will by no means catch and repair every error to your filesystems, but most common problems should be handled. If you delete an important file, there is currently no easy way to recover it—*fsck* can't do that for you. There is work
underway to provide an "undelete" utility in the Second Extended filesystem. Be
sure to keep backups, or use *rm -i* which always prompts before deleting a file.

Managing Swap Space

Swap space is a generic term for disk storage used to increase the amount of apparent memory available on the system. Under Linux, swap space is used to implement *paging*, a process whereby memory pages (a page is generally 4096 bytes) are written out to disk when physical memory is low, and read back into physical memory when needed. The process by which paging works is rather involved, but it is optimized for certain cases. The virtual memory subsystem under Linux allows memory pages to be shared between running programs—for example, if you have multiple copies of Emacs running simultaneously, there is only one copy of the Emacs code actually in memory. Also, text pages (those pages containing program code, not data) are usually read-only, and therefore not written to disk when swapped out. Those pages are instead directly freed from main memory and read from the original executable file when they are accessed again.

Of course, swap space cannot completely make up for a lack of physical RAM. Disk access is much slower than RAM access, by several orders of magnitude. Therefore, swap is useful primarily as a means to run a number of programs simultaneously that would not otherwise fit into physical RAM; if you are switching between these programs rapidly you'll notice a lag as pages are swapped to and from disk.

At any rate, Linux supports swap space in two forms: as a separate disk partition, or a file somewhere on your existing Linux filesystems. You can have up to 16 swap areas, with each swap area being a disk file or partition up to 128 megabytes in size. You math whizzes out there will realize that this allows up to 2 gigabytes of swap space. (If anyone has actually attempted to use this much swap, the author would love to hear about it, whether you're a math whiz or not.)

Note that using a swap partition can yield better performance, because the disk blocks are guaranteed to be contiguous. In the case of a swap file, however, the disk blocks may be scattered around the filesystem, which can be a serious performance hit in some cases. Many people use a swap file when they must add additional swap space temporarily—for example, if the system is thrashing because of lack of physical RAM and swap. Swap files are a good way to add swap on demand.

Chapter 2

Nearly all Linux systems utilize swap space of some kind, usually a single swap partition. In Chapter 2 we explained how to create a swap partition on your system during the Linux installation procedure. In this section we will describe how to add and remove swap files and partitions. If you already have swap space and are happy with it, this section may not be of interest to you.

How much swap space do you have? The *free* command will report information on system memory usage.

```
rutabaga% free
              total      used      free    shared    buffers
    Mem:      19308     17672      1636      8012     10820
    Swap:     16408         0     16408
```

All of the numbers here are reported in 1024-byte blocks. Here, we see a system with 19308 blocks (about 19 megabytes) of physical RAM, with 17672 (about 17 megabytes) currently in use. Note that your system actually has more physical RAM than that given in the "total" column; this number does not include the memory used by the kernel for its own sundry needs.

The "shared" column lists the amount of physical memory that is shared between multiple processes. Here, we see that about 8 megabytes of pages are being shared, which means that memory is being utilized very well. The "buffers" column shows the amount of memory being used by the kernel buffer cache. The buffer cache (described briefly in the previous section) is used to speed up disk operations, by allowing disk reads and writes to be serviced directly from memory. The buffer cache size will increase or decrease as memory usage on the system changes; this memory is reclaimed if it is needed by applications. Therefore, although we see that 17 megabytes of system memory is in use, not all of it is being used by application programs.

Below the numbers for physical RAM we see the total amount of swap, which is 16408 blocks (about 16 megabytes). In this case, none of the swap is being used— there is plenty of physical RAM available. If additional applications were started, parts of the buffer cache memory would be used to host them. Swap space is generally used as a last resort when the system can't reclaim physical memory in any other way.

Note that the amount of swap reported by *free* is somewhat less than the total size of your swap partitions and files. This is because several blocks of each swap area must be used to store a map of how each page in the swap area is being utilized. This overhead should be rather small; only a few kilobytes per swap area.

If you're considering creating a swap file, the *df* command can give you information on the amount of space remaining on your various filesystems. This command prints a list of filesystems, showing each one's size and what percentage of it is currently occupied.

Creating Swap Space

Chapter 2

The first step in adding additional swap is to create a file or partition to host the swap area. If you wish to create an additional swap partition, you can create the partition using the *fdisk* utility, as described in the section "Creating Linux Partitions" in Chapter 2.

In order to create a swap file, you'll need to open a file and write bytes to it equaling the amount of swap that you wish to add. One easy way to do this is with the *dd* command. For example, to create an 8-megabyte swap file, you can use the command

```
dd if=/dev/zero of=/swap bs=1024 count=8192
```

This will write 8192 blocks (8 megabytes) of data from */dev/zero* to the file */swap.* (*/dev/zero* is a special device in which read operations always return null bytes. It's something like the inverse of */dev/null.*) After creating a file of this size, it's a good idea to use the command

```
sync
```

to sync the filesystems in case of a system crash.

Chapter 2

Once you have created the swap file or partition, you can use the *mkswap* command to "format" the swap area. As described in the section "Creating the Swap Space" of Chapter 2, the format of the *mkswap* command is

```
mkswap -c device size
```
blocks

where *device* is the name of the swap partition or file, and *size* is the size of the swap area in ~~bytes.~~ The *-c* switch is optional and causes the swap area to be checked for bad blocks as it is formatted.

For example, for the swap file created above, you would use the command

```
mkswap -c /swap 8192
```

If the swap area is a partition, instead, you would substitute the name of the partition (such as */dev/hda3*) and the size of the partition, also in blocks.

After running *mkswap* on a swap file, you should use the *sync* command to ensure that the format information has been physically written to the new swap file. Running *sync* is not necessary when formatting a swap partition.

Enabling the Swap Space

In order for the new swap space to be utilized, you must enable it with the *swapon* command. For example, after creating the swap file above, and running *mkswap* and *sync*, we could use the command

```
swapon /swap
```

This adds the new swap area to the total amount of available swap; use the *free* command to verify that this is indeed the case. If you are using a new swap partition, you can enable it with a command such as

```
swapon /dev/hda3
```

if */dev/hda* is the name of the swap partition.

Like filesystems, swap areas are automatically enabled at boot time, using the *swapon −a* command from one of the system startup files (usually in */etc/rc.d/rc.S*). This command looks in the file */etc/fstab*, which, as you'll remember from the section "Mounting Filesystems," includes information on filesystems and swap areas. All entries in */etc/fstab* with the options field set to sw are enabled by *swapon −a*.

Therefore, if */etc/fstab* contains the entries:

```
# device       directory    type   options
/dev/hda3      none         swap   sw
/swap          none         swap   sw
```

then the two swap areas */dev/hda3* and */swap* will be enabled at boot time. For each new swap area, you should add such an entry to */etc/fstab*.

Disabling Swap Space

As is usually the case, undoing a task is easier than doing it. To disable swap space, simply use the command

```
swapoff device
```

where *device* is the name of the swap partition or file that you wish to disable. For example, to disable swapping on the device */dev/hda3*, use the command

```
swapoff /dev/hda3
```

If you wish to disable a swap file, you can simply remove the file, using *rm*, *after* using *swapoff.* Don't remove a swap file before disabling it; this can cause disaster.

If you have disabled a swap partition using *swapoff*, you are free to re-use that partition as you see fit, remove it using *fdisk*, whatever.

Also, if there is a corresponding entry for the swap area in */etc/fstab*, remove it. Otherwise, you'll get errors when you next reboot the system and the swap area can't be found.

Device Files

Device files allow user programs to access hardware devices on the system, through the kernel. They are not "files" per se, but look like files from the program's point of view—you can read from them, write to them, *mmap( )* onto them, and so forth. When you access such a device "file," the kernel recognizes the I/O request and passes it a device driver, which performs some operation, such as reading data from a serial port, or sending data to a sound card.

Device files (though inappropriately named, we will continue to use this term) provide a convenient way to access system resources without requiring the applications programmer to know how the underlying device works. Under Linux, as with most UNIX systems, device drivers themselves are part of the kernel. In the section "Building the Kernel" we show you how to build your own kernel, including only those device drivers for the hardware on your system.

Device files are located in the directory */dev* on nearly all UNIX-like systems. Each device on the system should have a corresponding entry in */dev*. For example, */dev/ttyS0* corresponds to the first serial port, known as COM1 under MS-DOS; */dev/hda2* corresponds to the second partition on the first IDE drive. In fact, there should be entries in */dev* for many devices that you do not have. The device files are generally created during system installation and include every possible device driver. They don't necessarily correspond to the actual hardware on your system.

There are a number of "pseudo-devices" in */dev* that don't correspond to any actual peripheral. For example, */dev/null* acts as a byte sink—any write request to */dev/null* will succeed, but the data written will be ignored. Similarly, we've already demonstrated the use of */dev/zero* to create a swap file; any read request on */dev/zero* simply returns null bytes.

When using *ls –l* to list device files in */dev*, you'll see something like the following:

```
brw-rw----   1 root     disk      3,   0 May 19 1994 /dev/hda
```

This is */dev/hda*, which corresponds to the first IDE drive. First of all, note that the first letter of the permissions field is b, which means that this is a block device file. (Recall that normal files have a - in this first column, directories a d, and so forth.) Device files are denoted either by b, for block devices, or c, for character devices. A block device is usually a peripheral such as a hard drive—data is read and written to the device as entire blocks (where the block size is determined by the device—it may not be 1024 bytes as we usually call "blocks" under Linux), and the device may be accessed randomly. In contrast, character devices are usually read or written sequentially, and I/O may be done as single bytes. An example of a character device is a serial port.

Also, note that the size field in the *ls –l* listing is replaced by two numbers, separated by a comma. The first value is the *major device number*, and the second is the *minor device number*. When a device file is accessed by a program, the kernel receives the I/O request in terms of the major and minor numbers of the device. The major number generally specifies a particular driver within the kernel, and the minor number specifies a particular device handled by that driver. For example, all serial port devices have the same major number, but different minor numbers. The kernel uses the major number to redirect an I/O request to the appropriate driver, and the driver uses the minor number to figure out which specific device to access.

The naming convention used by files in */dev* is, to put it bluntly, a complete mess. Because the kernel itself doesn't care what filenames are used in */dev* (it cares only about the major and minor numbers), the distribution maintainers, applications programmers, and device driver writers are free to choose names for a device file. Often, the person writing a device driver will suggest a name for the device, and later the name will be changed to accommodate other, similar devices. This can cause confusion and inconsistency as the system develops—hopefully, you won't encounter this problem unless you're working with newer device drivers, those that are under testing.

At any rate, the device files included in your original distribution should be accurate for the kernel version and device drivers included with that distribution. When you upgrade your kernel, or add additional device drivers (see the section "Building a New Kernel"), you may need to add a device file using the *mknod* command. The format of this command is

```
mknod -m permissions name type major minor
```

where

- *name* is the full pathname of the device to create, such as */dev/rft0*.

- *type* is either c for a character device or b for a block device.

- *major* is the major number of the device.

- *minor* is the minor number of the device.

- *−m permissions* is an optional argument that sets the permission bits of the new device file to *permissions*.

For example, let's say that you're adding a new device driver to the kernel, and the documentation says that you need to create the block device */dev/bogus*, major number 42, minor number 0. You would use the command

```
mknod /dev/bogus b 42 0
```

If you don't specify the *−m permissions* argument, the new device is given the permissions for a newly-created file, modified by your current umask—that is, usually 0644. To set the permissions for */dev/bogus* to 0666 instead, we would use

```
mknod -m 666 /dev/bogus b 42 0
```

You can also use *chmod* to set the permissions for a device file after creation.

Chapter 3

Why are device permissions important? Like any file, the permissions for a device file control who may access the raw device, and how. As we saw above, the device file for */dev/hda* has permissions 0660, which means that only the owner and users in the file's group (here, the group **disk** is used) may read and write directly to this device. (Permissions are introduced in "File Ownership and Permissions" in Chapter 3.)

In general, you don't want to give any user direct read and write access to certain devices—especially those devices corresponding to disk drives and partitions. Otherwise, anyone could, say, run *mkfs* on a drive partition and completely destroy all data on the system.

In the case of drives and partitions, write access is required to corrupt data in this way, but read access is a also breach of security—given read access to a raw device file corresponding to a disk partition, a user could peek in on other user's files. Likewise, the device file */dev/mem* corresponds to the system's physical memory (it's generally used only for extreme debugging purposes). Given read access, clever users could spy on other users' passwords, including the one belonging to **root**, as they are entered at login time.

Be sure that the permissions for any device that you add to the system correspond to how the device can and should be accessed by users. Devices such as serial ports, sound cards, and virtual consoles are generally safe for mortals to have access to, but most other devices on the system should be limited to use by **root** (and programs running setuid as **root**).

Many of the files found in */dev* are actually symbolic links (created using *ln −s*, in the usual way) to another device file. These links make it easier to access certain devices by using a more common name. For example, if you have a serial mouse, that mouse might be accessed through one of the device files */dev/cua0*, */dev/cua1*, */dev/cua2*, or */dev/cua3*, depending on which serial port the mouse is attached to. Many people create a link named */dev/mouse* to the appropriate serial device, as in:

```
ln −s /dev/cua2 /dev/mouse
```

In this way, we can access the mouse from */dev/mouse*, instead of having to remember which serial port it is on. This convention is also used for devices such as */dev/cdrom* and */dev/modem*. These files are usually symbolic links to a device file in */dev* corresponding to the actual CD-ROM or modem device.

To remove a device file, just use *rm*, as in:

```
rm /dev/bogus
```

Removing a device file does not remove the corresponding device driver from memory or from the kernel; it simply leaves you with no means to talk to a particular device driver. Similarly, adding a device file does not add a device driver to the system—in fact, you can add device files for drivers that don't even exist. Device files simply provide a "hook" into a particular device driver, should such a driver exist in the kernel.

Scheduling Jobs Using cron

The original purpose of the computer was to automate routine tasks. If you need to back up your disk at 1:00 AM every day, why should you have to enter the commands manually each time—particularly if it means getting out of bed? You should be able to tell the computer once to do it, and then forget about it. On UNIX systems, *cron* exists to perform this automating function.

Briefly, you use *cron* by running the *crontab* command and entering lines in a special format recognized by *cron*. Each line specifies a command to run and when to run it.

Behind your back, *crontab* saves your commands in a file bearing your username in the */usr/spool/cron/crontabs* directory. (For instance, my *crontab* file would be called */usr/spool/cron/crontabs/mdw*.) A daemon called *crond* reads this file regularly and executes the commands at the proper times. One of the *rc* files on your system starts up *crond* when the system boots. There actually is no command named *cron*, only the *crontab* utility and the *crond* daemon.

On some systems, use of *cron* is limited to the **root** user. In any case, let's look at a useful command that you might want to run as **root** and show how you'd specify it as a *crontab* entry. Suppose that every day you'd like to clean old files out of the */tmp* directory, which is supposed to serve as temporary storage for files created by lots of utilities.

Most systems remove the contents of */tmp* when the system reboots, but if you keep it up for a long time you may find it useful to use *cron* to check for old files (say, files that haven't been accessed in the past three days) and remove them. The command you want to enter is:

```
rm -f filename
```

But how do you know which `filename` to specify? You have to place the command inside a *find* command, which lists all files beneath a directory and performs the operation you specify on each one.

We've already seen the find command in the section "Incremental Backups." Here, we'll specify */tmp* as the directory to search, and use the *–atime* option to find files whose last access time is at least three days in the past. The *–exec* option means "execute the following command on every file we find."

```
find /tmp -atime 3 -exec rm -f {} \;
```

The command we are asking *find* to execute is *rm –f*, which we've already seen. The funny string {} is just a way of saying "Do it to each file that you find, according to the previous selection material." The string \; tells *find* that the *–exec* option is finished.

Now we have a command that removes old files from */tmp*. We still have to say how often it runs. The format used by *crontab* consists of six fields:

```
minute    hour    day    month    dayofweek    command
```

Fill the fields as follows:

1. Minute (specify from 0 to 59)

2. Hour (specify from 0 to 23)

3. Day of the month (specify from 1 to 31)

4. Month (specify from 1 to 12, or a name such as jan, feb, etc.)

5. Day of the week (specify from 0 to 6 where 0 is Sunday, or a name such as mon, tue, etc.)

6. Command (can be multiple words)

Figure 4-1 shows a *cron* entry with all the fields filled in. The command is a shell script, run with the Bourne shell *sh*. But the entry is not too realistic—the script runs only when all the conditions in the first five fields are true. That is, it has to run on a Sunday that falls on the 15th day of either January or July—not a common occurrence! So this is not a realistic example.

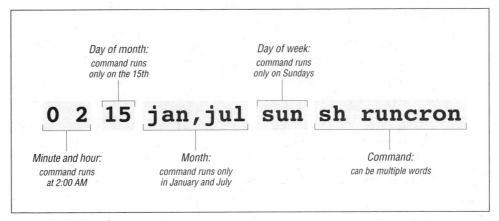

Figure 4–1. Sample cron entry

If you want a command to run every day at 1:00 AM, specify the minute as 0 and the hour as 1. The other three fields should be asterisks, which mean "every day and month at the given time." The complete line in *crontab* is:

```
0 1 * * * find /tmp -atime 3 -exec rm -f {} \;
```

Since there are a lot of fancy things you can do with the time fields, let's play with this command a bit more. Suppose you want to run the command just on the first day of each month, You would keep the first two fields, but add a 1 in the third field:

```
0 1 1 * * find /tmp -atime 3 -exec rm -f {} \;
```

To do it once a week on Monday, restore the third field to an asterisk but specify either 1 or mon as the fifth field:

```
0 1 * * mon find /tmp -atime 3 -exec rm -f {} \;
```

To get even more sophisticated, there are ways to specify multiple times in each field. Here, a comma means "run on the 1st and 15th day" of each month:

```
0 1 1,15 * * find /tmp -atime 3 -exec rm -f {} \;
```

while a hyphen means "run every day from the 1st through the 15th, inclusive":

```
0 1 1-15 * * find /tmp -atime 3 -exec rm -f {} \;
```

and a slash followed by a 5 means "run every fifth day" which comes out to the 1st, 6th, 11th, and so on:

```
0 1 */5 * * find /tmp -atime 3 -exec rm -f {} \;
```

Now we're ready to actually put the entry in our *crontab* file. Become **root** (since this is the kind of thing **root** should do) and enter the *crontab* command with the *−e* option for "edit":

```
rutabaga# crontab -e
```

By default, this command starts a *vi* edit session. If you'd like to use Emacs instead, you can specify this before you start *crontab*. For a Bourne-compliant shell, enter the command

```
rutabaga# export VISUAL=emacs
```

For the C shell:

```
rutabaga# setenv VISUAL emacs
```

The environment variable EDITOR also works in place of VISUAL for some versions of *crontab*.

Enter a line or two beginning with hash marks (#) to serve as comments explaining what you're doing, then put in your *crontab* entry:

```
# Remove files from /tmp that are 3 or more days old.  Runs at 1:00 AM
# each morning.
0 1 * * * find /tmp -atime 3 -exec rm -f {} \;
```

When you exit *vi*, the commands are saved. Look at your *crontab* entry by entering

```
rutabaga# crontab -l
```

Here's another example of a common type of command used in *crontab* files. It performs a tape backup of a directory. We assume that someone has put a tape in the drive before the command runs. First, an *mt* command makes sure that the tape in the */dev/rft0* device is rewound to the beginning. Then a *tar* command transfers all the files from the directory */src* to the tape. A semicolon is used to separate the commands; that is standard shell syntax.

```
# back up the /src directory once every two months.
0 2 1 */2 * mt -f /dev/rft0 rewind; tar cf /dev/rft0 /src
```

The first two fields ensure that the command runs at 2:00 AM, and the third field specifies the first day of the month. The fourth field specifies every two months. We could achieve the same effect, in a possibly more readable manner, by entering:

```
0 2 1 jan,mar,may,jul,sep,nov * mt -f /dev/rft0 rewind; tar cf /dev/rft0 /src
```

The section "Making Backups" explains how to do backups on a regular basis.

Another aspect you should always consider with *cron* is what happens to the output of the commands. *cron* saves up all the standard output and standard error, and sends it to the user as a mail message. In the example above, the mail goes to **root**, but that should be automatically be directed to you as the system administrator. Make sure the following line appears in */usr/lib/aliases*:

```
root: your-account-name
```

The following example uses *mailq* every two days to test whether there is any mail stuck in the mail queue, and sends the mail administrator the results by mail. If there is mail stuck in the mail queue, the report includes details about addressing and delivery problems, but otherwise the message is empty:

```
0 6 */2 * * mail -s "Tested Mail Queue for Stuck Email" postmaster < mailq -v
```

Probably you don't want to receive a mail message every day when everything is going normally. In the examples we've used so far, the commands do not produce any output unless they encounter errors. But you may want to get into the habit of redirecting the standard output to */dev/null*, or sending it to a log file like this (note the use of two > signs so that we don't wipe out previous output):

```
0 1 * * * find /tmp -atime 3 -exec rm -f {} \; >> /home/mdw/log
```

In this entry, we redirect the standard output, but allow the standard error to be sent as a mail message. This can be a nice feature, because we'll get a mail message if anything goes wrong. If you want to make sure you don't receive mail under any circumstances, redirect both the standard output and the standard error:

```
0 1 * * * find /tmp -atime 3 -exec rm -f {} \; >> /home/mdw/log 2>&1
```

When you save output in a log file, you get the problem of a file that grows continuously. You may want another *cron* entry that runs once a week or so, just to remove the file.

Only Bourne shell commands can be used in *crontab* entries. That means you can't use any of the convenient extensions recognized by *bash* and other modern shells, such as aliases or the use of ~ to mean "my home directory." You can use

$HOME, however—*cron* recognizes the $USER, $HOME, and $SHELL environment variables. Each command runs with your home directory as its current directory.

Some people like to specify absolute path names for commands, like */usr/bin/find* and */bin/rm*, in *crontab* entries. This ensures that the right command is always found, instead of relying on the PATH being set correctly.

If a command gets too long and complicated to put on a single line, write a shell script and invoke it from *cron*. Make sure the script is executable (use *chmod +x*) or execute it by using a shell like:

```
0 1 * * * sh runcron
```

As a system administrator, you often have to create *crontab* files for dummy users such as **news** or **uucp**. Running all utilities as **root** would be overkill and possibly dangerous, so these special users exist instead.

The choice of a user also affects file ownership: a *crontab* file for **news** should run files owned by **news**, and so on. In general, make sure that the utilities are owned by the user in whose name you create the *crontab* file.

Chapter 3

Also, think about who is going to use the output files you create. If a file is created by a *cron* entry running as **news**, you may have trouble reading the file later as another user. You may have to use *chown* or *chmod* in your *cron* script to make sure the file is usable later. These commands are discussed in the section "Changing the Owner, Group, and Permissions" in Chapter 3.

Since you can't log in as **news**, you can edit **news**'s crontab file as **root** using the command:

```
rutabaga# crontab -e news
```

Managing System Logs

The *syslogd* utility logs various kinds of system activity, such as debugging output from *sendmail* and warnings printed by the kernel. *syslogd* runs as a daemon and is usually started in one of the *rc* files at boot time.

The file */etc/syslog.conf* is used to control where *syslogd* records information. Such a file might look like the following:

```
*.info;*.notice    /var/adm/messages
mail.debug         /var/adm/maillog
*.warn             /var/adm/syslog
kern.emerg         /dev/console
```

The first field of each line lists the kinds of messages that should be logged, and the second field lists the location where they should be logged. The first field is of the format

```
facility.level [; facility.level ... ]
```

Where *facility* is the system application or facility generating the message, and *level* is the severity of the message.

For example, *facility* can be mail (for the mail daemon), kern (for the kernel), user (for user programs), or auth (for authentication programs such as *login* or *su*). An asterisk in this field specifies all facilities.

level can be (in increasing severity): debug, info, notice, warning, err, crit, alert, or emerg.

In the above */etc/syslog.conf*, we see that all messages of severity info and notice are logged to */var/adm/messages*, all debug messages from the mail daemon are logged in */var/adm/maillog*, and all warn messages are logged in */var/adm/syslog*. Also, any emerg warnings from the kernel are sent to the console (which is the current virtual console, or an *xterm* started with the −*C* option).

The messages logged by *syslogd* usually include the date, an indication of what process or facility delivered the message, and the message itself, all on one line. For example, a kernel error message indicating a problem with data on an *ext2fs* filesystem might appear in the log files as

```
Dec  1 21:03:35 loomer kernel: EXT2-fs error (device 3/2):
  ext2_check_blocks_bit map: Wrong free blocks count in super block,
  stored = 27202, counted = 27853
```

Similarly, if an *su* to the root account succeeds, you might see a log message such as

```
Dec 11 15:31:51 loomer su: mdw on /dev/ttyp3
```

Log files can be very important for tracking down system problems. If a log file grows too large you can delete it using *rm*; it will be re-created when *syslogd* starts up again.

Your system probably comes equipped with a running *syslogd* and a */etc/syslog.conf* that does the right thing. However, it's important to know where your log files are and what programs they represent. If you need to log many messages (say, debugging messages from the kernel, which can be very verbose) you can edit *syslog.conf* and tell *syslogd* to re-read its configuration file with the command

```
kill -HUP `cat < /etc/syslog.pid`
```

Note the use of backquotes to obtain the process ID of *syslogd*, contained in */etc/syslog.pid*.

Other system logs might be available as well. These include:

/var/adm/lastlog

This file contains binary data indicating the login times and duration for each user on the system; it is used by the *last* command to generate a listing of user logins. The output of *last* might look like:

```
mdw       tty3                         Sun Dec 11 15:25   still logged in
mdw       tty3                         Sun Dec 11 15:24 - 15:25  (00:00)
mdw       tty1                         Sun Dec 11 11:46   still logged in
reboot    ~                            Sun Dec 11 06:46
```

A record is also logged in */var/adm/lastlog* when the system is rebooted.

/etc/utmp

This is another binary file which contains information on the users currently logged into the system. It is used by commands such as *who*, *w*, and *finger* to produce information on who is logged in. For example, the *w* command might print:

```
 3:58pm  up  4:12,  5 users,  load average: 0.01, 0.02, 0.00
User      tty          login@  idle   JCPU   PCPU  what
mdw       ttyp3       11:46am   14                  -
mdw       ttyp2       11:46am           1           w
mdw       ttyp4       11:46am                       kermit
mdw       ttyp0       11:46am   14                  bash
```

w(1)

We see the login times for each user (in this case, one user logged in many times), as well as the command currently being used. The *w* man page describes all of the fields displayed.

/var/adm/wtmp

This file is of the same format as *utmp* but records previous logins, not just the current ones. It is similar in nature to *lastlog*, but is used by different programs (such as *finger*, to determine when a user was last logged in).

Note that the format of the *wtmp* and *utmp* files differs from system to system. Some programs may be compiled to expect one format, and others another format. For this reason, commands that use the files may produce confusing or inaccurate information—especially if the files become corrupted by a program that writes information to them in the wrong format.

Setting Terminal Attributes

setterm is a program that sets various characteristics of your terminal (say, each virtual console), such as the keyboard repeat rate, tab stops, and text colors.

Most people use this command to change the colors for each virtual console. In this way you can tell which virtual console you're currently looking at based on the text color.

For example, to change the color of the current terminal to white text on a blue background, use the command

```
$ setterm -foreground white -background blue
```

Some programs and actions cause the terminal attributes to be reset to their default values. In order to store the current set of attributes as the default, use

```
$ setterm -store
```

setterm(1)

setterm provides many options (most of which you will probably never use). See the *setterm* man page or use *setterm –help* for more information.

What To Do in an Emergency

It's not difficult to make a simple mistake as **root** that can cause real problems on your system, such as not being able to log in or loss of important files. This is especially true for novice system administrators who are beginning to explore the system. Nearly all new system admins learn their lessons "the hard way," by being forced to recover from a real emergency. In this section we'll give you some hints about what to do when the inevitable happens.

You should always be aware of preventative measures that can reduce the impact of such emergencies. For example, take backups of all important system files, if not the entire system. If you happen to have a Linux distribution on CD-ROM, the CD-ROM itself acts as a wonderful backup for most files (as long as you have a way to access the CD-ROM in a tight situation—more on this later). Backups are vital to recovering from many problems; don't let the many weeks of hard work configuring your Linux system go to waste.

Also, be sure to keep notes on your system configuration, such as your partition table entries, partition sizes and types, and filesystems. If you were to trash your partition table somehow, fixing the problem might be a simple matter of re-running *fdisk*, but this only helps as long as you can remember what your partition table used to look like.[*]

Of course, for any of the above measures to work, you'll need some way to boot the system and access your files, or recover from backups, in an emergency. This is best accomplished with an "emergency disk," or "root disk." Such a disk contains a small root filesystem with the basics required to run a Linux system completely from floppy—just the essential commands and system files, as well as tools that you can use to repair problems. Such a disk can be used by booting a kernel from another floppy (as discussed in "Using a Boot Floppy") and telling the kernel to use the emergency disk as the root filesystem.

---

[*] True story: The author once did this by booting a blank floppy, and had *no* record of the partition table contents. Needless to say, some guesswork was necessary to restore the partition table to its previous state!

Most distributions of Linux include such a boot/root floppy combination as the original install diskettes. The install disks usually contain a small Linux system, which can be accessed completely from floppy and used to install the software as well as perform basic system maintenance. Some systems include both the kernel and root filesystem on one floppy, but this severely limits the amount of files that can be stored on the emergency disk. How useful these disks are to you as a maintenance tool depends upon whether or not they actually contain the tools (such as *fsck*, *fdisk*, a small editor such as *vi*, and so on) necessary for problem recovery. Some distributions have such an elaborate installation process that the install floppies don't have room for much else.

At any rate, you can create such a root floppy yourself. Being able to do this from scratch requires an intimate knowledge of what's required to boot and use a Linux system, and exactly what can be trimmed down and cut out. For example, you could dispose of the startup programs *init*, *getty*, and *login*, as long as you know how to rig things so that the kernel starts a shell on the console instead of using a real boot procedure. (One way to do this is to have */etc/init* be a symbolic link to */sbin/bash*, all on the floppy filesystem.)

While we can't cover all of the details here, the first step in creating an emergency floppy is to use *mkfs* to create a filesystem on a floppy (see the section "Creating Filesystems"). You then mount the floppy and place whatever files on it that you'll need, including appropriate entries in */dev* (most of which can be copied from */dev* on your hard drive root filesystem). You'll also need a boot diskette, which merely contains a kernel. The kernel should have its root device set to */dev/fd0*, using *rdev*. This is covered in the section "Using a Boot Floppy." You'll also have to decide if you want the root floppy filesystem loaded into a RAMdisk (which can be set using *rdev* as well). If you have more than 4 megabytes of RAM, this is a good idea because it can free up the floppy drive to be used for, say, mounting another diskette containing additional tools. If you have two floppy drives you can do this without using a RAMdisk.

At any rate, the best place to start is your installation diskettes. If those diskettes don't contain all of the tools you need, create a filesystem on a separate floppy and place the missing programs on it. If you load the root filesystem from floppy into a RAMdisk, or have a second floppy drive, you can mount the other floppy to access your maintenance tools.

What tools do you need? In the following sections we'll talk about some common emergencies and how to recover from them—this should act as a guide to tell you what programs would be required for various situations.

Repairing Filesystems

As discussed in the section "Checking and Repairing Filesystems," you can use *fsck* to recover from several kinds of filesystem corruption. Most of these problems are relatively minor, however, and can be repaired by booting your system in the usual way, and running *fsck* from the hard drive. However, it is usually better to check and repair your root filesystem while it is unmounted. In this case it's easier to run *fsck* from an emergency floppy.

There are no differences running *fsck* from floppy than from the hard drive; the syntax is exactly the same as described earlier in the chapter. However, remember that *fsck* is usually a front-end to tools such as *fsck.ext2*. On other systems, you'll need to use *e2fsck* (for Second Extended Filesystems).

It is possible to corrupt a filesystem so that it cannot be mounted. This is usually the result of damage to the filesystem's *superblock*, which stores information about the filesystem as a whole. If the superblock is corrupted, the system won't be able to access the filesystem at all, and any attempt to mount it will fail (probably with an error to the effect of "can't read superblock").

Because of the importance of the superblock, the filesystem keeps backup copies of it at intervals on the filesystem. Second Extended Filesystems are divided into "block groups," where each group has, by default, 8192 blocks. Therefore, there are backup copies of the superblock at block offsets 8193, 16385 (that's 8193 × 2 + 1), 24577, and so on. If you use the *ext2* filesystem, check that the filesystem has 8192-block groups with the command

```
dumpe2fs device | more
```

(Of course, this will work only when the master superblock is intact.) This command will print a great deal of information about the filesystem, and you should see something like

```
Blocks per group:        8192     ———> ( 32768 )
```

If another offset is given, use it for computing offsets to the superblock copies, as mentioned above.

If you can't mount a filesystem because of superblock problems, chances are that *fsck* (or *e2fsck*) will fail as well. You can tell *e2fsck* to use one of the superblock copies instead to repair the filesystem. The command is

```
e2fsck -f -b offset device
```

where *offset* is the block offset to a superblock copy; usually this is 8193. The *−f* switch is used to force a check of the filesystem; when using superblock backups, the filesystem may appear "clean," in which case no check is needed. *−f* overrides this. For example, to repair the filesystem on */dev/hda2* with a bad superblock, we can say   *32768*

```
e2fsck -f -b 8193 /dev/hda2
```

Superblock copies save the day.

The above commands can be executed from an emergency floppy system and will hopefully allow you to mount your filesystems again.

Accessing Damaged Files

You might have a need to access the files on your hard drive filesystems when booting from an emergency floppy. In order to do this, simply use the *mount* command as described in the section "Mounting Filesystems," mounting your filesystems under a directory such as */mnt*. (This directory must exist on the root filesystem contained on the floppy.) For example,

```
mount -t ext2 /dev/hda2 /mnt
```

will allow us to access the files on the Second Extended filesystem stored on */dev/hda2* in the directory */mnt*. You can then access the files directly, and even execute programs from your hard drive filesystems. For example, if you wish to execute *vi* from the hard drive, normally found in */usr/bin/vi*, you would use the command

```
/mnt/usr/bin/vi filename
```

You could even place subdirectories of */mnt* on your path to make this easier.

Be sure to unmount your hard drive filesystems before rebooting the system. If your emergency disks don't have the ability to do a clean shutdown, unmount your filesystems explicitly with *umount*, to be safe.

One problem that is easily fixed by doing this is forgetting the **root** password, or trashing the contents of */etc/passwd*. In either case it might be impossible to log in to the system, or *su* to **root**. To repair this problem, boot from your emergency disks, mount your root filesystem under */mnt*, and edit */mnt/etc/passwd*. (It might be a good idea to keep a backup copy of this file somewhere, in case you delete it accidentally.) For example, to clear the **root** password altogether, change the entry for **root** to

```
root::0:0:The root of all evil:/:/bin/bash
```

Now **root** will have no password; you can reboot the system from hard drive and use the *passwd* command to reset it.

Another common problem is corrupt links to system shared libraries. The shared library images in */lib* are generally accessed through symbolic links such as */lib/libc.so.4*, which points to the actual library, */lib/libc.so.version*. If this link is removed or is pointing to the wrong place, many commands on the system won't run. You can fix this problem by mounting your hard drive filesystems, and re-linking the library with a command such as

```
cd /mnt/lib; ln -sf libc.so.4.5.26 libc.so.4
```

to force the *libc.so.4* link to point to *libc.so.4.5.26*. Remember that symbolic links use the pathname given on the *ln* command line. For this reason, the command

```
ln -sf /mnt/lib/libc.so.4.5.26 /mnt/lib/libc.so.4
```

won't do the right thing; *libc.so.4* will point to */mnt/lib/libc.so.4.5.26*. When you boot from the hard drive, */mnt/lib* can't be accessed, and the library won't be located. The first command works because the symbolic link points to a file in the same directory.

Restoring Files from Backup

If you have deleted important system files, it might be necessary to restore back-ups while booting from an emergency disk. For this reason, it's important to be sure that your emergency disk has the tools that you need to restore backups—this includes programs such as *tar* and *gzip*, as well as the drivers necessary to access the backup device. For instance, if your backups are made using the floppy tape device driver, be sure that the *ftape* module and *insmod* command are available on your emergency disk. See the section "Loadable Device Drivers" for more about this.

All that's required to restore backups to your hard drive filesystems is to mount those filesystems, as described above, and unpack the contents of the archives over those filesystems (using the appropriate *tar* and *gzip* commands, for example; see the section "Making Backups"). Remember that every time you restore a backup you will be overwriting other system files; be sure that you're doing every-thing correctly and not make the situation worse. With most archiving programs you can extract individual files from the archive.

Likewise, if you want to use your original CD-ROM to restore files, be sure that the kernel used on your emergency disks has the drivers necessary to access the CD-ROM drive. You can then mount the CD-ROM (remember the *mount* flags *−r −t iso9660*) and copy files from there.

The filesystems on your emergency disks should also contain important system files; if you have deleted one of these from your system it's easy to copy the lost file from the emergency disk to your hard drive filesystem.

CHAPTER FIVE

POWER TOOLS

In this chapter, we'll introduce a number of popular applications for Linux. We'll start with text editing, which underlies nearly every other activity on the system. (You need an editor to create a file of more than trivial size, whether it is a program to be compiled, a configuration file for your system, or a mail message to send to a friend.) On a related topic, we'll show you some text formatters that can make attractive documents.

Then we'll show you how to install and use the X Window System. We'll describe the features that give you access to files and programs developed for MS-DOS and Windows. These are the power tools that you need to be familiar with in your Linux toolbox. We'll touch on multimedia too, a hot topic nowadays. Nearly every major application that you'll use under Linux is available as free software.

Editing Files Using vi

In this section, we're going to cover the use of the *vi* text editor. *vi* was the first real screen-based editor for UNIX systems. It is also simple, small, and sleek. If you're a system administrator, learning *vi* can be invaluable—in many cases, larger editors such as Emacs won't be available in emergency situations (for instance, when booting Linux from a maintenance disk).

vi is based on the same principles as many other UNIX applications—that each program should provide a small, specific function and be able to interact with other programs. For example, *vi* doesn't include its own spell checker, or paragraph filler, but those features are provided by other programs which are easy to fire off from within *vi*. Therefore, *vi* itself is a bit limited, but is able to interact with other applications to provide virtually any functionality that you might want.

At first, *vi* may appear to be somewhat complex and unwieldy. However, its single-letter commands are very fast and powerful once you've learned them. In the next section we're going to describe Emacs, a much more flexible editor with an easier learning curve. Do keep in mind that knowing *vi* may be essential to you if you are in a situation when Emacs is not available, so we encourage you to learn the basics, as odd as they may seem.

Starting *vi*

Let's fire up *vi* and edit a file. The syntax for *vi* is

```
vi filename
```

For example,

```
eggplant$ vi test
```

will edit the file *test*. Your screen should look like:

```
~
~
~
~
~
~
"test" [New file]
```

The column of ~ characters indicates that you are at the end of the file.

Inserting Text and Moving Around

While using *vi*, at any one time you are in one of three modes of operation. These modes are known as *command mode*, *edit mode*, and *ex mode*.

After starting *vi*, you are in command mode. This mode allows you to use a number of (usually single-letter) commands to modify text, as we'll see soon. Text is actually inserted and modified within edit mode. To begin inserting text, press i (which will place you into edit mode) and begin typing.

```
Now is the time for all good men to come to the aid of the party.
~
~
~
~
~
```

While inserting text, you may type as many lines as you wish (pressing the Return key after each, of course), and you may correct mistakes using the Backspace key. To end edit mode, and return to command mode, press the Esc (escape) key).

While in command mode, you can use the arrow keys to move around the file. Alternatively, you may use h, j, k, and 1, which move the cursor left, down, up, and right respectively.

There are several ways to insert text other than using the i command. The a command (for "append") inserts text *after* the current cursor position. For example, use the left arrow key to move the cursor between the words "good" and "men."

```
Now is the time for all good_men to come to the aid of the party.
~
~
~
~
~
```

Press a, type "wo", and then press Esc to return to command mode.

```
Now is the time for all good women to come to the aid of the party.
~
~
~
~
~
```

To open a line below the current one, and begin inserting text, use the o command. Press o and type another line or two.

```
Now is the time for all good women to come to the aid of the party.
Afterwards, we'll go out for pizza and beer.
~
~
~
~
```

Remember that at any time you're either in command mode (where commands such as i, a, or o are valid), or in edit mode (where you're inserting text, followed by Esc to return to command mode). If you're not sure which mode you're in, press Esc. This takes you out of edit mode, if you are in it, and does nothing if you're already in command mode.

Deleting Text and Undoing Changes

From command mode, the x command deletes the character under the cursor. If you press x five times, you'll end up with:

```
Now is the time for all good women to come to the aid of the party.
Afterwards, we'll go out for pizza and_
~
~
~
~
```

Now press a and insert some text, followed by Esc:

```
Now is the time for all good women to come to the aid of the party.
Afterwards, we'll go out for pizza and Diet Coke._
~
~
~
~
```

You can delete entire lines using the command dd (that is, press d twice in a row). If your cursor is on the second line, dd will produce:

```
Now is the time for all good women to come to the aid of the party.
~
~
~
~
~
```

Text that is deleted may be re-inserted using the p command (for "put"). Pressing p now will return the deleted line to the buffer, after the current line. Using P (uppercase) instead will insert the text before the current line. By default, p and P insert text from the "undo buffer"; you can also yank and replace text from other buffers, as we'll see later.

The u command will undo the latest change (in this case, pressing u after dd is equivalent to p). If you inserted a large amount of text using the i command, pressing u immediately after returning to command mode would undo it.

To delete the word beneath the cursor, use the dw command. Place the cursor on the word "Diet" and type dw.

```
Now is the time for all good women to come to the aid of the party.
Afterwards, we'll go out for pizza and Coke.
~
~
~
~
```

Changing Text

You can replace text using the R command, which overwrites the text beginning at the cursor. Place the cursor on the first letter in "pizza," press R, and type:

```
Now is the time for all good women to come to the aid of the party.
Afterwards, we'll go out for burgers and fries.
~
~
~
~
```

The r command replaces the single character under the cursor. r does not place you in insert mode per se, so there is no reason to use Esc to return to command mode.

The ~ command changes the case of the letter under the cursor from upper to lowercase, and vice versa. If you place the cursor on the "o" in "Now" above, and repeatedly press ~, you'll end up with:

```
NOW IS THE TIME FOR ALL GOOD WOMEN TO COME TO THE AID OF THE PARTY.
Afterwards, we'll go out for burgers and fries.
~
~
~
~
```

Moving Commands

You already know how to use the arrow keys to move around the document. In addition, the w command moves the cursor to the beginning of the next word; b moves it to the beginning of the current word. The 0 (that's a zero) command moves the cursor to the beginning of the current line, and the $ command moves it to the end of the line.

When editing large files, you'll want to move forwards or backwards through the file a screenful at a time. Pressing Ctrl-F moves the cursor one screenful forward, and Ctrl-B moves it a screenful back.

In order to move the cursor to the end of the file, type G. You can also move to an arbitrary line: the command 10G would move the cursor to line 10 in the file. To move to the beginning of the file, use 1G.

Typing / followed by a pattern and the Return key causes you to jump to the first occurrence of that pattern in the text following the cursor. For example, placing the cursor on the first line of text in our example, and typing /burg will move the cursor to the beginning of the word "burgers." Using ? instead of / will search backwards through the file.

The pattern following a / or ? command is actually a *regular expression*. Regular expressions are a powerful way to specify patterns for search and replace operations, and are used by many UNIX utilites. (The manual page for *ed* describes regular expressions in some detail.) Using regular expressions, you could, for example, search for the next uppercase letter, using the command

```
/[A-Z]
```

Therefore, if the pattern that you're searching for is not a static string, regular expressions can be used to specify just what you want.

You can couple moving commands with other commands, such as deletion. For example, the command d$ will delete everything from the cursor to the end of the line; dG will delete everything from the cursor to the end of the file.

Saving Files and Quitting vi

Most of the commands dealing with files within *vi* are invoked from *ex mode*. *ex* mode is entered when you press the : key from command mode. This places the cursor on the last line of the display, allowing you to enter various extended commands.

For example, to write the file being edited, use the command :w. Typing : causes you to enter *ex* mode, and typing w followed by the Enter key completes the command. The command :wq writes the file and exits *vi*. (The command ZZ—from command mode, without the ":"—is equivalent to :wq.)

To quit *vi* without saving changes to the file, use the command :q!. Using :q alone will quit *vi*, but only if modifications to the file have been saved. The ! in :q! means to quit *vi*—and that you really mean it.

Editing Another File

To edit another file, use the :e command. For example, to stop editing *test*, and edit the file *foo* instead, use the command

```
NOW IS THE TIME FOR ALL GOOD WOMEN TO COME TO THE AID OF THE PARTY.
Afterwards, we'll go out for burgers and fries.
~
~
~
~
:e foo_
```

If you use :e without writing the file first, you'll get the error message

```
No write since last change (:edit! overrides)
```

At this point, you can use :w to save the original file, and then use :e, or you can use the command :e! test, which tells *vi* to edit the new file without saving changes to the original.

Including Other Files

If you use the :r command, you can include the contents of another file in the *vi* buffer. For example, the command

    :r foo.txt

would insert the contents of the file *foo.txt* just before the current cursor location.

Running Shell Commands

The :! command allows you to enter the name of a command, which will be executed within *vi*. For example, the command

    :! ls -F

will execute the *ls* command and display the results on your screen.

The :r! command is similar to :!, but includes the standard output of the command in the buffer. The command

    :r! ls -F

will produce

```
NOW IS THE TIME FOR ALL GOOD WOMEN TO COME TO THE AID OF THE PARTY.
Afterwards, we'll go out for burgers and fries.
letters/
misc/
papers/
~
```

If you need to execute a series of shell commands, it's often easier to use the suspend key (usually Ctrl-Z), provided that you're using a shell that supports job control, such as *tcsh* or *bash*.

Global Search and Replace

There are many more features of *vi* than we can document here; most of these features are simply implemented through combinations of the simple features we've seen. Here we'll present one or two other tidbits that most *vi* users find useful.

The command

    :[x,y]s/pattern/replacement/flags

will search for *pattern* between lines *x* and *y* in the buffer, and replace instances of *pattern* with the *replacement* text. *pattern* is a regular expression; *replacement* is literal text, but can contain several special characters to refer to elements in the original *pattern*. The following command replaces occurrences of weeble with wobble on lines 1 through 10 inclusive.

    :1,10s/weeble/wobble

Instead of giving line number specification, you can use the % symbol to refer to the entire file. Other special symbols can be used in place of *x* and *y*. $ refers to the last line of the file. If you leave either *x* or *y* blank, it refers to the current line.

Among the *flags* that you can use are g to replace *all* instances of *pattern* on each line, and c to ask for confirmation for each replacement. In most instances you will want to use the g flag, unless you want to replace only the first occurrence of *pattern* on each line.

You can also use *marks* to refer to lines. Marks are just single-letter names that are given to cursor locations within the document. Moving the cursor to a location in the file and typing ma will set the mark a at that point. (Marks may be named any of the letters a–z or A–Z.) You can move the cursor directly to the mark a with the command `a (with a backquote). Using a regular single quote (as in 'a) will move the cursor to the beginning of the line that the mark a is on.

Marks allow you to "remember" cursor locations which can be used to denote a region of text. For example, if you want to search-and-replace on a block of text, you can move the cursor to the beginning of the text, set a mark, move the cursor to the end of the text, and use the command:

    :'a,.s/weeble/wobble

where 'a refers to the line containing mark a, and . refers to the current line.

Moving Text, Registers

One way to copy and move text is to delete it (using the d or dd commands) and then replace it with the P command, as described above. For example, if you want to delete the 10 lines, starting with the line that contains the cursor, and paste them somewhere else, just use the command 10dd (to delete 10 lines), move the cursor to the new location for the text, and type p. You can copy text in this way as well: typing 10dd followed by P (at the same cursor location) will delete the text and immediately replace it. You can then paste the text elsewhere by moving the cursor and using p multiple times.

Similar to dd is the yy command, which "yanks" text without deleting it. You use p to paste the yanked text as with dd. The deletion and yank commands can be used on more general regions than lines. Recall that the d command deletes text through a move command; for example, d$ deletes text from the cursor to the end of the line. Similarly, y$ yanks text from the cursor to the end of the line.

Let's say that you want to yank (or delete) a region of text. This can be done with marks as well. Move the cursor to the beginning of the text to be yanked and set a mark, as in ma. Move the cursor to the end of the text to be yanked and use the command y`a. This will yank text from the cursor position to the mark a. (Remember that the command `a moves the cursor to the mark a.) Using d instead of y will delete the text from the cursor to the mark.

The most convenient way to cut, copy, and paste portions of text within *vi* is to use registers. A register is just a named temporary storage space for text that you wish to copy between locations, cut and paste within the document, and so forth.

Registers are given single letter names; any of the characters a–z or A–Z are valid. The " command (a quotation mark) is used to specify a register; it is followed by the name of the register, as in "a for register a.

For instance, if we move the cursor to the first line in our example:

```
NOW IS THE TIME FOR ALL GOOD WOMEN TO COME TO THE AID OF THE PARTY.
Afterwards, we'll go out for burgers and fries.
~
~
~
~
```

and use the command "ayy, the current line will be yanked into the register a. We can then move the cursor to the second line, and use the command "ap to paste the text from register a after the current line:

```
NOW IS THE TIME FOR ALL GOOD WOMEN TO COME TO THE AID OF THE PARTY.
Afterwards, we'll go out for burgers and fries.
NOW IS THE TIME FOR ALL GOOD WOMEN TO COME TO THE AID OF THE PARTY.
~
~
~
```

Similarly, the command "ay`a will yank text from the cursor to mark a into register a. Note that there is no correspondence between mark and register names!

Using registers allows you copy text between files. Just copy the text to a register, use the :e command to edit a new file, and then paste the text from the register.

Extending vi

vi is extensible in many ways. Most of the commands that we've introduced can be generalized to arbitrary regions of text. As we've already seen, commands such as d and y operate on the text from the cursor to a move operation such as $ or G. (dG deletes text from the cursor to the end of the file.) Many other commands operate on text through a move command in the same way. Using marks you can operate on any region of text.

As we mentioned before, *vi* is just a text editor; it doesn't have facilities for spell checking text, compiling programs, and other such features. However, *vi* is able to execute other programs, which you can use to extend the editor. The command

```
:x,y!command
```

will execute the named *command* with the text on lines *x* through *y* as standard input, and replace the lines with the standard output of the command. As with the s (search-and-replace) command, other specifications such as % and $ can be used for the line numbers.

Chapter 6

For example, let's say that you wanted to prepend a quote character (>) to all of the lines in a region of text. One way to do this is to write a short shell or Perl script (see Chapter 6, *Programming with Linux*) that reads lines of input and outputs those same lines with the quote character prepended. (Or use a *sed* command; there are many alternatives.) You can then send lines of text through this filter, which will replace them with the quoted text within *vi*. If the script is called *quote* just use a command such as

```
:'a,.!quote
```

which will quote the region of text between the cursor location and the mark a.

Be familiar with the various *ex* commands that are available. The :set command will allow you to set various options; for example, :set ai will turn on auto-indentation of text. (:set noai will turn it off.)

You can specify *ex* commands (such as :set) to execute when starting up *vi* in the file *.exrc* in your home directory. (The name of this file can be changed with the EXINIT environment variable.) For example, your *.exrc* file might contain:

```
set ai
```

to turn on auto-indentation. You don't need the : before *ex* commands in this file.

[18]
Learning vi

There are a number of good tutorials and references to *vi* available, both online as well as in print. The book *Learning the vi editor* by Linda Lamb and O'Reilly & Associates is a good place to look for more information. If you have Internet access, the *comp.editors vi* archives contain a number of reference and tutorial documents, as well as interesting *vi* hacks. **alf.uib.no:/pub/vi** is the archive home site. It is mirrored at *cs.uwp.edu* and elsewhere.

The Emacs Editor

Text editors are among the most important applications in the UNIX world. They are used so often that many people spend more time within an editor than anywhere else on their UNIX system. The same holds true for Linux.

The choice of an editor can be a religious one. Many editors exist, but the UNIX community has arranged itself into two major groups: the Emacs camp, and the *vi* camp. Actually, adherents to *vi* seem to be dwindling, perhaps because *vi* is an aging editor with a somewhat non-intuitive user interface. However, long-time users of *vi* (and single-finger typists) are able to use it much more efficiently than a more complex editor such as Emacs.

If *vi* is one end of the text editor spectrum, Emacs is the other. They are widely different in their design and philosophy. Emacs is the brainchild of Richard Stallman, founder of the Free Software Foundation and author of much of the GNU software.

Emacs is a very large system, with more features than any single UNIX application to date. It contains its own LISP language engine which you can use to write extensions and macros for the editor. (Many of the functions within Emacs are written in Emacs LISP). Emacs includes extensions for everything from compiling and debugging programs to reading and sending electronic mail to X Window System support and more. Emacs also includes its own online tutorial and documentation.

Firing It Up

Emacs is simply invoked as

```
$ emacs filename
```

For example, using the command *emacs wibble.txt*, you should see something like:

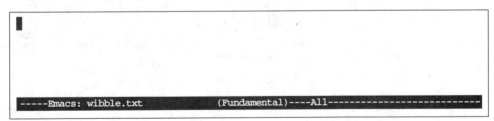

The mode line at the bottom indicates the name of the file as well as the type of buffer you're in (which here is Fundamental). Emacs supports many kinds of editing modes—Fundamental is the default for plain text files, but other modes exist for editing C and TEX source, modifying directories, etc. Each mode has certain key bindings and commands associated with it, as we'll see soon. Emacs typically determines the mode of the buffer based on the filename extension.

To the right of the buffer type is the word `All`, which means that you are currently looking at the entire file (which is empty). Typically you will see a percentage, which represents how far into the file you are. Usually in place of this a percentage is given, which represents how far into the file you are.

If you're running Emacs under the X Window System, a new window will be created for the editor, with a menu bar at the top, scrollbars, and other goodies. In the section "Emacs" we discuss Emacs's special features when used within X.

Simple Editing Commands

Emacs is much more straightforward than *vi* when it comes to basic text editing. The arrow keys should move the cursor around the buffer; if they don't (in case Emacs is not configured for your terminal), use the keys `Ctrl-P` (previous line), `Ctrl-N` (next line), `Ctrl-F` (forward character), and `Ctrl-B` (backwards character). Note that in Emacs lingo `C-p` means `Ctrl-p`, and `M-p` (or `Meta-p`) is equivalent to `Alt-p`. And, as you might guess, `C-M-p` means `Ctrl-Alt-p`.

If you find the Alt key uncomfortable, press Esc and then `p`. Pressing and releasing Esc is equivalent to holding down Alt.

Already we must take the first aside on our tour of Emacs. Literally every command and key within Emacs is customizable. That is, with a "default" Emacs configuration, `C-p` maps to the internal function *previous-line*, which moves the cursor (also called "point") to the previous line. However, you can easily rebind different keys to these functions, or write new functions and bind keys to them, and so forth. Unless otherwise stated, the keys that we introduce here work for the default Emacs configuration. Later we'll show you how to customize the keys for your own use.

Back to editing: Using the arrow keys or one of the equivalents given above will move the cursor around the current buffer. Just start typing text, and it will be inserted at the current cursor location. The Backspace or Delete key should delete text at the cursor. If it doesn't, we'll show a way to fix it in the section "Tailoring Emacs." Therefore you can begin to type:

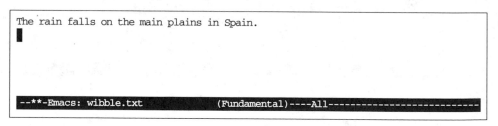

The keys C-a and C-e will move the cursor to the beginning and end of the current line, respectively. C-v will move forward a page; M-v will move back a page. There are many more basic editing commands, but we'll allow the Emacs online documentation (which we'll discuss shortly) to fill those in.

In order to get out of Emacs, use the command C-x C-c. This is the first of the extended commands that we've seen; many Emacs commands require several keys. C-x alone is a "prefix" to other keys. In this case pressing C-x followed by C-c will quit Emacs, first asking for confirmation if you want to quit without saving changes to the buffer.

You can use C-x C-s to save the current file, and C-x C-f to "find" another file to edit. For example, typing C-x C-f will present you with a prompt such as:

```
Find file: /home/loomer/mdw/.rV " "
```

where the current directory is displayed. After this you can type the name of the file to find. Pressing the Tab key will do filename completion similar to that used in *bash* and *tcsh*. For example, entering

```
Find file: /home/loomer/mdw/.bash.rV " "
```

and pressing Tab will open up another buffer, showing all possible completions, as so:

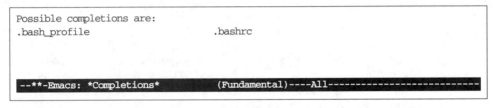

```
Possible completions are:
.bash_profile                    .bashrc



--**-Emacs: *Completions*        (Fundamental)----All---------------------------
```

After you complete the filename, the *Completions* buffer will go away and the new file will be displayed for editing. This is one example of how Emacs uses temporary buffers to present information.

Emacs allows you to use multiple buffers when editing text; each buffer may contain a different file that you're editing. When you load a file with C-x C-f, a new buffer is created to edit the file, but the original buffer isn't deleted.

You can switch to another buffer using the C-x b command, which will ask you for the name of the buffer (usually the name of the file within the buffer). For example, pressing C-x b will present the prompt:

```
Switch to buffer: (default wibble.txt)
```

The default buffer is the previous one visited. Press Enter to switch to the default buffer, or type another buffer name. Using C-x C-b will present a buffer list (in a buffer of its own), as so:

```
MR Buffer         Size  Mode          File
-- ------         ----  ----          ----
.   wibble.txt     44   Fundamental   /home/loomer/mdw/wibble.txt
    .bashrc       1763  Fundamental   /home/loomer/mdw/.bashrc
    *scratch*       0   Lisp Interaction
*   *Buffer List*  265  Buffer Menu
```

Popping up the buffer menu splits the Emacs screen into two "windows," which you can switch between using C-x o. More than two concurrent windows are possible as well. In order to view just one window at a time, switch to the appropriate one and press C-x 1. This hides all of the other windows, but you can switch to them later using the C-x b command just described. Using C-x k actually deletes a buffer from Emacs's memory.

Tutorial and Online Help

[16] GNU
Emacs manual

Already Emacs is looking a bit complex; that is simply because it's such a flexible system. Before we go any further it will be instructive to introduce Emacs's built-in online help and tutorial. This documentation has also been published in book form.

Using the C-h command will give you a list of help options on the last line of the display. Pressing C-h again will describe what they are. In particular, C-h followed by t will drop you into the Emacs tutorial. It should be quite self-explanatory, and an interactive tutorial about Emacs will tell you much more about the system than we can hope to cover here.

After going through the Emacs tutorial you should get accustomed to the Info system, where the rest of the Emacs documentation resides. C-h followed by i enters the Info reader. A mythical Info page might look like this:

```
File: intercal.info,  Node: Top,  Next: Instructions,  Up: (dir)

    This file documents the the Intercal interpreter for Linux.

  * Menu:

  * Instructions::     How to read this manual.
  * Overview::         Preliminary information.
  * Examples::         Example Intercal programs and bugs.
  * Concept Index::    Index of concepts.
```

As you see, text is presented along with a menu to other "nodes." Pressing m and then entering a node name from the menu will allow you to read that note. You can read nodes sequentially by pressing n, which jumps to the next node in the document (indicated by the information line at the top of the buffer). Here, the next node is Instructions, which is the first node in the menu.

Each node also has a link to the parent node (Up), which here is (dir), meaning the Info page directory. Pressing u will take you to the parent node. In addition, each node has a link to the previous node, if it exists (in this case, it does not). The p command moves to the previous node. The l command will return you to the node most recently visited.

Within Info, pressing ? will give you a list of commands, and pressing h will present you with a short tutorial on using the system. Since you're running Info within Emacs, you can use Emacs commands as well (such as C-x b to switch to another buffer).

Other online help is available within Emacs. Pressing C-h C-h will give you a list of help options. One of these is C-h k, after which you press a key, and documentation about the function that is bound to that key appears.

Deleting, Copying, and Moving Text

There are various ways to move and duplicate blocks of text within Emacs. These methods involve use of the *mark*, which is simply a "remembered" cursor location that you can set using various commands. The block of text between the current cursor location (*point*) and the mark is called the *region*.

The mark can be set using the key C-@ (or C-Space on most systems). Moving the cursor to a location and pressing C-@ sets the mark at that position. You can now move the cursor to another location within the document, and the region is defined as the text between mark and point.

Many Emacs commands operate on the region. The most important of these commands deal with deleting and yanking text. The command C-w will delete the current region and save it in the *kill ring*. The kill ring is a list of text blocks that have been deleted. You can then paste (*yank*) the text at another location, using the C-y command. (Note that the semantics of the term *yank* differ between *vi* and Emacs. In *vi*, "yanking" text is equivalent to adding it to the undo register without deleting it, while in Emacs, "yank" means to paste text.). Using the kill ring, you can paste not only the most recently deleted block of text, but also blocks of text that were deleted previously.

For example, type the following text into an Emacs buffer:

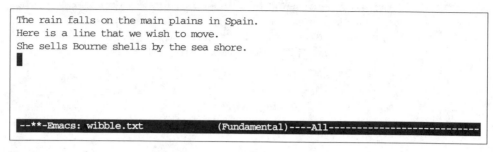

```
The rain falls on the main plains in Spain.
Here is a line that we wish to move.
She sells Bourne shells by the sea shore.
```
`--**-Emacs: wibble.txt                    (Fundamental)----All--------------------------`

Now, move the cursor to the beginning of the second line ("Here is a line..."), and set the mark with C-@. Move to the end of the line (with C-e), and delete the region, using C-w. The buffer should now look like:

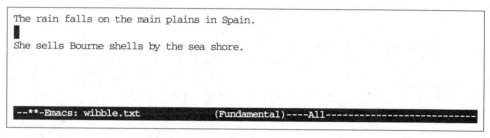

```
The rain falls on the main plains in Spain.

She sells Bourne shells by the sea shore.
```
`--**-Emacs: wibble.txt                    (Fundamental)----All--------------------------`

In order to yank the text just deleted, move the cursor to the end of the buffer, and press C-y. The line should be pasted at the new location:

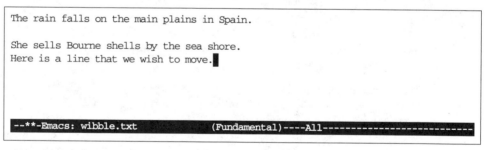

```
The rain falls on the main plains in Spain.

She sells Bourne shells by the sea shore.
Here is a line that we wish to move.
```
`--**-Emacs: wibble.txt                    (Fundamental)----All--------------------------`

Pressing C-y repeatedly will insert the text multiple times.

You can copy text in a similar fashion. Using M-w instead of C-w will copy the region into the kill ring without deleting it. (Remember that M- means holding down the Alt key, or pressing Esc before the w.)

Text that is deleted using other kill commands, such as C-k, is also added to the kill ring. This means that you don't need to set the mark and use C-w to move a block of text; any deletion command will do.

In order to recover previously-deleted blocks of text (which are saved on the kill ring), use the command M-y after yanking with C-y. M-y replaces the yanked text with the previous block from the kill ring. Pressing M-y repeatedly will cycle through the contents of the kill ring. This feature can be very useful if you wish to move or copy multiple blocks of text. Emacs also provides a more general *register* mechanism, similar to that found in *vi*, but use of the kill ring is versatile enough for most needs.

Searching and Replacing

The most common way to search for a string within Emacs is to press C-s. This starts what is called an *incremental search*. You then start entering the characters you are looking for. Each time you press a character, Emacs searches forward for a string matching everything you've typed so far. If you make a mistake, just press the Delete key and continue typing the right characters. If the string cannot be found, Emacs beeps. If you find an occurrence, but you want to keep searching for another one, press C-s again.

You can also search backward this way using the C-r key. Several other types of searches exist, including a regular expression search that you can invoke by pressing M-C-s. This lets you search for something like jo.*n, which matches names like John, Joan, and Johann. (By default, searches are not case-sensitive.)

To replace a string, enter M-%. You are prompted for the string that is currently in the buffer, and then the one you want to replace it with. Emacs displays each place in the buffer where the string lies, and asks you if you want to replace this occurrence. Press the Space bar to replace the string, the Delete key to skip this string, and a period to stop the search.

If you know that you want to replace all occurrences of a string that follow your current place in the buffer, without being queried for each one, enter M-x *string*. (The M-x key allows you to enter the name of an Emacs function and execute it, without use of a key binding. Many Emacs functions are available only via M-x, unless you bind them to keys yourself.) A regular expression can be replaced by entering M-x *regexp*.

Running Commands and Programming Within Emacs

Emacs provides interfaces for many programs, which you can run within an Emacs buffer. For example, Emacs modes exist for reading and sending electronic mail, reading Usenet news, compiling programs, and interacting with the shell. In this section we'll introduce some of these features.

To send electronic mail from within Emacs, use C-x m. This will open up a buffer that will allow you to compose and send an e-mail message.

```
To:
Subject:
--text follows this line--
█




-----Emacs: *mail*                    (Mail)----All-------------------------------
```

Simply enter your message within this buffer, and use C-c C-s to send it. You can also insert text from other buffers, extend the interface with your own Elisp functions, and so on.

RMAIL is Emacs's interface for reading electronic mail. Many users prefer it to other mail readers, because Emacs can be used directly as the editor for both sending and reading mail. To start RMAIL, use the command M-x rmail.

When you run RMAIL, Emacs will convert messages in your incoming mailbox to a special format that it uses to keep track of messages, and mail will be moved to the file *RMAIL* in your home directory. Therefore, be careful! Your incoming mail file will be converted to RMAIL format, and to convert it back (in case you don't want to use RMAIL as your mail reader), you need to use the M-x unrmail function.

When you start RMAIL, a buffer will be created, displaying the first message in your inbox. The n and p commands can be used to display the previous and next messages. (As with all Emacs modes, using C-h m will give you a summary of the available keys.) While you're viewing a message, the r key replies to that message, opening a mail buffer (as described above) with the header fields initialized. While in the mail buffer you can use C-c C-y to insert the original message.

Within RMAIL, the h command will display a summary of the messages in your mailbox, as so:

```
  11  17-Feb                     johnsonm@sunsite  Re: Which release?

  12  25-Feb                              schar  Vision Group meeting
  13  26-Feb                  okir@monad.swb.de  Re: Spaces in .ms?
  14  26-Feb           wirzeniu@cc.helsinki.fi  Re: LDP
--%%-Emacs: RMAIL-summary         (RMAIL Summary)----50%-------------------------
```

Several M-x commands are available in summary mode for sorting the list, and so forth. RMAIL commands such as n, p, and r may be used as well.

Similar to the RMAIL mail interface is GNUS, the Emacs-based newsreader, which you can start with the M-x gnus command. After startup (and a bit of chewing on your *.newsrc* file), a list of newsgroups will be presented, along with a count of unread articles for each.

```
   10: comp.os.linux.development
    0: cucs.system
   32: alt.fan.warlord
  195: alt.folklore.urban
--- GNUS: List of Newsgroups        (Newsgroup {cloyd.cs})--6%--------------------
```

Using the arrow keys, you can select a newsgroup that you wish to read. Press the Space bar to begin reading articles from that group. Two buffers will be displayed, one containing a list of articles, and the other displaying the current article. Using n and p will move to the next and previous articles, f and F will follow up to the current article (either with or without including the current article), and r and R will reply to the article via electronic mail. There are many other GNUS commands; use C-h m for a list. If you're used to a newsreader such as *rn*, GNUS will be somewhat familiar.

Emacs provides a number of modes for editing various types of files. For example, there is C mode, for editing C source code, and TEX mode, for editing (surprise) TEX source. Each of these modes boast features that make editing the appropriate type of file much easier.

For example, within C mode, you can use the command M-x compile which will by default run *make –k* in the current directory, and redirect errors to another buffer. For example, the compilation buffer may contain:

```
cd /home/loomer/mdw/pgmseq/
make -k
gcc -O -O2 -I. -I../include -c stream_load.c -o stream_load.o
stream_load.c:217: syntax error before `struct'
stream_load.c:217: parse error before `struct'
```

You can move the cursor to a line containing an error message, press C-c C-c, and the cursor will jump to that line in the corresponding source buffer (opening a buffer for the appropriate source file if one does not already exist). Now you can edit and compile programs entirely within Emacs.

Chapter 6

Emacs also provides a complete interface to the *gdb* debugger, which is described in the section "Using Emacs with gdb" in Chapter 6.

Usually, Emacs will select the appropriate mode for the buffer based on the filename extension. For example, editing a file with the extension *.c* in the filename will automatically select C mode for that buffer.

Shell mode is one of the most popular Emacs extensions. Shell mode allows you to interact with the shell in an Emacs buffer, using the command M-x shell. Editing shell command lines and using command history can be done with standard Emacs commands. You can also run single shell commands from Emacs using M-!. If you use M-|, instead, the contents of the current region will be piped to the given shell command as standard input. This is a general interface for running subprograms from within Emacs.

Tailoring Emacs

The Emacs online documentation should be sufficient to get you on the track to learning more about the system, and to growing accustomed to it. However, sometimes it can be hard to locate some of the most helpful hints for getting started. Here we'll present a rundown on certain customization options that many Emacs users choose to employ, to make life easier.

The Emacs personal customization file is *.emacs*, which should reside in your home directory. This file should contain code, written in Emacs LISP, which runs or defines functions to customize your Emacs environment. (If you've never written LISP before, don't worry—most customizations using it are quite simple.)

One of the most common things that users customize are key bindings. For instance, if you use Emacs to read your mail, you can bind the key C-c r to execute the rmail function. Put this in your *.emacs* file:

```
; Provide quick way to read mail.
(global-set-key "\C-cr" 'rmail)
```

Comments in Emacs Lisp start with a semicolon. The command that follows runs the command *global-set-key*. Now you don't have to type in the long sequence M-x rmail every time you get that little message Mail in your mode line. Just press the two characters C-c r. This will work anywhere in Emacs—no matter what mode your buffer is in—because it is "global."

You don't always want your key mappings to be global. As you use TEX mode, C mode, and other modes defined by Emacs, you'll find useful things that you'd like to do only in a single mode. Here, we define a simple Lisp function to insert some characters into C code, and then bind the function to a key for our convenience:

```
(defun start-if-block()
  (interactive)
  (insert "if () {\n}\n")
  (backward-char 6)
)
```

We start the function by declaring it "interactive" so that we can invoke it (otherwise, it would be used only internally by other functions). Then we use the *insert* function to put the following characters into our C buffer:

```
if () {
}
```

Strings in Emacs can contain standard C escape characters. Here we've used \n for a newline.

Now we have a template for an if block. To put on the ribbon and the bow, our function also moves backwards six characters so that point is within the parentheses, and we can immediately start typing an expression.

Our whole goal was to make it easy to insert these characters, so now let's bind our function to a key.

```
(define-key c-mode-map "\C-ci" 'start-if-block)
```

The *define-key* function binds a key to a function. By specifying `c-mode-map` we indicate that the key works only in C mode. There is also a `tex-mode-map` for TEX mode, a `lisp-mode-map` that you will want to know about if you play with your *.emacs* file a lot, and so on.

If you're interested in writing your own Emacs LISP functions, you should read the Info pages for *elisp*, which should be available on your system.

Now for a very important customization you may need. On many terminals the Backspace key sends the character C-h, which is the Emacs help key. To fix this, you should change the internal table that Emacs uses to interpret keys as follows:

```
(keyboard-translate ?\C-h ?\C-?)
```

Pretty cryptic code. \C-h is recognizable as the Control key pressed with h, which happens to produce the same ASCII code (8) as the Backspace key. \C-? represents the Delete key (ASCII code 127). Don't confuse this question mark with the question marks that precede each backslash. ?\C-h means "the ASCII code corresponding to \C-h." You could just as well specify 8 directly.

So now, both Backspace and C-h will delete. You've lost your help key. Therefore, another good customization would be to bind another key to C-h. Let's use C-\, which isn't used very often for anything else. You have to double the backslash when you specify it as a key.

```
(keyboard-translate ?\C-\\ ?\C-h)
```

xmodmap(1)

On the X Window System, there is a way to change the code sent by your Backspace key using the *xmodmap* command, but we'll have to leave it up to you to do your own research. It is not a completely portable solution (so we can't show you an example that we guarantee will work for you), and it may be too sweeping for your taste (it also changes the meaning of the Backspace key in your *xterm* shell and everywhere else).

There are other key bindings that you may wish to employ. For example, you may prefer to use the keys C-f and C-b to scroll forward (or backward) a page at a time, as in *vi*. In your *.emacs* file you might include the lines:

```
(global-set-key "\C-f" 'scroll-up)
(global-set-key "\C-b" 'scroll-down)
```

Again, we have to issue a caveat: be careful not to redefine keys that have other important uses. (One way to find out is to use C-h k to tell you what a key does in the current mode. You should also consider that the key may have definitions in other modes.) In particular, you'll lose access to a lot of functions if you rebind the *prefix keys* that start commands, such as C-x and C-c.

You can create your own prefix keys, if you really want to extend your current mode with lots of new commands. Use something like:

```
(global-unset-key "\C-d")
(global-set-key "\C-d\C-f" 'my-function)
```

First, we must unbind the C-d key (which simply deletes the character under the cursor), in order to use it as a prefix for other keys. Now, pressing C-d C-f will execute *my-function*.

You may also prefer to use another mode besides Fundamental or Text for editing "vanilla" files. Indented Text mode, for example, will automatically indent lines of text relative to the previous line (as with the :set ai function in *vi*). To turn on this mode by default, use:

```
; Default mode for editing text
(setq default-major-mode 'indented-text-mode)
```

You should also rebind the Return key to indent the next line of text:

```
(define-key indented-text-mode-map "\C-m" 'newline-and-indent)
```

Emacs also provides "minor" modes, which are modes that you can use along with major modes. For example, Overwrite mode is a minor mode that causes text to overwrite that in the buffer, instead of inserting it. To bind the key C-r to toggle Overwrite mode, use the command:

```
; Toggle overwrite mode.
(global-set-key "\C-r" 'overwrite-mode)
```

Another minor mode is Autofill, which will automatically wrap lines as you type them. That is, instead of pressing Return at the end of each line of text, you may continue typing and Emacs will automatically break the line for you. To enable Autofill mode, use the commands:

```
(setq text-mode-hook 'turn-on-auto-fill)
(setq fill-column 72)
```

This will turn on Autofill mode whenever you enter Text mode (through the *text-mode-hook* function). It also sets the point at which to break lines at 72 characters.

Text and Document Processing

In the first chapter, we mentioned briefly the various text processing systems available for Linux, and how they differ from word processing systems that you may be familiar with. While most word processors allow the user to enter text in a What-You-See-Is-What-You-Get environment, text processing systems have the user enter source text using a text formatting language, which can be modified with any text editor. (In fact, Emacs provides special modes for editing various types of text formatting languages.) Then, the source is processed into a printable (or viewable) document with the text processor itself.

In this section we'll talk about three of the most popular text processing systems for Linux: TEX, *groff,* and Texinfo.

TEX and LATEX

TEX is a professional text-processing system for all kinds of documents, articles, and books—especially those that contain a great deal of mathematics. It is somewhat of a "low-level" text processing language, for it describes to the system how to lay out text on the page, how it should be spaced, and so forth. TEX doesn't concern itself directly with higher-level elements of text such as chapters, sections, footnotes, and so forth (those things that you, the writer, care about the most). For this reason, TEX is known as a functional text formatting language (referring to the actual physical layout of text on a page), rather than a logical one (referring to logical elements such as chapters and sections). TEX was designed by Donald E. Knuth, one of the world's foremost experts in programming. One of Knuth's motives for developing TEX was to produce a typesetting system powerful enough to handle the mathematics formatting needs for his series of computer science textbooks. Knuth ended up taking an eight-year detour to finish TEX—most would agree that the result was well worth the wait.

Of course, TEX is very extensible, and it is possible to write macros for TEX which would allow writers to concern themselves primarily with the logical, rather then the physical, format of the document. In fact, a number of such macro packages have been developed—the most popular of which is LATEX, a set of extensions for TEX designed by Leslie Lamport. LATEX commands are concerned mostly with logical structure, but because LATEX is just a set of macros on top of TEX, you can use plain TEX commands as well. LATEX greatly simplifies the use of TEX, hiding most of the low-level functional features from the writer.

In order to write well-structured documents using TEX, you would either have to decide on a pre-built macro package such as LATEX, or develop your own (or use a combination of the two). In *The TEXbook,* Knuth presents his own set of macros that he used for production of the book. As you might expect, they include commands for beginning new chapters, sections, and the like—somewhat similar to their LATEX counterparts. In this section, we'll concentrate on the use of LATEX, which provides support for many types of documents: technical articles, manuals, books, letters, and so on. As with plain TEX, LATEX is extensible as well.

Learning the ropes

If you're never used a text formatting system before, there are a number of new concepts that you should be aware of. As we said, text processing systems start with a source document, which you enter with a plain text editor such as Emacs. The source is written in a text formatting language, which includes the text that you wish to appear in your document, as well as commands that tell the text processor how to format it. In the first chapter we gave a simple example of what the LaTeX language looks like and what kind of output it produces.

So, without further ado, let's dive in and see how to write a simple document, and format it, from start to finish. As a demonstration we'll show how to use LaTeX to write a short business letter. Sit down at your favorite text editor, and enter the following text into a file (without the line numbers, of course). Call it *letter.tex*:

```
1  \documentstyle{letter}
2  \address{755 Chmod Way \\ Apt 0x7F \\
3          Pipeline, N.M. 09915}
4  \signature{Boomer Petway}
5
6  \begin{document}
7  \begin{letter}{O'Reilly and Associates, Inc. \\
8               103 Morris Street Suite A \\
9               Sebastopol, C.A. 95472}
10
11 \opening{Dear Mr. O'Reilly,}
12
13 I would like to comment on the \LaTeX\ example as presented in
14 Chapter~5 of {\em Running Linux}. Although it was a valiant effort,
15 I find that the example falls somewhat short of what one might expect in
16 a discussion of text formatting systems. In a future edition of the book,
17 I suggest that you replace the example with one that is more instructive.
18
19 \closing{Thank you,}
20
21 \end{letter}
22 \end{document}
```

This is a complete LaTeX document for the business letter that we wish to send. As you can see, it contains the actual text of the letter, with a number of commands (using backslashes and braces) thrown in. Let's walk through it.

Line 1 uses the documentstyle command to specify the type of document that we're producing (which is a letter). Commands in LaTeX begin with a backslash and are followed by the actual command name, which is in this case documentstyle. Following the command name are any arguments, enclosed in braces. LaTeX supports several document styles, such as article, report, and book, and you can define your own. Specifying the document style defines global macros for use within the TeX document, such as the address and signature commands used on lines 2-4. As you might guess, the address and signature commands are used to specify your own address and name in the letter. The double-backslashes (\\) that appear in the address are used to generate linebreaks in the resulting output of the address.

A word about how LaTeX processes input: As with most text-formatting systems, whitespace, linebreaks, and other such features in the input source are not treated literally in the output. Therefore, you can break lines more or less wherever you please—when formatting paragraphs, LaTeX will fit the lines back together again. Of course, there are exceptions: blank lines in the input are used to begin new paragraphs, and there are commands to force LaTeX to treat the source text literally.

On line 6, the command \begin{document} is used to signify the beginning of the document as a whole. Everything enclosed within the \begin{document} and \end{document} on line 22 is considered part of the text to be formatted; anything before \begin{document} is called the *preamble* and is used to define formatting parameters before the actual body.

On lines 7-9, \begin{letter} is used to begin the actual letter. This is required because you may have many letters within a single source file, and a \begin{letter} is needed for each. This command takes as an argument the address of the intended recipient; as with the address command, double-backslashes are used to signify linebreaks in the address.

Line 11 uses the opening command to open the letter. Following on lines 12-18 is the actual body of the letter. As straightforward as it may seem, there are a few tricks hidden in the body as well. On line 13 the LaTeX command is used to generate the LaTeX logo. You'll notice that a backslash follows the LaTeX command as well as preceding it; the trailing backslash is used to force a space after the word "LaTeX." This is because TeX ignores spaces after command invocations, the command must be followed by a backslash and a space. (Otherwise, "LaTeX is fun" would appear as "LaTeXis fun.")

There are two quirks of note on line 14. First of all, there is a tilde (~) present between "Chapter" and "5," which is used to cause a space to appear between the two words, but to prevent a linebreak between them in the output (that is, to prevent "Chapter" from being on the end of a line, and "5" to be on the beginning of the next). You need only use the tilde to generate a space between two words that should be stuck together on the same line, as in Chapter~5 and Mr.~Jones. (In retrospect, we could have used the tilde in the \begin{letter} and opening commands, although it's doubtful that TeX would break a line anywhere within the address or the opening.)

The second thing to take note of on line 14 is the use of \em to generate *emphasized text* in the output. LaTeX supports various other fonts, including **boldface** \bf, and typewriter \tt.

Line 19 uses the closing command to close off the letter. This also has the effect of appending the signature used on line 4 after the closing in the output. Lines 21–22 use the commands \end{letter} and \end{document} to end the letter and document environments begun on lines 6 and 7.

You'll notice that none of the commands in the LaTeX source have anything to do with setting up margins, line spacing, or other functional issues of text formatting. That's all taken care of by the LaTeX macros on top of the TeX engine. LaTeX provides reasonable defaults for these parameters; if you wanted to change any of these formatting options, you could use other LaTeX commands (or lower-level TeX commands) to modify them.

We don't expect you to understand all of the intricacies of using LaTeX from such a limited example, although this should give you an idea of how a living, breathing LaTeX document looks. Now, let's format the document in order to print it out.

Formatting and printing

Believe it or not, the command used to format LaTeX source files into something printable is *latex*. After editing and saving *letter.tex*, above, you should be able to use the command:

```
eggplant$ latex letter
This is TeX, C Version 3.141
(letter.tex
LaTeX Version 2.09 <25 March 1992>
(/usr/TeX/lib/tex/macros/LaTeX/letter.sty
Standard Document Style `letter' <25 Mar 92>.
) [1] )
Output written on letter.dvi (1 page, 1152 bytes).
Transcript written on letter.log.
eggplant$
```

latex assumes the extension *.tex* for source files. Here, LaTeX has processed the source *letter.tex* and saved the results in the file *letter.dvi*. This is a "device-independent" file which can be used to generate printable output on a variety of printers. Various tools exist for converting *.dvi* files to PostScript, HP LaserJet, and other formats, as we'll see shortly.

Instead of immediately printing your letter, you may wish to preview it to be sure that everything looks right. If you're running the X Window System, you can use the *xdvi* command to preview *.dvi* files on your screen. What about printing the letter? First, you need to convert the *.dvi* to something that your printer can handle. DVI drivers exist for many printer types. Almost all of the program names begin with the three characters "dvi," as in *dvips*, *dvilj*, and so forth. If your system doesn't have one that you need, you will have to get the appropriate driver from the TeX archives, if you have Internet access. See the FAQ for *comp.text.tex* for details.

If you're lucky enough to have a PostScript printer, you can use *dvips* to generate PostScript from the *.dvi*:

```
eggplant$ dvips -o letter.ps letter.dvi
```

You can then print the PostScript using *lpr*. Or, to do this in one step:

```
eggplant$ dvips letter.dvi | lpr
```

In addition, *dvilj* will print *.dvi* files on HP LaserJet printers, and *eps* will print *.dvi* files on Epson-compatible printers.

If you can't seem to find a DVI driver for your printer, you might be able to use GhostScript to convert PostScript (produced by *dvips*) into something that you can print. Although some of GhostScript's fonts are less than optimal, it does allow you to use Adobe fonts (which you can obtain for MS-DOS, and use with GhostScript under Linux). GhostScript also provides an SVGA preview mode which you can use if you're not running X.

At any rate, after you manage to format and print the example letter, it should end up looking something like the following.

---

755 Chmod Way
Apt 0x7F
Pipeline, N.M. 09915

March 26, 1994

O'Reilly and Associates, Inc.
103 Morris Street Suite A
Sebastopol, C.A. 95472

Dear Mr. O'Reilly,

I would like to comment on your LATEX example as presented in Chapter 5 of *Running Linux*. Although it was a valiant effort, I find that the example falls somewhat short of what one might expect in a discussion of text formatting systems. In a future edition of the book, I suggest that you replace the example with one that is more instructive.

Thank you,

Boomer Petway

Further reading

[23] LATEX
[22] TEXbook
[24] Making
TEX Work

If LATEX seems right for your document-processing needs, and you have been able to get at least this initial example working and printed out, we suggest checking into Leslie Lamport's *LATEX User's Guide and Reference Manual*, which includes everything that you need to know about LATEX for formatting letters, articles, books, and more. If you're interested in hacking, or want to know more about the underlying workings of TEX (which can be invaluable), Donald Knuth's *The TEXbook* is the definitive guide to the system. Norman Walsh's *Making TEX Work* explains how to administer TEX and get it working with other programs.

comp.text.tex is the Usenet newsgroup for questions and information about these systems, although information found there assumes that you have access to TEX and LATEX documentation of some kind, such as the manuals mentioned above.

groff

Long before TEX there was *troff*, and later, *nroff*. These are text processing systems developed at Bell Labs for the original implementation of UNIX (in fact, the development of UNIX was spurred, in part, to support such a text-processing system). The first version of this text processor was called *roff* (for "runoff"); later came *troff*, which generated output for a particular typesetter in use at the time. *nroff* was a later version that became the standard text processor on UNIX systems everywhere. *groff* is GNU's implementation of *nroff* and *troff* that is used on Linux systems. It includes several extended features and drivers for a number of printing devices.

groff is capable of producing documents, articles, and books, much in the same vein as TEX. However, *groff* (as well as the original *nroff*) has one intrinsic feature that is absent from TEX and variants: the ability to produce plain-ASCII output. While TEX is great for producing documents to be printed, *groff* is able to produce plain ASCII to be viewed online (or printed directly as plain text on even the simplest of printers). If you're going to be producing documentation to be viewed online as well as in printed form, *groff* may be the way to go (although there are other alternatives as well—Texinfo, which is discussed later, being one).

groff also has the benefit of being much smaller than TEX; it requires fewer support files and executables than even a minimal TEX distribution.

One special application of *groff* is to format UNIX manual pages. If you're a UNIX programmer, you'll eventually need to write and produce manual pages of some kind. In this section we'll introduce the use of *groff* through the writing of a short manual page.

As with TEX, *groff* uses a particular text formatting language to describe how to process the text. This language is slightly more cryptic than TEX, but also less verbose. In addition, *groff* provides several macro packages that are used on top of the basic *groff* formatter; these macro packages are tailored to a particular type of document. For example, the mgs macros are an ideal choice for writing articles and papers, while the man macros are used for manual pages.

Writing a manual page

Writing manual pages with *groff* is actually quite simple. In order for your manual page to look like other manual pages, you need to follow several conventions in the source, which are presented below. In this example, we'll write a manual page for a mythical command *coffee*, which controls your networked coffee machine in various ways.

Enter the following source with your text editor, and save the result as *coffee.man*.

```
1  .TH COFFEE 1 "23 March 94"
2  .SH NAME
3  coffee \- Control remote coffee machine
4  .SH SYNOPSIS
5  \fBcoffee\fP [ -h | -b ] [ -t \fItype\fP ] \fIamount\fP
6  .SH DESCRIPTION
7  \fIcoffee\fP queues a request to the remote coffee machine at the
8  device \fB/dev/cf0\fR. The required \fIamount\fP argument specifies
9  the number of cups, generally between 0 and 15 on ISO standard
10 coffee machines.
11 .SS Options
12 .TP
13 \fB-h\fP
14 Brew hot coffee. Cold is the default.
15 .TP
16 \fB-b\fP
17 Burn coffee. Especially useful when executing \fIcoffee\fP on behalf
18 of your boss.
19 .TP
20 \fB-t \fItype\fR
21 Specify the type of coffee to brew, where \fItype\fP is one of
22 \fBcolombian\fP, \fBregular\fP, or \fBdecaf\fP.
23 .SH FILES
24 .TP
25 \fI/dev/cf0\fR
26 The remote coffee machine device
27 .SH "SEE ALSO"
28 milk(5), sugar(5)
29 .SH BUGS
30 May require human intervention if coffee supply is exhausted.
```

Don't let the amount of obscurity in this source file frighten you. It helps to know that the character sequences \fB, \fI, and \fR are used to change the font to bold-face, italics, and roman type, respectively. \fP sets the font to the one previously selected.

Other *groff* requests appear on lines beginning with a dot (.). On line 1, we see that the .TH request is used to set the title of the manual page to COFFEE and the manual section to 1. (Manual section 1 is used for user commands, section 2 is for system calls, and so forth.) The .TH request also sets the date of the last manual page revision.

On line 2, the .SH request is used to start a section entitled NAME. Note that almost all UNIX manual pages use the section progression NAME, SYNOPSIS, DESCRIPTION, FILES, SEE ALSO, NOTES, AUTHOR, and BUGS, with extra optional sections as needed. This is just a convention used when writing manual pages, and isn't enforced by the software at all.

Line 3 gives the name of the command and a short description, after a dash (\-). You should use this format for the NAME section so that your manual page can be added to the *whatis* database used by the *man –k* and *apropos* commands.

On lines 4-5 we give the synopsis of the command syntax for *coffee*. Note that italic type \fI...\fP is used to denote parameters on the command line, and that optional arguments are enclosed in square brackets.

Lines 6–10 give a brief description of the command. Italic type is generally used to denote commands, filenames, and user options. On line 11, a subsection named Options is started with the .SS request. Following this on lines 11-22 is a list of options, presented using a tagged list. Each item in the tagged list is marked with the .TP request; the line *after* .TP is the tag, after which follows the item text itself. For example, the source on lines 12-14:

```
.TP
\fB-h\fP
Brew hot coffee. Cold is the default.
```

will appear as the following in the output:

```
-h      Brew hot coffee. Cold is the default.
```

You should document each command-line option for your program in this way.

Lines 23–26 make up the FILES section of the manual page, which describes any files that the command might use to do its work. A tagged list using the .TP request is used for this as well.

On lines 27-28, the SEE ALSO section is given, which provides cross-references to other manual pages of note. Notice that the string "SEE ALSO" following the .SH request on line 27 is in quotes; this is because .SH uses the first whitespace-delimited argument as the section title. Therefore any section titles that are more than one word need to be enclosed in quotes to make up a single argument. Finally, on lines 29-30, the BUGS section is presented.

Formatting and installing the manual page

In order to format this manual page and view it on your screen, use the command

```
eggplant$ groff -Tascii -man coffee.man | more
```

The *–Tascii* option tells *groff* to produce plain-ASCII output; *–man* tells *groff* to use the manual page macro set. If all goes well, the manual page should be displayed as:

```
COFFEE(1)                                              COFFEE(1)


NAME
       coffee - Control remote coffee machine
```

```
SYNOPSIS
        coffee [ -h | -b ] [ -t type ] amount

DESCRIPTION
        coffee  queues  a  request to the remote coffee machine at
        the device /dev/cf0. The required amount  argument  speci-
        fies the number of cups, generally between 0 and 12 on ISO
        standard coffee machines.

    Options
        -h      Brew hot coffee. Cold is the default.

        -b      Burn coffee. Especially useful when executing  cof-
                fee on behalf of your boss.

        -t type
                Specify  the  type of coffee to brew, where type is
                one of colombian, regular, or decaf.

FILES
        /dev/cf0
                The remote coffee machine device

SEE ALSO
        milk(5), sugar(5)

BUGS
        May  require  human  intervention  if  coffee  supply  is
        exhausted.
```

As mentioned before, *groff* is capable of producing other types of output. Using the −*Tps* option in place of −*Tascii* will produce PostScript output that you can save to a file, view with Ghostview, or print on a PostScript printer. −*Tdvi* will produce device-independent *.dvi* output similar to that produced by TEX.

If you wish to make the manual page available for others to view on your system, you need to install the *groff* source in a directory that is present on the users' MAN-PATH. The location for standard manual pages is */usr/man*. The source for section 1 manual pages should therefore go in */usr/man/man1*. The command

```
eggplant$ cp coffee.man /usr/man/man1/coffee.1
```

installs this manual page in */usr/man* for all to use (note the use of the *.1* filename extension, instead of *.man*). When *man coffee* is subsequently invoked, the manual page will be automatically reformatted, and the viewable text saved in */usr/man/cat1/coffee.1.Z.*

Chapter 3

If you can't copy manual page sources directly to */usr/man*, you can create your own manual page directory tree and add it to your MANPATH. See the section "Manual Pages" in Chapter 3, *Basic UNIX Commands and Concepts.*

Texinfo

Texinfo is a text-formatting system used by the GNU project to produce both online documentation, in the form of hypertext Info pages, and printed manuals, through TEX. It is documented completely through its own Info pages, which are readable within Emacs (using the C-h i command) or a separate Info reader such as *info*. If the GNU Info pages are installed in your system, complete Texinfo documentation is contained therein. Just as you'll find yourself using *groff* to write a manual page, you'll use Texinfo to write an Info document.

Writing the Texinfo source

In this section we're going to present a simple Texinfo source file, chunks at a time, and describe what each chunk does as we go along.

Our Texinfo source file will be called *vacuum.texi*. As usual, you can enter the source using a plain text editor.

```
\input texinfo @c -*-texinfo-*-
@c %**start of header
@setfilename vacuum.info
@settitle The Empty Info File
@setchapternewpage odd
@c %**end of header
```

This is the header of the Texinfo source. The first line is a TEX command used to input the Texinfo macros when producing printed documentation. Commands in Texinfo begin with the at-sign, @. The @c command begins a comment; here, the comment -*-texinfo-*- is a tag that tells Emacs that this is a Texinfo source file, so that Emacs can set the proper major mode. (Major modes were discussed earlier, in the section "Tailoring Emacs.")

The comments @c %**start of header and @c %**end of header are used to denote the Texinfo header. This is required if you wish to format just a portion of the Texinfo file. The @setfilename command is used to specify the filename to use for the resulting Info file, @settitle sets the title of the document, and @setchapternewpage odd tells Texinfo to start new chapters on an odd-numbered page. These are just cookbook routines which should be used for all Texinfo files.

The next section of the source file sets up the title page, which is used when formatting the document using TEX. These commands should be self-explanatory.

```
@titlepage
@title Vacuum
@subtitle The Empty Info File
@author by Tab U. Larasa
@end titlepage
```

Now we move on to the body of the Texinfo source. The Info file is divided into *nodes*, where each node is somewhat like a "page" in the document. Each node has links to the next, previous, and parent nodes, and can be linked to other nodes as cross-references. You can think of each node as a chapter or section within the document, with a menu to nodes below it. For example, a chapter-level node will have a menu that lists the sections within the chapter. Each section node will point to the chapter-level node as its parent. Each section will also point to the previous and next section, if they exist. This is a little complicated, but will become clear when you see it in action.

Each node is given a short name. The topmost node is called Top. The @node command is used to start a node; it takes as arguments the node name, the name of the next node, the previous node, and the parent node. As noted above, the next and previous nodes should be nodes on the same hierarchical level. The parent node is the node above the current one in the node "tree" (for example, the parent of Section 2.1 in a document is Chapter 2). A sample node hierarchy is depicted in Figure 5-1.

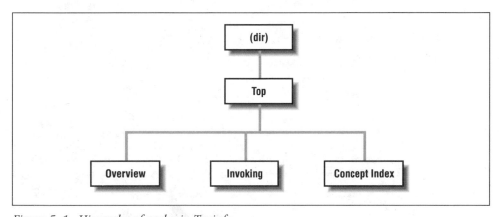

Figure 5-1. Hierarchy of nodes in Texinfo

Here is the source for the Top node:

```
@c      Node, Next, Previous, Up
@node Top ,         ,          , (dir)

@ifinfo
This Info file is a close approximation to a vacuum. It documents
absolutely nothing.
@end ifinfo

@menu
* Overview::            Overview of Vacuum
* Invoking::            How to use the Vacuum
* Concept Index::       Index of concepts
@end menu
```

The @node command is preceded by a comment, to remind us of the order of the arguments to @node. Here, Top has no previous or next node, so they are left blank. The parent node for Top is (dir), which denotes the system-wide Info page directory. Supposedly your Info file will be linked into the system's Info page tree, so you want the Top node to have a link back to the overall directory.

Following the @node command is an abstract for the overall document, enclosed in an @ifinfo...@end ifinfo pair. This is used because the actual text of the Top node should appear only in the Info file, not the TEX-generated printed document.

The @menu...@end menu commands demarcate the node's menu. Each menu entry includes a node name followed by a short description of the node. In this case, the menu points to the nodes Overview, Invoking, and Concept Index, the source for which appear later in the file. These three nodes are the three "chapters" in our document.

We continue with the Overview node, which is the first "chapter."

```
@c     Node,      Next,      Previous, Up
@node Overview, Invoking,           , Top
@chapter Overview of @code{vacuum}

@cindex Nothingness
@cindex Overview
@cindex Vacuum cleaners

A @code{vacuum} is a space entirely devoid of all matter. That means no
air, no empty beer cans, no dust, no nothing. Vacuums are usually found
in outer space. A vacuum cleaner is a device used to clean a vacuum.
See @xref{Invoking} for information on running @code{vacuum}.
```

The next node for Overview is Invoking, which is the second "chapter" node, and also the node to appear after Overview in the menu. Note that you can use just about any structure for your Texinfo documents; however, it is often useful to organize them so that nodes resemble chapters, sections, subsections, and so forth. It's up to you.

The @chapter command is used to begin a chapter, which has effect only when formatting the source with TEX. Similarly, the @section and @subsection commands are used to begin (you guessed it) sections and subsections in the resulting TEX document. The chapter (or section or subsection) name can be more descriptive than the brief name used for the node itself.

You'll notice that the @code... command is used in the chapter name. This is just one way to specify text to be emphasized in some way. @code should be used for the names of commands, as well as source code that appears in a program. This will cause the text within the @code... to be printed in constant-width type in the TEX output, and enclosed in quotes (like `this') in the Info file.

Following this are three @cindex commands, which are used to produce entries in the concept index at the end of the document. After this appears the actual text of the node. Again, @code is used to mark the name of the vacuum "command."

The @xref command is used to produce a cross-reference to another node, which the reader can follow with the f command in the Info-reader. @xref can also be used to make cross-references between other Texinfo documents. See the Texinfo documentation for a complete discussion.

Our next node is Invoking.

```
@node Invoking, Concept Index, Overview, Top
@chapter Running @code{vacuum}

@cindex Running @code{vacuum}
@code{vacuum} is executed as follows:

@example
vacuum @var{options} @dots{}
@end example
```

Here, @example...@end example is used to set off an example. Within the example, @var is used to denote a metavariable, a placeholder for a string provided by the user (in this case, the options given to the *vacuum* command). @dots{} produces an ellipsis. The example will appear as:

```
vacuum options ...
```

in the TEX-formatted document, and as

```
vacuum OPTIONS ...
```

in the Info file. Commands such as @code and @var provide emphasis which can be represented in different ways in the TEX and Info outputs.

Continuing the Invoking node, we have:

```
@cindex Options
@cindex Arguments
The following options are supported:

@cindex Getting help
@table @samp
@item -help
Print a summary of options.

@item -version
Print the version number for @code{vacuum}.

@cindex Empty vacuums
@item -empty
Produce a particularly empty vacuum. This is the default.
@end table
```

Here we have a table of the options that *vacuum* supposedly supports. The command `@table @samp` begins a two-column table (which ends up looking more like a tagged list), where each item is emphasized using the `@samp` command. `@samp` is similar to `@code` and `@var`, except that it's meant to be used for literal input, such as command-line options.

A normal Texinfo document would contain nodes for examples, information on reporting bugs, and much more, but for brevity we're going to wrap up this example with the final node, `Concept Index`. This is an index of concepts presented in the document, and is produced automatically with the `@printindex` command.

```
@node Concept Index, , Invoking, Top
@unnumbered Concept Index

@printindex cp
```

Here, `@printindex cp` tells the formatter to include the concept index at this point. There are other types of indices as well, such as a function index, command index, and so forth. All are generated with variants on the `@cindex` and `@printindex` commands.

The final three lines of our Texinfo source are

```
@shortcontents
@contents
@bye
```

This instructs the formatter to produce a "summary" table of contents (`@shortcontents`), a full table of contents (`@contents`), and to end formatting (`@bye`). `@shortcontents` produces a brief table of contents that lists only chapters and appendices. In reality only long manuals would require `@shortcontents` in addition to `@contents`.

Formatting Texinfo

To produce an Info file from the Texinfo source, use the *makeinfo* command. (This command, along with the other programs used to process Texinfo, are included in the Texinfo software distribution, which is sometimes bundled with Emacs.) The command

```
eggplant$ makeinfo vacuum.texi
```

will produce *vacuum.info* from *vacuum.texi*. *makeinfo* uses the output filename specified by the `@setfilename` in the source; you can change this using the *−o* option.

If the resulting Info file is large, *makeinfo* will split it into a series of files named *vacuum.info-1*, *vacuum.info-2*, and so on, where *vacuum.info* will be the "top-level" file that will point to the various split files. As long as all of the *vacuum.info* files are in the same directory, the Info reader should be able to find them.

You can also use the Emacs commands M-x makeinfo-region and M-x makeinfo-buffer to generate Info from the Texinfo source.

The Info file can now be viewed from within Emacs, using the C-h i command. Within Emacs Info-mode, you'll need to use the g command and specify the complete path to your Info file, as in:

```
Goto node: (/home/loomer/mdw/info/vacuum.info)Top
```

This is because Emacs usually looks for Info files only within its own Info directory (which may be */usr/local/emacs/info* on your system).

Another alternative is to use the Emacs-independent Info reader, *info*. The command

```
eggplant$ info -f vacuum.info
```

will invoke *info*, reading your new Info file.

If you wish to install the new Info page for all users on your system, you will need to add a link to it in the *dir* file in the Emacs *info* directory. The Texinfo documentation describes how to do this in detail.

To produce a printed document from the source, you will need to have TEX installed on your system. The Texinfo software comes with a TEX macro file, *texinfo.tex*, which includes all of the macros used by Texinfo for TEX formatting. If installed correctly, *texinfo.tex* should be in the TEX *inputs* directory on your system, where TEX can find it. If not, you can copy *texinfo.tex* to the directory where your Texinfo files reside.

First, process the Texinfo file using TEX:

```
eggplant$ tex vacuum.texi
```

This will produce a slew of files in your directory, some of which are associated with TEX, others of which are used to generate the index. The *texindex* command (which is included in the Texinfo package) is used to reformat the index into something that TEX can use. The next command to issue is therefore:

```
eggplant$ texindex vacuum.??
```

Using the ?? wildcard will run *texindex* on all files in the directory with two-letter extensions; these are the files produced by Texinfo for generating the index.

Finally, you need to re-format the Texinfo file using TEX, which will clear up cross-references and include the index.

```
eggplant$ tex vacuum.texi
```

This should leave you with *vacuum.dvi*, a device-independent file that you can now view with *xdvi* or convert into something printable. See the section "TEX and LATEX" earlier in the chapter for a discussion of how to print *.dvi* files.

As usual, there's much more to learn about this system. Texinfo has a complete set of Info pages of its own, which should be available in your Info reader. Or, now that you know the basics, you could format the Texinfo documentation sources yourself, using TEX. The *.texi* sources for the Texinfo documentation are found in the Texinfo source distribution.

The X Window System

We come now to the X Window System—one of the most powerful and important software packages available for Linux. If you've ever used X on a UNIX system before, you're in luck—there is very little that is different about running X under Linux than on other systems. And, if you've never had the occasion to use it before, never fear. Salvation is at hand.

It's difficult to describe the X Window System in a nutshell. X is a complete windowing graphics interface for UNIX systems. It provides a huge number of options to both the programmer and the user. For instance, there are at least half a dozen *window managers* available for X, each one offering a different interface for manipulating windows. By customizing the attributes of the window manager, you have complete control over how windows are placed on the screen, the colors and borders used to decorate them, and so forth.

X was originally developed by Project Athena at MIT and Digital Equipment Corporation. The current version of X is version 11 revision 6 (X11R6), which was first released in April 1994. Since the release of version 11, X has virtually taken over as the de facto standard for UNIX graphical environments. It is now developed and distributed by the X Consortium, an association that is composed of many large computer manufacturers.

Despite its commercial use, The X Window System remains distributable under a liberal license from the X Consortium. As such, a complete implementation of X is freely available for Linux systems. XFree86, an implementation of X for i386 UNIX systems, is the version used by Linux. It was derived from the X386 server on the MIT release tape, and includes many extensions and optimizations for popular video hardware used on Linux and other Intel-based UNIX systems.

In this section, we're going to (briefly) cover installation and configuration of X on your system, and then delve into the messy world of X customization from the user's point of view. We're also going to talk about a number of software applications that run under X, and give you a feel for using this powerful software without being intimidated by its complexity.

X Concepts

X is based on a client-server model in which the X *server* is a program that runs on your system and handles all access to the graphics hardware. An X *client* is an applications program that communicates with the server, sending it requests such as "draw a line" or "pay attention to keyboard input." The X server takes care of servicing these requests by drawing a line on the display, or sending user input (via the keyboard, mouse, whatever) to the client application. Examples of X clients are *xterm* (which emulates a terminal within a window), or *xman* (an X-based manual page reader).

It is important to note that X is a network-oriented graphics system. That is, X clients can run either locally (on the same system that the server is running), or remotely (on a system somewhere on a TCP/IP network). The X server listens to both local and remote network sockets for requests from clients. This feature is obviously quite powerful. If you have a connection to a TCP/IP network, you can log in to another system over the network, and run an X application there, directing it to display on your local X server.

Another concept to be aware of is X's idea of *window management*. Clients running under X are displayed within one or more *windows* on your screen. However, how windows are manipulated (placed on the display, resized, and so forth) and how they are decorated (the appearance of the window frames) is not controlled by the X server. Instead, it is handled by another X client called a *window manager* that runs concurrently with the other X clients. Your choice of window manager will decide to some extent how X as a whole looks and feels.

Hardware Requirements

As of XFree86 version 3.1, released in September 1994, the following video chipsets are supported. The documentation included with your video adaptor should specify the chipset used. If you are in the market for a new video card, or are buying a new machine that comes with a video card, have the vendor find out exactly what the make, model, and chipset of the video card is. This may require the vendor to call technical support on your behalf; vendors usually will be happy to do this. Many PC hardware vendors will state that the video card is a "standard SVGA card" which "should work" on your system. Explain that your software (mention Linux and XFree86!) does not support all video chipsets and that you must have detailed information.

You can also determine your videocard chipset by running the *SuperProbe* program included with the XFree86 distribution. This is covered in more detail below.

The following standard SVGA chipsets are supported:

- Tseng ET3000, ET4000AX, ET4000/W32

- Western Digital/Paradise PVGA1

- Western Digital WD90C00, WD90C10, WD90C11, WD90C24, WD90C30, WD90C31, WD90C33

- Genoa GVGA

- Trident TVGA8800CS, TVGA8900B, TVGA8900C, TVGA8900CL, TVGA9000, TVGA9000i, TVGA9100B, TVGA9200CX, TVGA9320, TVGA9400CX, TVGA9420

- ATI 18800, 18800-1, 28800-2, 28800-4, 28800-5, 28800-6, 68800-3, 68800-6, 68800AX, 68800LX, 88800

- NCR 77C22, 77C22E, 77C22E+

- Cirrus Logic CLGD5420, CLGD5422, CLGD5424, CLGD5426, CLGD5428, CLGD5429, CLGD5430, CLGD5434, CLGD6205, CLGD6215, CLGD6225, CLGD6235, CLGD6420

- Compaq AVGA

- OAK OTI067, OTI077

- Avance Logic AL2101

- MX MX68000, MX680010

- Video 7/Headland Technologies HT216-32

The following SVGA chipsets with accelerated features are also supported:

- 8514/A (and true clones)

- ATI Mach8, Mach32

- Cirrus CLGD5420, CLGD5422, CLGD5424, CLGD5426, CLGD5428, CLGD5429, CLGD5430, CLGD5434, CLGD6205, CLGD6215, CLGD6225, CLGD6235

- S3 86C911, 86C924, 86C801, 86C805, 86C805i, 86C928, 86C864, 86C964

- Western Digital WD90C31, WD90C33

- Weitek P9000

- IIT AGX-014, AGX-015, AGX-016

- Tseng ET4000/W32, ET4000/W32i, ET4000/W32p

Video cards using these chipsets are supported on all bus types, including VLB and PCI.

All of the above are supported in both 256 color and monochrome modes, with the exception of the Avance Logic, MX, and Video 7 chipsets, which are supported only in 256-color mode. If your video card has enough DRAM installed, many of the above chipsets are supported in 16 and 32 bits-per-pixel mode (specifically, some Mach32, P9000, S3, and Cirrus boards). The usual configuration is 8 bits per pixel (that is, 256 colors).

The monochrome server also supports generic VGA cards, the Hercules monochrome card, the Hyundai HGC1280, the Sigma LaserView, and the Apollo monochrome cards. On the Compaq AVGA, only 64k of video memory is supported for the monochrome server, and the GVGA has not been tested with more than 64k.

This list will undoubtedly expand as time passes. The release notes for the current version of XFree86 should contain the complete list of supported video chipsets.

One problem faced by the XFree86 developers is that some video card manufacturers use non-standard mechanisms for determining clock frequencies used to drive the card. Some of these manufacturers either don't release specifications describing how to program the card, or they require developers to sign a non-disclosure statement to obtain the information. This would obviously restrict the free distribution of the XFree86 software, something that the XFree86 development team is not willing to do. This had been a problem with cards manufactured by companies such as Diamond. Since release 3.1 of XFree86, however, Diamond has been working with the development team to provide free drivers for those cards.

The suggested setup for XFree86 under Linux is a 486 machine with at least 8 megabytes of RAM, and a video card with a chipset listed above. For optimal performance, we suggest using an accelerated card, such as an S3-chipset card. You should check the documentation for XFree86 and verify that your particular card is supported before taking the plunge and purchasing expensive hardware. Benchmark ratings comparisons for various video cards under XFree86 are posted to the Usenet newsgroups *comp.windows.x.i386unix* and *comp.os.linux.misc* regularly.

As a side note, my (Matt's) personal Linux system is a 486DX2-66, 20 megabytes of RAM, and is equipped with a VLB S3-864 chipset card with 2 megabytes of DRAM. I have run X benchmarks on this machine as well as on Sun Sparc IPX workstations. The Linux system is roughly 7 times faster than the Sparc IPX (for the curious, XFree86-3.1 under Linux, with this video card, runs at around 171,000 xstones; the Sparc IPX at around 24,000). In general, XFree86 on a Linux system with an accelerated SVGA card will give you much greater performance than that found on commercial UNIX workstations (which usually employ simple framebuffers for graphics).

Your machine will need at least 4 megabytes of physical RAM, and 16 megabytes of virtual RAM (for example, 8 megs physical and 8 megs swap). Remember that the more physical RAM that you have, the less that the system will swap to and from disk when memory is low. Because swapping is inherently slow (disks are very slow compared to memory), having 8 megabytes of RAM or more is necessary to run XFree86 comfortably. A system with 4 megabytes of physical RAM could run *much* (up to 10 times) more slowly than one with 8 megs or more.

Installing XFree86

The Linux binary distribution of XFree86 can be found on a number of FTP sites. On **sunsite.unc.edu**, it is found in the directory */pub/Linux/X11*. (At the time of this writing, the current version is 3.1; newer versions are released periodically).

It's quite likely that you obtained XFree86 as part of a Linux distribution, in which case downloading the software separately is not necessary. If you are downloading XFree86 directly, the following tables list the files in the XFree86-3.1 distribution.

One of the following servers is required:

File	Description
XF86-3.1-8514.tar.gz	Server for 8514-based boards
XF86-3.1-AGX.tar.gz	Server for AGX-based boards
XF86-3.1-Mach32.tar.gz	Server for Mach32-based boards
XF86-3.1-Mach8.tar.gz	Server for Mach8-based boards
XF86-3.1-Mono.tar.gz	Server for monochrome video modes
XF86-3.1-P9000.tar.gz	Server for P9000-based boards
XF86-3.1-S3.tar.gz	Server for S3-based boards
XF86-3.1-SVGA.tar.gz	Server for Super VGA-based boards
XF86-3.1-VGA16.tar.gz	Server for VGA/EGA-based boards
XF86-3.1-W32.tar.gz	Server for ET4000/W32-based boards

All of the following files are required:

File	Description
XF86-3.1-bin.tar.gz	The rest of the X11R6 binaries
XF86-3.1-cfg.tar.gz	Config files for *xdm, xinit,* and *fs*
XF86-3.1-doc.tar.gz	Documentation and manual pages
XF86-3.1-inc.tar.gz	Include files
XF86-3.1-lib.tar.gz	Shared X libraries and support files
XF86-3.1-fnt.tar.gz	Basic fonts

The following files are optional:

File	Description
XF86-3.1-ctrb.tar.gz	Selected *contrib* programs
XF86-3.1-extra.tar.gz	Extra XFree86 servers and binaries
XF86-3.1-lkit.tar.gz	Server linkkit for customization
XF86-3.1-fnt75.tar.gz	75-dpi screen fonts
XF86-3.1-fnt100.tar.gz	100-dpi screen fonts
XF86-3.1-fntbig.tar.gz	Large Kanji and other fonts
XF86-3.1-fntscl.tar.gz	Scaled fonts (Speedo, Type1)
XF86-3.1-man.tar.gz	Manual pages
XF86-3.1-pex.tar.gz	PEX binaries, includes, and libraries
XF86-3.1-slib.tar.gz	Static X libraries and support files
XF86-3.1-usrbin.tar.gz	Daemons which reside in */usr/bin*
XF86-3.1-xdmshdw.tar.gz	Shadow password version of *xdm*

The XFree86 directory should contain *README* files and installation notes for the current version.

Obtain the above files, create the directory */usr/X11R6* (as **root**), and unpack the files from */usr/X11R6* with a command such as:

```
# gzip -dc XF86-3.1-bin.tar.gz | tar xfB -
```

Remember that these tar files are packed relative to */usr/X11R6*, so it's important to unpack the files there.

After unpacking the files, you first need to link the file */usr/X11R6/bin/X* to the server that you're using. For example, if you wish to use the SVGA color server, */usr/bin/X11/X* should be linked to */usr/X11R6/bin/XF86_SVGA*. If you wish to use the monochrome server instead, relink this file to *XF86_MONO* with the command

```
# ln -sf /usr/X11R6/bin/XF86_MONO  /usr/X11R6/bin/X
```

The same holds true if you are using one of the other servers.

If you aren't sure which server to use, or don't know your video card chipset, you can run the *SuperProbe* program found in */usr/X11R6/bin* (included in the *XF86-3.1-bin* archive listed above). This program will attempt to determine your video chipset type and other information; write down its output for later reference.

You need to make sure that */usr/X11R6/bin* is on your path. This can be done by editing your system default */etc/profile* or */etc/csh.login* (based on the shell that you, or other users on your system, use). Or you can simply add the directory to your personal path by modifying */etc/.bashrc* or */etc/.cshrc*, based on your shell.

You also need to make sure that */usr/X11R6/lib* can be located by *ld.so*, the run-time linker. To do this, add the line

```
/usr/X11R6/lib
```

to the file */etc/ld.so.conf*, and run */sbin/ldconfig*, as **root**.

Configuring XFree86

Setting up XFree86 is not difficult in most cases. However, if you happen to be using hardware for which drivers are under development, or wish to obtain the best performance or resolution from an accelerated graphics card, configuring XFree86 can be somewhat time-consuming.

In this section we will describe how to create and edit the *XF86Config* file, which configures the XFree86 server. In many cases it is best to start out with a "basic" XFree86 configuration, one that uses a low resolution. A good choice is 640x480, which should be supported on all video cards and monitor types. Once you have XFree86 working at a lower, standard resolution, you can tweak the configuration to exploit the capabilities of your video hardware. The idea is that you want to make sure that XFree86 works at all on your system, and that something isn't wrong with your installation, before attempting the sometimes difficult task of setting up XFree86 for real use.

In addition to the information here, you should read the following documentation:

- The XFree86 documentation in */usr/X11R6/lib/X11/doc* (contained within the *XFree86-3.1-doc* package). You should especially see the file *README.Config*, which is an XFree86 configuration tutorial.

- The *README* file for your video chipset, if one exists, in the directory */usr/X11R6/lib/X11/doc*. These have names such as *README.Cirrus* and *README.S3*.

- The manual page for *XFree86*.

- The manual page for *XF86Config*.

- The manual page for the particular server that you are using (such as *XF86_SVGA* or *XF86_S3*).

The main configuration file you need to create is */usr/X11R6/lib/X11/XF86Config*. This file contains information on your mouse, video card parameters, and so on. The file *XF86Config.eg* is provided with the XFree86 distribution as an example. Copy this file to *XF86Config* and edit it as a starting point.

The *XF86Config* manual page explains the format of this file in detail. Read this manual page now, if you have not done so already.

We are going to present a sample *XF86Config* file, piece by piece. This file may not look exactly like the sample file included in the XFree86 distribution, but the structure is the same.

The *XF86Config* file format may change with each version of XFree86; this information is only valid for XFree86 version 3.1.

Also, you should not simply copy the configuration file listed here to your own system and attempt to use it. Attempting to use a configuration file that doesn't correspond to your hardware could drive the monitor at a frequency which is too high for it; there have been reports of monitors (especially fixed-frequency monitors) being damaged or destroyed by using an incorrectly configured *XF86Config* file. The bottom line is this: make absolutely sure that your *XF86Config* file corresponds to your hardware before you attempt to use it.

Each section of the *XF86Config* file is surrounded by the pair of lines Section "*section-name*"...EndSection. *The first part of the XF86Config* file is Files, which looks like this:

```
Section "Files"
    RgbPath     "/usr/X11R6/lib/X11/rgb"
    FontPath    "/usr/X11R6/lib/X11/fonts/misc/"
    FontPath    "/usr/X11R6/lib/X11/fonts/75dpi/"
EndSection
```

The RgbPath line sets the path to the X11R6 RGB color database, and each Font-Path line sets the path to a directory containing X11 fonts. In general you shouldn't have to modify these lines; just be sure that there is a FontPath entry for each font type that you have installed (i.e., for each directory in */usr/X11R6/lib/X11/fonts*).

The next section is ServerFlags, which specifies several global flags for the server. In general this section is empty.

```
Section "ServerFlags"
# Uncomment this to cause a core dump at the spot where a signal is
# received.  This may leave the console in an unusable state, but may
# provide a better stack trace in the core dump to aid in debugging
#    NoTrapSignals
# Uncomment this to disable the <Crtl><Alt><BS> server abort sequence
#    DontZap
EndSection
```

Here, we have all lines within the section commented out.

The next section is Keyboard.

```
Section "Keyboard"
     Protocol    "Standard"
     AutoRepeat  500 5
     ServerNumLock
EndSection
```

Other options are available as well—see the *XF86Config* file if you wish to modify the keyboard configuration. The above should work for most systems.

The next section is Pointer, which specifies parameters for the mouse device.

```
Section "Pointer"

     Protocol    "MouseSystems"
     Device      "/dev/mouse"

# Baudrate and SampleRate are only for some Logitech mice
#    BaudRate   9600
#    SampleRate 150

# Emulate3Buttons is an option for 2-button Microsoft mice
#    Emulate3Buttons

# ChordMiddle is an option for some 3-button Logitech mice
#    ChordMiddle

EndSection
```

The only options that you should concern yourself with now are Protocol and Device. Protocol specifies the mouse *protocol* that your mouse uses (not the make or brand of mouse). Valid types for Protocol (under Linux—there are other options available for other operating systems) are:

- BusMouse

- Logitech

- Microsoft

- MMSeries

- Mouseman

- MouseSystems

- PS/2

- MMHitTab

BusMouse should be used for the Logitech busmouse. Note that older Logitech mice should use Logitech, but newer Logitech mice use either Microsoft or Mouseman protocols. This is a case in which the protocol doesn't necessarily have anything to do with the make of the mouse.

Device specifies the device file where the mouse can be accessed. On most Linux systems, this is */dev/mouse*. */dev/mouse* is usually a link to the appropriate serial port (such as */dev/cua0*) for serial mice, or to the appropriate busmouse device for busmice. At any rate, be sure that the device file listed in Device exists.

The next section is Monitor, which specifies the characteristics of your monitor. As with other sections in the *XF86Config* file, there may be more than one Monitor section. This is useful if you have multiple monitors connected to a system, or use the same *XF86Config* file under multiple hardware configurations. In general though, you will need a single Monitor section.

```
Section "Monitor"

    Identifier  "CTX 5468 NI"

    # These values are for a CTX 5468NI only! Don't attempt to use
    # them with your monitor (unless you have this model)

    HorizSync    30-38,47-50
    VertRefresh  50-90

    # Modes: Name     dotclock  horiz              vert

    ModeLine "640x480"   25    640 664 760 800    480 491 493 525
    ModeLine "800x600"   36    800 824 896 1024   600 601 603 625
    ModeLine "1024x768"  65    1024 1088 1200 1328 768 783 789 818

EndSection
```

The Identifier line is used to give an arbitrary name to the Monitor entry. This can be any string; you will use it to refer to the Monitor entry later in the *XF86Config* file.

HorizSync specifies the valid horizontal sync frequencies for your monitor, in kHz. If you have a multisync monitor, this can be a range of values (or several comma-separated ranges), as seen above. If you have a fixed-frequency monitor, this will be a list of discrete values, such as:

```
HorizSync    31.5, 35.2, 37.9, 35.5, 48.95
```

Your monitor manual should list these values in the technical specifications section. If you do not have this information available, you should contact either the manufacturer or the vendor of your monitor to obtain it. There are other sources of information, as well; they are listed below.

VertRefresh specifies the valid vertical refresh rates (or vertical synchronization frequencies) for your monitor, in Hz. Like HorizSync, this can be a range or a list of discrete values; your monitor manual should list them.

HorizSync and VertRefresh are used only to double-check that the monitor resolutions you specify are in valid ranges. This reduces the chance that you will damage your monitor by attempting to drive it at a frequency for which it wasn't designed.

The ModeLine directive is used to specify a single resolution mode for your monitor. The format of ModeLine is

```
ModeLine name dot-clock horiz-values vert-values
```

name is an arbitrary string, which you will use to refer to the resolution mode later in the file. *dot-clock* is the driving clock frequency, or "dot clock" associated with the resolution mode. A dot clock is usually specified in MHz, and is the rate at which the video card must send pixels to the monitor at this resolution. *horiz-values* and *vert-values* are four numbers each, which specify when the electron gun of the monitor should fire, and when the horizontal and vertical sync pulses fire during a sweep.

How can you determine the ModeLine values for your monitor? The file *Video-Modes.doc*, included with the XFree86 distribution, describes in detail how to determine these values for each resolution mode that your monitor supports. First of all, *clock* must correspond to one of the dot clock values that your video card can produce. Later in the *XF86Config* file you will specify these clocks; you can use only video modes that have a *clock* value supported by your video card.

Two files included in the XFree86 distribution may include ModeLine data for your monitor. These files are *modeDB.txt* and *Monitors*, both of which are found in */usr/X11R6/lib/X11/doc*.

You should start with ModeLine values for the VESA standard monitor timings, which most monitors support. *modeDB.txt* includes timing values for VESA standard resolutions. In that file, you will see entries such as

```
# 640x480@60Hz Non-Interlaced mode
# Horizontal Sync = 31.5kHz
# Timing: H=(0.95us, 3.81us, 1.59us), V=(0.35ms, 0.064ms, 1.02ms)
#
# name         clock   horizontal timing     vertical timing      flags
  "640x480"    25.175  640  664  760  800    480  491  493  525
```

This is a VESA standard timing for a 640x480 video mode. It uses a dot clock of 25.175, which your video card must support to use this mode (more on this later).

To include this entry in the *XF86Config* file, you'd use the line

```
ModeLine "640x480" 25.175   640 664 760 800   480 491 493 525
```

Note that the *name* argument to ModeLine (in this case "640x480") is an arbitrary string—the convention is to name the mode after the resolution, but *name* can technically be anything descriptive that describes the mode to you.

For each ModeLine used, the server will check that the specifications for the mode fall within the range of values specified with HorizSync and VertRefresh. If they do not, the server will complain when you attempt to start up X (more on this later).

If the VESA standard timings do not work for you (you'll know after trying to use them later) then the files *modeDB.txt* and *Monitors* include specific mode values for many monitor types. You can create ModeLine entries from the values found in those two files as well. Be sure to use values only for the specific model of monitor that you have. Note that many 14 and 15-inch monitors cannot support higher resolution modes, and often resolutions of 1024x768 at low dot clocks. This means that if you can't find high resolution modes for your monitor in these files, then your monitor probably does not support those resolution modes.

If you are completely at a loss, and can't find working ModeLine values for your monitor, you can follow the instructions in the *VideoModes.doc* file included in the XFree86 distribution to generate ModeLine values from the specifications listed in your monitor's manual. While your mileage will certainly vary when attempting to generate ModeLine values by hand, this is a good place to look if you can't find the values that you need. *VideoModes.doc* also describes the format of the ModeLine directive and other aspects of the XFree86 server in gory detail.

Lastly, if you do obtain ModeLine values which are almost, but not quite, right, then it may be possible to simply modify the values slightly to obtain the desired result. For example, if while running XFree86 the image on the monitor is shifted slightly, or seems to "roll," you can follow the instructions in the *VideoModes.doc* file to try to fix these values. Also, be sure to check the knobs and controls on the monitor itself! In many cases it is necessary to change the horizontal or vertical size of the display after starting up XFree86 in order for the image to be centered and be of the appropriate size. Having these controls on the front of the monitor can certainly make life easier.

You shouldn't use monitor timing values or ModeLine values for monitors other than the model that you own. If you attempt to drive the monitor at a frequency for which it was not designed, you can damage or even destroy it.

The next section of the *XF86Config* file is Device, which specifies parameters for your video card. Here is an example:

```
Section "Device"
        Identifier "#9 GXE 64"

        # Nothing yet; we fill in these values later.


EndSection
```

This section defines properties for a particular video card. Identifier is an arbitrary string describing the card; you will use this string to refer to the card later.

Initially, you don't need to include anything in the Device section, except for Identifier. This is because we will be using the X server itself to probe for the properties of the video card, and entering them into the Device section later. The XFree86 server is capable of probing for the video chipset, clocks, RAMDAC, and amount of video RAM on the board.

Before we do this, however, we need to finish writing the *XF86Config* file. The next section is Screen, which specifies the monitor/video card combination to use for a particular server.

```
Section "Screen"
        Driver      "Accel"
        Device      "#9 GXE 64"
        Monitor     "CTX 5468 NI"
        Subsection "Display"
            Depth       16
            Modes       "1024x768" "800x600" "640x480"
            ViewPort    0 0
            Virtual     1024 768
        EndSubsection
EndSection
```

The Driver line specifies the X server that you will be using. The possible values for Driver are:

Accel
> For the *XF86_S3, XF86_Mach32, XF86_Mach8, XF86_8514, XF86_P9000, XF86_AGX,* and *XF86_W32* servers

SVGA

    For the *XF86_SVGA* server

VGA16

    For the *XF86_VGA16* server

VGA2

    For the *XF86_Mono* server

Mono

    For the non-VGA monochrome drivers in the *XF86_Mono* and *XF86_VGA16* servers

Chapter 3

Be sure that */usr/X11R6/bin/X* is a symbolic link to the server that you are using. (The section "Symbolic Links" in Chapter 3 shows you how to make a symbolic link.)

The Device line specifies the Identifier from the Device section. Above, we created a Device section with the line

```
Identifier "#9 GXE 64"
```

Therefore, we use "#9 GXE 64" on the Device line here.

Similarly, the Monitor line specifies the name of the Monitor section to be used with this server. Here, "CTX 5468 NI" is the Identifier used in the Monitor section described above.

Subsection "Display" defines several properties of the XFree86 server corresponding to your monitor/video card combination. The *XF86Config* file describes all of these options in detail; most of them are icing on the cake and are not necessary to get the system working.

The options that you should know about are:

Depth

    Defines the number of color planes—the number of bits per pixel. Usually, Depth is set to 8. For the VGA16 server, you would use a depth of 4, and for the monochrome server a depth of 1. If you are using an accelerated video card with enough memory to support more bits per pixel, you can set Depth to 16, 24, or 32. If you have problems with depths higher than 8, set it back to 8 and attempt to debug the problem later.

Modes

    This is the list of video mode names which have been defined using the ModeLine directive in the Monitor section. In the above section, we used ModeLines named "1024x768", "800x600", and "640x480", so we use a Modes line of

```
Modes     "1024x768" "800x600" "640x480"
```

The first mode listed on this line will be the default when XFree86 starts up. After XFree86 is running, you can switch between the modes listed here using the key combination Ctrl, Alt, and numeric + or Ctrl, Alt, and numeric –.

It might be best, when initially configuring XFree86, to use lower resolution video modes, such as 640x480, which tend to work on most systems. Once you have the basic configuration working you can modify *XF86Config* to support higher resolutions.

Virtual

Sets the virtual desktop size. XFree86 has the ability to use any additional memory on your video card to extend the size of your desktop. When you move the mouse pointer to the edge of the display, the desktop will scroll, bringing the additional space into view. Therefore, even if you are running at a lower video resolution such as 800x600, you can set Virtual to the total resolution that your video card can support. A 1-megabyte video card can support 1024x768 at a depth of 8 bits per pixel; a 2-megabyte card 1280x1024 at depth 8, or 1024x768 at depth 16. Of course, the entire area will not be visible at once, but it can still be used.

The Virtual feature is a nice way to utilize the memory of your video card, but it is rather limited. If you want to use a true virtual desktop, we suggest using *fvwm* instead. *fvwm* allows you to have rather large virtual desktops (implemented by hiding windows, and so forth, instead of actually storing the entire desktop in video memory at once). See the manual pages for *fvwm* for more details about this; most Linux systems use *fvwm* by default.

ViewPort

If you are using the Virtual option described above, ViewPort sets the coordinates of the upper-left-hand corner of the virtual desktop when XFree86 starts up. Virtual 0 0 is often used, putting the screen at the top left corner of the desktop; if this is unspecified then the desktop is centered on the virtual desktop display (which may be undesirable to you).

Many other options for this section exist; see the *XF86Config* manual page for a complete description. In practice these other options are not necessary to get XFree86 working initially.

Filling in Video Card Information

Your *XF86Config* file is now ready to go, with the exception of complete information on the video card. What we're going to do is use the X server to probe for the rest of this information and fill it into *XF86Config*.

Instead of probing for this information with the X server, you can find the *XF86Config* values for many cards in the files *modeDB.txt*, *AccelCards*, and *Devices*. These files are all in */usr/X11R6/lib/X11/doc*. In addition, there are various *README* files for certain chipsets. You should look in these files for information on your video card, and use that information (the clock values, chipset type, and any options) in the *XF86Config* file. If any information is missing, you can probe for it as described here.

In these examples we will demonstrate configuration for a #9 GXE 64 video card, which uses the XF86_S3 chipset. This card happens to be the one that the author uses, but the discussion here applies to any video card.

The first thing to do is to determine the video chipset used on the card. Running *SuperProbe* (found in */usr/X11R6/bin*) will tell you this information, but you need to know the chipset name as it is known to the X server.

To do this, run the command

```
# X -showconfig
```

This will give the chipset names known to your X server. (The manual pages for each X server list these as well.) For example, with the accelerated XF86_S3 server, we obtain:

```
XFree86 Version 3.1 / X Window System
(protocol Version 11, revision 0, vendor release 6000)
Operating System: Linux
Configured drivers:
  S3: accelerated server for S3 graphics adaptors (Patchlevel 0)
      mmio_928, s3_generic
```

The valid chipset names for this server are mmio_928 and s3_generic. The XF86_S3 manual page describes these chipsets and which videocards use them. In the case of the #9 GXE 64 video card, mmio_928 is appropriate.

If you don't know which chipset to use, the X server can probe it for you. To do this, run the command

```
# X -probeonly > /tmp/x.out 2>&1
```

if you use *bash* as your shell. If you use *csh*, try:

```
% X -probeonly >& /tmp/x.out
```

You should run this command while the system is unloaded, that is, while no other activity is occurring on the system. This command will also probe for your video card dot clocks (as seen below), and system load can throw off this calculation.

The output from the above command (in */tmp/x.out*) should contain lines such as the following:

```
XFree86 Version 3.1 / X Window System
(protocol Version 11, revision 0, vendor release 6000)
Operating System: Linux
```

```
Configured drivers:
  S3: accelerated server for S3 graphics adaptors (Patchlevel 0)
      mmio_928, s3_generic
        .
        .
        .
(--) S3: card type: 386/486 localbus
(--) S3: chipset:   864 rev. 0
(--) S3: chipset driver: mmio_928
```

Here, we see that the two valid chipsets for this server (XF86_S3) are mmio_928 and s3_generic. The server probed for and found a video card using the mmio_928 chipset driver.

In the Device section of the XF86Config file, add a Chipset line containing the name of the chipset you determined above. For example,

```
Section "Device"
        # We already had Identifier here...
        Identifier "#9 GXE 64"
        # Add this line:
        Chipset "mmio_928"
EndSection
```

Now we need to determine the driving clock frequencies used by the video card. A driving clock frequency, or dot clock, is simply a rate at which the video card can send pixels to the monitor. As we have seen, each monitor resolution has a dot clock associated with it. Now we need to determine which dot clocks are made available by the video card.

First you should look into the files (*modeDB.txt*, and so forth) mentioned above and see if your card's clocks are listed there. The dot clocks will usually be a list of 8 or 16 values, all of which are in MHz. For example, when looking at *mode-DB.txt* we see an entry for the Cardinal ET4000 video board, which looks like this:

```
# chip    ram    virtual    clocks                        default-mode  flags
  ET4000  1024   1024 768   25  28  38  36  40  45  32   0 "1024x768"
```

As we can see, the dot clocks for this card are 25, 28, 38, 36, 40, 45, 32, and 0 MHz.

In the Devices section of the *XF86Config* file, you should add a Clocks line containing the list of dot clocks for your card. For example, for the clocks above, we would add the line

```
Clocks 25 28 38 36 40 45 32 0
```

to the Devices section of the file, after Chipset. The order of the clocks is important! Don't re-sort the list of clocks or remove duplicates.

If you cannot find the dot clocks associated with your card, the X server can probe for these as well. Using the *X –probeonly* command described above, the output should contain lines that look like the following:

```
(--) S3: clocks: 25.18  28.32  38.02  36.15  40.33  45.32  32.00  00.00
```

We could then add a `Clocks` line containing all of these values, as printed. You can use more than one `Clocks` line in *XF86Config* should all of the values (sometimes there are more than 8 clock values printed) not fit onto one line. Again, be sure to keep the list of clocks in order as they are printed.

Be sure that there is no `Clocks` line (or that it is commented out) in the `Devices` section of the file when using *X –probeonly* to probe for the clocks. If there is a `Clocks` line present, the server will *not* probe for the clocks—it will use the values given in *XF86Config*.

Note that some accelerated video boards use a programmable clock chip. (See the `XF86_Accel` manual page for details; this generally applies to S3, AGX, and XGA-2 boards.) This chip essentially allows the X server to tell the card which dot clocks to use. If this is the case, then you may not find a list of dot clocks for the card in any of the above files. Or the list of dot clocks printed when using *X –probeonly* will contain only one or two discrete clock values, with the rest being duplicates or zero.

For boards that use a programmable clock chip, you would use a `ClockChip` line, instead of a `Clocks` line, in your *XF86Config* file. `ClockChip` gives the name of the clock chip as used by the video card; the manual pages for each server describe what these are. For example, in the file *README.S3*, we see that several S3-864 video cards use an "ICD2061A" clock chip, and that we should use the line

```
ClockChip "icd2061a"
```

instead of `Clocks` in the *XF86Config* file. As with `Clocks`, this line should go in the `Devices` section, after `Chipset`.

Similarly, some accelerated cards require you to specify the RAMDAC chip type in the *XF86Config* file, using a `Ramdac` line. The `XF86_Accel` manual page describes this option. Usually, the X server will correctly probe for the RAMDAC.

Some video card types require you to specify several options in the `Devices` section of *XF86Config*. These options will be described in the manual page for your server, as well as in the various files (such as *README.cirrus* or *README.S3*). These options are enabled using the `Option` line. For example, the #9 GXE 64 card requires two options:

```
Option "number_nine"
Option "dac_8_bit"
```

Usually, the X server will work without these options, but they are necessary to obtain the best performance. There are too many such options to list here, and they each depend on the particular video card being used. If you must use one of these options, fear not—the X server manual pages and various files in */usr/X11R6/lib/X11/doc* will tell you what they are.

So when you're finished, you should end up with a Devices section that looks something like this:

```
Section "Device"
        # Device section for the #9 GXE 64 only !
        Identifier "#9 GXE 64"
        Chipset "mmio_928"
        ClockChip "icd2061a"
        Option "number_nine"
        Option "dac_8_bit"
EndSection
```

This Device entry is valid only for a particular video card, the #9 GXE 64. It is given here only as an example. Most video cards will require a Clocks line, instead of ClockChip, as described above.

There are other options that you can include in the Devices entry. Check the X server manual pages for the gritty details, but the above should suffice for most systems.

Running XFree86

With your *XF86Config* file configured, you're ready to fire up the X server and give it a spin. First, be sure that */usr/X11R6/bin* is on your path.

The command to start up XFree86 is

```
startx
```

This is a front-end to *xinit* (in case you're used to using *xinit* on other UNIX systems).

This command will start the X server and run the commands found in the file *.xinitrc* in your home directory. *.xinitrc* is just a shell script containing X clients to run. If this file does not exist, the system default */usr/X11R6/lib/X11/xinit/xinitrc* will be used.

A standard *.xinitrc* file looks like this:

```
#!/bin/sh

xterm -fn 7x13bold -geometry 80x32+10+50 &
xterm -fn 9x15bold -geometry 80x34+30-10 &
oclock -geometry 70x70-7+7 &
xsetroot -solid midnightblue &

exec twm
```

This script will start up two *xterm* clients and an *oclock*, and set the root window (background) color to midnightblue. It will then start up *twm*, the window manager. Note that *twm* is executed with the shell's *exec* statement; this causes the *xinit* process to be replaced with *twm*. Once the *twm* process exits, the X server will shut down. You can cause *twm* to exit by using the root menus. Press mouse button 1 on the desktop background to display a pop-up menu, and then choose Exit Twm.

Be sure that the last command in *.xinitrc* is started with *exec*, and that it is not placed into the background (no ampersand on the end of the line). Otherwise the X server will shut down as soon as it has started the clients in the *.xinitrc* file. Alternatively, you can exit X by pressing Ctrl-Alt-Del in combination. This will kill the X server directly, exiting the window system.

The above is a very, very simple desktop configuration. Many wonderful programs and configurations are available with a bit of work on your *.xinitrc* file. For example, the *fvwm* window manager provides a virtual desktop, and you can customize colors, fonts, window sizes and positions, and so forth to your heart's content. Although the X Window System might appear to be simplistic at first, it is extremely powerful once you customize it for yourself.

[14] X User Guide

If you are new to the X Window System environment, we strongly suggest picking up a book such as *The X Window System User's Guide*.

Running Into Trouble

Often, something will not be quite right when you initially fire up the X server. This is almost always caused by a problem in your *XF86Config* file. Usually, the monitor timing values are off, or the video card dot clocks are set incorrectly. If your display seems to roll, or the edges are fuzzy, this is a clear indication that the monitor timing values or dot clocks are wrong. Also be sure that you are correctly specifying your video card chipset, as well as other options for the Device section of *XF86Config*. Be absolutely certain that you are using the right X server and that */usr/X11R6/bin/X* is a symbolic link to this server.

If all else fails, try to start X "bare"; that is, use a command such as:

```
X > /tmp/x.out 2>&1
```

You can then kill the X server (using the Ctrl-Alt-Del key combination) and examine the contents of */tmp/x.out*. The X server will report any warnings or errors—for example, if your video card doesn't have a dot clock corresponding to a mode supported by your monitor.

The file *VideoModes.doc* included in the XFree86 distribution contains many hints for tweaking the values in your *XF86Config* file.

Remember that you can use Ctrl, Alt, and numeric + or Ctrl, Alt, and numeric – to switch between the video modes listed on the Modes line of the Screen section of

XF86Config. If the highest resolution mode doesn't look right, try switching to lower resolutions. This will let you know, at least, that those parts of your X configuration are working correctly.

Also, check the vertical and horizontal size/hold knobs on your monitor. In many cases it is necessary to adjust these when starting up X. For example, if the display seems to be shifted slightly to one side, you can usually correct this using the monitor controls.

The Usenet newsgroup *comp.windows.x.i386unix* is devoted to discussions about XFree86. It might be a good idea to watch that newsgroup for postings relating to your video configuration—you might run across someone with the same problems as your own.

Customizing Your X Environment

Before we talk about various applications available for X, it's a good idea to discuss the rudiments of X customization, so that you're not forced to live with the (often unappealing) default configuration used on many systems.

xinit

You run X with the *startx* command. This is a front end for *xinit*, the program responsible for starting the X server (with reasonable options) and running various X clients that you specify. *xinit* (via *startx*) executes the shell script *.xinitrc* in your home directory. This script merely contains commands that you wish to run when starting X, such as *xterm*, *xclock*, and so on. If you don't have a *.xinitrc* file, the system default */usr/lib/X11/xinit/xinitrc* is used instead.

Below, we'll present a sample *.xinitrc* file, and explain what it does. You could use this as your own *.xinitrc*, or copy the system default *xinitrc* as a starting point.

```
 1  #!/bin/sh
 2  # Sample .xinitrc shell script
 3
 4  # Start xterms
 5  xterm -geometry 80x40+10+100 -fg black -bg white &
 6  xterm -geometry -20+10 -fn 7x13bold -fg darkslategray -bg white &
 7  xterm -geometry -20-30 -fn 7x13bold -fg black -bg white &
 8
 9  # Other useful X clients
10  oclock -geometry 70x70+5+5 &
11  xload -geometry 85x60+85+5 &
12  xbiff -geometry +200+5 &
13  xsetroot -solid darkslateblue &
14
15  # Start the window manager
16  exec fvwm
```

This should be quite straightforward, even if you're not familiar with X. The first two lines simply identify the shell script. Lines 5–7 start up three *xterm* clients (recall that *xterm* is a terminal emulator client). Other clients are started on lines 10–13, and on line 16 the window manager, *fvwm*, is started.

Running *startx* with this particular *.xinitrc* in place will give you something that looks like Figure 5-2.[*]

Figure 5–2. Screen created by sample .xinitrc file

Let's look at this in more detail. On line 5 we see that *xterm* is started with several options, *–geometry*, *–fg*, and *–bg*. Most X clients support these "standard" options, among others. The *–geometry* option allows you to specify the size and position of the window on the display. The geometry specification has the format

```
xsizexysize+xoffset+yoffset
```

In this case, the option *–geometry 80x40+10+100* causes the window to be placed at the location (10,100) on the screen (where (0,0) is the top-left corner), and to be 80 characters wide by 40 characters high. Note that *xterm* measures the size of

---

[*] All right, so it's not a work of art, but we needed something simple that would work correctly on most displays!

the window in *characters*, not pixels. The actual size of the window in pixels is determined by the font that is used.

The *–fg* and *–bg* arguments allow you to specify the foreground (text) and background colors for the *xterm* window, respectively. The colors used here are a rather boring black and white, but this should work on color and monochrome displays alike. Under X, colors are usually specified by name, although you can provide your own RGB values if you prefer. The list of color names (and corresponding RGB values) is given in the file */usr/lib/X11/rgb.txt*. (Running *xcolors* will display these colors, along with their names.)

Line 6 runs another *xterm*, although the arguments are slightly different:

```
xterm -geometry -20+10 -fn 7x13bold -fg darkslategray -bg white &
```

First of all, the geometry specification is just –20+10. Without size parameters, *xterm* will use the default, which is usually 80x25. Also, we see that the *xoffset* is prefixed with a –, instead of +. This causes the window to be placed 20 pixels from the *right* edge of the screen. Likewise, a geometry specification such as –20–30 (as is used on line 7) means to place the window 20 pixels from the right edge of the screen, and 30 pixels from the bottom. In this way, the placement of windows is less dependent on the particular resolution that you're using.

The *–fn* option on lines 6 and 7 specifies that the font used by *xterm* should be 7x13bold. Using the command *xlsfonts* will display a complete list of fonts on your system; the X client *xfontsel* will allow you to select fonts interactively—more about fonts later.

On line 10 we start an *oclock* client, which is a simple analog clock. Line 11 starts *xload*, which displays a graph of the system *load average* (number of running processes) that changes with time. Line 12 starts *xbiff*, which just lets you know when mail is waiting to be read. Finally, on line 13 we do away with the bland grey X background and replace it with a flashy darkslateblue. (Fear not; there is more fun to be had with X decor than this.)

You'll notice that each of the X clients started on lines 6–13 is executed in the background (the ampersand on the end of each line forces this). If you forget to background each client, *xinit* will execute the first *xterm*, wait for it to exit (usually, after you log out), execute the next *xterm*, and so on. Putting on the ampersands causes each client to start up concurrently.

What about line 16? Here, we start *fvwm*, a window manager used on many Linux systems. As we mentioned before, the window manager is responsible for decorating the windows, allowing you to place them with the mouse, and so forth. However, it is started with the command

```
exec fvwm
```

This causes the *fvwm* process to *replace* the *xinit* process. This way, once you kill *fvwm*,[*] the X server shuts down. This is equivalent to but more succinct than using the Ctrl-Alt-Del combination.

In general, you should put an ampersand after each X client started from *.xinitrc*, and *exec* the window manager at the end of the file. Of course, there are other ways of doing this, but many users employ this technique.

[14] X User
Guide

If you read the manual pages for *xterm* and the other X clients, you'll see many more command-line options than those described here. As we said, virtually everything about X is configurable. *fvwm* uses a configuration file of its own, *.fvwmrc*, described in its manual page. (If you have no *.fvwmrc* file, the system default */usr/lib/X11/fvwm/system.fvwmrc* is used instead.) The manual pages, as well as books on using X (such as O'Reilly's *X Window System User's Guide*), provide more information on configuring individual clients.

The X resource database

You can't use X for long without running into X resources—they are mentioned in virtually every manual page. X resources provide a more flexible and powerful way to configure X clients than using command-line options such as *–geometry* and *–fg*. They allow you to specify defaults for entire classes of clients; for example, we could set the default font for all invocations of *xterm* to 7x13bold, instead of specifying it on each command line.

Using X resources requires two steps. First, you must create a file containing your X resource defaults. Typically, this file is called *.Xdefaults*, and lives in your home directory. Secondly, you need to use *xrdb* to load the X resources into the server, which makes them available for use. In general, you run *xrdb* from your *.xinitrc* before starting any clients.

As a simple example, let's take the various command-line options used by the clients in the above sample *.xinitrc* and specify them as X resources instead. Afterwards we'll show you what kinds of changes need to be made to *.xinitrc* to make use of the resources.

First a few words about resources and how they work. Each X application is part of a certain *application class*. For example, *xterm* is a member of the XTerm class. *xclock* and *oclock* are both members of the Clock class. Setting resources for the Clock class affects all applications that are part of that class—because *xclock* (a square analog clock) and *oclock* (an oval analog clock) are similar, they belong to the same class and share the same resources. Most applications are members of their own exclusive class—*xload* is the only member of the XLoad class. However, if another *xload*-like application were to be written, it might be part of the XLoad class as well. Placing X clients into application classes allows you to set resources

---

[*] If you have experimented with *fvwm*, you'll notice that pressing the first mouse button while the cursor is on the background causes a menu to pop up. Selecting the Quit fvwm option from this menu will cause *fvwm* to exit.

for all applications in that class. (The manual page for each X client specifies the application class that the client belongs to.)

"Standard" X clients employ resources such as foreground, background, geometry, and font. Also, many X clients have specific resources of their own—for example, *xterm* defines the resource logFile, which allows you to specify a file in which to log the terminal session. Again, the manual pages for X clients specify which resources are available.

Moreover, resources themselves are arranged into a hierarchy of classes. For instance, the background resource is a member of the Background class. Resource classes allow many separate resources to be members of the same class, for which you can set resource values for the class as a whole. For example, the background resource usually determines the primary background color of a window. However, if an application window has several panels, or regions, you may wish to set the background for each panel separately. There might be resources such as background1, background2, and so on, for each panel, but they would all be members of the Background resource class. Setting the resource value for the Background class sets the value for all resources in that class.

In general, you won't need to concern yourself with the differences between resource classes and the resources within that class. In most cases it's easier to set resource values for an entire class (such as Background) instead of individual resources in that class.

Now, let's look at how resource values are set in the X resource database. A complete resource specification is of the form:[*]

    (ApplicationClass|applicationName)*(ResourceClass|resourceName) : value

The vertical bar means "choose one or the other." Let's say that you wanted to set the background color of an *xterm* window. The *complete* resource specification might be:

    xterm*background: darkslategray

However, this only sets a particular background resource (not all of the resources that might be in the Background class), and only for the *xterm* client when it is invoked as *xterm* (more on this later). Therefore, we might want to use resource classes instead:

    XTerm*Background: darkslategray

This resource specification will apply to *all xterm* clients, and all Background-class resources used by *xterm*.

---

[*] Actually, resource specifications have a much more complex syntax than this, and the rules used to determine resource and value bindings are somewhat involved. For simplification we are presenting a reasonable model for application resource settings—and direct curious readers to a good book on using X.

Now, let's look at translating the options given in the above *.xinitrc* file into application resources. Create a file in your home directory, called *.Xdefaults*. For the sample *.xinitrc* above, it should contain:

```
 1  Clock*Geometry:        70x70+5+5
 2  XLoad*Geometry:        85x50+85+5
 3  XBiff*Geometry:         +200+5
 4
 5  ! Defaults for all xterm clients
 6  XTerm*Foreground:      white
 7  XTerm*Background:      black
 8
 9  ! Specific xterms
10  xterm-1*Geometry:      80x40+10+110
11
12  xterm-2*Geometry:      -20+10
13  xterm-2*Font:          7x13bold
14  xterm-2*Background:    darkslategray
15
16  xterm-3*Geometry:      80x25-20-30
17  xterm-3*Font:          7x13bold
```

Lines 1–3 set the Geometry resource class for the Clock, XLoad, and XBiff application classes. On lines 6–7, we set the Foreground and Background resource classes for the XTerm class as whole. All *xterm* clients will use these values for Foreground and Background by default.

On lines 10–17, we set resources specific to each invocation of *xterm*. (This is necessary because not all of the *xterm*s are alike; they each have different geometry specifications, for example.) In this case, we have named the individual *xterm* invocations xterm-1, xterm-2, and xterm-3. As you can see, we set the Geometry resource for each on lines 10, 12, and 16. Also, we set the Font class for xterm-2 and xterm-3. And we set the Background class to darkslategray for xterm-2.

X resource binding rules work so that certain bindings have precedence over others. In this case, setting a resource for a specific invocation of *xterm* (as in "xterm-2*Background" on line 14) has precedence over the resource setting for the XTerm class as a whole (XTerm*Background on line 7). In general, bindings for an application or resource *class* have *lower* precedence than bindings for particular instances of that class. In this way, you can set defaults for the class as a whole, but override those defaults for particular instances of the class.

Now, let's look at the changes required to *.xinitrc* to use the X resources defined here. First, we need to add an *xrdb* command, which will load the application resources into the server. And, we can get rid of the various command-line options which the resources have replaced. To wit:

```
#!/bin/sh
# Sample .xinitrc shell script
```

```
# Load resources
xrdb -load $HOME/.Xdefaults

# Start xterms
xterm -name "xterm-1" &
xterm -name "xterm-2" &
xterm -name "xterm-3" &

# Other useful X clients
oclock &
xload &
xbiff &
xsetroot -solid darkslateblue &

# Start the window manager
exec fvwm
```

As you see, the *–name* argument given to the three instances of *xterm* lets us specify the application name that *xterm* will use for locating X resources. Most X clients don't support a *–name* argument; the name used is usually that which it was invoked with. However, because many users run several *xterm*s at once, it is helpful to distinguish between them when setting resources.

Now, you should be able to modify your X environment to some degree. Of course, knowing how to configure X depends partly on being familiar with the many X clients out there, as well as the window manager (and how to configure it). The rest of this section will present various X applications for Linux. We'll also look at a particular window manager, *fvwm*, in detail.

The fvwm Window Manager

Your choice of window manager determines, to a large extent, the look and feel of your X environment. Many window managers also provide menus, which allow you to start other X applications using the mouse, and a virtual desktop, which increases your overall desktop space considerably.

fvwm is a virtual desktop window manager used by many Linux users. It is based partially on the code for *twm*, the classic window manager included with the MIT X11 distribution. However, *fvwm* has been trimmed down and requires about half of the memory used by *twm*—welcome news for Linux systems with 8 megabytes or less of physical RAM. *fvwm* provides many features not available in other window managers, and for this reason (as well as the fact that it was developed specifically for Linux) we are covering it here.

Unlike *twm* and some other window managers, *fvwm* undergoes constant development. This means that some of the features described here may not be present in the same form in newer versions of the software. Refer to the manual page for *fvwm* to verify that the features presented here are available.

Among the features offered by *fvwm* are:

- About one-half to one-third the memory consumption of *twm*.

- A simple virtual desktop, which provides a *pager* (an overall "birds-eye" view of the desktop) and automatic desktop scrolling when the pointer reaches the screen boundary.

- Almost every mouse-based feature has a keyboard equivalent; this is useful when using X on laptops without a mouse or trackball.

- Support for color icons, using the XPM libraries.

- A programming interface for extensions, allowing you to add new features to *fvwm*. One extension included in the *fvwm* distribution is a button box that stays put on your root window. You can bind commands to each button, allowing you to point and click to start applications.

- Fully-configurable desktop menus, which appear when you press the mouse buttons.

- A Motif-like 3-D look and feel for window frames. In fact, *fvwm* includes options for Motif compatibility.

Among the most powerful *fvwm* features is the *virtual desktop*, which allows you to place windows on an area that is much larger than the actual size of the visible display. Using the mouse, you can switch (page) between areas of the virtual desktop. For example, when you move the mouse pointer to the right edge of the display, the desktop will shift a screenful to the left, bringing new windows into view. This way you can place windows across an area larger than your screen, viewing only a portion of the virtual desktop at a time.

A sample desktop using *fvwm* was shown in Figure 5-2 in the section "xinit." Each window is given a decorative frame, provided by *fvwm*, with titlebar buttons that are configurable. Later in this section we'll describe how to customize these to your liking.

The pager, in the top right-hand corner of the display, gives a "bird's-eye view" of the entire virtual desktop. The pager can also be used to move windows around the virtual desktop and to select the portion of the desktop currently in view.

Configuring fvwm

In order to use *fvwm*, you'll need to create a configuration file, *.fvwmrc*, in your home directory. In this section, we're going to present a number of features of *fvwm* and describe how to enable them from *.fvwmrc*. In order to get the full benefit of the window manager, you may need to include most of these items in your own *.fvwmrc*.

We must warn you that the syntax of some of the options have changed between different versions of *fvwm*; just check them against the manual page if you have problems. You may wish to use the system default *.fvwmrc* file (usually found in */usr/lib/X11/system.fvwmrc*) as a starting point.

The most basic *fvwm* customizations deal with colors and fonts used for window frames and menus. For example, you might include the following in your *.fvwmrc*:

```
# Set up colors
StdForeColor           white
StdBackColor           midnightblue
HiForeColor            white
HiBackColor            red
Font                   -adobe-helvetica-medium-r-normal-*-*-120-*
WindowFont             -adobe-helvetica-bold-r-normal-*-*-120-*
```

Some commands depend on which window is in *focus*, which means that it is receiving input. (Normally you just put the mouse in a window to make it the one in focus.) StdForeColor and StdBackColor are used for unfocused windows, menus, and the virtual desktop pager; HiForeColor and HiBackColor are used by the window in focus. The foreground color is generally used for text, while the background is used for the window frame itself. Be artistic! WindowFont names the font used by window title bars; Font is used by menus (and icons, unless you specify otherwise).

To get a list of all the colors defined on your system, enter the command:

eggplant$ **showrgb | more**

Most *fvwm* users also make use of the virtual desktop. In order to configure the virtual desktop, you should include lines such as the following in *.fvwmrc*:

```
# Configure virtual desktop
DeskTopSize    3x3
DeskTopScale   50
Pager          -10 -10
EdgeScroll     100 100
```

We want the size of the desktop (DeskTopSize) to be three screens wide by three screens high. DeskTopScale sets the scale to be used by the pager; in this case, windows in the pager will appear to be 1/50th of their actual size. Also, we enable the Pager and place it in the lower right-hand corner of the screen. The Pager window allows us to see the entire virtual desktop at once; clicking the mouse button in the pager will move the virtual desktop to that location.

EdgeScroll specifies the percentage by which the desktop should scroll when the pointer reaches the edge of the screen. Using EdgeScroll 100 100 causes the desktop to shift by an entire screen when we move the mouse cursor to the edge; this has the appearance of switching from one screen to an entirely different one. This way you can place windows across the entire virtual desktop and wander around the desktop using only the mouse.

The `Style` command can be used to set a whole slew of attributes for windows on your screen. For instance, to specify that the *xbiff* should always stay on top of other windows on the display, use the command:

```
Style "XBiff" StaysOnTop
```

Now, no other window is allowed to obscure *xbiff*. Besides `StaysOnTop`, other popular options to `Style` include:

- `NoTitle`, which prevents a window from having a decorative title on the top with its name. This option is often used for small windows like *xclock* and *xbiff*, especially if you don't expect to move or resize them.

- `NoBorder`, which prevents a window from having a border.

- `Sticky`, which makes a window stay in the same place on the screen when you shift the virtual desktop.

- `BoundaryWidth`, which sets the width in pixels of frames placed around windows by *fvwm*. The default used by *fvwm* is 6 pixels, which is quite wide.

Arguments to `Style` may be window titles or application class names. Older versions of *fvwm* don't have the `Style` command. Instead, they offer a variety of commands named `StaysOnTop`, `NoTitle`, and so on. You use them like this:

```
StaysOnTop XBiff
```

There are various *.fvwmrc* commands dealing with *icons*. As with other window managers, *fvwm* allows you to iconify a window, which replaces the window with a small icon containing the name of the window and possibly a picture depicting the type of window. *fvwm* supports both bitmaps and color pixmaps for icons.

```
IconFont    -adobe-helvetica-medium-r-*-*-*-120-*
IconPath    /usr/include/X11/bitmaps/
PixmapPath  /usr/include/X11/pixmaps/

IconBox     700 0 1080 50
Style "*" Icon unknown.xpm
Style "XTerm" Icon xterm.xpm
Style "Mosaic" Icon mosaic.xpm
```

`IconFont` specifies the font to use for icons. `IconPath` and `PixmapPath` specify colon-separated pathnames where icon images can be found; if you keep images in several directories, separate their pathnames with colons. `IconPath` specifies locations for bitmaps (XBM), and `PixmapPath` specifies locations for color pixmaps (XPM).

`IconBox` defines a region of the screen where icons should be placed. You can specify more than one `IconBox`, up to four, if you wish. In this case, icons should be placed in an invisible box defined by the top-left corner at location (700,0) and bottom-right corner at (1080,50).

Following `IconBox` are several `Style` commands that bind icon images to windows. In this case we want all `XTerm` windows to use *xterm.xpm*, and `Mosaic` to use *mosaic.xpm*. The name of the icon file can either be a full pathname, or a pathname relative to either `IconPath` or `PixmapPath`. The command

```
Style "*" Icon unknown.xpm
```

sets the default icon to *unknown.xpm*.

If your *fvwm* does not support the `Style` command, use commands such as:

```
Icon "" unknown.xpm
Icon "XTerm" xterm.xpm
Icon "Mosaic" mosaic.xpm
```

More advanced customizations

Most *fvwm* users include at least the above options in the *.fvwmrc* file. However, *fvwm* also provides the ability to configure the desktop menus, functions executed by the window title bar buttons, and so on. Here we'll introduce several of those features.

First, let's configure *fvwm* popup menus, which appear when pressing the mouse buttons on the root window. You can use these menus to execute commands, manipulate windows, and so on.

```
Popup "Xclients"
   Title    "Xclients"
   Exec     "Mosaic"         exec Mosaic &
   Exec     "xterm"          exec xterm &
   Exec     "emacs"          exec emacs -w &
   Nop      ""
   Exec     "eggplant"       exec xterm -e rlogin eggplant &
   Exec     "papaya"         exec xterm -e rlogin papaya &
   Nop      ""
   Exec     "screensaver"    exec xscreensaver-command -activate &
   Exec     "xcalc"          exec xcalc &
   Exec     "xman"           exec xman &
   Exec     "xlock"          exec xlock -mode rotor &
EndPopup
```

The menu is defined between the `Popup` and `EndPopup` lines. Each menu is given a name (in this case, "`Xclients`"), which is used to refer to the menu later.

The format of the menu is relatively self-explanatory. The `Title` command sets the menu title, and `Nop` causes a separator line to appear in the menu. The `Exec` function causes a command to be executed when the menu item is chosen. The first argument is the name of the item as it appears in the menu; the remaining arguments specify the command to be executed.

We define a second menu, called *fvwm*, which utilizes the *fvwm* window-manipulation functions.

```
Popup "Fvwm"
   Title   "Window Ops"
   Move    "Move Window"
   Resize  "Resize Window"
   Raise   "Raise Window"
   Lower   "Lower Window"
   Iconify "Iconify Window"
   Stick   "Stick Window"
   Nop     " "
   Popup   "Xclients"  Xclients
   Nop     " "
   Destroy "Destroy Window"
   Delete  "Delete Window"
   Nop     " "
   Exec    "Load Xdefaults"   exec xrdb -load $HOME/.Xdefaults
   Restart "Restart Fvwm"     fvwm
   Restart "Start twm"        twm
   Quit "Quit Fvwm"
EndPopup
```

Each of the built-in functions Move, Resize, Lower, and so on are described in the *fvwm* manual page. One function of note is Popup, which allows a previously-defined popup to be used as a sub-menu of the current menu. Here, we include the Xclients menu, defined above, as a sub-menu.

Also included here are commands for restarting *fvwm*, or starting another window manager (*twm*) in place of *fvwm*.

fvwm also allows you to modify the function of the mouse buttons in various contexts. The Mouse command is used for this, and takes the form

```
Mouse button context modifiers function
```

button is 1, 2, 3, or 0 (where 0 means "any button"). *context* specifies the region in which the mouse binding takes effect; *context* may be:

- R for the root window

- W for an application window

- S for a window frame

- F for a window frame corner

- T for a window title bar

- I for an icon window

- A digit from 0–9, specifying a particular titlebar button (described below)

- A for any context (except titlebar buttons)

- Any combination of the above

For example, the *context* TSIF specifies window titlebars, frames, and frame corners, as well as icon windows.

Using a digit from 0 through 9 in *context* binds the function to a window titlebar button. By default, there are two such buttons—one on the left edge of the titlebar, and one on the right. Binding mouse functions to other buttons causes them to be visible. Left titlebar buttons are given odd numbers (1, 3, 5, 7, and 9), and right titlebar buttons are given even numbers (2, 4, 6, 8, 0). Figure 5-3 shows a window with all buttons visible, with their corresponding numbers. Unless you bind mouse functions to each button, most of them will be invisible.

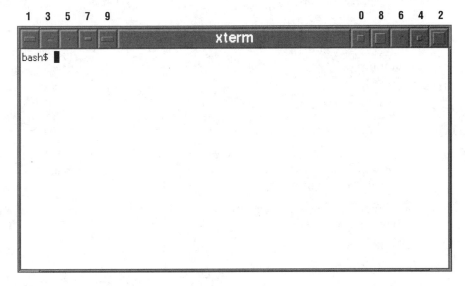

Figure 5–3. Buttons on fvwm titlebar

modifiers specifies various key combinations to be used in conjunction with the mouse button press. Valid *modifiers* are C for control, M for meta, S for shift, N for none, or A for any of the above. For example, setting *modifiers* to C means that the control key must be pressed while the mouse button is clicked.

Here are some examples of mouse bindings.

```
#       Button    Context Modifi  Function
Mouse 1           R       N       PopUp "Fvwm"
Mouse 2           R       N       PopUp "Xclients"
Mouse 3           R       N       WindowList
```

These lines bind each mouse button to one of the popup menus *fvwm* or Xclients, defined above, or the WindowList command, which is a popup menu containing entries for each window on the display.

```
# Window titlebar buttons
Mouse 1        1        N        Popup "Fvwm"
Mouse 1        3        N        Iconify
Mouse 1        4        N        Destroy
Mouse 1        2        N        Resize
```

Here we bind titlebar buttons 1, 3, 4, and 2 (two buttons on each side of the title-bar) to various functions. The leftmost titlebar button pops up the *fvwm* menu, the second left button iconifies the window, and so on. The *fvwm* manual page lists all of the available functions, such as Resize, Move, and RaiseLower.

You can also specify key bindings with the Key command. They are similar in syntax to mouse bindings:

```
Key key context modifiers function
```

with *context* and *modifiers* having the meanings given above. Here are some examples:

```
Key Up         A        C        Scroll +0    -100
Key Down       A        C        Scroll +0    +100
Key Left       A        C        Scroll -100 0
Key Right      A        C        Scroll +100 +0
```

These bindings cause Ctrl-*arrowkey* to scroll the desktop by a full page in the given direction. You can bind any key to an *fvwm* function in this way; for instance, the function keys are named F1, F2, and so on.

Read the *fvwm* manual page. As new versions are released, the syntax of the configuration file changes slightly, and new features are added periodically.

X Applications

There are thousands of programs available for X. They range from basic utilities (such as *xterm* and *xclock*, already discussed) to editors to programming aids to games to multimedia applications. The most that we can provide here is the thinnest slice of software available for X. In this section we'll present those applications that all X users should know how to use. These aren't necessarily the most exciting programs out there, but they should certainly be part of your toolbox.

[14] X User Guide

A more comprehensive explanation of X applications can be found in *The X Window System User's Guide*.

xterm—your home base

Let's start our exploration of X applications with the workhorse where you'll be spending most of your time—*xterm*. This is simply a window that contains a UNIX shell. It displays a prompt, accepts commands, and scrolls like a terminal.

Perhaps, like me, you are struck by the irony of buying a high-resolution color monitor, installing several megabytes of graphics software, and then being confronted by an emulation of an old VT100. But Linux is simply not a point-and-click operating system. There are plenty of nice graphical applications, but a lot of the time you'll want to manipulate text, and a command-line interface still offers the most powerful tools for doing that.

So let's take look at an *xterm* window. Figure 5-4 shows one where we've already entered a few commands. By the way, if you've read the section "Customizing Your X Environment," you may enjoy browsing some of the files in */usr/lib/X11/app-defaults*; they show the default behavior of X applications when you don't specify your own preferences.

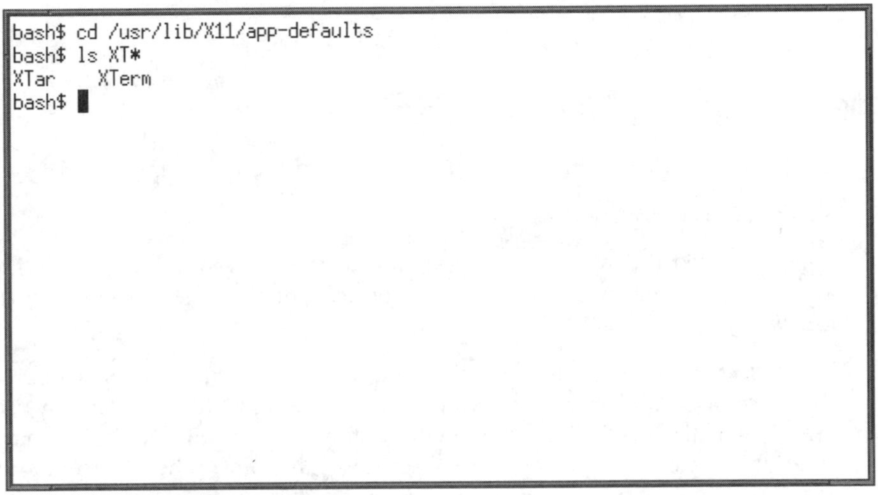

```
bash$ cd /usr/lib/X11/app-defaults
bash$ ls XT*
XTar    XTerm
bash$ █
```

Figure 5–4. xterm window

Starting up xterm

Maybe first we should explain how we created the *xterm* window. You can reproduce it through the command

```
eggplant$ xterm  -geometry 80x25-20-30  -fn 7x13bold  -sb  -name xterm-3
```

where the options mean:

–geometry 80x25-20-30
> The window is 80 characters wide and 25 characters high, located 20 pixels from the left edge of the screen and 30 pixels from the bottom.

–fn 7x13bold
> Text appears in a medium-sized bold font. (A large but limited set of fonts are available; we'll show you how to look at them in the section "Choosing a font.")

—sb
> A scrollbar is displayed.

—name xterm-3
> The string "xterm-3" appears in the title bar at the top of the window, and on the icon when you iconify the window..

But we don't want to go to the trouble of entering this long command every time we start an *xterm.* What we did (as you can see in the section "Customizing Your X Environment") was put the following options in our *.Xdefaults* file:

```
! Defaults for all xterm clients
  XTerm*scrollBar:             true

! Specific xterms
  xterm-3*Geometry:       80x25-20-30
  xterm-3*Font:           7x13bold
```

and when we logged in, our *.xinitrc* file issued the command:

```
xterm -name "xterm-3" &
```

which created the window. As you saw in the section "The fvwm Window Manager," you can easily set up a menu, mouse button, function key, etc. to start the *xterm.*

To close a window, enter "exit" or press Ctrl-D. If this seems dangerous to you (because you could lose your window by pressing Ctrl-D accidentally) start up the *xterm* with the *—ls* option, which stands for "login shell." Now you have to enter "logout" to close the window. (The option has some other consequences too. In the *bash* shell, it will cause your ~/.bash_profile file to run. In the C shell, it will cause your ~/.login file to run.)

Selections: cutting and pasting

Actually, xterm offers a good deal more than a VT100 terminal. One of its features is a powerful cut-and-paste capability.

Take another look at Figure 5-4. Let's say that we didn't really want the *app-defaults* directory; we wanted to look at the fonts in */usr/lib/X11/fonts* instead. (This is actually not too interesting; it was an arbitrary choice.)

First we'll choose the part of the *cd* command that interests us. Put the mouse just to the left of the c in cd. Press the left-most button, and drag the mouse until it highlights the slash following X11. The result is shown in Figure 5-5.

Did you include too many characters, or too few? That's all right, just hold down the Shift key and press the left-most mouse button anywhere in the highlighted area. Now you can make the highlighted area bigger or smaller.

```
bash$ cd /usr/lib/X11/app-defaults
bash$ ls XT*
XTar     XTerm
bash$ 
```

Figure 5–5. Selected text in xterm

When the highlighted area covers just the right number of characters, click the middle button. *xterm* pastes in what you've selected on the next command line. See the result in Figure 5-6.

```
bash$ cd /usr/lib/X11/app-defaults
bash$ ls XT*
XTar     XTerm
bash$ cd /usr/lib/X11/
```

Figure 5–6. xterm window after text is pasted

Now you can type in the remainder of the directory name "fonts" and press the return key to execute the command.

You can select anything you want in the window—output as well as input. To select whole words instead of characters, double click the left-most button. To select whole lines, triple click it. You can select multiple lines too. Selecting multiple lines is not useful when you're entering commands but is very convenient if you're using the *vi* editor and want to cut and paste a lot of text between windows.

Be careful if a long line wraps around; you will end up with a newline in the selection even though you didn't type the return key when you entered the line.

Scrolling

Eventually, as you type along in your *xterm*, previous commands will scroll off the top of the window. That's why we specified a scrollbar when we started the *xterm*. Using it is pretty simple (as it ought to be with any point-and-click tool) but there are a few neat tricks. By the way, the techniques you learn here should work in most applications that offer scrollbars. An X application is free to act anyway that the programmer designed it to, but most developers use the same conventions as *xterm* does.

First let's get a lot of text into our window. Issuing one of the following commands should suffice:

```
eggplant$ ls /bin
eggplant$ ls /usr/bin
eggplant$ cat ~/.*
```

Of course the output will go streaming by too fast to see. Now we can go back and look at it. If you look at the scrollbar area on the left side of the window, you'll see a little dark area near the bottom. Its size indicates how much of the output you can currently see, and its position shows you where you are (at the end).

Place the mouse in the scrollbar area, near the bottom, and press the right-most mouse button. This moves you one whole page upward; what used to be at the top of the screen is now at the bottom. If you click near the top of the screen, you move back by just a couple lines. If you click near the middle, you move back half a window at a time. Notice that the scrollbar moves up as you click the button.

To go back down, click the left-most mouse button. Again, clicking near the top moves you just a couple lines, while clicking near the bottom moves you a full window's length.

When you have a really big buffer of saved material, you may want to go to the beginning or end really fast. That's what the middle button is good for. Click anywhere in the scrollbar area, and you'll go to that part of the buffer. Therefore, click at the top to go to the beginning, and at the bottom to go to the end. Or click right on the scrollbar itself, hold down the button, and drag the scrollbar where you want to go.

Chapter 3

If you're a keyboard kind of person, you don't need to use the mouse to scroll. You can also hold down the Shift key and press the Page Up key to scroll backward, or the Page Down key to scroll forward. The keys work the same in a virtual console, by the way (see the section "Virtual Consoles" in Chapter 3).

You'll find that *xterm* does not save much output by default. To increase the number of lines that are saved, use the *–sl number* option or put an entry like the following in your *.Xdefaults* file:

```
XTerm*saveLines:                    400
```

Choosing fonts

Think your fonts are ugly or too small? There are plenty of others to choose from. Virtually every X application will let you choose the font used to display each kind of text (menus, etc.) You just have to know what their names are and what they look like.

To solve the first problem you can use the *xlsfonts* commands. Just as *ls* lists files, *xlsfonts* lists fonts. But if you enter the command without arguments, the volume of output will overwhelm you. It's better to figure out what types of fonts you need and just look at those.

Fonts on the X Window System have incredibly long names. A typical one is

```
-misc-fixed-bold-r-normal--13-100-100-100-c-70-iso8859-1
```

The hyphens divide the fonts into fields. For now, what interests us most is the field following the eleventh hyphen, where we see "c" in this example.

For *xterm* and many other applications, what you need is a *monospaced font*. That means a font where every character takes up the same amount of space, as opposed to *proportional fonts*, where an "m" is wider than an "i". Proportional fonts are great for displaying the output of a text processor like TEX, but they look horrible when they're used in a program that's not designed to handle the variety of spacing. When the eleventh field of the font name is "c" or "m" it represents a monospaced font.

Other fields can also help you make a choice. The third field tells you whether the font is medium (which means normal weight) or bold. The seventh field, which says 13 in the example above, gives you the size (actually the height of the largest character in pixels).

Now let's make up a specification and see whether our system has any fonts to match it. In *xlsfonts*, you specify a font through the *–fn* option and use an asterisk to match an arbitrary set of characters. If we want to match the third and eleventh fields exactly, and don't care what the other fields are, we enter:

```
eggplant$ xlsfonts -fn -*-*-bold-*-*-*-*-*-*-*-m-*-*
```

The first and second fields can be anything. But the third must be bold. The eleventh is also specified; it's an m. What we'll see is a list of monospaced bold fonts. If none exist, we'll get the message:

```
xlsfonts: pattern "-*-*-bold-*-*-*-*-*-*-*-m-*-*" unmatched
```

Now replace the m with a c and look for the rest of the monospaced fonts.

Actually, you don't have to use such complicated names. In our examples earlier in the chapter, we specified the short name 7x13bold. That kind of name is called an *alias*; it represents another name of the longer type. To see a short list of monospaced fonts using these aliases, enter

```
eggplant$ xlsfonts *x*
```

We've gone through a fair amount of trouble already, and all we have is a list of names. What do fonts actually look like? One simple way to try it is just to specify it in your *xterm* command:

```
eggplant$ xterm -fn -misc-fixed-bold-r-normal--13-100-100-100-c-70-iso8859-1
```

If you want to see every character in the font, use the *xfd* command, which stands for "X font display." It displays a grid with one rectangle for each character.

```
eggplant$ xfd -fn -misc-fixed-bold-r-normal--13-100-100-100-c-70-iso8859-1
```

When you find a font you like, cast it in concrete by putting it in your *.Xdefaults* file:

```
XTerm*Font:         7x13bold
```

Clocks

How can your screen be complete if it is unadorned by a little clock that tells you how much time you are wasting on customizing the screen's appearance? You can have a clock just the way you want it, square or round, analog or digital, big or small. You can even make it chime.

The *.xinit* file shown earlier in this chapter contains a line that starts *oclock*:

```
oclock -geometry 70x70+5+5 &
```

Refer to Figure 5-2 to see what this clock looks like. You may prefer the square outline of the *xclock* program:

```
xclock -geometry 150x150+5+5 &
```

Or perhaps a tiny digital clock at the bottom of your screen:

```
xclock -digital -geometry +10-10
```

oclock allows you to scatter more colors about, while *xclock* gives you more control over other aspects of the clock; see the manual pages for more information. To get a beep every half hour, invoke *xclock* with the *-chime* option.

The xbiff and xmh mail programs

The *xbiff* program just puts up a little picture of a mailbox that changes color and beeps whenever new mail arrives. A flag on the mailbox also goes up—a charming image from rural American life that we doubt exists anywhere within commuting distance of MIT, where *xbiff* is distributed.

You can change the pictures displayed by *xbiff* in your *.Xdefaults* file. The default bitmaps are `flagdown` when there's no mail waiting to be delivered, and `flagup` when mail is waiting. In the following two *.Xdefaults* entries, we change the bitmaps to an empty mailbox and one with a letter in it. Other predefined bitmaps can be found in */usr/local/X11/include/bitmaps*.

```
xbiff*emptyPixmap:          mailempty
xbiff*fullPixmap:           mailfull
```

If you find the *xbiff* beep distractingly loud or too soft, you can specify a different value through the *-volume* option. The range is 0 to 100, and the default is 33.

You can also hard-wire a value in your *.Xdefaults* file, as with most options in X applications:

```
xbiff*volume:          20
```

If you like scrollbars and buttons, you can use them to read and respond to your mail. The *xmh* program is a pretty full-featured mailer that offers the standard UNIX mailer options. You can store mail messages in different folders, view messages from a particular person or messages containing a particular word, etc. Since *xmh* is an interface to the character-based *mh* program, you need to have *mh* on your system.

Chapter 7

Most people seem to prefer a character-based mail reader like Elm or Pine, and you can do most of the same things within Emacs. We show you how to install Elm in Chapter 7, *Networking and Communications*. But here we'll show you the basics of *xmh* so you can decide whether to try it. Besides, it's worth learning the features of *xmh* because the other mailers offer similar ones—just the commands are different.

One nice feature of *xmh* is that you can see a list of mail messages at the same time that you read a message; you don't have to flip back and forth. Also, you can move messages from one folder to another without a lot of typing.

Before we start up *xmh*, let's increase the size of the windows, because the defaults tend to be too narrow. Put these lines in your *.Xdefaults* file:

```
Xmh*geometry              : 675x700
Xmh.clip*compGeometry     : 675x500
```

The first line sets the size of the main window that you will see in just a moment. The second sets the size of the composition window, where you write messages. Now start up the program:

```
eggplant$ xmh
```

A window like the one in Figure 5-7 appears. Since the format can be confusing when you're starting out, the figure explains what each element of the window is. There are already a lot of messages visible, and the little black box on the inbox button indicates that more are waiting to be read in.

Let's begin our mail session by reading in new mail. Put the mouse on the Table of Contents menu at the top. Hold down any of the buttons, pull the mouse down, and release the button over the Incorporate New Mail menu item.

If you like to use your keyboard instead of the mouse, this function and many others are bound to keys; in the X world, such keys are called accelerators. The key is a rather difficult stretch in this case (you'd better use two hands): you have to hold down the Shift and Alt keys at the same time and press "I".

The new mail should appear in the middle part of the window (the one bearing the label "inbox:all") with a plus sign next to the current message. The current

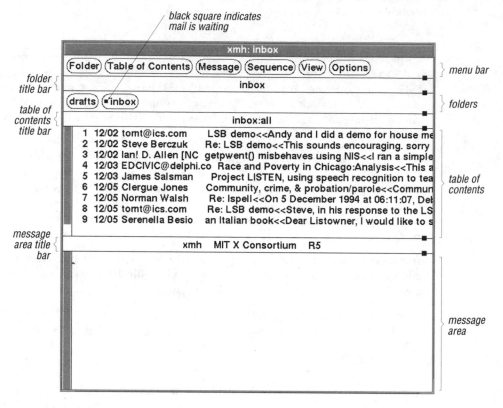

Figure 5-7. xmh window

message appears at the bottom of the window. Use the scrollbar to move down and read the message.

If you don't find the message exciting enough to continue taking up disk space, pull down the Message menu and choose Delete. You can achieve the same effect by pressing Alt-d. But the deletion is reversible; it doesn't become permanent until you choose Commit Changes from the Table of Contents menu or press Shift-Alt-C.

If you want to keep the message, you can go on to look at the next one by pulling down the Message menu and choosing the View Next Message item, or by pressing either Alt-Space or Alt-n. But just for fun, let's store the message in another folder. Folders let you keep track of messages on different subjects in different places.

Let's create a folder named "local." Just pull down the Folder menu and choose Create Folder (there's no accelerator key for this function). Type in "local" at the prompt and press the Return key. The folder now appears in an oval near the top of the window (see Figure 5-8).

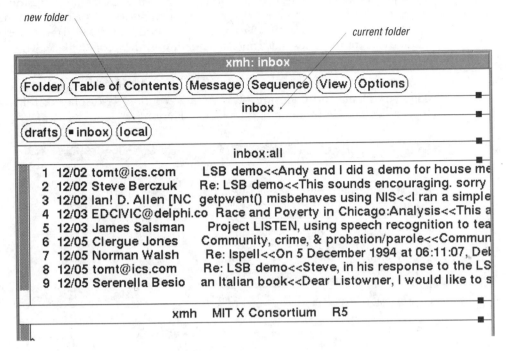

Figure 5-8. xmh window with new folder

You're not quite ready to file the mail away yet. Click on the new local folder. It's name replaces "inbox" in the label above the list of folders, meaning it's ready to receive messages. (One of the weaknesses of *xmh* is that it gives very subtle clues about what you've done and where you are; you really have to know what to look for.)

Now, to move the current message there, pull down the Message menu and choose Move. You can check to see that the operation was successful by pulling down the Folder menu and choosing Open Folder. This displays the contents of the local folder. Now click on the inbox oval and choose Open Folder again to return to your inbox.

To reply to a message, pull down the Message menu and choose Reply, or press Alt-r. To start a new message from scratch, pull down the Message menu and choose Compose Message. In either case, a new window appears. Unfortunately, unlike most UNIX mailers, *xmh* does not let you choose an editor. It makes you use a no-frills text editor developed as part of the X Window System. But it's not too bad; if you know Emacs, you'll find that a lot of the same commands work. When you are ready to send the message, press the Send button at the bottom of the window, then the Close Window button.

We'll just show one more very useful feature of *xmh*: the ability to restrict the messages displayed. You do this by specifying a string and a place that string should appear (the subject line, the "From" line, the body, and so on). All messages are hidden except the ones that contain the string in the proper place. There is also a mechanism for specifying a range of dates.

Suppose we want to view all messages about schools. Start by pulling down the Sequence menu and choosing Pick. A new window is displayed, full of options that we will not explore here. It looks like Figure 5-9.

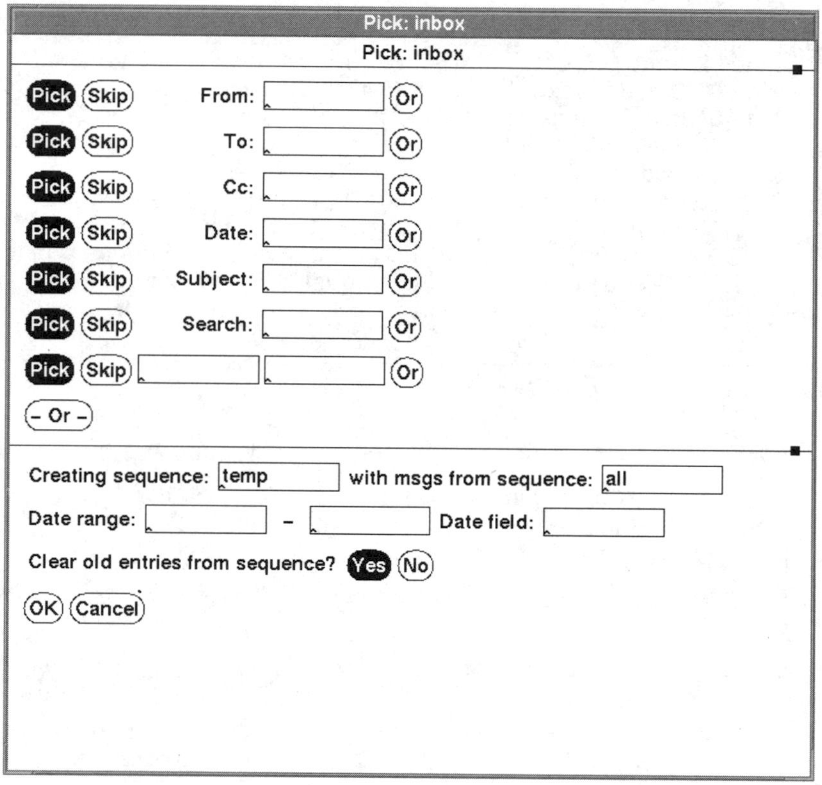

Figure 5–9. Pick window in xmh

Click on the box next to "Subject:" and type in "LSB". Also, you should give this sequence of messages a meaningful name so that you can find it later. Click on the box next to "Creating sequence," backspace to remove what's there, and type in "lsb". The result is shown in Figure 5-10. Finally, press the button on the bottom labeled OK. The window disappears and a new list of messages appears in the inbox.

To exit *xmh*, pull down the Folder menu and choose Close Window.

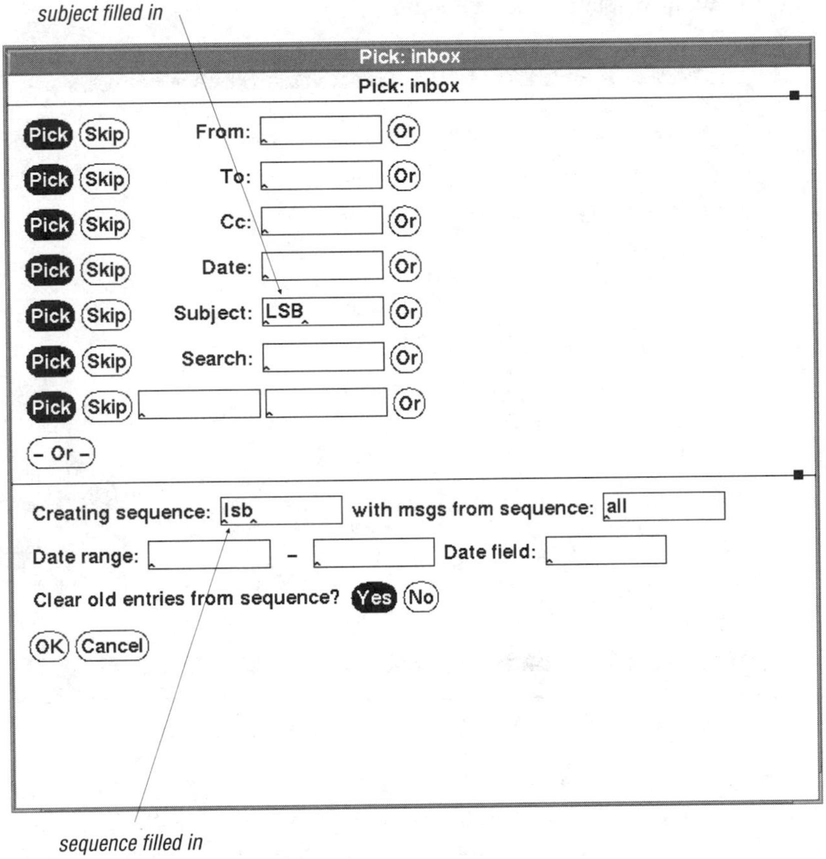

subject filled in

Figure 5-10. Pick window in xmh, filled in

Emacs

The X features in Emacs are getting spiffier and spiffier. Emacs version 19 includes pull-down menus, different typefaces for different parts of your window, and a complete integration of cut-and-paste functions with the X environment.

Let's start by defining some nice colors for different parts of the Emacs window. Try this command:

```
eggplant$ emacs  -bg ivory  -fg slateblue  -ms orangered  -cr brown
```

You are setting the background color, foreground color, mouse color, and cursor color respectively. The cursor is the little rectangle that appears in the window, representing what's called "point" in Emacs—the place where you type in text. We'll return to colors soon.

When you start Emacs, the menu bar on top and the scrollbar on the right side of the window stand out. See Figure 5-11.

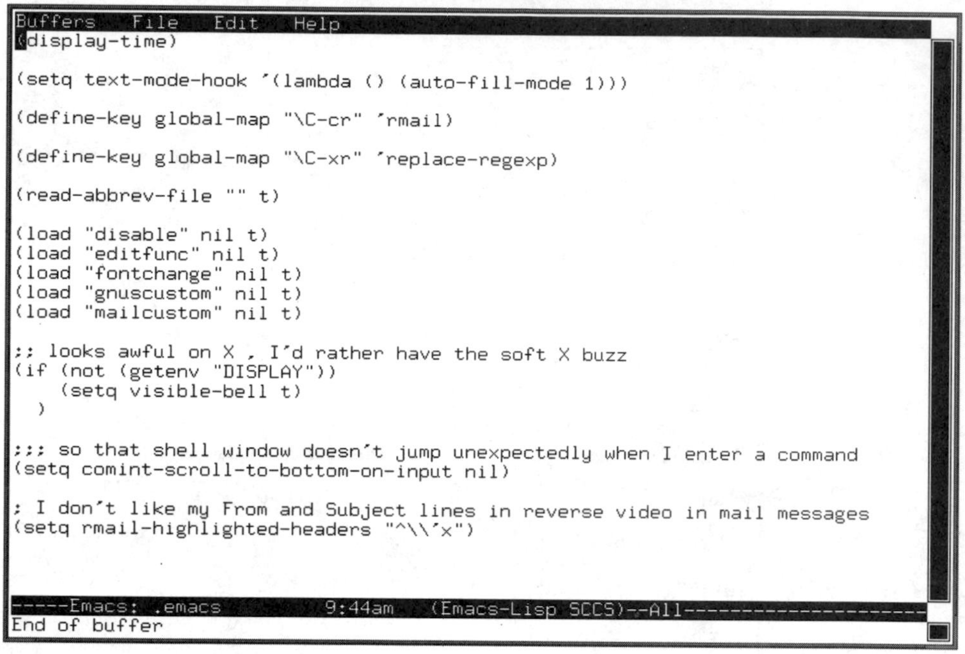

```
Buffers   File   Edit   Help
(display-time)

(setq text-mode-hook '(lambda () (auto-fill-mode 1)))

(define-key global-map "\C-cr" 'rmail)

(define-key global-map "\C-xr" 'replace-regexp)

(read-abbrev-file "" t)

(load "disable" nil t)
(load "editfunc" nil t)
(load "fontchange" nil t)
(load "gnuscustom" nil t)
(load "mailcustom" nil t)
;; looks awful on X , I'd rather have the soft X buzz
(if (not (getenv "DISPLAY"))
    (setq visible-bell t)
  )

;;; so that shell window doesn't jump unexpectedly when I enter a command
(setq comint-scroll-to-bottom-on-input nil)

; I don't like my From and Subject lines in reverse video in mail messages
(setq rmail-highlighted-headers "^\\'x")



-----Emacs: .emacs        9:44am   (Emacs-Lisp SCCS)--All-------------------
End of buffer
```

Figure 5-11. Emacs window

The scrollbar works just like the *xterm* scrollbar. The menu bar offers a lot of common functions. Some editing modes, like C and TEX, have their own pull-down menus. The menus are not documented, so you will just have to experiment and try to figure out which Emacs functions they correspond to.

When you want to use a function that doesn't have a simple key sequence—or you've forgotten the sequence—then the menus come in most handy, For instance, if you rarely use a regular expression search (a quite powerful feature, well worth studying) then the easiest way to invoke it is to pull down the Edit menu and choose Regexp Search from it.

Another useful menu item is Choose Next Paste on the Edit menu. This offers something you can't get any other way: a list of all the pieces of text you've cut recently. In other words, it shows you the kill ring. You can choose the text you want to paste in next, and the next time you press C-y (the Control key plus y) it's put in your buffer.

If you get tired of the scrollbar and the menu, put the following Lisp code in your *.emacs* file to make them go away:

```
(if (getenv "DISPLAY")
    (progn (menu-bar-mode -1)
           (scroll-bar-mode -1))
    )
```

The mouse is the next X feature with interesting possibilities. You can cut and paste text much the same way as in *xterm*. And you can do this between windows—so if you see some output in an *xterm* that you'd like to put in a file, you can copy it from the *xterm* and paste it into your Emacs buffer. Moreover, any text you cut the normal way (such as through C-w) goes into the same selection as text you cut with the mouse. So you can cut a few words from your Emacs buffer and paste them into an *xterm*.

The right-most mouse button works a little unusually. If you select text with the left-most button, you can click once on the right-most button to copy it. A second click removes it. To paste it back, press the middle button. The text goes just before the character that the mouse is on currently.

Make a mistake? That's all right; the undo command reverses it just as for any other Emacs function. (Choose Undo from the Edit menu or just press the C-_ key.)

If you really love mouse work, you can define the buttons to execute any functions you want, just as with keys. Try putting the following command in your *.emacs* file. When you hold down the Shift key and press the left-most button, a buffer for composing a mail message appears:

```
(define-key global-map [S-mouse-1] 'mail)
```

We don't recommend that you redefine the existing mouse functions, but the Shift, Control, and Meta keys offer plenty of unused possibilities. Combine S-, C-, and M- any way you want in your definitions:

```
(define-key global-map [S-C-mouse-1] 'mail)
```

Now let's play around a bit with windows. Emacs has had windows of its own for decades, of course, long before the X Window System existed. So an Emacs window is not the same as an X window. What X considers a window, Emacs calls a *frame*.

How would you like to edit in two frames at once? Press C-x52 and another frame appears. The new frame is simply another view onto the same editing session. You can edit different buffers in the two frames, but anything you do in one frame is reflected to the corresponding buffer in the other. If you exit Emacs by pressing C-x C-c, both frames disappear. So if you want to close just one frame, use C-x50.

To end our exploration of Emacs on the X Window System, we'll look at the exciting things you can do with colors. These can be changed during an Emacs session, which makes it easy to play around with different possibilities. Press M-x, then type in "set-background-color" and press the return key. At the prompt, type "ivory" or whatever other color you've chosen. (Emacs uses the convention M-x where we use Meta-x or Alt-x in the rest of the book.)

Be careful to make the foreground and background different enough so that you can see the text! In addition to set-background-color, Emacs offers set-foreground-color, set-cursor-color, and set-mouse-color.

This playing around may appear just cute, but it shows its true colors when you let Emacs highlight different parts of your buffer in different ways. For instance, when you are programming in C or Lisp, you can display strings, comments, function names, and keywords in different colors.

To set up color coding, you have to set font lock mode. The easiest way to do this is in your *.emacs* start-up file; add lines like the following:

```
(add-hook 'c-mode-hook '(lambda () (font-lock-mode 1)))
(add-hook 'c++-mode-hook '(lambda () (font-lock-mode 1)))
(add-hook 'lisp-mode-hook '(lambda () (font-lock-mode 1)))
(add-hook 'emacs-lisp-mode-hook '(lambda () (font-lock-mode 1)))
```

These rather complicated commands tell each major mode to set the font lock whenever you open a buffer in that mode. So whenever you edit a file ending with the suffix *.c*, for instance, you automatically set the font lock.

Next, you want to play with faces, which are the different kinds of text defined by Emacs. Press M-x and enter the command list-faces-display. You'll see a list like the following:

```
            bold abcdefghijklmnopqrstuvwxyz ABCDEFGHIJKLMNOPQRSTUVWXYZ
     bold-italic abcdefghijklmnopqrstuvwxyz ABCDEFGHIJKLMNOPQRSTUVWXYZ
         default abcdefghijklmnopqrstuvwxyz ABCDEFGHIJKLMNOPQRSTUVWXYZ
       highlight abcdefghijklmnopqrstuvwxyz ABCDEFGHIJKLMNOPQRSTUVWXYZ
          italic abcdefghijklmnopqrstuvwxyz ABCDEFGHIJKLMNOPQRSTUVWXYZ
        modeline abcdefghijklmnopqrstuvwxyz ABCDEFGHIJKLMNOPQRSTUVWXYZ
          region abcdefghijklmnopqrstuvwxyz ABCDEFGHIJKLMNOPQRSTUVWXYZ
secondary-selection abcdefghijklmnopqrstuvwxyz ABCDEFGHIJKLMNOPQRSTUVWXYZ
       underline abcdefghijklmnopqrstuvwxyz ABCDEFGHIJKLMNOPQRSTUVWXYZ
```

You can now set the background and foreground of each face interactively. For instance:

1. Enter M-x set-face-background.

2. Type "modeline" at the first prompt.

3. Type "lemonchiffon" at the second prompt.

You'll see the results immediately. Then set the foreground:

1. Enter M-x set-face-foreground.

2.   Type "modeline" at the first prompt.

3.   Type "green" at the second prompt.

No, that probably doesn't offer enough contrast for you to read the words. So do it again and use the color "maroon." That looks better.

Find a buffer with C or Lisp code in it and try setting each of the other faces. Faces are assigned rather arbitrarily to elements of the code. As you add colors, new dimensions will be revealed in your code. For instance, in C or C++ mode:

- Comments and preprocessor keywords appear in `italic` face

- Strings and include file names appear in `underline` face

- Function names and defined variables appear in `bold-italic` face

It probably looks best to reserve the bolder colors for short, rarely seen pieces of text.

When you find a set of colors you like, hard-wire them into your *.emacs* file by using the Lisp functions that correspond to the commands you've been experimenting with. Here's a sample set:

```
(set-background-color "ivory")
(set-foreground-color "slateblue")
(set-cursor-color "brown")
(set-mouse-color "orangered")
(set-face-foreground 'bold "black")
(set-face-background 'bold "lightpink")
(set-face-foreground 'bold-italic "red")
(set-face-background 'bold-italic "wheat")
(set-face-foreground 'italic "darkolivegreen")
(set-face-background 'modeline "lemonchiffon")
(set-face-foreground 'modeline "maroon")
(set-face-foreground 'underline "violet")
```

You can also set colors in your *.Xdefaults* file, but that takes a little more effort, so we won't bother to explain it here.

Ghostview—displaying PostScript

Adobe PostScript, as a standard in its own right, has become one of the most popular formats for exchanging documents in the computer world. Many academics distribute papers in PostScript format. The Linux Documentation Project offers its manuals in PostScript form, among others. This is useful for people who lack the time to format LaTeX input, or who have immense network bandwidth for transferring files. When you create documents of your own using *groff* or TeX, you'll want to be able to view them on a screen before you use up precious paper resources by printing them.

Ghostview, a GNU application, offers a pleasant environment for viewing PostScript on the X Window System. It's very simple. Invoke it with the name of the file to be displayed, for instance:

```
eggplant$ ghostview article.ps
```

The Ghostview window is huge; it can easily take up most of your screen. The first page of the document is displayed with a vertical scrollbar on the right and a horizontal one on the bottom. Menu options appear on the left side of the window, and page numbers just to their right.

Like most X applications, Ghostview offers both menu options and keys (accelerators) for common functions. Thus, to view the next page, you can pull down the Page menu and choose the Next option. Or you can just press the Space bar.

To go back to the previous page, choose Previous from the Page menu. To go to any page you want, press the middle button on its number in the number column. To exit, choose Quit from the File menu or just press q.

Documents from different countries often use different page sizes. The Ghostview default is the standard U.S. letter size (this can be overridden by comments in the PostScript file). You can specify a different size on the command line:

```
eggplant$ ghostview -a3 article.ps
```

or in your *.Xdefaults* file:

```
Ghostview*pageMedia:            A3
```

Finally, you can also choose a different size at run time from the Media menu.

Ghostview lets you enlarge or reduce the size of the page, a very useful feature for checking the details of your formatting work. (But be warned that fonts on the screen are different from the fonts on a printer, and therefore the exact layout of characters in Ghostview will not be the same as the layout in the hard copy.) To zoom in on a small part of the page, press any of the mouse buttons on it. (The right-most button enlarges the most; the left-most button the least.)

You can also change the default size for displaying the whole document by using the Magstep menu. The higher the number you choose, the more the document is enlarged. Negative numbers reduce the size of the document.

To print a page, choose Print from the File menu or just press p anywhere in the window. You are prompted to make sure that you've chosen the right printer; you can erase what is shown there and enter a different name. The name shown comes from your environment. So, if your printer is named "doorway," you should have issued a shell command in your start-up file like:

```
export PRINTER=doorway
```

You can also print several pages. Select individual ones by clicking on their numbers with the middle button. Or select the first page with the left-most button, and the last page with the right-most button; the whole range of pages will be printed when you press p.

xman: a point-and-click interface to manual pages

Manual pages, read through the *man* command, are the ultimate authority on a UNIX system. Other books can describe a significant percentage of any given command's functions—and can often describe them in a more readable fashion—but only the manual page has all the details. See the section "Manual Pages" in Chapter 3 for basic information about manual pages.

Chapter 3

Now there's a simple X interface to manual pages, in the *xman* command. As befits a tool that displays documents, it contains a pretty good description of itself. In order to see this documentation clearly, start up the program with a large page size:

```
eggplant$ xman -pagesize 650x600
```

What you see first is a tiny box with three buttons. Click on the Manual Page button to bring up the main screen, where you'll do most of your work.

Now you see the *xman* documentation. You'll have plenty of time to read this; for now, just pull down the Options menu and choose Search, or press Ctrl-S. (You can also display the options menu by holding down the Control key and pressing the left-most mouse button.) In the box that pops up, type in a command or function that you'd like to read about, then press the return key. The contents of the main window are replaced by the corresponding manual page.

If you don't know what to look for, try pulling down the Sections menu or pressing the Control key along with the middle button. Choose a section from the menu that appears. You'll see a long list of manual pages. Click the left-most button on one of them, and it will be displayed.

Another time-honored way to look for information is through the *apropos* command (discussed already in the section "Manual Pages" in Chapter 3. Press Ctrl-S again, type in a word about a subject you're interested in, and press the Apropos button. If any manual pages match that word, their names will be displayed along with short descriptions. Unfortunately, you can't call up their manual pages by clicking on them; that little convenience was left out of *xman*. You have to press Ctrl-S and type in the page that looks interesting.

Within a manual page, scrolling is easy. Use the Space bar or f to move down a page, b to move up. You can also use the scrollbar, just as in *xterm*.

Now you can read the documentation! Press the Help button on the small window that appeared when you started *xterm*. To exit the program, press Ctrl-Q or the Quit button, or choose Quit from the Options menu.

Linux, DOS, and Foreign OS Compatibility

Linux is a remarkably effective operating system that normally replaces MS-DOS. However, there are always those of us who want to have their cake and eat it, too. We want to continue to use other operating systems as well as Linux, or at least to exchange files directly with them. Linux satisfies such yearnings with internal enhancements that allow it to access foreign filesystems and act on their files, and with compatibility utilities that allow DOS to be invoked to run DOS applications, or a utility that allows Xenix binaries to be run on Linux without recompiling.

We use the term DOS semi-generically in this chapter to refer to any of the MS-DOS compatible OS's—MS-DOS, PC-DOS, and DR-DOS/Novell DOS—but not in the generic sense of Disk Operating System, unless specifically indicated otherwise.

Some of these utilities work very well, while others are perhaps "not ready for prime time." Still, development in this area is proceeding rapidly, and if you want to use some of these compatibility features, you should investigate the matter further. These tools will allow many who otherwise couldn't find out about Linux to try it out without first abandoning their reliable working platform, or without buying a second computer to play with.

You should be a little skeptical of some dreams of compatibility though. Just because something can be done, doesn't mean it is a great idea. As a practical matter, you might find for example that you need twice the disk storage in order to support two OS's and their associated files and applications programs, plus file conversion and graphic format conversion tools, and so on. You may find that hardware tuned for one OS won't be tuned for the other, and you will have to choose where to spend your cash.

For example, as we write this, MS-DOS supports 32-bit file read and write operations only on IDE drives, leaving SCSI drives with compromised performance, and also making the user rely on third-party-supplied drivers for the SCSI peripheral devices. On the other hand, Linux makes it easy to use the full power and expandability of SCSI-2 peripherals. While an SCSI controller supports up to seven of a broad variety of devices, the typical IDE controller supports only two IDE devices. Anything but disk drives and a few choices in CD-ROM drives are scarce).

The desire to have everything will probably continue to drive Linux developers, so we confidently expect that the fledgling AT-bus/Intel tools that we describe here be developed until they are stable and practical. Moreover, we expect similar developments to allow other OS's to coexist with Linux on other platforms, such as the Amiga, the Macintosh, and Intel and DEC Alpha systems running Windows NT.

Foreign Files and Directories

The ability of Linux to access foreign filesystems is a key factor in making it practical to keep more than one OS on a PC. Linux can already read and write to a number of different filesystems—more than any other OS we know of. This capability includes compatibility with filesystems of some UNIX work-alikes, such as Minix and Coherent, as well as the various DOS and OS/2 file systems, and such academically developed or research-oriented filesystems as Carnegie Mellon University's `afs` (Andrew File System). Linux can also access ISO 9660 CD-ROM filesystems, along with the Rock Ridge extensions that support long filenames.

Chapter 2
Chapter 4

You can add support for foreign filesystems when installing Linux, or by rebuilding the Linux kernel. These activities are described in the sections "Creating the Filesystems" in Chapter 2, *Obtaining and Installing Linux*, and "Building the Kernel" in Chapter 4, *Essential System Management*. Non-Linux partitions are mounted and seen as directories you can access. A DOS partition that serves you as your C: drive might be seen from Linux as */dosc*.

Clearly, the most important foreign filesystem that Linux currently can read from and write is the MS-DOS 16-bit FAT (File Allocation Table) filesystem. This is a truly practical feature. You can enjoy the power and speed of Linux without giving up special DOS applications that you need. For example, you could use graphics authoring software under DOS, and then access the graphics files under Linux (perhaps filtering them through a graphics conversion filter like *pbmplus*) and incorporate them into multimedia World Wide Web documents that you access with Mosaic or another multimedia browser. Or, you might use a favorite DOS communications package to retrieve a file that you will use under Linux.

Because you can also access DOS FAT-16 format diskettes under a number of other OS's as well as Linux (particularly in the 3.5 inch, 1.44 MB diskette format), you have the means for "sneakernet" file transfer between Linux and these OS's, which include DOS, Macintosh, Amiga, and various UNIXes. The FAT 16 filesystem, limited as it is, is the *lingua franca* of filesystem-based data transfer.

However, file formats are also a compatibility issue. System V UNIX has introduced several file formats to UNIX that are not shared across all UNIX implementations. Foreign file formats are addressed by iBCS2, an "Intel Binary Compatibility Standard" package that allows users to run many commercial applications on Linux.

While we don't tend to think of UNIX-type applications as foreign, incompatible file formats do prevent direct interchange of executable applications between some UNIX-type operating systems, even on the same hardware. The iBCS2 package supports the UNIX SVR4 ELF file link format, and the COFF common object file format (commonly used on UNIX SVR3 implementations and Xenix). Some applications packages for commercial Intel UNIX implementations have been demonstrated using iBCS2 (most notably Word Perfect, the most popular DOS word processor). iBCS2 seems to work fairly well, and it may eventually be added to standard Linux distributions.

iBCS2 recently was moved from alpha to beta distribution status. You can retrieve it from Linux archive sites, including **sunsite**, in */pub/linux/ALPHA/ibcs2*. However, it is not clear that iBCS2 is a significant package that will have a long-term influence to get people to use Linux. Many commercial developers have already identified Linux as far and away the fastest growing segment of the UNIX market, and are actively porting their applications to Linux or using it as a native development platform. Also, many Linux users would not consider buying software priced for use on commercial UNIXes because of the cost of the package, and because such a commercial package will almost certainly not be supported by the vendor when used under Linux rather than the intended (and supported) UNIX OS.

Utilities for Accessing DOS Filesystems: MTools

The MTools package is a suite of Linux tools that allow DOS files to be manipulated from within Linux. (The MTools *do not* provide Linux file manipulation features from DOS.) Some of the MTools may be made obsolete by the ability to build Linux with support for DOS filesystems, which you should do. But other tools remain useful.

Here are summaries of the MTools utilities; they are further documented in manual pages that are part of the distribution.

mattrib
Change attributes of a DOS file.

mcd
Change to a DOS directory.

mcopy
Copy files from Linux to DOS or from DOS to Linux.

mdel
Delete a DOS file.

mdir
Display a DOS directory.

mformat
Write a DOS FAT filesystem to a diskette.

mlabel
Write a DOS disk volume label to a DOS partition.

mmd
Create a DOS directory.

mrd
Remove a DOS directory.

mread
> Read a low-level DOS file to Linux.

mren
> Rename a DOS file.

mtype
> Display the contents of a DOS file.

mwrite
> Write a low-level format Linux file to DOS.

The Next Step: Binary Emulation

The most important compatibility target for Linux (at this time) is clearly the DOS market: MS-DOS, PC-DOS, Novell DOS, and Windows 3.1 and later. You can use the Linux MTools package to search DOS filesystems, read and copy files, and write to a DOS filesystem. Still, compatibility with DOS obviously requires a lot more than handling a DOS filesystem.

There are two main packages intended to provide Linux with the desired DOS compatibility. One is *dosemu* and the other is Wine. We discuss them both in this chapter because of their importance to the Linux community. Still, we have to remind you that as of the time of this writing, the announcement message for the current version of the *dosemu* package (0.52) advises "definitely still consider this ALPHA software." The Wine package is still described as "early alpha stage" development. Neither can be recommended as reliable solutions for running a DOS application under Linux. For that reason, you won't find them in many standard Linux distribution packages.

The development teams working on *dosemu* and Wine are delighted to encourage more developers to pitch in and help, but if you are simply an end-user, or are a programmer but don't have access to the Internet to get ready access to the developer community, these packages may not be right for you.

There are also emulators for the Apple II and CP/M operating systems. They originally were ports for other operating systems (such as MS-DOS) and have now been ported to Linux. You can get them from the usual Linux FTP sites that archive the emulator software, which are primarily **sunsite.unc.edu** and its mirror sites in the path */pub/Linux/system/emulators*.

A demo of a commercial (but low-priced) Macintosh emulator is also available from **sunsite.unc.edu**. You can find it in a file confusingly named *elinux199c.tar* (if they don't rename it when they see this comment), but it is called Executor/Linux. This is a Linux version of a package that has been offered for several years on NeXT machines, and for over a year on DOS machines. You might try it if only to gain the ability to read and write Mac diskette and SCSI disk formats that the demo package provides. (The developers of this product announced that they will release the source code for their Mac file browser to the public.) By running *tar* on the file, we found out that it is intended to be installed from the root directory.

If you want to keep up with developments on Executor/Linux, send mail to *majordomo@nacm.com* with nothing in the Subject: field, and with the message text of subscribe executor.

DOS Emulators: *dos* and *xdos*

First, we should make it clear that Linux's "DOS emulators," the *dosemu* and *xdos* packages, aren't really emulators. They can be considered virtual machines that allow DOS and applications running on DOS to execute in real mode (virtual 8086 mode) in a "compatibility box" environment that is similar to the operation of DOS on a standard Intel 80286 or 80386. Because a necessary element of the compatibility box is the virtual 8086, only chipsets that implement the Intel real mode will ever have *dosemu* or *xdos* ported to it. *xdos* is a development of *dosemu* adapted specifically to be run in an X Window, so for this discussion we'll focus primarily on *dosemu*.

You should have 8 MB of RAM to use *dosemu*, and it would be wise to also have a 12 MB swap partition set up on the hard disk.

dosemu emulates the BIOS, CMOS memory, XMS and EMS memory, disk services, keyboard, serial devices and printer, and other necessary machine functions, letting DOS work in this controlled environment. *dosemu* requires that you have a (licensed) copy of DOS. MS-DOS versions 3.3 through 6.22 are currently used in *dosemu* development, and Novell DOS (DR-DOS) 6 has also been used. Presumably one can also use comparable versions of IBM's PC-DOS. Graphics accelerators using the ET4000 chipset seem to be favored in *dosemu* development, and such video support as exists may appear first for this graphics chipset. However, the S3 chipset is also reasonably supported.

dosemu tries to trap DOS and BIOS system calls and handle them in Linux, but isn't always entirely successful. (Remember that Linux is a multitasking OS, and DOS is not; a hung DOS process could potentially bring Linux to its knees.) For example, DOS BIOS printer services are emulated with UNIX file I/O, with the output intended for a printer spooled to a corresponding Linux file. *dosemu* has problems with mouse support for some mice, particularly bus mouse systems.

We don't encourage you to use *dosemu* unless you are willing and able to contribute to the further development of the package, and have Internet access to work with the development team. However, *dosemu* appears to be useful enough and stable enough to justify discussing it as an installable package. You should be aware, though, that the development of documentation for *dosemu* lags behind the development of software. If you aren't involved in *dosemu* development you may find it difficult to use new features. They may not be that safe anyhow.

More recent versions of *dosemu* include some functions that were originally developed as part of Carnegie Mellon University's DOS emulator for Mach, so *dosemu* distributions include the very non-restrictive CMU copyright notice. This notice asks that developers who build software using CMU's work provide a copy of their work to CMU and allow CMU the right to use and redistribute it. (The copyright notice *requires* that their notice be reproduced and included in any distribution that uses their software, whether or not their code is modified.) You should honor CMU's copyright, so if you will participate in developing *dosemu*, be sure to read and observe their copyright notice.

The *dosemu* package includes scripts and utilities to install and maintain the package. *dosemu* is updated weekly, and each distribution includes a list of software known to run (or not to run) with the current release of the package.

Getting dosemu and xdos

The FTP sites guaranteed to maintain the latest public version of the *dosemu* package are **tsx-11.mit.edu** and **dspsun.eas.asu.edu**. The files can be found in the */pub/linux/ALPHA/dosemu* directory. ("Alpha" refers to the state of development of the application, not to a distribution for Alpha architecture Linux.) The most recent FAQ/HOWTO file for *dosemu* is found on the FTP site **dspsun.eas.asu.edu** in the */pub/dosemu* directory. However, the package can also be readily found on **sunsite.unc.edu** in the */pub/Linux/system/Emulators* directory, along with all other emulators for Linux.

The *xdos* package, for those determined to explore all corners of Linux, can be found on the FTP site **unix.hensa.ac.uk** in */pub/yggdrasil/usr/X386/bin/xdos*, and at **sunsite.unc.edu** in */pub/Linux/system/Emulators/dosemu*. The *xdos* package, while derived from *dosemu*, does not directly inform or control *dosemu* development. While it is planned for *dosemu* to provide windows support, it has not been determined that *xdos* will form a basis for this development.

A new utility called *garrot* was recently announced (in early alpha stage) by developer Thomas McWilliams (*tgm@netcom.com*) that allows you to minimize *dosemu*'s demand for CPU cycles when idle. *garrot* allows *dosemu* to be used with less impact on other ongoing Linux operations. *garrot.com* is run as a DOS command in the *dosemu* compatibility box and installs itself as a Linux daemon. You can FTP this utility from **sunsite.unc.edu** in the */pub/Linux/system/Emulators* directory.

dosemu support for compressed filesystems is still in development, and you may or may not be able to use *dosemu* with a DOS filesystem that implements data compression. *dosemu* can handle both Stacker and doublespace data compression modes, apparently, but not always without problems. (There have been problems using these with DOS at times, too, eh?) You may need a certain amount of disk space for a DOS partition, and if you don't have one, you either need to add a hard disk or at least repartition the hard disk. This implies re-installing Linux. The

MFS redirector feature of *dosemu* allows you to access a Linux directory as a DOS network filesystem, but is doesn't eliminate the need for disk storage for DOS.

As you update from one version of *dosemu* to a later version, you will probably find that you have to discard utilities, rebuild files and directories, and so on. This is fairly normal when using alpha or beta grade software, and isn't unheard of for released commercial products. It is one of the common joys of using beta software.

Installing and configuring dosemu

Before you install the *dosemu* package, you must first compile the Linux kernel with IPC (System V InterProcess Communication facilities). If you did not build Linux with IPC during the *config* process when installing Linux, you will have to rebuild the kernel to add the facilities before installing *dosemu*, which uses System V shared memory. We strongly recommend that you use a current release of Linux as a basis for running *dosemu*, and compile *dosemu* with a current *gcc* compiler and libraries. Linux 1.1.12 and later include the needed kernel support for *dosemu*, but you can update versions Linux 1.0.8 and later using a patch provided in the *dosemu* distribution if you don't want to replace a version of Linux you are using.

You must have *gcc* version 2.5.8 and *libc* version 4.5.21 or later at this time. Later versions of *dosemu* may require later versions of Linux, *gcc*, and C libraries.

To install *dosemu*, start by making a bootable DOS diskette for use in your A: drive. Here is a procedure using a formatted blank disk (if you already have a built DOS partition on your disk to work from):

```
C:> sys a:
C:> copy \dos\fdisk.exe a:
C:> copy \dos\sys.com a:
C:> dir a:
COMMAND.COM
FDISK.EXE
SYS.COM
```

These are the minimum files your bootable DOS diskette should have, but don't fill the disk with other files yet; you'll have to add some new *dosemu* utilities to this diskette.

Boot Linux and login as **root**. Place the *dosemu* package in the /root directory and unpack it. (The *dosemu* package name may vary from this example, whose name reflects downloading the file via DOS before copying it into the Linux filesystem.)

```
# gunzip dosem052.tgz
# tar -xvf dosemu052.tar
```

The files will unpack into the directories */var/lib/dosemu*, */usr/lib/libdosemu*, *dosemu0.52*, and subdirectories of *dosemu0.52*.

Now read the documentation. A *dosemu* HOWTO file comes with the distribution package, in the */dosemu0.52/doc* directory. Also, read the file *QuickStart* that comes with the distribution. If you need to rebuild your kernel to add IPC and DOS filesystem support, and to install a kernel patch, do it now.

A file named *DANG* ("Dosemu Novice's Altering Guide") contains notes for customizing source code. These are extracted automatically from the source code itself, at each release. Additionally, the *dos(1)* manual page describes the state of the *dos* command for your version of *dosemu*. There is a Texinfo document for *dosemu* (*dosemu.texinfo*) that lags well behind the current state of development of the package. It contains information useful in preparing to install the *dosemu* package.

Still as root, go to the *dosemu0.52* directory and verify that the distribution Makefile exists there. Enter the command

```
# make doeverything
```

If this fails with a message indicating "no rule to build a '.h' file", enter

```
# make install
```

Copy the */dosemu0.52/examples/exitemu.com* file to the bootable DOS disk you made earlier.

Copy the file */dosemu0.52/hdimage.dist* to */var/lib/dosemu/hdimage*. This is a DOS image file that will be made DOS-bootable from Linux as a DOS partition. From the */dosemu0.52* directory, copy the *./drivers/*.sys* files, *./commands/*.com* files, and *./commands/*.exe* files to a directory accessible to *dosemu*, such as */tmp*.

Copy */dosemu0.52/examples/config.dist*, the *dosemu* configuration file, to */etc/dosemu.conf*, and edit it. The first `disk` statement in the */etc/dosemu.conf* file should point to the file */var/lib/dosemu/hdimage*. The */etc/dosemu.conf* file contains lots of comments to assist you in configuring *dosemu*. An example of this file follows this procedure. You will need to provide information for location of the DOS partition on the hard disk that contains the bootable DOS system.

Set up the emulated drive. From the */dosemu0.52* directory, enter:

```
# dos -A
```

After a delay, DOS will boot and show a prompt:

```
A>
```

From the `A:` drive, view the `C:` drive to determine that you are using the emulated DOS disk image drive (specified as */var/lib/dosemu/hdimage*):

```
A> DIR C:
```

Enter:

```
A> FDISK /MBR C:
A> SYS C:
```

This adds the master boot record to the emulated C: drive and enables you to boot DOS directly from the *hdimage* file without using a diskette. Exit from DOS:

```
A> EXITEMU
```

Back at the Linux prompt, enter:

```
# dos
C> COPY \TMP\*.* .
```

You will be in your *dos* image file, and the copy command will collect files that *dosemu* uses into the *dos* image file.

Chapter 3

Now try switching virtual consoles while running *dos* with the usual Alt-F1 through Alt-F6 function keys. (Virtual consoles are described in the section "Virtual Consoles" in Chapter 3.) If this doesn't work properly, you can try using Ctrl-Alt-*functionkey* to switch virtual consoles. Then exit *dosemu*:

```
C> EXITEMU
#
```

Undoubtedly, you will want to perform additional tuning to get just the DOS configuration you want. Just edit */etc/dosemu.conf* to make further adjustments; they take effect when you next run *dos*. This lets you quickly solve problems that occur with specific DOS software, terminal modes, sound system support, and the like. You can add pointers to additional DOS directories on hard disks. You will have to use */usr/lib/dosemu/mkpartition* if you will use disk compression on a DOS partition (but don't use compression on the Linux *dos* image file). You may want to run *dosemu* in a 25-line X terminal window, or use a virtual console for DOS. You may need to restrict access privileges to DOS if you have a heavily taxed Linux system.

Sample dosemu configuration file

The *dosemu* configuration file, */etc/dosemu.conf,* looks like Example 5-1 when it is first unpacked. (This file came from *dosemu* version 0.52; your version may differ).

Example 5-1: dosemu Configuration File

```
# Linux dosemu 0.51 configuration file.
# Updated to include QuickStart documentation 5/10/94 by Mark Rejhon
# James MacLean, jmaclean@fox.nstn.ns.ca, 12/31/93
# Robert Sanders, gt8134b@prism.gatech.edu, 5/16/93
# NOTICE:
#    - Although QuickStart information is included in this file, you
#        should refer to the documentation in the "doc" subdirectory of the
```

Example 5-1: dosemu Configuration File (continued)

```
#        DOSEMU distribution, wherever possible.
#     - This configuration file is designed to be used as a base to make
#        it easier for you to set up DOSEMU for your specific system.
#     - Configuration options between lace brackets { } can be split onto
#        multiple lines.
#     - Comments start with # or ; in column 1. (beginning of a line)
#     - Send Email to the jmaclean address above if you find any errors.
#************************** DEBUG *****************************************
#
# QuickStart:
#     This section is of interest mainly to programmers.  This is useful if
#     you are having problems with DOSEMU and you want to enclose debug info
#     when you make bug reports to a member of the DOSEMU development team.
#     Simply set desired flags to "on" or "off", then redirect stderr of
#     DOSEMU to a file using "dos 2>debug" to record the debug information
#     if desired.  Skip this section if you're only starting to set up.
#
debug { config  off     disk    off     warning off     hardware off
        port    off     read    off     general off     IPC      off
        video   off     write   off     xms     off     ems      off
        serial  off     keyb    off     dpmi    off
        printer off     mouse   off
      }
#************************** MISCELLANOUS *********************************
#
#   Want startup DOSEMU banner messages?  Of course :-)
dosbanner on
#
#   timint is necessary for many programs to work.
timint on
#************************** KEYBOARD ************************************
#
# QuickStart:
#     With the "layout" keyword, you can specify your country's keyboard
#     layout.  The following layouts are implemented:
#         finnish             us          dvorak        sf
#         finnish_latin1      uk          sg            sf_latin1
#         gr                  dk          sg_latin1     es
#         gr_latin1           dk_latin1   fr            es_latin1
#         be                  no          fr_latin1
#     The us-layout is selected by default if the "layout" keyword is omitted.
#
#     The keyword "keybint" allows more accurate of keyboard interrupts,
#     It is a bit unstable, but makes keyboard work better when set to "on".
#     The keyword "rawkeyboard" allows for accurate keyboard emulation for
#     DOS programs, and is only activated when DOSEMU starts up at the
#     console.  It only becomes a problem when DOSEMU prematurely exits
#     with a "Segmentation Fault" fatal error, because the keyboard would
#     have not been reset properly.  In that case, you would have to reboot
#     your Linux system remotely, or using the RESET button.  In reality,
```

Example 5–1: dosemu Configuration File (continued)

```
#     this should never happen.  But if it does, please do report to the
#     dosemu development team, of the problem and detailed circumstances,
#     we're trying our best!  If you don't need near complete keyboard
#     emulation (needed by major software package), set it to "off"
keyboard {  layout us  keybint on  rawkeyboard on  }
# keyboard {  layout gr-latin1  keybint on  rawkeyboard on  }
#
#     If DOSEMU speed is unimportant, and CPU time is very valuable to you,
#     you may want to set HogThreshold to a non-zero value.  This means
#     the number of keypress requests in a row before CPU time is given
#     away from DOSEMU.  A good value to use could be 10000.
#     A zero disables CPU hogging detection via keyboard requests.
#
HogThreshold 0
#*************************** SERIAL ************************************
#
# QuickStart:
#     You can specify up to 4 simultaneous serial ports here.
#     If more than one ports have the same IRQ, only one of those ports
#     can be used at the same time.  Also, you can specify the com port,
#     base address, irq, and device path!  The defaults are:
#         COM1 default is base 0x03F8, irq 4, and device /dev/cua0
#         COM2 default is base 0x02F8, irq 3, and device /dev/cua1
#         COM3 default is base 0x03E8, irq 4, and device /dev/cua2
#         COM4 default is base 0x02E8, irq 3, and device /dev/cua3
#     If the "com" keyword is omitted, the next unused COM port is assigned.
#     Also, remember, these are only how you want the ports to be emulated
#     in DOSEMU.  That means what is COM3 on IRQ 5 in real DOS, can become
#     COM1 on IRQ 4 in DOSEMU!
#     Also, as an example of defaults, these two lines are functionally equal:
#     serial {  com 1  mouse  }
#     serial {  com 1  mouse  base 0x03F8  irq 4  device /dev/cua0  }
#
#     If you want to use a serial mouse with DOSEMU, the "mouse" keyword
#     should be specified in only one of the serial lines.  (For PS/2
#     mice, it is not necessary, and device path is in mouse line instead)
#     Uncomment/modify any of the following if you want to support a modem:
#     (or any other serial device.)
#serial {  com 1  device /dev/modem  }
#serial {  com 2  device /dev/modem  }
#serial {  com 3  device /dev/modem  }
#serial {  com 4  device /dev/modem  }
#serial {  com 3  base 0x03E8  irq 5  device /dev/cua2  }
#     If you have a non-PS/2 mouse, uncomment/modify one of the following.
#serial {  mouse  com 1  device /dev/mouse  }
#serial {  mouse  com 2  device /dev/mouse  }
#
#     What type is your mouse?  Uncomment one of the following.
#     Use the 'internaldriver' option with ps2 and busmouse options.
#mouse {  microsoft  }
```

Example 5-1: dosemu Configuration File (continued)

```
#mouse { logitech }
#mouse { mmseries }
#mouse { mouseman }
#mouse { hitachi }
#mouse { mousesystems }
#mouse { busmouse }
#mouse { ps2  device /dev/mouse internaldriver }
#    The following line won't run for now, but I hope it will sometimes
#mouse { mousesystems device /dev/mouse internaldriver cleardtr }
#************************* NETWORKING SUPPORT ***************************
#
#    Turn the following option 'on' if you require IPX/SPX emulation.
#    Therefore, there is no need to load IPX.COM within the DOS session.
#    The following option does not emulate LSL.COM, IPXODI.COM, etc.
#    NOTE: MUST HAVE IPX PROTOCOL ENABLED IN KERNEL !!
ipxsupport off
#
#    Enable Novell 8137->raw 802.3 translation hack in new packet driver.
#pktdriver novell_hack
#************************* VIDEO ***************************************
#
# !!WARNING!!: A LOT OF THIS VIDEO CODE IS ALPHA!  IF YOU ENABLE GRAPHICS
# ON AN INCOMPATIBLE ADAPTOR, YOU COULD GET A BLANK SCREEN OR MESSY SCREEN
# EVEN AFTER EXITING DOSEMU.  JUST REBOOT (BLINDLY) AND THEN MODIFY CONFIG.
# QuickStart:
#    Start with only text video using the following line, to get started.
#    then when DOSEMU is running, you can set up a better video configuration.
#
video { vga  console }          # Use this line, if you are using VGA
# video { cga  console }        # Use this line, if you are using CGA
# video { ega  console }        # Use this line, if you are using EGA
# video { mda  console }        # Use this line, if you are using MDA
# Even more basic, like on an xterm or over serial, use one of the
# following :
#
#    For Xterm
# video { vga chunks 25 }
#    For serial at 2400 baud
# video { vga chunks 200 }
# QuickStart Notes for Graphics:
#    - If your VGA-Bios resides at E000-EFFF, turn off video BIOS shadow
#      for this address range and add the statement vbios_seg 0xe000
#      to the correct vios-statement, see the example below
#    - Set "allowvideoportaccess on" earlier in this configuration file
#      if DOSEMU wont boot properly, such as hanging with a blank screen,
#      beeping, or the video card bootup message.
#    - Video BIOS shadowing (in your CMOS setup) at C000-CFFF must be disabled.
#
#      *> CAUTION <*: TURN OFF VIDEO BIOS SHADOWING BEFORE ENABLING GRAPHICS!
#
```

Example 5-1: dosemu Configuration File (continued)

```
#    It may be necessary to set this to "on" if DOSEMU can't boot up properly
#    on your system when it's set "off" and when graphics are enabled.
#    Note: May interfere with serial ports when using certain video boards.
allowvideoportaccess on
#
#    Any 100% compatible standard VGA card _MAY_ work with this:
#video { vga  console  graphics }
#
#    If your VGA-BIOS is at segment E000, this may work for you:
#video { vga  console  graphics  vbios_seg 0xe000 }
#
#    Trident SVGA with 1 megabyte on board
#video { vga  console  graphics  chipset trident  memsize 1024 }
#
#    Diamond SVGA
#video { vga  console  graphics  chipset diamond }
#
#    ET4000 SVGA card with 1 megabyte on board:
#video { vga  console  graphics  chipset et4000  memsize 1024 }
#
#    S3-based SVGA video card with 1 megabyte on board:
#video { vga  console  graphics  chipset s3  memsize 1024 }
#*************************** MISCALLANEOUS ***************************
#
# QuickStart:
#    For "mathco", set this to "on" to enable the coprocessor during DOSEMU.
#    This really only has an effect on kernels prior to 1.0.3.
#    For "cpu", set this to the CPU you want recognized during DOSEMU.
#    For "bootA"/"bootC", set this to the bootup drive you want to use.
#    It is strongly recommended you start with "bootA" to get DOSEMU
#    going, and during configuration of DOSEMU to recognize hard disks.
#
mathco on              # Math coprocessor valid values:  on  off
cpu 80386              # CPU emulation valid values:  80286  80386  80486
bootA                  # Startup drive valid values:  bootA  bootC
#*********************** MEMORY *****************************************
#
# QuickStart:
#    These are memory parameters, stated in number of kilobytes.
#    If you get lots of disk swapping while DOSEMU runs, you should
#    reduce these values.  Also, DPMI is still somewhat unstable,
#    (as of early April 1994) so be careful with DPMI parameters.
#
xms 1024               # XMS size in K,  or "off"
ems 1024               # EMS size in K,  or "off"
dpmi off               # DPMI size in K, or "off"  Be careful with DPMI!
#********************** PORT ACCESS ************************************
#
# !!WARNING!!: GIVING ACCESS TO PORTS IS BOTH A SECURITY CONCERN AND
# SOME PORTS ARE DANGEROUS TO USE.  PLEASE SKIP THIS SECTION, AND
```

Example 5-1: dosemu Configuration File (continued)

```
# DON'T FIDDLE WITH THIS SECTION UNLESS YOU KNOW WHAT YOU'RE DOING.
#
# ports { 0x388 0x389 }  # for SimEarth
# ports { 0x21e 0x22e 0x23e 0x24e 0x25e 0x26e 0x27e 0x28e 0x29e } # for jill
#****************** SPEAKER ******************************************
#
# These keywords are allowable on the "speaker" line:
#   native      Enable DOSEMU direct access to the speaker ports.
#   emulated    Enable simple beeps at the terminal.
#   off         Disable speaker emulation.
#
speaker native        # or "off" or "emulated"
#****************** HARD DISKS ****************************************
#
# !!WARNING!!: DAMAGE MIGHT RESULT TO YOUR HARD DISK (LINUX AND/OR DOS)
# IF YOU FIDDLE WITH THIS SECTION WITHOUT KNOWING WHAT YOU'RE DOING!
#
# QuickStart:
#    The best way to get started is to start with a boot floppy, and set
#    "bootA" above in the configuration.  Keep using the boot floppy
#    while you are setting this hard disk configuration up for DOSEMU,
#    and testing by using DIR C: or something like that.
#    If you want DOSEMU to be able to access a DOS partition, the
#    safer type of access is "partition" access, because "wholedisk"
#    access gives DOSEMU write access to a whole physical disk,
#    including any vulnerable Linux partitions on that drive!
#    !!! IMPORTANT !!!
#    You must not have LILO installed on the partition for dosemu to boot off.
#    As of 04/26/94, doublespace and stacker 3.1 will work with wholedisk
#    or partition only access.  Stacker 4.0 has been reported to work with
#    wholedisk access.  If you want to use disk compression using partition
#    access, you will need to use the "mkpartition" command included with
#    dosemu to create a partition table datafile for dosemu.
#    Please read the documentation in the "doc" subdirectory for info
#    on how to set up access to real hard disk.
#
#    "image" specifies a hard disk image file.
#    "partition" specifies partition access, with device and partition number.
#    "wholedisk" specifies full access to entire hard drive.
#    "readonly" for read only access.  A good idea to set up with.
#
#disk { image "/var/lib/dosemu/hdimage" }   # use diskimage file.
#disk { partition "/dev/hda1" 1 readonly }  # 1st partition on 1st IDE.
#disk { partition "/dev/sda2" 1 readonly }  # 1st partition on 2nd SCSI.
#disk { wholedisk "/dev/hda" }              # Entire disk drive unit
#****************** DOSEMU BOOT ****************************************
#
#    Use the following option to boot from the specified file, and then
#    once booted, have bootoff execute in autoexec.bat. Thanks Ted :-).
#    Notice it follows a typical floppy spec. To create this file use
```

Example 5-1: dosemu Configuration File (continued)

```
#       dd if=/dev/fd0 of=/var/lib/dosemu/bdisk bs=16k
#
#bootdisk { heads 2 sectors 18 tracks 80 threeinch file /var/lib/dosemu/bdisk }
#
#       Specify extensions for the CONFIG and AUTOEXEC files.  If the below
#       are uncommented, the extensions become CONFIG.EMU and AUTOEXEC.EMU.
#       NOTE: this feature may affect file naming even after boot time.
#       If you use MSDOS 6+, you may want to use a CONFIG.SYS menu instead.
#
#EmuSys EMU
#EmuBat EMU
#******************** FLOPPY DISKS ****************************************
#
# QuickStart:
#       This part is fairly easy.  Make sure that the first (/dev/fd0) and
#       second (/dev/fd1) floppy drives are of the correct size, "threeinch"
#       and/or "fiveinch".  A floppy disk image can be used instead, however.
#
#       FOR SAFETY, UNMOUNT ALL FLOPPY DRIVES FROM YOUR FILESYSTEM BEFORE
#       STARTING UP DOSEMU!  DAMAGE TO THE FLOPPY MAY RESULT OTHERWISE!
#
floppy { device /dev/fd0 threeinch }
floppy { device /dev/fd1 fiveinch }
#floppy { heads 2  sectors 18  tracks 80
#          threeinch  file /var/lib/dosemu/diskimage }
#
#       If floppy disk speed is very important, uncomment the following
#       line.  However, this makes the floppy drive a bit unstable.  This
#       is best used if the floppies are write-protected.
#
#FastFloppy on
#******************** PRINTERS ****************************************
#
# QuickStart:
#       Printer is emulated by piping printer data to a file or via a unix
#       command such as "lpr".  Don't bother fiddling with this configuration
#       until you've got DOSEMU up and running already.
#
#printer { options "%s"  command "lpr"  timeout 20 }
#printer { options "-p %s"  command "lpr"  timeout 10 }    # pr format it
#printer { file "lpt3" }
```

Windows Emulation: WINE

Wine is the most ambitious DOS compatibility package, and it bears tremendous
potential value to the Linux community. Wine is inspired by the Windows Application Binary Interface (WABI), which originally was developed by Sun Microsystems
to allow Microsoft Windows packages to be run directly on Solaris. WABI has been
licensed by Sun to other System V ports to the Intel PC, and a WABI development

group comprised of several UNIX vendors guides further development of WABI. No Linux vendor (that we are aware of) is a member of the WABI development group. However, the WABI specifications are made available to the public, and the Linux *dosemu* team has applied them to the Wine development effort. Wine is being developed for Linux, NetBSD, and FreeBSD at this time, and commercial vendor support is also being sought.

You need at least 8 MB of RAM to use Wine, and at least a 12 MB swap partition set up on the hard disk.

Wine consists primarily of a program loader that loads and executes 16-bit MS Windows application binaries, and an emulation library that translates calls to MS Windows functions and translates them into Linux and X Window System function calls. As the Wine FAQ notes, Wine means either "WINdows Emulator, or Wine Is Not an Emulator. Both are right." When Wine is fully developed, most Windows applications will run under Wine in the Linux/X environment, and will run about as fast under under Wine as they do under windows. Maybe faster. A Linux-supported graphics coprocessor makes a big difference in performance of the X Window System, and therefore makes a big difference to Wine performance.

Wine ultimately will not require that you have Microsoft Windows, or even a DOS partition on your system. Currently, however, both a (Linux-mounted) uncompressed DOS partition, DOS, and an MS-Windows binary are required so that Wine can locate Windows applications. Wine is filesystem-independent, and can be used on any Linux (or UNIX) filesystem. You also must use the X Window System to run Wine; Wine is invoked from a window opened by your favorite Linux window manager:

```
wine /dospartition/winapp.exe
```

where *dospartition* is the Linux-mounted DOS partition name (usually something like */dosc* or */dos/c*), and *winapp.exe* is a windows-based executable.

We can't encourage you to use Wine unless you are a programmer who will contribute to the further development of this ambitious package. Wine is very much in alpha-stage development. As of this writing, Wine implements more than 40 percent of the MS-Windows application programming interface (API) functions. Because we think you won't be able to use Wine effectively at this stage unless you are a programmer with Internet access, in this edition of the book we omit discussing how to install and configure Wine.

You can join the Wine developers' mailing list by contacting the Wine Project Manager, Bob Amstadt (*bob@amscons.com*). If you aren't willing to be a developer, please don't try to to join this mailing list. You can track Wine development on the newsgroup *comp.emulators.ms-windows.wine*. Bob will gladly accept money and equipment to further the development effort, of course.

You can FTP the current Wine package from the **sunsite.unc.edu** FTP site in the directory */pub/Linux/system/Emulators*, and at some other Linux FTP sites. The

Wine distribution is updated weekly, and each distribution includes a list of software known to run (or not to run) with the current release of the package.

When the current 16-bit Windows applications are well supported, and when 32-bit Windows95 is released, work will continue in order to support Windows95 and Windows NT applications. Currently this isn't an issue, as all Windows applications are available for the 16-bit Windows environment.

Using Multimedia on Linux

Linux, installed on the correct hardware, provides an excellent platform for developing and using multimedia documents and applications. In this section we discuss considerations in setting up your Linux system for multimedia documents. These might range from hypertext, to printed matter and graphics, to interactive video and audio. We don't try to discuss multimedia software development in this section—that deserves a separate book—but we do discuss fundamental issues that are of interest to the applications developer as well as to the multimedia document developer and consumer.

Your requirements for both hardware and software are directly determined by the type of multimedia documents you want to create. You can accomplish a lot even with a very limited budget. If you select the right approach, you can augment and extend your initial multimedia work when you have a more capable system, rather than discarding it. We discuss the structured documentation philosophy that allows you to continually develop and enhance your documents rather than replace them as more powerful hardware and software becomes common for multimedia presentation. Finally, we offer a strategy for implementing a structured documentation philosophy that will continue to meet your needs as your skills and goals expand.

Hardware

If all you wish to do is create hypertext, the basic Linux requirements are sufficient. You don't even need to run the X Window System. If you wish to include much in the way of graphics, or if you want to use system audio, you may have much more serious requirements. You can actually create effective multimedia documents with a system that is inadequate for satisfactory presentation of that document.

First, let's examine the physical elements of a PC Linux system and how they affect your ability to create and display multimedia documents. Then we'll summarize the minimum requirements for creating and presenting various levels of multimedia document sophistication.

Motherboard

The ISA (AT bus) 16-bit motherboard is the bottom end performer for your multimedia platform. A 16-bit motherboard without an expansion bus such as a local-bus slot is probably a bit too slow for satisfactory graphics performance, unless you are using a graphics card with a dedicated graphics coprocessor on it. Even then, you will probably be unable to perform smooth video and animation.

If your multimedia requirements do not include video sequences, a basic 16-bit motherboard can provide adequate multimedia performance. Some motherboards allow you to increase the bus speed from the base 8MHz rate to 10 or even 12.5 MHz. This is an effective way to improve graphics performance if all your cards are able to cope with the accelerated bus clock. If you are buying a new motherboard, however, don't get one without localbus slots conforming to either VLB or PCI specifications. Today that also means getting a 486 or Pentium processor, since development of 386 motherboards has pretty much stopped.

Processor

The 386SX central processing unit (CPU) is the slowest CPU that Linux will run on, and it is adequate for creating hypertext. If you wish to format large text documents into a graphic form, or incorporate and manipulate graphic file forms such as X bitmaps or PostScript files, however, you may find that you need a math processing unit (MPU). This is a separate processor on Intel 386SX, 386, and 486SX systems, and on most clone systems as well. Even an 80287-class MPU (supported on some 386/486SX motherboards) will provide a significant boost in performance to many graphic formatting applications over a "bare" CPU without MPU support.

If you haven't yet bought a system for multimedia use, you should strongly consider getting a system that has a CPU with integral MPU circuitry, such as the Intel 80486 or Pentium. Note that popular clone CPUs often do not provide integral math circuitry. Their math performance, even with an external MPU, may suffer in comparison with a processor that incorporates mathematics processing circuitry. That aside, a number of multimedia products do not use an MPU, and in that case, it really doesn't matter whether or not a math coprocessor is installed. Also, while it may be important to have an MPU to create page layouts and format graphics, it is less important for displaying them. This function is more dependent on your graphics card performance, as discussed below.

Memory

If you want to do multimedia development beyond hypertext and the occasional graphic, you should plan to use more memory than the base 8MB requirement it requires for that purpose. 16MB should be adequate for developing and displaying any multimedia document, though more memory can be used effectively to buffer large amounts of data for rapid access and presentation.

Audio systems

The heart of your audio system is the audio card. Most audio cards are rather unsophisticated, which would be deplorable if more applications actually needed good audio performance. But high quality audio is not a priority in the current generation of multimedia applications. Most audio cards currently are 16-bit cards that provide waveform generation that is SoundBlaster-compatible. Your audio card should meet this minimum requirement and have stereo input and output jacks. You may have additional requirements depending on your intended multimedia presentation purposes, and most current generation cards offer enhancements oriented toward one or another of the contending computer audio standards. They also often provide DOS software to permit you to use these enhanced features. But you may also have to convert the audio files from one format to another to use them effectively in the Linux environment.

Increasingly, sound cards provide enhanced sound-sampling features that you may wish to use, or have chips that provide sophisticated sound generation capabilities. Most of these features are currently unsupported except through some software package that may lock you in—probably on DOS or OS/2 rather than on Linux.

Don't despair, though, if you want to use these capabilities. A number of Linux device driver developers and applications programmers continue to broaden support for features of a number of different sound cards under Linux. Check the Linux Hardware FAQ and the Linux SOUND HOWTO for the latest information on utilities and drivers to support the features you need. Currently available Linux utilities provide support for sound generation, recording, and playback on various SoundBlaster, Pro Audio, Gravis, and other ISA bus audio cards. Using audio file conversion utilities, you may also convert and use sound sample files retrieved from Internet FTP sites, created by MIDI synthesizers, or taken from audio CDs, and incorporate them into your multimedia document in a form usable by your presentation software.

Graphics board and display

For anything but plain text, you need at least VGA-level (640 by 480 pixel) graphics. Luckily, this fundamental baseline is supported by nearly all PC systems that can run Linux, and is a resolution that can also be used on Macintosh systems, Amigas, and other non-Intel architectures too. If you are developing documents to be portable, you should probably support this mode, even if you provide higher resolutions. 640 by 480 pixel resolution easily exceeds requirements for video, especially if 16.7 million colors can be used—even 256 colors is adequate in this resolution if the colors are carefully managed.

Today, however, 640 by 480 resolution may seem inadequate for still images. You may prefer to support a higher resolution, such as 800 by 600, 256-color mode, or 1024 by 768 resolution in monochrome or color. Whatever resolution you select, it will simplify your portability and graphics conversion issues if you stay with a display mode that uses a 4:3 horizontal/vertical pixel ratio. (This provides a "square pixel" display that, for example, allows 90 degree image rotation without turning your squares to rectangles and your circles to ovals.) The bottom line is that your graphics card and display must support your intended graphics display resolution.

There are countless combinations of graphics card and display that you may have in a PC. We assume that you will use the X Window System, and thus the XFree86 package, if you wish to develop or use graphics in your multimedia documents. It is enticing to use the highest possible resolution in a windowing environment because that lets you more effectively use multiple windows. However, as you get into the higher resolutions, the performance of both the graphics card and the display become significant limiting factors, and either or both can cripple multimedia graphics performance. Beyond 800 by 600 resolution, display system costs also begin to escalate rapidly.

We recommend that you use a graphics card with a popular graphics accelerator chipset that XFree86 supports, such as the ET4000 or the S3, on the best, highest bandwidth bus that your motherboard supports. These are available for well under US $200. Other, better-performing chipsets are also now supported. You can find the latest listings for supported graphics boards and chipsets in the XFree86 FAQ or the Linux Hardware FAQ. Such a graphics coprocessor will offer non-interlaced resolution of 1024 by 768 or better.

Data has to be loaded to the graphics coprocessor via the system bus, and this is also a bottleneck. If you have an EISA bus system or a VLB or PCI local bus slot on your motherboard, you can easily get much better performance than the standard 16-bit ISA card. You might have to use such an enhanced bus to achieve adequate performance if you want to display animation or computer video images.

Most of these accelerated graphics cards provide 1MB of graphics memory on the board. If you are doing animation or resolutions above 1024 by 768 pixels, or are using many colors, you may prefer a graphics board that permits you to have 2MB or more of video RAM.

Your monitor often sets the limit on your system's graphics performance, and there are cost thresholds that set the parameters of your display performance. Your base color or monochrome monitor has a 14-inch display (measured diagonally from corner to corner). If this display has a reasonably small dot pitch (.28 mm, or better, .26 mm) it can present a 1024 by 768 resolution at this display size. For multimedia use, you may want a larger display, even if the dot pitch is larger.

A 17-inch display offers a viewing area 50 percent larger than that of a 14-inch display. Even at equal resolutions, the image is much more satisfying on the larger display. For resolutions greater than 14 inches, you should forget about monochrome monitors. In years past, large monochrome displays of 1600 by 1200 pixels and 21 inches were available, but these products have all but disappeared as the cost of large color displays have dropped. There are a handful of good

15-inch color displays available, and the next step up is the 17-inch color display. Many of these displays are capable of displaying 1600 by 1200 resolution or higher; most larger displays don't offer resolutions higher than this. Of course, within limits, bigger is still perceived to be better.

The size of the display is only part of the issue though. A smaller monitor with finer dot pitch may be better than a larger display with a larger dot pitch, especially if the pixels are bright and clearly defined and the display tube is "flat."

A major contributor to high resolution imaging is the display horizontal scan rate. This rate sets the display refresh rate and the maximum non-interlaced resolution for the display. If the refresh rate is not high enough at a given resolution, annoying screen flicker can cause eye fatigue, especially when you view graphics that have fine lines. If you are using extensive graphics at 1024 by 768 resolution, you will want a scan rate of 76kHz or higher. Remember, too, that your graphics adaptor must supply an input frequency that allows your display to perform at the desired frequency. Here's how to determine the ability of a monitor to provide the horizontal scan rate that you need—generally, higher is better:

1. Divide the monitor's horizontal scan rate in Hertz by the number of horizontal lines in the resolution setting (768 for a resolution of 1024 by 768 pixels, for example). This gives you a theoretical refresh rate.

2. Multiply the theoretical refresh rate by an adjustment factor of .96. This factor compensates for the necessary time that the monitor's electron gun takes to reposition itself, from the bottom of the screen at the end of a scan, back to the top to begin the next scan. The result is a reasonable approximation of the actual refresh rate.

When examining your graphics card and your display, you may find that you can achieve certain graphic modes using more than one scan rate. You may have to tune your XFree86 configuration in order to specify the highest effective scan rate that your graphics card and display can jointly support for a given mode. This will usually result in the best possible display for the resolution, though you may find unwelcome harmonic flicker effects at some frequencies that interact with fluorescent lighting, or that performance at the edge of a monitor's tolerance may be jittery.

Structured Multimedia Documents

Effective multimedia documents are "structured documents." They have elements that can be presented in different ways, depending on the output devices that are available to the user.

For example, a structured multimedia document might be formatted for the printed page with 1-inch margins, 10-point roman font, 6 lines of text per vertical inch of display, graphics presented as black on white monochrome images, and footnotes printed at the bottom of the page in which the footnote marker occurs. The identical document might be displayed on a multimedia computer system in a window wider than it is tall, with no margins preserved, and with footnotes not revealed unless an icon is selected using the mouse, which would cause the footnote text to pop up in a secondary window. The graphics might be in color or monochrome depending on the display, and at a resolution appropriate to the scale of the window; clicking on the graphic might initiate a segment of video with audio accompaniment. Viewing the same document with a character-based display and no window system might cause the text to be formatted for a 24-line, 80-character wide display, with footnotes appearing immediately following the paragraph containing the footnote marker.

Another characteristic of a structured document is that it "lives." It can be adapted, linked to, and used in ways the original author never considered. The user, by applying features of the presentation software, controls the access and presentation of the document, and can extend the document by creating additional documentation through techniques such as indexing, annotation, creating links to other documents, and the like. All that is required to do this effectively is to have a document conform to a well-defined structure that is standard enough for developers of "formatting" software to accommodate.

This isn't pie-in-the-sky: structured documents have been around in some form for years, implemented as textual databases and mailing lists, Hypercard stacks, UNIX manual pages, and so on. Structured documents do not specify the appearance of the document or data stream (such as the RTF format, TeX, and *troff*) or map the presentation of an image on a defined plane surface (as do page description languages like HPGL and PostScript). The explicit mapping used by these older standards prevents the document from "living": it cannot be easily adapted for a wide range of output devices.

In 1986 a major international standard was adopted, ISO 8879, which defined the Standard Generalized Markup Language (SGML). This standard is now widely adopted in the publishing industry, and its promise in allowing flexibility in presentation is finally being realized.

In an SGML document, the content of a document—text, images, audio sequences, etc.—is contained in structural elements. Thus, you might have text organized into paragraphs and lists, those elements contained in sections and chapters. A Document Type Description, or DTD, defines what structural organization is permitted. (A book must contain at least one chapter; a chapter must have a title and at least one paragraph of text and may contain an image; an image can contain other images and one or more audio streams, etc.)

Computer industry publishers and some general publishers are creating books and online help systems from SGML-tagged documents. Admittedly, the technology is still expensive and complicated for developing large, complex documents, but you can use SGML today without studying musty spell books and learning dread incantations.

In the last two years, the Internet has exploded with documents created using World Wide Web (WWW) technology. The concept behind the World Wide Web is that documents around the world can be referenced and linked to each other on the Internet.

Using a WWW browser (a presentation utility) you can access a document at a site in London, England that contains a reference to another document in Helsinki, Finland. The browser treats the reference as a link, and if you select that link, the document is retrieved for you. You've just traveled the world with the click of a mouse! WWW browsers are becoming pretty sophisticated. There are a number of Linux/UNIX browsers that support WWW technology, and some have been ported to DOS, VMS, Macintosh, and other operating systems.

Chapter 7

The vast interlinked network of WWW documents is implemented through a structured document tagging language called HTML (HyperText Markup Language). A tutorial for writing in HTML appears in "Writing HTML Documents" in Chapter 7. While the original HTML implementation was only semi-structured (it allowed documents to be structured but did not require it), HTML 2.0, a second generation of the HTML language, permits you to create fully structured WWW documents that can also be fully SGML-compliant.

HTML 2.0 allows you to include various graphics, animation, audio, and other special output file formats in your structured document. One under-appreciated feature of HTML is that you can use the technology locally to create and display multimedia documents maintained on a hard disk or CD-ROM. You can also link the local documents to other WWW files on the Internet.

## CHAPTER SIX

PROGRAMMING WITH LINUX

There's much more to Linux than simply using the system. One of the benefits of free software is that it can be modified to suit the user's needs. This applies equally to the many free applications available for Linux and to the Linux kernel itself.

Linux supports an advanced programming interface, using GNU compilers and tools such as the *gcc* compiler, the *gdb* debugger, and so on. A number of other programming languages, including Perl, Tcl/Tk, and LISP, are also supported. Whatever your programming needs, Linux is a great choice for developing UNIX applications. Because the complete source code for the libraries and Linux kernel are provided, those programmers who need to delve into the system internals are able to do so.[*]

Chapter 5

Linux is an ideal platform for developing software to run under the X Window System. The Linux X distribution, as described in the section "The X Window System" in Chapter 5, *Power Tools*, is a complete implementation with everything that you need to develop and support X applications. Programming for X itself is portable across applications, so the X-specific portions of your application should compile cleanly on other UNIX systems.

In this chapter, we'll explore the Linux programming environment, and give you a nickel tour of the many facilities it provides. Half of the trick to UNIX programming is just knowing what tools are available, and how to use them effectively. Often the most useful features of these tools are not obvious to new users.

Since C programming is the basis of most large projects and the language common to most modern programmers—not only on UNIX, but on many other systems as well—we'll start out telling you what tools are available for that. The first few sections of the chapter assume that you are already a C programmer.

---

[*] On a variety of UNIX systems, the author has repeatedly found available documentation to be insufficient. With Linux, you are able to explore the very source code for the kernel, libraries, and system utilities. Having access to source code is more important than most programmers would think.

But several other tools are emerging as important resources, especially for system administration. We'll examine two in this chapter: Perl and Tcl/Tk. They are both scripting languages like the UNIX shells, taking care of grunt work like memory allocation so you can concentrate on your task. But both Perl and Tcl/Tk offer a degree of sophistication that makes them more powerful than shell scripts and appropriate for many programming tasks.

We'll wrap up the chapter by offering an introduction to debugging in C, and a number of other auxiliary tools that C programmers will find useful.

Programming with gcc

The C programming language is by far the most used in UNIX software development. Perhaps this is because the UNIX system itself was originally developed in C—it is the native tongue of UNIX. UNIX C compilers have traditionally defined the interface standards for other languages and tools, such as linkers, debuggers, and so on. Conventions set forth by the original C compilers have remained fairly consistent across the UNIX programming board. To know the C compiler is to know the UNIX system itself. Before we get too abstract, let's get to details.

The GNU C compiler, *gcc*, is one of the most versatile and advanced compilers around. Unlike other C compilers (such as those shipped with the original AT&T or BSD distributions, or from various third-party vendors), *gcc* supports all of the modern C standards currently in use—such as the ANSI C standard—as well as many extensions specific to *gcc* itself. Happily, however, *gcc* provides features to make it compatible with older C compilers and older styles of C programming.

gcc is also a C++ compiler. For those of you who prefer the obscure object-oriented environment, C++ is supported with all of the bells and whistles—including AT&T 3.0 C++ features, such as method templates. Complete C++ class libraries are provided as well, such as the *iostream* library familiar to many programmers.

For those with a taste for the particularly esoteric, *gcc* also supports Objective-C, an object-oriented C spinoff that never gained much popularity. But the fun doesn't stop there, as we'll see.

In this section, we're going to cover the use of *gcc* to compile and link programs under Linux. We assume that you are familiar with programming in C/C++, but we don't assume that you're accustomed to the UNIX programming environment. That's what we'll introduce you to here.

Quick Overview

Before imparting to you all of the gritty details of *gcc* itself, we're going to present a simple example and walk through the steps of what happens when you compile a C program on a UNIX system.

Let's say that you have the following bit of code, an encore of the much-overused "Hello, World!" program (not that it bears repeating):

```
#include <stdio.h>
int main() {
  (void)printf("Hello, World!\n");
  return 0; /* Just to be nice */
}
```

To compile this program into a living, breathing executable, there are several steps. Most of these steps can be accomplished through a single *gcc* command, but the specifics are left for later in the chapter.

First, the *gcc* compiler must generate an *object file* from the above *source code*. The object file is essentially the machine-code equivalent of the C source. It contains code to set up the *main()* calling stack, a call to the mysterious *printf()* function, and code to return the value of 0.

The next step is to *link* the object file to produce an executable. As you might guess, this is done by the *linker*. The job of the linker is to take object files, merge them with code from libraries, and spit out an executable. The object code from the above source does not make up a complete executable. First and foremost, the code for *printf()* must be linked in. Also, various initialization routines, invisible to the mortal programmer, must be appended to the executable.

Where does the code for *printf()* come from? The libraries. It is impossible to talk for long about *gcc* without making mention of them. A library is essentially a collection of many object files, including an index. When looking for the code for *printf()*, the linker looks at the index for each library it's been told to link against. It finds the object file containing the *printf()* function, and extracts that object file (the entire object file, which may contain much more than just the *printf()* function) and links it to the executable.

In reality, things are more complicated than this. As we have said, Linux supports two kinds of libraries—*static* and *shared*. What we have described above are static libraries—libraries where the actual code for called subroutines is appended to the executable. However, the code for subroutines such as *printf()* can be quite lengthy. Because many programs use common subroutines from the libraries, it doesn't make sense for each executable to contain its own copy of the library code. That's where shared libraries come in.

With shared libraries, all of the common subroutine code is contained in a single library "image file" on disk. When a program is linked with a shared library, "stub code," instead of actual subroutine code, is appended to the executable. This stub code tells the program loader where to find the library code on disk, in the image file, at run time. Therefore, when our friendly "Hello, World!" program is executed, the program loader notices that the program has been linked against a shared library. It then finds the shared library image and loads code for library routines, such as *printf()*, along with the code for the program itself. The stub code tells the loader where to find the code for *printf()* in the image file.

Even this is an oversimplification of what's really going on. Linux shared libraries use "jump tables" that allow the libraries to be upgraded, and their contents to be jumbled around, without requiring the executables using these libraries to be relinked. The stub code in the executable itself actually looks up another reference in the library itself—in the jump table. In this way, the library contents and the corresponding jump tables can be changed, but the executable stub code can remain the same.

But don't allow yourself to be befuddled by all of this abstract information. In time, we'll approach a real-life example and show you how to compile, link, and debug your programs. It's actually very simple—most of the details are taken care of for you by the *gcc* compiler itself. However, it helps to have an understanding of what's going on behind the scenes.

gcc Features

gcc has more features than we could possibly enumerate here. Below, we present a short list, and refer the curious to the *gcc* manual page and info document, which will undoubtedly give you an eyeful of interesting information about this compiler. Later in this section, we'll give you a comprehensive overview of the most useful *gcc* features to get you started. This in hand, you should be able to figure out for yourself how to get the many other facilities to work to your advantage.

For starters, *gcc* supports the "standard" C syntax currently in use, specified for the most part by the ANSI C standard. The most important feature of this standard is function prototyping. That is, when defining a function *foo()*, which returns an int and takes two arguments, a (of type char *) and b (of type double), the function may be defined like this:

```
int foo(char *a, double b) {
  /* your code here... */
}
```

This is in contrast to the older, non-prototype function definition syntax, which looks like:

```
int foo(a, b)
char *a;
double b;
{
  /* your code here... */
}
```

which is also supported by *gcc*. Of course, ANSI C defines many other conventions, but this is the one that is most obvious to the new programmer. Anyone familiar to C programming style in modern books such as the second edition of Kernighan and Ritchie's *The C Programming Language* will be able to program using *gcc* with no problem. (C compilers shipped on some other UNIX systems do not support ANSI features such as prototyping.)

[42] C Progr.
Language

The *gcc* compiler boasts quite an impressive optimizer. Whereas most C compilers allow you to use the single switch *–O* to specify optimization, *gcc* supports multiple *levels* of optimization. At the highest level of optimization, *gcc* will pull tricks out of its sleeve such as allowing code and static data to be shared. That is, if you have a static string in your program such as "Hello, World!", and the ASCII encoding of that string happens to coincide with a sequence of instruction code in your program, *gcc* will allow the string data and the corresponding code to share the same storage. How's that for clever?

Of course, *gcc* allows you to compile debugging information into object files, which aids a debugger (and hence, the programmer) in tracing through the program. The compiler will insert markers in the object file allowing the debugger to locate specific lines, variables, and functions in the compiled program. Therefore, when using a debugger such as *gdb* (which we'll talk about later in the chapter), you can step through the compiled program and view the original source text simultaneously.

Among the other tricks offered by *gcc* is the ability to generate assembly code with the flick of a switch (literally). Instead of telling *gcc* to compile your source to machine code, you can ask it to stop at the assembly-language level, which is much easier for humans to comprehend. This happens to be a nice way to learn the intricacies of protected-mode assembly programming under Linux—write some C code, have *gcc* translate it into assembler for you, and study that.

gcc includes its own assembler (which can be used independently of *gcc*), just in case you're wondering how this assembly-language code might get assembled. In fact, you can include inline assembly code in your C source, in case you need to invoke some particularly nasty magic but don't want to write exclusively in assembly.

Basic gcc Usage

By now, you must be itching to know how to invoke all of these wonderful features. It is important, especially to novice UNIX and C programmers, to know how to use *gcc* effectively. Using a command-line compiler such as *gcc* is quite different from, say, using a development system such as Borland C under MS-DOS. Even though the language syntax itself is similar, the methods used to compile and link programs are not at all the same.

Returning to our innocent-looking "Hello, World!" example, above, how would you go about compiling and linking this program?

The first step, of course, is to enter the source code. This is simply accomplished with a text editor, such as Emacs or *vi*. The would-be programmer should enter the source code and save it in a file named something like *hello.c*. (As with most C compilers, *gcc* is picky about the filename extension—that is how it can distinguish C source from assembly source from object files and so on. The *.c* extension should be used for standard C source.)

To compile and link the program to the executable *hello*, the programmer would use the command

```
papaya$ gcc -o hello hello.c
```

and (barring any errors), in one fell swoop, *gcc* would compile the source into an object file, link against the appropriate libraries, and spit out the executable *hello*, ready-to-run. In fact, the wary programmer might want to test it:

```
papaya$ hello
Hello, World!
papaya$
```

As friendly as can be expected.

Obviously, quite a few things took place behind the scenes when executing this single *gcc* command. First of all, *gcc* had to compile your source file, *hello.c*, into an object file, *hello.o*. Next, it had to link *hello.o* against the standard libraries and produce an executable.

By default, *gcc* assumes that not only do you want to compile the source files that you specify, but also that you want them linked together (with each other and with the standard libraries) to produce an executable. First, *gcc* compiles any source files into object files. Next, it automatically invokes the linker to glue all of the object files and libraries into an executable. (That's right, the linker is a separate program, called *ld*, not part of *gcc* itself—although it can be said that *gcc* and *ld* are close friends.) *gcc* also knows about the "standard" libraries used by most programs, and tells *ld* to link against them. You can, of course, override these defaults in various ways.

You can pass multiple filenames in one *gcc* command, but on large projects you'll find it more natural to compile a few files at a time and keep the *.o* object files around. If you want only to compile a source file into an object file and forego the linking process, use the *-c* switch with *gcc*, as in:

```
papaya$ gcc -c hello.c
```

This will produce the object file *hello.o*, and nothing else.

By default, the linker produces an executable named, of all things, *a.out*. By using the *-o* switch with *gcc*, you can force the resulting executable to be named something different, in this case, *hello*. This is just a bit of left-over gunk from early implementations of UNIX, and nothing to write home about.

Using Multiple Source Files

The next step on your path to *gcc* enlightenment is to understand how to compile programs using multiple source files. Let's say that you have a program consisting of two source files, *foo.c* and *bar.c*. Naturally, you would use one or more header files (such as *foo.h*) containing function declarations shared between the two programs. In this way, code in *foo.c* will know about functions in *bar.c*, and vice versa.

To compile these two source files and link them together (along with the libraries, of course) to produce the executable *baz*, you'd use the command

```
papaya$ gcc -o baz foo.c bar.c
```

This is roughly equivalent to the three commands:

```
papaya$ gcc -c foo.c
papaya$ gcc -c bar.c
papaya$ gcc -o baz foo.o bar.o
```

gcc acts as a nice front-end to the linker and other "hidden" utilities invoked during compilation.

Of course, compiling a program using multiple source files in one command can be very time consuming. If you had, say, five or more source files in your program, the *gcc* command given above would recompile *each* source file in turn before linking the executable. This can be a large waste of time, especially if you only made modifications to a single source file since last compilation. There would be no reason to recompile the other source files, as their up-to-date object files are still intact.

The answer to this problem is to use a project manager such as *make*. We'll talk about *make* later in the chapter, in the section "Makefiles."

Optimizing

Telling *gcc* to optimize your code as it compiles is a simple matter; just use the −*O* switch on the *gcc* command line:

```
papaya$ gcc -O -o fishsticks fishsticks.c
```

As we mentioned not long ago, *gcc* supports different levels of optimization. Using −*O2* instead of −*O* will turn on several "expensive" optimizations which may cause compilation to run more slowly, but will (hopefully) greatly enhance performance of your code.

You may notice in your dealings with Linux that a number of programs are compiled using the switch −*O6* (the Linux kernel being a good example). The current version of *gcc* does not support optimization up to −*O6*, so this defaults to (presently) the equivalent of −*O2*. However, −*O6* is sometimes used for compatibility with future versions of *gcc*, to ensure that the greatest level of optimization will be used.

Enabling Debugging Code

The *–g* switch to *gcc* turns on debugging code in your compiled object files. That is, extra information is added to the object file, as well as the resulting executable, allowing the program to be traced with a debugger such as *gdb* (which we'll get to later in the chapter—no worries). The downside to using debug code is that it greatly increases the size of the resulting object files. Also, programs enabled for debugging must be linked with static libraries, which causes further binary gloat. It's usually best to use *–g* only while developing and testing your programs, and to leave it out for the "final" compilation.

Happily, debug-enabled code is not incompatible with code optimization. This means that you can safely use the command

```
papaya$ gcc -O -g -o mumble mumble.c
```

However, certain optimizations enabled by *–O* or *–O2* may cause the program to appear to behave erratically while under the guise of a debugger. It is usually best to use either *–O* or *–g*, not both.

More Fun with Libraries

Before we leave the realm of *gcc*, a few words on linking and libraries are in order. For one thing, it's easy for you to create your own libraries. If you have a set of routines that you use often, you may wish to group them together into a set of source files, compile each source file into an object file, and then create a library from the object files. This saves you the time of having to compile these routines individually for each program that you use them in.

Let's say that you have a set of source files, containing oft-used routines, such as:

```
float square(float x) {
  /* Code for square()... */
}

int factorial(int x, int n) {
  /* Code for factorial()... */
}
```

and so on (of course, the *gcc* standard libraries provide analogues to these common routines, so don't be misled by our choice of example). Furthermore, let's say that the code for *square()* is in the file *square.c* and that the code for *factorial()* is in *factorial.c*. Simple enough, right?

To produce a library containing these routines, all that you have to do is compile each source file, as so:

papaya$ `gcc -c square.c factorial.c`

which will leave you with *square.o* and *factorial.o*. Next, you create a library from the object files. As it turns out, a library is just an archive file created using *ar* (a close counterpart to *tar*). Let's call our library *libstuff.a*, and create it this way:

papaya$ `ar r libstuff.a square.o factorial.o`

When updating a library such as this, you may need to delete the old *libstuff.a*, if it exists. The last step is to generate an index for the library, which enables the linker to find routines within the library. To do this, use the *ranlib* command, as so:

papaya$ `ranlib libstuff.a`

This command adds information to the library itself; no separate index file is created.

Now you have *libstuff.a*, a static library containing your routines. Before you can link programs against it, you'll need to create a header file describing the contents of the library. For example, we could create *libstuff.h* with the contents:

```
/* libstuff.h: routines in libstuff.a */
extern float square(float);
extern int factorial(int, int);
```

Every source file that uses routines from *libstuff.a* should #include "libstuff.h", as you would do with standard header files.

Now that we have our library and header file, how to we compile programs to use them? First of all, we need to put the library and header file somewhere that the compiler can find them. Many users place personal libraries in the directory *lib* in their home directory, and personal include files under *include*. Assuming that we have done so, we can compile the mythical program *wibble.c* using the command:

papaya$ `gcc -I../include -L../lib -o wibble wibble.c -lstuff`

The *−I* option tells *gcc* to add the directory *../include* to the *include path* which it uses to search for include files. *−L* is similar, in that it tells *gcc* to add the directory *../lib* to the *library path*.

The last argument on the command line is *−lstuff*, which tells the linker to link against the library *libstuff.a* (wherever it may be along the library path). The *lib* at the beginning of the filename is assumed for libraries.

Any time that you wish to link against libraries other than the standard ones, you should use the *−l* switch on the *gcc* command line. For example, if you wish to use math routines (specified in *math.h*), you should add *−lm* to the end of the *gcc* command, which will link against *libm*. Note, however, that the *order* of *−l* options is significant. For example, if our *libstuff* library used routines found in *libm*, you must include *−lm* after *−lstuff* on the command line:

```
papaya$ gcc -I../include -L../lib -o wibble wibble.c -lstuff -lm
```

This will force the linker to link *libm* after *libstuff*, allowing those unresolved references in *libstuff* to be taken care of.

Where does *gcc* look for libraries? By default, libraries are searched for in a number of locations, the most important of which is */usr/lib*. If you take a glance at the contents of */usr/lib*, you'll notice it contains many library files—some of which have filenames ending in *.a*, others ending in *.sa*. As it turns out, the *.a* files are static libraries, as is the case with our *libstuff.a*. The *.sa* files are shared library stubs—containing only the "stub code" necessary for runtime dynamic linking for programs that use shared libraries.

We can almost guess your next question. Where does the actual code for shared libraries exist? At run time, the program loader looks for shared library images in several places, including */lib*. If you look at */lib*, you'll see files such as *libc.so.4.4.4*. This is the image file containing the code for the *libc* shared library (one of the standard libraries, which most programs are linked against). The file */usr/lib/libc.sa* contains the stubs for this library.

By default, the linker attempts to link against shared libraries. However, there are several cases in which static libraries are used. If you enable debugging code with *−g*, the program will be linked against the static libraries. You can also specify that static libraries should be linked by using the *−static* switch with *gcc*.

Using C++

If you prefer object-oriented programming, *gcc* provides complete support for C++ as well as Objective-C. There are only a few considerations that you need to be aware of when doing C++ programming with *gcc*.

First of all, C++ source filenames should end in the extension *.C* or *.cc*. This is to distinguish them from regular C source filenames, which end in *.c*.

Secondly, the *g++* shell script should be used in lieu of *gcc* when compiling C++ code. *g++* is simply a shell script that invokes *gcc* with a number of additional arguments, specifying to link against the C++ standard libraries, for example. *g++* takes the same arguments and options as *gcc*.

If you do not use *g++*, you'll need to be sure to link against the C++ libraries in order to use any of the basic C++ classes, such as the cout and cin I/O objects. Also be sure that you have actually installed the C++ libraries and include files. Some distributions contain only the standard C libraries. *gcc* will be able to compile your C++ programs fine, but without the C++ libraries you'll end up with linker errors whenever you attempt to use standard objects.

Makefiles

Sometime during your life with Linux you will probably have to deal with *make*, even if you don't plan to do any programming. It's likely that you'll want to patch and rebuild the kernel, and that involves running *make*. If you're lucky, you won't have to muck with the makefiles—but we've tried to direct this book toward unlucky people as well. So in this section we'll to explain enough of the subtle syntax of *make* so that you're not intimidated by a makefile.

[51] make

[52] GNU make

For some of our examples we'll draw on the current makefile for the Linux kernel. It exploits a lot of extensions in the powerful GNU version of *make*, so we'll describe some of those as well as the standard *make* features. A good introduction to *make* is provided in *Managing Projects with make* by Andrew Oram and Steve Talbott. GNU extensions are well-documented by the GNU *make* manual.

Most users see *make* as a way to build object files and libraries from sources and to build executables from object files. More conceptually, *make* is a general-purpose program which builds *targets* from *prerequisites*. The target can be a program executable, a PostScript document, or whatever. The prerequisites can be C code, a TEX text file, and so on.

While you can write simple shell scripts to execute *gcc* commands building an executable program, *make* is special in that it knows which targets need only be rebuilt and which don't. An object file needs to be recompiled only if its corresponding source has changed.

For example, say you have a program that consists of three C source files. If you were to build the executable using the command:

```
papaya$ gcc -o foo foo.c bar.c baz.c
```

each time you changed any of the source files, all three would be recompiled and relinked into the executable. If you only changed one source file, this is a real waste of time (especially if the program in question is much larger than a handful of sources). What you really want to do is only recompile the one source file that changed into an object file, and relink all of the object files in the program to form the executable. *make* can automate this process for you.

What make Does

The basic goal of *make* is to let you build a file in small steps. If a lot of source files make up the final executable, you can change one and rebuild the executable without having to recompile everything. In order to give you this flexibility, *make* records what files you need to do your build.

Here's a trivial makefile. Call it *makefile* or *Makefile* and keep it in the same directory as the source files.

```
edimh: main.o edit.o
        gcc -o edimh main.o edit.o

main.o: main.c
        gcc -c main.c

edit.o: edit.c
        gcc -c edit.c
```

This file builds a program named *edimh* from two source files named *main.c* and *edit.c*. You aren't restricted to C programming in a makefile; the commands could be anything.

Three entries appear in the file. Each contains a *dependency line* that shows how a file is built. Thus the first line says that *edimh* (the name before the colon) is built from the two object files *main.o* and *edit.o* (the names after the colon). What this line tells *make* is that it should execute the following *gcc* line whenever one of those object files change. The lines containing commands have to begin with tabs (not spaces).

The command:

```
papaya$ make edimh
```

will execute the *gcc* line if there isn't currently any file named *edimh*. But the *gcc* line will also execute if *edimh* exists but one of the object files is newer. Here, *edimh* is called a *target*. The files after the colon are called either *dependents* or *prerequisites*.

The next two entries perform the same service for the object files. *main.o* is built if it doesn't exist or if the associated source file *main.c* is newer. *edit.o* is built from *edit.c*.

How does *make* know if a file is new? It looks at the timestamp, which the filesystem associates with every file. You can see timestamps by issuing the *ls –l* command. Since the timestamp is accurate to one second, it reliably tells *make* whether you've edited a source file since the latest compilation, or have compiled an object file since the executable was last built.

Let's try out the makefile and see what it does:

```
papaya$ make edimh
gcc -c main.c
gcc -c edit.c
gcc -o edimh main.o edit.o
```

If we edit *main.c* and reissue the command, it rebuilds only the necessary files, saving us some time:

```
papaya$ make edimh
gcc -c main.c
gcc -o edimh main.o edit.o
```


It doesn't matter what order the three entries are in the makefile. *make* figures out which files depend on which, and executes all the commands in the right order. Putting the entry for *edimh* first is convenient, because that becomes the file built by default. In other words, typing make is the same as typing make edimh.

Here's a more extensive makefile. See if you can figure out what it does.

```
install: all
        mv edimh /usr/local
        mv readimh /usr/local

all: edimh readimh

readimh: read.o edit.o
        gcc -o readimh main.o read.o

edimh: main.o edit.o
        gcc -o edimh main.o edit.o

main.o: main.c
        gcc -c main.c

edit.o: edit.c
        gcc -c edit.c

read.o: read.c
        gcc -c read.c
```

First we see the target install. This is never going to generate a file; it's called a *phony target* because it exists just so you can execute the commands listed under it. But before install runs, all has to run, because install depends on all. (Remember, the order of the entries in the file doesn't matter.)

So *make* turns to the all target. There are no commands under it (this is perfectly legal), but it depends on edimh and readimh. These are real files; each is an executable program. So *make* keeps tracing back through the list of dependencies until it arrives at the .c files, which don't depend on anything else. Then it painstakingly rebuilds each of the targets.

Here is a sample run (you may need root privilege to install the files in the */usr/local* directory):

```
papaya$ make install
gcc -c main.c
gcc -c edit.c
gcc -o edimh main.o edit.o
gcc -c read.c
gcc -o readimh main.o read.o
mv edimh /usr/local
mv readimh /usr/local
```

So the effect of this makefile is to do a complete build and install. First it builds the files needed to create *edimh*. Then it builds the additional object file that it needs to create *readmh*. With those two executables created, the all target is satisfied. Now *make* can go on to build the install target, which means moving the two executables to their final home.

Many makefiles, including the ones that build Linux, contain a variety of phony targets to do routine activities. For instance, the makefile for the Linux kernel includes commands to remove temporary files:

```
clean:  archclean
        rm -f kernel/ksyms.lst
        rm -f core `find . -name '*.[oas]' -print`
        .
        .
        .
```

and to create a list of object files and the header files they depend on (this is a complicated but important task—if a header file changes, you want to make sure the files that refer to it are recompiled):

```
depend dep:
        touch tools/version.h
        for i in init/*.c;do echo -n "init/";$(CPP) -M $$i;done > .tmpdepend
        .
        .
        .
```

Some of these shell commands get pretty complicated; we'll look at makefile commands later in this chapter, in the section "Multiple Commands."

Some Syntax Rules

The hardest thing about maintaining makefiles, at least if you're new to them, is getting the syntax right. OK, let's be straight about it, the syntax of *make* is really stupid. If you use spaces where you're supposed to use tabs or vice versa, your makefile blows up. And the error messages are really confusing.

 Always put a tab at the beginning of a command. Not spaces. And don't use a tab before any other line.

You can place a hash mark (#) anywhere on a line to start a comment. Everything after the hash mark is ignored.

If you put a backslash at the end of a line, it continues on the next line. That works for long commands, and other types of makefile lines too.

Now let's look at some of the powerful features of *make*, which form a kind of programming language of their own.

Macros

When people use a filename or other string more than once in a makefile, they tend to assign it to a macro. That's simply a string that *make* expands to another string. For instance, you could change the beginning of our trivial makefile to read:

```
OBJECTS = main.o edit.o

edimh: $(OBJECTS)
        gcc -o edimh $(OBJECTS)
```

When *make* runs, it simply plugs in main.o edit.o wherever you specify $(OBJECTS). If you have to add another object file to the project, you just specify it on the first line of the file. The dependency line and command will then be updated correspondingly.

Don't forget the parentheses when you refer to $(OBJECTS). Macros may resemble shell variables like $HOME and $PATH, but they're not the same.

One macro can be defined in terms of another macro, so you could say something like:

```
ROOT = /usr/local
HEADERS = $(ROOT)/include
SOURCES = $(ROOT)/src
```

In this case, HEADERS evaluates to the directory */usr/local/include* and SOURCES to */usr/local/src*. If you are installing this package on your system and don't want it to be in */usr/local*, just choose another name and change the line that defines ROOT.

By the way, you don't have to use uppercase names for macros, but that's a universal convention.

An extension in GNU make allows you to add to the definition of a macro. This uses a := string in place of an equal sign:

```
DRIVERS        =drivers/block/block.a

ifdef CONFIG_SCSI
DRIVERS := $(DRIVERS) drivers/scsi/scsi.a
endif
```

The first line is a normal macro definition, setting the DRIVERS macro to drivers/block/block.a. The next definition adds the file drivers/scsi/scsi.a. But it takes effect only if the macro CONFIG_SCSI is defined. The full definition in that case becomes:

```
drivers/block/block.a drivers/scsi/scsi.a
```

So how do you define CONFIG_SCSI? You could put it in the makefile, assigning any string you want:

```
CONFIG_SCSI = yes
```

But you'll probably find it easier to define it on the *make* command line. Here's how to do it:

```
papaya$ make CONFIG_SCSI=yes target_name
```

One subtlety of using macros is that you can leave them undefined. If no one defines them, then a null string is substituted (that is, you end up with nothing where the macro is supposed to be). But this also give you the option of defining the macro as an environment variable. For instance, if you don't define CONFIG_SCSI in the makefile, you could put this in your *.bashrc* file, for use with the *bash* shell:

```
export CONFIG_SCSI=yes
```

Or put this in *.cshrc* if you use *csh* or *tcsh*:

```
setenv CONFIG_SCSI yes
```

All your builds will then have CONFIG_SCSI defined.

Suffix Rules and Pattern Rules

For something as routine as building an object file from a source file, you don't want to specify every single dependency in your makefile. And you don't have to. UNIX compilers enforce a simple standard (compile a file ending in the suffix *.c* to create a file ending in the suffix *.o*) and *make* provides a feature called suffix rules to cover all such files.

Here's a simple suffix rule to compile a C source file, which you could put in your makefile:

```
.c.o:
        gcc -c ${CFLAGS} $<
```

The .c.o: line means "use a *.c* input file to build a *.o* file." CFLAGS is a macro where you can plug in any compiler options you want: –g for debugging, for instance, or –O for optimization. The string $< is a cryptic way of saying "the input file." So the name of your *.c* file is plugged in when *make* executes this command.

Here's a sample run using this suffix rule. The command line passes both the –g option and the –O option:

```
papaya$ make CFLAGS="-O -g" edit.o
gcc -c -O -g edit.c
```

You actually don't have to specify this suffix rule in your makefile, because something very similar is already built into *make*. It even uses CFLAGS, so you can determine the options used for compiling just by setting that variable. The make-file used to build the Linux kernel currently contains the following definition, a whole slew of *gcc* options:

```
CFLAGS = -Wall -Wstrict-prototypes -O2 -fomit-frame-pointer -pipe
```

While we're discussing compiler flags, one set is seen so often that it's worth a special mention. This is the *−D* option, which is used to define symbols in the source code. Since there are all kinds of commonly used symbols appearing in #ifdefs, you may need to pass lots of such options to your makefile, such as *−DDEBUG* or *−DBSD*. If you do this on the *make* command line, be sure to put quotation marks or apostrophes around the whole set. This is because you want the shell to pass the set to your makefile as one argument:

```
papaya$ make CFLAGS="-DDEBUG -DBSD" ...
```

GNU *make* offers something called pattern rules, which are even better than suffix rules. A pattern rule uses a percent sign to mean "any string." So C source files would be compiled using a rule like the following:

```
%.o: %.c
        gcc -c -o $@ $(CFLAGS) $<
```

Here the output file *%.o* comes first, and the input file *%.c* comes after a colon. In short, a pattern rule is just like a regular dependency line, but it contains percent signs instead of exact filenames.

We see the $< string to refer to the input file, but we also see $@, which refers to the output file. So the name of the .o file is plugged in there. Both of these are built-in macros; *make* defines them every time it executes an entry.

Another common built-in macro is $*, which refers to the name of the input file stripped of the suffix. So if the input file is *edit.c*, the string $*.s would evaluate to *edit.s* (an assembly language source file).

Here's something useful you can do with a pattern rule that you can't do with a suffix rule—you add the string _dbg to the name of the output file, so you can tell later that you compiled it with debugging information:

```
%_dbg.o: %.c
        gcc -c -g -o $@ $(CFLAGS) $<

DEBUG_OBJECTS = main_dbg.o edit_dbg.o

edimh_dbg: $(DEBUG_OBJECTS)
        gcc -o $@ $(DEBUG_OBJECTS)
```

Now you can build all your objects in two different ways: one with debugging information and one without. They'll have different filenames, so you can keep them in one directory.

```
papaya$ make edimh_dbg
gcc -c -g -o main_dbg.o  main.c
gcc -c -g -o edit_dbg.o  edit.c
gcc -o edimh_dbg  main_dbg.o edit_dbg.o
```

Multiple Commands

Any shell commands can be executed in a makefile. But things can get kind of complicated because *make* executes each command in a separate shell. So this would not work:

```
target:
        cd obj
        HOST_DIR=/home/e
        mv *.o $HOST_DIR
```

Neither the *cd* command nor the definition of the variable HOST_DIR have any effect on subsequent commands. You have to string everything together into one command. The shell uses a semicolon as a separator between commands, so you can combine them all on one line like this:

```
target:
        cd obj ; HOST_DIR=/home/e ; mv *.o $$HOST_DIR
```

One more change: to define and use a shell variable within the command, you have to double the dollar sign. This lets *make* know that you mean it to be a shell variable, not a macro.

You may find the file easier to read if you break the semicolon-separated commands onto multiple lines, using backslashes so that *make* considers them one line:

```
target:
        cd obj ; \
        HOST_DIR=/home/e ; \
        mv *.o $$HOST_DIR
```

Complicated, but now it should make sense to you.

Sometimes makefiles contain their own *make* commands; this is called recursive *make*. It looks like this:

```
linuxsubdirs: dummy
        set -e; for i in $(SUBDIRS); do $(MAKE) -C $$i; done
```

The macro $(MAKE) invokes *make*. There are a few reasons for nesting makes. One reason, which applies to the above example, is to perform builds in multiple directories (each of these other directories has to contain its own makefile). Another reason is to define macros on the command line, so you can do builds with a variety of macro definitions.

GNU *make* offers another powerful interface to the shell as an extension. You can issue a shell command and assign its output to a macro. A couple of examples can be found in the Linux kernel makefile, but we'll just show a simple example here:

```
HOST_NAME = $(shell uname -n)
```

This assigns the name of your network node—the output of the *uname –n* command—to the macro HOST_NAME.

make offers a couple of conventions that you may occasionally want to use. One is to put an at-sign before a command, which keeps *make* from echoing the command when it's executed:

```
@if [ -x /bin/dnsdomainname ]; then \
   echo #define LINUX_COMPILE_DOMAIN \"`dnsdomainname`\"; \
 else \
   echo #define LINUX_COMPILE_DOMAIN \"`domainname`\"; \
 fi >> tools/version.h
```

Another convention is to put a hyphen before a command, which tells make to keep going even if the command fails. This may be useful if you want to continue after an *mv* or *cp* command fails:

```
- mv edimh /usr/local
- mv readimh /usr/local
```

Including Other Makefiles

Large projects tend to break parts of their makefiles into separate files. This makes it easy for different makefiles in different directories to share things, particularly macro definitions. The line

```
include filename
```

reads in the contents of *filename*. You can see this in the Linux kernel makefile, for instance:

```
include .depend
```

If you look in the file *.depend*, you'll find a bunch of makefile entries—to be exact, lines declaring that object files depend on header files. (By the way, *.depend* might not exist yet—it has to be created by another entry in the makefile.)

Sometimes include lines refer to macros instead of filenames, as in:

```
include ${INC_FILE}
```

In this case, INC_FILE must be defined either as an environment variable or as a macro. Doing things this way gives you more control over which file is used.

Using Perl

Perl may very well be the best thing to happen to the UNIX programming environment in years. It is worth the price of admission to Linux alone. Perl is a text and file manipulation language, originally intended to scan large amounts of text, process it, and produce nicely-formatted reports from that data. However, as Perl has matured, it has developed into an all-purpose scripting language, capable of doing everything from managing processes to communicating via TCP/IP over a network. Perl is free software developed by Larry Wall, the UNIX guru that brought us the *rn* newsreader and various popular tools such as *patch*.

Perl's main strength is that it incorporates the most widely-used features of languages such as C, *sed*, *awk*, and various shells into a single interpreted script language. In the past, getting a complicated job done was a matter of juggling these various languages into complex arrangements, often entailing *sed* scripts piping into *awk* scripts piping into shell scripts and eventually piping into a C program. Perl gets rid of the common UNIX philosophy of using many small tools to handle small parts of one large problem. Instead, Perl does it all, and it provides many different ways of doing the same thing. In fact, this chapter was written by an AI program developed in Perl. (Just kidding, Larry.)

Perl provides a nice programming interface to many features that were sometimes difficult to use in other languages. For example, a common task of many UNIX system administration scripts is to scan a large amount of text, cut fields out of each line of text based on a pattern (usually represented as a *regular expression*), and produce a report based on the data. Let's say that you want to process the output of the UNIX *last* command, which displays a record of login times for all users on the system, as so:

```
mdw        ttypf   loomer.vpizza.co Sun Jan 16 15:30 - 15:54   (00:23)
larry      ttyp1   muadib.oit.unc.e Sun Jan 16 15:11 - 15:12   (00:00)
mkjohnson ttyp4    mallard.vpizza.c Sun Jan 16 14:34 - 14:37   (00:03)
jem        ttyq2   mallard.vpizza.c Sun Jan 16 13:55 - 13:59   (00:03)
linus      ftp     kruuna.helsinki. Sun Jan 16 13:51 - 13:51   (00:00)
linus      ftp     kruuna.helsinki. Sun Jan 16 13:47 - 13:47   (00:00)
```

If we wanted to count up the total login time for each user (given in parentheses in the last field), we could write a *sed* script to splice the time values from the input, an *awk* script to sort the data for each user and add up the times, and another *awk* script to produce a report based on the accumulated data. Or, we could write a somewhat complex C program to do the entire task—complex because, as any C programmer knows, text-processing functions within C are somewhat limited.

However, this task can be easily accomplished by a simple Perl script. The facilities of input/output, regular expression pattern matching, sorting by associative arrays, and number crunching are all easily accessed from a Perl program with little overhead. Perl programs are generally short and to-the-point, without a lot of technical mumbo-jumbo getting in the way of what you want your program to actually *do*.

Using Perl under Linux is really no different than on any other UNIX system. Several good books on Perl already exist, including *Programming Perl*, by Larry Wall and Randal L. Schwartz, and *Learning Perl*, by Randal L. Schwartz, both from O'Reilly & Associates. Nevertheless, we think that Perl is such a great tool that it deserves something in the way of an introduction. After all, Perl is free software, as is Linux—they go hand-in-hand.

A Sample Program

What we really like about Perl is that it lets you immediately jump to the task at hand—you don't have to write extensive code to set up data structures, open files or pipes, allocate space for data, and so on. All of these features are taken care of for you in a very friendly way.

The example put forward above will serve to introduce many of the basic features of Perl. First, we'll give the entire script (complete with comments) and then a description of how it works. This script reads the output of the *last* command (see the example above) and prints an entry for each user on the system, describing the total login time and number of logins for each. (Line numbers are printed to the left of each line for reference.)

```
1       #!/usr/local/bin/perl
2
3       while (<STDIN>) {    # While we have input...
4         # Find lines and save username, login time
5         if (/^(\S*)\s*.*\((.*):(.*)\)$/) {
6           # Increment total hours, minutes, and logins
7           $hours{$1} += $2;
8           $minutes{$1} += $3;
9           $logins{$1}++;
10        }
11      }
12
13      # For each user in the array...
14      foreach $user (sort(keys %hours)) {
15        # Calculate hours from total minutes
16        $hours{$user} += int($minutes{$user} / 60);
17        $minutes{$user} %= 60;
18        # Print the information for this user
19        print "User $user, total login time ";
20        # Perl has printf, too
21        printf "%02d:%02d, ", $hours{$user}, $minutes{$user};
22        print "total logins $logins{$user}.\n";
23      }
```

Line 1 is there to tell the loader that this script should be executed through Perl, not as a shell script. Line 3 is the beginning of the program. It is the head of a simple while loop, which C and shell programmers will be familiar with—the code within the braces from lines 4–10 should be executed while a certain expression is true. However, the conditional expression "<STDIN>" looks funny. Actually, this expression is true whenever there is input on the STDIN filehandle—which refers to standard input, as you might guess.

Perl reads input one line at a time (unless you tell it to do otherwise). It also reads by default from standard input, again, unless you tell it to do otherwise. Therefore, this while loop will continuously read lines from standard input, until there are no lines left to be read.

The evil-looking mess on line 5 is just an if statement. As with most programming languages, the code within the braces (on lines 6–9) will be executed if the expression that follows the if is true. But what is this expression? "/^(\S*)\s*.*\((.*):(.*)\)$/"? Those readers familiar with UNIX tools such as *grep* and *sed* will peg this immediately as a *regular expression*—a cryptic but useful way to represent a pattern to be matched in the input text. Regular expressions are usually found between delimiting slashes (/.../).

This particular regular expression matches lines of the form:

```
mdw        ttypf     loomer.vpizza.co Sun Jan 16 15:30 - 15:54  (00:23)
```

This expression also "remembers" the username (mdw) and the total login time for this entry (00:23). You needn't worry about the expression itself—building regular expressions is a complex subject. For now, all that you need to know is that this if statement finds lines of the form given above, and splices out the username and login time for processing. The username is assigned to the variable $1, the hours to the variable $2, and the minutes to $3. (Variables in Perl begin with the $ character, but unlike the shell, the $ must be used when assigning to the variable as well.) This assignment is done by the regular expression match itself (anything enclosed in parenthesis in a regular expression is saved for later use to one of the variables $1 through $9).

Lines 6–9 actually process these three pieces of information. And they do it in an interesting way: through the use of an *associative array*. Whereas a normal array is indexed with a number as a subscript, an associative array is indexed by an arbitrary string. This lends itself to many powerful applications—it allows you to associate one set of data with another set of data gathered on the fly. In our short program, the keys are the usernames, gathered from the output of *last*. We maintain three associative arrays, all indexed by username: hours, which records the total number of hours that the user logged in; minutes, which records the number of minutes; and logins, which records the total number of logins.

As an example, referencing the variable $hours{'mdw'} will return the total number of hours that the user mdw was logged in. Similarly, if the username mdw is stored in the variable $1, referencing $hours{$1} would produce the same effect.

In lines 6–9, we increment the values of these arrays according to the data on the present line of input. For example, given the input line:

```
jem       ttyq2    mallard.vpizza.c Sun Jan 16 13:55 - 13:59  (00:03)
```

line 7 increments the value of the hours array, indexed with $1 (the username, jem), by the number of hours that jem was logged in (stored in the variable $2). The Perl increment operator += is equivalent to the corresponding C operator. Line 8 increments the value of minutes for the appropriate user similarly. Line 9 increments the value of the logins array by one, using the ++ operator.

Associative arrays are one of the most useful features of Perl. They allow you to build up complex databases while parsing text. It would be nearly impossible to use a standard array for this same task—we would first have to count the number of users in the input stream, and then allocate an array of the appropriate size, assigning a position in the array to each user (through the use of a hash function or some other indexing scheme). An associative array, however, allows you to index data directly using strings, and without regard for the size of the array in question. (Of course, performance issues always arise when attempting to use large arrays, but for most applications this isn't a problem.)

Let's move on. Line 14 uses the Perl foreach statement, which you may be used to if you write shell scripts. (The foreach loop actually breaks down into a for loop, much like that found in C.) Here, in each iteration of the loop, the variable $user is assigned the next value in the list given by the expression sort(keys %hours). %hours simply refers to the *entire* associative array hours that we have constructed. The function keys returns a list of all of the keys used to index the array, which is in this case a list of usernames. Finally, the sort function sorts the list returned by keys. Therefore, we are looping over a sorted list of usernames, assigning each username in turn to the variable $user.

Lines 16 and 17 simply correct for situations where the number of minutes is greater than 60—it determines the total number of hours contained in the minutes entry for this user and increments hours accordingly. The int function returns the integral portion of its argument. (Yes, Perl can handle floating-point numbers as well—that's why use of int is necessary.)

Finally, lines 19–22 print the total login time and number of logins for each user. The simple print function just prints its arguments, like the *awk* function of the same name. Note that variable evaluation can be done within a print statement, as on lines 19 and 22. However, if you want to do some fancy text formatting, you will need to use the printf function (which is just like its C equivalent). In this case, we wish to set the minimum output length of the hours and minutes values for this user to 2 characters wide, and to left-pad the output with zeroes. To do this, we use the printf command on line 21.

If this script is saved in the file `logintime`, we can execute it as follows:

```
papaya$ last | logintime
User johnsonm, total login time 01:07, total logins 11.
User kibo, total login time 00:42, total logins 3.
User linus, total login time 98:50, total logins 208.
User mdw, total login time 153:03, total logins 290.
papaya$
```

Of course, this example doesn't serve well as a Perl tutorial, but it should give you some idea of what it can do. We encourage you to read one of the excellent Perl books out there to learn more.

More Features

The previous example introduced the most commonly-used Perl features by demonstrating a living, breathing program. There is much more where that came from—in the way of both well-known and not-so-well-known features.

As we mentioned, Perl provides a report-generation mechanism beyond the standard `print` and `printf` functions. Using this feature, the programmer defines a report "format" which describes how each page of the report will look. For example, we could have included the following format definition in our example:

```
format STDOUT_TOP =
User               Total login time      Total logins
-------------      --------------------  -------------------
.
format STDOUT =
@<<<<<<<<<<<<<< @<<<<<<<<            @####
$user,          $thetime,           $logins{$user}
.
```

The `STDOUT_TOP` definition describes the header of the report, to be printed at the top of each page of output. The `STDOUT` format describes the look of each line of output. Each field is described beginning with the `@` character; `@<<<<` specifies a left-justified text field, and `@####` specifies a numeric field. The line below the field definitions gives the names of the variables to use in printing the fields. Here, we have used the variable `$thetime` to store the formatted time-string.

To use this report for the output, we replace lines 19–22 in the original script with the following:

```
$thetime = sprintf("%02d:%02d", $hours{$user}, $minutes{$user});
write;
```

The first line uses the `sprintf` function to format the time string and save it in the variable `$thetime`; the second line is a `write` command which tells Perl to go off and use the given report format to print a line of output.

Using this report format, we'll get something looking like:

```
User            Total login time      Total logins
--------------  --------------------  --------------------
johnsonm        01:07                      11
kibo            00:42                       3
linus           98:50                     208
mdw             153:03                    290
```

Using other report formats we can achieve different (and better-looking) results.

Another abstruse feature of Perl is its ability to (more or less) directly access several UNIX system calls, including interprocess communications. For example, Perl provides the functions msgctl, msgget, msgsnd, and msgrcv from System V IPC. Perl also supports the BSD socket implementation, allowing communications via TCP/IP directly from a Perl program. No longer is C the exclusive language of networking daemons and clients. A Perl program loaded with IPC features can be very powerful indeed—especially considering that many client-server implementations call for advanced text-processing features such as those provided by Perl. It is generally easier to parse protocol commands transmitted between client and server from a Perl script, rather than writing a complex C program to do the work.

As an example, take the well-known SMTP daemon, which handles the sending and receiving of electronic mail. The SMTP protocol uses internal commands such as "recv from" and "mail to" in order for the client to communicate with the server. Either the client or the server, or both, can be written in Perl, and can have full access to Perl's text and file manipulation features as well as the vital socket communication functions.

As a far-out example of the kinds of things that Perl and IPC can do, Larry Wall was reportedly considering rewriting the *rn* newsreader entirely in Perl.

Pros and Cons

One of the features of (some might say "problems with") Perl is the ability to abbreviate—and obfuscate—code considerably. In the above script we have used several common shortcuts. For example, input into the Perl script is read into the variable $_. However, most operations act on the variable $_ by default, so it's usually not necessary to reference $_ by name.

Perl also gives you several ways of doing the same thing, which can, of course, be either a blessing or a curse depending on how you look at it. In *Programming Perl*, Larry Wall gives the following example of a short program that simply prints its standard input. All of the following statements are equivalent:

```
while ($_ = <STDIN>) { print; }
while (<STDIN>) { print; }
for (;<STDIN>;) { print; }
print while $_ = <STDIN>;
print while <STDIN>;
```

The programmer can use the syntax that is most appropriate for the situation at hand.

Perl is very popular, and not just because it is useful. Because Perl provides much in the way of eccentricity, it gives hackers something to play with, so to speak. Perl programmers are constantly outdoing each other with trickier bits of code. Perl lends itself to interesting kludges, neat hacks, and both very good and very bad programming. UNIX programmers see it as a challenging medium to work with—because Perl is relatively new, not all of the possibilities have been exploited. Even if you find Perl too baroque for your taste, there is still something to be said for its artistry. The ability to call oneself a "Perl hacker" is a point of pride within the UNIX community.

Shell Programming

Chapter 3

In the section "Shells" in Chapter 3, *Basic UNIX Commands and Concepts*, we discussed the various shells available for Linux, but something should be said about them in terms of programming. The differences come through most clearly when it comes to writing shell scripts. The Bourne Shell and C Shell command languages are slightly different, but the distinction is not obvious with most normal interactive use. In fact, many of the distinctions only arise when you attempt to use bizarre, little-known features of either shell such as word substitution or some of the more oblique parameter expansion functions.

The most notable difference between Bourne shells and C Shells is the form of the various flow-control structures, including if... then and while loops. In the Bourne shell, an if... then takes the form

```
if list
then
   commands
elif list
then
   commands
else
   commands
fi
```

where *list* is just a sequence of commands (more generally called "pipelines") to be used as the conditional expression for the if and elif (short for "else if") commands. The conditional is considered to be true if the exit status of the *list* is zero (unlike boolean expressions in C, in shell terminology an exit status of zero indicates successful completion). The *commands* enclosed in the conditionals are simply commands to execute if the appropriate *list* is true. The then after each *list* must be on a new line to distinguish it from the *list* itself; alternately, you can terminate the *list* with a ;. The same holds true for the *commands*.

An example is:

```
if [ "$PS1" ]; then
  PS1="\h:\w% "
fi
```

This sequence checks to see whether the shell is a login shell (that is, whether the prompt variable PS1 is set) and if so, resets the prompt to "\h:\w% ", which is a prompt expansion standing for the hostname followed by the current working directory, for example:

```
loomer:/home/loomer/mdw%
```

The "[...]" conditional appearing after the if is a *bash* built-in command, short-hand for *test*. The *test* command and its abbreviated equivalent provide a convenient mechanism for testing values of shell variables, string equivalence, and so forth. Instead of using [...], you could call any set of commands after the if, as long as the last command's exit value indicated the value of the conditional.

Under *tcsh*, an if... then compound statement looks like the following:

```
if (expression) then
  commands
else if (expression) then
  commands
else
  commands
endif
```

The difference here is that the *expression* after the if is an arithmetic or logical expression evaluated internally by *tcsh*, while with *bash* the conditional expression is a command, the truth of which is based on the exit status. Within *bash*, using *test* or [...] is similar to an arithmetic expression as used in *tcsh*.

With *tcsh*, however, if you wish to run external commands within the *expression*, you must enclose the command in braces: {command}.

The equivalent of the above *bash* sequence in *tcsh* is:

```
if ($?prompt) then
  set prompt="%m:%/%% "
endif
```

where *tcsh*'s own prompt special characters have been used. As you can see, *tcsh* boasts a command syntax similar to the C language, and expressions are arithmetically and logically oriented. In *bash*, however, almost everything is an actual command, and expressions are evaluated in terms of exit status values. There are analogous features in either shell, but the approach is slightly different.

A similar change exists with the `while` loop. In *bash*, this takes the form

```
while list
do
    commands
done
```

You can negate the effect by replacing the word `while` with `until`. Again, `list` is just a command pipeline to be executed, and the exit status determines the result (zero for success, nonzero for failure). Under *tcsh* the loop looks like

```
while (expression)
    commands
end
```

where *expression* is a logical expression to be evaluated within *tcsh*.

bash(1)
tcsh(1)

The above should be enough to get a head start on understanding the overall differences of shell scripts under *bash* and *tcsh*. We encourage you to read the *bash* and *tcsh* manual pages (although they barely serve as a tutorial; more as a reference) and Info pages, if you have them available. Various books and tutorials on using these two shells are available as well—in fact, any book on shell programming will do, and you can interpolate the advanced features of *bash* and *tcsh* over the standard Bourne and C shells using the manual pages.

Programming in Tcl and Tk

Tool Command Language, or Tcl, (pronounced "tickle") is a simple, interpreted language that is similar, in some respects, to the Bourne shell or Perl. The real benefit of Tcl is that it can be extended as well as embedded in other applications. It is particularly popular when used with the Tk extension, which offers about the simplest interface you could get to program with windows.

By "extended," we mean that you can add new commands to the Tcl language, simply by writing a few routines in C. By "embedded," we mean that you can link a C program to the Tcl libraries, giving that program full access to the Tcl language. Whereas most Tcl programs are written as scripts and executed by a precompiled Tcl interpreter, you can include the interpreter routines in your own application.

For example, let's say that you wanted to write a command-driven debugger similar in nature to *gdb*. The debugger would present a prompt and allow users to enter commands such as *step* and *breakpoint*.

If the command syntax for your debugger is simple, you could easily write your own routines, in C, to read a command and process it. However, this approach becomes much more complex when you wish to allow the user to define variables, macros, new functions, and so forth.

Instead of writing these routines from scratch, it is quite easy to embed a Tcl interpreter in your debugger application. Every command entered by the user would be handled by the interpreter routines. These routines are available as a set of C library functions.

The Tcl language itself includes many, many commands of its own. It provides control structures such as while and for loops, the ability to define functions, string and list manipulation routines, arithmetic functions, and so forth.

On top of these core Tcl routines, your debugger must provide additional commands—such as the aforementioned *step* and *breakpoint.* You would implement these commands in C within your application and tell the Tcl interpreter how to use them.

Now, your debugger application has all of the power of Tcl at its fingertips. For example, the user customization file for the debugger could be a simple Tcl script. Within this script, the user can define new functions and variables, using Tcl's built-in support for these features.

Chapter 5

Among the many extensions to Tcl is Tk, which provides many commands allowing your application to utilize the X Window System as a user interface. (X is introduced in the section "The X Window System" in Chapter 5.) Writing X-based applications as a Tk script is surprisingly easy. For example, the following Tcl/Tk application displays a text entry widget in which a filename may be entered. It then runs an *xterm* containing a *vi* process to edit the file.

```
#!/usr/local/bin/wish -f

# Create a label widget, named .l
label .l -text "Filename:"
# Create an entry widget, named .e
entry .e -relief sunken -width 30 -textvariable fname

# Place the two widgets into the application window
pack .l -side left
pack .e -side left -padx 1m -pady 1m

# When the return key is pressed in the entry widget, run xterm
bind .e <Return> {
  exec xterm -e vi $fname
}
```

We will explain the syntax of this script shortly, but for now you can see that in less than 20 lines of code, we have developed a reasonably complex X application. When this script is executed, it will look like Figure 6-1.

For Tcl applications that use only the core Tcl routines, the pre-compiled interpreter *tclsh* is provided. This interpreter simply reads Tcl commands and executes them, one by one. In the case of our debugger application, we would write a new program which is linked to the Tcl interpreter library routines.

Figure 6-1. Simple Tk-generated window

Likewise, for Tk applications that use only the standard set of Tcl commands and Tk widgets, the *wish* (window shell) interpreter is provided. *wish* is used to execute the above script, as you can see. If you wanted to implement new Tcl commands or Tk widgets, you could write a C program and link it to the Tcl and Tk libraries. In this section, we will introduce you to writing simple Tcl and Tk scripts, for execution under *tclsh* or *wish*.

Crash Course in Tcl

The Tcl language is very easy to learn. If you are at all familiar with other scripting languages such as the Bourne or C shell, Tcl/Tk will pose no threat to you.

[50] Tcl/Tk

For this reason, we will not spend a great deal of time on the Tcl language itself. It is very straightforward and can be learned with the help of the various Tcl manual pages, or John Ousterhout's excellent book, *Tcl and the Tk Toolkit*. This book describes not only how to write Tcl and Tk scripts, but also how to use the Tcl/Tk libraries in your own applications.

Let's start with a simple example. The following Tcl script will count the lines in the given filename.

```
 1  #!/usr/local/bin/tclsh -f
 2
 3  if {$argc != 1} {
 4     error "lc <filename>"
 5  }
 6
 7  set thefile [open [lindex $argv 0] r]
 8  set count 0
 9
10  while {[gets $thefile line] >= 0} {
11     set count [expr $count + 1]
12  }
13
14  puts "Read $count lines."
```

Lines 3–5 use a simple if statement to ensure that there is one argument to the script—that being the filename containing lines to count. The if command takes two arguments—an expression and a block of code to execute if the expression evaluates as true. (Like C, zero indicates false, nonzero indicates true.)

Each of the arguments to the if command are contained in braces. Braces are simply used to group a set of words (or lines) together as a single argument. Although

this syntax may remind you of C or Perl, Tcl's command-parsing behavior is actually quite simple. For example, it allows a command argument (here, the body of
code on lines 3–5 containing the `error` command) to span multiple lines only if
the opening brace is at the end of a line. If we had written the `if` command as

```
if {$argc != 1}
  { error "lc <filename>" }
```

Tcl would have given us the error:

```
Error: wrong # args: no script following "$argc != 1" argument
wrong # args: no script following "$argc != 1" argument
    while executing
"if {$argc != 1} "
    (file "./lc.tcl" line 3)
```

In other words, Tcl doesn't know that the second argument to `if` is on the following line.

The body of the `if` command, on line 4, uses the `error` command to display an
error message and exit the Tcl script.

On line 7, we open the file given as the first command-line argument, and assign
the resulting file pointer to the variable `thefile`. The `set` command is used to
assign values to variables. This is because all Tcl commands must begin with a
command name; we can't set the variable `a` to 1 using something like:

```
a = 1
```

because `a` refers to a variable, not a command. Instead, we use

```
set a 1
```

Later, to refer to the value of the variable `a`, we would use `$a`.

The first argument to `set` is the name of the variable to assign, and the second
argument is the value. Here, we have

```
set thefile [open [lindex $argv 0] r]
```

Square brackets `[...]` are used to specify a *subscript*, a sequence of commands to
nest within the current command. The subscript is executed, and its return value
substituted in its place.

For example, let's look at the subscript

```
open [lindex $argv 0] r
```

This script executes the `open` command to open the file given as its first argument.
The second argument, `r`, indicates that the file should be opened for reading.

The first argument to open is the subscript

```
lindex $argv 0
```

The lindex command is used to index a list, or array, of items. In this case, we wish to obtain the 0th element of the $argv array, which contains the command-line arguments to the program, minus the command name itself. (This is unlike the use of argv in C programs.) Therefore, the 0th element of $argv is the first command-line argument.

Let's say that we named our script *lc.tcl*, and invoked it as

```
eggplant$ lc.tcl /etc/passwd
```

Therefore, within the command

```
set thefile [open [lindex $argv 0] r]
```

the nested subscript

```
open [lindex $argv 0] r
```

will be replaced with

```
open "/etc/passwd" r
```

which will, in turn, be replaced with the value of the file pointer corresponding to */etc/passwd*. The net result is that the file pointer value is assigned to the variable thefile.

On line 8, we set the variable count to 0, which will act as our line counter.

Lines 10–12 contain a simple while loop, which repeatedly reads lines from the file until EOF.

```
while {[gets $thefile line] >= 0} {
  set count [expr $count + 1]
}
```

As we can see, the while command takes two arguments: a condition and a block of code to execute while the condition is true. Here, the loop condition is

```
[gets $thefile line] >= 0
```

We see the subscript

```
gets $thefile line
```

which executes the gets command. This reads a single line from the file pointer $thefile, and assigns it to the variable line. gets returns the count of the number of characters read, or -1 if EOF is reached. Therefore, the while loop will continuously read lines from the file until gets returns a value less than zero.

The body of the while loop is

```
set count [expr $count + 1]
```

which increments the value of count. Remember that Tcl commands must begin with a command name. Therefore, arithmetic expressions are handled using the expr command. Here, the subscript

```
expr $count + 1
```

returns the value of the variable count plus 1. This is the canonical way to increment variables within Tcl.

Finally, on line 14, we see

```
puts "Read $count lines."
```

which uses the puts command to display a string to standard output.

Here is a sample run of this script:

```
eggplant$ lc.tcl /etc/passwd
Read 144 lines.
```

Writing Tk Applications

Even the basic Tcl knowledge given in the previous section is enough to allow you to write applications using Tk, the Tcl extensions for the X Window System. Tk is essentially a collection of Tcl commands that create and manipulate X widgets—such as buttons, scrollbars, menus, and so forth. As we will see, Tk is extremely versatile and greatly simplifies the task of building a graphical user interface under X.

In this section, we'll tour Tk through a simple application which allows the user to draw within a "canvas" widget. The canvas widget is a generic graphics widget with support for many types of objects, such as ovals, lines, text, and so forth. In this application, we'll use a canvas widget interactively to draw pictures using ovals and rectangles. When executed, this application looks something like Figure 6-2.

Let's walk through the source for our application, *draw.tcl.*

```
#!/usr/local/bin/wish -f
# Global variables, used to keep track of objects and positions
set oval_count 0
set rect_count 0
set orig_x 0
set orig_y 0
```

No sweat here—we simply initialize a few variables that will be used to keep track of the oval and rectangle objects that we create, as well as the location of the object as created.

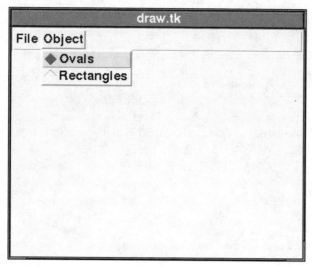

Figure 6-2. Window displayed by Tk program

The next portion of the source may be a bit daunting at first.

```
# This procedure enables ovals.
proc set_oval {} {
  # Allow us to access these global variables
  global oval_count orig_x orig_y

  # When button-1 is pressed, create an oval
  bind .c <ButtonPress-1> {
    set orig_x %x
    set orig_y %y
    set oval_count [expr $oval_count + 1]
    .c create oval %x %y %x %y -tags "oval$oval_count" -fill red
  }

  # When we drag button 1, delete the current oval and replace it
  bind .c <B1-Motion> {
    .c delete "oval$oval_count"
    .c create oval $orig_x $orig_y %x %y -tags "oval$oval_count" -fill red
  }
}
```

Here, we are defining a procedure named set_oval using the Tcl proc command. The first argument to proc is the list of arguments that the procedure will take—in this case, there are none. The second argument is the body of the procedure itself. This procedure will be invoked when we select the "Ovals" item from the "Objects" menu, which is configured below.

The first thing that set_oval does is declare the variables oval_count, orig_x, and orig_y to be globals—otherwise, Tcl would assume that we were using these variables locally within the procedure.

The next task is to bind an action to a ButtonPress event in the canvas widget, which we will be drawing into. This widget is named .c and is created below. Tk widgets are named hierarchically. The widget . (a period) refers to the main application window. Any widgets created within that window are given names beginning with a period, such as .c (for a canvas widget), .mbar (for a menu bar), and so on. Of course, the programmer is allowed to choose widget names, but those names must begin with a period. As we will see later, widgets may be contained within other widgets—for example, a menu is contained within a menu bar. A widget namcd

```
.mbar.file.menu
```

might refer to the menu menu contained within the menu item file contained within the menu bar .mbar. This will be demonstrated below.

The bind command is used to create an event binding for a particular widget. (An *event* is simply a "message" generated by the X server in response to a user action. For example, when the user presses mouse button 1 within a certain window, that window is sent a ButtonPress-1 event.) The first argument to bind is the widget in which to create the binding, and the second argument is the code to execute when that event occurs.

In this case, we wish to start drawing an oval whenever the user presses mouse button 1 in the canvas widget. The code of the binding sets the variables orig_x and orig_y to %x and %y, respectively. Within a binding, %x and %y refer to the x and y coordinates of the event in question. In this case, this would be the cursor position where the mouse button was pressed. We wish to save this location when the oval is resized. In addition, we increment the oval_count variable.

The ButtonPress-1 binding also executes the command

```
.c create oval %x %y %x %y -tags "oval$oval_count" -fill red
```

This creates an oval object within the canvas widget .c. The upper-left-hand and lower-right-hand coordinates of the oval are given as %x and %y, the location of the ButtonPress event. We fill the oval with the color red.

The -tags option to the canvas create command assigns a "name" to the newly-created oval object. In this way, we can refer to this particular oval on the canvas widget by its name. To ensure that each oval has a unique name, we use the oval_count variable, which is incremented each time an oval is created.

When the mouse is dragged with button 1 pressed, we wish to resize the oval as created. This is accomplished by setting a binding for the B1-Motion event in the canvas widget. This binding executes the two commands

```
.c delete "oval$oval_count"
.c create oval $orig_x $orig_y %x %y -tags "oval$oval_count" -fill red
```

The canvas delete command deletes the object named by the given tag. We then re-create the oval at its original upper-left-hand corner position, but with the new lower-right-hand corner given by the location of the B1-Motion event. In other words, we are replacing the original oval object with a new oval with different coordinates, corresponding to the position of the mouse. This effectively resizes the oval as the mouse moves across the canvas widget with button 1 pressed.

We define an analogous set_rect function, which is nearly identical to the above, but creates canvas rectangle objects instead.

```
# Identical to set_oval, but uses rectangles
proc set_rect {} {
  global rect_count orig_x orig_y
  bind .c <ButtonPress-1> {
    set orig_x %x
    set orig_y %y
    set rect_count [expr $rect_count + 1]
    .c create rectangle %x %y %x %y -tags "rect$rect_count" -fill blue
  }
  bind .c <B1-Motion> {
    .c delete "rect$rect_count"
    .c create rectangle $orig_x $orig_y %x %y -tags "rect$rect_count" \
      -fill blue
  }
}
```

Another way to draw rectangles and ovals would be to have a generic "draw object" function that uses a variable, say $objtype, to keep track of the current object type. The menu settings (described below) would be used to select the object type by setting the value of this variable. In the drawing function, we could simply use a canvas command such as

```
.c create $objtype %x %y %x %y -tags "obj$obj_count" -fill blue
```

However, this assumes that all objects will be drawn in the same way (by clicking on one position and dragging the mouse to size the object). Using separate functions for each object type allows us to specialize the interface for each if we wish to do so.

Now we are ready to define the various widgets that make up our application. First, we need to create a frame widget to be used as a menu bar. A frame widget merely acts as a container for other widgets.

```
# Create a frame widget to be used as a menubar.
frame .mbar -relief groove -bd 3
pack .mbar -side top -expand yes -fill x
```

Here, we create a frame widget named .mbar. The -relief option specifies the display style for this widget—in this case, we wish the menu bar to appear as though it has a "groove" running along its perimeter. The –bd option sets the width of the widget's border, which in this case defines the width of the groove.

The pack command is used to place widgets within the application window, or within other widgets. It is one kind of "geometry manager" available for Tk. In order for a widget to be displayed within the application, a geometry manager must be called to place the widget. pack is provided with Tcl/Tk, and is versatile enough for almost any application. pack allows you to specify how widgets should be placed relative to one another, without having to specify absolute locations.

In this case, we pack the .mbar widget into the top edge of its parent widget, which is . (the main application window). The –fill x option tells pack that the widget should be allocated the entire width of the window in which it is contained; the –expand option specifies that the widget should "grow" to fill that space. If you are interested in the intricacies of pack, the Tk pack manual page provides a great deal of detail.

Next, we create two menubutton widgets within this menu bar—the File and Object menus.

```
# Create two menu items
menubutton .mbar.file -text "File" -menu .mbar.file.menu
menubutton .mbar.obj -text "Object" -menu .mbar.obj.menu
pack .mbar.file .mbar.obj -side left
```

The two widgets in question are named .mbar.file and .mbar.obj. Therefore, each widget is a direct child of the .mbar widget, not the main application window. When we pack the two widgets, they are packed into the left side of their parent, the menu bar.

The –menu option to the menubutton command specifies the menu widget that should be displayed when this pulldown menu is selected. We will create the .mbar.file.menu and .mbar.obj.menu widgets below.

```
# Create the file menu, and add a single "Quit" item to it
menu .mbar.file.menu
.mbar.file.menu add command -label "Quit" -command { exit }
```

First, we create the File menu itself, and add a single command item to it. A command item is like a button—when selected, the code given by the –command option is executed. In this case, selecting this option will exit the Tk script.

```
# Create the object menu, and add two radiobutton objects to it
menu .mbar.obj.menu
.mbar.obj.menu add radiobutton -label "Ovals" -variable objtype \
    -command { set_oval }
.mbar.obj.menu add radiobutton -label "Rectangles" -variable objtype \
    -command { set_rect }
```

Here, we create the Objects menu, and add two objects of type radiobutton to it. Radiobuttons define a set of options where only one of the options may be selected at a given time. For example, when Ovals is selected, it will be highlighted in the menu, and Rectangles unhighlighted.

In order to "link" the two radiobuttons (so that only one may be selected at a time), we use the −variable option to specify a "dummy" variable which keeps track of the current setting of the radio buttons. The −variable option may be used in conjunction with −value, which assigns a value to the named variable when the menu item is selected. Instead, we choose to execute a procedure (specified with the −command option) when the menu item is selected, which precludes the need for −value.

Next, we create our canvas widget, and pack it into the application window.

```
# Create the canvas .c
canvas .c
pack .c -side top
```

Finally, we enable the Ovals option by artificially invoking the corresponding menu item. This is exactly what happens when the user selects the menu item using the mouse.

```
# Turn on ovals, by invoking the first item in the object menu
.mbar.obj.menu invoke 0
```

Here, in a few dozen lines of code, we have a complete, relatively complex X application. There are many easy ways to extend this program—for example, by adding new object types, allowing the user to save and load "pictures" created with it, and so on. In fact, the canvas widget even supports an option to dump a PostScript image of its contents, which can be used for printing.

Using Tcl and Tk in Other Applications

As mentioned previously, you can use Tcl and Tk with other programs written in languages such as C or Perl. Writing a complex program as a Tcl/Tk script is possible, but would probably be slower than coding it in a compiled language because Tcl is interpreted. Although Perl is interpreted as well, Perl is suited to many tasks that are more difficult to accomplish in Tcl or C.

The canonical way to use Tcl and Tk with a C program is to link the Tcl and Tk libraries with the C code. Tcl and Tk provide simple *.a* static libraries, as well as shared *.so* libraries on some systems. The Tcl interpreter is implemented as a series of functions that your program calls.

The idea is that you implement new Tcl commands as C functions, and the Tcl interpreter calls those functions when one of those commands is used. To do this you must structure your program to initialize the Tcl interpreter and use a Tcl "main loop," which reads Tcl commands from some location (such as a file) and executes them. This is roughly equivalent to building your own *tclsh* or *wish* interpreter with a few extra Tcl/Tk commands implemented in C.

This may not be the best solution for all applications. First of all, it requires some of your program to be restructured, and the Tcl interpreter ends up controlling the application—not the other way around. Also, unless you use shared Tcl and Tk libraries, having a complete Tcl/Tk interpreter embedded in your application can make the binary quite large—well over a megabyte. Also, your application may depend on some kind of Tcl script to drive it, which means that the executable itself is not enough to use the complete application—you need the driving script as well.

Another solution is to write an application in C or Perl that executes the *wish* interpreter as a separate process and communicates with it via pipes. In this case, you will need two pipes: one for the C program to write commands to *wish*, and another for the C program to read responses from *wish*. This can be done with a single pipe, but synchronization becomes more difficult. For example, responses from *wish* may be asynchronous—generated from user events such as a button press—which makes the use of a single pipe a bit complex. *

The most straightforward way of setting this up is to write a C function that does the following (in pseudocode):

```
Create two pipes by calling pipe() twice;
Use fork() to start a child process;
    In the child process,
        close the read end of one pipe and the write end of another;
        Use dup2() to duplicate stdin and stdout to the appropriate pipes;
        Use execlp() to start wish;
    In the parent process;
        close the read end of the write pipe, and the write end of the read pipe;
        Use fdopen() on each pipe to get a FILE descriptor for use with fprintf()
            and fscanf();
```

Of course, you'll need some knowledge of UNIX systems programming to use the above example, but it's provided here for the adventurous.

The parent process (your C application) can now write Tcl/Tk commands to the write pipe, and read responses from *wish* on the read pipe. The *select* function can be used to poll for data on the read pipe, in case you want your application to keep processing while waiting for data from the *wish* interpreter.

This way, we treat *wish* as a "server" for X Window System routines. Your program would send widget creation commands down the write pipe. *wish* could be told to print a string to standard output when a response is required from the application. For example, a button widget could be created that prints the string "okay pressed" when pressed by the user. Your program would read this string on the read pipe and respond to it. Other parts of the application could be controlled by

---

* Remember that a pipe is a simple one-way data stream used to communicate from one process to another. The shell allows you to use single pipes between commands, as in *cat foo.txt.gz | gunzip -c | more.*

wish without your application's knowledge. The computing-intensive, speed-critical parts of the application would be coded in C, and the interface handled by *wish*.

[43] Advanced
Programming

Hopefully, the overview here should be enough to give you an idea of how to write a C or Perl program that uses *wish* in this way. It's a good idea to read a book on UNIX systems programming that talks about interprocess communication using pipes, such as *Advanced Programming in The Unix Environment.*

Other Languages

There are many other popular (and not-so-popular) languages available for Linux. For the most part, however, these work identically on Linux as on other UNIX systems, so there's not much in the way of news there. There are also so many of them that we can't cover them in much detail here. We do want to let you know what's out there, however, and explain some of the differences between the various languages and compilers.

LISP is an interpreted language used in many applications, ranging from artificial intelligence to statistics. It is a language used primarily in computer science, because it defines a very clean, logical interface to working with algorithms. (It also uses a lot of parentheses, which is something that computer scientists are always fond of.) It is a functional programming language and is very generalized. Many operations are defined in terms of recursion instead of linear loops. Expressions are hierarchical, and data is represented by lists of items.

There are several LISP interpreters available for Linux. Emacs contains its own dialect of LISP, called Elisp, which is a fairly complete implementation in itself. Elisp has many features that allow it to interact directly with Emacs—input and output through Emacs buffers, for example—but it may be used for non-Emacs-related applications as well.

Also available is CLISP, a Common LISP implementation by Bruno Haible of Karlsruhe University and Michael Stoll of Munich University. It includes an interpreter, a compiler, and a subset of CLOS (Common LISP Object System, an object-oriented extension to LISP). CLX, a Common LISP interface to the X Window System, is also available, and runs under CLISP. CLX will allow you to write X-based applications in LISP. Austin Kyoto Common LISP, another LISP implementation, is available and compatible with CLX as well.

SWI-Prolog, a very complete Prolog implementation by Jan Wielemaker of the University of Amsterdam, is also available. Prolog is a logic-based language, allowing you to make logical assertions, and defining heuristics for validating those assertions and making decisions based on them. It is a very useful language for AI applications.

Also available are several Scheme interpreters, including MIT Scheme, a complete Scheme interpreter conforming to the R^4 standard. Scheme is a dialect of LISP that has a cleaner, more general programming model. It is a good LISP dialect for computer science applications and for studying algorithms.

At least two implementations of Ada are available—AdaEd, an Ada interpreter, and GNAT, the GNU Ada Translator. GNAT acts as a front-end to Ada, translating it into C for compilation.

Along the same vein, two other popular language translators exist for Linux—*p2c*, a Pascal-to-C translator, and *f2c*, a FORTRAN-to-C translator. If you're concerned that these translators won't function as well as bona fide compilers, don't be. Both *p2c* and *f2c* have proven to be robust and useful for heavy Pascal and FORTRAN use.

f2c is FORTRAN-77 compliant, and a number of tools are available for it as well. *ftnchek* is a FORTRAN "checker," similar to *lint*. Both the LAPACK numerical methods library and the *mpfun* multi-precision FORTRAN library have been ported to Linux using *f2c*. *toolpack* is a collection of FORTRAN tools such as a source code pretty-printer, a precision converter, and a portability checker.

Among the miscellaneous other languages available for Linux are interpreters for APL, Rexx, Forth, and a Simula-to-C translator. The GNU versions of the compiler tools *lex* and *yacc* (renamed to *flex* and *bison*, respectively) have also been ported to Linux. *lex* and *yacc* are invaluable for creating any kind of parser or translator, most commonly used when writing compilers.

Debugging with gdb

Are you one of those programmers who scoff at the very idea of using a debugger to trace through code? Is your philosophy that if the code is too complex for even the programmer to understand it, then you deserve no mercy when it comes to bugs? Do you step through your code, mentally, using a magnifying glass and a toothpick? More often than not, are bugs usually caused by a single-character omission, such as using the = operator when you mean +=?

Then perhaps you should meet *gdb*—the GNU debugger. Whether or not you know it, *gdb* is your friend. It can locate obscure and difficult-to-find bugs that result in core dumps, memory leaks, and erratic behavior (both for the program and the programmer). Sometimes even the most harmless-looking glitches in your code can cause everything to go haywire, and without the aid of a debugger like *gdb* finding, these problems can be nearly impossible—especially for programs longer than a few hundred lines. In this section, we'll introduce you to the most useful features of *gdb* by way of examples. There's a book on *gdb*, too—the Free Software Foundation's *Debugging with GDB*.

[55] gdb

gdb is capable of either debugging programs as they run, or examining the cause for a program crash with a core dump. Programs debugged at run time with *gdb* can either be executed from within *gdb* itself, or run separately—that is, *gdb* can attach itself to an already-running process to examine it. First, we'll discuss how to debug programs running within *gdb*, and then move on to attaching to running processes and examining core dumps.

Tracing a Program

Our first example is a program called *trymh* that detects edges in a grayscale image. *trymh* takes as input an image file, does some calculations on the data, and spits out another image file. Unfortunately, it crashes whenever it is invoked, as so:

```
papaya$ trymh < image00.pgm > image00.pbm
Segmentation fault (core dumped)
```

Now, using *gdb* we could analyze the resulting core file, but for this example we'll show how to trace the program as it runs, instead. *

Before we can use *gdb* to trace through the executable *trymh*, we need to ensure that it has been compiled with debugging code (see the section "Enabling Debugging Code" earlier in the chapter). To do so, we should compile *trymh* using the –*g* switch with *gcc*.

Note that enabling optimization (–*O*) with debug code (–*g*) is not illegal, but not recommended. The problem is that *gcc* is too smart for its own good. For example, if you have two identical lines of code in two different places in a function, *gdb* may unexpectedly jump to the second occurrence of the line, instead of the first, as expected. This is because *gcc* combined the two lines into a single line of machine code used in both instances.

Some of the automatic optimizations performed by *gcc* can be very confusing when using a debugger. To turn off *all* optimization (even optimizations performed without specifying –*O*), use the –*OO* (that's *dash-oh-zero*) option with *gcc*.

Now we can fire up *gdb* to see what the problem might be:

```
papaya$ gdb trymh
GDB is free software and you are welcome to distribute copies of it
 under certain conditions; type "show copying" to see the conditions.
There is absolutely no warranty for GDB; type "show warranty" for details.
GDB 4.8, Copyright 1993 Free Software Foundation, Inc...
 (gdb)
```

Now *gdb* is waiting for a command. (The command *help* will display information on the available commands.) The first thing that we want to do is start running the program so that we can observe its behavior. However, if we immediately use the *run* command, the program will simply execute until it exits or crashes.

First, we need to set a *breakpoint* somewhere in the program. A breakpoint is just a location in the program where *gdb* should stop and allow us to control

---

* The sample programs in this section are not programs that you're likely to run into anywhere; they were thrown together by the author for purposes of demonstration.

execution of the program. For the sake of simplicity, let's set a breakpoint on the first line of actual code, so that the program stops just as it begins to execute. The *list* command is used to display several lines of code (an amount which is variable) at a time.

```
(gdb) list
12          main() {
13
14              FloatImage inimage;
15              FloatImage outimage;
16              BinaryImage binimage;
17              int i,j;
18
19              inimage = (FloatImage)imLoadF(IMAGE_FLOAT,stdin);
20              outimage = laplacian_float(inimage);
21
(gdb) break 19
Breakpoint 1 at 0x289c: file trymh.c, line 19.
(gdb)
```

A breakpoint is now set at line 19 in the current source file. You can set many breakpoints in the program; breakpoints may be conditional (that is, triggered only when a certain expression is true), unconditional, delayed, temporarily disabled, and so on. You may set breakpoints on a particular line of code, a particular function, a set of functions, and a slew of other ways. You may also set a *watchpoint*, using the *watch* command, which is similar to a breakpoint but is triggered whenever a certain event takes place—not necessarily at a specific line of code within the program. We'll talk more about breakpoints and watchpoints later in the chapter.

Next, we use the *run* command to start the program running. *run* takes as arguments the same arguments that you'd give *trymh* on the command line—this can include shell wildcards, input/output redirection, and so on, as the command is passed to */bin/sh* for execution.

```
(gdb) run < image00.pgm > image00.pfm
Starting program: /amd/dusk/d/mdw/vis/src/trymh < image00.pgm > image00.pfm

Breakpoint 1, main () at trymh.c:19
19              inimage = (FloatImage)imLoadF(IMAGE_FLOAT,stdin);
(gdb)
```

As expected, the breakpoint is reached immediately at the first line of code. We can now take over.

The most useful program-stepping commands are *next* and *step*. Both commands execute the next line of code in the program, except that *step* will descend into any function calls in the program, and *next* will step only to the next line of code *in the same function. next* will quietly execute any function calls that it steps over, but not descend in their code for us to examine.

imLoadF is a function to load an image from a disk file. We know that this function is not at fault (you'll have to trust us on that one), so we wish to step over it using the *next* command.

```
(gdb) next
20              outimage = laplacian_float(inimage);
(gdb)
```

Here, we are interested in tracing into the suspicious-looking *laplacian_float* function, so we use the *step* command.

```
(gdb) step
laplacian_float (fim=0x0) at laplacian.c:21
21              i = 20.0;
(gdb)
```

Let's use the *list* command to get some idea of where we are:

```
(gdb) list
16              FloatImage laplacian_float(FloatImage fim) {
17
18                  FloatImage mask;
19                  float i;
20
21                  i = 20.0;
22                  mask=(FloatImage)imNew(IMAGE_FLOAT,3,3);
23                  imRef(mask,0,0) = imRef(mask,2,0) = imRef(mask,0,2) = 1.0;
24                  imRef(mask,2,2) = 1.0; imRef(mask,1,0) = imRef(mask,0,1) = i/5;
25                  imRef(mask,2,1) = imRef(mask,1,2) = i/5; imRef(mask,1,1) = -i;
(gdb) list
26
27                  return convolveFloatWithFloat(fim,mask);
28              }
(gdb)
```

As you can see, using *list* multiple times just displays more of the code. Because we don't want to *step* manually through this code, and we're not interested in the *imNew* function on line 22, let's continue execution until line 27. For this, we use the *until* command:

```
(gdb) until 27
laplacian_float (fim=0x0) at laplacian.c:27
27                  return convolveFloatWithFloat(fim,mask);
(gdb)
```

Before we step into the *convolveFloatWithFloat* function, let's be sure that the two parameters, fim and mask, are valid. The *print* command will examine the value of a variable.

```
(gdb) print mask
$1 = (struct {...} *) 0xe838
(gdb) print fim
```

```
$2 = (struct {...} *) 0x0
(gdb)
```

mask looks fine, but fim, the input image, is null! Obviously, *laplacian_float* was passed a null pointer instead of a valid image. If you have been paying close attention, you would have noticed this as we entered *laplacian_float*, above.

Instead of stepping deeper into the program (as it's apparent that something has already gone wrong), let's continue execution until the current function returns. The *finish* command will accomplish this.

```
(gdb) finish
Run till exit from #0  laplacian_float (fim=0x0) at laplacian.c:27
0x28c0 in main () at trymh.c:20
20          outimage = laplacian_float(inimage);
Value returned is $3 = (struct {...} *) 0x0
(gdb)
```

Now we're back in *main*. To determine the source of the problem, let's examine the values of some variables.

```
(gdb) list
15          FloatImage outimage;
16          BinaryImage binimage;
17          int i,j;
18
19          inimage = (FloatImage)imLoadF(IMAGE_FLOAT,stdin);
20          outimage = laplacian_float(inimage);
21
22          binimage = marr_hildreth(outimage);
23          if  (binimage == NULL) {
24            fprintf(stderr,"trymh: binimage returned NULL\n");
(gdb) print inimage
$6 = (struct {...} *) 0x0
(gdb)
```

The variable inimage, containing the input image returned from *imLoadF*, is null. Passing a null pointer into the image manipulation routines certainly would cause a core dump, in this case. However, we know *imLoadF* to be tried and true, so what's the problem?

As it turns out, our library function *imLoadF* will return NULL on failure—if the input format is bad, for example. Because we never check the return value of *imLoadF* before passing it along to *laplacian_float*, the program goes haywire when inimage is assigned NULL. To correct the problem we simply insert code to cause the problem to exit with an error message if *imLoadF* returns a null pointer.

To quit *gdb*, just use the command *quit*. Unless the program has finished execution, *gdb* will complain that the program is still running.

```
(gdb) quit
The program is running.  Quit anyway (and kill it)? (y or n) y
papaya$
```

In the following sections we examine some specific features provided by the debugger, given the general picture just presented.

Examining a Core File

Do you hate it when a program crashes, and spites you again by leaving a ten-megabyte core file in your working directory, wasting much-needed space? Don't be so quick to delete that core file—it can be very helpful. A core file is just a dump of the memory image of a process at the time of the crash. You can use the core file with *gdb* to examine the state of your program (such as the values of variables and data) and determine the cause for failure.

The core file is written to disk by the operating system whenever certain failures occur. The most frequent reason for a crash and subsequent core dump is a memory violation—that is, trying to read or write memory that your program does not have access to. For example, attempting to write data into a null pointer can cause a "segmentation fault," which is essentially a fancy way to say "you screwed up."

However, not all such memory errors will cause immediate crashes. For example, you may overwrite memory in some way, but the program will continue to run, not knowing the difference between actual data and instructions or garbage. Subtle memory violations can cause programs to behave erratically. The author once witnessed a bug that would cause the program to jump randomly around, but without tracing it with *gdb*, it would still appear to be working normally. The only evidence of a bug was that the program was returning output that meant, roughly, that two and two did not add up to four. Sure enough, the bug was an attempt to write one too many characters into a block of allocated memory. That single-byte error caused hours of grief.

You can prevent these kinds of memory problems (even the best programmers make these mistakes!) using the Checker package, a set of memory management routines which replaces the commonly-used *malloc( )* and *free( )* functions. We'll talk about Checker in the section "Using Checker."

However, if your program does cause a memory fault, it will crash and dump core. Under Linux, core files are named *core.name*, where *name* is the name of the executable that crashed. For example, if the program *trymh* were to crash and dump core, the core file would be named *core.trymh*. The core file appears in the current working directory of the running process, which is usually the working directory of the shell that started the program, but on occasion programs may change their own working directory.

Some shells provide facilities for controlling whether or not core files are written. Under *bash*, for example, the default behavior is not to write core files at all. In order to enable core file output, you should use the command

```
ulimit -c unlimited
```

probably in your *.bashrc* initialization file. You can specify a maximum size for core files other than unlimited, but truncated core files may not be of use when debugging applications.

Also, in order for a core file to be useful, the program must be compiled with debugging code enabled, as described in the previous section. Most binaries on your system will not contain debugging code, so the core file will be of limited value.

Our example for using *gdb* with a core file is yet another mythical program called *cross*. Like *trymh* in the previous section, *cross* takes as input an image file, does some calculations on it, and outputs another image file. However, when running *cross*, we get a segmentation fault:

```
papaya$ cross < image30.pfm > image30.pbm
Segmentation fault (core dumped)
papaya$
```

To invoke *gdb* for use with a core file, you must not only specify the core file-name, but also the name of the executable that goes along with that core file. This is because the core file itself does not contain all of the information necessary to debug.

```
papaya$ gdb cross core.cross
GDB is free software and you are welcome to distribute copies of it
  under certain conditions; type "show copying" to see the conditions.
There is absolutely no warranty for GDB; type "show warranty" for details.
GDB 4.8, Copyright 1993 Free Software Foundation, Inc...
Core was generated by `cross'.
Program terminated with signal 11, Segmentation fault.
#0  0x2494 in crossings (image=0xc7c8) at cross.c:31
31                 if ((image[i][j] >= 0) &&
(gdb)
```

gdb tells us that the core file terminated with signal 11. A *signal* is a kind of message that is sent to a running program from the kernel, the user, or the program itself. Signals are generally used to terminate a program (and possibly cause it to dump core). For example, when you type the interrupt character, a signal is sent to the running program, which will probably kill it.

In this case, signal 11 was sent to the running *cross* process by the kernel when *cross* attempted to read or write to memory that it did not have access to. This signal caused *cross* to die and dump core. *gdb* says that the illegal memory reference occurred on line 31 of the source file *cross.c*.

```
(gdb) list
26              xmax = imGetWidth(image)-1;
27              ymax = imGetHeight(image)-1;
28
29              for (j=1; j<xmax; j++) {
30                for (i=1; i<ymax; i++) {
31                  if ((image[i][j] >= 0) &&
32                     (image[i-1][j-1] < 0) ||
33                     (image[i-1][j] < 0) ||
34                     (image[i-1][j+1] < 0) ||
35                     (image[i][j-1] < 0) ||
(gdb)
```

Here, we see several things. First of all, there is a loop across the two index variables i and j, presumably in order to do calculations on the input image. Line 31 is an attempt to reference data from image[i][j], a two-dimensional array. When a program dumps core while attempting to access data from an array, it's usually a sign that one of the indices is out of bounds. Let's check them.

```
(gdb) print i
$1 = 1
(gdb) print j
$2 = 1194
(gdb) print xmax
$3 = 1551
(gdb) print ymax
$4 = 1194
(gdb)
```

Here we see the problem. The program was attempting to reference element image[1][1194], however, the array extends only to image[1550][1193] (remember that arrays in C are indexed from 0 to *max*-1). In other words, we attempted to read the 1195th row of an image that only has 1194 rows.

If we look at lines 29 and 30, above, we see the problem: the values xmax and ymax are reversed. The variable j should range from 1 to ymax (because it is the row index of the array), and i should range from 1 to xmax. Fixing the two for loops on lines 29 and 30 corrects the problem.

Let's say that your program is crashing within a function that is called from many different locations, and you want to determine where the function was invoked from, and what situation led up to the crash. The *backtrace* command will display the *call stack* of the program at the time of failure.

The call stack is just the list of functions that led up to the current one. For example, if the program starts in function *main*, which calls function *foo*, which calls *bamf*, the call stack will look like:

```
(gdb) backtrace
#0  0x1384 in bamf () at goop.c:31
#1  0x4280 in foo () at goop.c:48
```

```
#2  0x218 in main () at goop.c:116
(gdb)
```

As each function is called, it pushes certain data onto the stack, such as saved registers, function arguments, local variables, and so forth. Each function has a certain amount of space allocated on the stack for its use. The chunk of memory on the stack for a particular function is called a *stack frame*, and the call stack is just the ordered list of stack frames.

In the following example, we are looking at a core file for an X-based animation program. Using *backtrace* gives us:

```
(gdb) backtrace
#0  0x602b4982 in _end ()
#1  0xbffff934 in _end ()
#2  0x13c6 in stream_drawimage (wgt=0x38330000, sn=4) at stream_display.c:94
#3  0x1497 in stream_refresh_all () at stream_display.c:116
#4  0x49c in control_update_all () at control_init.c:73
#5  0x224 in play_timeout (Cannot access memory at address 0x602b7676.
(gdb)
```

This is a list of stack frames for the process. The most recently called function is frame 0, which is the "function" *_end* in this case. Here, we see that *play_timeout* called *control_update_all*, which called *stream_refresh_all*, and so on. Somehow, the program jumped to *_end*, where it crashed.

However, *_end* is not a function—it is simply a label that specifies the end of the process data segment. When a program branches to an address such as *_end*, which is not a real function, it is a sign that something must have caused the process to go haywire, corrupting the call stack. (This is known in hacker jargon as "jumping to hyperspace.") In fact, the error "Cannot access memory at address 0x602b7676" is another indication that something bizarre has occurred.

We can see, however, that the last "real" function that was called was *stream_drawimage*, and we might guess that it is the source of the problem. To examine the state of *stream_drawimage*, we need to select its stack frame (frame number 2), using the *frame* command.

```
(gdb) frame 2
#2  0x13c6 in stream_drawimage (wgt=0x38330000, sn=4) at stream_display.c:94
94          XCopyArea(mydisplay,streams[sn].frames[currentframe],XtWindow(wgt),
(gdb) list
91
92          printf("CopyArea frame %d, sn %d, wid %d\n",currentframe,sn,wgt);
93
94          XCopyArea(mydisplay,streams[sn].frames[currentframe],XtWindow(wgt),
95              picGC,0,0,streams[sn].width,streams[sn].height,0,0);
(gdb)
```

Well, not knowing anything else about the program at hand, we can't see anything wrong here, unless the variable sn (being used as an index into the array streams) is out of range. From the output of *frame*, we see that *stream_drawimage* was called with an sn parameter of 4. (Function parameters are displayed in the output of *backtrace*, as well as whenever we change frames.)

Let's move up another frame, to *stream_refresh_all*, to see how *stream_display* was called. To do this, we can use the *up* command, which selects the stack frame above the current one.

```
(gdb) up
#3  0x1497 in stream_refresh_all () at stream_display.c:116
116             stream_drawimage(streams[i].drawbox,i);
(gdb) list
113     void stream_refresh_all(void) {
114         int i;
115         for (i=0; i<=numstreams; i++) {
116             stream_drawimage(streams[i].drawbox,i);
117
(gdb) print i
$2 = 4
(gdb) print numstreams
$3 = 4
(gdb)
```

Here, we see that the index variable i is looping from 0 to numstreams, and indeed i here is 4, the second parameter to *stream_drawimage*. However, numstreams is also 4. What's going on?

The for loop on line 115 looks funny—it should read

```
for (i=0; i<numstreams; i++) {
```

The error is the use of the <= comparison operator. The streams array is indexed from 0 to numstreams-1, not from 0 to numstreams. This simple off-by-one error caused the program to go berserk.

As you can see, using *gdb* with a core dump allows you to browse through the image of a crashed program to find bugs. Never again will you delete those pesky core files, right?

Debugging a Running Program

gdb is also capable of debugging a program that is already running, allowing you to interrupt it, examine it, and then return the process to its regularly scheduled execution. This is very similar to running a program from within *gdb*, and there are only a few new commands to learn.

The *attach* attaches *gdb* to a running process. In order to use *attach* you must also have access to the executable that corresponds to the process.

For example, if you have started the program *pgmseq* with process ID 254, you can start up *gdb* with:

```
papaya$ gdb pgmseq
```

and once inside *gdb* use the command

```
(gdb) attach 254
Attaching program `/home/loomer/mdw/pgmseq/pgmseq', pid 254
__select (nd=4, in=0xbffff96c, out=0xbffff94c, ex=0xbffff92c, tv=0x0)
    at __select.c:22
__select.c:22: No such file or directory.
(gdb)
```

(The "No such file or directory" error is given because *gdb* can't locate the source file for *__select*. This is often the case with system calls and library functions, and it's not anything to worry about.) Alternately, you can start *gdb* with the command

```
papaya$ gdb pgmseq 254
```

Once *gdb* attaches to the running process, it will temporarily suspend the program and let you take over, issuing *gdb* commands. Or you can set a breakpoint or watchpoint (with the *break* and *watch* commands), and use *continue* to cause the program to continue execution until the breakpoint is triggered.

The *detach* command will detach *gdb* from the running process. You can then use *attach* again, on another process, if necessary. If you find a bug, you can *detach* the current process, make changes to the source, recompile, and use the *file* command to load the new executable into *gdb*. You can then start the new version of the program and use the *attach* command to debug it. All without leaving *gdb*!

In fact, *gdb* will allow you to debug three programs concurrently: one running directly under *gdb*, one tracing with a core file, and one running as an independent process. The *target* command allows you to select which one you wish to debug.

Changing and Examining Data

To examine the values of variables in your program, you can use the *print*, *x*, and *ptype* commands. The *print* command is the most commonly-used data inspection command; it takes as an argument an expression in the source language (usually C or C++), and returns its value. For example:

```
(gdb) print mydisplay
$10 = (struct _XDisplay *) 0x9c800
(gdb)
```

This displays the value of the variable mydisplay, as well as an indication of its type. Because this variable is a pointer, you can examine its contents by dereferencing the pointer, as you would in C:

```
(gdb) print *mydisplay
$11 = {ext_data = 0x0, free_funcs = 0x99c20, fd = 5, lock = 0,
  proto_major_version = 11, proto_minor_version = 0,
  vendor = 0x9dff0 "XFree86", resource_base = 41943040,
  ...
  error_vec = 0x0, cms = {defaultCCCs = 0xa3d80 "", clientCmaps = 0x991a0 "'",
    perVisualIntensityMaps = 0x0}, conn_checker = 0, im_filters = 0x0}
(gdb)
```

mydisplay is an extensive structure used by X programs—we have abbreviated the output for your reading enjoyment.

print can print the value of just about any expression, including C function calls (which it executes on the fly, within the context of the running program):

```
(gdb) print getpid()
$11 = 138
(gdb)
```

Of course, not all functions may be called in this manner. Only those functions which have been linked to the running program may be called. If a function has not been linked to the program and you attempt to call it, *gdb* will complain that there is no such symbol in the current context.

More complicated expressions may be used as arguments to *print* as well, including assignments to variables. For example,

```
(gdb) print mydisplay->vendor = ``Linux''
$19 = 0x9de70 "Linux"
(gdb)
```

will assign the value of the vendor member of the mydisplay structure the value "Linux" instead of "XFree86" (a useless modification, but interesting nonetheless). In this way, you can interactively change data in a running program to correct errant behavior or test uncommon situations.

Note that after each *print* command, the value displayed is assigned to one of the *gdb* convenience registers, which are *gdb* internal variables that may be handy for you to use. For example, to recall the value of mydisplay, above, we need to merely print the value of $10.

```
(gdb) print $10
$21 = (struct _XDisplay *) 0x9c800
(gdb)
```

You may also use expressions such as typecasts with the *print* command. Almost anything goes.

The *ptype* command will give you detailed (and often long-winded) information about a variable's type, or the definition of a struct or typedef. To get a full definition for the struct _XDisplay used by the mydisplay variable, we use

```
(gdb) ptype mydisplay
type = struct _XDisplay {
    struct _XExtData *ext_data;
    struct _XFreeFuncs *free_funcs;
    int fd;
    int lock;
    int proto_major_version;
    ...
    struct _XIMFilter *im_filters;
} *
(gdb)
```

If you're interested in examining memory on a more fundamental level, beyond the petty confines of defined types, you can use the *x* command. *x* takes a memory address as an argument. If you give it a variable, it will use the *value* of that variable as the address.

x also takes a count and a type specification as an optional argument. The count is the number of objects of the given type to display. For example, x/100x 0x4200 will display 100 bytes of data, represented in hexadecimal format, at the address 0x4200. Use *help x* to get a description of the various output formats.

To examine the value of mydisplay->vendor, we can use

```
(gdb) x mydisplay->vendor
0x9de70 <_end+35376>:    76 'L'
(gdb) x/6c mydisplay->vendor
0x9de70 <_end+35376>:    76 'L'  105 'i' 110 'n' 117 'u' 120 'x' 0 '\000'
(gdb) x/s mydisplay->vendor
0x9de70 <_end+35376>:    "Linux"
(gdb)
```

The first field of each line gives the absolute address of the data. The second represents the address as some symbol (in this case, _end) plus an offset in bytes. The remaining fields give the actual value of memory at that address, first in decimal, then as an ASCII character. As described above you can force *x* to print the data in other formats.

Getting Information

The *info* command provides information about the status of the program being debugged. There are many sub-commands under *info*; use *help info* to see them all. For example, *info program* will display the execution status of the program.

```
(gdb) info program
Using the running image of child process 138.
Program stopped at 0x9e.
```

```
It stopped at breakpoint 1.
(gdb)
```

Another useful command is *info locals*, which will display the names and values of all local variables in the current function.

```
(gdb) info locals
inimage = (struct {...} *) 0x2000
outimage = (struct {...} *) 0x8000
(gdb)
```

This is a rather cursory description of the variables. The *print* or *x* commands can be used to describe them further.

Similarly, *info variables* will display a list of all known variables in the program, ordered by source file. Note that many of the variables displayed will be from sources outside of your actual program—for example, the names of variables used within the library code will be displayed. The values for these variables are not displayed, because the list is culled more or less directly from the executable's symbol table. Only those local variables in the current stack frame, and global (static) variables are actually accessible from *gdb*.

info address will give you information about exactly where a certain variable is stored. For example:

```
(gdb) info address inimage
Symbol "inimage" is a local variable at frame offset -20.
(gdb)
```

By "frame offset," *gdb* means that *inimage* is stored 20 bytes below the top of the stack frame.

You can get information on the current frame using the *info frame* command, as so:

```
(gdb) info frame
Stack level 0, frame at 0xbffffaa8:
 eip = 0x9e in main (main.c:44); saved eip 0x34
 source language c.
 Arglist at 0xbffffaa8, args: argc=1, argv=0xbffffabc
 Locals at 0xbffffaa8, Previous frame's sp is 0x0
 Saved registers:
  ebx at 0xbffffaa0, ebp at 0xbffffaa8, esi at 0xbffffaa4, eip at 0xbffffaac
(gdb)
```

This kind of information is useful if you're debugging at the assembly language level with the *disass*, *nexti*, and *stepi* commands (see the section "Instruction-level debugging").

Miscellaneous Features

We have barely scratched the surface about what *gdb* can do. It is an amazing program with a lot of power—we have only introduced you to the most commonly-used commands. In this section we'll look at other features of *gdb*, and then send you on your way.

gdb(1)

[55] gdb
Chapter 5

If you're interested in learning more about *gdb*, we encourage you to read the *gdb* manual page and the Free Software Foundation manual. The manual is also available as an online info file (info files may be read under Emacs, or using the *info* reader; see the section "Tutorial and Online Help" in Chapter 5 for details).

Breakpoints and watchpoints

As promised, we're going to demonstrate further use of breakpoints and watchpoints. Breakpoints may be set with the *break* command; similarly, watchpoints may be set with the *watch* command. The only difference between the two is that breakpoints must break at a particular location in the program—on a certain line of code, for example—and watchpoints may be triggered whenever a certain expression is true, regardless of location within the program. Though powerful, watchpoints can be horribly inefficient—any time the state of the program changes, all watchpoints must be reevaluated.

When a breakpoint or watchpoint is triggered, *gdb* suspends the program and returns control to you. Breakpoints and watchpoints are meant to allow you to run the program (using the *run* and *continue* commands) and stop only in certain situations—saving you the trouble of using many *next* and *step* commands to walk through the program manually.

There are many ways to set a breakpoint in the program. You can specify a line number, as in *break 20*. Or, you can specify a particular function, as in *break stream_unload*. You can also specify a line number in another source file, as in *break foo.c:38*. Use *help break* to see the complete syntax.

Breakpoints may be conditional—that is, the breakpoint will trigger only when a certain expression is true. For example, using the command

```
break 184 if (status == 0)
```

will set a conditional breakpoint at line 184 in the current source file, which will trigger only when the variable status is zero. The variable status must be either a global variable, or a local variable in the current stack frame. The expression may be any valid expression in the source language that *gdb* understands, identical to the expressions used by the *print* command. You can change the breakpoint condition (if it is conditional) using the *condition* command.

Using the command *info break* will give you a list of all breakpoints and watchpoints and their status. This is to allow you to delete or disable breakpoints, using the commands *clear*, *delete*, or *disable*. A disabled breakpoint is merely inactive, until you reenable it (with the *enable* command)—on the other hand, a breakpoint which has been deleted is gone from the list of breakpoints for good. You can also specify that a breakpoint be enabled once—meaning that once it is triggered, it will be disabled again—or enabled once and then deleted.

To set a watchpoint, just use the *watch* command, as in

```
watch (numticks < 1024 && incoming != clear)
```

Watchpoint conditions may be any valid source expression, as with conditional breakpoints.

Instruction-level debugging

gdb is capable of debugging on the processor instruction level, allowing you to watch the innards of your program with great scrutiny. However, understanding what you see requires not only knowledge of the processor architecture and assembly language, but also some gist of how the operating system sets up process address space. For example, it helps to understand the conventions used for setting up stack frames, calling functions, passing parameters and return values, and so on. Any book on protected-mode 80386/80486 programming can fill you in on these details. But be warned: protected-mode programming on this processor is quite different from real-mode programming (as is used in the MS-DOS world). Be sure that you're reading about native *protected-mode* 386 programming, or else you might subject yourself to terminal confusion.

The primary *gdb* commands used for instruction-level debugging are *nexti*, *stepi*, and *disass*. *nexti* is equivalent to *next*, except that it steps to the next instruction, not the next source line. Similarly, *stepi* is the instruction-level analogue of *step*.

The *disass* command displays a disassembly of an address range that you supply. This address range may be specified by literal address or function name. For example, to display a disassembly of the function *play_timeout*, use the command

```
(gdb) disass play_timeout
Dump of assembler code for function play_timeout:
to 0x2ac:
0x21c <play_timeout>:            pushl   %ebp
0x21d <play_timeout+1>:          movl    %esp,%ebp
0x21f <play_timeout+3>:          call    0x494 <control_update_all>
0x224 <play_timeout+8>:          movl    0x952f4,%eax
0x229 <play_timeout+13>:         decl    %eax
0x22a <play_timeout+14>:         cmpl    %eax,0x9530c
0x230 <play_timeout+20>:         jne     0x24c <play_timeout+48>
0x232 <play_timeout+22>:         jmp     0x29c <play_timeout+128>
0x234 <play_timeout+24>:         nop
0x235 <play_timeout+25>:         nop
...
```

```
    0x2a8 <play_timeout+140>:      addb   %al,(%eax)
    0x2aa <play_timeout+142>:      addb   %al,(%eax)
    (gdb)
```

This is equivalent to using the command *disass 0x21c* (where 0x21c is the literal address of the beginning of *play_timeout.*

You can specify an optional second argument to *disass,* which will be used as the address to end the disassembly dump with. Using *disass 0x21c 0x232* will only display the first 7 lines of the assembly listing above (the instruction starting with 0x232 itself will not be displayed).

If you use *nexti* and *stepi* often, you may wish to use the command

```
    display/i $pc
```

This will cause the current instruction to be displayed after every *nexti* or *stepi* command. *display* specifies variables to watch or commands to execute after every stepping command. $pc is a *gdb* internal register that corresponds to the processor's program counter, pointing to the current instruction.

Using Emacs with gdb

Chapter 5

Emacs (described in the section "The Emacs Editor" in Chapter 5) provides a debugging mode that lets you run *gdb*—or another debugger—within the integrated program-tracing environment provided by Emacs. This so-called "Grand Unified Debugger" library is very powerful, and will allow you to debug and edit your programs entirely within Emacs.

To start *gdb* under Emacs, use the Emacs command M-x gdb, and give the name of the executable to debug as the argument. A buffer will be created for *gdb* interaction, which is similar to using *gdb* alone. You can then use *core-file* to load a core file, or *attach* to attach to a running process, if you wish.

Whenever you step to a new frame (for example, when you first trigger a breakpoint), *gdb* opens a separate window which displays the source corresponding to the current stack frame. This buffer may be used to edit the source text just as you normally would with Emacs, but the current source line is highlighted with an arrow (the characters "=>"). This allows you to watch the source in one window, and execute *gdb* commands in the other.

Within the debugging window, there are several special key sequences that can be used. They are fairly long, though, so it's not clear that you'll find them more convenient than just entering *gdb* commands directly. Some of the more common commands include:

C-x C-a C-s
    The equivalent of a *gdb step* command, updating the source window appropriately.

```
C-x C-a C-i
```
    The equivalent of a *stepi* command.

```
C-x C-a C-n
```
    The equivalent of a *next* command.

```
C-x C-a C-r
```
    The equivalent of a *continue* command.

```
C-x C-a <
```
    The equivalent of an *up* command.

```
C-x C-a >
```
    The equivalent of a *down* command.

If you do type in commands in the traditional manner, you can use M-p to move backwards to previously issued commands, and M-n to move forward. You can also move around in the buffer using Emacs commands for searching, cursor movement, and so on. All in all, using *gdb* within Emacs is much more convenient than using it from the shell.

In addition, you may edit the source text in the *gdb* source buffer; the prefix arrow will not be present in the source when it is saved.

Emacs is very customizable, and there are many extensions to this *gdb* interface that you could write yourself. You could define Emacs keys for other commonly-used *gdb* commands, or change the behavior of the source window. (For example, you could cause all breakpoints to be highlighted in some fashion, or provide keys to disable or clear breakpoints).

Programming Tools

Along with languages and compilers, there is a plethora of programming tools out there, including libraries, interface builders, debuggers, and other utilities to aid the programming process. In this section we'll talk about some of the most interesting bells and whistles of these tools to let you know what's out there.

Debuggers

There are several interactive debuggers available for Linux. The de facto standard debugger is *gdb*, which we covered in detail.

In addition to *gdb*, there are several other debuggers, each with features very similar to *gdb*. *xxgdb* is a version of *gdb* with an X Window System interface similar to that found on the *xdbx* debugger on other UNIX systems. This X-based interface provides a window that contains several panes. One pane looks like the regular *gdb* text interface, allowing you to input commands manually to interact with the system. Another pane automatically displays the current source file, along with a marker displaying the current line. You can use the source pane to set and select breakpoints, browse the source, and so on, while typing commands directly to *gdb*. A number of buttons are provided on the *xxgdb* window as well, implementing frequently-used commands such as *step*, *next*, and so on. This way, you can use the mouse in conjunction with the keyboard to debug your program within an easy-to-use X interface.

Another debugger similar to *xxgdb* is UPS, an X-based debugger which has been ported to a number of UNIX platforms. UPS is much simpler than *xxgdb* and doesn't provide the same features, but it is a good debugger nonetheless and has a less demanding learning curve than *gdb*. It is adequate enough for most applications and straightforward debugging needs.

Profiling and Performance Tools

There are several utilities out there that allow you to monitor and rate the performance of your program. These tools can help you to locate bottlenecks in your code—places where performance is lacking. These tools will also give you a run-down on the call structure of your program, indicating what functions are called, from where, and how often. (Everything you ever wanted to know about your program, but were afraid to ask.)

gprof is a profiling utility that will give you a very detailed listing of the running statistics for your program, including how often each function was called, from where, the total amount of time that each function required, and so forth.

In order to use *gprof* with a program, you must compile the program using the *–pg* option with *gcc*. This adds profiling information to the object file, and links the executable with standard libraries that have profiling information enabled.

Having compiled the program to profile with *–pg*, simply run it. If it exits normally the file *gmon.out* will be written to the working directory of the program. This file contains profiling information for the run and can be used with *gprof* to display a table of statistics.

As an example, let's take a program called *getstat*, which gathers statistics about an image file. First, we compile *getstat* with *–pg*, and run it:

```
papaya$ getstat image11.pgm > stats.dat
papaya$ ls -l gmon.out
-rw-------   1 mdw        mdw          54448 Feb  5 17:00 gmon.out
papaya$
```

Indeed, the profiling information was written to *gmon.out*.

To examine the profiling data, we run *gprof* and give it the name of the executable and the profiling file *gmon.out*:

```
papaya$ gprof getstat gmon.out
```

If you do not specify the name of the profiling file, *gprof* assumes the name *gmon.out*. It will also assume the executable name *a.out* if you do not specify that, either.

gprof output is rather verbose, so you may want to redirect it to a file or pipe it through a pager. It comes in two parts. The first part is the "flat profile," which gives a one-line entry for each function, listing the percentage of time spent in that function, the time (in seconds) used to execute that function, the number of calls to the function, and other information. For example:

```
Each sample counts as 0.01 seconds.
  %   cumulative   self              self     total
 time   seconds   seconds    calls  ms/call  ms/call  name
45.11    27.49     27.49       41   670.51   903.13  GetComponent
16.25    37.40      9.91                              mcount
10.72    43.93      6.54  1811863     0.00     0.00  Push
10.33    50.23      6.30  1811863     0.00     0.00  Pop
 5.87    53.81      3.58       40    89.50   247.06  stackstats
 4.92    56.81      3.00  1811863     0.00     0.00  TrimNeighbors
```

If any of the fields are blank in the output, *gprof* was unable to determine any further information about that function. This is usually caused by not compiling parts of the code with the *–pg* option—for example, if you call routines in non-standard libraries that haven't been compiled with *–pg*, *gprof* won't be able to gather much information about those routines. In the above output, the function *mcount* probably hasn't been compiled with profiling enabled.

As we can see, 45.11% of the total running time was spent in the function *GetComponent*—which amounts to 27.49 seconds. But is this because *GetComponent* is horribly inefficient, or because *GetComponent* itself called many other slow functions? The functions *Push* and *Pop* were called many, many times during execution—could they be the culprits? [*]

The second part of the *gprof* report can help us here. It gives a detailed "call graph" describing which functions called other functions, and how many times. For example:

```
index % time    self  children    called     name
                                               <spontaneous>
[1]     92.7    0.00    47.30                 start [1]
                0.01    47.29       1/1            main [2]
                0.00     0.00       1/2            on_exit [53]
                0.00     0.00       1/1            exit [172]
```

The first column of the call graph is the index—a unique number given to every function, allowing you to find other functions in the graph. Here, the first function, *start*, is called implicitly when the program begins. *start* required 92.7% of the total running time (47.30 seconds), including its children, but required very little time to run itself. This is because *start* is the parent of all other functions in the program,

---

[*] Always a possibility where the author's code is concerned!

including *main*—it makes sense that *start* plus its children should require that percentage of time.

The call graph normally displays the children as well as the parents of each function in the graph. Here, we can see that *start* called the functions *main, on_exit,* and *exit* (listed below the line for *start*). However, there are no parents (normally listed above *start*)—instead, we see the ominous word <spontaneous>. This means that *gprof* was unable to determine the parent function of *start*—more than likely because *start* was not called from within the program itself, but kicked off by the operating system.

Skipping down to the entry for *GetComponent,* or function-under-suspect, we see the following:

```
index % time    self  children    called     name
                0.67    0.23       1/41           GetFirstComponent [12]
               26.82    9.30      40/41           GetNextComponent [5]
[4]     72.6   27.49    9.54       41         GetComponent [4]
                6.54    0.00 1811863/1811863      Push [7]
                3.00    0.00 1811863/1811863      TrimNeighbors [9]
                0.00    0.00       1/1            InitStack [54]
```

The parent functions of *GetComponent* were *GetFirstComponent* and *GetNextComponent,* and its children were *Push, TrimNeighbors,* and *InitStack.* As we can see, *GetComponent* was called 41 times—one time from *GetFirstComponent* and 40 times from *GetNextComponent.* The *gprof* output contains notes that describe the report in more detail.

GetComponent itself does require over 27.49 seconds to run—only 9.54 seconds are spent executing the children of *GetComponent* (including the many calls to *Push* and *TrimNeighbors!*). So it looks as though *GetComponent* and possibly its parent *GetNextComponent* need some tuning—the oft-called *Push* function is not the sole cause of the problem.

gprof is also capable of keeping track of recursive calls and "cycles" of called functions, and indicating the amount of time required for each call. Of course, using *gprof* effectively requires that all code to be profiled is compiled with the *–pg* option. It also requires a knowledge of the program that you're attempting to profile—*gprof* can only tell you so much about what's going on. It's up to the programmer to optimize inefficient code.

One last note about *gprof*: running it on a program that calls only a few functions, and runs very quickly, may not give you meaningful results. The units used for timing execution are usually rather coarse—maybe one-hundredth of a second—and if many functions in your program run more quickly than that *gprof* will be unable to distinguish between their respective running times (rounding them to the nearest hundredth of a second). In order to get good profiling information, you may need to run your program under unusual circumstances—for example, giving it an unusually large data set to churn on, as in the above example.

If *gprof* is more than you need, *calls* is a program that will display a tree of all function calls in your C source code. This can be useful to generate either an index of all called functions, or to produce a high-level hierarchical report of the structure of a program.

Use of *calls* is very simple. You simply tell it the names of the source files to map out, and a function-call tree is displayed. For example,

```
papaya$ calls scan.c
   1    level1 [scan.c]
   2         getid [scan.c]
   3              getc
   4              eatwhite [scan.c]
   5                   getc
   6                   ungetc
   7              strcmp
   8         eatwhite [see line 4]
   9         balance [scan.c]
  10              eatwhite [see line 4]
```

By default, *calls* lists only one instance of each called function at each level of the tree (so that if *printf* is called five times in a given function, it is listed only once). The *−a* switch will print all instances. *calls* has several other options as well; using *calls −h* will give you a summary.

Using strace

strace is a tool that displays the system calls being executed by a running program. This can be extremely useful for real-time monitoring of a program's activity— although it does take some knowledge of programming at the system-call level. For example, when the library routine *printf* is used within a program, *strace* displays information only about the underlying *write* system call when it is executed. Also, *strace* can be quite verbose—many, many system calls are executed within a program that the programmer may not be aware of. However, *strace* is a good way to quickly determine the cause for a program crash or other strange failure.

Take the "Hello, World!" program given earlier in the chapter. Running *strace* on the executable *hello* gives us:

```
papaya$ strace hello
uselib("/lib/ld.so") = 0
open("/etc/ld.so.conf", RDONLY, 0) = 3
fstat(3, [dev 3 2 ino 4143 nlnks 1 ...]) = 0
read(3, "/usr/local/lib\n/usr/X386/lib\n", 29) = 29
close(3) = 0
access("/usr/local/lib/libc.so.4", 0) = -1 (No such file or directory)
access("/usr/X386/lib/libc.so.4", 0) = -1 (No such file or directory)
access("/usr/lib/libc.so.4", 0) = -1 (No such file or directory)
access("/lib/libc.so.4", 0) = 0
uselib("/lib/libc.so.4") = 0
```

```
munmap(0x62f00000, , 16384, ) = 0
brk(0) = 0x2000
fstat(1, [dev 3 2 ino 24040 nlnks 1 ...]) = 0
brk(5000) = 0x5000
brk(6000) = 0x6000
ioctl(1, TCGETS, 0xbffff80c) = 0
write(1, "Hello, World!\n", 14) = 14
Hello, World!
exit(0) = ?
papaya$
```

This may be much more than you expected to see from a simple program. Let's walk through it, briefly, to explain what's going on.

The first *uselib* call is embedded in the executable; it loads the *ld.so* library used by programs linked with shared libraries. The *open* system call opens the *ld.so* configuration file, which is subsequently *read* and *close*d. The four calls to *access* are an attempt to find the shared library image *libc.so.4* which the program was linked with. On the fourth try (a "library path" is searched for each shared library image), the file is found in */lib/libc.so.4*, and a *uselib* call is made to load the library.

The calls to *munmap* (which unmaps a memory-mapped portion of a file) and *brk* (which allocates memory on the heap) set up the memory image of the running process. The *ioctl* call is the result of a *tcgetattr* library call, which retrieves the terminal attributes before attempting to write to it. Finally, the *write* call prints our friendly message to the terminal, and *exit* ends the program.

strace sends its output to standard error, so you can redirect it to a file separately from the actual output of the program (usually on standard output). As you can see, *strace* tells you not only the names of the system calls, but also their parameters (expressed as well-known constant names, if possible, instead of just numerics) and return values.

make and imake

We have already introduced *make*, the project manager used to compile projects, among other things. One problem with *make* is that Makefiles aren't always easy to write. When large projects are involved, writing a Makefile with cases for each particular kind of source file can be tedious. Even with the built-in *make* defaults, this is often more work than should be necessary.

One solution is to use *imake*, an extension to *make* based on the use of the C preprocessor. *imake* is simply a Makefile generator—you write an Imakefile that *imake* converts to a robust Makefile. *imake* is used by programs in the X Window System distribution, but is not limited to use by X applications.

We should note at this point that *imake* can simplify the process of writing Makefiles, especially for compiling C programs. However, *make* is much more generally applicable than for this task. For example, you can use *make* to automatically format documents using *groff* or TEX. In this case, you need the flexibility of *make* alone, and *imake* may not be the best solution.

Here is a sample Imakefile that will build two programs, *laplacian* and *getstat*. At the top of the Imakefile, options for the entire compilation are specified (*imake* has its own defaults for these, but they aren't always useful). Following that, variables are defined for each program to be compiled, and the *imake* macros `AllTarget` and `NormalProgramTarget` are used to create Makefile rules for compiling these programs.

```
# Linker options:
LDOPTIONS = -L/usr/local/lib -L../lib
# The C compiler to use:
CC = gcc
# Flags to be used with gcc:
CFLAGS = -I. -I$(HOME)/include -g
# Local and system libraries to link against:
LOCAL_LIBRARIES = -lvistuff
SYS_LIBRARIES = -lm

# Specify the sources in the SRCS variable, and the corresponding object
# files in the variable LAP_OBJS.
SRCS = laplacian.c laplacian-main.c
LAP_OBJS = laplacian.o laplacian-main.o

# Create rules for building laplacian.
AllTarget(laplacian)
NormalProgramTarget(laplacian,$(LAP_OBJS),,$(LOCAL_LIBRARIES),$(SYS_LIBRARIES))

# Do the same thing for getstat. Note that SRCS can be redefined for each
# target, but LAP_OBJS can't, so we use a unique name for each target.
SRCS = getstat.c getstat-main.c component.c
GS_OBJS = getstat.o getstat-main.o component.o

AllTarget(getstat)
NormalProgramTarget(getstat,$(GS_OBJS),,$(LOCAL_LIBRARIES),$(SYS_LIBRARIES))
```

Note that we must use a different variable for the object files for each target, although `SRCS` can be redefined for each.

In order to translate the Imakefile into a Makefile, use the command *xmkmf*. *xmkmf* will simply run *imake* with the correct options to do the translation correctly, using the default *imake* macros (such as `AllTarget` and `NormalProgramTarget`). You can then issue *make* to compile the program.

```
papaya$ xmkmf
mv Makefile Makefile.bak
imake -DUseInstalled -I/usr/X386/lib/X11/config
papaya$
```

imake(1)
xmkmf(1)
[53]imake

If you want to use your own *imake* macros, you can invoke it by hand using the appropriate options. The *imake* and *xmkmf* manual pages should fill in the gaps. *Software Portability with imake* by Paul DuBois is another guide to the system.

If you find *imake* too complex for your taste, other "Makefile makers" are available as well, such as *ICmake*, which generates Makefiles using a macro language very much resembling C.

Using Checker

Checker is a replacement for the various memory-allocation routines such as *malloc*, *realloc*, and *free* used by C programs. It provides smarter memory-allocation procedures and code to detect illegal memory accesses and common faults, such as attempting to free a block of memory more than once. Checker will display detailed error messages if your program attempts any kind of hazardous memory access, helping you to catch segmentation faults in your program before they happen. It is also capable of detecting memory leaks—for example, places in the code where new memory is *malloc*ed without being *free*d after use.

Checker is not just a replacement for *malloc* and friends. It also inserts code into your program to verify all memory reads and writes. It is very robust, and therefore somewhat slower than using the regular *malloc* routines. Checker is meant to be used during program development and testing—once all potential memory-corrupting bugs have been fixed, you can link your program with the standard libraries.

For example, take the following program, which allocates some memory and attempts to do various nasty things with it:

```
#include <malloc.h>
int main() {
  char *thememory, ch;

  thememory=(char *)malloc(10*sizeof(char));

  ch=thememory[1];       /* Attempt to read uninitialized memory */
  thememory[12]=' ';     /* Attempt to write after the block */
  ch=thememory[-2];      /* Attempt to read before the block */
}
```

We simply compile this program with the *–lchecker* option, which will link it with the Checker libraries. Upon running it, we get the following error messages (among others):

```
From Checker:
        Memory access error
        When Reading at address 0x10033
        inside the heap
        1 bytes after the begin of the block
```

```
From Checker:
        Memory access error
        When Writing at address 0x1003e
        inside the heap
        2 bytes after the end of the block
From Checker:
        Memory access error
        When Reading at address 0x10030
        inside the heap
        2 bytes before the begin of the block
```

For each memory violation, Checker reports an error and gives us information on what happened. The actual Checker error messages include information on where the program is executing as well as where the memory block was allocated. You can coax even more information out of Checker if you wish—and along with a debugger such as *gdb* problems are not difficult to pinpoint. *

Checker also provides a garbage collector and detector that you can call from within your program. In brief, the garbage detector will inform you of any memory leaks—places where a function *malloc*ed a block of memory, but forgot to *free* it before returning. The garbage collector routine will walk through the heap and clean up the results of these leaks. You can also call the garbage collector and detector manually when running the program from within *gdb* (as *gdb* allows you to directly call functions during execution).

Interface Building Tools

A number of applications and libraries let you easily generate a user interface for your applications under the X Window System. If you do not want to bother with the complexity of the X programming interface, using one of these simple interface-building tools may be the answer for you. There are also tools for producing a text-based interface for programs that don't require X.

The classic X programming model has attempted to be as general as possible, providing only the bare minimum of interface restrictions and assumptions. This allows programmers to build their own interface "from scratch," as the core X libraries don't make any assumptions about the interface in advance. The X Toolkit Intrinsics (Xt) provides a rudimentary set of interface widgets (such as simple buttons, scrollbars, and the like), as well as a general interface for writing your own widgets if necessary. Unfortunately this can require a great deal of work for programmers who would rather use a set of pre-made interface routines. A number of Xt widget sets and programming libraries are available for Linux, all of which make the user interface easier to program.

In addition, the commercial Motif library and widget set is available from several vendors for an inexpensive single-user license fee. Also available is the XView

---

* We have edited the output somewhat, in order to remove extraneous information and to increase readability for the purpose of the example.

library and widget interface, which is another alternative to using Xt for building interfaces under X. XView and Motif are two sets of X-based programming libraries which in some ways are easier to program than the X Toolkit Intrinsics. Many applications are available that utilize Motif and XView, such as XVhelp (a system for generating interactive hypertext help for your program). Binaries statically linked with Motif may be distributed freely and used by people who don't own Motif itself.

Among the widget sets and interface libraries for X are:

- *Xm++*, a set of C++ wrappers for the Athena and Motif widget sets (for those programmers who prefer the object-oriented C++ programming model)

- *fwf*, a set of Xt widgets from the Free Widget Foundation

- Xaw3D, a modified version of the standard Athena widget set which provides a 3-D, Motif-like look and feel

Many people complain that the Athena widgets are too plain in appearance. Xaw3D is completely compatible with the standard Athena set and can even be used to replace the Athena libraries on your system, giving all programs that use Athena widgets a modern look. Xaw3D also provides a few widgets not found in the Athena set, such as a layout widget with a TEX-like interface for specifying the position of child widgets.

Another excellent package for building X-based applications is wxWindows, a set of libraries and tools for writing applications for X as well as Microsoft Windows 3.1 (under MS-DOS). wxWindows allows you to use the same C++ source for generating applications for XView, Motif, and Microsoft Windows, with support for Windows NT and text-based interface on the way. It provides a great many features, including menu bars, toolbars, pens, brushes, fonts, icons, Encapsulated PostScript generation (for printing), a hypertext help system, complete documentation, and more. It is available from many Linux archive sites, and requires either Motif or XView to develop X-based applications under Linux.

Many programmers are finding that building a user interface, even with a complete set of widgets and routines in C, requires much overhead and can be quite difficult. This is a question of flexibility versus ease of programming—the easier the interface is to build, the less control the programmer has over it. Many programmers are finding that pre-built widgets are adequate enough for their needs, so the loss in flexibility is not a problem.

One of the problems with interface generation and X programming is that it is very difficult to generalize the most widely-used elements of a user interface into a simple programming model. For example, many programs use features such as buttons, dialog boxes, pull-down menus, and so forth, but almost every program uses these "widgets" in a different context. In simplifying the creation of a graphical interface, generators tend to make assumptions about what you'll want. For example, it is simple enough to specify that a button, when pressed, should execute a certain procedure within your program, but what if you want the button to execute some specialized behavior that the programming interface does not allow for? For example, what if you wanted the button to have a different effect when pressed with mouse button 2 instead of mouse button 1? If the interface-building system does not allow for this degree of generality, it is not of much use to programmers who need a powerful, customized interface.

The Tcl/Tk programming interface described earlier in the chapter is growing in popularity, partly because it is so simple to use and does provide a good amount of flexibility. Because Tcl and Tk routines are able to be called from interpreted "scripts" as well as internally from a C program, it is not difficult to tie the interface features provided by this language and toolkit to functionality in the program. Using Tcl and Tk is on the whole less demanding than learning to program Xlib and Xt (along with the myriad of widget sets) directly.

TclMotif, a version of Tcl bound with the popular Motif widget set, is also available for Linux. The Motif widgets are widely acclaimed to be easy to program and pleasant to use. The advantage of TclMotif is that the binary is freely distributable although Motif itself is a commercial product. Therefore, you do not have to own Motif to use TclMotif. TclMotif will in effect let you write programs that use Motif widgets and routines, through the Tcl interface. A statically-linked binary is available on a number of Linux FTP sites, and from other sources. If you want to recompile TclMotif itself, for some reason, you would need to own Motif in order to do so.

Wafe is another version of Tcl/Tk which includes the Athena widgets and miscellaneous other tools that make the programming model easier to use. If you are accustomed to programming Xt with the Athena widgets, but want to move to Tcl and Tk, Wafe is a good place to start.

Tcl and Tk will allow you to generate an X-based interface complete with windows, buttons, menus, scrollbars, and the like, around your existing program. The interface may be accessed from a Tcl script (as described in the section "Writing Tk Applications") or from within a C program.

Another interface-building tool much like Tcl and Tk is *xtpanel*. *xtpanel* is meant primarily to generate an X interface "wrapper" around an existing text-based program. *xtpanel* allows you to set up a window with various panes, text editing regions, buttons, scrollbars, and so on, and bind the actions of these widgets to features in the program. For example, one could use *xtpanel* to produce an X-based interface for the *gdb* debugger, similar to *xxgdb*. You could define a "step" button which, when pressed, would send the *step* command to the regular *gdb* interface. A text-editing pane could be defined to interact with *gdb* in the regular way. Of course, doing something more complex like setting up a source-view pane would be difficult using something as general as *xtpanel*.

If you require a nice text-based interface for a program, there are several options. The GNU *getline* library is a set of routines that provide advanced command-line

Chapter 3

editing, prompting, command history, and other features used by many programs. As an example, both *bash* and *gdb* use the *getline* library to read user input. *getline* provides the Emacs and *vi*-like command-line editing features found in *bash* and similar programs. (The use of command-line editing within *bash* is described in the section "Typing Shortcuts" in Chapter 3.)

Another option is to write a set of Emacs interface routines for your program. An example of this is the *gdb* Emacs interface, which sets up multiple windows, special key sequences, and so on, within Emacs. (The interface is discussed in the section "Using Emacs with gdb.") No changes were required to *gdb* code in order to implement this—look at the Emacs library file *gdb.el* for hints on how this was accomplished. Emacs allows you to start up a subprogram within a text buffer, and provides many routines for parsing and processing text within that buffer. For example, within the Emacs *gdb* interface, the *gdb* source listing output is captured by Emacs and turned into a command that displays the current line of code in another window. Routines written in Emacs Lisp process the *gdb* output and take certain actions based on it.

The advantage to using Emacs to interact with text-based programs is that Emacs is a very powerful and customizable user interface within itself. The user can easily redefine keys and commands to fit his or her own needs—you don't need to provide these customization features yourself. As long as the text interface of the program is straightforward enough to interact with Emacs, this is not difficult to accomplish. In addition, many users prefer to do virtually everything within Emacs—from reading electronic mail and news, to compiling and debugging programs. Giving your program an Emacs front-end will allow it to be used more easily by people with this mindset. It will also allow your program to interact with other programs running under Emacs—for example, text can easily be cut and pasted between different Emacs text buffers. You can even write entire programs using Emacs Lisp, if you wish.

Revision Control Tools

RCS (Revision Control System) has been ported to Linux. This is a set of programs that allow you to maintain a "library" of files that record a history of revisions, allow source file locking (in case several people are working on the same project), and automatically keep track of source file version numbers. RCS is generally used with program source code files, but is general enough to be applicable to any type of file where multiple revisions must be maintained.

Why bother with revision control? Many large projects require some kind of revision control in order to keep track of many tiny complex changes to the system. For example, attempting to maintain a program with a thousand source files and a team of several dozen programmers would be nearly impossible without using something like RCS. With RCS, you can ensure that only one person may modify a given source file at any one time, and all changes are checked in along with a log message detailing the change.

RCS is based on the concept of an *RCS file*, a file which acts as a "library" where source files are "checked in" and "checked out." Let's say that you have a source file *foo.c* that you want to maintain with RCS. The RCS filename would be *foo.c,v* by default. The RCS file contains a history of revisions to the file, allowing you to extract any previous checked-in version of the file. Each revision is tagged with a log message that you provide.

When you check in a file with RCS, the revisions are added to the RCS file, and the original file is deleted by default. In order to access the original file, you must check it out from the RCS file. When you're editing a file, you generally don't want someone else to be able to edit it at the same time. Therefore, RCS places a lock on the file when you check it out for editing. A locked file may only be modified by the user who checks it out (this is accomplished through file permissions). Once you're done making changes to the source, you check it back in, which allows anyone working on the project to check it back out again, for further work. Checking out a file as unlocked does not subject it to these restrictions; generally, files are checked out as locked only when they are to be edited, but checked out as unlocked just for reading (for example, to use the source file in a program build).

RCS automatically keeps track of all previous revisions in the RCS file, and assigns incremental version numbers to each new revision that you check in. You can also specify a version number of your own when checking in a file with RCS; this allows you to start a new "revision branch" so that multiple projects can stem from different revisions of the same file. This is a good way to share code between projects, but assure that changes made to one branch won't be reflected in others.

Here's an example. Take the source file *foo.c*, which contains our friendly program:

```
#include <stdio.h>

void main(void) {
  printf("Hello, world!");
}
```

The first step is to check it into RCS, with the *ci* command.

```
papaya$ ci foo.c
foo.c,v  <--  foo.c
enter description, terminated with single '.' or end of file:
NOTE: This is NOT the log message!
>> Hello world source code
>> .
initial revision: 1.1
done
papaya$
```

The RCS file *foo.c,v* is created, and *foo.c* is removed.

In order to work on the source file again, use the *co* command to check it out. For example,

```
papaya$ co -l foo.c
foo.c,v  -->  foo.c
revision 1.1 (locked)
done
papaya$
```

will check out *foo.c* (from *foo.c,v*) and lock it. Locking the file allows you to edit it, and to check it back in. If you only need to check the file out in order to read it (for example, to issue a *make*), you can leave the *–l* switch off of the *co* command to check it out unlocked. You can't check in a file unless it is locked first (or it has never been checked in before, as above).

Now, you can make some changes to the source and check it back in when done. In many cases, you'll want to always have the file checked out, and use *ci* to merely record your most recent revisions in the RCS file and bump the version number. For this, you can use the *–l* switch with *ci*, as so:

```
papaya$ ci -l foo.c
foo.c,v  <--  foo.c
new revision: 1.2; previous revision: 1.1
enter log message, terminated with single '.' or end of file:
>> Changed printf call
>> .
done
papaya$
```

which will automatically check out the file, locked, after checking it in. This is a useful way to keep track of revisions if you're the only one working on a project.

If you use RCS often, you may not like all of those unsightly *foo.c,v* RCS files cluttering up your directory. If you create the subdirectory *RCS* within your project directory, *ci* and *co* will place the RCS files there, out of the way from the rest of the source.

In addition, RCS keeps track of all previous revisions of your file. For instance, if you make a change to your program that causes it to break in some way, and want to revert to the previous version to "undo" your changes and retrace your steps, you can specify a particular version number to check out with *co*. For example:

```
papaya$ co -l1.1 foo.c
foo.c,v  -->  foo.c
revision 1.1 (locked)
writable foo.c exists; remove it? [ny](n): y
done
papaya$
```

will check out version 1.1 of the file *foo.c*. You can use the program *rlog* to print the revision history of a particular file; this displays your revision log entries (entered with *ci*) along with other information such as the date, the user who checked in the revision, and so forth.

RCS will automatically update embedded "keyword strings" in your source file at checkout time. For example, if you have the string

```
/* $Header$ */
```

in the source file, *co* will replace it with an informative line about the revision date, version number, and so forth, as in

```
/* $Header: /work/linux/hitch/programming/tools/RCS/rcs.tex
         1.2 1994/12/04 15:19:31 mdw Exp mdw $ */
```

This line was broken to fit on the page, but in actuality it is supposed to be all on one line.

Other keywords exist as well, such as $Author$, $Date$, and Log (the latter will keep a complete record of the log entries for each revision embedded in the source file).

Many programmers place a static string within each source file that can be used to identify the version of the program after it has been compiled. For example, within each source file in your program, you can place the line

```
static char rcsid[] = "\@(#)$Header$";
```

co will replace the keyword $Header$ with a string of the form given above. This static string will survive in the executable, and the *what* command can be used to display these strings in a given binary. For example, after compiling *foo.c* into the executable *foo*, we can use the command

```
papaya$ what foo
foo:
        $Header: /work/linux/hitch/programming/tools/RCS/rcs.tex
                1.2 1994/12/04 15:19:31 mdw Exp mdw $
papaya$
```

what picks out strings beginning with the characters @(#) in a file and displays them. If you have a program that has been compiled from many source files and libraries, and don't know how up-to-date each of the components are, you can use *what* to display a version string for each source file used to compile the binary.

ci(1)
co(1)
rcs(1)

RCS has several other programs in its suite, including *rcs*, used for maintaining RCS files. Among other things, *rcs* can give other users permission to check out sources from an RCS file. See the manual pages for *ci*, *co*, and *rcs* for more information.

Patching Files

Let's say that you're trying to maintain a program that is updated periodically, but the program contains many source files, and releasing a complete source distribution with every update is just infeasible. The best way to incrementally update source files is with *patch*, a program by Larry Wall, author of Perl.

patch is a program that can be used to make context-dependent changes in a file in order to update that file from one version to the next. This way, when your program changes, you simply release a patch file against the source, which the user can apply with *patch* to get the newest version. For example, Linus Torvalds usually releases new Linux kernel versions as patch files (unless the changes from one version to the next are so extreme that a complete source distribution is warranted).

A nice feature of *patch* is that it will apply updates in context—that is, if you have made changes to the source yourself, but still wish to get the changes in the patch-file update, usually *patch* will be able to figure out the right location in the original file to apply the changes. This way, your version of the original source files don't need to correspond exactly to those that the patchfile was made against.

In order to make a patchfile, the program *diff* is used, which can produce "context diffs" between two files. For example, take our overused "Hello World" source code, given below:

```
/* hello.c version 1.0 by Norbert Ebersol */
#include <stdio.h>

void main() {
  printf("Hello, World!");
  exit(0);
}
```

Let's say that you were to update this source, as in the following:

```
/* hello.c version 2.0 */
/* (c)1994 Norbert Ebersol */
#include <stdio.h>

int main() {
  printf("Hello, Mother Earth!\n");
  return 0;
}
```

If you want to produce a patchfile to update the original *hello.c* to the newest version, use *diff* with the *–c* option:

```
papaya$ diff –c hello.c.old hello.c > hello.patch
```

This will produce the patchfile *hello.patch* that describes how to convert the original *hello.c* (here, saved in the file *hello.c.old*) to the new version. You can distribute this patchfile to anyone who has the original version of "Hello, World" and they can use *patch* to update it.

Using *patch* is quite simple; in most cases, you simply run it with the patchfile as input:

```
papaya$ patch < hello.patch
Hmm...  Looks like a new-style context diff to me...
The text leading up to this was:
--------------------------
|*** hello.c.old      Sun Feb  6 15:30:52 1994
|--- hello.c    Sun Feb  6 15:32:21 1994
--------------------------
Patching file hello.c using Plan A...
Hunk #1 succeeded at 1.
done
papaya$
```

patch will warn you if it appears as though the patch has already been applied. If we tried to apply the patchfile again, *patch* would ask us if we wanted to assume that *–R* was enabled—which will *reverse* the patch. This is a good way to back out patches that you didn't intend to apply. *patch* also saves the original version of each file that it updates in a backup file, usually named *filename~* (the filename with a tilde appended).

In many cases, you'll want to update not only a single source file, but an entire directory tree of sources. *patch* allows many files to be updated from a single diff. Let's say that you have two directory trees, *hello.old* and *hello*, which contain the sources for the old and new versions of a program, respectively. To make a patch file for the entire tree, use the *–r* switch with *diff*:

```
papaya$ diff –cr hello.old hello > hello.patch
```

Now, let's move to the system where the software needs to be updated. Assuming that the original source is contained in the directory *hello*, you can apply the patch with

```
papaya$ patch –p0 < hello.patch
```

patch(1)

The *–p0* switch tells *patch* to preserve the pathnames of files to be updated (so it will know to look in the *hello* directory for the source). If you have the source to be patched saved in a directory named differently than that given in the patchfile, you may need to use the *–p* option. See the *patch* manual page for details about this.

Indenting Code

If you're terrible at indenting code, and find the idea of an editor that automatically indents code for you on-the-fly a bit annoying, you can use the *indent* program to pretty-print your code after you're done writing it. *indent* is a very smart C code formatter, and has many options allowing you to specify just what kind of indentation style you wish to use.

Take the terribly-formatted source below:

```
double fact (double n) { if (n==1) return 1;
else return (n*fact(n-1)); }
void main () {
printf("Factorial 5 is %f.\n",fact(5));
printf("Factorial 10 is %f.\n",fact(10)); exit (0); }
```

Running *indent* on this source produces the relatively beautiful:

```
#include <math.h>

double
fact (double n)
{
  if (n == 1)
    return 1;
  else
    return (n * fact (n - 1));
}
void
main ()
{
  printf ("Factorial 5 is %f.\n", fact (5));
  printf ("Factorial 10 is %f.\n", fact (10));
  exit (0);
}
```

Not only are lines indented well, but whitespace is added around operators and function parameters to make them more readable. There are many ways to specify how the output of *indent* will look—if you're not fond of this particular indentation style, *indent* can accommodate you.

indent can also produce *troff* code from a source file, suitable for printing or for inclusion in a technical document. This code will have such nice features as italicized comments, boldfaced keywords, and so on. Using a command such as

```
papaya$ indent -troff foo.c | groff -mindent
```

will produce *troff* code and format it with *groff.*

## CHAPTER SEVEN

NETWORKING AND COMMUNICATIONS

S o, you've staked out your homestead on the Linux frontier and installed and configured your system. What next? Eventually you'll want to communicate with other systems—Linux and otherwise—and the Pony Express isn't going to suffice.

Fortunately, Linux supports a number of methods for data communication and networking. This includes serial communications, TCP/IP, and UUCP. In this chapter we will discuss how to configure your system to communicate with the world.

[3] Network Admin Guide

Linux Network Administrator's Guide, available from the Linux Documentation Project (see Appendix A, *Sources of Linux Information*), and also published by O'Reilly & Associates, is a complete guide to configuring TCP/IP and UUCP networking under Linux. For a detailed account of the information presented here, we refer you to that book.

Networking with TCP/IP

Linux supports a full implementation of the TCP/IP (Transmission Control Protocol/Internet Protocol) networking protocols. TCP/IP has become the most successful mechanism for networking computers worldwide. With Linux and an Ethernet card, you can network your machine to a local area network or (with the proper network connections) to the Internet—the worldwide TCP/IP network.

Hooking up a small local area network of UNIX machines is easy. It simply requires an Ethernet controller in each machine and the appropriate Ethernet cables and other hardware. Or if your business or university provides access to the Internet, you can easily add your Linux machine to this network.

Linux TCP/IP support has had its ups and downs. After all, implementing an entire protocol stack from scratch isn't something that one does for fun on a weekend. On the other hand, the Linux TCP/IP code has benefited greatly from the hoard of beta testers and developers to have crossed its path, and as time has progressed many bugs and configuration problems have fallen in their wake.

The current implementation of TCP/IP and related protocols for Linux is called "NET-2." This has no relationship to the so-called NET-2 release of BSD UNIX; instead, "NET-2" in this context means the second implementation of TCP/IP for Linux. Before NET-2 came (no surprise here) NET-1, which was phased out around kernel version 0.99.pl10. NET-2 supports nearly all of the features that you'd expect from a UNIX TCP/IP implementation, and a wide range of networking hardware.

Linux NET-2 also supports SLIP—Serial Line Internet Protocol. SLIP allows you to have dialup Internet access using a modem. If your business or university provides SLIP access, you can dial in to the SLIP server and put your machine on the Internet over the phone line. Alternatively, if your Linux machine also has Ethernet access to the Internet, you can configure it as a SLIP server.

[73] NET-2-HOWTO
[74] Ethernet HOWTO

Besides the *Linux Network Administrator's Guide*, the Linux NET-2 HOWTO contains more or less complete information on configuring TCP/IP and SLIP for Linux. The Linux Ethernet HOWTO is a related document that describes configuration of various Ethernet card drivers for Linux.

Also of interest is *TCP/IP Network Administration* by Craig Hunt. It contains complete information on using and configuring TCP/IP on UNIX systems. If you plan to set up a network of Linux machines or do any serious TCP/IP hacking, you should have the background in network administration presented by that book.

TCP/IP Concepts

In order to fully appreciate (and utilize) the power of TCP/IP, you should be familiar with its underlying principles. Transmission Control Protocol/Internet Protocol is a suite of *protocols* (the magic buzzword for this chapter) which define how machines should communicate with each other via a network, as well as internally to other layers of the protocol suite. For the theoretical background of the Internet protocols, the best source of information is the first volume of Douglas Comer's *Internetworking with TCP/IP*.

[33] Internetworking

TCP/IP was originally developed for use on the Advanced Research Projects Agency network, ARPAnet, which was funded to support military and computer science research. Therefore, you may hear TCP/IP being referred to as the "DARPA Internet Protocols." Since then, many other TCP/IP networks have come into use, such as the National Science Foundation's NSFNET, as well as thousands of other local and regional networks around the world. All of these networks are interconnected into a single conglomerate known as the Internet.

On a TCP/IP network, each machine is assigned an *IP address*, which is a 32-bit number uniquely identifying the machine. You need to know a little about IP addresses to structure your network and assign addresses to hosts. The IP address is usually represented as a dotted quad: four numbers in decimal notation, separated by dots. As an example, the IP address 0x80114b14 (in hexadecimal) can be written 128.17.75.20.

The IP address is divided into two parts: the network address and the host address. The network address consists of the higher-order bits of the address, and the host address of the remaining bits. (In general, each *host* is a separate machine on the network.) The size of these two fields depends upon the type of network in question. For example, on a Class B network (for which the first byte of the IP address is between 128 to 191), the first two bytes of the address identify the network, and the remaining two bytes identify the host. See Figure 7-1. For the example address given above, the network address is 128.17, and the host address is 75.20. To put this another way, the machine with IP address 128.17.75.20 is host number 75.20 on the network 128.17.

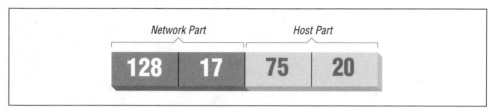

Figure 7-1. IP address

In addition, the host portion of the IP address may be subdivided to allow for a *subnetwork address.* Subnetworking allows large networks to be divided into smaller subnets, each of which may be maintained independently. For example, an organization may allocate a single Class B network, which provides two bytes of host information—up to 65534 hosts on the network. The organization may then wish to dole out the responsibility of maintaining portions of the network, so that each subnetwork is handled by a different department. Using subnetworking, the organization can specify, for example, that the first byte of the host address (that is, the third byte of the overall IP address) is the subnet address, and the second byte is the host address for that subnetwork. See Figure 7-2. In this case, the IP address 128.17.75.20 identifies host number 20 on subnetwork 75 of network 128.17. *

Processes (either on the same machine or on different machines) that wish to communicate via TCP/IP generally specify the destination machine's IP address, as well as a *port address.* The destination IP address is used, of course, to route data from one machine to the destination machine. The port address is a 16-bit number that specifies a particular service or application on the destination machine that should receive the data. Port numbers can be thought of as office numbers at a large office building: the entire building has a single IP address, but each business has a separate office there.

---

* Why not 65536, instead? For reasons to be discussed later, a host address of 0 or 255 is invalid.

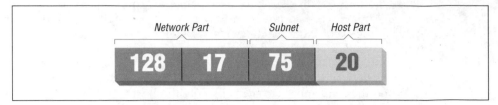

Figure 7–2. IP address with subnet

Here's a real-life example of how IP addresses and port numbers are used. The *tel-net* program allows a user on one machine to start a login session on another. On the remote machine, there is the *telnet* "daemon," *telnetd*, which is listening to a specific port for incoming connections (in this case, the port number is 27). [*]

The user executing *telnet* specifies the address of the machine to log in to, and the *telnet* program attempts to open a connection to port 27 on the remote machine. If it is successful, *telnet* and *telnetd* are able to communicate with each other to provide the remote login for the user in question.

Note that the *telnet* client on the local machine has a port address of its own. This port address is allocated to the client dynamically, when it begins execution. This is because the remote *telnetd* doesn't need to know the port number of the incoming *telnet* client beforehand. When the client initiates the connection, part of the information that it sends to *telnetd* is its port number. *telnetd* can be thought of as a business with a well-known mailing address. Any customers that wish to correspond with the *telnetd* running on a particular machine need to know not only the IP address of the machine to talk to (the address of the *telnetd* office building), but also the port number where *telnetd* can be found (the particular office within the building). The address and port number of the *telnet* client are included as part of the "return address" on the envelope containing the letter.

The TCP/IP family contains a number of protocols. Transmission Control Protocol (TCP) is responsible for providing reliable, connection-oriented communications between two processes, which may be running on different machines on the network. User Datagram Protocol (UDP) is similar to TCP except that it provides connectionless, unreliable service. Processes that use UDP must implement their own acknowledgment and synchronization routines if necessary.

TCP and UDP transmit and receive data in units known as *packets*. Each packet contains a chunk of information to send to another machine, as well as a header specifying the destination and source port addresses.

Internet Protocol (IP) sits beneath TCP and UDP in the protocol hierarchy. It is responsible for transmitting and routing TCP or UDP packets via the network. In order to do so, IP wraps each TCP or UDP packet within another packet (known

---

[*] On many systems, *telnetd* is not always listening to port 27; the Internet services daemon *inetd* is listening on its behalf. For now, let's sweep that detail under the carpet.

as an IP *datagram*), which includes a header with routing and destination information. The IP datagram header includes the IP address of the source and destination machines.

Note that IP doesn't know anything about port addresses; those are the responsibility of TCP and UDP. Similarly, TCP and UDP don't deal with IP addresses, which (as the name implies) are only IP's concern. As you can see, the above metaphor with return addresses and envelopes is quite accurate: each packet can be thought of as a letter contained within an envelope. TCP and UDP wrap the letter in an envelope with the source and destination port numbers (office numbers) written on it.

IP acts as the mailroom for the office building sending the letter. IP receives the envelope and wraps it in yet another envelope, with the IP address (office building address) of both the destination and the source affixed. The post office (which we haven't discussed quite yet) delivers the letter to the appropriate office building. There, the mailroom unwraps the outer envelope and hands it to TCP/UDP, which delivers the letter to the appropriate office based on the port number (written on the inner envelope). Each envelope has a return address which IP and TCP/UDP use to reply to the letter.

In order to make the specification of machines on the Internet more humane, network hosts are often given a name as well as an IP address. The Domain Name Service (DNS) takes care of translating hostnames to IP addresses, and vice versa, as well as handling the distribution of the name-to-IP address database across the entire Internet. Using hostnames also allows the IP address associated with a machine to change (for example, if the machine is moved to a different network), without having to worry that others won't be able to "find" the machine once the address changes. The DNS record for the machine is simply updated with the new IP address, and all references to the machine, by name, will continue to work.

[3] Network
Admin Guide
[34] TCP/IP

[35] DNS
and BIND

DNS is an enormous, worldwide distributed database. Each organization maintains a piece of the database, listing the machines in the organization. If you find yourself in the position of maintaining the list for your organization, you can get help from the *Linux Network Administrator's Guide* or *TCP/IP Network Administration*. If those aren't enough, you can really get the full scoop from the book *DNS and BIND*.

For the purposes of most administration, all you need to know is that a daemon called *named* (pronounced "name-dee") has to run on your system. This daemon is your window onto DNS.

Now, we might ask ourselves how a packet gets from one machine (office building) to another. This is the actual job of IP, as well as a number of other protocols that aid IP in its task. Besides managing IP datagrams on each host (as the mailroom), IP is also responsible for routing packets between hosts.

Before we can discuss how routing works, we must explain the model upon which TCP/IP networks are built. A network is just a set of machines that are connected together through some physical network medium—such as Ethernet or serial lines. In TCP/IP terms, each network has its own methods for handling routing and packet transfer internally.

Networks are connected to each other via *gateways*. A gateway is a host that has direct connections to two or more networks; the gateway can then exchange information between the networks, and route packets from one network to another. For instance, a gateway might be a workstation with more than one Ethernet interface. Each interface is connected to a different network, and the operating system uses this connectivity to allow the machine to act as a gateway.

In order to make our discussion more concrete, let's introduce an imaginary network, made up of the machines **eggplant**, **papaya**, **apricot**, and **zucchini**. Figure 7-3 depicts the configuration of these machines on the network. Note that **papaya** is connected to another network as well, which includes the machines **pineapple** and **pear**. These machines have the respective IP addresses:

Hostname	IP address
eggplant	128.17.75.20
apricot	128.17.75.12
zucchini	128.17.75.37
papaya	128.17.75.98, 128.17.112.3
pear	128.17.112.21
pineapple	128.17.112.40, 128.17.30.1

As you can see, **papaya** has two IP addresses—one on the 128.17.75 subnetwork, and another on the 128.17.112 subnetwork. **pineapple** has two IP addresses as well—one on 128.17.112, and another on 128.7.30.

IP uses the network portion of the IP address to determine how to route packets between machines. In order to do this, each machine on the network has a *routing table*, which contains a list of networks and the gateway machine for that network. To route a packet to a particular machine, IP looks at the network portion of the destination address. If there is an entry for that network in the routing table, IP routes the packet through the appropriate gateway. Otherwise, IP routes the packet through the "default" gateway given in the routing table.

Routing tables can contain entries for specific machines, as well as for networks. In addition, each machine has a routing table entry for itself.

Let's examine the routing table for **eggplant**. Using the command *netstat −rn*, we see the following:

```
eggplant:$ netstat -rn
Kernel routing table
Destination net/address   Gateway address        Flags RefCnt    Use Iface
128.17.75.0               128.17.75.20           UN        0   20417 eth0
default                   128.17.75.98           UGN       0   20417 eth0
```

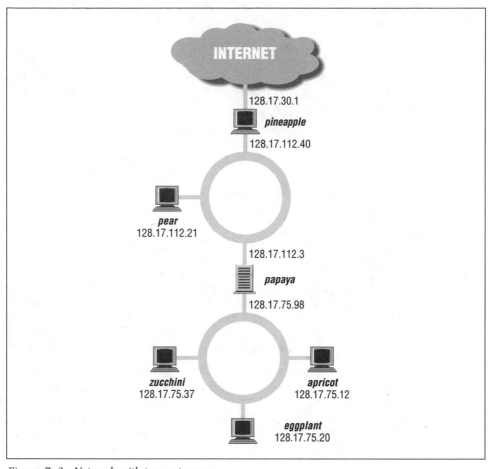

Figure 7–3. Network with two gateways

127.0.0.1	127.0.0.1	UH	0	268 lo
128.17.75.20	127.0.0.1	UH	0	268 lo

The first column displays the destination networks (and hosts) that the routing table includes. The first entry is for the network 128.17.75 (note that the host address is 0 for network entries), which is the network that **eggplant** lives on. Any packets sent to this network should be routed through 128.17.75.20, which is the IP address of **eggplant**. In general, a machine's route to its own network is through itself.

The Flags column of the routing table gives information on the destination address for this entry; U specifies that the route is "up," N that the destination is a network, and so on. The RefCnt and Use columns give statistics on the use of this route, and Iface lists the network device used for the route. On Linux systems,

Ethernet interfaces are named *eth0*, *eth1*, and so on. *lo* is the loopback device, discussed shortly.

The second entry in the routing table is the default route, which applies to all packets destined for networks or hosts for which there is no entry in the table. In this case, the default route is through **papaya**, which can be considered the door to the outside world. Every machine on the 128.17.75 subnet must go through **papaya** to talk to machines on any other network.

The third entry in the table is for the address 127.0.0.1, which is the *loopback* address. This address is used when a machine wants to make a TCP/IP connection to itself. It uses the *lo* device as its interface, which prevents loopback connections from using the Ethernet (via the *eth0* interface). In this way network bandwidth is not wasted when a machine wishes to talk to itself.

The last entry in the routing table is for the IP address 128.17.75.20, which is the **eggplant** host's own address. As we can see, it uses 127.0.0.1 as its gateway. This way, any time **eggplant** makes a TCP/IP connection to itself, the loopback address is used as the gateway, and the *lo* network device is used.

Let's say that **eggplant** wants to send a packet to **zucchini**. The IP datagram will contain a source address of 128.17.75.20, and a destination address of 128.17.75.37. IP determines that the network portion of the destination address is 128.17.75, and uses the routing table entry for 128.17.75.0 accordingly. The packet is sent directly to the network, which **zucchini** receives and is able to process.

What happens if **eggplant** wants to send packets to a machine not on the local network, such as **pear**? In this case, the destination address is 128.17.112.21. IP attempts to find a route for the 128.17.112 network in the routing tables, but none exists, so it selects the default route, through **papaya**. **papaya** receives the packet and looks up the destination address in its own routing tables. The routing table for **papaya** might look like this:

Destination net/address	Gateway address	Flags	RefCnt	Use	Iface
128.17.75.0	128.17.75.98	UN	0	20417	eth0
128.17.112.0	128.17.112.3	UN	0	20417	eth1
default	128.17.112.40	UGN	0	20417	eth1
127.0.0.1	127.0.0.1	UH	0	268	lo
128.17.75.98	127.0.0.1	UH	0	268	lo

As you can see, **papaya** is connected to the 128.17.75 network through its *eth0* device, and to 128.17.112 through *eth1*. The default route is through **pineapple**, which is a gateway to the Wild Blue Yonder (as far as **papaya** is concerned).

Once **papaya** receives a packet destined for **pear**, it sees that the destination address is on the network 128.17.112 and routes that packet to the network using the second entry in the routing table, given above.

Similarly, if **eggplant** wanted to send packets to machines outside of the local organization, it would route packets through **papaya** (its gateway). **papaya** would, in turn, route outgoing packets through **pineapple**, and so forth. Packets are handed from one gateway to the next until they reach the intended destination network. This is the basic structure upon which the Internet is based: A seemingly infinite chain of networks, interconnected via gateways.

Hardware Requirements

You can use Linux TCP/IP without any networking hardware at all—configuring "loopback" mode allows you to talk to yourself. This is necessary for some applications and games that use the "loopback" network device.

However, if you want to use Linux with an Ethernet TCP/IP network, you need one of the following Ethernet cards:

3com
    3c503, 3c503/16;

Novell
    NE1000, NE2000;

Western Digital
    WD8003, WD8013;

Hewlett-Packard
    HP27245, HP27247, and HP27250.

The following clones are reported to work:

WD-80x3 clones
    LANNET LEC-45

NE2000 clones
    Alta Combo, Artisoft LANtastic AE-2, Asante Etherpak 2001/2003, D-Link Ethernet II, LTC E-NET/16 P/N 8300-200-002, Network Solutions HE-203, SVEC 4 Dimension Ethernet, 4-Dimension FD0490 EtherBoard 16, and D-Link DE-600, SMC Elite 16.

[74] Ethernet HOWTO

See the Linux Ethernet HOWTO for a more complete discussion of Linux Ethernet hardware compatibility.

Linux also supports SLIP, which allows you to use a modem to access the Internet over the phone line. In this case, you'll need a modem compatible with your SLIP server—for example, many servers require a 14.4bps V.32bis modem.

Configuring TCP/IP with Ethernet

In this section, we discuss how to configure an Ethernet TCP/IP connection on a Linux system. Presumably this system will be part of a local network of machines that are already running TCP/IP—in which case your gateway, name server, and so forth are already configured and available.

The following information applies primarily to Ethernet connections. If you're planning to use SLIP, read this section to understand the concepts, and follow the SLIP-specific instructions in the section "SLIP Configuration."

On the other hand, you may wish to set up an entire LAN of Linux machines (or a mix of Linux machines and other systems). In this case, you'll have to take care of a number of other issues not discussed here. This includes setting up a name server for yourself, as well as a gateway machine if your network is to be connected to other networks. If your network is to be connected to the Internet, you'll also have to obtain IP addresses and related information from your access provider.

In short, the method described here should work for many Linux systems configured for an existing LAN—but certainly not all. For further details we direct you to a book on TCP/IP network administration, such as those mentioned at the beginning of this chapter.

First of all, we assume that your Linux system has the necessary TCP/IP software installed. This includes basic clients such as *telnet* and *ftp*, system administration commands such as *ifconfig* and *route* (usually found in */etc* or */sbin*), and networking configuration files (such as */etc/hosts*). The other Linux-related networking documents described above explain how to go about installing the Linux networking software if you do not have it already.

Chapter 4

We also assume that your kernel has been configured and compiled with TCP/IP support enabled. See the section "Building a New Kernel" in Chapter 4, *Essential System Management*, for information on compiling your kernel. To enable networking, you must answer "yes" to the appropriate questions during the *make config* step, rebuild the kernel, and boot from it.

Once this has been done, you must modify a number of configuration files used by NET-2. For the most part this is a simple procedure. Unfortunately, however, there is wide disagreement between Linux distributions as to where the various TCP/IP configuration files and support programs should go. Much of the time, they can be found in */etc*, but in other cases may be found in */usr/etc*, */usr/etc/inet*, or other bizarre locations. In the worst case, you'll have to use the *find* command to locate the files on your system. Also note that not all distributions keep the NET-2 configuration files and software in the same location—they may be spread across several directories.

This section also assumes use of one Ethernet device on the system. These instructions should be fairly easy to extrapolate if your system has more than one network connection (and hence acts as a gateway).

Here, we also discuss configuration for loopback-only systems (systems with no Ethernet or SLIP connection). If you have no network access, you may wish to configure your system for loopback-only TCP/IP so that you can use applications that support it.

Your network configuration

Before you can configure TCP/IP, you need to determine the following information about your network setup. In most cases, your local network administrator or network access provider can provide you with this information.

- Your IP address. This is the unique machine address in dotted-decimal format. An example is 128.17.75.98. Your network admins will provide you with this number.

    If you're configuring loopback mode (i.e., no SLIP, no Ethernet card, just TCP/IP connections to your own machine), your IP address is 127.0.0.1.

- Your subnetwork mask. This is a dotted quad, similar to the IP address, which determines which portion of the IP address specifies the subnetwork number, and which portion specifies the host on that subnet.

    The subnetwork mask is a pattern of bits, which, when bitwise-ANDed with an IP address on your network, will tell you which subnet that address belongs to. For example, your subnet mask might be 255.255.255.0. If your IP address is 128.17.75.20, the subnetwork portion of your address is 128.17.75.

    We distinguish here between "network address" and "subnetwork address." Remember that for Class B addresses, the first two bytes (here, 128.17) specify the network, and the second two bytes the host. With a subnet mask of 255.255.255.0, however, 128.17.75 is considered the entire subnet address (e.g., subnetwork 75 of network 128.17), and 20 the host address.

    Your network administrators choose the subnet mask and therefore can provide you with this information.

    This applies as well to the loopback device. Since the loopback address is always 127.0.0.1, the netmask for this device is always 255.0.0.0.

- Your subnetwork address. This is the subnet portion of your IP address, as determined by the subnet mask. For example, if your subnet mask is 255.255.255.0 and your IP address 128.17.75.20, your subnet address is 128.17.75.0.

    Loopback-only systems don't have a subnet address.

- Your broadcast address. This address is used to broadcast packets to every machine on your subnet. In general, this is equal to your subnet address (see above) with 255 replaced as the host address. For subnet address 128.17.75.0, the broadcast address is 128.17.75.255. Similarly, for subnet address 128.17.0.0, the broadcast address is 128.17.255.255.

    Note that some systems use the subnet address itself as the broadcast address. If you have any doubt, check with your network administrators.

    Loopback-only systems do not have a broadcast address.

- The IP address of your gateway. This is the address of the machine that acts as the default route to the outside world. In fact, you may have more than one gateway address—for example, if your network is connected directly to several other networks. However, only one of these will act as the *default* route. (Recall the example in the previous section, where the 128.17.112.0 network is connected both to 128.17.75.0 through **papaya**, and to the outside world through **pineapple**.)

  Your network administrators will provide you with the IP addresses of any gateways on your network, as well as the networks that they connect to. Later, you will use this information with the *route* command to include entries in the routing table for each gateway.

  Loopback-only systems do not have a gateway address. The same is true for isolated networks.

- The IP address of your name server. This is the address of the machine that handles hostname-to-address translations for your machine. Your network administrators will provide you with this information.

  You may wish to run your own name server (by configuring and running *named*). However, unless you absolutely must run your own name server (for example, if there is no other name server available on your local network), we suggest using the name server address provided by your network admins. At any rate, most books on TCP/IP configuration include information on running *named*.

  Naturally, loopback-only systems have no name server address.

The networking rc files

rc files are system-wide resource configuration scripts executed at boot time by *init*. They run basic system daemons (such as *sendmail, crond*, etc.) and are used to configure network parameters. *rc* files are usually found in the directory */etc*, but other systems may keep them in */etc/rc.d*.

Here, we're going to describe the *rc* files used to configure TCP/IP: *rc.inet1* and *rc.inet2*. *rc.inet1* is used to configure the basic network parameters (such as IP addresses and routing information), and *rc.inet2* fires up the TCP/IP daemons (*telnetd, ftpd*, and so forth).

Many systems combine these two files into one, usually called *rc.inet* or *rc.net*. The actual filenames used don't matter, as long as the corresponding files perform the appropriate network configuration and are executed at boot time by *init*.

init uses the file */etc/inittab* to determine what processes to run at boot time. In order to run the files */etc/rc.d/rc.inet1* and */etc/rc.d/rc.inet2* from *init*, */etc/inittab* might include entries such as

```
n1:123456:wait:/etc/rc.d/rc.inet1
n2:123456:wait:/etc/rc.d/rc.inet2
```

Chapter 4

The *inittab* file is described in the section "init and inittab" in Chapter 4. The first field gives a unique two-character identifier for each entry. The second field lists the runlevels in which the scripts are run; on this system, we initialize networking in runlevels 1 through 6. The word wait in the third field tells *init* to wait until the script has finished execution before continuing. The last field gives the name of the script to run.

On many systems, a single *rc* script is executed for multi-user runlevels. For example, *inittab* might contain

```
rc:123456:wait:/etc/rc.d/rc.M
```

/etc/rc.d/rc.M would then, in turn, execute *rc.inet1* and *rc.inet2*.

While you are first setting up your network configuration, you may wish to run *rc.inet1* and *rc.inet2* by hand (as **root**) in order to debug any problems. Later you can include entries for them in another *rc* file or in */etc/inittab*.

As mentioned above, *rc.inet1* configures the basic network interface. This includes your IP and network address, and the routing table information for your system. Two programs are used to configure these parameters: *ifconfig* and *route*. Both of these are usually found in */etc*.

ifconfig is used for configuring the network device interface with certain parameters, such as the IP address, subnetwork mask, broadcast address, and the like. *route* is used to create and modify entries in the routing table.

For most configurations, an *rc.inet1* file similar to the following should work. You will, of course, have to edit this for your own system. Do *not* use the sample IP and network addresses listed here; they may correspond to an actual machine on the Internet.

```
#!/bin/sh
# This is /etc/rc.d/rc.inet1 - Configure the TCP/IP interfaces

# First, configure the loopback device

HOSTNAME=`hostname`

/etc/ifconfig lo 127.0.0.1      # uses default netmask 255.0.0.0
/etc/route add 127.0.0.1        # a route to point to the loopback device

# Next, configure the ethernet device. If you're only using loopback or
# SLIP, comment out the rest of these lines.
```

```
# Edit for your setup.
IPADDR="128.17.75.20"          # REPLACE with your IP address
NETMASK="255.255.255.0"        # REPLACE with your subnet mask
NETWORK="128.17.75.0"          # REPLACE with your network address
BROADCAST="128.17.75.255"      # REPLACE with your broadcast address
GATEWAY="128.17.75.98"         # REPLACE with your default gateway address

# Configure the eth0 device to use information above
/etc/ifconfig eth0 ${IPADDR} netmask ${NETMASK} broadcast ${BROADCAST}

# Add a route for our own network
/etc/route add ${NETWORK}

# Add a route to the default gateway
/etc/route add default gw ${GATEWAY} metric 1

# End of Ethernet Configuration
```

As you can see, the format of the *ifconfig* command is

```
ifconfig interface device options...
```

For example:

```
ifconfig lo 127.0.0.1
```

assigns the *lo* (loopback) device the IP address 127.0.0.1, and

```
ifconfig eth0 127.17.75.20
```

assigns the *eth0* (first Ethernet) device the address 127.17.75.20.

In addition to specifying the address, Ethernet devices usually require that the subnetwork mask be set with the *netmask* option, and the broadcast address set with *broadcast*.

The format of the *route* command, as used here, is

```
route add [ -net | -host ] destination [ gw gateway ]
[ metric metric ] options
```

Where *destination* is the destination address for this route (or the keyword default), *gateway* the IP address of the gateway for this route, and *metric* is the metric number for the route (discussed below).

We use *route* to add entries to the routing table. You should add a route for the loopback device (as seen above), for your local network, and for your default gateway. For example, if our default gateway is 128.17.75.98, we would use the command

```
route add default gw 128.17.75.98
```

route takes several options. Using *-net* or *-host* before *destination* will tell *route* that the destination is a network or specific host, respectively. (In most cases, routes point to networks, but in some situations you may have an independent machine that requires its own route. You would use –*host* for such a routing table entry.)

The `metric` option is used to specify a *metric value* for this route. Metric values are used when there is more than one route to a specific location, and the system must make a decision about which to use. Routes with lower metric values are preferred. In this case, we set the metric value for our default route to 1, which will force that route to be preferred over all others.

How could there possibly be more than one route to a particular location? First of all, you may use multiple *route* commands in *rc.inet1* for a particular destination— if you have more than one gateway to a particular network, for example. However, your routing tables may dynamically acquire additional entries in them if you run *routed* (discussed further below). If you run *routed*, other systems may broadcast routing information to machines on the network, causing extra routing table entries to be created on your machine. By setting the `metric` value for your default route to 1, you ensure that any new routing table entries will not supersede the preference of your default gateway.

You should read the manual pages for *ifconfig* and *route*, which describe the syntax of these commands in detail. There may be other options to *ifconfig* and *route* that are pertinent to your configuration.

Let's move on. *rc.inet2* is used to run various daemons used by the TCP/IP suite. These are not necessary in order for your system to talk to the network, and are therefore relegated to a separate *rc* file. In most cases you should attempt to configure *rc.inet1*, and ensure that your system is able to send and receive packets from the network, before bothering to configure *rc.inet2*.

Among the daemons executed by *rc.inet2* are *inetd*, *syslogd*, and *routed*. The version of *rc.inet2* on your system may currently start a number of other servers, but we suggest commenting these out while you are debugging your network configuration.

The most important of these servers is *inetd*, which acts as the "operator" for other system daemons. It sits in the background and listens to certain network ports for incoming connections. When a connection is made, *inetd* spawns off a copy of the appropriate daemon for that port. For example, when an incoming *telnet* connection is made, *inetd* forks *in.telnetd*, which handles the *telnet* connection from there. This is simpler and more efficient than running individual copies of each daemon. This way, network daemons are executed on demand.

syslogd is the system logging daemon—it accumulates log messages from various applications and stores them into log files based on the configuration information in */etc/syslogd.conf.*

routed is a server used to maintain dynamic routing information. When your system attempts to send packets to another network, it may require additional routing table entries in order to do so. *routed* takes care of manipulating the routing table without the need for user intervention.

Here is a sample *rc.inet2* that starts up *syslogd*, *inetd*, and *routed*.

```
#! /bin/sh
# Sample /etc/rc.d/rc.inet2

# Start syslogd
if [ -f /etc/syslogd ]
then
     /etc/syslogd
fi

# Start inetd
if [ -f /etc/inetd ]
then
     /etc/inetd
fi

# Start routed
if [ -f /etc/routed ]
then
     /etc/routed -q
fi
```

Among the various additional servers that you may want to start in *rc.inet2* is *named*. *named* is a name server—it is responsible for translating (local) IP addresses to names, and vice versa. If you don't have a name server elsewhere on the network, or if you want to provide local machine names to other machines in your domain, it may be necessary to run *named*. *named* configuration is somewhat complex and requires planning; we refer interested readers to *DNS and BIND*.

[35] DNS
and BIND

/etc/hosts

/etc/hosts contains a list of IP addresses and the hostnames that they correspond to. In general, */etc/hosts* contains entries only for your local machine, and perhaps other "important" machines (such as your name server or gateway). Your local name server will provide address-to-name mappings for other machines on the network transparently.

For example, if your machine is **eggplant.veggie.com** with the IP address 128.17.75.20, your */etc/hosts* would look like this:

```
127.0.0.1              localhost
128.17.75.20           eggplant.veggie.com eggplant
```

If you're only using loopback, the only line in */etc/hosts* should be for the address 127.0.0.1.

/etc/networks

The */etc/networks* file lists the names and addresses of your own and other networks. It is used by the *route* command, and allows you to specify a network by name, instead of by address.

Every network you wish to add a route to using the *route* command (generally called from *rc.inet1*—see above) *must* have an entry in */etc/networks*.

As an example:

```
default       0.0.0.0       # default route    - mandatory
loopnet       127.0.0.0     # loopback network - mandatory
veggie-net    128.17.75.0   # Modify for your own network address
```

Now, instead of using the command

```
route add 128.17.75.20
```

we can use

```
route add veggie-net
```

Nevertheless, you must have an entry for each network route in */etc/networks*, whether you opt to use the name with the *route* command or not.

/etc/host.conf

The */etc/hosts* file specifies how your system will resolve hostnames. It should contain the two lines:

```
order hosts,bind
multi on
```

These lines tell the resolve libraries to first check the */etc/hosts* file for any names to lookup, and then ask the name server (if one is present). The multi entry allows you to have multiple IP addresses for a given machine name in */etc/hosts*.

/etc/resolv.conf

This file configures the name resolver, specifying the address of your name server (if any) and your DNS domain name. Your domain name is your fully-qualified hostname (if you're a registered machine on the Internet, for example) with the hostname chopped off. That is, if your full hostname is **loomer.vpizza.com**, your domain name is just **vpizza.com**. Your network administrators will provide you with your domain name if you are unsure.

For example, the machine **eggplant.veggie.com** with a name server at address 128.17.75.55 would have the following lines in */etc/resolv.conf*:

```
domain      veggie.com
nameserver  128.17.75.55 .
```

You can specify more than one name server—each must have a `nameserver` line of its own in *resolv.conf*.

Setting your hostname

You should set your system hostname with the *hostname* command. This is usually executed from */etc/rc* or */etc/rc.local*; simply search your system *rc* files to determine where it is invoked. For example, if your (full) hostname is **eggplant.veggie.com**, edit the appropriate *rc* file to execute the command: */bin/hostname eggplant.veggie.com*. Note that the *hostname* executable may be found in a directory other than */bin* on your system.

Trying it out

Once you have the various networking configuration files modified for your system, you should be able to reboot (using a TCP/IP-enabled kernel) and attempt to use the network.

When first booting the system, you may wish to disable execution of *rc.inet1* and *rc.inet2*, and run them by hand once the system is up. This will allow you to catch any error messages, modify the scripts, and retry. Once you have things working you can enable the scripts from */etc/inittab*.

One good way of testing network connectivity is to simply *telnet* to another host. You should first try to connect to another host on your local network, and if this works, attempt to connect to hosts on other networks. The former will test your connection to the local subnet; the latter, your connection to the rest of the world through your gateway.

You may be able to connect to remote machines, via the gateway, whereas connecting to machines on the subnet fails. This is a sign that there is a problem with your subnetwork mask or the routing table entry for the local network.

When attempting to connect to other machines, you should first try to connect using only the IP address of the remote host. If this seems to work, but connecting via hostname does not, then there may be a problem with your name server configuration (e.g., */etc/resolv.conf* and */etc/host.conf*) or with your route to the name server.

The most common source of network trouble is an ill-configured routing table. You can use the command

```
netstat -rn
```

to display the routing table; in the previous section we described the format of the routing tables as displayed by this command. The *netstat* manual page provides additional insight as well. Using *netstat* without the *−n* option will force it to display host and network entries by name, instead of address.

route(8)

To debug your routing tables, you can either edit *rc.inet1*, and reboot, or use the *route* command by hand to add or delete entries. The manual page for *route* describes the full syntax of this command. Note that simply editing *rc.inet1* and re-executing it will not clear out old entries in the routing table; you must either reboot, or use *route del* to delete the entries.

If absolutely nothing seems to work, then there may be a problem with your Ethernet device configuration. First, be sure that your Ethernet card was detected, at the appropriate address and/or IRQ, at boot time. The kernel boot messages will give you this information; if you are using *syslogd*, then kernel boot-time messages are also saved in a file such as */var/adm/messages*.

[74] Ethernet
HOWTO

If detection of your Ethernet card is faulty, you may have to modify kernel parameters to fix it. The Linux Ethernet HOWTO includes much information on debugging Ethernet card configurations. In many cases, the fix is as simple as specifying the appropriate IRQ and port address at the LILO boot prompt. For example, booting via LILO with the command

```
lilo: linux ether=9,0x300,0,1,eth0
```

will select IRQ 9, base address 0x300, and the external transceiver (the fourth value of 1) for the *eth0* device. To use the internal transceiver (if your card supports both types), change the fourth value of the `ether` option to 0.

Also, don't overlook the possibility that your Ethernet card is damaged or incorrectly connected to your machine or the network. A bad Ethernet card or cable can cause no end of trouble, including intermittent network failures, system crashes, and so forth. When you're at the end of your rope, consider replacing the Ethernet card and/or cable to determine if this is the source of the problem. [*]

If your Ethernet card is detected, but the system is still having problems talking to the network, the device configuration with *ifconfig* may be to blame. Be sure that you have specified the appropriate IP address, broadcast address, and subnet mask for your machine. Invoking *ifconfig* with no arguments will display information on your Ethernet device configuration.

---

* The author once spent three hours trying to determine why the kernel wouldn't recognize an Ethernet card at boot time. As it turned out, the 16-bit card was plugged into an 8-bit slot—mea culpa.

SLIP Configuration

SLIP (Serial Line Internet Protocol) allows you to use TCP/IP over a serial line, be it a phone line, with a dialup modem, or a leased asynchronous line of some sort. To use SLIP you'll need access to a dial-in SLIP server in your area. Many universities and businesses provide SLIP access for a modest fee.

SLIP is quite unlike Ethernet, in that there are only two machines on the "network"—the SLIP host (that's you) and the SLIP server. For this reason, SLIP is often referred to as a "point-to-point" connection. A different protocol embodying this idea, known as PPP (Point-to-Point Protocol) has also been implemented for Linux. PPP configuration is described in the *Linux Network Administrator's Guide*.

[3] Network Admin Guide

There are two major SLIP-related programs available—*dip* and *slattach*. Both of these programs are used to initiate a SLIP connection over a serial device. You have to use one of these programs in order to enable SLIP—it will not suffice to dial up the SLIP server (with a communications program such as *kermit*) and issue *ifconfig* and *route* commands. This is because *dip* and *slattach* issue a certain *ioctl()* system call to seize control of the serial device to be used as a SLIP interface.

dip can be used to dial up a SLIP server, do some handshaking to log in to the server (exchanging your username and password, for example) and then initiate the SLIP connection over the open serial line. *slattach*, on the other hand, does very little other than grab the serial device for use by SLIP. It is useful if you have a permanent line to your SLIP server and no modem dialup or handshaking is necessary to initiate the connection.

dip can also be used to configure your Linux system as a SLIP server, where other machines can dial in and connect to the network through a secondary Ethernet connection on your machine. The documentation and manual page for *dip* provide more information on this procedure.

When you initiate a connection to a SLIP server, the SLIP server will give you an IP address based on (usually) one of two methods. Some SLIP servers allocate "static" IP addresses—in which case your IP address will be the same every time you connect to the server. However, other SLIP servers allocate IP addresses dynamically—in which case you receive a different IP address each time you connect. In this case, the server usually prints the values of your IP and gateway addresses when you connect. *dip* is capable of reading these values from the server login session and using them to configure the SLIP device.

Essentially, configuring a SLIP connection is just like configuring for loopback or Ethernet. The main differences are discussed below. Read the previous section on configuring the basic TCP/IP files, and apply the changes described here.

Static IP address SLIP connections using dip

If you are using a static-allocation SLIP server, you may want to include entries for your IP address and hostname in */etc/hosts*. (Your network administrators will tell you what your IP address and official hostname are.) Also, you should configure the *rc.inet2*, *host.conf*, and *resolv.conf* files as discussed in the section "Configuring TCP/IP with Ethernet."

You will also need to configure *rc.inet1*. However, include the *ifconfig* and *route* commands only for the loopback device. If you use *dip* to connect to the SLIP server, it will execute the appropriate *ifconfig* and *route* commands for the SLIP device for you. (If you're using *slattach*, on the other hand, you *will* need to include *ifconfig/route* commands in *rc.inet1* for the SLIP device—see below.)

dip should configure your routing tables appropriately for the SLIP connection when you connect. In some cases, however, the behavior of *dip* may not be correct for your configuration, and you'll have to run *ifconfig* or *route* commands by hand after connecting to the server. This is most easily done from within a shell script that runs *dip* and immediately executes the appropriate configuration commands. You can then execute this shell script to initiate your SLIP connection.

In most cases, the gateway for your machine is the IP address of the SLIP server itself. You may know this address beforehand, or the gateway address will be printed by the SLIP server when you connect. In the latter case, the *dip* chat script (described below) can obtain this information from the SLIP server.

ifconfig may require use of the *pointopoint* argument if *dip* doesn't configure the interface correctly. For example, if your SLIP server address is 128.17.75.98, and your IP address is 128.17.75.2, you may need to run the command

```
ifconfig sl0 128.17.75.2 pointopoint 128.17.75.98
```

as **root**, after connecting with *dip*. The manual page for *ifconfig* will come in handy.

Note that SLIP device names used with the *ifconfig* and *route* commands are *sl0*, *sl1* and so on (as opposed to *eth0*, *eth1*, etc. for Ethernet devices).

In the section "Using dip" below, we explain how to configure *dip* to connect to the SLIP server.

Static IP address SLIP connections using slattach

If you have a leased line or cable running directly to your SLIP server, there is no need to use *dip* to initiate a connection. *slattach* can be used to configure the SLIP device instead.

In this case, your */etc/rc.inet1* file should look something like the following:

```
#!/bin/sh
IPADDR="128.17.75.2"          # Replace with your IP address
REMADDR="128.17.75.98"        # Replace with your SLIP server address

# Modify the following for the appropriate serial device for the SLIP
# connection:
slattach -p cslip -s 19200 /dev/ttyS0
/etc/ifconfig sl0 $IPADDR pointopoint $REMADDR up
/etc/route add default gw $REMADDR
```

slattach allocates the first unallocated SLIP device (*sl0*, *sl1*, etc.) to the serial line specified.

Note that the first parameter to *slattach* is the SLIP protocol to use. At present the only valid values are `slip` and `cslip`. `slip` is regular SLIP, as you would expect, and `cslip` is SLIP with datagram header compression. In most cases you should use `cslip`; however, if you seem to be having problems with this, you may want to fall back to `slip`.

Dynamic IP address SLIP connections using dip

If your SLIP server allocates an IP address dynamically, you certainly don't know your address in advance—therefore, you can't include an entry for it in */etc/hosts*. (You should, however, include an entry for your host with the loopback address 127.0.0.1.)

Many SLIP servers print the host IP address (as well as the server's address) at connection time. For example, one type of SLIP server prints a message such as

```
Your IP address is 128.253.154.44.
Server address is 128.253.154.2.
```

dip can capture these numbers from the output of the server and use them to configure the SLIP device.

See the previous section for information on configuring your various TCP/IP files for use with SLIP.

Using dip

To use *dip*, you'll need to write a "chat script" that contains a list of commands used to communicate with the SLIP server at login time. These commands can automatically send your username/password to the server, as well as get information on your IP address from the server.

Example 7-1 is a sample *dip* chat script for use with a dynamic IP address server. For static servers, you will need to set the variables `$local` and `$remote` to the values of your local IP address and server IP address, respectively, at the top of the script. The comments in the sample script below explain what to do.

Example 7-1: Sample chat Script

```
main:
  # Set Maximum Transfer Unit. This is the maximum size of packets
  # transmitted on the SLIP device. Many SLIP servers use either 1500 or
  # 1006; check with your network admins when in doubt.
  get $mtu 1500

  # If you are using a static SLIP server, set the address for your machine
  # ($local) and the remote server ($remote). These lines are commented out
  # for dynamic SLIP servers.
  # get $local eggplant.veggie.com
  # get $remote slipserver.veggie.com

  # Make the SLIP route the default route on your system.
  default

  # Set the desired serial port and speed.
  port cua03
  speed 38400

  # Reset the modem and terminal line. If this causes trouble for you,
  # comment it out.
  reset

  # Prepare for dialing. Replace the following with your
  # modem initialization string.
  send ATT&C1&D2N3&Q5%M3%C1N1W1L1S48=7\r
  wait OK 2
  if $errlvl != 0 goto error
  # Dial the SLIP server
  dial 5551234
  if $errlvl != 0 goto error
  wait CONNECT 60
  if $errlvl != 0 goto error

  # We are connected.  Log in to the system.
login:
  sleep 3
  send \r\n\r\n
  # Wait for the login prompt
  wait login: 10
  if $errlvl != 0 goto error

  # Send your username
  send USERNAME\n

  # Wait for password prompt
  wait ord: 5
  if $errlvl != 0 goto error

  # Send password.
```

Example 7-1: Sample chat Script (continued)

```
send PASSWORD\n

# Wait for SLIP server ready prompt
wait annex: 30
if $errlvl != 0 goto error

# Send commands to SLIP server to initiate connection.
send slip\n
wait Annex 30

# Get the remote IP address from the SLIP server. The `get...remote'
# command reads text in the form xxx.xxx.xxx.xxx, and assigns it
# to the variable given as the second argument (here, $remote).
# Comment out the following lines if you use a static SLIP server.

get $remote remote
if $errlvl != 0 goto error
wait Your 30

# Get local IP address from SLIP server, assign to variable $local.
get $local remote
if $errlvl != 0 goto error

# Fire up the SLIP connection
done:
    print CONNECTED to $remote at $rmtip
    print GATEWAY address $rmtip
    print LOCAL address $local

# Use compressed-header SLIP. Change this to "mode SLIP" if your
# server does not support this.
mode CSLIP
goto exit

error:
    print SLIP to $remote failed.

exit:
    # Done.
```

dip automatically executes *ifconfig* and *route* commands based on the values of the variables $local and $remote. Here, those variables are assigned using the *get...remote* command, which obtains text from the SLIP server and assigns it to the named variable.

If the *ifconfig* and *route* commands that *dip* uses don't work, you can either execute the correct commands in a shell script after running *dip*, or modify the source for *dip* itself. Running *dip* with the −*v* option will print debugging information while the connection is being made, which should help you to determine where things might be going awry.

Now, in order to run *dip* and open the SLIP connection, you can use a command such as:

```
/etc/dip/dip -v /etc/dip/mychat 2>&1
```

Where the various *dip* files and the chat script (*mychat.dip*) are stored in */etc/dip*.

Once *dip* has completed making the connection, it will remain running as a background process. You should be able to use *telnet, ftp*, and so forth over your SLIP connection.

To hang up the SLIP connection, you can simply kill the *dip* process. Some versions of *dip* trap several signals, so you may need to use kill -9 to achieve the desired effect.

The above discussion should be enough to get you well on your way to talking to the network, either via Ethernet or SLIP. Again, we strongly suggest looking into a book on TCP/IP network configuration, especially if your network has special routing considerations. When in doubt, check with your network administrators—configuring TCP/IP under Linux is no different than on other implementations of UNIX.

The World Wide Web

The World Wide Web (WWW) is a relative newcomer to the Internet information hierarchy. The WWW project's goal is to unite the many disparate services available on the Internet into a single, worldwide multimedia hypertext space. Although this may seem very abstract to you now, the WWW is best understood by using it. In this section we'll show you how to access the WWW with your Linux machine. We'll also describe how to configure your own WWW server to provide documents to the Web.

The World Wide Web project was started in 1989 by Tim Berners-Lee at the European Center for Particle Physics (CERN). The original goal of the project was to allow groups of researchers in the particle physics community to share many kinds of information through a single, homogeneous interface.

Before the WWW, each type of information available via the Internet was provided by its own unique client-server pair. For example, to retrieve files via FTP, one used the *ftp* client, which connected to the *ftpd* daemon on the server machine. Gopher, Usenet news, finger information, and so forth all required their own individual clients. The differences between operating systems and machine architectures compounded the problem—in theory, these details should be hidden from the user who is trying to access the information.

The WWW provides a single abstraction for the many kinds of information available from the Internet. One uses a single WWW "client"—such as NCSA Mosaic or Lynx—to access the WWW. On the Web, information is provided as documents (also known as "pages"), where each document may have links to others.

Chapter 5

Documents may be located on any machine on the Internet that is configured to provide WWW access. Representing information in this way is commonly referred to as "hypertext," which is a very important concept underlying the entire Web. The section "Using Multimedia on Linux" in Chapter 5, *Power Tools*, describes the concept of hypertext in more detail.

For example, the Linux Documentation Project provides various Linux-related documents via the Web. The LDP "Home Page," which resides on **sunsite.unc.edu**, contains links to a number of other Linux-related pages around the world. The LDP Home Page is shown in Figure 7-4.

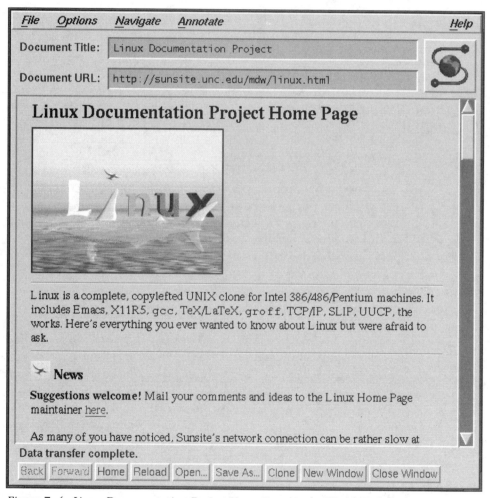

Figure 7–4. Linux Documentation Project Home Page on the World Wide Web

The highlighted regions of text in the document are links. When the user selects a link (for example, by clicking on the text with the mouse), the document pointed to by the link is retrieved. The documents can reside on virtually any machine on the Internet; the actual "locations" of WWW documents are hidden from the user.

Many of the documents available via the Web are in the form of multimedia hypertext pages, as seen above. These pages may contain links to pictures, sounds, MPEG video files, PostScript documents, and much more. This multimedia information is provided by a protocol known as HTTP—HyperText Transfer Protocol. The WWW is also capable of accessing documents provided via FTP, Gopher, Usenet news, and so on.

For example, when accessing a document via HTTP, you are likely to see a page such as that displayed in Figure 7-4—with embedded pictures, links to other pages, and so on. When accessing a document via FTP, you might see a directory listing of the FTP server, as seen in Figure 7-5. Clicking on a link in the FTP document will either retrieve the selected file or display the contents of another directory.

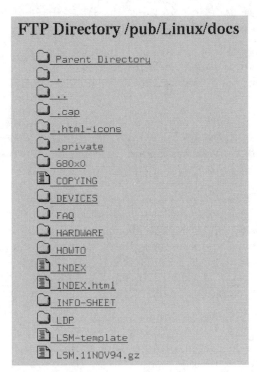

Figure 7–5. FTP directory displayed by Mosaic

Given this kind of abstraction, we need a way to refer to documents available on the Web. *Universal Resource Locators*, or URLs, are the answer. A URL is simply a "pathname" uniquely identifying a WWW document, including the machine that it resides on, the filename of the document, and the protocol used to access it (FTP, HTTP, etc.). For example, the Linux Documentation Project's Home Page can be accessed with the URL

```
http://sunsite.unc.edu/mdw/linux.html
```

Let's break this down. The first part of the URL, `http:`, identifies the protocol used for the document, which in this case is HTTP. The second part of the URL, `//sunsite.unc.edu`, identifies the machine where the document is provided. The final portion of the URL, `/mdw/linux.html`, is the logical pathname to the document on **sunsite.unc.edu**. This is similar to a UNIX pathname—it identifies the file *linux.html* in the directory *mdw*. Therefore, to access the LDP home page, you would simply fire up a WWW client and tell it to access the URL *http://sunsite.unc.edu/mdw/linux.html*. What could be easier?

To access a file via anonymous FTP, we can use a URL such as

```
ftp://tsx-11.mit.edu/pub/linux/docs/FAQ
```

This URL will retrieve the Linux FAQ on **tsx-11.mit.edu**. Using this URL with your WWW client is identical to using the *ftp* client to fetch the file by hand.

The best way to understand the Web is to explore it. In the following section we'll explain how to get started with a WWW client. Later in the chapter, we'll cover how to configure your own machine as a WWW server for providing documents to the rest of the Web.

Of course, in order to access the Web, you'll need a machine with direct Internet access (via either Ethernet or SLIP). In the following sections, we assume that you have already configured TCP/IP on your system and that you can successfully use clients such as *telnet* and *ftp*.

Using NCSA Mosaic

NCSA Mosaic is one of the most popular WWW clients. Versions are available for the Macintosh, Microsoft Windows, and, of course, the X Window System on UNIX machines. As you would expect there is a Linux binary version available, which you can obtain from nearly any Linux-related FTP site. The original Mosaic distribution can be obtained from **ftp.ncsa.uiuc.edu**.

NCSA Mosaic has an interesting license. It is not distributed under the GNU GPL. Anyone may freely download Mosaic from NCSA's FTP site, but companies may not redistribute Mosaic in source or binary form without licensing it from the National Center for Supercomputing Applications (NCSA). The bottom line is that commercial distributions of Linux (e.g., CD-ROMs or diskettes available via mail order) cannot include NCSA Mosaic without paying a license fee. Therefore, chances are you'll have to download Mosaic—it won't be found on your CD-ROM distribution of Linux. Supposedly, if you're going to access the WWW, your machine already has Internet access, so downloading Mosaic via FTP is no problem.[*]

Here, we assume that you're using a networked Linux machine running X, and that you have obtained a copy of Mosaic. As stated before, your machine must be configured to use TCP/IP, and you should be able to use clients such as *telnet* and *ftp*.

Starting Mosaic is simple. Run the command

```
eggplant$ Mosaic url
```

where *url* is the Universal Resource Locator for the document that you wish to view. If you don't specify a URL, Mosaic should display the NCSA Mosaic Home Page as shown in Figure 7-6.

The NCSA Home Page is a good place to start if you're interested in Web exploration. It contains links to information about Mosaic itself, as well as demonstration documents showing off the power of the Web. (See the section "Navigating the Web," later in the chapter, for more information on finding your way around the Web.)

While using Mosaic, you can scroll the document using the scrollbars on the edge of the window. Alternatively, you can use the Space bar and Delete key to move back and forth by pages, or the arrow keys to scroll the document in smaller steps.

Links will appear as highlighted text (usually in blue, on color systems, or under-lined on monochrome). To follow a link, simply click on it with the mouse. Mosaic remembers the links that you have followed; after you have selected a link it will appear in a darker color (or with dotted underlines) in the future.

Keep in mind that retrieving documents on the Web can be slow at times. This depends on the speed of the network connection from your site to the server, as well as the traffic on the network at the time. In some cases, WWW sites may be so loaded that they simply refuse connections; if this is the case, Mosaic will display an appropriate error message. At the bottom edge of the Mosaic window, a status report will be displayed, and while a transfer is taking place, the NCSA Mosaic logo in the upper-right-hand corner of the window will spin. Clicking on the logo will interrupt the transfer, in case the site seems to be down or the network connection is very slow.

Note that many documents contain inline images—for example, the Mosaic banner displayed at the top of the Mosaic Home Page. If you happen to be using a slow network connection, you can select *Delay Image Loading* from the *Options* menu, which will cause these images to be displayed as small icons in the document. Clicking on such an icon will load the actual image at that time.

---

* See the NCSA Mosaic Licensing FAQ, available via anonymous FTP from **ftp.ncsa.uiuc.edu** in *Mosaic/LICENSING.FAQ*, if you have questions.

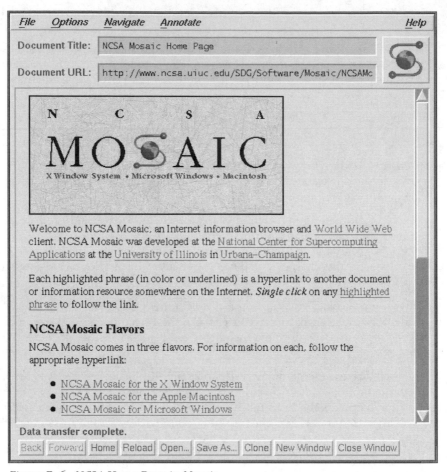

Figure 7–6. NCSA Home Page in Mosaic

As you traverse links within Mosaic, each document is saved in the "window history," which can be recalled using the *Window History...* item from the *Navigate* menu. Pressing the *Back* button at the lower edge of the Mosaic window will move you back through the window history to previously-visited documents. Similarly, the *Forward* button will move you forward through the history.

Many Mosaic commands have "hotkey" equivalents. For example, pressing b is equivalent to pressing the *Back* button, f is equivalent to *Forward*, and h will display the window history list.

You can save oft-accessed URLs in the Mosaic "hotlist." Whenever you are viewing a document that you might want to return to later, choose *Add Current to Hotlist* from the *Navigate* menu. You can display your hotlist by choosing the *Hotlist...* item from this menu, or by pressing H. Figure 7-7 shows what the hotlist looks like. Double-clicking on any item in the window will retrieve the corresponding document from the Web.

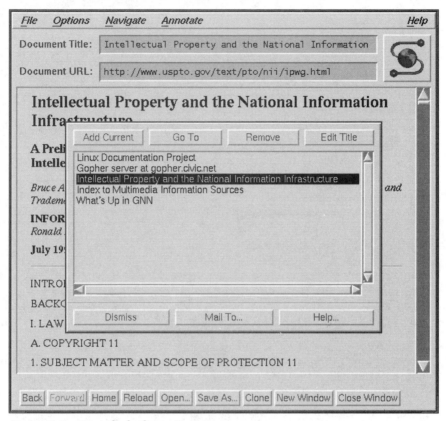

Figure 7–7. Using the hotlist in Mosaic

As mentioned previously, you can access new URLs by running *Mosaic* with the URL as the argument. However, you can also select *Open URL...* from the *File* menu. Just type the name of the URL into the text entry field, press enter, and the corresponding document will be retrieved.

Note that Mosaic allows you to cut and paste text from the document window and text entry fields (for example, from the *Open URL* window), as you would with *xterm*. That is, dragging the mouse while holding down button 1 will select a region of text; pressing mouse button 2 will paste the text at the cursor location. You can cut and paste text between other X applications, such as *xterm*, as well. In this way, if you have a URL name in an *xterm* window, you can select it from the *xterm* and paste it into the *Open URL* window.

If you select *Fancy Selections* from the *Options* window, text selected from the Mosaic document window will retain its formatting (e.g., line breaks, list bullets, and so forth) when pasted elsewhere.

As you can see, Mosaic is a powerful application with many options. There are many ways to customize Mosaic's behavior—however, many of the customization details tend to change from release to release. Fortunately, NCSA has provided complete documentation for Mosaic on-line, via the Web (where else?). If you select *About...* from the *Help* menu, you will be presented with the top-level page for Mosaic's online documentation. Therein you will find descriptions of Mosaic's other many features, as well as instructions on how to customize its behavior to taste. *The Mosaic Handbook for the X Window System* also provides a guide to the use and customization of Mosaic.

[19] Mosaic

Mosaic is not the only browser that reads World Wide Web documents. Another versatile one is Lynx. It is a text-based browser, so you miss the pictures when you use it. But this makes it fast, and you may find it convenient. You can also use it without the X Window System.

Navigating the Web

The World Wide Web is growing at a tremendous rate. In fact, by the time you read this book, the Web may have completely changed in appearance from the descriptions given here. Thousands of WWW servers have emerged in the first year or so of the Web's existence.

As the Web expands to encompass countless servers from all over the world, it becomes much more difficult to find the information that's out there. Unless you happen to run across a URL or hyperlink to an interesting site, how can you locate information by subject?

Fortunately, a number of services have appeared on the Web to simplify this task. While none of these services provide a *complete* listing of WWW sites, the high degree of connectivity on the Web ensures that if whatever you're looking for is out there, you'll find it.

First, keep in mind that the Web is a dynamic place. We've made every attempt to certify that the information here is current, but by the time you read this book, it may be the case that several of these links have moved, or no longer exist.

A good place to start is the NCSA *Internet Resources Meta-Index*, which lists directories and indices for various services available via the Web. This includes WWW, Gopher, WAIS, and FTP sites. The URL for the Meta-Index is

```
http://www.ncsa.uiuc.edu/SDG/Software/Mosaic/MetaIndex.html
```

This can also be accessed from the *Internet Resources Meta-Index* item of the NCSA Mosaic *Navigate* menu.

Administrators of new WWW sites are encouraged to send an announcement of their service to NCSA. These announcements are presented in the NCSA Mosaic "What's New" page, at

```
http://www.ncsa.uiuc.edu/SDG/Software/Mosaic/Docs/whats-new.html
```

You can think of the What's New page as the World Wide Web newspaper. It's updated nearly every day with listings of new services. The What's New listings are archived at the Centre Universitaire d'Informatique (CUI), University of Geneva "W3 Catalog," at

```
http://cui_www.unige.ch/w3catalog
```

This is a forms-based page that allows you to enter keywords, or a regular expression, which will be used to search the What's New listings. You'll be presented with a list of announcements that matched the search.

Another interesting project is the World Wide Web Worm, one of the many "robots" that scour the Web, accumulating URLs and document titles. You can then search the listings of Web sites that the Worm gathers. You can access the Worm via the URL

```
http://www.cs.colorado.edu/home/mcbryan/WWWW.html
```

Note that because of the computational intensity required to run the Worm, its databases are updated only every few months or so.

There are other WWW robots, or "spiders," similar in nature to the World Wide Web Worm. This URL lists a number of them:

```
http://web.nexor.co.uk/mak/doc/robots/active.html
```

O'Reilly & Associates publishes the *Global Network Navigator* (*GNN*), a Web-based magazine and information resource. This magazine is provided free-of-charge via the WWW. It includes, among other things, a WWW-based interface to *The Whole Internet Catalog*, a directory of Internet resources by subject. *The Whole Internet Catalog* is a great place to find topical information on the Internet. You can access the *Global Network Navigator* directory at the URL

```
http://nearnet.gnn.com/gnn/GNNhome.html
```

There are dozens of other resources that can be used to search the Web, or the Internet in general, for information about a particular subject. The CUI "W3 Search Engines" page accumulates interfaces to many of them, including the World Wide Web Worm, *The Whole Internet Catalog*, and other indices mentioned above. The W3 Search Engines page is located at the URL

```
http://cui_www.unige.ch/meta-index.html
```

If you're at a loss about which index to try, this is a good place to start. This page includes search engines for Gopher, Usenet, and various other kinds of information, as well as Web sites.

Configuring Your Own WWW Server

Now that you've seen what the Web has to provide, you're ready to set up your own gas station on the information superhighway. Running your own WWW server is easy. It consists of two tasks: configuring the *httpd* daemon and writing documents to provide on the server.

httpd is the daemon that services HTTP requests on your machine. Any document accessed with an *http:* URL will be retrieved using *httpd*. Likewise, *ftp:* URLs will be accessed using *ftpd*, *gopher:* URLs using *gopherd*, etc. There is no single "WWW daemon"; each URL type uses a separate daemon to request information from the server.

There are several HTTP servers available. The one discussed here is the NCSA *httpd*, which is easy to configure and very flexible. In this section we'll discuss how to install and configure the basic aspects of this version of *httpd*. Later in the chapter we talk about how to write your own documents in HTML (the markup language used by WWW pages), as well as more advanced aspects of server configuration, such as providing interactive fill-out forms.

The first step, of course, is to obtain a Linux *httpd* binary. Your Linux distribution may come with *httpd* installed. Alternately, you can obtain a Linux binary from one of the various archive sites. If all else fails you can obtain the *httpd* sources from NCSA and build it yourself.

To find out more about NCSA *httpd* and how to obtain it, see the URL

```
http://hoohoo.ncsa.uiuc.edu
```

[37] Internet Services

which contains complete documentation for the software. *Managing Internet Information Services* describes the setup and administration of a WWW server, as well as mailing lists, gopher sites, and other services.

When installing the binary *httpd* package, you'll end up with the *httpd* executable, as well as several support directories:

cgi-bin

Contains executables for various Common Gateway Interface programs. These programs service requests from interactive forms used on your server. This is discussed in more detail in the section "Writing the CGI script."

cgi-src

Contains sources for the programs in *cgi-bin*.

conf

Contains the configuration files for *httpd*. We discuss how to modify these files later.

icons

> Contains icon images that can be used to decorate your HTML pages. This will be discussed in the section "Writing HTML Documents."

logs

> Holds log files stored by the server.

support

> Contains miscellaneous utilities.

These files are usually stored together under a single server root directory, such as */etc/httpd*. Under this scheme, the server binary itself is */etc/httpd/httpd*, the configuration files stored in */etc/httpd/conf*, and so on.

Our task now is to modify the configuration files in the *conf* subdirectory. You should notice four files in this directory: *access.conf-dist*, *httpd.conf-dist*, *mime.types*, and *srm.conf-dist*. You will copy the files with names ending in *-dist* and modify them for your own system. For example, *access.conf-dist* will be copied to *access.conf* and edited.

At *http://hoohoo.ncsa.uiuc.edu* you will find complete documentation on how to configure *httpd*. Here, we'll present sample configuration files that correspond to an actual running *httpd*.

httpd.conf

The file *httpd.conf* is the main server configuration file. First, copy *httpd.conf-dist* to *httpd.conf*, and edit it. Below, a sample *httpd.conf* is presented, with comments explaining each field.

```
# Sample httpd.conf

# Run httpd as a standalone server
ServerType standalone

# Port 80 is the standard httpd port, but you must run the server as
# root for ports numbered below 1023.
Port 80

# The user ID that httpd will run as. Make sure that 'nobody' is listed
# in /etc/passwd
User nobody

# The address where the server's administrator can be reached.
ServerAdmin mdw@zucchini.veggie.org

# The directory where the httpd support directories are located
ServerRoot /etc/httpd

# Locations of server log files. These pathnames are assumed to be relative
# to ServerRoot, unless they begin with '/'.
```

```
ErrorLog logs/httpd.errs
TransferLog logs/httpd.access
PidFile logs/httpd.pid

# The hostname to return as the server location. This must be an actual,
# registered hostname. For example, we may have httpd running on a
# machine aliased to 'www.veggie.org', where the canonical hostname
# is something different.
ServerName www.veggie.org
```

The ServerType directive is used to specify how the server will run—either as a standalone daemon (as seen here), or from *inetd*. For various reasons, it's usually best to run *httpd* in standalone mode. Otherwise, *inetd* must spawn a new instance of *httpd* for each incoming connection.

One tricky item here is the port number specification. You may wish to run *httpd* as a user other than **root** (that is, you may not have root access on the machine in question, and wish to run *httpd* as yourself). In this case, you must use a port numbered 1024 or above. For example, if we specify

```
Port 2112
```

then we may run *httpd* as a regular user. In this case, HTTP URLs to this machine must be specified as

```
http://www.veggie.org:2112/...
```

If no port number is given in the URL (as is the usual case), port 80 is assumed.

srm.conf

srm.conf is the Server Resource Map file. It configures a number of facilities provided by the server—for example, the directory where HTML documents will be stored on your system, or what directory the various CGI binaries may be located in. Let's walk through a sample *srm.conf*.

```
# The directory where HTML documents will be held.
DocumentRoot /usr/local/html_docs
# Personal directory for each user where HTML documents will be held.

UserDir public_html
```

Here, we specify the DocumentRoot directory, where documents to be provided via HTTP will be stored. These documents are written in IITML, the HyperText Markup Language. This markup language is discussed in the section "Writing HTML Documents." For example, if someone were to access the URL

```
http://www.veggie.org/fruits.html
```

the actual file accessed would be */usr/local/html_docs/fruits.html*.

The UserDir directive specifies a directory that each user may create in his or her
home directory for storing public HTML files. For example, if we were to use the
URL

```
http://www.veggie.org/~mdw/linux-info.html
```

the actual file accessed would be *~mdw/public_html/linux-info.html*.

```
# If a URL is received with a directory but no filename, retrieve this
# file as the index (if it exists).
DirectoryIndex index.html


# Turn on 'fancy' directory indexes
FancyIndexing on
```

Here, we enable the indexing features of *httpd*. In this case, if a client attempts to
access a directory URL, the file *index.html* in that directory is returned, if it exists.
Otherwise, *httpd* will generate a "fancy" index, with icons representing various file
types. Figure 7-8 shows an example of such an index.

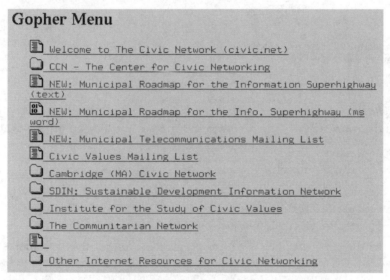

Figure 7–8. Gopher directory with fancy index icons in Mosaic

Icons are assigned using the AddIcon directive, as seen here:

```
# Set up various icons for use with fancy indexes, by filename
# E.g., we use DocumentRoot/icons/movie.xbm for files ending in .mpg and .qt
AddIcon /icons/movie.xbm .mpg
AddIcon /icons/back.xbm ..
AddIcon /icons/menu.xbm ^^DIRECTORY^^
AddIcon /icons/blank.xbm ^^BLANKICON^^
DefaultIcon /icons/unknown.xbm
```

The icon filenames (such as */icons/movie.xbm*) are relative to `DocumentRoot` by default. (There are other ways to specify pathnames to documents and icons—for example, by using aliases. This is discussed below.) There is also an `AddIconBy-Type` directive, which will let you specify an icon for a document based on the document's MIME type. See the section "An aside: MIME types" for more information about this.

The optional `ReadmeName` and `HeaderName` directives specify the names of files to be included in the index generated by *httpd*.

```
ReadmeName README
HeaderName HEADER
```

Here, if the file *README.html* exists in the current directory, it will be appended to the index. The file *README* will be appended if *README.html* does not exist. Likewise, *HEADER.html* or *HEADER* will be included at the top of the index generated by *httpd*. You can use these files to describe the contents of a particular directory when an index is requested by the client.

```
# Local access filename
AccessFileName .htaccess

# Default MIME type for documents
DefaultType text/plain
```

The `AccessFileName` directive specifies the name of the *local access file* for each directory. (This is described below, along with the discussion about the *access.conf* file.) The `DefaultType` directive specifies the MIME type for documents not listed in *mime.types*. This is described further in the section "An aside: MIME types."

```
# Set location of icons
Alias /icons/ /usr/local/html/icons/

# Set location of CGI binaries
ScriptAlias /cgi-bin/ /usr/local/html/cgi-bin/
```

The `Alias` directive specifies a pathname alias for any of the documents listed in *srm.conf*, or accessed by a URL. Earlier, we used the `AddIcon` directive to set icon names using pathnames such as */icons/movie.xbm*. Here, we specify that the pathname */icons/* should be translated to */usr/local/html/icons/*. Therefore, the various icon files should be stored in the latter directory. You can use `Alias` to set aliases for other pathnames as well.

The `ScriptAlias` directive is similar in nature, but sets the actual location of CGI scripts on the system. Here, we wish to store scripts in the directory */usr/local/html/cgi-bin/*. Any time a URL is used with a leading directory component of */cgi-bin/*, it will be translated into the actual directory name. More information on CGI and scripts is included in the section "Writing the CGI script."

access.conf

The last configuration file that requires your immediate attention is *access.conf*, which is the global access configuration file for *httpd*. It specifies which files may be accessed, and in what ways. You may also have a per-directory access configuration file if you require greater specificity. (Recall that we used the `AccessFile-Name` directive in *srm.conf* to set the local access file for each directory to *.htaccess*.)

Here is a sample *access.conf* file. It consists of a number of <Directory> items, each of which specifies the options and attributes for a particular directory.

```
# Set options for the cgi-bin script directory.
<Directory /usr/local/html/cgi-bin>
Options Indexes FollowSymLinks
</Directory>
```

Here, we specify that the CGI script directory should have the access options `Indexes` and `FollowSymLinks`. There are a number of access options available. These include:

`FollowSymLinks`

Symbolic links in this directory should be followed to retrieve the documents they point to.

`SymLinkIfOwnerMatch`

Similar to `FollowSymLinks`, but follow only if the owner of the symbolic link and its target are identical.

`ExecCGI`

Allow the execution of CGI scripts from this directory.

`Indexes`

Allow indexes to be generated from this directory.

`None`

Disable all options for this directory.

`All`

Enable all options for this directory.

There are other options as well; see the *httpd* documentation for details.

Below, we enable several options and other attributes for */usr/local/html*, the directory containing our HTML documents.

```
<Directory /usr/local/html>

Options Indexes FollowSymLinks

# Allow the local access file, .htaccess, to override any attributes
# listed here
```

```
AllowOverride All

# Access restrictions for documents in this directory
<Limit GET>
order allow,deny
allow from all
</Limit>

</Directory>
```

Here, we turn on the `Indexes` and `FollowSymLinks` options for this directory. The `AllowOverride` option allows the local access file in each directory (*.htaccess*, set in *srm.conf*) to override any of the attributes given here. The *.htaccess* file has the same format as the global *access.conf*, but applies only to the directory in which it is located. This way, we can specify attributes for particular directories by including a *.htaccess* file in those directories, instead of listing the attributes in the global file.

The primary use for local access files is to allow individual users to set the access permissions for personal HTML directories (such as ~/*public_html*) themselves without having to ask the system administrator to modify the global access file. There are security issues associated with this, however. For example, a user might enable access permissions in his or her own directory such that any client can run expensive server-side CGI scripts. By disabling the `AllowOverride` feature, users will not be able to get around the access attributes specified in the global *access.conf.* This can be done by using

```
AllowOverride None
```

which effectively disables local *.htaccess* files.

The `<Limit GET>` field is used to specify access rules for clients attempting to retrieve documents from this server. In this case, we specify `order allow,deny`, which means that `allow` rules should be evaluated before `deny` rules. We then instate the rule `allow from all`, which simply means any host may retrieve documents from the server. If you wish to deny access from a particular machine or domain, you could add the line

```
deny from .nuts.com biffnet.biffs-house.us
```

The first entry denies access from all sites in the **nuts.com** domain. The second denies access from the site **biffnet.biffs-house.us**.

Starting httpd

Now you're ready to run *httpd*, allowing your machine to service HTTP URLs. As mentioned previously, you can run *httpd* from *inetd* or as a standalone server. Here, we describe how to run *httpd* in standalone mode.

All that's required to start *httpd* is to run the command

```
httpd -f configuration-file
```

where *configuration-file* is the pathname of *httpd.conf.* For example:

```
/etc/httpd/httpd -f /etc/httpd/conf/httpd.conf
```

will start up *httpd*, with configuration files found in */etc/httpd/conf.*

Watch the *httpd* error logs (the location of which is given in *httpd.conf*) for any errors that might occur when trying to start up the server, or when accessing documents. Remember that you must run *httpd* as **root** if it is to use a port numbered 1023 or less. Once you have *httpd* working to your satisfaction, you can start it automatically at boot time by including the appropriate *httpd* command line in one of your system *rc* files, such as */etc/rc.d/rc.local.*

Before you can request documents via HTTP from your Web client, you'll need to write them. This is the subject of the next section.

Writing HTML Documents

Documents requested by HTTP may be in several forms. These forms include images, PostScript files, sounds, MPEG movies, and so forth. The *mime.types* configuration file describes the document types that *httpd* understands.

The most common type of document serviced by HTTP is a HyperText Markup Language (HTML) file. HTML documents support text, links to other documents, inline images, and so forth. Most documents that you'll see on the Web are written in HTML.

HTML is surprisingly easy to learn. With the tutorial included here, you should be on your way to writing HTML documents and providing information to the Web in less than an hour.

Many tools allow you to convert other markup languages (such as LATEX, Microsoft RTF, and so forth) to HTML, and vice-versa. If you have particularly long documents in another formatting language that you wish to provide on the Web, it might be easier to convert them automatically to HTML, or provide a PostScript or DVI image of the documents instead.

The canonical source for HTML information is the URL

```
http://www.ncsa.uiuc.edu/General/Internet/WWW/HTMLPrimer.html
```

[19] Mosaic

which is a Beginner's Guide to writing HTML documents. Here, we'll present the essentials of HTML to get you up to speed. *The Mosaic Handbook for the X Window System* also contains a tutorial on HTML.

HTML basics

If you're used to other formatting languages such as TEX, HTML will appear to be quite simple in comparison. Here is a minimal HTML document:

```
<title>Ye Olde Generic HTML Document</title>
<h1>Writing HTML for Fun and Profit</h1>

Although writing HTML documents may not be a common source
of income, <em>authors</em> tend to bend the rules in this
respect.

<p> The advantage? It's really too easy for words.
```

Chapter 5

Within HTML documents, *elements* are denoted by a <tag>...</tag> pair.[*]

As you can see, we begin the document with

```
<title>Ye Olde Generic HTML Document</title>
```

which defines the title for this document. Immediately following the title is an <h1> element, which is a top-level heading. Under NCSA Mosaic for X, the title will generally appear in the *Document Title* window, and the heading within the document itself.

All HTML documents must have a title, but headings are, of course, optional. To HTML, a heading is just a portion of text that is set in a larger and/or bolder font. It has no bearing on the actual document structure.

HTML supports six levels of headings:

```
<h1>First-level heading</h1>
<h2>Second-level heading</h2>
...
<h6>Sixth-level heading</h6>
```

Following the heading is the body of the document. As you can see, we use the <em> tag to emphasize text:

```
...of income, <em>authors</em> tend to bend the rules in this...
```

Paragraphs are separated with a <p> tag. HTML ignores blank lines and indentation in the document. Therefore, to skip a line and begin a new paragraph, using <p> is necessary (unlike TEX, for example, which causes paragraph breaks at blank lines).

---

* HTML is really an SGML (Standard Generalized Markup Language) DTD. SGML defines the <tag>...</tag> conventions. See the section "Using Multimedia on Linux" in Chapter 5.

Viewing the document

Before we go much further with HTML, let's describe how to look at your first work of hypertext art. Most WWW browsers will allow you to open a local HTML document and view it. For example, under NCSA Mosaic, selecting *Open Local* from the *File* menu will allow you to view an HTML file. Other browsers, such as Lynx, provide similar mechanisms. You should first save your HTML document in a file (such as *sample.html*) and view it with your WWW browser.

When viewed in NCSA Mosaic, our sample document will look like Figure 7-9. As you can see, Mosaic does the actual "text formatting" for you—all that is required on your end is to write the document and point your Web browser at it.

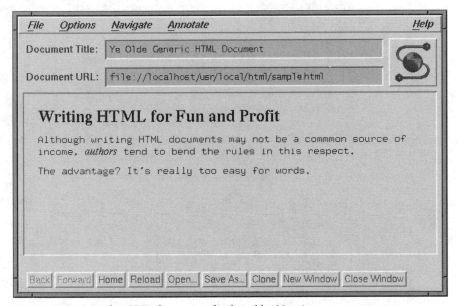

Figure 7–9. Sample HTML document displayed by Mosaic

It's also quite easy to make your new HTML documents available via the Web. Assuming that you have configured *httpd* as described in the previous section, you can place the HTML file in the *httpd* DocumentRoot directory (in our case, this was */usr/local/html*).

Therefore, assuming the above document is saved as */usr/local/html/sample.html*, and *httpd* is running on your system, anyone can access the document by opening the URL

```
http://www.veggie.org/sample.html
```

with a WWW browser.[*]

---

[*] Of course, substituting your own hostname for **www.veggie.org**.

Note that you can create directories, symbolic links, and so forth within the Docu-mentRoot directory. Any HTTP URLs to your system will access filenames that are relative to DocumentRoot. So if we create the directory */usr/local/html/my-docs* and place *sample.html* there, the corresponding URL is

```
http://www.veggie.org/my-docs/sample.html
```

Using links

In order to refer to other documents, or sections within the same document, *links* are used within the HTML source. For example,

```
<p> You can find more information about HTML
<a href="http://info.cern.ch/hypertext/WWW/MarkUp/MarkUp.html"> here </a>.
```

Within Mosaic, this sentence will look like Figure 7-10.

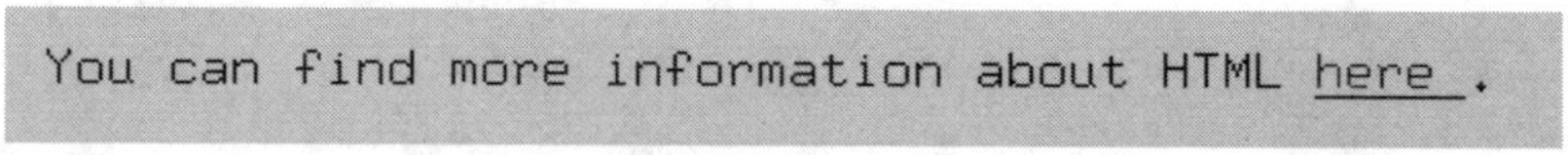

```
You can find more information about HTML here .
```

Figure 7–10. Link displayed by Mosaic

The word "here" is highlighted, indicating that it is a link. Clicking on the link within Mosaic will retrieve the document pointed to by the URL

```
http://info.cern.ch/hypertext/WWW/MarkUp/MarkUp.html
```

The <a> element is known as an *anchor*—it specifies a link that is associated with a particular region of text (in this case, the word "here").

This is what is known as an *absolute link*. That is, the URL includes the complete machine and pathname specification. For documents on the same machine, you should use *relative links*, such as

```
<p> You can also access the <a href="gardening.html">Vegetable Gardening
    Home Page</a>.
```

URL names in relative links are relative to the directory in which the current HTML document is located. The *type* of URL (e.g., *http*, *ftp*, and so on) is assumed to be identical to that of the URL of the current document. That is, if the above text is found within the document

```
http://www.veggie.org/my-docs/sample.html
```

then the link points to the URL

```
http://www.veggie.org/my-docs/gardening.html
```

If the filename used in a relative link begins with a slash (/), as in

```
Click <a href="/info/veggie.html">here</a> for more information.
```

then the URL is assumed to be relative to the DocumentRoot directory. In this case, the URL is equivalent to

```
http://www.veggie.org/info/veggie.html
```

Relative links can also point to the parent directory, as in:

```
<a href="../plants/plants.html">Here</a> is more about plants.
```

The use of relative links is very important for documents that are related. They will allow you to rearrange the directory hierarchy of HTML files without rendering all of your links obsolete. However, when accessing unrelated documents on the same system, it might be best to use an absolute link. In this way, the location of your document does not depend on the location of others on the same system.

You can also use links to refer to sections within the same document. For example, the link

```
See <a href="#Genetics">below</a> for information on
genetically-engineered vegetables.
```

will refer to the location within the current document, tagged as so:

```
<a name="Genetics">
<h1>Genetically Engineered Vegetables: Our Specialty</h1> </a>
```

Here, the anchor uses the name option, instead of href. In addition, the text within the anchor is the entire heading name. It's not required that you use headings as name anchors, but it usually makes sense to do so when you want to have cross-references to other "sections" of the document. For instance, when a user selects the link pointing to this anchor, they will see the section heading

Genetically Engineered Vegetables: Our Specialty

at the top of the Mosaic document window.

Links can also refer to particular locations within other documents. For example:

```
<a href="tomatoes.html#Genetics">Here</a> is more information on
our mutated tomatoes.
```

refers to the section labeled with <a name="Genetics"> in the document *tomatoes.html.*

As you might guess, you are not limited to making links to other HTML documents. Links can point to image files, sounds, PostScript files, as well as other URL types such as FTP, Gopher, or WAIS services. In short, any valid URL can serve as a link. For example:

```
Click <a href="ftp://ftp.veggie.org/pub/">here</a> to access our
anonymous FTP archive.
```

provides a link to the named FTP URL.

An aside: MIME types

When you link to images or sounds, the range of valid image and sound types that you may use depends on the abilities of the client. For example, when accessing the URL

```
http://www.veggie.org/pics/artichoke.gif
```

the WWW client will be responsible for running a separate program to display the image. However, the server providing the image must be able to tell the client what type of data the incoming image is. This is handled by the *mime.types* file, in the *httpd* configuration directory. This file contains lines such as

```
image/gif                gif
image/jpeg               jpeg jpg jpe
audio/basic              au snd
application/postscript   ai eps ps
text/html                html
text/plain               txt
```

The first field in each line defines the MIME type name for the document in question. MIME stands for *Multipurpose Internet Mail Extensions*. As the named suggests, it was originally developed for electronic mail. It is a standard for transporting documents that contain data other than plain printable ASCII text.

The remaining fields indicate filename extensions that the MIME type corresponds to. In this case, any filenames ending in *.gif* are treated as image/gif type documents.

When the client (say, NCSA Mosaic) retrieves a document, it also gets information on the MIME type associated with it from the server. In this way, the client knows how to deal with the document. For text/html documents, NCSA Mosaic will simply format the HTML source text and display it in the document window. For image/gif documents, Mosaic will run a separate image viewer, such as *xv*. Similarly, application/postscript documents are viewed using Ghostview, on most UNIX systems.

How individual MIME types are dealt with is up to the Web client. NCSA Mosaic provides an option that allows you to specify a program to be run to process documents of a particular type.

This is the purpose of the `DefaultType` directive used in the *srm.conf* file. We use:

```
DefaultType    text/plain
```

If the server is unable to determine the type of document, it will assume `text/plain`, which is used for unformatted text files. NCSA Mosaic displays these text files in a constant-width font in the document window.

Inline images

One of the nicer features provided by HTML is the ability to include images directly in the document. This is accomplished with the `<img>` element:

```
<img src="pics/logo.gif"> Our stylish logo, in full color.
```

This will embed the image pointed to by the relative URL `pics/logo.gif` in the document, as seen in Figure 7-11. Absolute URLs can be used with `<img>` as well.

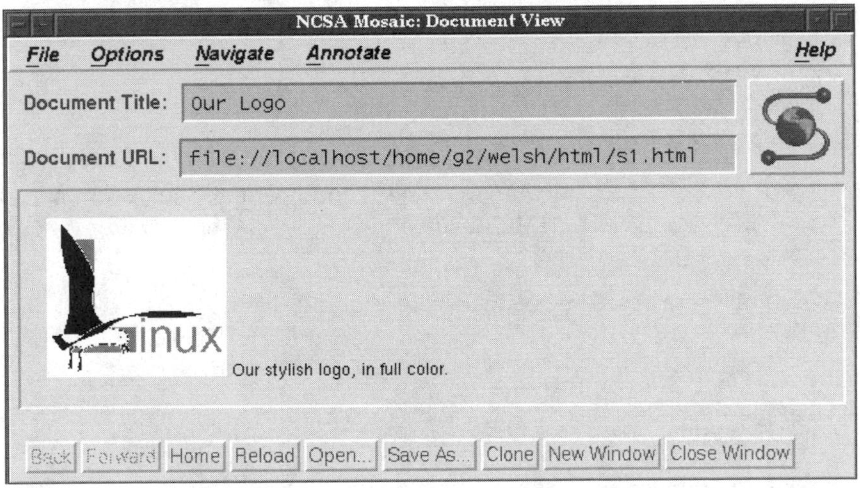

Figure 7-11. Image displayed by Mosaic

In theory, the `<img>` element can be used to embed "any" document into the current one. However, it is most commonly used for small images. The kind of images that can be inlined depends on the particular browser being used. GIF and X Bitmap format images seem to be universally accepted. However, note that not all clients are capable of displaying inline images—most notably text-based clients such as Lynx.

You can also use `<img>` within an anchor, as in:

```
<a href="zucchini.html">
<img src="pics/zuke.gif"> Zucchinis (also known as Courgettes) </a>
```

Both image and text will be included in the anchor, as seen in Figure 7-12. Selecting either will access the URL *zucchini.html.*

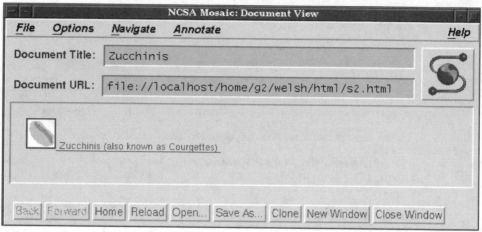

Figure 7-12. Image and link displayed by Mosaic

More HTML features

Obviously, you need much more than section headings, links, and inline images to write nicely-formatted HTML documents. HTML provides many other text layout features.

A numbered list can be obtained with the `<ol>` element, using `<li>` for each item in the list.

```
Zucchinis have the following nice features:
<ol>
<li> They're green.
<li> They're crunchy.
<li> They taste great in salads.
</ol>
```

This list will appear as shown in Figure 7-13 when formatted by Mosaic.

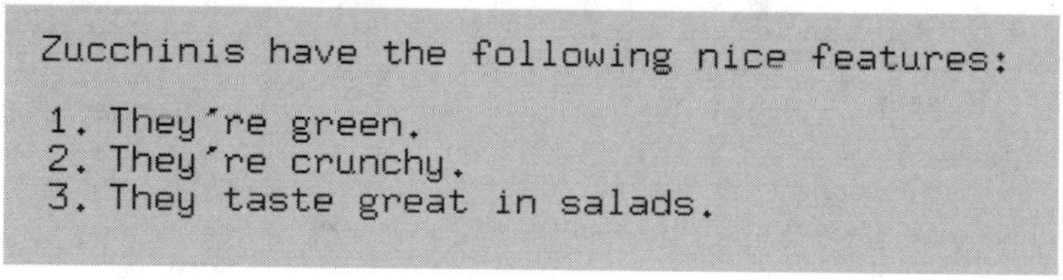

```
Zucchinis have the following nice features:

1. They're green.
2. They're crunchy.
3. They taste great in salads.
```

Figure 7-13. List displayed by Mosaic

An unnumbered list can be obtained by using <ul> in place of <ol>. Unnumbered list items are marked with bullets, instead of incremental numbers.

Lists can be nested as well. When unnumbered lists are nested, the bullet style usually changes at each level, as in Figure 7-14. The HTML source used to produce this list is:

```
Here is an example of a nested list.
<ul>
<li> The first item.
<li> The second item.
    <ul>
    <li> The first nested item.
    <li> Another item.
        <ul>
        <li> Yet another level of nesting.
        </ul>
    </ul>
</ul>
```

The indentation used is strictly to make the source easier to read; feel free to use whatever indentation style you deem appropriate.

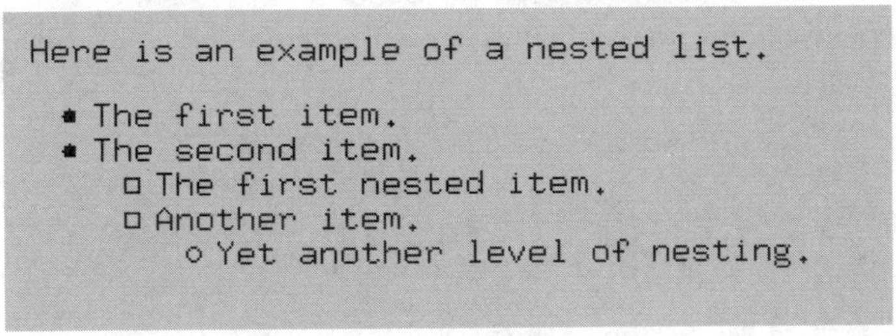

Figure 7-14. Nested lists displayed by Mosaic

Various types of text emphasis are available. We've already seen <em>, which usually causes words to be placed in italics. Note that how these items are displayed depends entirely on the client. The most commonly-used emphasis tags are:

<em>   Emphasized text, usually rendered as italics.

<code>   Program source code, usually rendered in a constant-width font.

<samp>   Sample output from a program, also in constant-width.

<kbd>   User keyboard input.

<strong>   For strong emphasis, usually in boldface.

Here is an example that uses several of these elements.

```
<p> <em>Amazing</em>, she thought. The <kbd>find</kbd> command can be
used for almost <strong>anything!</strong>
```

This is displayed within Mosaic as seen in Figure 7-15.

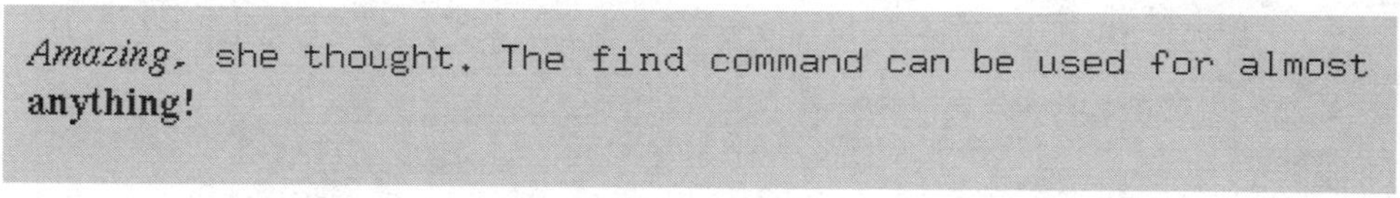

Amazing, she thought. The find command can be used for almost
anything!

Figure 7–15. Fonts displayed by Mosaic

Note that <code>, <samp>, and <kbd> are all usually displayed as a constant-width typewriter font. However, it is important to distinquish between different types of *logical* emphasis in documents. In this way, we can change the typeface used to display <kbd> items (for example, to a slanted font), but allow <code> and <samp> to remain the same.

HTML also provides the <b>, <i>, and <tt> tags to produce boldface, italics, and constant-width text, respectively, should you wish to specify fonts directly.

The <pre> element allows you to include "preformatted" or "verbatim" text within an HTML document.

```
The source code for <code>hello.c</code> is as follows.
<pre>
#include &lt;stdio.h&gt;

void main() {
  printf("Hello, world!");
}
</pre>
```

This text will be displayed as seen in Figure 7-16.

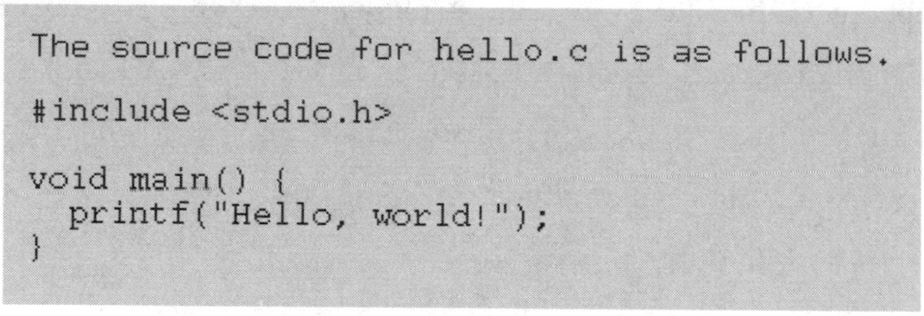

```
The source code for hello.c is as follows.

#include <stdio.h>

void main() {
  printf("Hello, world!");
}
```

Figure 7–16. Preformatted text displayed by Mosaic

Note the use of < to obtain <, and > to obtain >. This is necessary because the < and > characters have a special meaning within HTML documents. Even within a <pre> element, this is necessary.

Other special characters are available as well, including:

"   To obtain a double-quote: "

&   To obtain an ampersand: &

é   To obtain an acute-accented *e*: é

ö   To obtain an *o*-umlaut: ö

The complete HTML specification, located at

    http://info.cern.ch/hypertext/WWW/MarkUp/MarkUp.html

lists all of the available codes.

You'll often seen a horizontal rule used in HTML documents to visually divide the page. This is obtained with the <hr> element, as so:

```
All right, I dare you to cross this line:
<p><hr>
<p> All right, I dare you to cross this one:
<p><hr>
```

Finally, the <address> element is often used at the end of HTML documents to specify the name and address of the author, or maintainer, of the page. For example,

```
<p><hr><p>
<address>Mr. P. Head, potatoe@veggie.org</address>
```

Many people link the name within the <address> item to a personal home page.

Finding out more

There are many other sources of HTML information on the Web—in fact, HTML is all around you. The *On HTML...* item from the NCSA Mosaic *Help* menu will take you to the aforementioned HTML Primer. This page has links to other HTML information as well.

Within Mosaic, you can view the HTML source for any document on the Web. While viewing the document in question, select the *View Source* option from the *File* menu. This will give you an inside look at how the page was written. The Lynx Web browser provides a similar option, in the form of the backslash (\) command.

Building Interactive Forms

As mentioned in previous sections, Mosaic and NCSA *httpd* include support for *forms*, which allow the user to provide input (in the form of text entry fields, buttons, menus, and so forth) to a script, executed on the server. For example, one fill-out form might include a text field for entering a username. Submitting the form would cause the server to run a *finger* script, displaying the output as an HTML document.

The ability to use forms depends on the capabilities of both the WWW client and *httpd* server. Not all Web clients can view forms; in general, NCSA Mosaic version 2.0 or later is needed. Also, not all implementations of *httpd* understand forms. We suggest using NCSA *httpd*, discussed earlier in this chapter, which provides extensive forms support.

The canonical example of an interactive form is one in which users can send electronic mail to the maintainer of the form page. In this section, through the use of this example, we'll demonstrate how to write forms and the server scripts that are executed by them.

The form HTML document

The first step in building a form is to write an HTML document which corresponds to the form itself. These HTML pages contain a <form> element, which in turn contains several other elements denoting buttons, text entry fields, and so forth.

For an in-depth discussion of the HTML specification for fill-out forms, see the URL

    http://www.ncsa.uiuc.edu/SDG/Software/Mosaic/Docs/fill-out-forms/overview.html

Here, we present a small cross-section of what forms can do. For an extensive example of forms use, see the URL

    http://www.cm.cf.ac.uk/Movies/moviequery.html

which is a comprehensive database of information on over 30,000 movies, allowing you to search by title, genre, actors, directors, and so forth.

Here is the HTML document for our simple mail form:

```
1   <title>Ye Olde Generic Mail Form</title>
2   <h1>Send mail to me</h1>
3   <p>You can use this form to send me mail.
4
5   <p><hr><p>
6   <form method="POST" action="/cgi-bin/mailer.pl">
7   <input name="from"> Your email address<p>
8   <input name="subject"> Subject<p>
9   <input type=hidden name="to" value="mdw@veggie.org">
10  <hr>
```

```
11 Enter message body below:<br>
12 <hr>
13 <textarea name="body" cols=60 rows=12></textarea><p>
14 <hr>
15 <input type=submit value="Send mail"><p>
16 </form>
```

When viewed within NCSA Mosaic, this form looks like Figure 7-17.

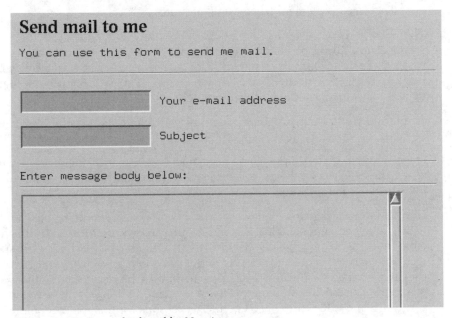

Figure 7-17. Form displayed by Mosaic

As you can see, the form uses several new features of HTML. Let's walk through the file and describe them all.

Line 6 uses the <form> element, which encloses the entire form itself. There are several options, or attributes, associated with the <form> element.

The method attribute specifies the means by which form information is sent to the server script. Valid methods are GET and POST. The GET method passes information as command-line arguments to the server script; the POST method passes information to the script's standard input. This option has bearing only on how you implement your server script; for various reasons it's strongly suggested that you use the POST method.

The action attribute specifies the URL of the script that this form will execute on the server. Recall that CGI scripts are usually stored in the *cgi-bin* subdirectory of the *httpd* ServerRoot directory.

Here, we specify that the script

```
/cgi-bin/mailer.pl
```

should be executed when the form is submitted. The next section will describe how to write this script.

Lines 7–9 use the `<input>` element. This is the most common element found within a form—it specifies some kind of input item, such as a text field, button, or checkbox. The `<input>` element has several attributes.

The `name` attribute specifies a unique string used to identify this element to the server script. The `type` attribute specifies the type of input element. Its value can be `text`, `radio`, `checkbox`, `password`, `submit`, `reset`, or `hidden`. If no `type` is specified (as on lines 7 and 8), `text` is the default. The `value` attribute specifies the default value associated with this input item.

Several other attributes for `input` are also available; these set the maximum length of input for text entry fields, and so forth.

Lines 7 and 8 define input elements named `"from"` and `"subject"`, both of type `text`. These text entry fields will be used to enter the sender's email address and the subject of the message.

Line 9 defines a `hidden` element named `"to"`, which sets the email address that mail should be sent to. This is a "trick" that allows us to specify the recipient's email address within the HTML form itself. Otherwise, we'd have to specify the recipient address within the server script (*mailer.pl*), which would require each user that wished to use the mail form to have a private copy of the script. This way, any user on the system can use the script, as long as he specifies his own address as the value of the `"to"` item. The reasons for this will become clear in the next section, where we discuss the *mailer.pl* script itself.

On line 13, we use the `<textarea>` element. This element denotes a multiline text entry field, with scrollbars on the right and bottom edges. As with `<input>`, the `name` attribute is used to name the element. The `cols` and `rows` attributes are used to set the size of the `textarea`.

Note that unlike `<input>`, the `<textarea>` element has a corresponding `</textarea>` end-tag on the same line. Any text that appears between `<textarea>` and `</textarea>` is used as the default contents of the entry field.

On line 15, we use another `<input>` element, of type `submit`. This defines a button which, when pressed, submits the form and runs the server script associated with it. The `value` attribute is used to specify the text of the button as displayed; in this case, it is `"Send mail"`.

Finally, on line 16, we end the form with a `</form>` end-tag.

Multiple forms can be used within a single HTML document; however, you cannot nest one `<form>` within another.

Writing the CGI script

Scripts executed by forms use the CGI (Common Gateway Interface) convention, which specifies how data is passed from the form to the script. At this point, it is not important to understand the details of the CGI specification; however, you should be aware that data is passed to scripts as a set of name/value pairs. For example, given our sample form, let's say that the user entered the address

```
bsmarks@norelco.com
```

in the "from" <input> field. The value bsmarks@norelco.com would then be associated with the name "from" when passed to the script.

As mentioned above, the mechanism by which these name/value pairs are passed to the server script depends upon the form method (GET or POST) used. In general, name/value pairs are encoded in the form

```
action?name=val&name=val&...
```

and passed to the server script either on the command line (in the case of GET-method forms) or as standard input (in the case of POST-method forms). In addition, certain characters (such as =, &, and so on) must be escaped, and several environment variables are used to pass certain parameters to the script.

Server scripts can be written in practically any language, such as C, Perl, or even shell scripts. Because decoding the name/value pairs within a C program can be a bit harrowing, we instead show how to implement a script in Perl, whose text-processing facilities are more suited for this task. The NCSA *httpd* distribution includes C source code for a number of sample CGI scripts. These can be found in the *cgi-src* subdirectory of the server.

Example 7-2 is the Perl script *mailer.pl.*

Example 7-2: CGI Script to Parse Mail Message

```
#!/usr/local/bin/perl

require "cgi.pl"; # Get CGI-parsing routines

# Parse form data
&ReadParse;

# Print header of output (in HTML form)
print STDOUT "Content-type: text/html\n\n";
print STDOUT "<title>Mail form results</title>";
print STDOUT "<h1>Mail form results</h1>";

open (MAIL,"|/usr/lib/sendmail $to") ||
   die "<p>Error: Couldn't execute sendmail.\n";

print MAIL "To: $in{'to'}\n";
```

Example 7–2: CGI Script to Parse Mail Message (continued)

```
print MAIL "From: $in{'from'}\n";
print MAIL "subject: $in{'subject'}\n\n";
print MAIL "$in{'body'}\n";
close MAIL;

print STDOUT "<p>All right, mailed the following to <tt>$to</tt>:\n";
print STDOUT "<p><pre>";
print STDOUT "To: $in{'to'}\n";
print STDOUT "From: $in{'from'}\n";
print STDOUT "subject: $in{'subject'}\n\n";
print STDOUT "$in{'body'}\n";
print STDOUT "</pre>";
```

Chapter 6

If you're new to Perl, refer to the introduction given in Chapter 6, *Programming with Linux*. However, you need not be a Perl wizard to follow this code.

This script first loads the routines in *cgi.pl* (given below), which includes the Read-Parse subroutine. ReadParse reads the name/value pairs from the form, and places them into an associative array named %in. (It also places each *name=val* pair into the linear array @in.) For example, if we wish to obtain the value of the "from" entry item, we can access the variable

```
$in{'from'}
```

After calling ReadParse, *mailer.pl* prints several strings to standard output. Note that CGI scripts output their data in HTML format (although this is not strictly necessary). The first line printed by the script should read

```
Content-type: text/html
```

This is to inform the server of the MIME type of data coming from the script.

The script then opens a pipe to */usr/lib/sendmail* with which to send the mail message. (If you use a mail handler other than *sendmail* on your system, this should be modified.) We then pass the message to *sendmail*, prefixing it with an appropriate header containing the To:, From:, and Subject: fields derived from the data given on the form.

After closing the pipe to *sendmail*, we print the message as sent to standard output to allow the user to verify that the message was processed correctly.

The file *cgi.pl* contains the ReadParse routine. It is shown in Example 7-3.

Example 7–3: CGI Script for Parsing WWW Forms

```
#!/usr/local/bin/perl

# Routines for parsing CGI forms data within Perl
# Derived from code by Steven E. Brenner, <S.E.Brenner@bioc.cam.ac.uk>
# Copyright 1993 Steven E. Brenner
```

Example 7–3: CGI Script for Parsing WWW Forms (continued)

```perl
# Permission granted to use and modify this library so long as the
# copyright above is maintained, modifications are documented, and
# credit is given for any use of the library.

# ReadParse
# Reads in GET or POST data, converts it to unescaped text, and puts
# one key=value in each member of the list "@in"
# Also creates key/value pairs in %in, using '\0' to separate multiple
# selections.

# If a variable-glob parameter (e.g., *cgi_input) is passed to ReadParse,
# information is stored there, rather than in $in, @in, and %in.

sub ReadParse {
    if (@_) {
        local (*in) = @_;
    }

    local ($i, $loc, $key, $val);

    # Read in text
    if ($ENV{'REQUEST_METHOD'} eq "GET") {
        $in = $ENV{'QUERY_STRING'};
    } elsif ($ENV{'REQUEST_METHOD'} eq "POST") {
        for ($i = 0; $i < $ENV{'CONTENT_LENGTH'}; $i++) {
            $in .= getc;
        }
    }

    @in = split(/&/,$in);

    foreach $i (0 .. $#in) {
        # Convert plus's to spaces
        $in[$i] =~ s/\+/ /g;

        # Convert %XX from hex numbers to alphanumeric
        $in[$i] =~ s/%(..)/pack("c",hex($1))/ge;

        # Split into key and value.
        $loc = index($in[$i],"=");
        $key = substr($in[$i],0,$loc);
        $val = substr($in[$i],$loc+1);
        $in{$key} .= '\0' if (defined($in{$key})); # \0 is the multiple separator
        $in{$key} .= $val;
    }
    return 1;

}
1; #return true
```

This code takes care of the mundane aspects of processing input from forms—splitting the name/value pairs, loading them into arrays, conversion of special characters, and so forth. You need not completely understand this code to use it effectively.

Keep in mind that there are always security issues at work when dealing with HTML-based forms. Be certain that your scripts cannot be used to execute unauthorized processes on your system. If your server scripts are CPU-intensive, you might want to limit access to them to prevent heavy system load. In general, be sure that you know what you're doing when providing forms on your WWW server.

Electronic Mail

Electronic mail (email) is one of the most desirable features of a computer system. You can send and receive email on your Linux system locally between users on the host and between hosts on a network. You have to set up three classes of software to provide email service. These are the mail user agent or mailer, the mail transport agent (MTA), and the transport protocol.

The mailer provides the user interface for displaying mail, writing new messages, and filing messages away. Linux offers you many choices for mailers. They are always being improved, and a particular mailer may provide features such as the ability to serve as a newsreader, or to serve as a World Wide Web hypertext document browser.

The mailer relies on the MTA to route mail from one user to another, whether locally or across systems. The MTA in turn uses a transport protocol, usually either UUCP or SMTP (Simple Mail Transport Protocol), to provide the medium for mail transfer.

You have a number of software choices for setting up email on a Linux host. We can't describe all the available email solutions, but we do describe how to set up one practical solution. We document what we think is the most popular Linux solution at this time: the Elm mailer (version 2.4 at the time of this writing) with the *smail* (*smail3.1*) mail transport agent. These are relatively simple to configure but provide all the features that most users need. For the sake of simplicity, we assume that your Linux host is connected to a mail host that is fully capable of Internet mail routing.

The smail Mail Transport Agent

There are two major mail transport agents (MTAs) available on Linux, *smail* and *sendmail*. They both support the SMTP and UUCP protocols for handling mail. The *sendmail* package has been around for a long time. It is generally considered somewhat more difficult to use than *smail*, but it is thoroughly documented in the book *sendmail*, by Costales, Allman, and Rickert. The *smail* package is reportedly easier to configure and manage than *sendmail*, and is perhaps more robust on systems with limited memory. It is very popular on Linux. We've decided to go with the most popular Linux MTA, *smail*, and describe its essential configuration and use here. However, if you need to configure a mail host that has many connections and handles lots of mail, you really need to use *sendmail*.

smail can be invoked in many modes by a specific invocation name that establishes its special uses. For example, *smail* can be invoked as *rmail*, and it replaces the original *rmail* in that function. It can be invoked as a daemon process (*smtpd*, *in.smtpd*) and also replaces other mail utilities, such as *mailq*. *smail* is compatible with the *sendmail* MTA and interfaces satisfactorily with it.

Olaf Kirsch's *Linux Network Administrator's Guide* provides information specific to installing *smail* on Linux hosts. Also, the *smail3* package has an excellent guide to installing and maintaining *smail*, entitled *Smail—Installation and Administration Guide*, by Karr and Noll. Finally, you should also print out the manual pages for *smail*, which describe in detail all the configuration files and directories that *smail* uses.

The *smail* package is bundled with some Linux distributions. On the distributions that bundle *smail*, most use the Linux installation script to perform basic configuration of *smail* as well. One problem with this approach is that you probably will need to periodically update your *smail* installation, and there is no convenient script to do this unless you reinstall Linux at the same time. Another problem is that some major Linux distributions seem to miss some detail or another in configuring the *smail* utilities, so that you need to go in and add a file link, edit a resource file, or something of the kind.

But take heart: even though patches are applied and features are added, your same old *smail* configuration files will almost always continue to work just fine. You usually only need to update your binaries to stay up-to-date.

That's the good news. The bad news is that different distributions of *smail* install the files in different places. If you grab a set of binaries from an FTP site and install it over your obsolete installation, you might find that you have one version of *smail* installed in */usr/bin* and another in */sbin*. Because *smail* is intended to function as a number of mail utilities through the use of file links, this kind of inconsistency can cause real problems with your installation.

If you build a distribution from scratch, though, you may find that it is a generic installation that isn't tailored for Linux. (However, a generic UNIX FTP site is likely to have the full set of documentation that seems to be missing from the Linux sites we've checked.)

What can you do? Well, if you take a distribution from a particular FTP site, it might help to stick with that site, even if it means you don't get the latest and greatest update at the earliest possible instant. This works particularly well if the site is a binary distribution site—your configuration files will be left untouched. Or you can just jump in and install updated files, and then use *find* or *whereis* to sort out tangled up links and duplicated files. In any case, you will likely find that even if your Linux installation script installed and configured *smail* correctly on your system, you don't like all the selected behaviors. If this is the case, often your best bet is to simply edit the *smail* configuration file for your system.

Getting and installing smail

An excellent FTP site that contains an up-to-date Linux binary distribution (at the time of this writing) is **qiclab.scn.rain.com**. The *smail* package can be found in */pub/network/smail/smail-linuxbin-3.1.29.tar.gz*. The specific filename will presumably change with each update to the source files, but the path will probably remain the same.

For a Linux source distribution of *smail*, we like the FTP site **ftp.cyberspace.com**. The distribution package is kept in */pub/unix/linux/slackware/contrib/smail.tgz* and must be gunzipped and untarred. To install this distribution:

1. FTP the file in binary mode.

2. Move the file to the Linux root directory, as */smail.tar.gz*.

3. Run *gunzip* on the file, which will result in a file named *smail.tar*.

4. Execute *tar –xvf smail.tar* on the file in the root directory. The *smail.tar* unpacks into a directory tree.

Chapter 4

The section "Archive and Compression Utilities" in Chapter 4 tells you all you need to know about *gunzip* and *tar*.

If you should run across a package called *smailcfg* when browsing an FTP site, you might think it is a configuration utility for *smail*. It is not; it is a configuration utility for *sendmail*.

Configuring a Linux-installed smail package

Some Linux distributions come with *smail* already packaged, and it is installed when you run the Linux installation program. Linux systems typically install the various parts of the *smail* package to the following directories: */bin, /usr/bin, /usr/lib/smail, /usr/man/man?*. The *smail* configuration may be stored in */var/lib/smail/config*.

Many of the variables that *smail* uses will be assigned based on information collected from the Linux configuration. If you installed Linux with TCP/IP, for example, *smail* will be configured to use SMTP with it. There are some *smail* variables that you will still need to set, however. These include:

postmaster

> Supply a user ID on the local system to be the postmaster. The mail adminis-
> trator on the system is normally the designated postmaster. It is almost a moral
> obligation of a system on an open network (with links beyond a LAN) to have
> a designated postmaster. If there is a problem with email on a system, any
> user (anywhere) should be able to send a message to postmaster@*hostname* to
> have it investigated. In the most rudimentary system, the postmaster can be
> the root user, but it is preferable for the mail for postmaster to be assigned to
> an ordinary user ID. (Some systems set up a "phony" account for the postmas-
> ter, so the duties can be rotated.)

smart_path

> This is an important variable to set, especially when you are a fledgling mail
> host. smart_path should be the name of the "smart host" to which your system
> routes all mail that it doesn't already know how to deliver. In the simplest
> setup, anything that isn't local mail is routed to the smart_path host you spec-
> ify. If you have a connection to an Internet host, it should be your smart host.

visible_name

> This variable specifies a name that *smail* will use as the return address for all
> mail sent by your host. For example, if your full hostname was **deus.x-
> machina.org** you might prefer the visible name to be **x-machina.org**. A user on
> the host **deus** would have his or her "From" address set to *user@x-
> machina.org* instead of *user@deus.x-machina.org*. This is especially useful if
> there are several hosts that users on the local net have accounts on, or if
> names of specific host systems in the domain change.

smart_user

> The smart_user isn't necessarily a user. You can leave smart_user with no
> value assigned, in which case any mail that cannot be delivered will be
> bounced (returned to sender). If you assign a user ID to be smart_user,
> improperly addressed mail sent to your system will be forwarded to the
> smart_user. Often, smart_user is the same user as postmaster, but for a small
> system, it is probably best to bounce the mail. smart_user is intended to allow
> manual rerouting of mail when a user moves, loses an account, etc. It has little
> use on a system with few users.

smail(5)

There are additional variables that you can set. The online manual page describes
them all in its discussion of the *config* file. Your distribution might not contain the
documents in printable form, but you should print your own if you need to, by
entering one of the following commands. (The first generates plain text for every
printer, the second assumes your default printer is a PostScript device.)

```
$ man 5 smail | col -b | lpr
$ gtroff -man /usr/man/man5/smail.5 | ghostscript | lpr
```

The Slackware distribution includes an *smail* configuration script that you can run
(as root, from the */usr/lib/smail* directory) to install a prepared Linux *smail* binary,

[3] Network
Admin Guide

if your Linux installation uses the same directories. This script has been used with other Linux *smail* distributions. The file is */usr/lib/smail/tools.linux/config.* You can retrieve it from a Slackware Linux FTP site or from any Linux site that has it. On the other hand, all you really need is *smail(5)* and your trusty ASCII editor to fix up your */var/lib/smail/config* file. (Though we would also use the *Linux Network Administrator's Guide* and the *Smail—Installation and Administration Guide.*)

Configuring smail

[66] Mail
HOWTO

For an overview of the email system you are setting up, you should first read the current Linux Electronic Mail HOWTO file. Fortunately, *smail* default values for the Linux *smail* distribution are decent, and the *mkconfig* script largely automates the remaining *smail* installation issues. With any luck you can accept all default values and just run *smail* "out of the box."

Look for a *README* text file in the current distribution. You should begin by reading this file if it exists. On a typical Linux distribution of *smail*, the *README* file is found in */usr/lib/smail/linux.tools/README.* The README file describes the release and provides any special notes and general instructions for installing and configuring the current version of the software.

smail EDITME file

The first step in configuring *smail* from a Linux distribution is to go to the */usr/lib/smail/linux.tools* directory, and copy the *EDITME-dist* file to *EDITME.* Then, edit the *EDITME* file to alter any variables that you need to. Some of the values you can assign in *EDITME* are better handled in a later step, when you will run */usr/lib/smail/linux.tools/mkconfig* to complete the *smail* installation. Variable assignments in the *EDITME* file are in the form of `variable=value`. The following are variables that you might wish to give special attention to in the *EDITME* file:

OS_TYPE=linux
> The OS_TYPE should already have a value of `linux` if you are using a standard Linux distribution of *smail.* Check this just in case.

HAVE=HDB_UUCP
> If you've installed some other UUCP package than the usual Taylor UUCP, you should study the comments about the HAVE variable. For Taylor UUCP you don't want to set a value for HAVE.

UUCP_ZONE
> If you are on a UUCP network and you are *not* going to be on the Internet, look at the comments on the UUCP_ZONE variable. You may need to set UUCP_ZONE=true to achieve the address handling behavior you want for certain UUCP networks.

DOMAINS

> You may need to set DOMAINS to a domain name if you did not perform a standard Linux installation and configuration. If you have, though, you will probably want to omit setting DOMAINS in the *EDITME* file and make any changes you need when you run *mkconfig.*

SMAIL_BIN_DIR

> Linux will normally set */usr/bin* as the SMAIL_BIN_DIR value. This variable establishes the path to the primary mailer on the system. If you've put your primary mailer somewhere else, you'll have to change the value of SMAIL_BIN_DIR.

LIB_DIR

> Linux normally sets */usr/lib/smail* as the LIB_DIR path. LIB_DIR is the path for *smail* files. If you put *smail* files somewhere other than */usr/lib/smail,* you need either to change LIB_DIR to reflect this, or to link the directory you use to */usr/lib/smail.*

NEWALIASES

> The *mkaliases* command can function as the *newaliases* utility if you set this variable; otherwise you must invoke the utility as *mkaliases*. The default behavior is the latter. If you want to enable invocation as *newaliases*, the argument to NEWALIASES should be set to the path of the *newaliases* command.

UUCP_SYSTEM_FILE

> If you are using a UUCP package other than Taylor UUCP, you may need to set this variable to something different from its current value. Currently it is set as UUCP_SYSTEM_FILE=/usr/lib/uucp/Systems, which is typical for a BNU or HoneyDanBer UUCP distribution.

SPOOL_DIRS

> By default, SPOOL_DIRS is set to */usr/spool/smail,* but you may want to have more than one spool directory available if you think you will need more inodes to handle the volume of pending mail or if you can change the directory specified. To specify more than one spooling directory, enter each spooling directory's path, separated by a colon character. If you have set aside a fast disk drive for spooling operations, you may need to change the path to use in order to place the primary spooling directory in that mounted path. For example, if your fast disk drive is mounted as */var/spool,* then you might have something like:

```
SPOOL_DIRS=/var/spool/smail:/usr/spool/smail
```

NEWS_SPOOL_DIR

> This is normally set to */usr/spool/news;* considerations are similar to SPOOL_DIRS variable. Except, of course, that Netnews volume is getting huge, so you really might need more spooling directories...

The mkconfig file

After you are satisfied with the state of your *EDITME* file (and in fact, you may have determined that you did not need to set any special values in an *EDITME* file), you are ready to run */usr/lib/smail/tools.linux/mkconfig*. This utility creates a supplementary file that overrides or supplements other *smail* variables; the file is */usr/lib/smail/tools.linux/config.state*. We'll provide responses to a few of these questions and show you the resulting output file. These are the considerations you should be ready to resolve when *mkconfig* is run:

Extra hostnames

    mkconfig will already know about a hostname if you installed Linux using one of the standard distributions, or if you gave a value in the *EDITME* file. Now you are asked if you want your host to be known by multiple hostnames. This is useful if the host is on more than one network, for example. For our configuration run, the host value was already set to **pond.walden.com** (composed from the hostname value of **pond** and from the domain name value of **walden.com**). I (Lar) answered the query by entering an additional hostname of **pond.conserve.org**, because we'd like to be known to some correspondents on the outside by that domain name.

System's visible name

    You can set the visible name to something other than the actual hostname. The purpose of this is to provide a single visible mailing address for mail coming from a cluster of machines. You should specify the machine that all mail coming from outside the local network will be sent to. If the visible name value isn't set, the primary host and domain names form the name used.

Smart host

    This is a very important consideration; you should have a *smart host*, which is a host to which you route all mail that you don't know how to deliver. If you don't answer this question when you run *mkconfig*, you should edit the */usr/lib/smail/config* file to provide this data when you are ready to designate a smart host. We responded to this query with **ruby.ora.com**, because we are using it as our connection to the outside world.

Smart transport

    This specifies the preferred mail transport medium; the default is TCP.

Smart user

    This is for email wizards who can figure out forwarding addresses for misrouted mail. You should probably leave it unset, so mail that is routed to an unknown user on the local host is bounced back to the sender.

Postmaster

    Someone should take responsibility for email. If you are performing *mkconfig*, you are probably "it" and you should provide your own user ID in response to this. If the postmaster isn't designated, all mail sent to postmaster goes to the root user. We supplied lark as the user ID for postmaster.

Primary mailer

Basically, *mkconfig* checks to see if */bin/mail* exists, and if it does (as it does on most Linux systems) it regretfully accepts this as the primary mailer. You can edit your customization file to use some other mailer that you have, like Elm.

The file that resulted from the interactive *mkconfig* procedure looks like this:

```
more_hostnames=pond.walden.com:pond.conserve.org
visible_name=
smart_path=ruby.ora.com
smart_user=
postmaster=lark
```

Final smail installation notes

When your *smail* installation is complete, make sure you remove or rename any existing *rmail*, *sendmail*, or other commands that *smail* is intended to replace on your system. (The *smail* installation script probably already has created these links, but you need to verify the situation; if you had existing utilities, they may not have been replaced with links to *smail*.) Create the *smail* links that are needed to all of its many roles, so programs that depend on these utilities can find them:

```
# ln /usr/bin/smail /usr/bin/mailq
# ln /usr/bin/smail /usr/bin/rmail
# ln /usr/bin/smail /usr/bin/rsmtp
# ln /usr/bin/smail /usr/bin/runq
# ln /usr/bin/smail /usr/sbin/sendmail
# ln /usr/bin/smail /usr/bin/smtpd
# ln /usr/bin/smail /usr/bin/mkaliases
```

[3] Network
Admin Guide

When you have established these links, the utilities that rely on them can be configured for full network operation. For good instructions on that process, refer to (of course) the *Linux Network Administrator's Guide*.

If *smail* is configured correctly on your system, there is a line in the */etc/services* file that says:

```
smtp        25/tcp        mail
```

There is also a line in the */etc/services* file that says:

```
smtp    stream  tcp    nowait  root  /usr/sbin/tcpd  /usr/bin/rsmtp -bs
```

smail runtime configuration files

The *smail* binary is preconfigured and needs only minor tuning. Usually the changes can be made through the *EDITME* script, the *linux.tools/config* script, or directly to the */var/lib/smail/config* file. Normally, you need no other configuration, but there are some other files that *smail* can use to alter configuration at run time. If you should ever need any of these, build them according to "Setting Up Runtime Configuration Files" in *Smail—Installation and Administration Guide.* Also use *smail(5)* to provide information about the meanings of the variables you set.

A second host configuration file, */private/usr/lib/smail/config,* can be used to redefine mailer behavior on a local workstation. This is intended for use on a LAN, in cases where your local system might need to behave differently from the central *smail* configuration file that controls the site as a whole.

The *directors, routers,* and *transports* files can be used to redefine attributes of the *smail* director, router, or transport MTA functions. Again, these normally apply to LAN and multi-pathed network connections.

A *methods* file can be used in conjunction with runtime configuration files to assign different transport protocols to use with different hosts. This isn't necessary for mixed UUCP and TCP/IP use, but it can be employed when you want to do something unusual, such as using an SMTP protocol over UUCP or a UUCP batch protocol over TCP/IP. The technique can be very useful but is not for the novice mail administrator.

A *qualify* file can be used to tell a host the domain to route mail to if a bare hostname is given as a mail address. This is an easily abused feature and should normally be avoided. However, it can be useful in defining UUCP mail routing to a UUCP system that keeps full and accurate UUCP maps (with the cooperation of that host's mail administrator).

A *retry* file can be used to modify retry and timeout behavior of *smail.* This file can be used to set minimum delivery intervals, maximum durations, and the number of attempts separately for each target domain that the mail host connects to. Its use is beyond the scope of this book, but you may need to know about this file at some point.

Mail Transport Protocol

Your choices for transport medium are limited. In order to have Internet mail connectivity, you will have to adopt a transport protocol that is acceptable to the administrators of the particular Internet host you connect with. This might be TCP/IP if your host can be connected through an Ethernet or ISDN connection to an Internet host. Otherwise, you will use a serial protocol. SLIP or UUCP may be used through a dedicated serial line or a modem connection. The *Linux Network Administrator's Guide* provides detailed descriptions and configuration instructions for the use of transport protocols on your system, and should be your guide for this purpose.

Other Email Administrative Issues

In this section we describe tasks, services, and some additional utilities involved in managing the electronic mail system you are setting up.

Getting an Internet mail feed

You should normally use only one Internet host for getting all your mail. It is possible to use a more complex arrangement, but it is frowned upon because of the possibility of setting up loops—virtual Sargasso Seas of lost network information—so that mail is routed in circles, passing over and over through the same machines until they "time out" by exceeding the limit on the number of machines they can pass through.

Registering an address

You need to register an Internet domain name for your system if you will be accessible from the Internet. You may have the domain name of your Internet connecting host, but you could have some other domain name entirely. It doesn't matter; the domain name system (DNS) database will indicate that mail for your domain will be routed to your Internet host connection. We call this host your *gateway* connection. (If your system routes all mail only back to this gateway connection, your system is called a *leaf* system.)

In turn, the gateway host that connects you to the Internet normally holds your MX (mail exchanger) record. A host that holds an MX record for a system acts as the mail forwarder to that system. It must know the exact paths to deliver mail to all the machines in your domain, if you use more than one host as a mail host. The gateway host connects directly to your system, generally either by Ethernet or by UUCP connection over a switched telephone line.

Your own mail host should be configured so that all email not sent to the local host, or not otherwise sent directly to a host you connect to, is routed to your Internet mail gateway, which is your "smart host."

The *Linux Network Administrator's Guide* tells how to register domain names, fill out MX records, and configure both sides of the gateway-leaf mail connection. Two other books that can help you manage your Internet connection are *TCP/IP Network Administration* and *DNS and BIND*.

Mail system maintenance

You should set up a *cron* task to occasionally check the the mail queue (usually */var/spool/smail*) and force an attempt to deliver mail that wasn't previously delivered for some reason. Mail can be queued because a host was temporarily unreachable, or a file system was full, or for myriad other little reasons. *cron* is discussed in the section "Scheduling Jobs Using cron" in Chapter 4.

Chapter 4

The mail administrator also should occasionally check the mail queue and make sure that there are no messages "stuck" there:

```
$ mailq -v
```

This generates a report on mail in the queue, along with log information that will inform you if there is a persistent mail delivery problem.

Installing Elm

Now you can get mail to your system, and it is sitting in a spool directory waiting to be read. Your last job is to install a mailer that provides a convenient interface for reading, composing, and filing mail messages.

The Elm mailer was created by Dave Taylor, of the Elm Development Group, and continues to be developed through the Usenet Community Trust. Copyrights on Elm are held by Dave Taylor and the Usenet Community Trust.

Elm isn't the most powerful mailer available, but it is robust and suits the needs of most users. It has a simple user interface with menus and built-in help. Most other screen-oriented mailers available on Linux support much the same basic mailer features, using a similar display interface. Once you know Elm, you can easily switch to another mailer if you find one more to your taste.

In this discussion, we mention different directories and files that Elm uses. These are defaults; the mail administrator can set up some different location, and each Elm user can change the setup of files and directories.

Preparing for installation

Before you install Elm, you should already have set up communications links to any UUCP and TCP/IP hosts that you will exchange mail with directly. If these connections change, you may have to reinstall Elm or edit some files. During installation, you should be prepared to supply the Elm configuration program with essential data about the host domain name and system name, about the routing of mail, etc. Specific information you need includes:

Domain name
> If you are on the Internet, you need to register a domain name, or (more commonly) become part of an established domain—probably the domain of the host that will provide you with mail service and holds your MX record.

Hostname
> The name of the mail host you are configuring.

Absolute name
> The complete hostname, including the domain.

Locking methods
> Elm uses mail spool files, and sometimes it needs to lock files. Elm can support UUCP "dotlock," locking, BSD *flock* locking, and System V *fcntl* locking. Linux possesses both *fcntl* and *flock* functions. If you are also using UUCP on your system, you need "dotlock" and you should also enable at least *fcntl* locking. Elm will ask you interactively when you run *Configure* what forms of locking to support.

Content-length control
> MTAs can now transmit binary messages embedded in email. However, to do so they cannot tolerate changes in message content by mailers. A Content-Length: header is used to specify the message length, and you should allow this header to be used. However, honoring Content-Length: headers requires that the mailer not insert escapes or buffering characters in front of instances of the text string "Front" occurring at the start of a line.

Dot message termination
> By default, Elm turns off dot-termination of mail (where a line containing only a . causes the mailer to end the message). You don't want dot termination if content-length control is enabled, which you probably want to allow in the brave new multimedia world.

[3] Network Admin Guide

Before using *Configure* to install Elm, read the *Elm Configuration Guide* to make sure you have the answers you need to complete the process successfully. There are a number of lesser issues to decide in addition to the issues just mentioned. Some of them require knowledge of your Linux filetree, so you should investigate these first to avoid having to abort or reinstall later. You may also find it useful to refer to the chapter in the *Linux Network Administrator's Guide* that gives an introduction to electronic mail, for a broader view of electronic mail issues, including mail addressing and routing and use of UUCP as a mail routing agent.

If you reinstall Elm from an earlier version, you may need to replace system alias files and have all the users replace their alias files. A *newalias* command is provided for the purpose and should be run by each Elm user.

Installation

First, get the latest released sources for Elm and put the source files in a build directory, such as */usr/local/bin/elm2.4*. Elm may have been included with your Linux distribution and could have been built when installing or reinstalling the Linux package. If this is the case, you should test the installation to make sure it is complete and up-to-date.

At least one major distribution of Linux that includes the Elm package includes only the executable and omits example configuration files and installation instructions. You can get the rest of the package (including documentation) through FTP sites that have the full package. These are not necessarily Linux source sites.

The Elm package contains a *Configure* shell script that you should run to install Elm. A file named *Instruct* contains fundamental directions for installing the current version of Elm on your system, but probably doesn't tell you the information you should have on hand when you run *Configure*. We'll try to tell you key information you will need to know, but if we miss something, reinstallation of Elm is as easy as running *Configure* again. From your Elm build directory, as the root user, execute *Configure*.

```
# sh Configure
```

Configure interactively installs localized configuration files.

Next, you need to build the Elm document set.

```
# make documentation
```

Then run a full make process, building a logfile and showing messages in case of *make* errors.

```
# make all > MAKELOG 2>&1 &
# tail -f MAKELOG
```

This assumes you are using the *bash* shell. If you use *csh* or *tcsh*, enter the *make* command this way:

```
% make all >& MAKELOG &
```

This process will take a while. On successful completion, you should find most of these commands in */usr/bin*: *answer*, *arepdaemon*, *autoreply*, *checkalias*, *elm*, *fastmail*, *filter*, *frm*, *listalias*, *messages*, *newalias*, *newmail*, *printmail*, and *readmsg*. There should also be equivalent online reference pages in */usr/man/man1* and */usr/man/man8*.

Next, install your software on the system.

```
# make install
```

As of the time of this writing (Elm version 2.4) there is a known security risk with *arepdaemon* and *autoreply*. These should be removed from your system. The manual pages for these utilities should also be removed before you update your *whatis* database by running *makewhatis*.

Before running Elm, read and dispose of any queued mail for the root user. You will be testing the Elm configuration as root, and you don't want to lose any pending messages.

Now test your installation by running Elm. First, check for correct detection of no existing mail (still as the root user):

```
# elm -z
```

Elm should display the message no mail and exit. (If there is mail for root, Elm will come up in interactive mode and list the messages at the Index screen.)

Next, check for correct mailbox handling. (Elm creates a test mail folder when it installs.)

```
# elm -f test/test.mail
```

Exit without marking any messages for deletion. Elm should prompt you for correct handling of the messages.

Assume a non-privileged user identity and run *elm −z*. Elm should not load unless there is pending mail. If there is pending mail and you have not previously had Elm installed (don't have a *$HOME/.elm* directory), Elm should prompt you to create the directory. You need to edit the *SYSTEM_ALIASES* file to set up at least one alias, defining the identity of the system postmaster so that mail sent to the postmaster at your site is handled correctly. Then, the *newaliases* command must be run to set up the aliases table. The procedure is described in the *Elm Configuration Guide* for your version of Elm.

Once you are satisfied that Elm is configured and installed properly, you can propagate the installation of Elm on your whole LAN, if you maintain mail services on more than one host. The directions for the make process are included in the *Instruct* file of the Elm distribution.

Elm documentation

There is a set of documents for Elm that may be useful to you in tuning Elm or building up scripts for advanced mail management. The Elm document set on your system most likely matches the version of Elm you are running, which is a critical advantage. These are guides in the Elm document set:

Elm User's Guide
> Provides some history of Elm, fundamental usage, and credits for contributors to the continued development of Elm. Provides basic usage information, but is thin on concepts, some of which are described in the *Elm Reference Guide* or in other guides. Unless your version of Elm is later than version 2.4, you probably won't need this except to satisfy your curiosity.

Elm Reference Guide
> Discusses Elm and the options within the Elm environment, Elm advanced features and debugging, tailoring the *elmrc* options file, and more. Provides some of the conceptual information that the Elm User's Guide omits, as well as useful practical and conceptual information on various Elm features and utilities.

This volume can be handy when configuring Elm. Contains some information of interest only to mail administrators.

Elm Alias User's Guide
Tells how to set up and maintain mail aliases in Elm, and the related files.

Elm Filter System User's Guide
Tells how to use Elm mail filter utilities to automate some mail handling.

Elm Configuration Guide
Discusses all the available options of the current version of Elm, to help you fine-tune your configuration. You can get into trouble relying only on this volume, so if you decide to tinker with some of the more arcane options, I recommend that you change them one by one and test the results, rather than making wholesale changes. This volume is of practical interest to mail administrators, though, who should use it in conjunction with a printout of a complete *elmrc* file and the *sysdefs.h* file on the system.

Elm Forms Mode Guide
Describes the use of AT&T Mail Forms, which Elm supports. This feature isn't useful to most Elm mail users, but if you need the feature, you need this guide as well.

Elm reference pages
Elm has online reference pages that you can access using the *man* command for each utility that you can invoke from the command line, and a reference page that describes files that Elm creates and uses in mail management. These are always useful, and you should use them generously at any time. They describe the command-line options for each command and provide technical detail that may not be available anywhere else. Some sites may keep these files built in printable form as well, in PostScript, text, or other format, so you can have them at hand for personal reference.

Elm also contains internal help, which is stored in a set of files that you can print for convenient hardcopy reference. These files are:

elm-help.0
Help for Elm Actions (internal commands) available from the Index screen.

elm-help.1
Help for Elm Options (user customization) menu.

elm-help.2
Help for the Elm Alias menu.

elm-help.3
Help for Elm Actions available from the message display screen.

File Transfer and Remote Terminal Software

One of the more important issues to resolve in using a stand-alone Linux system has to be that of file transfer and remote file operations. We cover solutions here that offer useful alternatives and enrichments to TCP/IP and UUCP. C-Kermit and Zmodem utilities move beyond traditional UNIX solutions by providing interaction with a broad variety of non-UNIX hosts and by extending the types of file operations and interactive operating modes that can be performed through serial communications.

C-Kermit

If you aren't on the Internet, or you have to communicate with someone who has a modem but is not on the Internet, you need a telecommunications program. Everyone should have at least one of these on the system, because someday there will be a need to exchange files with another system whose only access to the rest of the world is a serial communications line.

One of the oldest and most widespread communications packages is Kermit. The C-Kermit package is a full-featured UNIX data communications package that evolved from earlier Kermit implementations. In addition to providing file transfer and (nowadays) many more services as well, C-Kermit is not limited to serial port communications. C-Kermit can use TCP/IP and X.25 data links.

Among the services provided by C-Kermit are:

- File transfer of text and binary files

- Full terminal emulation using the most popular terminal types

- TELNET services

- Configuration of modems and other communications devices

- Support for multiple character sets and translation between character sets

While Kermit is freely available, licensing restrictions keep it from being a part of standard Linux distributions. We think this is a regrettable omission, because Kermit is the "king" of communications between dissimilar computer systems. Kermit has been ported to more than 150 different computer platforms. To understand why it is not in Linux distributions, a history of its development is helpful.

The Kermit file transfer protocol was designed in 1981 by the Columbia University Center of Computing Activities, in New York City. The specification for the Kermit protocol is published and can be freely implemented by developers of communications applications. The Trustees of Columbia University own the copyright to Kermit, and thus control its official development, though anyone can add features or adapt Kermit for their own use. C-Kermit is one of many applications using the Kermit protocol. It was written in the C language in 1985 by Frank da Cruz at

Columbia University, with the assistance and input of hundreds of developers around the world.

The development of Kermit foreshadowed the GNU Project and the Linux development effort in developing an effective model for public software development and refinement. Columbia University has used their copyright control benevolently. They have allowed the Kermit development team to develop, refine, extend, and define Kermit in an era that conspicuously lacked open data communications standards, while also making stable Kermit software freely available for use on an impressive variety of platforms.

Well, "it isn't easy being green" as Kermit the Frog has observed in song. Columbia University requires that vendors who sell Kermit for profit explicitly receive written permission to do so, and also that complete documentation be bundled with the software. Since the Kermit manual is large, its cost puts Kermit outside the price range for a Linux distribution.

Still, if you want to make sure your Linux system can interchange files reliably between a variety of different host systems running user environments ranging from AmigaDOS to ZetaLISP, we think C-Kermit is the right software to use. C-Kermit's terminal mode even allows you to retrieve files from a host that doesn't have Kermit installed, by letting you capture a file that is "displayed" to the Kermit "terminal." C-Kermit also allows alternative data transfer protocols, controlling Zmodem transfer by using the *sz* and *rz* commands.

Because Kermit isn't part of standard Linux distributions, you'll have to FTP it or get it from someone who has it. We tell you where to get C-Kermit below in the section "Getting C-Kermit." The version of C-Kermit described generally in this section is the current release at the time of writing: version 5A, edit 190.

Getting C-Kermit

You can get complete C-Kermit source by anonymous FTP from the official **kermit.columbia.edu** FTP site in */kermit/c-kermit/cku*.** files, which you can FTP in text mode. You will probably prefer to get the compressed, tarred package for the UNIX version of C-Kermit, which is found in */kermit/archives/cku*.tar.Z*. (The asterisk represents the edit level of the current release—190 for the UNIX version of C-Kermit at the time of this writing.) See Appendix C, *FTP Tutorial and Site List*, for directions on using FTP, and the section "Archive and Compression Utilities" in Chapter 4 for information on uncompressing files and using *tar*.

Appendix C
Chapter 4

You can also get a (usually) current release of the UNIX version of C-Kermit from other archive sites around the world, such as **src.honeywell.com** (in */kermit*) or **beetle.murdoch.edu.au** (in */pub/solaris2/src/kermit*).

You can also order Kermit on a variety of media directly from the Kermit Distribution Department of Columbia University. Call them at +1 212 854 3703 to verify that the medium and format you need for your operating system is available.

Columbia charges a distribution fee to cover materials and labor, as well as shipping. Their mailing address is:

Attn: Kermit Distribution, Dept CI
Columbia University, Center for Computing Activities
612 W. 115th Street
New York, NY 10025, USA

Installation and configuration

We assume that you are the system administrator installing C-Kermit on your system. If you are not, you may still install C-Kermit, perhaps in your own *$HOME/bin* directory, or in */usr/local/bin* if your administrator allows you to install software packages for general use on your system. However, because C-Kermit is used for direct communications between systems, your system or network administrator should be made aware that you want to install and use C-Kermit if it isn't already on your system. There are system security and virus protection issues involving both your system and the systems you access.

When you have the C-Kermit package ready to install on your system, locate a directory to put the files that you will use to build C-Kermit. For example (as root) you might create a build directory like this:

```
# mkdir /usr/local/bin/kermit5a
```

Move the software package to the build directory you have created. If you received your distribution by FTP, it probably is in a compressed and tarred form that you will have to reconstitute:

```
# gunzip ckermit5A.tar.Z
# tar -vxf ckermit5A.tar
```

The unpacked files are numerous and potentially confusing. The C-Kermit files typically begin with the *ck* prefix, with generic C-Kermit files having a *ckc* or *cke* prefix and UNIX C-Kermit files having a *cku* prefix. Document files have the *.doc* suffix, or the *.bwr* ("beware") suffix for notes and warnings, with an occasional announcement file having a *.ann* suffix. There may be other document files having a *.blp* suffix (help files), and a *.nr* ("nroff") manual page. For the most part, you can ignore these files for now, unless you want to tinker with C-Kermit source or have some unexpected problem with your installation.

You probably won't have any problem installing C-Kermit if you begin by reading the *READ.ME* file and *ckuaaaa.doc* file for your distribution, and then the *ckuins.doc* file. One of the Linux makefile options is probably correct for your Linux installation, and you need only invoke the *make* command (as the root user) with the correct argument.

There is probably a historic *Makefile* file in the distribution that you should not try to use. (Remove or rename it.) There should be a contemporary *makefile* file that already contains the configuration information you need to successfully build C-Kermit for your Linux system. If this file does not exist, copy the *ckuker.mak* file to *makefile* and use it. You can see any existing make options for Linux installations by using your editor and searching for "linux" in the makefile.

Because the makefile tunes the installation of C-Kermit to your system, you should compile C-Kermit on your system rather than importing a pre-compiled version, if possible.

The makefile that comes with the standard C-Kermit distribution offers at least four different compilations for Linux. There is one for the usual serial connection, one that also supports TCP/IP network connections, and static linking versions of those options. All versions will probably compile on your system without alteration using *make* and *gcc*, and they will probably be configured to suit the vast majority of Linux systems.

To *make* a standard serial Kermit protocol version of C-Kermit, enter:

```
# make linux
```

If you also want *kermit* to be able to use TCP/IP communications links, enter:

```
# make linuxtcp
```

For a statically-linked *kermit* able to use TCP/IP communications links, enter:

```
# make linuxtcps
```

(You probably shouldn't build a statically-linked *kermit* unless you need to make a portable distribution. It's a lot bigger than the version that uses shared libraries.)

If your *make* process fails with compiler errors identified as being associated with *linux/serial.h*, then clean up the directory:

```
# make clean
```

and repeat the *make* process, appending the argument `KFLAGS=-DNOHISPEED` to the original *make* command you used.

```
# make linuxtcp KFLAGS=-DNOHISPEED
```

The configuration document file for your distribution, *ckuins.doc*, discusses additional *make* options if you wish to do more elaborate installations such as configuring a system-wide Kermit initialization file. It also gives procedures for testing the resulting executable file *wermit*.

By default the Linux *make* script configures *kermit* to use the UUCP file locking mechanism (temporary *.lck* files). The script tries to figure out the directory where the UUCP lock files are kept and specifies the same directory, to ensure that there are no collisions between users simultaneously using both Kermit and UUCP.

After a successful *make* process, the resulting executable files are *wermit* and *wart*. After you have tested *wermit* and are satisfied with it, set its permissions appropriately and put it in the normal execution path:

```
# chmod 755 wermit
# mv wermit /usr/local/bin/kermit
```

The *wart* executable that you find in your *make* directory is a substitute for the UNIX *lex* utility that is used during the *make* process, and you probably don't need to keep it. To clean up both the object files and the *wart* executable after you have run the *make* process, enter:

```
# make clean
```

You have other files that you should install on your system in appropriate places. If your Linux installation did not already include a reference page online for C-Kermit 5A, then you will want to set up the reference page and put it on the system to use:

```
# chmod 644 ckuker.nr
# mv ckuker.nr /usr/man/man1/kermit.1
```

If you don't put your C-Kermit files in the expected locations, you may need to edit the *kermit.1* manual page to indicate the correct paths for the C-Kermit example files (in the FILES section). You should probably put your C-Kermit example files in the */usr/local/lib/kermit* directory. These files should be put in the directory: *ckermit.ini, ckermod.ini, ckermit.kdd, ckermit.kdd, ckermit.ksd, ckermit.ksd, ckedemo.ini, ckevt.ini, ckurzsz, ckcker.upd, ckcker.bwr,* and *ckuker.bwr*. Make sure you set the permissions so that these files are readable by all; they are example code and configuration files that users copy to customize their *kermit* installation.

One implementation of the UNIX version of C-Kermit, for Solaris, has support for X.25 communications as well as TCP/IP and the Kermit serial protocol. If you need X.25, it would be a significant contribution to the Linux and Kermit communities to complete a C-Kermit build that implements X.25 on Linux hosts.

Using C-Kermit interactively

C-Kermit is an interactive program that provides subcommands you invoke from within the program. You must know the necessary connection data to reach the remote system: the port, modem data, and phone number to dial for switched serial communications, or the Internet address for TCP/IP connection.

To start C-Kermit interactively, simply enter:

```
$ kermit
```

You can also include some command-line options, as described below. C-Kermit displays a greeting message followed by a prompt, which is typically `C-Kermit>` (but you can change it). If you include "action" options on the command line, however, C-Kermit operates in a non-interactive mode. It performs actions specified by flags and arguments to the *kermit* command and then returns you to your shell command line.

Having entered *kermit* in interactive mode, the next thing you probably want to know is how to get out of it. You can enter either *quit* or *exit* to exit. C-Kermit automatically closes files and cleans up after itself when it exits.

Next, you will probably use *set* commands to set the proper modem, transfer speed, and other properties of the connection. You will use the *dial* command to connect to a system over a phone line, and a *send* or *receive* command to transfer a file.

You don't have to enter the complete text of a command in order for C-Kermit to act correctly; you only need to enter enough of the command to be unambiguous as to how it will complete. You could enter *exi* or *ex*, and C-Kermit would know you mean *exit*. If you don't provide enough information, C-Kermit will prompt you for completion.

Okay, you have the rudiments. Let's take a tour of the main uses of Kermit.

File transfer

Kermit is used primarily for file transfer, using the *send, msend,* and *receive* commands. We'll walk you through a complete example of accessing a system and retrieving files. We are starting here in the user's home directory.

Start by invoking Kermit.

```
$ kermit
C-Kermit 5A(190), 10 Dec 94, Linux 1.0.9
Type ? or HELP for help
Linux Kermit>
```

First, specify the parameters for communication. This includes the type of modem (Hayes), the device to use (*dev/modem*), the port speed, the parity (8 bits, no parity), and the time to wait before giving up. Of course, you have to do some research to determine what is supported by the modems at each end of your own connection. The following parameters just happened to work for the session we were using as an example.

```
Linux Kermit> set modem hayes
Linux Kermit> set line /dev/modem
Linux Kermit> set speed 9600
Linux Kermit> set parity none
Linux Kermit> set dial timeout 60
```

Make the call.

```
Linux Kermit> dial 1-508-555-5000
Dialing 1-508-555-5000
Device=dev/modem, modem=hayes, speed=9600
Call completed.
```

Access the system.

```
Linux Kermit> connect
Welcome to the World.
Login: mdw
Password: Enter password here-it will not be echoed.
You have new mail.
world$
```

Now you're logged in to **world**. To create a file for transfer, we'll run off a manual page.

```
world$ cd working
world$ man kermit | col -b > kermit.1
```

Start Kermit on the remote system.

```
world$ kermit
C-Kermit 5A(189), 30 Jun 93, Silicon Graphics IRIX 4.0
Type ? or HELP for help
```

Change the remote prompt. This is optional but recommended, so that you can remember you're on the remote system.

```
C-Kermit> set prompt {world-k> }
world-k>
```

Now send a file.

```
world-k> send kermit.1
```

Switch temporarily to your local system in order to receive the file. To switch between systems, enter a Ctrl-backslash character followed by c. The *r* command receives the sent file.

```
world-k> ^\c
Linux Kermit> r
```

Return to the remote system and exit Kermit. You will then be back at the shell prompt on the remote system.

```
Linux Kermit> ^\c
world-k> exit
world$
```

Copy some files to the work directory.

```
world$ cp ../bin/lp* .
```

Start remote Kermit again.

```
world$ kermit
C-Kermit 5A(189), 30 Jun 93, Silicon Graphics IRIX 4.0
Type ? or HELP for help
C-Kermit>
```

Get binary files.

```
C-Kermit> set file type binary
C-Kermit> mget lp*
```

Switch back to the local system and receive the files. Then return to the remote system and exit Kermit.

```
C-Kermit> ^\c
Linux Kermit> receive
Linux Kermit> ^\c
C-Kermit> exit
world$
```

Log off the remote system. You might have to use *logout* instead of *exit*.

```
world$ exit
Communications disconnect (back at local system)
Linux Kermit>
```

Leave Kermit.

```
Linux Kermit> exit
$
```

In the following example, we use Kermit on an Internet host over TCP/IP.

```
world$ kermit
C-Kermit 5A(189), 30 Jun 94, Silicon Graphics IRIX 4.0
Type ? or HELP for help
C-Kermit>
```

Specify the remote host's name as the port for TCP communications, and connect to the remote host. Log in just as on any UNIX system.

```
C-Kermit> set port tcp pond.walden.com
C-Kermit> connect
Linux 1.0.9
login: mdw
password: Enter password
pond$
```

Start Kermit on the remote system.

```
pond$ kermit
C-Kermit 5A(190), 10 Dec 94, Linux 1.0.9
Type ? or HELP for help
Linux Kermit>
```

Change to the directory where files are stored, and send some TEX files.

```
Linux Kermit> cd /book/linux
Linux Kermit> msend *.tex
```

Now pop back to the local system temporarily to receive the files. Use Ctrl-backslash followed by c.

```
Linux Kermit> ^\c
Linux Kermit> receive
```

Return to the remote host to exit Kermit.

```
Linux Kermit> ^\c
Linux Kermit> exit
pond$
```

Exit from the shell on the remote system, returning to Kermit on the local system.

```
pond$ exit
Communications disconnect (back at local system)
```

Finally, exit from the local Kermit. You will return to your local shell prompt.

```
C-Kermit> exit
world$
```

In the following session, we'll use Kermit to log on to a remote system and transfer a text file without using any communications utility on the remote system. The trick is to display a file on the screen, and to use Kermit's log facility to capture the screen.

```
pond$ kermit
C-Kermit 5A(190), 10 Dec 94, Linux 1.0.9
Type ? or HELP for help
Linux Kermit>
```

Set the communication parameters and make the telephone call.

```
Linux Kermit> set modem hayes
Linux Kermit> set line /dev/modem
Linux Kermit> set speed 19200
Linux Kermit> set parity none
Linux Kermit> set dial timeout 60
Linux Kermit> dial 1-617-739-9753
Dialing 1-617-739-9753
Device=dev/modem, modem=hayes, speed=9600
```

```
Call completed.
Linux Kermit>
```

Connect to the remote system and log in.

```
Linux Kermit> connect
Welcome to the World.
Login: mdw
Password: Enter password
world$
```

Change to the directory where the desired file *elm.rc* is located.

```
world$ cd /usr/local/lib
```

What we're going to do now is display the file through the *cat* command, with logging enabled on our local system. Type the *cat* command, but do not press the Return key yet. Instead, switch back to the local system through Ctrl-backslash followed by c.

```
world$ cat elm.rc^\c
Linux Kermit>
```

Open a file to store the session in.

```
Linux Kermit> log session sample.elm.rc
```

Return to the remote host, where the *cat* command is waiting, and press Return to execute it.

```
Linux Kermit> connect
world$ cat elm.rc
```

At this point, when you press Return, the file *elm.rc* is scrolled to the Kermit display, and simultaneously logged to the file previously specified: *sample.elm.rc* on the local host. When the command is done, switch to the local host to turn off logging.

```
world$ ^\c
Linux Kermit> close session
```

Leave Kermit.

```
Linux Kermit> exit
pond$
```

The contents of the file have been trapped to the log file. All that is required is to discard the extra line at the end of the file, which will consist of the system prompt returned at the end of the *cat* command.

Terminal connection

When you issue the *connect* command within Kermit, you have entered a terminal emulation state. C-Kermit defaults to emulating the vt100 terminal. You can change many of the characteristics of the terminal, including the character set, newline mode, and key mapping.

You can see your main terminal settings by issuing the Kermit *show terminal* command. In terminal mode (called *connect mode* in Kermit documentation), the default escape character is Ctrl-backslash. You've already seen this used with a following c character to exit from connect mode. It may seem awkward to enter at first, but you'll quickly get used to it.

You can get the status of a current connect session by entering Ctrl-backslash followed by s. The result might look something like this:

```
C-Kermit> ^\s
Connected through /dev/ttyh5, speed 19200
Terminal bytesize: 7, Command bytesize: 7, Parity: none
Terminal echo: remote
Carrier Detect        (CD):   On
Dataset Ready         (DSR):  Off
Clear To Send         (CTS):  Off
Ring Indicator        (RI):   Off
Data Terminal Ready   (DTR):  On
Request to Send       (RTS):  On
C-Kermit>
```

From connect mode, you can suspend Kermit and exit to a shell by entering Ctrl-backslash followed by an exclamation mark or at-sign (! or @). Other commands you can enter after a Ctrl-backslash include:

b   Sends a break signal.

l   Sends a break signal on a networked connection.

h   Tells Kermit to hang up.

Customizing C-Kermit for your use

C-Kermit normally configures itself according to the Kermit configuration commands that it reads in its initialization file *$HOME/.kermrc* before it performs any other commands. Most Linux sites, when they install C-Kermit, allow the user configuration file to control configuration.

However, the administrator may have configured Kermit to use a system-wide configuration file instead. This file is probably stored in */usr/local/lib/kermit/ckermit.ini.* Your system administrator may or may not have configured C-Kermit to allow a user's local configuration file, when one exists, to override the system-wide initialization file.

Should your site be one of the more liberal ones, you can set up your own *$HOME/.kermrc* file by copying the system *ckermit.ini* file. For example:

```
$ cp /usr/local/lib/kermit/ckermit.ini ~/.kermrc
```

This file will hold standard Kermit configuration information. You can modify it, or a second configuration file that overrides values stored in the standard configuration file, *$HOME/.mykermrc*. You can copy an example of this file and then adapt it:

```
# cp /usr/local/lib/kermit/ckermod.ini ~/.mykermrc
```

By modifying the *$HOME/.mykermrc* file instead of your *.kermrc* file, you can rapidly isolate and debug customizations you make to your *kermit* operation. Using the –*Y* command-line flag, you can force the active initialization file(s) to be left unread. You can also specify an alternative initialization file for C-Kermit to use by supplying the path as the argument to the –*y* option to *kermit*.

You won't usually want to change most of the settings in the basic configuration file. However, you probably do have some preferences for file transfer protocols, terminal settings, macro definitions, and the like. We recommend that you copy */usr/local/lib/kermit/ckermod.ini* into *$HOME/.mykermrc* and put your customizations in it. Don't get overly ambitious—make your changes as you need them, and test each change to make sure it does what you want. If you make too many changes at once, you can have a hard time figuring out what went wrong if something doesn't work correctly.

The Kermit customization file has a simple format. Mostly it contains *set* commands that establish things like modem types, line speeds, and which serial port to use. It may also contain messages to display to the user, contained in echo lines. Comments are text following a semicolon on a line. The file might look something like this:

```
set modem telebit      ; Use Trailblazer initialization
set line /dev/modem    ; /dev/modem is DOS com1 here
set speed 9600         ; speed limit for this old war horse
dial 1170              ; turn off Call Waiting service.

echo Call Waiting has been turned off so your session won't be interrupted.
echo Ready for 'dial' instruction: provide the full number to dial.
```

Documentation

[41] C-Kermit

C-Kermit has many more features than we can describe here, some of which may never come to your attention unless you read about them. It takes a thick book to cover C-Kermit properly, and fortunately a good one exists: *Using C-Kermit: Communication software for UNIX, VMS, OS/2, AOS/VS, OS-9, Amiga, Atari ST.* A German version is also available: *C-Kermit—Einfuehrung und Referenz.* (For the MS-DOS version of Kermit, there are books published in English, German, Japanese, and probably other languages, but we'll try to stick to Linux here. But the various versions of Kermit distributed through Columbia University all operate similarly, so the commands learned for one package generally apply to the other implementations.)

A terse configuration guide to C-Kermit is included with the distribution files, as well as a manual page for online reference. The document files for C-Kermit may be stored for your use in */usr/local/lib/kermit*.

The **kermit.columbia.edu** FTP site also has some German and Portuguese documentation for earlier versions of Kermit that will still be useful, as well as text of articles published about Kermit, and information about use of Kermit by blind and print-handicapped users, etc. These documents are stored in */kermit/doc*.

Since Kermit isn't part of a standard Linux distribution, and you really ought to use a book to take advantage of all the features of C-Kermit, we'll provide a little extra contact info on how to get the manual you need.

In Asia
Digital Press in Singapore: +65.220.3684.

In Australia
Digital Press in Chatswood, New South Wales: +61.2.372.5511.

In Canada
Logan Brothers, in Winnipeg, Manitoba: +1.800.665.1148; or Digital Press at the U.S.A. office.

In Europe
For *Using C-Kermit*: Digital Press in Rushden, England: +44.993.58521. For *C-Kermit—Einfuehrung und Referenz*: Verlag Heinz Heise, Hannover, Germany: +49.05.11.53.52-0.

In the U.S.A.
Digital Press in Woburn, Massachusetts: +1.800.366.2665.

You can get additional C-Kermit help and information about updates and problems with the package on the Internet by reading postings to the *comp.protocols.kermit* newsgroup. You can subscribe to the *Info-Kermit Digest* electronic journal (which is also posted to *comp.protocols.kermit*) by sending a message to the mail server with the body text:

```
subscribe: your-name
```

to the (Internet) address *listserv@cuvma.cc.columbia.edu* or (BITnet or EARN) *LISTSERV@CUVMA.BITNET.*

Internal help

kermit(1C)

Aside from the *kermit* manual page, C-Kermit has an excellent online help mechanism that you can invoke during interactive use. Just enter ? (question mark) at any point during your use of *kermit*. The interactive help provides a message, a list of the possible actions, or a list of sendable or retrievable files (whatever is appropriate). Here are examples of how you can use help.

? This results in a long list of available commands you can enter at this level of the program—a menu. For more information on one of the commands, you can specify the command, followed by a question mark.

set ?
A question mark following a primary command asks for a listing of the available options that can follow that command.

s? C-Kermit lists the commands beginning with the letter "s." The list might include

```
send server set show space statistics stop stay
```

se?
C-Kermit lists the commands beginning with the letters "se." The list might include:

```
send server set
```

Because the question mark invokes help in Kermit, you need to escape it with a backslash character (\) if you want to pass the question mark as part of the actual command, where it serves as a wildcard character. For example, if you wanted to get the files named *megadoom.h* and *megadoom.c* from another system, you could retrieve them by entering:

```
C-Kermit> get megadoom.\?
```

However, if you instead entered the command:

```
C-Kermit> get megadoom.?
```

C-Kermit would try to respond helpfully, something like:

```
File(s) to get, one of the following:
megadoom.bak    megadoom.c    megadoom.exe    megadoom.h
```

From the command line you can also enter the *help* or *man* command. This will provide you with pages of information describing how the help system works with your version of Kermit.

Kermit as server

Kermit's *remote services* are an advanced feature that simplifies transfer of large numbers of files, add or remove files from a host, and so on. While we won't cover this feature here, you need to know that it exists as an administrator of a system accessible from other sites.

When C-Kermit is in server mode, a Kermit at another site establishes a connection with it and executes a series of Kermit commands, which can be set up as a script using Kermit's internal scripting language.

By default, all Kermit server services are enabled. You can check which Kermit server features are enabled by entering the command *show server* from the C-Kermit prompt. The interchange might look something like this:

```
C-Kermit> show server
Function            Status
 GET                enabled
 SEND               enabled
 REMOTE CD/CWD      enabled
 REMOTE DELETE      disabled
 REMOTE DIRECTORY   enabled
 REMOTE HOST        disabled
 REMOTE SET         disabled
 REMOTE SPACE       enabled
 REMOTE TYPE        enabled
 REMOTE WHO         disabled
 BYE                disabled
 FINISH             enabled
```

(These services are described briefly below.)

The Kermit administrator can disable any of the remote services using the *disable* command. A change in service mode must be made before C-Kermit server mode is entered; it only becomes effective the next time C-Kermit is put in server mode. A disabled service can be re-enabled by using the *enable* command. The following are the server facilities, which you can control with the *enable* and *disable* Kermit commands:

bye
  Allows Kermit to be switched out of server mode.

cd Allows the user to change directories using the *cwd* or *cd* Kermit command.

delete
  Allows remote *delete* commands to be executed.

directory
  Controls the display of directory information to remote users.

finish
>   Allows Kermit to exit from server mode.

get Controls download access to the server's files.

host
>   Controls whether the C-Kermit server can be switched into Host mode. Some of the remote server features can also be accessed in Host mode. If you want to control those features, you have to issue *disable host*. The remote features accessible from Host mode are *delete*, *directory*, *space*, *type*, and *who*.

send
>   Controls whether the server will accept files sent by another Kermit instance.

set Controls whether the remote user is allowed to change Kermit features controlled by the *set* command.

space
>   Controls whether the server gives out information about the available storage space in the Kermit-controlled directories.

type
>   Controls whether a remote Kermit user is allowed to display the Kermit-controlled files.

who
>   Determines whether a remote user is able to gather information about a local user.

If you are concerned about Kermit security, you will control these features in the system-wide C-Kermit initialization file in */usr/local/lib/kermit/ckermit.ini*.

More C-Kermit features: a superficial survey

[41] C-Kermit
We don't have space to show you the full power and flexibility of C-Kermit here. However, you should be aware of some of these features. They are fully documented in *Using C-Kermit*.

International character set support
>   Though C-Kermit uses ASCII characters for its user interface, you can set up C-Kermit to use a variety of different character sets for Romance, Cyrillic, and Japanese character sets. All you need is an 8-bit (no parity) data link. The Latin1-ISO, Latin2-ISO, Cyrillic-ISO, and Japanese-EUC character sets are supported. C-Kermit also supports character translation and ASCII approximation; that is, received non-ASCII characters can be presented as phonetical ASCII equivalents.

Macros, variables, etc.
>   C-Kermit has a rich programming language with which you can prepare scripts and save them in files for invocation on demand. This can greatly

simplify repetitive and complex tasks. C-Kermit recognizes a number of variables for system configuration information or environment characteristics. The programming language supports conditional statements, case statements, GOTOs and structured programming elements, file handling, and built-in functions.

Curses
> C-Kermit supports use of the *curses* library for terminal mapping.

Zmodem File Transfer

The Zmodem protocol is a robust and fast data transfer protocol. It includes 32-bit cyclic redundancy checking (CRC) to ensure error-free data transfer. On UNIX platforms, the RZSZ package provides the dominant tools for implementing Zmodem protocols. Related protocols such as Xmodem and Ymodem are also supported by commands that are part of the RZSZ package.

These commands are available in the current RZSZ package:

rz Receive files using the Zmodem batch protocol. If the sending program doesn't send Zmodem protocol files within 50 seconds, *rz* switches to *rb* mode.

rb Receive files using the Ymodem or Ymodem-g protocol. *rb* is an alternative invocation for the *rz* command.

rx Receive a file using the Xmodem protocol.

sz Send files using the Zmodem batch protocol.

sb Send files using either the Ymodem or Ymodem-g protocol. *sb* is an alternative invocation for the *sz* command.

sx Send a file using the Xmodem protocol.

sz provides automatic downloading in response to an incoming *rz* request, and *rz* automatically processes incoming Ymodem or Zmodem files. *sz* can also be used as a filter to send standard input to the receiving host. The RZSZ tools display information about the file transfers, including projections of transmission time, incremental crash recovery, recognition of wildcard file selection arguments, and user notification on completion of transfer. Because most popular PC terminal emulation packages (Professional-YAM, ZCOMM, ProComm, Telix, and a host of others) support Zmodem transfer, the RZSZ package makes it very simple to transfer files between Linux systems, DOS, Macintosh, VMS, and other operating systems.

Interestingly, although some Linux distributions include the *sz* and *rz* commands, they may omit portions of the RZSZ package (including the manual pages). So we'll give you some FTP sites to get the whole package in the next section.

Most of the time you won't need to use Xmodem or Ymodem, so we will restrict our discussion to the *sz* and *rz* features.

Getting RZSZ

The RZSZ package isn't acknowledged as such in the Linux tools, which may mean that you won't find the whole package collected and compiled for Linux. However, using *archie* we were able to find a number of sites that carry it for a number of operating systems, including FreeBSD FTP sites. Sources for the package are kept in *comp.sources.unix\volume12* at FTP sites that archive the standard UNIX source files, including **ftp.cs.umn.edu** and **plaza.aarnet.edu.au**. Sources are also available at **ftp.cc.utexas.edu** in */source/comm/Zmodem*.

The primary source for state-of-the-art RZSZ is **ftp.cs.pdx.edu** maintained in directory */pub/zmodem* by Chuck Forsberg. You can also get it from the TeleGodzilla BBS, in Portland, Oregon, U.S.A., which you can call at +1-503-621-3746. A listing of files available for downloading from the BBS is kept in */usr/spool/uucppublic/FILES*. This BBS (*omen.uucp*) is maintained by Omen Technology, Inc., 17505-V Northwest Sauvie Island Road, Portland, OR 97231.

Omen Technology offers a hardcopy manual for the RZSZ package (as well as detailed documentation for the ZCOMM and Professional-YAM packages) that you can buy if the manual pages seem insufficient. You can order it from their voice number, +1-503-621-3406. Please take care not to dial up the voice number by modem! Finally, unregistered rz/sz users can call 900-737-RTFM for technical support. Omen Technology reports that almost all technical support problems with rz/sz are caused by the network, OS kernel bugs, or problems with third party comm programs, not the rz/sz code itself.

Sending and Receiving Files

Most communications programs can invoke *rz* and *sz* automatically. You can also connect to a remote system, log in, and manually invoke *sz* with the flags you want to use. Zmodem automatically downloads the files to your home system using the same filenames. (Zmodem tools aren't clever about file names, so when you download to DOS, be careful about getting files with names that can't be squeezed into the *filename.ext* DOS filename limit. If you transfer *filename.extension*, it will arrive on your DOS host converted to *filename.ext*, which is probably OK. But, if you try to transfer *filename.more.extension*, most Zmodem utilities will give up, probably with a misleading message that the transfer completed.)

One of the most confusing things about Zmodem transfer is determining the command to use to perform the transfer. You have to remember which system you are invoking the command from, and which system contains the files to transfer. A consistent way to perform Zmodem transfer is to always invoke the transfer on the remote host, whether uploading (sending to the remote host) or downloading (receiving from the remote host). For example, if you were logged in to a remote host (using C-Kermit, or Telix, whatever) and wanted to send some text files from that system to your home system, you might enter something like this:

```
$ sz -a *.txt
```

sz would queue the files and successively send them back to the local system. The *-a* option stands for "ASCII," and ensures that carriage returns and newlines appear as they should on the system where the file ends up.

On the other hand, if you want to upload some files (receive them on the remote host), you would simply enter the command:

```
$ rz
```

The remote system would then prompt something like:

```
rz ready to begin transfer, type "sz file ..." to your modem program
**B0100000023be50
```

rz waits patiently for you to switch back to the local host and give it a Zmodem send command, using *sz* directly, or through the software you are using. For example, if you called the remote host using ProComm, you would press Page Up and select Z)modem transfer from the pop-up menu, and then enter the files to send on the input line ProComm provides.

When sending files from a Macintosh system to a UNIX or Linux host via Zmodem protocol, remember that the filenames cannot have spaces in them.

The following command checks some text files, and sends only the *.txt* and *.doc* files that exist on both systems and that are newer on the sending system. Conversion of UNIX newlines to DOS-style carriage return/linefeed is performed automatically by most receiving zmodem packages.

```
$ sz -Yan *.txt *.doc
```

In many versions (not all, unfortunately) you can pipe the output of a process from a remote host to *sz* using a dash argument (*sz –*), and *sz* automatically sends the file on to you. A file name for the output is generated by putting an *s* in front of the process ID of the process that pipes the standard input to *sz*, and appending a *.sz* suffix. For example, to get a printout of the *sz.1* manual page on the remote system (versions of *sz* software vary, of course), you might enter:

```
man sz | col -b | sz -
```

where col –b strips out the backspacing that was put into the formatted output by the *man* command to implement highlighting and underscoring on the display. The dash argument to *sz* tells it to send the file back to your local system. When you get offline and check, you might find the file saved locally as something like *\tmp\s7750.sz*. (The *\tmp* directory is the most common receiving directory that a given communications program uses, unless the current directory is used.)

Summary of rz and sz options

Because of the poor prevailing state of RZSZ documentation in the standard Linux distributions, and because RZSZ tools don't have interactive help, we're providing you with summaries of the important flags for using the Zmodem protocol for file transfer. However, you should get the manual pages and possibly other documentation you need from an FTP site or a BBS; see the section "Getting RZSZ." When you use RZSZ on another system, you should be aware that the utilities may have been modified to support additional features, or to disable standard features. Check the local documentation.

The *rz* utility recognizes the following flags:

−+ Append to any existing file of the same name, rather than overwriting it. (This can cause a malformed file if you are re-transmitting an interrupted Zmodem transfer.)

−*a* Receive ASCII text. Convert files to UNIX newline conventions, stripping carriage returns and all characters beginning with a Ctrl-Z (The end-of-file character for the CP/M OS).

−*b* Receive binary. Save the file in exactly the form it was received.

−*D* Discard output. Send data to */dev/null*; this is useful for tests.

−*e* Escape the control characters. By default, *sz* escapes just XON, XOFF, and (in older versions) DLE. This option forces the sending Zmodem program to escape others as well.

−*p* Protect destination files. Skip Zmodem transfer if a destination file of the same name already exists. (Be aware that this will prevent completion of an interrupted Zmodem transfer.)

−*q* Quiet exchange. Suppresses informational messages to standard output.

−*t n*

Change timeout to *n* tenths of seconds.

−*v* Verbose. Not like a typical UNIX utility "verbose." This flag causes a list of transferred filenames to be appended to a log file, normally */tmp/rzlog*. If multiple −*v* flags are used, additional information is also stored to the log.

Now for *sz*. Most *sz* options are simply passed to the receiving program that performs the operation. Not all Zmodem receiving programs can execute the requested options. If *sz* is invoked with the $SHELL environment variable set to a restricted shell (*rsh* for example), it restricts pathnames to the current directory and to the value of the $PUBDIR variable if set (often used with UUCP), as well as subdirectories of these directories.

The meanings of the most common *sz* options are:

−+ Append. Have the Zmodem receiver utility append the transmitted data to an existing file.

−a Send ASCII text. Convert each newline character (UNIX style) in the transmitted file to a carriage return/linefeed (DOS style). Be aware, though, that at least one popular PC communications package does not do this conversion correctly.

−b Binary transfer. Transfer the file without any translation, and tell the receiving Zmodem program not to make any translation.

−d Divert path. This tries to compensate for file and path name incompatibilities between systems. (It's more reliable to rename files before you send them, though.) All periods (.) in a filename are changed to path-subpath separators in the transmitted pathname. (In UNIX, change to / characters, and in DOS, change to backslashes. A file named *foobar.bazbuzzy*, for example, is transmitted as *foobar/bazbuzzy*.) If a stem filename has more than 8 characters, a period is inserted to allow up to 11 characters. For example, a UNIX file named *foo.barbazbuzzy* would be transmitted as *foo/barbazbuzzy*, but when received by the DOS Zmodem program would be stored as *foo\barbazbu.zzy*. (If the file is longer than that, and the receiving program cannot handle the length, the file is truncated at the limit—depending on the "wisdom" of the DOS Zmodem program.)

−e Escape control characters.

−f Full path. Directory prefixes are usually omitted; this forces the entire path to be sent in the transmitted filename.

−L *bytes*
   Set the Zmodem subpacket length in bytes. (These are not the same as Xmodem, Ymodem, or Kermit packets.) The default packet length is 128 below 300 baud, 256 above 300 baud, or 1024 above 2400 baud. A larger packet gives slightly higher throughput, while a smaller packet speeds error recovery. This isn't worth messing with for modern modems that implement an error-correcting protocol in hardware.

−l *num*
   Set the packet length in bytes. The receiver acknowledges correct data every *num* characters, where *num* is a value between 32 and 1024. You can use this to avoid overrun when XOFF flow control is lacking between the systems.

−n Newer file preservation. Send the file if the destination file of the same name does not exist, and overwrite the destination file only if the source file is newer than the destination file.

−N Newer/longer file preservation. Send the file if the destination file of the same name does not exist, and overwrite the destination file only if the source file is newer or longer than the destination file.

−*p* Protect destination files. Don't transfer the file if the destination file exists.

−*q* Quiet. Suppresses reporting to the standard error.

−*r* Resume. An interrupted file transfer is resumed. If the source file is longer than the destination file, the transfer begins at the offset in the source file that equals the length of the destination file. (This mode is automatically assumed in some Zmodem receiving programs.)

−*t num*

Timeout. Set the timeout to *num* tenths of seconds.

−*u* Unlink. Break file links after successful transmission. Conveniently implements a way to "collect" files to a directory they can all be sent from.

−*w bytes*

Window size. Limits the transmit window size to the specified number of bytes to impose flow control and limit buffering.

−*v* Verbose. Appends the list of transmitted filenames to the */tmp/szlog* record. Extra −*v* options cause additional information about the transfer to be added to the record.

−*y* Yes, overwrite. Tells the receiving Zmodem program to overwrite any existing files having the same name.

−*Y* Yes, overwrite, but... Tells the receiving Zmodem program to overwrite any existing file with the same name, but skip sending source files that have a file with the same pathname on the destination system.

Some Zmodem usage notes

You can invoke *sz* with a special terminal test mode:

```
$ sz -TT
```

This form of invocation causes *sz* to output all 256 8-bit character code combinations to your terminal. If you are having problems transferring files intact, this command lets you isolate the character codes that are being trapped by the operating systems.

Calling an RZSZ utility from most versions of the UUCP *cu* usually fails, because most *cu* implementations contend for characters from the modem with RZSZ tools. (C-Kermit apparently now can call RZSZ, but this is a new feature that we haven't tried.)

Other Interesting Packages

There are several other packages commonly available on Linux systems that you may be interested in using. You can find out about them by reading the appropriate HOWTO files and other accompanying documentation.

The *term* utility is a client/server system that allows you to multiplex your serial line—that is, you can log in multiple times over a single dialup connection. *term* includes additional features allowing you to run network clients (such as *telnet*, *ftp*, and Mosaic) over the serial line. You can even use *term* to display remote X Window System clients on your local machine. So you can simultaneously run a remote X session, download files, and send mail, for example. This capability is most useful if your modem can handle high-speed data transfer; you can get comfortable performance with a 28.8kbps (preferably v.34 compliant) modem.

term is somewhat like SLIP (discussed in the section "SLIP Configuration") but *term* can be executed as a normal user—no need for root access on either the client or server side, and no need for a special SLIP dialin server.

To use *term*, you need a dialin shell account on a UNIX system. You build the *term* software both on that UNIX system and on your Linux machine. You dial in to the remote system and execute *term* there; it will now handle all data to and from your dialin connection. On your local machine, you place the communications program (such as Kermit) in the background and execute *term* to control the dialin connection from your Linux system. The two instances of *term* are now communicating over the modem line.

To log in to the remote session over the *term*-controlled line, you can use *trsh*. This starts a remote shell over the modem line. You can run *trsh* many times (in different windows or virtual consoles), starting multiple logins to the remote machine for example.

You can also use various network clients with *term*. These include *telnet*, *ftp*, mail readers, and the like. These clients must be specially compiled to use *term*. Many of them are available for Linux. In order for them to work, the remote system must be·connected to the Internet (or another local network)—the network requests are redirected to the remote system over the modem line. This way, it appears as though your system is connected to the network; you can *telnet* or *ftp* to any other system on the Internet directly from your Linux machine. The WWW browser Mosaic, discussed in the section "Using NCSA Mosaic," works with *term* as well.

[75] Term HOWTO

The Linux Term HOWTO describes this system in detail; many Linux distributions come with *term* as an optional software package.

Two other packages are worth mentioning. *pcomm* is a data communications package that intentionally resembles the ProComm for DOS package, the most popular DOS communications package. *Seyon* offers a powerful suite of terminal emulation and data communications tools.

If we've missed your favorite file transfer or data communications tool, we apologize. This is certainly an area where available Linux tools offer an embarrassment of riches. On the other hand, if you are clinging to more primitive utilities, we hope this guide has given you the opportunity to learn and use more powerful tools.

Networking with UUCP

UUCP is a venerable UNIX-to-UNIX communications package that was invented at Bell Laboratories by Mike Lesk in the mid-1970s to enable serial data transfer between UNIX hosts. It was rewritten by Mike Lesk and Dave Nowitz in 1978 and distributed with Version 7 UNIX. People have freely re-implemented and added to UUCP over the years, and now it is a whole suite of utilities that provide:

- File transfer between hosts

- A communications protocol and carrier medium for email and network news

- Communications device control

- A way to execute programs on remote hosts

- Utilities for managing the files and utilities that comprise UUCP

UUCP has been described as standing for "UNIX-to-UNIX-copy" but this more accurately applies to the *uucp* program specifically. Some describe UUCP as the "UNIX-to-UNIX Communications Protocol" but rarely actually intend to refer to the G protocol that is UUCP's contribution to communications protocols. It is best to think of UUCP as the "UNIX-to-UNIX Communications Package." The central idea of UUCP is that it allows a user to cause one computer to automatically call up another one (locally or remotely) to transfer files (including email and newsgroup files) or execute commands on the remote system (whether through a direct serial connection or through a switched connection through the telephone system). A system administrator must configure UUCP to appropriately accept UUCP calls, select protocols, make UUCP calls, control modems, handle mail and Netnews routing and files, control access by ID and timeframe, and so on. Then a user can issue (for example) a *uucp* command to transfer a file, or a *uux* command to execute a command on a remote system.

The Value of UUCP

UUCP made cheap computer networks a reality. From the genesis of Usenet in 1979, UUCP provided the decentralized message distribution model for exchanging network news that was adopted by the ARPAnet, and which allowed it to become the Internet. Today UUCP is still very important for networks around the world, particularly in regions that lack dedicated high-bandwidth data links.

Thus, UUCP networks are found throughout Africa, Central America, and South America, serving people that still cannot get to the Internet directly. Wide-area UUCP networks thrive everywhere, such as UUCPnet in the United States and EUnet and Relcom in Europe. Many network service providers connect UUCP hosts and their users with the Internet. UUCP is also popular with users of home systems to exchange data with host systems at their offices and schools, and with other home systems and small businesses.

UUCP is available in some form for just about every UNIX-like operating system, and for many other operating systems as well. Because it is so widely used, many other software applications, such as the Waffle bulletin board system for MS-DOS, have been made compatible with it.

UUCP and Security

UUCP was originally conceived for internal (in-house) use, so it has features that might have not have been chosen for a wide area network (WAN) environment in today's more hostile era of system crackers, viruses, and network worms. When you use UUCP, you should be aware of computer system security risks and the concerns they raise with service providers. It is increasingly difficult to find administrators of host systems who are willing to provide strangers or casual acquaintances with a UUCP connection. Those that do may block the use of UUCP remote execution features and restrict your access to mail and news service. They may permit file transfer if you are lucky. Don't take your responsibilities as a user or system administrator casually, even if you believe in free system access. Once you have a UUCP link with another system, each system in the UUCP virtual network becomes more vulnerable to security breaches.

If you are setting up a UUCP system and are ready to approach a system or network administrator to ask for a UUCP connection, you may find it very helpful to reassure the administrator that you are sensitive to the security issue. You may have to always poll the other system, or always have that system call yours, depending on the particular security and access concerns of the administrator. Remember, too, that you will probably have to connect through a telephone line that was installed for remote login by system users. Be prepared to agree to limit your UUCP access to low-demand periods; a connecting host may block UUCP access during some time periods or when critical system resources are strained. Most UUCP service providers will also limit your UUCP command execution capabilities.

Switched line connections do have some security advantages as well. An intruder cannot rapidly pass from one host to another, but must instead use indirect invasion techniques, such as finding out user passwords and UUCP access strings, and looking for IDs on one system that may be used on another.

Individual hosts on a UUCP network are also less susceptible to virus and worm attack than many non-switched networks. This is partly because of the limited connection path, and partly because of the diversity of host operating systems and UUCP software that may be found on a UUCP network. Your Linux system could be on a UUCP virtual network that includes hosts running UNIX (in many flavors), MS-DOS, VMS, Amiga OS, and more, using a variety of UUCP and UUCP-compatible software.

After making sure that physical access and passwords are secure, your first line of defense against remote attack is to carefully set access and ownership for all executable programs and the control files that implement UUCP. These should have the minimum read, write, and access privileges necessary to allow them to work.

[3] Network Admin Guide [59] Practical UNIX Security

UUCP security is discussed in fair detail in Olaf Kirch's *Linux Network Administrator's Guide*, which you should have if you install or manage UUCP on Linux. For a good treatise on general security for your Linux system, try *Practical UNIX Security* by Simson Garfinkel and Gene Spafford; a detailed discussion of UUCP security is contained in the UUCP chapter of that book.

[38] Using UUCP [39] Managing UUCP

Of course, UUCP is too complex to describe in detail for you here; whole books have been written for both the user and the administrator. Here we try to give you an understanding of the strengths and limits of UUCP. An excellent pair of books on UUCP are *Using UUCP and Usenet* and *Managing UUCP and Usenet*, both from O'Reilly & Associates. Unfortunately, these books do not yet cover Taylor UUCP.

The best method for getting immediate support is to post to the *comp.mail.uucp* newsgroup, if you have access to this resource.

Hardware Requirements

UUCP normally uses a serial port for communications, generally with a modem. This is the funnel through which you must stuff all of your data. UUCP performance can be seriously limited if a serial port or modem is not up to snuff.

You probably have two serial ports on your host system. Normally, in order to run the X Window System, you need one serial port for your mouse (unless you have a bus mouse); or you might use a serial port to connect a terminal to your system. If you need to connect with more than one other host at a given time, you may very much need a high-performance multi-port serial communications board.

The performance of a serial port directly depends on the UART chip (Universal Asynchronous Receiver/Transmitter) that controls it. If that UART is of an older type, you may be limited to data transfer rates under 38.8kbps, which even a 14.4kbps modem (using data compression) may saturate. If you have an up-to-date chip for each serial port you use, you can easily support data transfer rates of 115kbps—more than enough to shift the bottleneck to the modem.

You can inexpensively replace an obsolete UART with the latest 16550A UART, and if you will depend heavily on serial communications you should do this. (You can tell the type of UART you have by invoking the MSD command from DOS.)

You should replace any 8250 or 16450 UART with a 16550A UART. If you have a 16550 UART, you needn't bother to replace it unless you are having saturation problems with a very high performance modem or a null modem serial connection.

You can directly connect local systems from serial port to serial port using a null-modem cable. This fast and cheap way to set up a UUCP link between local hosts may be as close as you need to get to having your own LAN. A null-modem cable is a serial cable under 50 feet (15 meters) in length, with wiring cross-connected to enable full data control without use of a modem. Null-modem cables, and null-modem adapters (so-called "modem eliminators") that connect to a standard serial cable, are readily available at most computer stores. You can also prepare your own. A wiring diagram for null-modem connection is provided in Figure 7-18 and Figure 7-19.

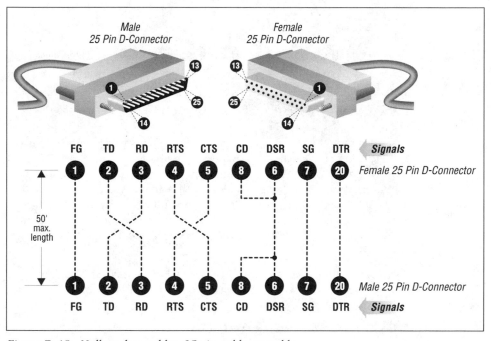

Figure 7–18. Null modem cables, 25 pin cable assembly

The TD and RD signals are swapped. The CTS and RTS signals are also swapped. CD and DSR are combined and passed through. DTR and SG are simply passed through. FG is passed through on a 25pin cable (this can be omitted) but RI on the 9 pin cable is not passed through. If you examine the pinouts and observe these signal handling rules, you can also construct a 9-25 pin hybrid null-modem cable.

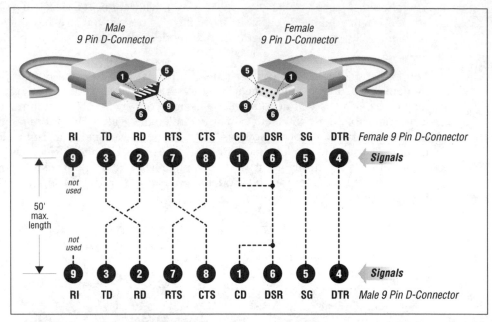

Figure 7–19. Null modem cables, 9 pin cable assembly

A host system with multiple serial ports can connect several UUCP hosts at a time, and relay files and commands between them. For example, a UUCP user might use *uuxqt* (a UUCP remote execution program) to make another UUCP host system immediately start communication with a third system. To allow this, the intermediate host must have used two ports simultaneously: one to receive the *uuxqt* command from the first system, and another to communicate with the third host. Having more than one phone line can be very beneficial on a heavily used UUCP host.

[3] Network Admin Guide

Under some circumstances you may use UUCP across ISDN or Ethernet links. See the *Linux Network Administrator's Guide* for a discussion of this topic.

UUCP Flavors and Features

Three important UUCP packages exist for UNIX-like systems. They use different files and administrative tools, but offer basically the same features and are functionally compatible. (That is, two hosts using different UUCP packages can still communicate with one another.)

The first implementation is Version 2 UUCP, whose history can be traced back to Mike Lesk's original AT&T version. Lesk's original UUCP—"Version 1" if you will—was never part of a UNIX distribution. So Version 2 was the first general UNIX distribution of UUCP, created by Lesk and Dave Nowitz at Bell Laboratories in 1978 and distributed with Version 7 UNIX. You can get Version 2-style UUCP utilities from FTP sites for BSD software.

Some deficiencies in Version 2 were identified at a design meeting on UUCP at Bell Laboratories in 1983, held to address problems discovered during the development and growth of Usenet. After this meeting, a new version of UNIX called BNU (Basic Networking Utilities) was developed by P. Honeyman, D.A. Nowitz, and B.E. Redman. In their honor, BNU is also popularly known as "HoneyDanBer UUCP."

Taylor UUCP, which is the UUCP most closely associated with Linux, is the new kid on the block. It offers some management and communications enhancements that are largely unused because only the Taylor UUCP package has them. Normally Taylor UUCP is compiled as a BNU UUCP package on a Linux host. That's what we recommend, too, unless you are already comfortable with another UUCP flavor.

BNU is easier to manage than plain Version 2 UUCP. BNU was the first package to implement some of the features so necessary to the desktop user, including bi-directional modem support and robust dial-up support for switched line communications. However, developers of Version 2 have generally modernized it and added utilities to make it functionally comparable to BNU. (Don't automatically assume that BNU is better than some of the updated Version 2 UUCP packages.) Additional freeware UUCP utilities can be used to enhance or customize your implementation, whichever version of UUCP you may use.

UUCP Remote Command Execution

Remote command execution is a very convenient feature in a LAN where access from outside intruders is not a concern. This UUCP feature allows you to take advantage of special capabilities of a remote UUCP-connected host. For example, you might send PostScript files to a remote host and then queue them for printing on that system's PostScript printer. Or you could access an Internet-connected host system and execute an *archie* query operation to find an FTPMAIL site that will send you requested files through email.

As mentioned earlier, the down-side of this convenience is the security threat that this form of access brings to the remotely accessed host system. Most hosts that permit remote execution at all will limit that access to a few utilities. They will try to provide what the small user on an isolated personal computer needs—for instance, email, Netnews, and commands that allow UUCP functions to be relayed. (For example, a system that normally queues mail for UUCP transfer late at night may allow a remote user to initiate *uucico* for an immediate UUCP connection and file exchange with a third host.)

Mail on UUCP Systems

For over a decade, one of the main things UUCP has been used for is the exchange of electronic mail. Here we'll explain the rather complicated mechanics. Things may happen somewhat differently in some pseudo-UUCP packages, particularly on non-UNIX systems.

This is how mail is typically processed between UUCP systems:

1. A user directly or indirectly invokes the *mail* program, and sends a message.

2. The mail program invokes the *uux* command. This stores the mail into a directory along with everybody else's (called "spooling" the mail) and invokes the *uucico* program. Because UUCP is going to control the transfer of mail, *uucico* starts in master mode. The other side will be in slave mode.

3. *uucico* checks configuration files to find out when it is allowed to dial the remote system. When the time arrives, *uucico* looks for queued UUCP files; assigns a file lock on the mail file to the remote host to which the mail is to be routed; and uses the assigned device to call the remote system, connects, and logs in.

4. The remote system starts a slave *uucico* daemon, which identifies its system to the master *uucico* daemon and negotiates a transfer protocol to use.

5. The master *uucico* daemon sends the files that are queued for the remote host.

6. The master on the local system switches to slave mode, while the receiving system switches to master mode.

7. The remote system's *uucico* (now the master) sends any queued UUCP files waiting to go to the local system.

8. When each *uucico* daemon reports to the other that it has no more UUCP work to do with that host, they break the connection (hang up).

9. The *uucico* of a system that receives mail then invokes the *rmail* program to deliver the mail to the user's mailbox on the system.

A word about UUCP addressing is necessary here. Traditional UUCP addressing, called "bang addressing," consists of the hostname followed by an exclamation mark (a "bang" character) and the user ID of the mail recipient. For example, you might mail a file named *missive* to joeuser on a UUCP host named **icarus** that your system connects to by sending it this way:

```
$ mail icarus!joeuser < missive
```

csh and *csh*-clone shell users have to escape the bang character with a backslash so that the shell won't attempt to treat it as an operator. For example, `phaeton\!joeuser` instead of `phaeton!joeuser`.

If you needed to send a message to a host named **phaeton** that you haven't got a direct UUCP connection to, but which the host **icarus** connects to, you could send something like:

```
$ mail icarus!phaeton!joeuser < missive
```

You probably noticed that this is a crude way to mail a file that you have already prepared. You might just have well bypassed *mail* and said:

```
$ uuto missive icarus!phaeton!joeuser
```

Or you might have composed the mail using Elm or some other mailer, which would in turn have called the *mail* program.

Now let's assume you have a minimally smart mail system configured on your Linux host. Your mail setup doesn't know anything about sending mail on the Internet, for example, but your system connects via UUCP to the host **phaeton**. This in turn connects via UUCP to a host named **kingkong.com**, which is on the Internet and can route the mail on the Internet. You might send your mail to jackie at **bigcompany.com** using this address:

```
icarus!phaeton!kingkong.com%jackie@bigcompany.com
```

The mail is routed according to the bangpath information. When it gets to the host whose name is terminated by the percent sign (**%**), that host re-reads the address to the right of the percent sign and forwards it to *jackie@bigcompany.com*. Your mileage may vary. OK, sorry to have had to say that, but when you mix addressing forms, you are at the mercy of how the mail routing programs (typically *send-mail* or *smail*) on all the intermediate hosts are configured to handle the mail—and they may not be configured correctly.

Newsgroups on UUCP Systems

The first publicly accessible network news was distributed over UUCP. But now there's probably more network news (Netnews) on the Internet alone than your PC can handle with UUCP (or any serial connection). Because Netnews can impose heavy processing and storage loads on a UUCP host, and adds significant administrative overhead, some UUCP hosts do not provide this service.

[39]
Managing
UUCP

Administrators that set up a UUCP system to handle Netnews usually focus on local newsgroups and subjects of special interest to users of the local UUCP system. For novice news administrators, we recommend a modest beginning to Netnews service. You can set up local newsgroups that aren't part of the global distribution, such as a newsgroup about the local UUCP net itself. This lets you solve your news processing and distribution problems before announcing your existence on *news.newsites* and connecting to the larger net (and encountering new problems). Nobody who must manage UUCP-based newsfeeds should try to do so without having *Managing UUCP and Usenet* as a reference.

The news administrator has to select the newsreading software that will be supported on the UUCP host, and this will vary depending on what the administrator is comfortable with. The most broadly used newsreader is probably *readnews*, but many sites are moving to more modern *threaded* newsreaders such as *trn* or *nn*. A threaded newsreader allows the reader to follow a "thread of conversation" through a newsgroup, starting with an article and continuing with followup postings on the same topic. This is often preferred over the original newsreader habit of presenting the news articles in a first in, first out sequence (which threaded newsreaders also allow).

If you are a fan of some particular user interface, you might prefer a newsreader that provides a common interface for both Netnews and mail. The pair of utilities *xrn* and *xmh*, for example, provide a common application interface and filesystem to the *rn* newsreader and the MH mail utilities. A devoted Emacs user might use Gnews, GNUS, C-News, MH, or some other newsreader from within the Emacs environment. Such personal preferences usually come at a cost—you may have to "support yourself." Administrators usually don't have time to devote to supporting software that is not broadly used by other system users.

Because each newsreader you might use is so different, you will need to ask your administrator what to use on your system. If you have a strong preference for one newsreader over another, you will be pleased to find that there are a large variety of freely usable newsreaders available that can be compiled for Linux. Now that multimedia mail is becoming relatively common, you might consider using a package that supports MIME, the Multimedia Internet Mail Extensions. Such packages should be able to take advantage of the available graphics and audio resources on your system, and gracefully handle embedded multimedia data that your system cannot properly present.

As diverse as the available newsreaders are, most of them do observe a few common traditions. Subscription to newsgroups is handled through a *news resource* file in your home directory called *.newsrc*. If this file does not exist, it is normally created by a newsreader program the first time you invoke the newsreader command. The *.newsrc* file normally contains a list of newsgroups available on the system, indicating whether or not you are subscribed to each one and which articles in it you have read already. Because just about all newsreaders follow this convention, you can use different newsreaders in different environments (for example, *xrn* from an X environment, and *rn* from an ANSI console) without losing track of what newsgroups you want to read and which articles you've already read.

SOURCES OF LINUX INFORMATION

This appendix contains information on various online sources of Linux information. All of these documents are available either in printed form, or electronically from the Internet or BBS systems. Many Linux distributions also include much of this documentation in the distribution itself, so after you have installed Linux these files may be present on your system. The Bibliography lists a number of books and other materials that relate to topics we have discussed in this book.

Online Documents

Appendix C
Appendix D

These documents should be available on any of the Linux FTP archive sites (see Appendix C, *FTP Tutorial and Site List*, for a list). If you do not have direct access to FTP, you may be able to locate these documents on other online services (such as CompuServe, local BBSes, and so on). Appendix D, *Bulletin Board Access to Linux*, lists BBSes that carry Linux materials.

If you have access to Internet mail, you can use the *ftpmail* service to receive these documents. See Appendix C for more information.

In particular, the following documents may be found on **sunsite.unc.edu** in the directory */pub/Linux/docs*. Many sites mirror this directory; however, if you're unable to locate a mirror site near you, this is a good one to fall back on. HOW-TOs and Linux Documentation Project manuals are listed in the Bibliography, which also lists other useful documents.

You can also access Linux files and documentation using *gopher*. Just point your *gopher* client to port 70 on **sunsite.unc.edu**, and follow the menus to the Linux archive. This is a good way to browse Linux documentation interactively.

The Linux Frequently Asked Questions List
The Linux Frequently Asked Questions list, or "FAQ," is a list of common questions (and answers!) about Linux. This document is meant to provide a general source of information about Linux, common problems and solutions, and a list of other sources of information. Every new Linux user should read this document. It is available in a number of formats, including plain ASCII, PostScript, and Lout typesetter format. The Linux FAQ is maintained by Ian Jackson, *ijackson@nyx.cs.du.edu.*

The Linux META-FAQ

The META-FAQ is a collection of "metaquestions" about Linux; that is, sources of information about the Linux system and other general topics. It is a good starting place for the Internet user wishing to find more information about the system. It is maintained by Michael K. Johnson, *johnsonm@sunsite.unc.edu*.

The Linux INFO-SHEET

The Linux INFO-SHEET is a technical introduction to the Linux system. It gives an overview of the system's features and available software, and also provides a list of other sources of Linux information. The format and content is similar in nature to the META-FAQ; incidentally, it is also maintained by Michael K. Johnson.

The Linux Software Map

The Linux Software Map is a list of many applications available for Linux, where to get them, who maintains them, and so forth. It is far from complete—to compile a complete list of Linux software would be nearly impossible. However, it does include many of the most popular Linux software packages. If you can't find a particular application to suit your needs, the LSM is a good place to start. It is maintained by Jeff Kopmanis, *jeffk@msen.com*.

The Linux HOWTO Index

The Linux HOWTOs are a collection of "how to" documents, each describing in detail a certain aspect of the Linux system. They are maintained by Matt Welsh, *mdw@sunsite.unc.edu*. The HOWTO Index lists the HOWTO documents which are available. See the Bibliography for a partial list of HOWTOs.

Other online documents

If you browse the *docs* subdirectory of any Linux FTP site, you'll see many other documents which are not listed here: a slew of FAQ's, interesting tidbits, and other important information. This miscellany is difficult to categorize here; if you don't see what you're looking for on the list above, just take a look at one of the Linux archive sites listed in Appendix C.

Linux Documentation Project Manuals

The Linux Documentation Project is working on developing a set of manuals and other documentation for Linux, including manual pages. These manuals are in various stages of development, and any help revising and updating them is greatly appreciated. If you have questions about the LDP, please contact Matt Welsh (*mdw@sunsite.unc.edu*).

These books are available via anonymous FTP from a number of Linux archive sites, including **sunsite.unc.edu** in the directory */pub/Linux/docs/LDP*. A number of commercial distributors are selling printed copies of these books; you may already be able to find the LDP manuals on the shelves of your local bookstore. A complete list of manuals can be found in the Bibliography.

Requests For Comments

Proposals, standards, and other information have historically been passed around the Internet community through documents called Requests for Comments. All RFCs are available via anonymous FTP from **nic.ddn.mil**, **ftp.uu.net**, and a number of other sites around the world. To obtain an RFC via email, send a message to *service@nic.ddn.mil* with the text

```
send RFC-number.TXT
```

in the subject header line. The Bibliography lists a number of RFCs that interest Linux network administrators and users.

LINUX VENDOR LIST

This appendix lists contact information for a number of vendors who sell Linux on diskette, tape, and CD-ROM. Many of them provide Linux documentation, support, and other services as well. This is by no means a complete listing; if you purchased this book in printed form, it's very possible that the vendor or publishing company also provides Linux software and services.

The author makes no guarantee as to the accuracy of any of the information listed in this Appendix. This information is included here only as a service to readers, not as an advertisement for any particular organization.

Fintronic Linux Systems
1360 Willow Rd., Suite 205
Menlo Park, CA 94025 USA
Tel: +1 415 325-4474
Fax: +1 415 325-4908
linux@fintronic.com

InfoMagic, Inc.
PO Box 30370
Flagstaff, AZ 86003-0370 USA
Tel: +1 800 800-6613, +1 602 526-9565
Fax: +1 602 526-9573
Orders@InfoMagic.com

Lasermoon Ltd
2a Beaconsfield Road, Fareham,
Hants, England. PO16 0QB.
Tel: +44 (0) 329 826444.
Fax: +44 (0) 329 825936.
info@lasermoon.co.uk

Linux Journal
P.O. Box 85867
Seattle, WA 98145-1867 USA
Tel: +1 206 527-3385
Fax: +1 206 527-2806
linux@ssc.com

Linux Systems Labs
18300 Tara Drive
Clinton Twp, MI 48036 USA
Tel: +1 313 954-2829, +1 800 432-0556
Fax: +1 313 954-2806
info@lsl.com

Morse Telecommunication, Inc.
26 East Park Avenue, Suite 240
Long Beach, NY 11561 USA
Tel: +1 800 60-MORSE
Fax: +1 516 889-8665
Linux@morse.net

Nascent Technology
Linux from Nascent CDROM
P.O. Box 60669
Sunnyvale CA 94088-0669 USA
Tel: +1 408 737-9500
Fax: +1 408 241-9390
nascent@netcom.com

Red Hat Software
P.O. Box 4325
Chapel Hill, NC 27515 USA
Tel: +1 919 309-9560
redhat@redhat.com

SW Technology
251 West Renner Suite 229
Richardson, TX 75080 USA
Tel: +1 214 907-0871
swt@netcom.com

Takelap Systems Ltd.
The Reddings, Court Robin Lane,
Llangwm, Usk, Gwent, United Kingdom NP5 1ET
Tel: +44 (0)291 650357
Fax: +44 (0)291 650500
info@ddrive.demon.co.uk

Trans-Ameritech Enterprises, Inc.
2342A Walsh Ave
Santa Clara, CA 95051 USA
Tel: +1 408 727-3883
roman@trans-ameritech.com

Unifix Software GmbH
Postfach 4918
D-38039 Braunschweig
Germany
Tel: +49 (0)531 515161
Fax: +49 (0)531 515162

Yggdrasil Computing, Incorporated
4880 Stevens Creek Blvd., Suite 205
San Jose, CA 95129-1034 USA
Tel: +1 800 261-6630, +1 408 261-6630
Fax: +1 408 261-6631
info@yggdrasil.com

FTP Tutorial and Site List

FTP (*File Transfer Protocol*) is the set of programs used for transferring files between systems on the Internet. Most UNIX, VMS, and MS-DOS systems on the Internet have a program called *ftp* which you use to transfer these files, and if you have Internet access, the best way to download the Linux software is by using *ftp*. This appendix covers basic *ftp* usage—of course, there are many more functions and uses of *ftp* than are given here. The *Whole Internet User's Guide and Catalog* gives everything you need to know about *ftp*.

[29] Whole
Internet

At the end of this appendix there is a listing of FTP sites where Linux software can be found. Also, if you don't have direct Internet access but are able to exchange electronic mail with the Internet, information on using the *ftpmail* service is included below.

If you're using an MS-DOS, UNIX, or VMS system to download files from the Internet, then *ftp* is a command-driven program. However, there are other implementations of *ftp* out there, such as the Macintosh version (called *Fetch*) with a nice menu-driven interface, which is quite self-explanatory. Even if you're not using the command-driven version of *ftp*, the information given here should help.

ftp can be used to both upload (send) or download (receive) files from other Internet sites. In most situations, you're going to be downloading software. On the Internet there are a large number of publicly-available *FTP archive sites*, machines which allow anyone to *ftp* to them and download free software. One such archive site is **sunsite.unc.edu**, which has a lot of Sun Microsystems software, and acts as one of the main Linux sites. In addition, FTP archive sites *mirror* software to each other—that is, software uploaded to one site will be automatically copied over to a number of other sites. So don't be surprised if you see the exact same files on many different archive sites.

Starting ftp

Note that in the examples printed below I'm only showing the most important information, and what you see may differ. Also, commands in **bold** represent commands that you type; everything else is screen output.

To start *ftp* and connect to a site, simply use the command

```
ftp hostname
```

where *hostname* is the name of the site you are connecting to. For example, to connect to the mythical site **shoop.vpizza.com** we can use the command

```
ftp shoop.vpizza.com
```

Logging In

When *ftp* starts up we should see something like

```
Connected to shoop.vpizza.com.
220 Shoop.vpizza.com FTPD ready at 15 Dec 1992 08:20:42 EDT
Name (shoop.vpizza.com:mdw):
```

Here, *ftp* is asking us to give the username that we want to log in as on **shoop.vpizza.com**. The default here is mdw, which is my username on the system I'm using FTP from. Since I don't have an account on **shoop.vpizza.com** I can't log in as myself. Instead, to access publicly-available software on an FTP site, I log in as anonymous, and give my Internet email address (if I have one) as the password. So, I would type

```
Name (shoop.vpizza.com:mdw): anonymous
331-Guest login ok, send e-mail address as password.
Password: mdw@sunsite.unc.edu
230- Welcome to shoop.vpizza.com.
230- Virtual Pizza Delivery[tm]: Download pizza in 30 cycles or less
230- or you get it FREE!
ftp>
```

Of course, you should give your email address, instead of mine, and it won't echo to the screen as you're typing it (since it's technically a "password"). *ftp* should allow us to log in, and we'll be ready to download software.

Poking Around

Okay, we're in. ftp> is our prompt, and the *ftp* program is waiting for commands. There are a few basic commands you need to know about. First, the commands

```
ls file
```

and

```
dir file
```

both give file listings (where *file* is an optional argument specifying a particular filename to list). The difference is that *ls* usually gives a short listing and *dir* gives a longer listing (that is, with more information on the sizes of the files, dates of

Chapter 3

modification, and so on). The *dir* output is like that of the UNIX command *ls –l*, discussed in the section "Listing Files" of Chapter 3, *Basic UNIX Commands and Concepts*.

The command

    cd *directory*

will move to the given directory (just like the *cd* command on UNIX or MS-DOS systems). You can use the command

    cdup

to change to the parent directory (the directory above the current one).

The command

    help *command*

will give help on the given *ftp command* (such as *ls* or *cd*). If no command is specified, *ftp* will list all of the available commands.

If we type *dir* at this point we'll see an initial directory listing of where we are:

```
ftp> dir
200 PORT command successful.
150 Opening ASCII mode data connection for /bin/ls.
total 1337
dr-xr-xr-x  2 root     wheel        512 Aug 13 13:55 bin
drwxr-xr-x  2 root     wheel        512 Aug 13 13:58 dev
drwxr-xr-x  2 root     wheel        512 Jan 25 17:35 etc
drwxr-xr-x 19 root     wheel       1024 Jan 27 21:39 pub
drwxrwx-wx  4 root     ftp-admi    1024 Feb  6 22:10 uploads
drwxr-xr-x  3 root     wheel        512 Mar 11  1992 usr
226 Transfer complete.
921 bytes received in 0.24 seconds (3.7 Kbytes/s)
ftp>
```

Each of these entries is a directory, not an individual file that we can download (specified by the d in the first column of the listing). On most FTP archive sites, the publicly available software is under the directory */pub*, so let's go there:

```
ftp> cd pub
ftp> dir
200 PORT command successful.
150 ASCII data connection for /bin/ls (128.84.181.1,4525) (0 bytes).
total 846
-rw-r--r--  1 root     staff       1433 Jul 12  1988 README
-r--r--r--  1 3807     staff      15586 May 13  1991 US.TXT.2
-rw-r--r--  1 539      staff      52664 Feb 20  1991 altenergy
-r--r--r--  1 65534    65534      56456 Dec 17  1990 ataxx.tar.Z
-rw-r--r--  1 root     other    2013041 Jul  3  1991 gesyps.tar.Z
-rw-r--r--  1 432      staff      41831 Jan 30  1989 gnexe.arc
-rw-rw-rw-  1 615      staff      50315 Apr 16  1992 linpack.tar.Z
```

```
-r--r--r--    1 root     wheel        12168 Dec 25  1990 localtime.o
-rw-r--r--    1 root     staff         7035 Aug 27  1986 manualslist
drwxr-xr-x    2 2195     staff          512 Mar 10 00:48 mdw
-rw-r--r--    1 root     staff         5593 Jul 19  1988 t.out.h
226 ASCII Transfer complete.
2443 bytes received in 0.35 seconds (6.8 Kbytes/s)
ftp>
```

Here we can see a number of (interesting?) files, one of which is called *README*, which we should download (most FTP sites have a *README* file in the */pub* directory).

Downloading Files

Before downloading files, there are a few things that you need to take care of.

- **Turn on hash mark printing.** *Hash marks* are printed to the screen as files are being transferred; they let you know how far along the transfer is, and that your connection hasn't hung up (so you don't sit for 20 minutes, thinking that you're still downloading a file). In general, a hash mark appears as a pound sign (#), and one is printed for every 1024 or 8192 bytes transferred, depending on your system.

  To turn on hash mark printing, give the command *hash*:

  ```
  ftp> hash
  Hash mark printing on (8192 bytes/hash mark).
  ftp>
  ```

- **Determine the type of file that you are downloading.** As far as FTP is concerned, files come in two flavors: *binary* and *text*. Most of the files that you'll be downloading are binary files: that is, programs, compressed files, archive files, and so on. However, many files (such as *README*s and so on) are text files.

  Why does the file type matter? Only because on some systems (such as MS-DOS systems), certain characters in a text file, such as carriage returns, need to be converted so that the file will be readable. While transferring in binary mode, no conversion is done—the file is simply transferred byte after byte.

  The commands *bin* and *ascii* set the transfer mode to binary and text, respectively. *When in doubt, always use binary mode to transfer files.* If you try to transfer a binary file in text mode, you'll corrupt the file, and it will be unusable. (This is one of the most common mistakes made when using FTP.) However, you can use text mode for plain text files (whose filenames often end in *.txt*).

  For our example, we're downloading the file *README*, which is most likely a text file, so we use the command

```
ftp> ascii
200 Type set to A.
ftp>
```

- **Set your local directory.** Your *local directory* is the directory on your system where you want the downloaded files to end up. While the *cd* command changes the remote directory (on the remote machine that you're FTPing to), the *lcd* command changes the local directory.

For example, to set the local directory to */home/db/mdw/tmp*, use the command

```
ftp> lcd /home/db/mdw/tmp
Local directory now /home/db/mdw/tmp
ftp>
```

Now you're ready to actually download the file. The command

```
get remote-name local-name
```

is used for this, where *remote-name* is the name of the file on the remote machine, and *local-name* is the name that you wish to give the file on your local machine. The *local-name* argument is optional; by default, the local filename is the same as the remote one. However, if for example you're downloading the file *README*, and you already have a *README* in your local directory, you'll want to give a different *local-filename* so that the first one isn't overwritten.

For our example, to download the file *README*, we simply use

```
ftp> get README
200 PORT command successful.
150 ASCII data connection for README (128.84.181.1,4527) (1433 bytes).
#
226 ASCII Transfer complete.
local: README remote: README
1493 bytes received in 0.03 seconds (49 Kbytes/s)
ftp>
```

Quitting ftp

To end your FTP session, simply use the command

```
quit
```

The command

```
close
```

can be used to close the connection with the current remote FTP site; the *open* command can then be used to start a session with another site (without quitting the FTP program altogether).

```
ftp> close
221 Goodbye.
ftp> quit
```

Using ftpmail

ftpmail is a service that allows you to obtain files from FTP archive sites via Internet electronic mail. If you don't have direct Internet access, but are able to send mail to the Internet (from a service such as CompuServe, for example), *ftpmail* is a good way to get files from FTP archive sites. Unfortunately, *ftpmail* can be slow, especially when sending large jobs. Before attempting to download large amounts of software using *ftpmail*, be sure that your mail spool will be able to handle the incoming traffic. Many systems keep quotas on incoming electronic mail, and may delete your account if your mail exceeds this quota. Just use common sense.

sunsite.unc.edu, one of the major Linux FTP archive sites, is home to an *ftpmail* server. To use this service, send electronic mail to

```
ftpmail@sunsite.unc.edu
```

with a message body containing only the word

```
help
```

This will send you back a list of *ftpmail* commands and a brief tutorial on using the system.

For example, to get a listing of Linux files found on **sunsite.unc.edu**, send mail to the above address containing the text

```
open sunsite.unc.edu
cd /pub/Linux
dir
quit
```

You may use the *ftpmail* service to connect to any FTP archive site; you are not limited to **sunsite.unc.edu**. The next section lists a number of Linux FTP archives.

Linux FTP Site List

Table C-1 is a listing of the most well-known FTP archive sites that carry the Linux software. Keep in mind that many other sites mirror these, and more than likely you'll run into Linux on a number of sites not on this list.

Table C–1: Linux FTP Sites

Site name	IP Address	Directory
tsx-11.mit.edu	18.172.1.2	/pub/linux
sunsite.unc.edu	152.2.22.81	/pub/Linux
nic.funet.fi	128.214.6.100	/pub/OS/Linux
ftp.mcc.ac.uk	130.88.200.7	/pub/linux
fgb1.fgb.mw.tu-muenchen.de	129.187.200.1	/pub/linux
ftp.informatik.tu-muenchen.de	131.159.0.110	/pub/Linux
ftp.dfv.rwth-aachen.de	137.226.4.105	/pub/linux
ftp.informatik.rwth-aachen.de	137.226.112.172	/pub/Linux
ftp.ibp.fr	132.227.60.2	/pub/linux
kirk.bond.edu.au	131.244.1.1	/pub/OS/Linux
ftp.uu.net	137.39.1.9	/systems/unix/linux
wuarchive.wustl.edu	128.252.135.4	/systems/linux
ftp.win.tue.nl	131.155.70.100	/pub/linux
ftp.stack.urc.tue.nl	131.155.2.71	/pub/linux
ftp.ibr.cs.tu-bs.de	134.169.34.15	/pub/os/linux
ftp.denet.dk	129.142.6.74	/pub/OS/linux

src.doc.ic.ac.uk

tsx-11.mit.edu, **sunsite.unc.edu**, and **nic.funet.fi** are the "home sites" for the Linux software, where most of the new software is uploaded. Most of the other sites on the list mirror some combination of these three. To reduce network traffic, choose a site that is geographically closest to you.

SunSite Northern Europe at Imperial College.

BULLETIN BOARD ACCESS TO LINUX

This appendix is a listing of bulletin board systems (BBSes) that carry Linux files. It was prepared from the 45th version of the list—the last edition we were able to pull together before this book went to press—dated December 8, 1994. We provide this listing because some of you simply don't have Internet access. However, for those of you that do, you can get the current listing by FTP at **ftp.cs.tu-berlin** in the file */pub/linux/Local/docs/linuxbbs.45.gz*.

If you access a BBS site that keeps a version of this list, it is probably stored under the name `linuxbbs.num`. This version, for example, would have been *linuxbbs.45*, or if stored in a zip-compressed form, *linuxbbs.45z*. LinuxNet and File-net BBSes carry this list.

Linux BBS Listings

The listings are separated by country, alphabetized by state, and sorted within those sections by the completeness of their Linux archives (if known). The listings are in a regular, structured format. The key to the listing is:

Format

```
State YYY  BBS Name          Phone Number    Modem Speed  Online time
       5   City              Other data
```

In the listing, the State entry is a postal service code for a province, state, borough, canton, district, or other defined region in the country. YYY represents the response to three questions about the accessibility of Linux files to users, as described below under "Access." 5 represents a numeric value that indicates the quantity or thoroughness of the Linux archives, as described below under "Rating system." An Online time listing of 24h indicates that the system is always available (00:00-24:00). In practical fact, most Fidonet BBSes observe a brief down-time each night for transfer of email and files with other systems and for system maintenance.

Access

The three letters after the State entry indicate whether the site:

- Allows free access to Linux files.

- Allows FREQ file requests, for Fidonet email of files not kept locally.

- Allows the download of Linux related files on first access to the BBS.

Rating system
We took the liberty of rephrasing the original words of the rating system.

5   The site is thorough—it has "pretty much everything you need."

4   The site is a respectable Linux source site.

3   The site is a fairly good Linux source site.

2   The Linux basics, perhaps a little more, are available.

1   Only a smattering of Linux files are available.

And now for the BBS list.

Australia

```
ACT YNY posgate.apana.org.au  +61-(06)-285-1701  V32bis      24h
      3 Canberra              Internet (APANA)

NSW YYN Linux-Support-Oz      +61-2-418-8750    v.32bis 14.4k 24h
      5 Sydney                Internet/Usenet
NSW NYY 500cc Formula 1 BBS   +61-2-550-4317     V.32bis     24h
      4 Sydney                -
NSW NNY Krikkit One PAU       +61.49.423565  2400  AET11:00-19:00
      2 Newcastle             APANA, slackware soon

VIC NNY Suburbia Multiline    +61-3-596-8366     14.4k       24h
      2 Melbourne             suburbia.apana.org.au

  -   YNY Desire BBS          +61-7-371-1190      14.4k V32bis 24h
      4 Brisbane              APANA (desire.apana.org.au)
```

Austria

```
W   YYY Galaktische Archive +43.222.830-38-04 16.8 ZYX 19:00-7:00
      4 Wien                 Fido 2:310/77
```

Belgium

```
  -   YYY In Limbo           +32-2-582-66-50 ZyX19.2 V.32bis 24h
      3-4 Lennik             +32-2-582-71-77   Fidonet 2:291/702
```

Brazil

```
SP  YNY Wintech BBS        +55-011-5238883    V32bis/V42bis 24h
    2 Sao Paulo            -
```

Canada

We've omitted +1 from the Canada listings.

```
AB  Y-Y Logical Solutions  299-9900 to 9911    2400bps      24h
    5 -                    14.4 K lines: 299-9912 to 9913,
                           16.8k USR v32bis: 299-9914 to 9917
AB  NNN WorldGate/VALIS 403-444-7685           14.4k V32bis 24h
    5 Edmonton         Internet, other Lines: 481-8584, 489-4064
AB  NNN Magic BBS          403-569-2882 14.4k HST/Telebit/MNP 24h
    3 Calgary             Internet/Usenet

AB  YYY Cameo Gateway      403-249-6008      14.4k HST v.42 24h
    - Calgary           Fidonet 1:134/63 & Emergnet 31:31/10
AB  NYN Cameo Gateway 2    403-242-7527         19.2k       24h
    - Calgary          Fidonet 1:134/500 & Emergnet 31:4331/50
AB  YYY Calgary Message Line 403-249-6560       14.4k       24h
    - Calgary             Fidonet 1:134/66

BC  YYY Serendipity        604-599-3820      14.4k v.32b  24h
    5 Richmond            Fidonet 1:153/916, SLS, Slackware
ON  YNY Mark's Linux BBS   613-829-1941       V.Fast 24k bps 24h
    5 Ottawa             Internet, UUCP, second line: 829-4553
ON  YNY The Void           613-731-4909         1200-16.8k  24h
    4 Ottawa             Fidonet: 1:163/273.5, SLS

QC  YNY Radio Free Nyongwa 514-524-0829       v.32bis ZyXEL 24h
    2 Montreal            USENET, Fido
QC  YNY Smegheads BBS      514-457-0093    14.4k V32b, V42b 24h
    2 Montreal         USENET, UUCP, Yggdrasil, login: guest
```

Czech Republic

```
-   YNY Super 7            +42-2421-8007      V32bis w/ASL 24h
    5 Prague              Internet vseedu.vse.cz
```

Finland

```
-   YNY Dream World BBS    +358 21 4389 843    9600/ARQ     24h
    4 Raisio              USENET dream.nullnet.fi
-   YNY Valhalla          +358-(9)52-181-299     14.4k      24h
    4 Kotka Finland    UseNet valhall.nullnet.fi no time limits
```

France

```
69  NYY Stdin              +33-72345437 (UUCP) V32bis      24h
     5 Lyon, Rhone         +33-72345072 (FidoNet 134:323/8)
-   NNY Modula      +33-1-4043-0124, -4530-1248 HST 14.4 V32bis 24h
     5 Paris             Michel Parlebas. no fee for Linux files
-   NNN Libernet BBS       33-1-402-290-93    V32b           24h
     5 Paris               Usenet (info@remcomp.fdn.org)

-   -NY BBS-FDN            +33-1-48-89-58-59 V32bis,V42bis 24h
     4 Paris               Internet
-   NNY Zenux             +33-78361001     V32b 24.4k Zoom 24h
     3 Lyon                Internet Mail/News

-   YYY Cafard Naum        +33-51701632           V.Fast 28.8k 24h
     2 Nantes, Yann Dupont Gdx BBS under Linux, +33-5170163
-   YNY Brasil             +33-1-44670844       V32bis         24h
     2 Paris, Laurent Chemla BBS under Linux (xbbs)
-   NYY Le Lien            +33-72089879       HST 14.4/V32bis 24h
     - Lyon, Pascal Valette  FidoNet 2:323/5
```

Germany

```
BAY NYN Fiffis Inn BBS     +49-89-570-13-53    ZyX+ 19.2k   24h
     5 Munich              Fido 2:246/69, LinuxNet, magic: LINUX
BAY YYY BMS               +49-951-952-00-51 ZyX 19.2bps+ISDN 24h
     5 Bamberg             952-00-31 LinuxNet, Fido 2:2490/3001

BAY YYY Asterix            +49-7424-91241 ZyX 19.2k V32bis 24h
     4 78554 Aixheim       Fido 2:246/8012
BAY YYY Die Box Passau 1+2 +49-851-555-96 19.2k V32terbo 8:00-NMH
     4 Passau              Fido 2:2494/21                   MET
BAY YYY Die Box Passau 3   +49-851-950-468 V.110/X.75 8:00-NMH
     4 Passau              Fido 2:2494/23, ISDN      MET

BAY YYY Die Box Passau 4   +49-851-950-462  V32b ZyX  8:00-NMH
     4 Passau              Fido 2:2494/22                   MET
BAY YNY Greenie            +49-89-324-33-28   ZyX 16.8      24h
     4 Munich              FREQ soon, gert@greenie.muc.de
          UUCP: machine greenie, login: nuucp, ~/green.files.Z

BAY YNY The Bingo BBS      +49-89-637-84-29   ZyX 19.2k     24h
     - Munich              Fido 2:2480/180.12
BAY NNY incubus            +49-931-781464    V32bis Vterbo 24h
     - Wuerzburg           Usenet, Z-Netz

BAY NNY Cyber-Park         +49-9621-23030      28.8k VFast  24h
     - 92224 Amberg        Fido 2:2494/508 VNET 46:9691/311
BAY YNY bino          +49-9187-41403          ZyX19.2 V32bis 24h
     - -                Usenet. sunsite/tsx-11 mirror, login: gast
          UUCP: machine bino, login nuucp, password nuucp, ~/00-find.z
```

```
BLN YYY lupo Rasca Gmelch +49-30-335-63-28 Z16 V32bis MET16-23:00
      4 Berlin                Fido 2:2410/305.4 Linuxnet login: guest
                  UUCP: machine lupo, login: nuucp, password: nuucp
BLN NYY INTERWORLD           +49-30-251-37-71  14.4k         24h
      5 Berlin                   Internet (prepared)

BRG YYY xffo                 +49-335-528-441       ZyX 19.2k     24h
      - Frankfurt (Oder)  Filelist: index Fido 2:2410/904, Z-Netz
              USENET xffo.sh.sub.de, UUCP: login nuucp, passwd nuucp

BW  NYY Fractal Zone/Maass +49-721-863-066         ZyX 16.8k  24h
      5 Karlsruhe          Fido 2:2476/462, LinuxNet magic: LINUX
BW  YYY CRYSTAL BBS          +49-7152-240-86    HST 14.4k    24h
      5 Leonberg            Fido 2:2407/3, LinuxNet

BW  YYY Echoblaster BBS #2   +49-7142-212-35 V32b 8-20:00,23-2:00
      5 Bietigheim          Fido 2:2407/40, LinuxNet
BW  NYN LinuxServer +49-711-756-275   HST16.8k 8:30-17:50,19-2:00
      5 Stuttgart   P. Berger Fido 2:2407/34, LinuxNet, Slackware

BW  NYY Rising Sun BBS    +49-7147-3845 ZyX16.8k V32b 05:30-02:30
      4 Sachsenheim      Fido 2:2407/41, LinuxNet
BW  NYY Rising Sun BBS       +49-7147-143-47      HST DS 14.4k 24h
      4 Sachsenheim      Fido 2:2407/410, LinuxNet, max. 90min

HB  YYY oytix.north.de       +49-421-396-57-62  V.fast       24h
      4 Bremen    mike@oytix.north.de, login "gast" (ZyX: AT&N17)

HES YNY BHT-BOX           +49-6648-3553          19.2k ZyX    24h
      4 Wartenburg       Usenet, bht-box.zer.de, 2. Line: 37333
          ISDN: +49-6648-91-00-50 or +49-6648-91-00-55
HES NYY Radio Bornheim      +49-69-493-08-30    ZyX19.2k     24h
      2 Frankfurt/Main      Fido 2:2461/332, LinuxNet Slackware

HH  YNY umibox              +49-4152-824-93     ZyX 16.8k    24h
      5 Geesthacht          USENET, bbs login: guest (no passwd)
HH  YNY troehl             +49-40-792-99-61     ZyX 19.2k    24h
      5 Hamburg             BBS login: gast   see /pub/Index.gz
              UUCP: machine troehl, login nuucp, password nuucp

NDS YYY Linux Server/A. Braukmann +49-441-592-963 ZyX 16.8k   24h
      5 Oldenburg           Fido 2:2426/2120, LinuxNet

NDS YYY MM's Spielebox       +49-5323-3515    ZyX 16.8k V32b 24h
      5 Clausthal-Zfd.      Fido 2:2437/120, SLS 1.03, SLT
NDS YYY MM's Spielebox +49-5323-3540           9.6k          24h
      5 Clausthal-Zfd.  Fido 2:2437/122, filelist magic: NEWLINUX
NDS YNY Harry's Box         +49-5132-825-928   ZyX 16.8k    24h
      5 Lehrte              BBS login: gast, password: gast
              UUCP: machine seneca, login nuucp, password nuucp
              sunsite mirror,  files /pub/find.ALL.z
```

```
NDS YYY OtE Bremen/R. Roeber  +49-421-557-97-05..8 ZyX 14.4k  24h
      3 Bremen                Fido 2:2426/3020..3, LinuxNet
NDS YNY LinuxBox Northeim     +49-5551-952-202 14.4k MET:0:00-23:00
      3 Northeim LinuxNet, Internet: peges.werries.de login: mbox

NRW YYY hippo.fido.de         +49-241-875-090     14.4k 4:30-18:00
      5 Aachen                Fido 2:2452/110  Slackware 19-24:00
NRW YYY hippo-isdn.fido.de +49-241-879-04-20                24h
      5 Aachen                    ISDN 64k X.75/38.4k V.110
                         Fido 2:2452/111  Slackware

NRW YNY Needful Things        +49-231-656-783   ZyX 16.8k   24h
      5 Dortmund              (soon: Fido and FREQ's)
NRW YYY Zaphods BBS/C.Lueders +49-228-262-894   HST V32b    24h
      5 Bonn                  Fido 2:2453/30, Slackware

NRW YYY Zaphods BBS           +49-228-229-147   HST V32b    24h
      5 Bonn                  Fido 2:2453/30, Slackware
NRW YYY Zaphods BBS ISDN      +49-228-911-10-41  64k V110/X75 24h
      5 Bonn                  Fido 2:2453/30, Slackware

NRW NNY MITROPA               +49-203-482-319      ZyX+ 19.2k   24h
      5 Duisburg              Internet, BBS under Linux (login: bbs)
NRW YNY asgard                +49-271-317-40-28 19.2k       24h
      5 Siegen                Usenet asgard.si.sub.de
NRW YNY Bigcomm Linux-Box     +49-211-398-52-58 ZyX+ 19.2k   24h
      5 Duesseldorf           Usenet, LinuxNet, Slackware Mirror

NRW YYY UB-HOFF /A. Hoffmann +49-203-584-155    ZyX+ 19.2k 24h
      3 Duisburg              Fido 2:242/37, SLS1.0
NRW YYY POLLUX /N. Szepanowski +49-2842-551-40    14.4k      24h
      3 Kamp-Lintfort         Fido 2:243/2007, SLS, C/C++ stuff
NRW YNY IUS                   +49-203-871-666 (5 Leitungen) 14.4k 24h
      - Duisburg              Internet, ISDN line: 8780222 - X.75 64k

SHL YYY FORMEL-Box            +49-4191-2846  ZyX 16.8k 5:30-03:30
      5 Kaltenkirchen         Fido 2:240/4005, LinuxNet

THU YNY AS-Node Jena          +49-3641-33-14-96 ZyX16.8      24h
      2 Jena                  ring, hangup, wait 10s, call again

-   NYY IRD-BBS Schoeningen   +49-5352-58200     14.4k      24h
      4 Schoeningen           Fido 2:241/560, UseNet
```

Hong Kong

```
-   NNY OLISC UNIX BBS        +852-429-6157      ZyX19.2     24h
    2-3 Hong Kong             UUCP, Inetnet, USENET, Uniboard BBS
```

Ireland

```
-   NNY Ireland On-Line      +353-91-92722       19.2 ZyX      24h
      5 Galway               +353-1-671-5185 Usenet/Inet @iol.ie
-   N?Y Nemesis' Dungeon +353-1-324755 or 326900 14.4k v32bis 24h
      3 Dublin          Fidonet 2:263/150
-   NNN DUBBS               +353-1-6789000      19.2 ZyXEL    24h
      1 Dublin, Ireland    Fidonet 2:263/167
```

Italy

```
-   YYY Nixnet             +39-862-316-950 V.FC,V32bis,V42bis 24h
      5 L'Aquila          Fidonet 2:335/613, Linuxnet
-   NYY nonsolosoftware    +39 51 6140772     V32bis,V42bis 24h
      5 Bologna           Fidonet 2:332/407
-   NYY nonsolopoint       +39 51 432904       ZyX19.2k      24h
      5 Bologna           Fidonet 2:332/417

-   NYY OneWay BBS         +39 2 4491062      V32bis/V42bis 24h
      4 Milano            Fidonet 2:331/333, Virnet
-   NYY DOC!               +39 41 5905472     V32bis/V42bis 24h
      4 Mogliano Veneto   Fidonet 2:333/503
-   YYY Sierra BBS         +39 6 39721568      ZyX19.2k      24h
      2 Roma              Fidonet 2:335/336
```

Netherlands

```
-   YNY DownTown BBS Lelystad +31-3200-48852      14.4k        24h
      5 Lelystad             Fido 2:512/155, UUCP
-   YYY Filosoft/PROGRAMMERS +31-50-412288       14.4k v.32bis 24h
      5 Groningen            50-426071 2400bps  Fido 2:282/517
-   YYY MUGNET Intl-Openworld +31-1720-42580      V-fast 115k  24h
    4-5 Alphen a/d Rijn    UUCP, -30979 Worldblazer, -19339 V-fast
```

New Zealand

```
-   YYY mserve.kiwi.gen.nz +64-9-366-44-62 ZyX16.8k, 28.8k 24h
      5 Auckland           usenet (login as linux)
-   NYY BugBoard           +64-4-526-4840    ZyX16.8 V32bis 24h
      3 Wellington         FidoNet 3:771/375
```

Russia

```
-   YNY sci                +7-831-234-3045     ZyX16.8       24h
    -   Nizhny Novgorod  Fido 2:5015/13, anonymous SLIP, GDX BBS
```

Singapore

```
-   YNY linuxpub            +65-583-6023       14.4k V42    24h
    5 -                     UUCP, Usenet, no download limits
-   YYY The Controversy     +65-560-6040 14.4k V.32bis/HST 24h
    3 -                     Fidonet 6:600/201
ROS YNY temasek             +65-270-4552       14.4k        24h
    - Gillman Heights       FidoNet, Rime, UUCP, Usenet
```

South Africa

```
-   NYY Pats System     +27-12-333-2049    14.4k v.32bis/HST 24h
    3 Pretoria          Fidonet 5:71-1/36
```

Sweden

```
-   YYY Gunship BBS     +46-31-693306      28.8k HST DS 24h
    - Gothenburg        Fidonet 2:203/117
```

Switzerland

```
-   YYY Baboon BBS          +41-62-511726        28.8k        24h
    5 Strengelback          Fido 2:301/520 /521 /551
-   NYY Baerengraben        +41-31-9340131       28.8k        24h
    4 Stettlen              Fido 2:301/502 /552
-   YYY Eulen Bbs           +41-1-4319649        19.2k        24h
    4 Zuerich               Fido 2:301/710
-   YYY The Best Bbs!       +41-1-2915606        19.2k        24h
    4 Zuerich               Fido 2:301/714
-   YYY Zuerich Live BBS    +41-1-4312321        19.2k        24h
    4 Zuerich               Fido 2:301/801 /850
-   YYY Gonisoft BBS        +41-22-7576185       19.2k        24h
    2 Bernex                Fido 2:301/320 /321
-   YYY ALPHANET            +41-38-41-40-81      V32bis       24h
    - Colombier             UUCP: login with "nuucp" (~/ls-laR.gz)
```

United Kingdom

```
ESU YNY POLUX Meridian BBS  +44-1273-588-924   14.4k V32bis 24h
    4 Peacehaven            -
-   NYN The Purple Tentacle +44-1734-266974    HST/V32bis   24h
    4 Reading               Fidonet 2:252/305
-   YYY On The Beach        +44-1273-600996    14.4k/16.8k  24h
    4 Brighton              Fidonet 2:441/122
-   NYY Pale Kat            +44-1291-650567    V32bis       24h
    4 Gwent                 Morse Winter 94 CD
-   YYY DarcWorld           +44-1865-377724    V32b/V42b    24h
    3 Oxford                Fidonet
```

United States of America

We've omitted +1 from the USA listings.

```
CA  YYY The Programmer's Corner 707-765-1431    14.4 V.32bis 24h
    4 Petaluma              USENET
CA  NNY Citrus Grove Public Access 916-381-5822 ZyX16.8/14.4 24h
    3 Sacramento               citrus.sac.ca.us
CA  YNY Beacons Beach BBS      619-632-2486    14.4k       24h
    3 Encinitas             Internet (email, Usenet), Slackware
CA  YNY Station Zebra         408-730-1092    14.4k V32bis 24h
    3 Sunnyvale             Usenet (ftp.saigon.com)

CA  YNY Southland BBS         818-793-9108         14.4k   24h
    2 Pasadena              UUCP, Slackware
CA  -YY The Rogue's Guild     818-347-4291      HST16.8 V32b 24h
    - Woodland Hills        Fido 1:102/812, Slackware, SLS

CO  YNY The Roman Catacombs   303-429-8914    14.4k, ZyX19.2k 24h
    - Denver               Internet, USENET

DC  YNY When Gravity Fails    202-686-9086    14.4k        24h
    5 Washington            -
DC  YYY Powderhorn BBS        202-562-8239    14.4k        24h
    3 Washington            Fido 1:109/195, SurvNet

FL  YYY Acquired Knowledge    305-720-3669    14.4k v.32bis 24h
    5 Fort Lauderdale       Internet (UUCP)
FL  YNY Amaranth BBS          904-456-2003    V32bis/V42bis 24h
    5 Pensacola             Internet amaranth.com

FL  NYY Slut Club        813-975-2603 USR/DS 16.8K HST/14.4K 24h
    5 Tampa               Fido 1:377/42
FL  Y?Y Southeastern DataLink 813-572-6817      28.8kbps    24h
    5 Tampa Bay             Fidonet, UUCP
FL  YYY The Computer Mechanic 813-546-0977    14.4k v.32bis 24h
    3 St. Petersburg        FIDONET

GA  YYY Information Overload  404-471-1549  SR V32b V32t Vfc 24h
    5 Riverdale             Fido 1:133/308
GA  YNY Ronin BBS            404-436-5676       14.4 HST/DS 24h
    2 -                     RIME ,Intelec, Smartnet, and more!

ID  YYY Rocky Mountain HUB    208-232-3405    38.4k        24h
    4 Pocatello             Fido,SLNet,CinemaNet,etc

IL  YNY UNIX USER            708-208-5980    14.4k        24h
    4 Batavia               USENET, Internet mail
IL  YNY World Trade Center II 708-481-3946    14.4k DS/HST 24h
    4 Chicago               wires@gnu.ai.mit.edu /Linux99.13
```

```
IN  NNY Digital Underground  812-941-9427       14.4k v.32bis 24h
     5 -                     USENET News Feed
IN  YNY The Point            812-246-8032          28.8k Hayes 24h
     4 Sellersberg           Internet

MA  YYY WayStar BBS    508-481-7147  V.32bis/V.FC/USR/HST 16.8K 24h
     5 Marlborough    Fido 1:333/14..16, other lines: -7293, -8371

MA  YNY VWIS Linux Support BBS 508-793-1570       9600          24h
     4 Worcester            -

MD  N?N Programmer's Corner  301-596-1180       9600          24h
     5 Columbia             RIME
MD  YNY WaterDeep BBS        410-614-2190       9600 v.32     24h
     5 Baltimore            -
MD  YYY Outpost23            301-475-8721       14.4k         24h
     3 Morganza             UUCP, open to any unix system

ME  YNY Harbor Heights BBS   207-663-0931       14.4k         24h
     5 Boothbay Harbor      -

MN  YYY Operating System BBS 612-378-2126       28.8k V.FC    24h
     4 Minneapolis          FidoNet

MN  YNY Part-Time BBS        612-544-5552       14.4k v.32bis 24h
     - Plymouth             tgales@empros.com

MO  NNY The Sole Survivor    314-846-2702    14.4k v.32bis    24h
     5 St. Louis            WWIVnet, WWIVlink, +more

NC  YNY Digital Designs      919-423-4216       14.4k,23k     24h
     4 Hope Mills           -

NJ  YNY Dan's Domain         201-301-0499       14.4k         24h
     4 Madison              Internet via UUCP
NJ  YNY WEFUNK, Mothership Connection 908-940-1012  38.4k     24h
     4 Franklin Park, NJ    -

NJ  YNY Steve Leon's         201-886-8041       14.4k         24h
     3 Cliffside Park       -
NJ  YYY Dwight-Englewood BBS 201-569-3543       9600 v.42     24h
     3 Englewood, NJ        USENET

NY  NYY Prism BBS            914-344-0350       14.4k         24h
     5 Middletown           Fido 1:272/38, Sysop: Janis Kracht
NY  YNY The Wizzard's Cave   516-483-5841       14.4k V32/V42 24h
     5 East Meadow          Usenet
NY  N?Y ShadowGuard          516-244-7064       9600          24h
   4-5 -                     -

NY  YYY The Laboratory  212-927-4980 16.8k HST, 14.4k v.32bis 24h
   3-4 -                   Fido 1:278/707
NY  YNY The Vector Board     716-544-1863/2645  14.4k         24h
     1 -                    sysop: Jim Lill, jpll@vectorbd.com
```

```
NY  YYY hpacv.com              212-924-9681      14.4k         24h
    -   New York              Internet
NY  YYY Manhatten College BBS 718-796-9531      14.4k V32bis 24h
    -   New York                  Fido 1:2603/508
NY  YYY Valhalla          516-321-6819          14.4k HST v.32 24h
    -   Babylon              Fido (1:107/255), UseNet (die.linet.org)

OH  NNY Akademia Pana Kleksa  216-481-1960     WorldBlazer  24h
    3   Cleveland             Internet: wariat.org
OH  Y?? Horizon Systems       216-899-1086|1293 USR v.32|2400 24h
    -   Westlake              -

OK  YYY Hermit Hideout        918-342-3410  16.8HST V32t V32bis 24h
    4   Claremore             Fido 1:170/300

OR  YYY Intermittent Connect  503-344-9838  14.4k HST v.32bis 24h
    5   Eugene, Ore           1:152/35 f'req LINUX for a list
OR  YYY the void 503-251-3808                  v.32bis       24h
    4   Portland Fido 1:105/366, Usenet altreal.egg.com Slackware

PA  NNY Centre Programmers Uni 814-353-0566 14.4k V.32bis/HST 24h
    5   Bellefonte, PA            -
PA  YNY Allentown Technical    610-432-5699 14.4k v.32/v.42bis 24h
    4   Allentown             WWIVNet 2055

TX  YNY alaree                512-575-5554 14.4k v32b/v42b/LAPM 24h
    5   Victoria              USENET, Slackware 1.1.1, BSD
TX  YNY uss.lonestar.org      214-424-9705      14.4k         24h
    5   Plano                 USENET, UUCP, tsx-11.mit.edu mirror

TX  YYY Chrysalis             214-690-9296      14.4k         24h
    4   Dallas                Usenet
TX  YYY CyberVille            817-249-6261      9600          24h
    3   -                     Fido 1:130/78

TX  YYY tIME sTARTS nOW       817-332-5336      V32b/V.FC     24h
    -   Fort Worth            Fido 1:130/908, djh@netcom.com
TX  YNY Solor Soyuz Zaibatsu  512-458-6084        -           24h
    -   Austin                'The Wired Society', guest account

VA  YN? Georgia Peach BBS     804-727-0399      14.4k         24h
    1   Newport News          -

VT  YYY Socialism_OnLine!     802-626-4103      28.8k V.FC    24h
    5   Sheffield             Fido 1:325/806
VT  YNY Relax                 802-453-4458      V.FC 28.8k    24h
    4   Bristol               USENET

WA  NN? Blarg! Online Service 206-784-9681      28.8k         24h
    5   Seattle               Internet
WA  YNY quark     206-748-9878                  28.8 v.Fast   24h
    4             BBS running Linux/SysAdmin quark!enyaw@efn.org
WA  YYY Top Hat BBS           206-244-9661      14.4k         24h
    2   -                     Fido 1:343/40
```

```
WI  YYY Sevenex PubAcc. Linux 414-843-4169        9600 v32    24h
      5 Paddock Lake          Fido 1:154/12, sevenex.sol.net, CDs
WI  NNY Exec PC               414-789-4360         14.4k       24h
      2 Milwaukee             Slackware, 140 phone lines
```

Reporting BBS Listing Changes

The listing we adapted and presented here is not maintained by us or by the publisher. Any additions or corrections to the list (not to our adaptation) should be sent to Rasca Gmelch at one of the following electronic addresses:

Internet
  rasca@marie.physik.tu-berlin.de

FidoNet
  2:2410/305.4

If filing a report on for a new or significantly changed BBS, please use this reporting format:

```
                                      BBS Name:
                                  Phone Number:
                                        Online:
                                       Expires:
                          Modem Speed (CCITT):
          City / Country / State (include region code):
    Whatever Networks it is on (i.e. FidoNet, etc.):
          First Time access to D/L Linux Files (Y/N):
              Allow File Requests - Fido-style (Y/N):
                    Free Access to Linux Files (Y/N):
                                BBS Rating (1-5):
```

Our thanks is extended to Rasca Gmelch for providing this valuable service to the communities of Linux and BBS users around the world.

THE GNU GENERAL PUBLIC LICENSE

Printed below is the GNU General Public License (the *GPL* or *copyleft*), under which Linux is licensed. It is reproduced here to clear up some of the confusion about Linux's copyright status—Linux is *not* shareware, and it is *not* in the public domain. The bulk of the Linux kernel is copyright \copyright 1993 by Linus Torvalds, and other software and parts of the kernel are copyrighted by their authors. Thus, Linux *is* copyrighted; however, you may redistribute it under the terms of the GPL printed below.

GNU GENERAL PUBLIC LICENSE
Version 2, June 1991

Copyright © 1989, 1991 Free Software Foundation, Inc. 675 Mass Ave, Cambridge, MA 02139, USA. Everyone is permitted to copy and distribute verbatim copies of this license document, but changing it is not allowed.

Preamble

The licenses for most software are designed to take away your freedom to share and change it. By contrast, the GNU General Public License is intended to guarantee your freedom to share and change free software—to make sure the software is free for all its users. This General Public License applies to most of the Free Software Foundation's software and to any other program whose authors commit to using it. (Some other Free Software Foundation software is covered by the GNU Library General Public License instead.) You can apply it to your programs, too.

When we speak of free software, we are referring to freedom, not price. Our General Public Licenses are designed to make sure that you have the freedom to distribute copies of free software (and charge for this service if you wish), that you receive source code or can get it if you want it, that you can change the software or use pieces of it in new free programs; and that you know you can do these things.

To protect your rights, we need to make restrictions that forbid anyone to deny you these rights or to ask you to surrender the rights. These restrictions translate to certain responsibilities for you if you distribute copies of the software, or if you modify it.

For example, if you distribute copies of such a program, whether gratis or for a fee, you must give the recipients all the rights that you have. You must make sure that they, too, receive or can get the source code. And you must show them these terms so they know their rights.

We protect your rights with two steps: (1) copyright the software, and (2) offer you this license which gives you legal permission to copy, distribute and/or modify the software.

Also, for each author's protection and ours, we want to make certain that everyone understands that there is no warranty for this free software. If the software is modified by someone else and passed on, we want its recipients to know that what they have is not the original, so that any problems introduced by others will not reflect on the original authors' reputations.

Finally, any free program is threatened constantly by software patents. We wish to avoid the danger that redistributors of a free program will individually obtain patent licenses, in effect making the program proprietary. To prevent this, we have made it clear that any patent must be licensed for everyone's free use or not licensed at all.

The precise terms and conditions for copying, distribution and modification follow.

Terms and Conditions for Copying, Distribution, and Modification

1. This License applies to any program or other work which contains a notice placed by the copyright holder saying it may be distributed under the terms of this General Public License. The "Program", below, refers to any such program or work, and a "work based on the Program" means either the Program or any derivative work under copyright law: that is to say, a work containing the Program or a portion of it, either verbatim or with modifications and/or translated into another language. (Hereinafter, translation is included without limitation in the term "modification".) Each licensee is addressed as "you".

    Activities other than copying, distribution and modification are not covered by this License; they are outside its scope. The act of running the Program is not restricted, and the output from the Program is covered only if its contents constitute a work based on the Program (independent of having been made by running the Program). Whether that is true depends on what the Program does.

2. You may copy and distribute verbatim copies of the Program's source code as you receive it, in any medium, provided that you conspicuously and

appropriately publish on each copy an appropriate copyright notice and disclaimer of warranty; keep intact all the notices that refer to this License and to the absence of any warranty; and give any other recipients of the Program a copy of this License along with the Program.

You may charge a fee for the physical act of transferring a copy, and you may at your option offer warranty protection in exchange for a fee.

3. You may modify your copy or copies of the Program or any portion of it, thus forming a work based on the Program, and copy and distribute such modifications or work under the terms of Section 1 above, provided that you also meet all of these conditions:

    a. You must cause the modified files to carry prominent notices stating that you changed the files and the date of any change.

    b. You must cause any work that you distribute or publish, that in whole or in part contains or is derived from the Program or any part thereof, to be licensed as a whole at no charge to all third parties under the terms of this License.

    c. If the modified program normally reads commands interactively when run, you must cause it, when started running for such interactive use in the most ordinary way, to print or display an announcement including an appropriate copyright notice and a notice that there is no warranty (or else, saying that you provide a warranty) and that users may redistribute the program under these conditions, and telling the user how to view a copy of this License. (Exception: if the Program itself is interactive but does not normally print such an announcement, your work based on the Program is not required to print an announcement.)

These requirements apply to the modified work as a whole. If identifiable sections of that work are not derived from the Program, and can be reasonably considered independent and separate works in themselves, then this License, and its terms, do not apply to those sections when you distribute them as separate works. But when you distribute the same sections as part of a whole which is a work based on the Program, the distribution of the whole must be on the terms of this License, whose permissions for other licensees extend to the entire whole, and thus to each and every part regardless of who wrote it.

Thus, it is not the intent of this section to claim rights or contest your rights to work written entirely by you; rather, the intent is to exercise the right to control the distribution of derivative or collective works based on the Program.

In addition, mere aggregation of another work not based on the Program with the Program (or with a work based on the Program) on a volume of a storage or distribution medium does not bring the other work under the scope of this License.

4. You may copy and distribute the Program (or a work based on it, under Section 2) in object code or executable form under the terms of Sections 1 and 2 above provided that you also do one of the following:

   a. Accompany it with the complete corresponding machine-readable source code, which must be distributed under the terms of Sections 1 and 2 above on a medium customarily used for software interchange; or,

   b. Accompany it with a written offer, valid for at least three years, to give any third party, for a charge no more than your cost of physically performing source distribution, a complete machine-readable copy of the corresponding source code, to be distributed under the terms of Sections 1 and 2 above on a medium customarily used for software interchange; or,

   c. Accompany it with the information you received as to the offer to distribute corresponding source code. (This alternative is allowed only for noncommercial distribution and only if you received the program in object code or executable form with such an offer, in accord with Subsection b above.)

   The source code for a work means the preferred form of the work for making modifications to it. For an executable work, complete source code means all the source code for all modules it contains, plus any associated interface definition files, plus the scripts used to control compilation and installation of the executable. However, as a special exception, the source code distributed need not include anything that is normally distributed (in either source or binary form) with the major components (compiler, kernel, and so on) of the operating system on which the executable runs, unless that component itself accompanies the executable.

   If distribution of executable or object code is made by offering access to copy from a designated place, then offering equivalent access to copy the source code from the same place counts as distribution of the source code, even though third parties are not compelled to copy the source along with the object code.

5. You may not copy, modify, sublicense, or distribute the Program except as expressly provided under this License. Any attempt otherwise to copy, modify, sublicense or distribute the Program is void, and will automatically terminate your rights under this License. However, parties who have received copies, or rights, from you under this License will not have their licenses terminated so long as such parties remain in full compliance.

6. You are not required to accept this License, since you have not signed it. However, nothing else grants you permission to modify or distribute the Program or its derivative works. These actions are prohibited by law if you do not accept this License. Therefore, by modifying or distributing the Program (or any work based on the Program), you indicate your acceptance of this

License to do so, and all its terms and conditions for copying, distributing or modifying the Program or works based on it.

7. Each time you redistribute the Program (or any work based on the Program), the recipient automatically receives a license from the original licensor to copy, distribute or modify the Program subject to these terms and conditions. You may not impose any further restrictions on the recipients' exercise of the rights granted herein. You are not responsible for enforcing compliance by third parties to this License.

8. If, as a consequence of a court judgment or allegation of patent infringement or for any other reason (not limited to patent issues), conditions are imposed on you (whether by court order, agreement or otherwise) that contradict the conditions of this License, they do not excuse you from the conditions of this License. If you cannot distribute so as to satisfy simultaneously your obligations under this License and any other pertinent obligations, then as a consequence you may not distribute the Program at all. For example, if a patent license would not permit royalty-free redistribution of the Program by all those who receive copies directly or indirectly through you, then the only way you could satisfy both it and this License would be to refrain entirely from distribution of the Program.

    If any portion of this section is held invalid or unenforceable under any particular circumstance, the balance of the section is intended to apply and the section as a whole is intended to apply in other circumstances.

    It is not the purpose of this section to induce you to infringe any patents or other property right claims or to contest validity of any such claims; this section has the sole purpose of protecting the integrity of the free software distribution system, which is implemented by public license practices. Many people have made generous contributions to the wide range of software distributed through that system in reliance on consistent application of that system; it is up to the author/donor to decide if he or she is willing to distribute software through any other system and a licensee cannot impose that choice.

    This section is intended to make thoroughly clear what is believed to be a consequence of the rest of this License.

9. If the distribution and/or use of the Program is restricted in certain countries either by patents or by copyrighted interfaces, the original copyright holder who places the Program under this License may add an explicit geographical distribution limitation excluding those countries, so that distribution is permitted only in or among countries not thus excluded. In such case, this License incorporates the limitation as if written in the body of this License.

10. The Free Software Foundation may publish revised and/or new versions of the General Public License from time to time. Such new versions will be similar in spirit to the present version, but may differ in detail to address new problems or concerns.

Each version is given a distinguishing version number. If the Program specifies a version number of this License which applies to it and "any later version", you have the option of following the terms and conditions either of that version or of any later version published by the Free Software Foundation. If the Program does not specify a version number of this License, you may choose any version ever published by the Free Software Foundation.

11. If you wish to incorporate parts of the Program into other free programs whose distribution conditions are different, write to the author to ask for permission. For software which is copyrighted by the Free Software Foundation, write to the Free Software Foundation; we sometimes make exceptions for this. Our decision will be guided by the two goals of preserving the free status of all derivatives of our free software and of promoting the sharing and reuse of software generally.

12. NO WARRANTY

BECAUSE THE PROGRAM IS LICENSED FREE OF CHARGE, THERE IS NO WARRANTY FOR THE PROGRAM, TO THE EXTENT PERMITTED BY APPLICABLE LAW. EXCEPT WHEN OTHERWISE STATED IN WRITING THE COPYRIGHT HOLDERS AND/OR OTHER PARTIES PROVIDE THE PROGRAM "AS IS" WITHOUT WARRANTY OF ANY KIND, EITHER EXPRESSED OR IMPLIED, INCLUDING, BUT NOT LIMITED TO, THE IMPLIED WARRANTIES OF MERCHANTABILITY AND FITNESS FOR A PARTICULAR PURPOSE. THE ENTIRE RISK AS TO THE QUALITY AND PERFORMANCE OF THE PROGRAM IS WITH YOU. SHOULD THE PROGRAM PROVE DEFECTIVE, YOU ASSUME THE COST OF ALL NECESSARY SERVICING, REPAIR OR CORRECTION.

13. IN NO EVENT UNLESS REQUIRED BY APPLICABLE LAW OR AGREED TO IN WRITING WILL ANY COPYRIGHT HOLDER, OR ANY OTHER PARTY WHO MAY MODIFY AND/OR REDISTRIBUTE THE PROGRAM AS PERMITTED ABOVE, BE LIABLE TO YOU FOR DAMAGES, INCLUDING ANY GENERAL, SPECIAL, INCIDENTAL OR CONSEQUENTIAL DAMAGES ARISING OUT OF THE USE OR INABILITY TO USE THE PROGRAM (INCLUDING BUT NOT LIMITED TO LOSS OF DATA OR DATA BEING RENDERED INACCURATE OR LOSSES SUSTAINED BY YOU OR THIRD PARTIES OR A FAILURE OF THE PROGRAM TO OPERATE WITH ANY OTHER PROGRAMS), EVEN IF SUCH HOLDER OR OTHER PARTY HAS BEEN ADVISED OF THE POSSIBILITY OF SUCH DAMAGES.

END OF TERMS AND CONDITIONS

Appendix: How to Apply These Terms to Your New Programs

If you develop a new program, and you want it to be of the greatest possible use to the public, the best way to achieve this is to make it free software which everyone can redistribute and change under these terms.

To do so, attach the following notices to the program. It is safest to attach them to the start of each source file to most effectively convey the exclusion of warranty; and each file should have at least the "copyright" line and a pointer to where the full notice is found.

> *<one line to give the program's name and a brief idea of what it does.>* Copyright © 19yy *<name of author>*

> This program is free software; you can redistribute it and/or modify it under the terms of the GNU General Public License as published by the Free Software Foundation; either version 2 of the License, or (at your option) any later version.

> This program is distributed in the hope that it will be useful, but WITHOUT ANY WARRANTY; without even the implied warranty of MERCHANTABILITY or FITNESS FOR A PARTICULAR PURPOSE. See the GNU General Public License for more details.

> You should have received a copy of the GNU General Public License along with this program; if not, write to the Free Software Foundation, Inc., 675 Mass Ave, Cambridge, MA 02139, USA.

Also add information on how to contact you by electronic and paper mail.

If the program is interactive, make it output a short notice like this when it starts in an interactive mode:

```
Gnomovision version 69, Copyright (C) 19yy name of author
Gnomovision comes with ABSOLUTELY NO WARRANTY; for details type `show w'.
This is free software, and you are welcome to redistribute it
under certain conditions; type `show c' for details.
```

The hypothetical commands "show w" and "show c" should show the appropriate parts of the General Public License. Of course, the commands you use may be called something other than "show w" and "show c"; they could even be mouse-clicks or menu items—whatever suits your program.

You should also get your employer (if you work as a programmer) or your school, if any, to sign a "copyright disclaimer" for the program, if necessary. Here is a sample; alter the names:

> Yoyodyne, Inc., hereby disclaims all copyright interest in the program 'Gnomovision' (which makes passes at compilers) written by James Hacker.

> *<signature of Ty Coon>*, 1 April 1989 Ty Coon, President of Vice

This General Public License does not permit incorporating your program into proprietary programs. If your program is a subroutine library, you may consider it more useful to permit linking proprietary applications with the library. If this is what you want to do, use the GNU Library General Public License instead of this License.

BIBLIOGRAPHY

Linux Documentation Project Manuals

[1] Welsh, Matt. *Linux Installation and Getting Started*.

A user's guide for Linux, a prototype for this book. The manual is targeted primarily for the UNIX novice, and as such does not contain the broad scope of information that is in this book. If you are new to UNIX and need more information, *Linux Installation and Getting Started* is a great place to look.

[2] Wirzenius, Lars. *The Linux System Administrator's Guide*.

This is a guide to running and configuring a Linux system. There are many issues relating to systems administration that are specific to Linux, such as needs for supporting a user community, filesystem maintenance, backups, and more. This guide covers many of them.

[3] Kirch, Olaf. *Linux Network Administrator's Guide*.

An extensive and complete guide to networking under Linux, including TCP/IP, UUCP, SLIP, and more. This book is a very good read; it contains a wealth of information on many subjects, clarifying the many confusing aspects of network configuration. It has been published by O'Reilly & Associates as a companion volume to this book.

[4] Johnson, Michael. *The Linux Kernel Hacker's Guide*.

The gritty details of kernel hacking and development under Linux. Linux is unique in that the complete kernel source is available. This book opens the doors to developers who wish to add or modify features within the kernel. This guide also contains comprehensive coverage of kernel concepts and conventions used by Linux.

UNIX and UNIX Shells

[5] McGilton, Henry, and Morgan, Rachel. *Introducing the UNIX System*. McGraw-Hill. 1983.

A classic, used by many people as their first guide to UNIX.

[6] Hahn, Harley. *A Student's Guide to Unix.* McGraw-Hill. 1993.

A popular and very approachable introduction to using UNIX.

[7] Todino, Grace, Strang, John, and Peek, Jerry. *Learning the UNIX Operating System.* O'Reilly & Associates. 1993.

A good introductory book on learning the UNIX operating system. Most of the information should be applicable to Linux as well. I suggest reading this book if you're new to UNIX and really want to get started with using your new system. Introduces basic networking commands, email, and the X Window System to novice users.

[8] Computer Systems Research Group, UC Berkeley. *4.4BSD-Lite CD-ROM Companion: Domestic Edition.* The USENIX Association and O'Reilly & Associates. 1994.

Provides the U.S. version of the University of California, Berkeley's 4.4BSD-Lite release on CD with utilities and support libraries, plus additional documentation and enhancements for the U.S. market. Particularly useful for programmers. 4.4BSD-Lite is the last version of the BSD operating system, minus some code that is in dispute with UNIX Software Labs.

[9] Computer Systems Research Group, UC Berkeley. *4.4BSD-Lite CD-ROM Companion: International Edition.* The USENIX Association and O'Reilly & Associates. 1994.

Provides the international version of 4.4BSD-Lite release on CD with utilities and support libraries, plus additional documentation and enhancements for the international market. The international version lacks some material in the U.S. version that could not be exported.

[10] Computer Systems Research Group, UC Berkeley. *4.4BSD User's Reference Manual.* The USENIX Association and O'Reilly & Associates. 1994.

Manual pages for more than 275 user programs comprising the user portion of the 4.4BSD UNIX release, including documentation for popular games and other information. Many commands are identical to those in other UNIX versions. Also documents important freeware programs such as Perl, GNU Emacs, compress, and kerberos.

[11] Rosenblatt, Bill. *Learning the Korn Shell.* O'Reilly & Associates. 1993.

Introduces the Korn shell, as a user interface and as a programming language. Useful for bash and zsh users, too. Includes practical programming examples and a *kshdb* Korn shell debugger.

[12] O'Reilly & Associates, Inc. *UNIX in a Nutshell: Berkeley Edition*. O'Reilly & Associates. 1990.

A quick-reference for BSD UNIX commands, through BSD 4.3. Many BSD utilities are used on Linux.

[13] Gilly, Daniel, and O'Reilly & Associates, Inc. *UNIX in a Nutshell: System V Edition*. O'Reilly & Associates. 1992.

A quick-reference for System V UNIX through SVR 5.4, Solaris 2.0. Summarizes all commands and options, along with generous descriptions and examples that put the commands in context.

[14] Quercia, Valerie, and O'Reilly, Tim. *Volume 3: X Window System User's Guide Standard Edition*. O'Reilly & Associates. 1993.

A complete tutorial and reference guide to using the X Window System. If you installed X on your Linux system, and want to know how to get the most out of it, you should read this book. Unlike some windowing systems, a lot of the power provided by X is not obvious at first sight. Even after using X for several years I learned some things by reading through this book. Includes the *twm* window manager. Revised for X11 Release 5.

Applications and Technologies

[15] Computer Systems Research Group, UC Berkeley. *4.4BSD User's Supplementary Documents*. The USENIX Association and O'Reilly & Associates. 1994.

Provides technical papers ("supplementary documents") documenting UNIX tools developed to solve common problems. Documents "user" tools, including text editors and formatting packages, and covers shell programming fundamentals.

[16] Stallman, Richard M. *Emacs manual*. Free Software Foundation.

A description of the widely used and powerful GNU Emacs editor by the software's creators. The same as the comprehensive online info documentation.

[17] Cameron, Debra, and Rosenblatt, Bill. *Learning GNU Emacs*. O'Reilly & Associates. 1991.

Provides a congenial introduction to GNU Emacs. Includes a brief introduction to Emacs customization, and to GNU Emacs LISP programming.

[18] Lamb, Linda. *Learning the vi Editor*. O'Reilly & Associates. 1990.

Provides a complete guide to text editing with the standard features of *vi*, an editor available on nearly every UNIX system and now on some non-UNIX operating systems (in the form of Elvis, Vile, and other clones). Covers use of the *ex* command (mode) and advanced features of *vi*. It's often important to know and be able to use *vi*, because you won't always have access to a "real" editor such as Emacs.

[19] Dougherty, Dale, Koman, Richard, and Ferguson, Paula. *The Mosaic Handbook for the X Window System*. O'Reilly & Associates. 1994.

A description of the World Wide Web and an in-depth guide to using Mosaic. Includes a chapter on HTML. Contains a CD with Mosaic V2.4 for the X Window System, and a subscription to the *Global Network Navigator* (*GNN*).

[20] Dougherty, Dale. *sed & awk*. O'Reilly & Associates. 1990.

Describes the use of *sed* and *awk* as powerful editors to create and modify text files. *sed* and *awk* are stream editors that can process multiple files and save many hours of repetitive work in achieving the same result using a standard text editor.

[21] Peek, Jerry, Loukides, Mike, O'Reilly, Tim, et al. *UNIX Power Tools*. O'Reilly & Associates. 1993.

Offers UNIX utility tips, tricks, concepts, and freeware. Covers add-on utilities and how to take advantage of clever features in the most popular UNIX utilities. A CD-ROM with source and popular binaries is included.

[22] Knuth, Donald E. *The TEXbook*. Addison-Wesley Publishing Co. 1984.

Provides the first, and still definitive, reference to the TEX text formatting language. By the creator of TEX.

[23] Lamport, Leslie. *LATEX—A Document Preparation System*. Addison-Wesley Publishing Co. 1986.

A very readable guide to the LATEX extension to TEX, by the creator of LATEX.

[24] Walsh, Norman. *Making TEX Work*. O'Reilly & Associates. 1994.

Describes how to use TEX to create professional-quality typeset text, mathematical equations, and provide output for different languages using different character sets. Describes all the software that actually lets you build, run, and use TEX to best advantage on your platform, be it Linux, DOS, OS/2, or whatever.

[25] van Herwijnen, Eric. *Practical SGML*. Kluwer Academic Publishers. 1994.

Provides an excellent introduction of the use of Standard Generalized Markup Language (ISO 8879-1986) for creation of structured documents. There are several flawed books on this subject, but this one is just about right.

[26] Goldfarb, Charles F. *The SGML Handbook*. Clarendon Press. 1990.

Provides the authoritative "Bible" on Standard Generalized Markup Language. Contains the complete text of the standard for SGML, ISO 8879-1986, with the author's annotations. Charles Goldfarb is the father of SGML and was chair of the committee that developed the standard. This book is expensive, but costs less than ISO 8879 alone. It is an essential resource for the serious SGML tools or documentation systems developer.

[27] Barron, David, and Rees, Mike. *Text Processing and Typesetting with UNIX*. Addison-Wesley Publishing Co. 1987.

Describes typesetting with *nroff* and *troff*, using the *–ms* and *–mm* macro packages, and related typesetting utilities *tbl* and *eqn* and the whole set of UNIX Software Labs' Documenter's Workbench (DWB) utilities. Tells how to create and modify macros, and discusses other useful UNIX tools for text manipulation and management. Does not cover the GNU *groff* implementation specifically, but no published volume does.

The Internet

[28] Estrada, Susan. *Connecting to the Internet: An O'Reilly Buyer's Guide*. O'Reilly & Associates. 1993.

Explains how to determine the level of Internet service you need, and how to find, evaluate, and connect with local access providers and the services they offer.

[29] Krol, Ed. *The Whole Internet User's Guide and Catalog, second edition*. O'Reilly & Associates. 1994.

Provides a comprehensive, bestselling introduction to the Internet. This book pays special attention to tools for helping you find World Wide Web information, and covers email, file transfer, remote login, and network news. Useful to novices and veterans. Includes a quick-reference card. The electronic version of the Catalog portion of this book is accessible online through the *Global Network Navigator* homepage. See "Internet Resources" below.

[30] Kehoe, Brendan P. *Zen and the Art of the Internet: A Beginner's Guide*. PTR Prentice Hall. 1993.

Introduction to the Internet, aimed at the novice user. It covers topics ranging from email to Usenet news to Internet folklore. An electronic text version of the first edition (1992) of this book is available via anonymous FTP, and may be freely distributed and printed. See "Internet Resources" below.

[31] Quarterman, John S. *The Matrix: Computer Networks and Conferencing Systems Worldwide*. Digital Press.

A massive listing of different networks around the world.

[32] Frey, Donnalyn, and Adams, Rick. *!%@:: A Directory of Electronic Mail Addressing and Networks*. O'Reilly & Associates. 1994.

Charts significant networks that comprise the Internet, describes their services, and provides contact information.

Networks and Communications

[33] Comer, Douglas R. *Internetworking with TCP/IP, Volume 1: Principles, Protocols, Architecture*. Prentice-Hall International. 1991.

Provides a comprehensive background for understanding the Internet suite of protocols and how they are used in modern networking.

[34] Hunt, Craig. *TCP/IP Network Administration*. O'Reilly & Associates. 1992.

A complete guide to setting up and running a TCP/IP network. While this book is not Linux-specific, roughly 90% of it is applicable to Linux. Coupled with the Linux NET-2-HOWTO and *Linux Network Administrator's Guide*, this is a great book discussing the concepts and technical details of managing TCP/IP. Covers setting up your network, configuring network applications, mail routing and address resolution, and issues in troubleshooting and security.

[35] Liu, Cricket, and Albitz, Paul. *DNS and BIND*. O'Reilly & Associates. 1992.

Provides thorough treatment of the Internet Domain Name System (DNS) and of the UNIX implementation: Berkeley Internet Name Domain (BIND). An important resource if you're a system administrator, because this book shows how to set up and maintain the DNS software on your network.

[36] Stern, Hal. *Managing NFS and NIS*. O'Reilly & Associates. 1992.

Describes management of NFS, the Network File System, and NIS, the Network Information System, for system administrators who need to set up and manage a network filesystem installation and network information services. Includes PC/NFS and automounter configuration.

[37] Liu, Cricket, Peek, Jerry, Jones, Russ, Buus, Bryan, and Nye, Adrian. *Managing Internet Information Services*. O'Reilly & Associates. 1994.

Tells system administrators how to set up servers for the World Wide Web, Gopher, FTP, Finger, Telnet, WAIS, and mailing lists.

[38] Todino, Grace, and Dougherty, Dale. *Using UUCP and Usenet*. O'Reilly & Associates. 1991.

Shows users how to communicate with both UNIX and non-UNIX systems using UUCP and *cu* or *tip*, and how to read news and post articles. This handbook assumes that UUCP is already running at your site.

[39] Todino, Grace, and O'Reilly, Tim. *Managing UUCP and Usenet*. O'Reilly & Associates. 1992.

This book covers how to install and configure UUCP networking software, including configuration for USENET news. If you're at all interested in using UUCP or accessing USENET news on your system, this book is a must-read. Unfortunately, it doesn't cover Taylor UUCP yet.

[40] Costales, Bryan, Allman, Eric, and Rickert, Neil. *sendmail*. O'Reilly & Associates. 1993.

A hefty and possibly intimidating book, but really a fine and complete description of how to configure sendmail. Includes extensive reference material.

[41] da Cruz, Frank, and Gianone, Christine M. *Using C-Kermit*. Digital Press. 1993.

A comprehensive guide to the use of the Kermit communications package, with particular emphasis on the powerful and portable C-Kermit implementation, available for just about any operating system and as C language source code. C-Kermit's copyright by Columbia University, New York, retains some restrictions on distribution, so this package isn't included in standard Linux distributions. However, it is readily available from FTP sites, and an important package for any host system that provides public access.

Programming Languages and Utilities

[42] Kernighan, Brian, and Ritchie, Dennis. *The C Programming Language*. Prentice Hall. 1988.

The classic reference on the C language, by its creators. Updated to cover ANSI C in the second edition.

[43] Stevens, Richard. *Advanced Programming in the Unix Environment*. Addison-Wesley Publising Co. 1992.

A large book introducing and describing the use of UNIX system calls in detail.

[44] Stallman, Richard M. *Using GNU CC*. Free Software Foundation.

A discussion of the many *gcc* command options, language extensions, and other considerations in using the GNU C compiler.

[45] Computer Systems Research Group, UC Berkeley. *4.4BSD Programmer's Reference Manual*. The USENIX Association and O'Reilly & Associates. 1994.

Provides sections 2 through 5 of the BSD release 4.4 online reference pages (manual pages) collection, for system calls, libraries, and file formats. Also useful for Linux and other UNIX implementations.

[46] Computer Systems Research Group, UC Berkeley. *4.4BSD Programmer's Supplementary Documents*. The USENIX Association and O'Reilly & Associates. 1994.

Provides traditional "Supplementary Documents" that are authoritative for many UNIX programs, and is particularly useful for programmers. Contains original Bell and BSD research papers, documenting the UNIX programming environment, plus current papers on new 4.4BSD features. Includes a two-part tutorial on interprocess communication (IPC) under 4.4BSD. Useful even for System V and Xenix operating systems.

[47] Kochan, Stephen, and Wood, Patrick. *Unix Shell Programming*. Hayden Press. 1990.

A well-known guide to writing shell scripts.

[48] Schwartz, Randal L. *Learning Perl*. O'Reilly & Associates. 1993.

Provides a hands-on tutorial designed to get you writing useful Perl scripts as quickly as possible. Perl provides a portable replacement (UNIX, DOS, and other operating systems) for shell programming that incorporates a superset of *sed* and *awk* functionality.

[49] Wall, Larry, and Schwartz, Randal L. *Programming Perl*. O'Reilly & Associates. 1991.

Provides an authoritative guide to the powerful and portable Perl programming language, co-authored by its creator, Larry Wall.

[50] Ousterhout, John K. *Tcl and the Tk Toolkit*. Addison-Wesley Publishing Co. 1994.

Written by the inventor of Tcl and Tk, this book fully describes the languages. Most of it is devoted to a discussion of Tk commands and widgets. Also tells how to embed Tcl and Tk in C programs.

[51] Oram, Andrew, and Talbott, Steve. *Managing Projects with make*. O'Reilly & Associates. 1991.

Describes all the basic features of the *make* utility and provides guidelines to programmers on using *make* for managing large compilation projects.

[52] Stallman, Richard M., and McGrath, Roland. *GNU Make manual*. Free Software Foundation.

A guide to the powerful GNU version of the *make* utility, both basic use and advanced features.

[53] DuBois, Paul. *Software Portability with imake*. O'Reilly & Associates. 1993.

Describes the *imake* utility, which works with *make* to let code be compiled and installed on different UNIX machines.

[54] Lewine, Donald. *POSIX Programmer's Guide*. O'Reilly & Associates. 1991.

Explains the X/Open POSIX standards and is a reference for the POSIX.1 programming library, helping you write more portable programs. Linux is intended to be POSIX-compliant, though its compliance is uncertified.

[55] Stallman, Richard M., and Pesch, Roland H. *Debugging with GDB*. Free Software Foundation.

Describes how to use the *gdb* debugger, the standard debugger on Linux and probably the most popular debugger in the UNIX world.

System Administration

[56] Nemeth, Evi, Snyder, Garth, and Seebass, Scott. *Unix System Administration Handbook*. Prentice Hall.

The most frequently recommended book on the subject.

[57] Frisch, Aeleen. *Essential System Administration*. O'Reilly & Associates. 1991.

Guides you through the system administration tasks on a UNIX system.

[58] Computer Systems Research Group, UC Berkeley, and O'Reilly & Associates, Inc. *4.4BSD System Manager's Manual*. O'Reilly & Associates. 1994.

This volume includes manual pages for system administration commands (section eight of the online reference manual), plus papers on many system administration utilities and tasks—all of interest to serious UNIX administrators. The original concise UNIX papers remain the definitive work for many UNIX topics.

[59] Garfinkel, Simson, and Spafford, Gene. *Practical UNIX Security*. O'Reilly & Associates. 1991.

This is an excellent book on UNIX system security. It taught me quite a few things that I didn't know, even with several years of UNIX system administration experience. As most UNIX books, this book is geared for large systems, but almost all of the content is relevant to Linux. Explains network security (including UUCP, NFS, Kerberos, and fire-wall machines) in detail.

[60] Mui, Linda, and Pearce, Eric. *Volume 8: X Window System Administrator's Guide*. O'Reilly & Associates). 1992.

Covers detailed system administration guidance for the X Window System and X-based networks, for anyone who must administer X. Can be purchased with or without a CD.

Personal Computer Hardware

[61] Grossbrenner, Alfred, and Anis, Nick. *Grossbrenner's Complete Hard Disk Handbook*. Osborne McGraw-Hill. 1990.

Provides an authoritative guide to hard disk selection, hardware, management, performance tuning, troubleshooting, and data recovery on personal computers for MFM, RLL, ATA (IDE), SCSI, and ESDI drives. This edition, which may be superseded, doesn't deal with EIDE specifically. Includes manufacturer contact information. Includes DOS utilities on diskette.

[62] Rosch, Winn L. *The Winn L. Rosch Hardware Bible*. Brady Publishing Div. Macmillan Computer Publishing. 1994.

Comprehensive guide to PC components and peripherals. You will find this book useful when purchasing, maintaining, repairing, and upgrading PCs. Though oriented primarily toward the Intel and clone systems, it is broadly useful because it covers technology, theory, and practice in computer architecture. It is applicable to all significant personal computer systems, as well as containing information specific to the ISA, EISA, and Microchannel systems (and the various secondary buses). This book can probably tell you what you need to know about microprocessors, memory, modems, MIDI and more.

HOWTOs

[63] *Linux Installation HOWTO*, by Matt Welsh.

Describes how to obtain and install a distribution of Linux, similar to the information presented in Chapter 2, *Obtaining and Installing Linux*.

[64] *The Linux Distribution HOWTO*, by Matt Welsh.

A list of Linux distributions available via mail order and anonymous FTP. It also includes information on other Linux-related goodies and services. Appendix B, *Linux Vendor List*, is a condensed version of the list in the Distribution HOWTO.

[65] *The Linux XFree86 HOWTO*, by Helmut Geyer.

This document describes how to install and configure the X Window System software for Linux. See Chapter 5, *Power Tools*, for more about the X Window System.

[66] *The Linux Electronic Mail HOWTO*, by Vince Skahan.

Basic directions on setting up both *smail* and *sendmail* (through the convenient extension known as sendmail+IDA). Also offers some help on mailers, particularly Elm.

[67] *The Linux News HOWTO*, by Vince Skahan.

Instructions on installing Cnews, InterNetNews (INN), and several newsreaders. Also contains many frequently-asked questions about reading and posting news.

[68] *The Linux UUCP HOWTO*, by Vince Skahan.

A brief introduction to installing UUCP.

[69] *The Linux Hardware HOWTO*, by Tawei Wan.

Contains an extensive list of hardware supported by Linux. While this list is far from complete, it should give you a general picture of which hardware devices should be supported by the system.

[70] *The Linux SCSI HOWTO*, by Drew Eckhardt.

A complete guide to configuration and use of SCSI devices under Linux, such as hard drives, tape drives and CD-ROM.

[71] *The Linux Ftape HOWTO*, by Kai Harrekilde-Petersen.

Describes the installation and use of the "floppy tape" driver that works on QIC-80 and QIC-40 compatible drives. This driver lets you attach tape drives to a floppy disk controller.

[72] *The Linux CD-ROM HOWTO*, by Jeff Tranter.

Lists supported CD-ROM drives and explains how to install, configure, and read from a drive. Also describes some useful utilities that can be used with a CD-ROM drive.

[73] *The Linux NET-2-HOWTO*, by Terry Dawson.

The Linux NET-2-HOWTO describes installation, setup, and configuration of the "NET-2" TCP/IP software under Linux, including SLIP. If you want to use TCP/IP on your Linux system, this document is a must read.

[74] *The Linux Ethernet HOWTO*, by Paul Gortmaker.

Closely related to the NET-2-HOWTO, the Ethernet HOWTO describes the various Ethernet devices supported by Linux, and explains how to configure each of them for use by the Linux TCP/IP software.

[75] *The Linux Term HOWTO*, by Bill Reynolds, and Patrick Reijnen.

Tells you how to install and use the *term* communications package, which allows you to run multiple login sessions over a serial line.

[76] *The Linux Printing HOWTO*, by Grant Taylor, and Brian McCauley.

Describes how to configure printing software under Linux, such as *lpr*. Configuration of printers and printing software under UNIX can be very confusing at times; this document sheds some light on the subject.

Internet Requests For Comments

[77] RFC 1597. *Address Allocation for Private Internets*. Rekhter, Y., Watson, T. J., and et al.

This RFC lists the IP network numbers private organizations can use internally without having to register these network numbers with the Internet Assigned Numbers Authority (IANA). The document also discusses the advantages and disadvantages of using these numbers.

[78] RFC 1340. *Assigned Numbers*. Postel, J., and Reynolds, J.

The Assigned Numbers RFC defines the meaning of numbers used in various protocols such as the port numbers standard TCP and UDP servers are known to listen on, and the protocol numbers used in the IP datagram header.

[79] RFC 1144. *Compressing TCP/IP headers for low-speed serial links*. Jacobson, V.

This document describes the algorithm used to compress TCP/IP headers in CSLIP and PPP.

[80] RFC 1033. *Domain Administrators Operations Guide*. Lottor, M.

Together with its companion RFCs, RFC 1034, and RFC 1035, this is the definitive source on DNS, the Domain Name System.

[81] RFC 1034. *Domain Names—Concepts and Facilities*. Mockapetris, P.V.

A companion to RFC 1033.

[82] RFC 1035. *Domain Names—Implementation and Specification*. Mockapetris, P.V.

A companion to RFC 1033.

[83] RFC 974. *Mail Routing and the Domain System*. Partridge, C.

This RFC describes mail routing on the Internet. Read this for the full story about MX records...

[84] RFC 977. *Network News Transfer Protocol*. Kantor, B., and Lapsley, P.

The definition of NNTP, the common news transport used on the Internet.

[85] RFC 1094. *NFS: Network File System Protocol specification*. Nowicki, B.

The formal specification of the NFS and mount protocols (version 2).

[86] RFC 1055. *Nonstandard for Transmission of IP Datagrams over Serial Lines: SLIP*. Romkey, J.L.

Describes SLIP, the Serial Line Internet Protocol.

[87] RFC 1057. *RPC: Remote Procedure Call Protocol Specification: Version 2*. Sun Microsystems, Inc.

The formal specification of the encoding used for remote procedure calls, which underlie both NFS and NIS.

[88] RFC 1058. *Routing Information Protocol*. Hedrick, C.L.

Describes RIP, which is used to exchange dynamic routing information within LANs and MANs.

[89] RFC 1535. *A Security Problem and Proposed Correction with Widely Deployed DNS Software*. Gavron,, E.

This RFC discusses a security problem with the default search list used by older versions of the BIND resolver library.

[90] RFC 1036. *Standard for the Interchange of USENET messages*. Adams, R., and Horton, M.R.

This RFC describes the format of Usenet News messages, and how they are exchanged on the Internet as well as on UUCP networks. A revision of this RFC is expected to be released in the near future.

[91] RFC 822. *Standard for the Format of ARPA Internet text messages.* Crocker, D.

This is the definitive source of wisdom regarding, well, RFC-conformant mail. Everyone knows it, few have really read it.

[92] RFC 821. *Simple Mail Transfer Protocol.* Postel, J.B.

Defines SMTP, the mail transport protocol over TCP/IP.

INDEX

Checker, 379-380
    use with gdb debugger, 380
checking filesystems, 182
    fsck command, 184
    when superblock is corrupted, 201
chgrp command, 101
chmod command
    absolute mode, 102
    example, 78, 101-103
chown command, 101
    example, 136
chsh command, 87
ci command, 384
class, X resources, 264
client, X Window System, 242, 274
client/server file, 106
CLISP, 354
co command, 385
Coherent filesystem, 29, 175
colors
    customizing windows, 269
    Emacs foreground and background, 287
    Emacs text faces, 288
    foreground and background, 263
    listing available, 269
    ls command, 84
    virtual console, 198
Columbia University, 464
command completion, 89
command line editing, 89
    selecting vi behavior, 90
    VISUAL environment variable, 90
commands
    basic UNIX, 82
    built-in, 95
    defined, 94
    executing automatically through cron,
        191
    in makefile, 332
    issuing within Emacs, 223
    issuing within vi, 211, 214
    location on system, 94
    not found, 95
    putting in pop-up menu, 271
    showrgb, 269
comments
    in /etc/fstab file, 65
    in C-Kermit customization file, 474

    in crontab file, 194
    in Emacs Lisp customization file, 224
    in makefiles, 328
    in texinfo files, 236
commercial support, 39
compatibility
    shared libraries, 155
    with MS-DOS, 292-308
compiling
    basic example, 320
    library searching, 324
    process of, 317
    within Emacs, 223
compress command, 139
compression
    afio command, 151
    and dosemu DOS emulator, 297
    graphics files, 137
    kernel, 169
    Linux kernel, 114
    of archives, 144, 151
    uncompressing, 137
    using gzip, 137
configuration
    disks and filesystems, 50-51, 55-60
    dosemu DOS emulator, 300
    electronic mail (smail), 450-456
    inittab file, 124-126
    LILO, 117
    SLIP, 410-415
    smail, 451
    swap space, 59, 185-188
    TCP/IP networking, 399-409
    World Wide Web server, 424-448
Configure command
    Elm mailer setup, 459
    example, 460
console
    in lilo.conf file, 117
    setting attributes, 198
    to get system messages, 196
    VGA text mode, 117, 121
    virtual, 82, 198
control-panel command, 63
conventions, typographic, xxi
copying Linux, 20-21, 28, 523-530
copyright, 20-21, 523-530
core files, 360-364

About the Authors

Matt Welsh is a systems programmer and all-around UNIX hacker, currently working with the Cornell University Robotics and Vision Laboratory in Ithaca, New York. He is the coordinator of the Linux Documentation Project and author of several Linux-related works, including the book *Linux Installation and Getting Started* (available for free via the Internet). He also writes for *Linux Journal* and moderates the USENET newsgroup *comp.os.linux.announce*. Apart from Linux, his interests cover operating systems design, including distributed systems and virtual memory management. Because of this, Matt's load average is usually quite high, and he page faults often.

Lar Kaufman is a documentation consultant living in Concord, Massachusetts. He began writing about UNIX in 1983 and since then has written on System V, BSD, Mach, OSF/1, and now Linux. His hobbies include interactive media as art/literature, homebuilt and antique aircraft (he's a licensed aircraft mechanic), and natural history. Formerly a BBS operator, in 1987 Lar founded the Fidonet echoes (newsgroups) Biosphere and BioNews. He is currently leading a project to establish a global biological conservation network, using a Linux host as the mail, news, and file server.

Colophon

Our look is the result of reader comments, our own experimentation, and feedback from distribution channels. Distinctive covers complement our distinctive approach to technical topics, breathing personality and life into potentially dry subjects.

Edie Freedman designed the cover of *Running Linux*. The cover image, of a rider on a bucking horse, is adapted from a 19th-century engraving from *Marvels of the New West: A Vivid Portrayal of the Stupendous Marvels in the Vast Wonderland West of the Missouri River*, by William Thayer (The Henry Bill Publishing Co., Norwich, CT, 1888).

Thayer quotes a stockman who gives this description of a bucking horse: "When a horse bucks he puts his head down between his legs, arches his back like an angry cat, and springs into the air with all his legs at once, coming down again with a frightful jar, and he sometimes keeps on repeating the performance until he is completely worn out with the excursion. The rider is apt to feel rather worn out too by that time, if he has kept his seat, which is not a very easy matter, especially if the horse is a real scientific bucker, and puts a kind of side action into every jump. The double girth commonly attached to these Mexican saddles is useful for keeping the saddle in its place during one of those bouts, but there is no doubt that they frequently make a horse buck who would not do so with a single girth. With some animals you can never draw up the flank girth without setting them bucking."

The cover layout was produced with Quark XPress 3.3 and Adobe Photoshop 2.5 software, using the ITC Garamond Condensed font.

Jennifer Niederst and Edie Freedman designed the interior layouts. Chapter opening graphics are from the Dover Pictorial Archive and *Marvels of the New West*. Interior fonts are Adobe ITC Garamond and Adobe Courier. Text was prepared in SGML using the DocBook 2.1 DTD. The print version of this book was created by translating the SGML source into a set of gtroff macros using a filter developed at ORA by Norman Walsh. Steve Talbott designed and wrote the underlying macro set on the basis of the GNU gtroff -gs macros; Lenny Muellner adapted them to SGML and implemented the book design. The GNU groff text formatter version 1.08 was used to generate PostScript output.

The illustrations that appear in the book were created in Aldus Freehand 4.0 by Chris Reilley.

SYSTEM ADMINISTRATION

Books from O'Reilly & Associates, Inc.

Fall/Winter 1994-95

"Good reference books make a system administrator's job much easier. However, finding useful books about system administration is a challenge, and I'm constantly on the lookout. In general, I have found that almost anything published by O'Reilly & Associates is worth having if you are interested in the topic."

—*Dinah McNutt,* UNIX Review

TCP/IP Network Administration

By Craig Hunt
1st Edition August 1992
502 pages, ISBN 0-937175-82-X

A complete guide to setting up and running a TCP/IP network for administrators of networks of systems or lone home systems that access the Internet. It starts with the fundamentals: what the protocols do and how they work, how to request a network address and a name (the forms needed are included in an appendix), and how to set up your network. Beyond basic setup, the book discusses how to configure important network applications, including sendmail, the r* commands, and some simple setups for NIS and NFS. There are also chapters on troubleshooting and security. In addition, this book covers several important packages that are available from the Net (such as *gated*). Covers BSD and System V TCP/IP implementations.

"Whether you're putting a network together, trying to figure out why an existing one doesn't work, or wanting to understand the one you've got a little better, *TCP/IP Network Administration* is the definitive volume on the subject."
—Tom Yager, *Byte*

Managing Internet Information Services

By Cricket Liu, Jerry Peek, Russ Jones,
Bryan Buus & Adrian Nye
1st Edition Fall 1994 (est.)
400 pages (est.), ISBN 1-56592-062-7

This comprehensive guide describes how to set up information services to make them available over the Internet. It discusses why a company would wnat to offer Internet services, provides complete coverage of all popular services, and tells how to select which ones to provide. Most of the book describes how to set up email services and FTP, Gopher, and World Wide Web servers.

"Managing Internet Information Services has long been needed in the Internet community, as well as in many organizations with IP-based networks. Although many on the Internet are quite savvy when it comes to administering these types of tools, MIIS will allow a much larger community to join in and perhaps provide more diverse information. This book will be a welcome addition to my Internet shelf."
—Robert H'obbes' Zakon, MITRE Corporation

Linux Network Administrator's Guide

By Olaf Kirch
1st Edition Fall 1994 (est.)
400 pages (est.), ISBN 1-56592-087-2

A UNIX-compatible operating system that runs on personal computers, Linux is a pinnacle within the free software movement. It is based on a kernel developed by Finnish student Linus Torvalds and is distributed on the Net or on low-cost disks, along with a complete set of UNIX libraries, popular free software utilities, and traditional layered products like NFS and the X Window System.

Networking is a fundamental part of Linux. Whether you want a simple UUCP connection or a full LAN with NFS and NIS, you are going to have to build a network.

Linux Network Administration Guide by Olaf Kirch is one of the most successful books to come from the Linux Documentation Project. It touches on all the essential networking software included with Linux, plus some hardware considerations. Topics include serial connections, UUCP, routing and DNS, mail and News, SLIP and PPP, NFS, and NIS.

DNS and BIND

By Paul Albitz & Cricket Liu
1st Edition October 1992
418 pages, ISBN 1-56592-010-4

DNS and BIND contains all you need to know about the Internet's Domain Name System (DNS) and the Berkeley Internet Name Domain (BIND), its UNIX implementation. The Domain Name System is the Internet's "phone book"; it's a database that tracks important information (in particular, names and addresses) for every computer on the Internet.

If you're a system administrator, this book will show you how to set up and maintain the DNS software on your network.

"*DNS and BIND* contains a lot of useful information that you'll never find written down anywhere else. And since it's written in a crisp style, you can pretty much use the book as your primary BIND reference."
—Marshall Rose, *ConneXions*

sendmail

By Bryan Costales, with Eric Allman & Neil Rickert
1st Edition November 1993
830 pages, ISBN 1-56592-056-2

This Nutshell Handbook® is far and away the most comprehensive book ever written on sendmail, the program that acts like a traffic cop in routing and delivering mail on UNIX-based networks. Although sendmail is used on almost every UNIX system, it's one of the last great uncharted territories—and most difficult utilities to learn—in UNIX system administration. This book provides a complete sendmail tutorial, plus extensive reference material on every aspect of the program. It covers IDA sendmail, the latest version (V8) from Berkeley, and the standard versions available on most systems.

"The program and its rule description file, sendmail.cf, have long been regarded as the pit of coals that separated the mild Unix system administrators from the real fire walkers. Now, sendmail syntax, testing, hidden rules, and other mysteries are revealed. Costales, Allman, and Rickert are the indisputable authorities to do the text."
—Ben Smith, *Byte Magazine*

Essential System Administration

By Æleen Frisch
1st Edition October 1991
466 pages, ISBN 0-937175-80-3

Like any other multi-user system, UNIX requires some care and feeding. *Essential System Administration* tells you how. This book strips away the myth and confusion surrounding this important topic and provides a compact, manageable introduction to the tasks faced by anyone responsible for a UNIX system.

If you use a stand-alone UNIX system, whether it's a PC or a workstation, you know how much you need this book: on these systems the fine line between a user and an administrator has vanished. Either you're both or you're in trouble. If you routinely provide administrative support for a larger shared system or a network of workstations, you will find this book indispensable. Even if you aren't directly responsible for system administration, you will find that understanding basic administrative functions greatly increases your ability to use UNIX effectively.

Computer Security Basics

By Deborah Russell & G.T. Gangemi Sr.
1st Edition July 1991
464 pages, ISBN 0-937175-71-4

There's a lot more consciousness of security today, but not a lot of understanding of what it means and how far it should go. This handbook describes complicated concepts, such as trusted systems, encryption, and mandatory access control, in simple terms. For example, most U.S. government equipment acquisitions now require Orange Book (Trusted Computer System Evaluation Criteria) certification. A lot of people have a vague feeling that they ought to know about the Orange Book, but few make the effort to track it down and read it. *Computer Security Basics* contains a more readable introduction to the Orange Book—why it exists, what it contains, and what the different security levels are all about—than any other book or government publication.

"A very well-rounded book, filled with concise, authoritative information...written with the user in mind, but still at a level to be an excellent professional reference."
—Mitch Wright, System Administrator, I-NET, Inc.

Practical UNIX Security

By Simson Garfinkel & Gene Spafford
1st Edition June 1991
512 pages, ISBN 0-937175-72-2

Tells system administrators how to make their UNIX system—either System V or BSD—as secure as it possibly can be without going to trusted system technology. The book describes UNIX concepts and how they enforce security, tells how to defend against and handle security breaches, and explains network security (including UUCP, NFS, Kerberos, and firewall machines) in detail. If you are a UNIX system administrator or user who deals with security, you need this book.

"The book could easily become a standard desktop reference for anyone involved in system administration. In general, its comprehensive treatment of UNIX security issues will enlighten anyone with an interest in the topic."
—Paul Clark, Trusted Information Systems

PGP: Pretty Good Privacy

By Simson Garfinkel
1st Edition Winter 1994-95 (est.)
250 pages (est.), ISBN 1-56592-098-8

PGP, which stands for Pretty Good Privacy, is a free and widely available program that lets you protect files and electronic mail. Written by Phil Zimmermann and released in 1991, PGP works on virtually every platform and has become very popular both in the U.S. and abroad. Because it uses state-of-the-art public key cryptography, PGP can be used to authenticate messages, as well as keep them secret. With PGP, you can digitally "sign"a message when you send it. By checking the digital signature at the other end, the recipient can be sure that the message was not changed during transmission and that the message actually came from you. The ability to protect the secrecy and authenticity of messages in this way is a vital part of being able to conduct business on the Internet.

PGP: Pretty Good Privacy is both a readable technical users guide and a fascinating behind-the-scenes look at cryptography and privacy. Part I of the book describes how to use PGP: protecting files and email, creating and using keys, signing messages, certifying and distributing keys, and using key servers. Part II provides background on cryptography, battles against public key patents and U.S. government export restrictions, and other aspects of the ongoing public debates about privacy and free speech.

System Performance Tuning

By Mike Loukides
1st Edition November 1990
336 pages, ISBN 0-937175-60-9

System Performance Tuning answers the fundamental question: How can I get my computer to do more work without buying more hardware? Some performance problems do require you to buy a bigger or faster computer, but many can be solved simply by making better use of the resources you already have.

"This book is a 'must' for anyone who has an interest in making their UNIX system run faster and more efficiently. It deals effectively with a complex subject that could require a multi-volume series."
—Stephan M. Chan, *ComUNIXation*

Managing UUCP and Usenet

By Grace Todino & Tim O'Reilly
10th Edition January 1992
368 pages, ISBN 0-937175-93-5

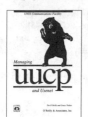

For all its widespread use, UUCP is one of the most difficult UNIX utilities to master. This book is for system administrators who want to install and manage UUCP and Usenet software.

"Don't even TRY to install UUCP without it!"—Usenet message 456@nitrex.UUCP

"If you are contemplating or struggling with connecting your system to the Internet via UUCP or planning even a passing contact with Usenet News Groups, this book should be on your shelf. Our highest recommendation."
—*Boardwatch Magazine*

Managing NFS and NIS

By Hal Stern
1st Edition June 1991
436 pages, ISBN 0-937175-75-7

Managing NFS and NIS is for system administrators who need to set up or manage a network filesystem installation. NFS (Network Filesystem) is probably running at any site that has two or more UNIX systems. NIS (Network Information System) is a distributed database used to manage a network of computers. The only practical book devoted entirely to these subjects, this guide is a "must-have" for anyone interested in UNIX networking.

termcap & terminfo

By John Strang, Linda Mui & Tim O'Reilly
3rd Edition April 1988
270 pages, ISBN 0-937175-22-6

For UNIX system administrators and programmers. This handbook provides information on writing and debugging terminal descriptions, as well as terminal initialization, for the two UNIX terminal databases.

"I've been working with both termcap and terminfo for years now, and I was confident that I had a handle on them, but reading this remarkable little book gave me some valuable new insights into terminal setting in UNIX."
—*Root Journal*

X Window System Administrator's Guide: Volume 8

By Linda Mui & Eric Pearce
1st Edition October 1992
372, pages, ISBN 0-937175-83-8

As X moves out of the hacker's domain and into the real world, users can't be expected to master all the ins and outs of setting up and administering their own X software. That will increasingly become the domain of system administrators. Even for experienced system administrators X raises many issues, both because of subtle changes in the standard UNIX way of doing things and because X blurs the boundaries between different platforms. Under X, users can run applications across the network on systems with different resources (including fonts, colors, and screen size). Many of these issues are poorly understood, and the technology for dealing with them is in rapid flux.

This book is the first and only book devoted to the issues of system administration for X and X-based networks, written not just for UNIX system administrators, but for anyone faced with the job of administering X (including those running X on stand-alone workstations).

Note: The CD that used to be offered with this book is now sold separately, allowing system administrators to purchase the book and the CD-ROM in quantities they choose. *The X Companion CD for R6*, estimated release November 1994.

The X Companion CD for R6

By O'Reilly & Associates
1st Edition Fall 1994 (est.)
(Includes CD-ROM plus 80-page guide)
ISBN 1-56592-084-8

The X CD-ROM contains precompiled binaries for X11, Release 6 (X11R6) for Sun4, Solaris, HP-UX on the HP700, DEC Alpha, IBM RS6000, and other industry-standard platforms. It includes X11R6 source code from the "core" and "contrib" directories and X11R5 source code from the "core"and "contrib" directories. The CD also provides examples from the O'Reilly *X Window System* series and *The X Resource* journal.

The package includes an 80-page booklet describing the contents of the CD-ROM, how to install the R6 binaries, and how to build X11 for other platforms. O'Reilly and Associates used to offer this CD-ROM with Volume 8, *X Window System Administrator's Guide*) of the *X Window System* series. Offering it separately allows system administrators to purchase the book and the CD-ROM in any quantities they choose.

AUDIOTAPES

O'Reilly now offers audiotapes based on interviews with people who are making a profound impact in the world of the Internet. Here we give you a quick overview of what's available. For details on our audiotape collection, send email to **audio@ora.com**.

"Ever listen to one of those five-minute-long news pieces being broadcast on National Public Radio's 'All Things Considered' and wish they were doing an in-depth story on new technology? Well, your wishes are answered." —Byte

Global Network Operations

Carl Malamud interviews Brian Carpenter, Bernhard Stockman, Mike O'Dell & Geoff Huston
Released Spring 1994
Duration: 2 hours, ISBN 1-56592-993-4

What does it take to actually run a network? In these four interviews, Carl Malamud explores some of the technical and operational issues faced by Internet service providers around the world.

Brian Carpenter is the director for networking at CERN, the high-energy physics laboratory in Geneva, Switzerland. Physicists are some of the world's most active Internet users, and its global user base makes CERN one of the world's most network-intensive sites. Carpenter discusses how he deals with issues such as the OSI and DECnet Phase V protocols and his views on the future of the Internet.

Bernhard Stockman is one of the founders and the technical manager of the European Backbone (EBONE). EBONE has proven to be the first effective transit backbone for Europe and has been a leader in the deployment of CIDR, BGP-4, and other key technologies.

Mike O'Dell is vice president of research at UUNET Technologies. O'Dell has a long record of involvement in data communications, ranging from his service as a telco lab employee, an engineer on several key projects, and a member of the USENIX board to now helping define new services for one of the largest commercial IP service providers.

Geoff Huston is the director of the Australian Academic Research Network (AARNET). AARNET is known as one of the most progressive regional networks, rapidly adopting new services for its users. Huston talks about how networking in Australia has flourished despite astronomically high rates for long-distance lines.

The Future of the Internet Protocol

Carl Malamud interviews Steve Deering, Bob Braden, Christian Huitema, Bob Hinden, Peter Ford, Steve Casner, Bernhard Stockman & Noel Chiappa
Released Spring 1994
Duration: 4 hours, ISBN 1-56592-996-9

The explosion of interest in the Internet is stressing what was originally designed as a research and education network. The sheer number of users is requiring new strategies for Internet address allocation; multimedia applications are requiring greater bandwidth and strategies such as "resource reservation" to provide synchronous end-to-end service.

In this series of eight interviews, Carl Malamud talks to some of the researchers who are working to define how the underlying technology of the Internet will need to evolve in order to meet the demands of the next five to ten years.

Give these tapes a try if you're intrigued by such topics as Internet "multicasting" of audio and video, or think your job might one day depend on understanding some of the following buzzwords:

- IPNG (Internet Protocol Next Generation)
- SIP (Simple Internet Protocol)
- TUBA (TCP and UDP with Big Addresses)
- CLNP (Connectionless Network Protocol)
- CIDR (Classless Inter-Domain Routing)

or if you are just interested in getting to know more about the people who are shaping the future.

Mobile IP Networking

Carl Malamud interviews Phil Karn & Jun Murai
Released Spring 1994
Duration: 1 hour, ISBN 1-56592-994-2

Phil Karn is the father of the KA9Q publicly available imple-mentation of TCP/IP for DOS (which has also been used as the basis for the software in many commercial Internet routers). KA9Q was originally developed to allow "packet radio," that is, TCP/IP over ham radio bands. Phil's current research focus is on commercial applications of wireless data communications.

Jun Murai is one of the most distinguished researchers in the Internet community. Murai is a professor at Keio University and the founder of the Japanese WIDE Internet. Murai talks about his research projects, which range from satellite-based IP multicasting to a massive testbed for mobile computing at the Fujisawa campus of Keio University.

Networked Information and Online Libraries

Carl Malamud interviews Peter Deutsch & Cliff Lynch
Released September 1993
Duration: 1 hour, ISBN 1-56592-998-5

Peter Deutsch, president of Bunyip Information Services, was one of the co-developers of Archie. In this interview Peter talks about his philosophy for services and compares Archie to X.500. He also talks about what kind of standards we need for networked information retrieval.

Cliff Lynch is currently the director of library automation for the University of California. He discusses issues behind online publishing, such as SGML and the democratization of publish-ing on the Internet.

European Networking

Carl Malamud interviews Glenn Kowack & Rob Blokzijl
Released September 1993
Duration: 1 hour, ISBN 1-56592-999-3

Glenn Kowack is chief executive of EUnet, the network that's bringing the Internet to the people of Europe. Glenn talks about EUnet's populist business model and the politics of European networking.

Rob Blokzijl is the network manager for NIKHEF, the Dutch Institute of High Energy Physics. Rob talks about RIPE, the IP user's group for Europe, and the nuts and bolts of European network coordination.

Security and Networks

Carl Malamud interviews Jeff Schiller & John Romkey
Released September 1993
Duration: 1 hour, ISBN 1-56592-997-7

Jeff Schiller is the manager of MIT's campus network and is one of the Internet's leading security experts. Here, he talks about Privacy Enhanced Mail (PEM), the difficulty of policing the Internet, and whether horses or computers are more useful to criminals.

John Romkey has been a long-time TCP/IP developer and was recently named to the Internet Architecture Board. In this wide-ranging interview, John talks about the famous "ToasterNet" demo at InterOp, what kind of Internet security he'd like to see put in place, and what Internet applications of the future might look like.

John Perry Barlow
Notable Speeches of the Information Age

USENIX Conference Keynote Address
San Francisco, CA; January 17, 1994
Duration: 1.5 hours, ISBN 1-56592-992-6

John Perry Barlow—retired Wyoming cattle rancher, a lyricist for the Grateful Dead since 1971— holds a degree in comparative religion from Wesleyan University. He also happens to be a recognized authority on computer security, virtual reality, digitized intellectual property, and the social and legal conditions arising in the global network of computers.

In 1990 Barlow co-founded the Electronic Frontier Foundation with Mitch Kapor and currently serves as chair of its executive committee. He writes and lectures on subjects relating to digital technology and society and is a contributing editor to *Communications of the ACM*, *NeXTWorld*, *Microtimes*, *Mondo 2000*, *Wired*, and other publications.

In his keynote address to the Winter 1994 USENIX Conference, Barlow talks of recent developments in the national information infrastructure, telecom-munications regulation, cryptography, globalization of the Internet, intellectual property, and the settlement of Cyberspace. The talk explores the premise that "architecture is politics": that the technology adopted for the coming "information superhighway" will help to determine what is carried on it, and that if the electronic frontier of the Internet is not to be replaced by electronic strip malls, we need to make sure that our technological choices favor bi-directional communication and open platforms.

Side A contains the keynote;
Side B contains a question and answer period.

O'Reilly & Associates—
GLOBAL NETWORK NAVIGATOR

The Global Network Navigator (GNN)™ is a unique kind of information service that makes the Internet easy and enjoyable to use. We organize access to the vast information resources of the Internet so that you can find what you want. We also help you understand the Internet and the many ways you can explore it.

In GNN you'll find:

Navigating the Net with GNN

 The *Whole Internet Catalog* contains a descriptive listing of the most useful Net resources and services with live links to those resources.

 The *GNN Business Pages* are where you'll learn about companies who have established a presence on the Internet and use its worldwide reach to help educate consumers.

 The *Internet Help Desk* helps folks who are new to the Net orient themselves and gets them started on the road to Internet exploration.

News

 NetNews is a weekly publication that reports on the news of the Internet, with weekly feature articles that focus on Internet trends and special events. The Sports, Weather, and Comix Pages round out the news.

Special Interest Publications

Whether you're planning a trip or are just interested in reading about the journeys of others, you'll find that the *Travelers' Center* contains a rich collection of feature articles and ongoing columns about travel. In the *Travelers' Center*, you can link to many helpful and informative travel-related Internet resources.

The *Personal Finance Center* is the place to go for information about money management and investment on the Internet. Whether you're an old pro at playing the market or are thinking about investing for the first time, you'll read articles and discover Internet resources that will help you to think of the Internet as a personal finance information tool.

All in all, GNN helps you get more value for the time you spend on the Internet.

 The Best of the Web

GNN received "Honorable Mention" for **"Best Overall Site," "Best Entertainment Service,"** and "**Most Important Service Concept**."

The *GNN NetNews* received "Honorable Mention" for "**Best Document Design**."

Subscribe Today

GNN is available over the Internet as a subscription service. To get complete information about subscribing to GNN, send email to **info@gnn.com**. If you have access to a World Wide Web browser such as Mosaic or Lynx, you can use the following URL to register online: `http://gnn.com/`

If you use a browser that does not support online forms, you can retrieve an email version of the registration form automatically by sending email to **form@gnn.com**. Fill this form out and send it back to us by email, and we will confirm your registration.

O'Reilly on the Net—
ONLINE PROGRAM GUIDE

O'Reilly & Associates offers extensive information through our online resources. If you've got Internet access, we invite you to come and explore our little neck-of-the-woods.

Online Resource Center

Most comprehensive among our online offerings is the O'Reilly Resource Center. Here, you'll find detailed information and descriptions on all O'Reilly products: titles, prices, tables of contents, indexes, author bios, CD-ROM directory listings, reviews... you can even view images of the products themselves. We also supply helpful ordering information: how to contact us, how to order online, distributors and bookstores around the world, discounts, upgrades, etc. In addition, we provide informative literature in the field, featuring articles, interviews, bibliographies, and columns that help you stay informed and abreast.

 The Best of the Web

The *O'Reilly Resource Center* was voted "**Best Commercial Site**" by users participating in "Best of the Web '94."

To access ORA's Online Resource Center:

Point your Web browser (e.g., `mosaic` or `lynx`) to:
`http://gnn.com/ora/`

For the plaintext version, `telnet` or `gopher` to:
`gopher.ora.com`
(telnetters login: `gopher`)

FTP

The example files and programs in many of our books are available electronically via FTP.

To obtain example files and programs from O'Reilly texts:

`ftp` to:
`ftp.uu.net`
`cd published/oreilly`

or
`ftp.ora.com`

Ora-news

An easy way to stay informed of the latest projects and products from O'Reilly & Associates is to subscribe to "ora-news," our electronic news service. Subscribers receive email as soon as the information breaks.

To subscribe to "ora-news":

Send email to:
listproc@online.ora.com

and put the following information on the first line of your message (not in "Subject"):
subscribe ora-news "your name" **of** "your company"

For example:
subscribe ora-news Jim Dandy of Mighty Fine Enterprises

Email

Many other helpful customer services are provided via email. Here's a few of the most popular and useful.

Useful email addresses

nuts@ora.com
For general questions and information.

bookquestions@ora.com
For technical questions, or corrections, concerning book contents.

order@ora.com
To order books online and for ordering questions.

catalog@ora.com
To receive a free copy of our magazine/catalog, "ora.com" (please include a snailmail address).

Snailmail and phones

O'Reilly & Associates, Inc.
103A Morris Street, Sebastopol, CA 95472
Inquiries: 707-829-0515, 800-998-9938
Credit card orders: 800-889-8969
FAX: 707-829-0104

TO ORDER: **800-889-8969** (CREDIT CARD ORDERS ONLY); **ORDER@ORA.COM**

O'Reilly & Associates—
INTERNATIONAL DISTRIBUTORS

Customers outside North America can now order O'Reilly & Associates books through the following distributors. They offer our international customers faster order processing, more bookstores, increased representation at tradeshows worldwide, and the high quality, responsive service our customers have come to expect.

EUROPE, MIDDLE EAST, AND AFRICA

(except Germany, Switzerland, and Austria)

INQUIRIES
International Thomson Publishing Europe
Berkshire House
168-173 High Holborn
London WC1V 7AA
United Kingdom
Telephone: 44-71-497-1422
Fax: 44-71-497-1426
Email: ora.orders@itpuk.co.uk

ORDERS
International Thomson Publishing Services, Ltd.
Cheriton House, North Way
Andover, Hampshire SP10 5BE
United Kingdom
Telephone: 44-264-342-832 (UK orders)
Telephone: 44-264-342-806 (outside UK)
Fax: 44-264-364418 (UK orders)
Fax: 44-264-342761 (outside UK)

GERMANY, SWITZERLAND, AND AUSTRIA

International Thomson Publishing GmbH
O'Reilly-International Thomson Verlag
Attn: Mr. G. Miske
Königswinterer Strasse 418
53227 Bonn
Germany
Telephone: 49-228-970240
Fax: 49-228-441342
Email: gerd@orade.ora.com

THE AMERICAS, JAPAN, AND OCEANIA

O'Reilly & Associates, Inc.
103A Morris Street
Sebastopol, CA 95472 U.S.A.
Telephone: 707-829-0515
Telephone: 800-998-9938 (U.S. & Canada)
Fax: 707-829-0104
Email: order@ora.com

ASIA

(except Japan)

INQUIRIES
International Thomson Publishing Asia
221 Henderson Road
#05 10 Henderson Building
Singapore 0315
Telephone: 65-272-6496
Fax: 65-272-6498

ORDERS
Telephone: 65-268-7867
Fax: 65-268-6727

AUSTRALIA

WoodsLane Pty. Ltd.
Unit 8, 101 Darley Street (P.O. Box 935)
Mona Vale NSW 2103
Australia
Telephone: 61-2-979-5944
Fax: 61-2-997-3348
Email: woods@tmx.mhs.oz.au

NEW ZEALAND

WoodsLane New Zealand Ltd.
21 Cooks Street (P.O. Box 575)
Wanganui, New Zealand
Telephone: 64-6-347-6543
Fax: 64-6-345-4840
Email: woods@tmx.mhs.oz.au

pwd command prompt via

```
PS1 = "\`pwd\`$ "
```

Here's a page we encourage readers to tear out...

O'REILLY WOULD LIKE TO HEAR FROM YOU

Please send me the following:

❏ *ora.com*

O'Reilly's magazine/catalog, containing behind-the-scenes articles and interviews on the technology we write about, and a complete listing of O'Reilly books and products.

❏ *Global Network Navigator*™
Information and subscription.

Please print legibly

Which book did this card come from?

_____

Where did you buy this book?
❏ Bookstore   ❏ Direct from O'Reilly
❏ Bundled with hardware/software   ❏ Class/seminar

Your job description: ❏ SysAdmin   ❏ Programmer
❏ Other _____

What computer system do you use?   ❏ UNIX
❏ MAC ❏ DOS(PC) ❏ Other _____

Name _____ Company/Organization Name _____

Address _____

City _____ State _____ Zip/Postal Code _____ Country _____

Telephone _____ Internet or other email address (specify network) _____

Nineteenth century wood engraving
of the horned owl from the O'Reilly
& Associates Nutshell Handbook®
Learning the UNIX Operating System

POST CARD

O'Reilly & Associates, Inc., 103A Morris Street, Sebastopol, CA 95472-9902

PLACE
STAMP
HERE

NO POSTAGE
NECESSARY IF
MAILED IN THE
UNITED STATES

BUSINESS REPLY MAIL

FIRST CLASS MAIL   PERMIT NO. 80   SEBASTOPOL, CA

Postage will be paid by addressee

O'Reilly & Associates, Inc.
103A Morris Street
Sebastopol, CA 95472-9902